FOREIGN AND COMMONWEALTH OFFICE

DOCUMENTS ON BRITISH POLICY OVERSEAS

EDITED BY

K.A. HAMILTON, Ph.D.

AND

P. SALMON, Ph.D.

SERIES III

Volume V

Routledge
Taylor & Francis Group

LONDON AND NEW YORK

First published 2006
by Routledge, an imprint of Taylor & Francis
2 Park Square, Milton Park, Abingdon, Oxon OX14 4RN

Simultaneously published in the USA and Canada
by Routledge
270 Madison Ave, New York, NY 10016

Routledge is an imprint of the Taylor & Francis Group, an informa business

Printed and bound in Great Britain by Biddles Ltd, King's Lynn

Publisher's note
This book has been produced from camera-ready copy supplied by the author.

British Library Cataloguing in Publication Data
A catalogue record for this book is available from the British Library

Library of Congress Cataloging in Publication Data
A catalog record for this book has been requested

ISBN10: 0–714–65114–1 (hbk)
ISBN10: 0–203–49627–2 (ebk)

ISBN13: 978–0–714–65114–9 (hbk)
ISBN13: 978–0–203–49627–5 (ebk)

DOCUMENTS ON BRITISH POLICY OVERSEAS

Series III, Volume V

The Southern Flank in Crisis, 1973–1976

WHITEHALL HISTORIES: FOREIGN AND COMMONWEALTH OFFICE PUBLICATIONS
Series Editors: Keith Hamilton and Patrick Salmon
ISSN: 1471-2083

FCO historians are responsible for editing *Documents on British Policy Overseas* (DBPO) and for overseeing the publication of FCO Internal Histories.

DBPO comprises three series of diplomatic documents, focusing on major themes in foreign policy since 1945, and drawn principally from the records of the Foreign and Commonwealth Office. The latest volumes, published in Series III, contain archival material which would otherwise be unavailable to the public.

FCO Internal Histories are occasional studies by former serving officials, commissioned to provide background information for members of the FCO, to point out possible lessons for the future and to evaluate how well objectives were met in a particular episode or crisis. They are not written for publication, but some Internal Histories, which offer fresh insights into British diplomacy, are now being declassified for publication by Whitehall History Publishing in association with Routledge.

Latest published volumes:

Britain and China, 1945-1950
Documents on British Policy Overseas, Series I, Volume VIII
S.R. Ashton, G. Bennett and K.A. Hamilton (eds)

Britain and the Soviet Union, 1968-1972
Documents on British Policy Overseas, Series III, Volume I
G. Bennett and K.A. Hamilton (eds)

The Conference on Security and Cooperation in Europe, 1972-1975
Documents on British Policy Overseas, Series III, Volume II
G. Bennett and K.A. Hamilton (eds)

Détente in Europe, 1972-1976
Documents on British Policy Overseas, Series III, Volume III
G. Bennett and K.A. Hamilton (eds)

The Year of Europe: America, Europe and the Energy Crisis, 1972-1974
Documents on British Policy Overseas, Series III, Volume IV
K.A. Hamilton and P. Salmon (eds)

PREFACE

Previous Series III volumes have to a large extent focussed upon British diplomacy in a period associated with an easing of East-West tensions in Europe. In the eyes of some observers this *détente* signalled the end of the Cold War. But during the mid-1970s members of the North Atlantic Treaty Organisation (NATO) had also to reckon with an increasingly unstable situation on the Alliance's southern flank which the Soviet Union seemed likely to exploit to its advantage. The collapse of the Caetano régime in Portugal, General Franco's death in Spain, a *coup d'état* in Cyprus, followed by Turkey's military intervention and the threat of a Græco-Turkish war, exposed NATO's vulnerability in a region in which Moscow was already expanding its strategic presence. Moreover, while in France and Italy Communist parties appeared set to make electoral gains, the prospective demise of Marshal Tito, Yugoslavia's ageing communist President, encouraged speculation over the consequences of domestic dissension in the Balkans. The British Government was, as the documents in this volume reveal, far from averse to all political change in southern Europe. Dictatorships in Portugal and Greece were regarded by Ministers as an embarrassment to NATO, and for many in Britain, particularly those on the political left, General Franco remained an unhappy reminder of events of an earlier decade. The transition from authoritarian rule to democracy nonetheless required careful handling: the revolution in Portugal seemed at one stage destined to end in rule by a pro-Soviet cabal, and Labour politicians in Britain were distinctly cautious in responding to the gradualist approach adopted by General Franco's successors towards the reform process in Spain. In the case of Greece, the restoration of democracy was intimately connected with developments in Cyprus, and was regarded in London as one of the few favourable results of a conflict which British diplomats strove to contain and, far less successfully, to resolve.

Cyprus: Prelude to Crisis

British policy towards Cyprus during 1973-75, the main theme of the first three chapters of this volume, was conditioned by Britain's historic links with the island, the presence of British forces there, and commitments undertaken when the Republic of Cyprus was established in 1960. Cyprus had achieved its independence from Britain after an armed struggle waged by elements of the ethnic Greek population of the island with the aim of securing union (*enosis*) with Greece. This was opposed by the island's Turkish Cypriot minority, who had come to favour partition (*taksim*) as an alternative to continued British rule. But the settlement resulting from the Zürich and London accords of February 1959, and elaborated in the Republic's Constitution and three treaties—the Treaty of Guarantee, the Treaty of Establishment and the Treaty of Alliance—all of which came into operation on 16 August 1960, represented a compromise between the divergent aspirations of the Greek and Turkish Cypriot communities, and the political and strategic interests of Britain, Greece and Turkey. The latter three powers jointly guaranteed the Republic's independence and integrity and 'the state of affairs established by the Basic Articles of the Constitution'. HMG also retained, under the Treaty of Establishment, two Sovereign Base Areas (SBAs) at Akrotiri and Dhekelia along with certain military rights and facilities on the territory of the Republic. And the Treaty of Alliance amongst Greece, Turkey and Cyprus provided for the establishment of a tripartite headquarters on the island, with military contingents of 950 Greeks and 650 Turks for the Republic's defence and the training of its army.

Cyprus's new constitutional arrangements never commanded the degree of popular support required to ensure their full and effective implementation. Greek Cypriots considered excessive the privileges granted to the Turkish Cypriot community, who made up no more than 18.2 per cent of the island's population, whilst the Turks insisted on the application of their rights in detail. The two communities were at odds over the composition of the army and the public services, the modalities of fiscal legislation, the future of the separate Turkish Cypriot municipalities established prior to independence, and the powers and status of the Turkish Cypriot Vice-President of the Republic. In December 1963 proposals presented by Archbishop Makarios, the President of the Republic, for the radical amendment of the Constitution along lines favoured by the Greek Cypriots were rejected by the Turkish Government. That same month violence erupted between the two communities. Fearing Turkish military action, Archbishop Makarios agreed that British forces might intervene from the SBAs. A ceasefire followed in Nicosia, and a 'Green Line' was established demarcating a neutral zone between the Greek and Turkish quarters of the capital. But a conference in London between the guarantor powers and representatives of the two Cypriot communities ended in disagreement, and in the wake of further intercommunal strife, the United Nations (UN) Security Council resolved in March 1964 on the creation of a multinational UN Peacekeeping Force in Cyprus (UNFICYP). Archbishop Makarios also introduced conscription and began the formation of a National Guard commanded by Greek officers, including General G. Grivas, who in the 1950s had led the guerrilla war against the British colonial administration.

Subsequent endeavours on the part of the United States and the UN to promote a comprehensive settlement of the Cyprus problem met with little success. And a group of colonels who seized power in Athens on 21 April 1967, some of whom had previously served in Cyprus, was unable to win Turkish approval for their proposals for *enosis*. Population movements within the island meanwhile resulted in the concentration of over half the Turkish Cypriot community in dispersed and disconnected enclaves. Subjected to economic blockade, these were defended by full-time 'fighter' units assisted by mainland Turkish officers. This was hardly conducive to the achievement of political stability, and in the autumn of 1967 heavy fighting between the National Guard and Turkish Cypriots near the village of Korphinou provoked a confrontation between Greece and Turkey. The Greek junta finally responded to Turkish pressure by recalling General Grivas, and an American brokered understanding between Athens and Ankara was followed by the withdrawal of 12,000 Greek troops from Cyprus and the lifting of the last economic restrictions on the Turkish Cypriot enclaves. Henceforth, progress towards an accommodation on the island's future seemed to depend on talks which began in June 1968 between Mr. G.J. Clerides, the President of the Cyprus House of Representatives, and Mr. R. Denktash, the President of the Turkish Cypriot Chamber. These were conducted under the auspices of the UN and were in the words of Mr. S.L.J. Olver, Britain's High Commissioner in Nicosia from March 1973, 'intended to find a fresh, mutually acceptable constitution for a sovereign independent and unitary Republic of Cyprus' (No. 1).

The talks were nonetheless beset by difficulties, and British diplomats were far from optimistic about a fresh round inaugurated in June 1972 by Dr. K. Waldheim, the UN Secretary-General, in which the representatives of the two communities were joined by his Special Representative, Sr. B.F. Osorio-Tafall, and Greek and Turkish constitutional advisers. Mr. Olver summarised the conflicting aims of the two communities in a despatch of 24 October 1973. 'The differences', he observed, 'spring from the Turkish Cypriots' fear for their physical security and for their continuation as a community, as against the Greek Cypriots' desire for a Greek dominated State which would have complete freedom of action internationally.' The Turks wanted full control of their own affairs through local autonomy and recognition of their status as partners in a bi-communal state; and the Greeks appeared determined to resist any measures which might lead to the establishment of a cantonal or federal system. But Mr. Olver doubted if either the Turkish Cypriots or the mainland Turks saw partition as a satisfactory solution to the Cyprus problem: the establishment of a mini-state would cause considerable dislocation and distress, and Ankara would not wish the island, or any part of it, to come under Greek or other potentially hostile control. He likewise thought that, while Greek Cypriots still hankered after *enosis* in the guise of 'self-determination', Archbishop Makarios would in practice work for the continued independence of the Republic. Time seemed, in any case, to be on the side of the Greek Cypriots, and their poorer Turkish neighbours could do little other than 'sit tight in the hope that something [would] turn up'. Perhaps, Mr. Olver speculated, 'the Greek Cypriot community will tear themselves to pieces or Archbishop Makarios will be removed from power' (*ibid*).

Support for Archbishop Makarios amongst the Greek Cypriot community was certainly far from universal. His critics increasingly saw him as an obstacle to *enosis* and, after his return to Cyprus in September 1971, General Grivas, set about waging a violent campaign against the Archbishop and his followers. But Mr. Olver thought Archbishop Makarios would still be able to present any deadlock in the intercommunal talks as a 'result of his determination not to sacrifice the Greek Cypriot birthright to the Turks'. He also assumed that the Turkish Government would seek to damp down separatist tendencies amongst the Turkish Cypriot community, since the declaration of a mini-state could only add to Turkey's 'burden both internationally and in practical terms'. Indeed, Mr. Olver thought it possible that the Greek and Turkish Governments might resume their former dialogue on Cyprus, on the understanding that any agreed understanding would be submitted to an island-wide plebiscite. But in the autumn of 1973 he considered the best contribution Britain could make to the continuing talks was that of applying 'quiet diplomatic pressure towards moderation and a settlement in Nicosia, Athens and Ankara' (*ibid.*).

During the following nine months HMG's policy towards the intercommunal talks remained what the Minister-Counsellor at the Greek Embassy in London defined as that 'of telling both sides that they hoped they would reach an agreement, while at the same time we asserted that we would accept any agreement reached between them' (No. 3). Meanwhile, little progress was made towards bridging the gap separating the Greek- and Turkish-Cypriot delegations. Papers prepared by Mr. Clerides and Mr. Denktash on local government in Cyprus revealed that their views were diametrically opposed, with the former seeking to reserve the lion's share of authority for the state, and the latter demanding the fullest possible local autonomy for his community (*ibid.*). The talks were regarded as a 'useful safety-valve', but by the end of February 1974 Mr. Olver was of the opinion that neither side thought they could provide any real solution to the problem. Political changes in Ankara and Athens seemed also to reduce the scope for diplomatic manoeuvre. The formation in January 1974 of a new coalition government in Turkey, headed by Mr. B. Eçevit of the Republican People's Party, was soon followed by the publication of a programme affirming Ankara's belief that the 'most appropriate solution' for Cyprus would be a 'federal system to maintain the equal sovereignty status of the Turkish community'. In conversation with Mr. Olver, Mr. Inhan, the Deputy Head of Mission of the Turkish Embassy in Nicosia, suggested that some degree of population transfer aimed at achieving a greater geographical concentration of Turkish Cypriots might provide the basis for a 'federation' (No. 4). But the concept of 'federalism' was anathema to the Greek and Cyprus Governments. Moreover, the overthrow of the six-year old dictatorship of Colonel G. Papadopoulos by a military *coup d'état* on 25 November 1973 had resulted in the installation in Athens of a régime which was even less disposed to compromise than its predecessor. Behind a façade of civilian government, power was effectively exercised by Brigadier D. Ioannides, the leader of the *coup*, and his associates included officers whose past links with General Grivas boded ill for future relations between Athens and Nicosia. 'Above all', noted Sir R. Hooper, Britain's Ambassador to Greece, 'this is a régime of inexperienced and largely unsophisticated men with some xenophobic tendencies' (No. 2).

Greece's new leaders had few friends in London. Bilateral relations between Britain and the régime of the Greek colonels had rarely, if ever, been close. In opposition the Labour Party had been particularly critical of the absence of democracy in Greece, and following the General Election of 28 February the incoming Labour Government registered its disapproval of the political situation there by cancelling the planned visit of two Royal Navy warships to Athens on 15 March (No. 5). Sir R. Hooper questioned the wisdom of this course. He thought that only the United States (US) disposed of sufficient means to make pressure effective, and that Britain, by acting on its own, or in conjunction with its European allies and partners, ran the risk not only of failing to achieve its objective, but of seeing what it was bound to lose commercially and in other ways picked up by others who were less scrupulous politically (No. 6). The new régime in Athens, nevertheless, seemed unlikely to make for peace and political stability in the eastern Mediterranean. And although the two months following General Grivas's death on 27 January were remarkably calm in Cyprus, by mid-March Mr. Olver was reporting upon a 'wave of rumours about sinister doings inside and outside the island'. The leadership of Cyprus's pro-Moscow communist party, AKEL, alleged that Greece and its NATO allies were plotting to impose a federal solution and/or partition, and that a prerequisite to this would be a *coup d'état* 'accompanied by the physical [and/or] political liquidation of the Archbishop'. Perhaps more disturbing from the British point of view were the suspicions harboured by Cyprus's pro-Western Foreign Minister that the Americans were backing EOKA (No. 8). British diplomats were nonetheless surprised when the Soviet Government delivered *démarches* in Ankara, Athens, London and Washington, expressing its concern over the hostility of 'extremist circles in Greece' towards Cyprus's independence (No. 7).

Mr. Olver could personally see no reason for suspecting the Greek Government of being involved in a plot against Archbishop Makarios. Indeed, he found it difficult to see how Greek interests could be served by promoting unrest in Cyprus, given that this could only strengthen those very left-wing forces which the Athens régime feared and give the Turks 'further excuse for intransigence in the talks' (No. 8). The latter were already close to stalling. By the end of March the two sides had made progress towards achieving agreement on most issues, including local autonomy. However, the nearer they had come to a settlement, the more sharply focussed had become the remaining sticking points. On 2 April Mr. Clerides challenged Mr. Denktash on Turkey's 'federalist' aspirations, Mr. Denktash made an evasive reply and, following a further wrangle over the precise basis of the talks, they were adjourned *sine die*. Archbishop Makarios evidently felt that the *status quo* could be maintained for a considerable time. But Mr. Olver was pessimistic. The intercommunal peace was, he believed, 'essentially fragile'; and Turkish 'impatience' could, he predicted, 'produce a situation which could escalate into real trouble', Moreover, Græco-Turkish differences over oil-drilling rights in the Aegean made it unlikely that either Ankara or Athens would give any fresh impetus to the talks. On the contrary, Sir R. Hooper feared that any personal influence the Greek Foreign Minister, Mr. S. Tetenes, might have over his country's policy towards Cyprus would be exerted in favour of a tough line, partly because his own inclinations lay in that direction, partly because he thought it might be 'a good way of sucking up to the military and hanging on to his job', and perhaps also because he thought 'that the best prescription for uniting the nation behind a shaky and unpopular government would be a good old row with the Turks over Cyprus' (No. 9).

During the spring of 1974 relations between Greece and Turkey steadily deteriorated. A Turkish gunboat was alleged to have intruded into Greek waters, Turkish aircraft overflew Greek territory, and these developments were accompanied by a bellicose and anti-Turkish press campaign in Athens. The Greeks also began making military preparations. But as Sir R. Hooper pointed out in a telegram of 15 May, the Greek Government had 'no rational interest in a conflict with Turkey which the more sober must realise would inevitably end in disaster for Greece'. The danger was that a régime whose decision-making processes were uncertain might all too easily allow a minor incident to escalate into a major clash (No. 12). Already under pressure from its supporters to promote democratic change in Greece, Britain's new Labour administration sought consultations with the Americans. During a visit to Washington in May Mr. R. Hattersley, Minister of State at the FCO, discussed the matter with Mr. A. Hartman, Assistant Secretary for European Affairs in the State Department, and other US officials (Nos. 13 and 108). The US Embassy in Athens had so far appeared to adopt an 'attitude of studied relaxation' towards the situation in the Aegean (No. 12), and Mr. Hartman explained that, despite American concern over the composition of the régime in Athens, Dr. H.A. Kissinger, the US Secretary of State, was 'reluctant to say anything in public about the desirability of a return to democracy in Greece'. Indeed, although Mr. Hattersley was keen to follow up Mr. Hartman's suggestion that Britain and the US should work out a joint strategy on Greece, Dr. Kissinger was evidently unprepared to consider raising the subject during the forthcoming NATO Ministerial meeting planned for Ottawa in June. According to Mr. Hartman, Dr. Kissinger 'believed firmly that any change for the better must be left for the Greeks to bring about themselves', and he had no wish to add to the problems which the US already had in the eastern Mediterranean. By early June, the Greeks in any case seemed ready to adopt a less rigid stance in their maritime dispute with Turkey (Nos. 13 and 14).

Meanwhile, the situation in Cyprus showed few signs of improving. The intercommunal talks which recommenced on 11 June were, in Mr. Olver's words, soon 'sputtering', neither side believing that they could produce a satisfactory solution. Mr. Olver was not, however, of the opinion that the maintenance of the *status quo* was a 'nice cosy option' which would suit everyone. In the absence of any bold Government initiative aimed at ending discrimination, Turkish Cypriot separatism had 'markedly hardened'. The Turkish community could not afford to stand still, and the last few years had witnessed steady progress towards the establishment of a fully autonomous separate Turkish Cypriot Administration. And Archbishop Makarios had already indicated that he thought Ankara might consider declaring a separate state. Under the impression that they might be 'nearing a point of no return—or rather, no return until there [had] been another cathartic outburst', Mr. Olver envisaged various courses which might facilitate a settlement. These included calls for goodwill, patience, etc. by other powers, and further intervention on the part of the UN. In a letter to Mr. Goodison of 19 June, he also suggested that, since the personal hostility of Mr. Denktash and Archbishop Markarios was a major element in the current deadlock, an attempt to promote a reconciliation between them, or the removal of one of them, might be a step in the right direction. Ironically, he thought that in practice this would mean jettisoning Mr. Denktash: the 'removal of Makarios in the foreseeable future—short of assassination—can I think be ruled out' (No. 16).

One other option which Mr. Olver considered impractical in the short-term was an agreement between Ankara and Athens on the terms of a Cyprus settlement. Greece and Turkey seemed unlikely to be able to patch up an accord (*ibid.*), and speculation regarding a comprehensive agreement covering an exchange of populations and the possible cession of Aegean islands to Turkey seemed no more than fantasy (No. 15). But, in addition, relations between the Greek Junta and Archbishop Makarios remained far from good. The Archbishop suspected Athens of being behind a renewed wave of EOKA-B violence in Cyprus, and he disagreed with Greece's military leaders over the composition and role of the largely Greek-officered Cyprus National Guard. The Greeks, for their part, probably saw EOKA-B as a 'threat and constraint on the Archbishop, and as a check on the growth of Communist influence in Cyprus' (No. 16). Archbishop Makarios was, however, in no mood to compromise. In an open letter of 2 July to the Greek President, General Gizikis, he accused Athens of conspiring to seize power in Cyprus and demanded the immediate withdrawal of 650 Greek officers from the National Guard. He also made his acceptance of a Greek invitation to visit Athens conditional on Greece first complying with his demands. Mr. E. Lagakos, the Greek Ambassador in Nicosia, was clearly disturbed by these developments, and in conversation with Mr. Olver on 10 July 'came pretty near ... to admitting that the Junta might have been plotting against Makarios'. Mr. Lagakos and Mr. Olver dismissed talk of a *coup*, but both agreed that the 'assassination of the Archbishop remained a possibility'. 'The next move', Mr. Olver noted on 11 July, 'is now with Athens. We can only hope it will not be a rash one' (No. 17).

The Cyprus coup, Turkey's intervention and the Geneva Conference

On the morning of 15 July the Cyprus National Guard launched an attack upon the Presidential Palace in Nicosia. Archbishop Makarios evaded capture, fleeing to Paphos from where he was taken by RAF helicopter to the British SBA at Akrotiri. Meanwhile, Nicos Sampson, a right-wing journalist and former leader of an EOKA execution squad was sworn in as President of the Republic. From the first, it was readily assumed by British officials that the Greek officers in the National Guard were responsible for the *coup d'état*. And, fully alive to the severe strains that the situation in Cyprus could place upon the Atlantic Alliance, Mr. Callaghan sought from Greece a public reaffirmation of its respect for the island's independence and integrity, and urged the Turks to restrain from intervention. Like the Americans, the British were also anxious to avoid internationalising the problem through premature reference to the UN Security Council. Mr. R.A. Fyjis-Walker, Counsellor in the British Embassy in Ankara, thought that the Turks would only intervene forcefully in Cyprus if they believed a declaration of *enosis* imminent or the Turkish Cypriots came under real attack (No. 21). But in a message delivered to Mr. Hattersley on 16 July Mr. H.E. Isik, the Acting Turkish Foreign Minister, called for Anglo-Turkish consultations and suggested joint action by British and Turkish forces to remove the 'threat directed against the independence of Cyprus' (*ibid.*).

Mr. Callaghan and senior FCO officials considered the possibility of British forces being used to restore Archbishop Makarios to power on the morning of 17 July. But when asked whether this was feasible, Ministry of Defence (MoD) representatives said the 'provisional answer was probably Yes if the only opposition was the National Guard': much 'would depend on the attitude of the population and the extent of a possible internal security problem' (No. 22). Meanwhile, Mr. Olver, who had learned that *HMS Hermes* was proceeding towards Cyprus, telegraphed to warn Mr. Callaghan that Archbishop Makarios's restoration by force 'would be very far from popular and would cause more problems locally than it would solve' (No. 23). The Archbishop seemed equally averse to forceful intervention. Following his arrival in London, he told Mr. Callaghan on the afternoon of the 17th, that if the Greeks were to withdraw their officers from the National Guard and withdraw their support, Mr. Sampson would fall from power. It was therefore 'for Britain and Turkey to press the Greeks in every way about their evaluation of the situation and to seek to restore the *status quo* before the coup' (No. 24). This appears to have been in line with Mr. Callaghan's thinking. He, nonetheless, considered the Americans to be in a better position to influence the régime in Athens, and during telephone conversations with Dr. Kissinger, he urged him to take the lead. 'As regards the Greeks', Mr. Callaghan observed, 'he intended to keep them in a state of uncertainty about our intentions and felt that this plus substantial pressure from the Americans might force the Greeks to back down' (No. 25). The danger was that, in the absence of an agreement on common or concerted action amongst the guarantor powers, the Turks might claim to exercise the right reserved to them in the Treaty of Guarantee of 1960 and act independently in Cyprus.

The arrival in London of Mr. Eçevit and Mr. Isik provided HMG with a clearer understanding of Turkey's position. During discussions with the Prime Minister, Mr. H. Wilson, and Mr. Callaghan on the evening of 17 July, Mr. Eçevit explained that the Turks regarded the new situation 'as a form of unnamed Enosis', adding that he wanted Britain and the United States to join Turkey in warning Greece of the violation of Cyprus's independence, and in requesting the withdrawal of Greek forces from the island under UN supervision. After stressing Turkey's primary interest in the safety of the Turkish-Cypriot community, for which it required 'secure access to the sea', Mr. Eçevit said that there must be a more effective Turkish presence and asked the British to permit the despatch of Turkish forces to Cyprus through the SBAs. 'The alternative', he stated, 'was unilateral action by Turkey, which he felt would be inevitable later if not sooner—later would be worse and bloodier.' This was contrary to Mr. Callaghan's preference for diplomatic action. But while Mr. Callaghan ruled out allowing Turkish forces free passage through the SBAs, Mr. Eçevit rejected his proposal for tripartite talks between the British, Greek and Turkish leaders. Mr. Eçevit insisted that he could not consider Greece, 'an aggressor nation', as a guarantor, and his colleagues sought a joint statement condemning its conduct (*ibid.*).

In Mr. Callaghan's view a tripartite meeting of the guarantor powers was one means by which pressure could be exercised on the Greeks. Another was through the UN Security Council, where Archbishop Makarios was hoping to secure international backing. But while Mr. Callaghan considered the Americans most capable of influencing the government in Athens, he found Dr. Kissinger in no mood to 'rush the deliberations of the Security Council, which would lead to support for Makarios from all quarters and give him a carte blanche even to seek Soviet aid' (*ibid.*). In a telephone conversation with Sir P. Ramsbotham, Britain's Ambassador in Washington, Dr. Kissinger insisted that, although he was against the Sampson régime, he would prefer to see it replaced by one headed by Mr. Clerides, and that he thought it 'unwise ... to go all-out for Makarios at this stage'. There was, he observed, a danger that by 'acting precipitately', the British would risk becoming embroiled in a civil war which might end by 'strengthening the communist position in Cyprus'. He was likewise opposed to demanding the withdrawal of Greek National Guard officers from Cyprus, who he felt had 'at least acted as a forces against communist infiltration in Cyprus' (No. 26). Mr. Callaghan was disappointed by Dr. Kissinger's attitude. During a meeting with US Under-Secretary of State Mr. J.J. Sisco, whom Dr. Kissinger despatched to London on 18 July, Mr. Callagahan welcomed the idea of a 'viable negotiating package' to be worked out with the Greeks and Turks, but added that pressure on the Greeks to remove the officers was intended to stop the Turks moving. 'The danger of creeping *Enosis* could', he remarked, 'lead to the Turkish hawks coming out on top—although probably not too soon' (No. 27).

Mr. Callaghan reiterated this point in a personal message he sent to Dr. Kissinger on 19 July. In this he further defined the policy he would like to see the British and US Governments pursue. They should, he proposed: (1) continue to assert the legitimacy of Archbishop Makarios as Cyprus President; (2) work for the disappearance of the Sampson régime; (3) enter into discussions with the Greeks and Turks on future military arrangements within Cyprus; (4) consider other possible modifications in the Cyprus Constitution; (5) exert 'very great pressure' on the Greeks; and (6) accept that there would have eventually to be a UN resolution. But Dr. Kissinger's response was cautious. He felt that they should not precipitate the downfall of the *de facto* situation until there was a viable alternative, and that pressure could only be exerted on the Greeks once they had a better idea of what was acceptable to the Turks (No. 29). All this, however, was of little relevance. Sir H. Phillips, the British Ambassador in Ankara, had already warned Mr. Callaghan on the evening of 19 July that if Mr. Sisco, who was *en route* for Ankara, were to arrive 'empty-handed', the Turkish Government might resort to force in Cyprus. Eight hours later, he informed the FCO that he had learned from Mr. Günes, that in the absence of any 'concrete proposals' from Mr. Sisco for resolving the situation in Cyprus, the Turkish Government had decided to send troops to the island under Article 4 of the Treaty of Guarantee (No. 30).

Faced by Turkey's military intervention, news of which reached London during the early hours of 20 July, Mr. Callaghan sought: first, to persuade the Turks to limit the fighting, accept an early ceasefire, and issue a statement of intent on their desire to return to constitutional rule in Cyprus; and secondly, to prevent the Greek Government from escalating the situation or intervening by force. He planned to invite the Greeks and Turks to talks in London with a view to reducing tension and returning Cyprus to constitutional rule, which 'must mean the removal of Sampson. Meanwhile, Dr. Kissinger, who shared these aims and objectives, despatched Mr. Sisco to Athens with a view to urging the Greek Government to abandon Mr. Sampson (No. 31). But the Greeks at first showed few signs of being amenable to persuasion. In response to Turkey's intervention they mobilised their forces, and demanded that Turkey's military action cease and that its forces withdraw to the Turkish Cypriot enclaves. Reports from Washington also indicated that the Greeks were threatening that Turkey's failure to meet these terms would result in war and a proclamation of *enosis* with Cyprus. In any event, Mr. S. Kypraios, Greece's Acting Foreign Minister, made Greek participation in talks in London conditional on a ceasefire in Cyprus (No. 32), and in a subsequent telephone conversation with Mr. Callaghan hinted that without one the Greeks might 'do something really reckless'. The UN Security Council meanwhile passed Resolution 353 calling for a halt to the fighting and talks amongst the guarantor powers, and demanding an end to foreign military intervention in Cyprus and the withdrawal of foreign military personnel (No. 33). It was not, however, until 22 July that Mr. Sisco, armed with a threat to withhold US arms supplies, succeeded in persuading Athens and Ankara to accept a ceasefire (Nos. 35 and 36).

Mr. Callaghan hoped that this would permit tripartite talks between himself and the Greek and Turkish Foreign Ministers (No. 37). But the ceasefire was fragile and slow to take effect. Turkish commanders in Cyprus were evidently anxious to improve their military position, and in one notable instance British forces had to be sent to assist UNFICYP in deterring a threat to Nicosia airport (No. 40). The collapse of the military Junta in Athens, soon followed by Mr. Clerides's replacement of Mr. Sampson as 'President' of Cyprus, also delayed talks (Nos. 38 and 39). When they at last began on 25 July in Geneva, the British had very limited objectives. They had neither the desire nor the power to impose a solution, and felt the most they could hope was that they would be able to reinforce the ceasefire, ensure the restoration of peaceful conditions, and achieve an agreement on the 'establishment of continuing machinery at working level' (No. 40). From the start, Mr. Callaghan found the discussions 'heavy going', with the Greeks and Turks locked in a seemingly interminable wrangling. He tried 'to bring home to the Turks that they would have to concede something and to the Greeks that they would have to accept less than they hoped for if the Conference was to continue'. But, as he confessed on 26 July, his 'principal achievement' during the first full day of the talks was that of dissuading Mr. Mavros, the new Greek Foreign Minister, from carrying out his regularly uttered threat to leave Geneva and return to Athens (No. 41). The negotiations which continued for six days in all, and which were directed largely towards the drafting of a tripartite Declaration, never proved less than arduous. The main bone of contention was the text referring to the future withdrawal of Turkish forces from Cyprus. The Greeks, basing themselves on Resolution 353, wanted inclusion in the Declaration of a commitment to the withdrawal of all military personnel in Cyprus, other than those there by international agreement; and the Turks desired a text which would make the removal of their forces dependent on the achievement of a 'final solution' to the Cyprus problem.

Mr. Callaghan, although sympathetic to Greek demands, sought to promote a compromise formula which would refer to the withdrawal of forces with the least possible delay and after consideration of the constitutional problems. The negotiations were, however, complicated by Mr. Günes's evident reluctance to commit himself without prior consultation with Mr. Eçevit. Thus, much to Mr. Callaghan's irritation, at 4.30 a.m. on 29 July, after a twelve hour session during which the three Foreign Ministers had gone through each of the passages of the draft Declaration and when agreement seemed close, Mr. Günes insisted on referring the whole matter back to Ankara. In a subsequent telephone conversation Mr. Callaghan was 'pretty rough with Eçevit' (No. 45). And, later that morning, after Ankara's revision of a fresh formula he had worked out with Mr. Günes, Mr. Callaghan delivered a 'diplomatic ultimatum' warning Mr. Günes that either the Turks reverted to the original formula by 9.30 p.m. local time on the 30th, or he would leave Geneva and make the reasons for his departure publicly clear (No. 46). Mr. Callaghan also sought American assistance and, following further telephone conversations between Dr. Kissinger and Mr. Eçevit, the Turks signalled their acceptance of a formula affirming that Resolution 353 should be implemented 'in the shortest possible time' and 'within the framework of a just and lasting solution acceptable to all the parties concerned' (No. 47). On this basis a tripartite Declaration was finally agreed on the afternoon of 30 July providing for a second stage of the Conference to begin in Geneva on 8 August, with representatives of the two Cypriot communities joining those of the guarantor powers a few days later. This, however, still left undecided the extent and nature of a buffer zone separating Turkish and Greek Cypriot forces on the island (No. 49).

The Geneva Declaration also foresaw an enlarged role for UNFICYP in protecting Turkish enclaves and policing mixed Greek and Turkish Cypriot villages. But in seeking UN Security Council approval, Dr. Waldheim had first to overcome a Soviet veto (No. 50). Already in a telegram of 19 July Mr. J.A. Dobbs, Minister in the British Embassy in Moscow, had advised Mr. Callaghan that the 'overriding Soviet objective' in Cyprus would be to prevent any change in the island which could lead to an additional NATO presence in the eastern Mediterranean. And he predicted that, while the Russians would seek to exploit the crisis in order to weaken the Alliance's southern flank, unless new factors emerged, they would 'huff and puff as strenuously as usual but in concrete terms ... behave with caution' (No. 29). This proved to be the case and, despite Western fears that they might look towards introducing an Eastern contingent into UNFICYP, the Soviet delegation finally gave its support to a Resolution endorsing the Geneva Declaration on 1 August (No. 50). Nonetheless, Sir J. Killick, a Deputy Under-Secretary (DUS) and former Ambassador in Moscow, thought that 'the main Soviet aim at the moment must be to find some means of controlling events, or at least influencing them significantly' and that when the Geneva Conference reconvened they would try to make their presence felt (No. 51).

It was originally expected that although Mr. Callaghan would be present at Geneva during the first five or so days of Stage II of the talks, the dialogue would thereafter continue at official level. HMG's immediate objectives were to achieve as much progress as possible towards making the ceasefire and buffer zone arrangements stick, to give impetus to constitutional negotiations, and to establish satisfactory machinery for the continuation of discussions with periodic Ministerial involvement. In the long run, the British hoped to disengage gradually from the prominent role accorded them by the 1960 agreements and the Geneva Declaration, to avoid perpetuating UNFICYP at its present level, and to keep open their options on the SBAs. They were also convinced that the best way of reaching a new constitutional settlement was 'to do it quickly before the problem again congeal[ed]'. A steering brief prepared for the UK delegation to the talks suggested that 'HMG's basic objectives could in the right circumstances, be secured by any of the variants of double ENOSIS'. This, however, was unlikely to be achieved satisfactorily in the foreseeable future, not least because the internal situation was 'not yet right for the consolidation of the two communities in wholly separate enclaves nor [were] there natural boundaries which might provide a stable frontier'. For the moment the only feasible course seemed to be to work with Athens and Ankara 'to promote a bi-communal system, with a greater degree of Turkish Cypriot autonomy than foreseen in the 1960 Constitution and less intermingling of populations' (No. 53).

A forced transfer of the Greek Cypriot population out of the Turkish-occupied Kyrenia area appeared already to be taking place. Such evictions Mr. Olver was anxious to contest. But he also believed that the area so far taken by the Turks fell far short of their hopes and plans, and he feared that unless the negotiating momentum were kept up they might find in a local incident a pretext for resuming their advance (No. 52). There was evidence that Turkish troops had in places moved beyond their positions of 30 July, and meanwhile, according to Mr. Günes, Turkish-Cypriot villages had been abandoned by their inhabitants, and others were either occupied, or under threat of occupation, by the National Guard (No. 55). All this seemed to suggest a need for haste. On 9 August Mr. Günes impressed on Mr. Callaghan that his Government wanted an early agreement on certain principles for a 'final solution on the Cyprus problem', and that the only solution was to create within a united republic 'two (and only two) administrative autonomous regions'. He added that the present area occupied by Turkish forces constituted only one twenty-fifth of the island, and that the Turkish autonomous region he envisaged must be in northern Cyprus. For his part, Mr. Callaghan was inclined to think that there might be scope for some kind of compromise based on Mr. Clerides's suggestion for 'functional', as opposed to 'regional', federalism. Evidently anxious to avoid forcing the new administration in Athens, headed by Mr. C. Karamanlis, into a humiliating settlement, he tried to persuade Mr. Günes that progress in the Conference must depend on the Turks demonstrating their readiness to begin troop withdrawals from Cyprus. He could not, however, have been encouraged in this course by a report relayed to him from London that the Turks were planning to extend their military occupation from east of Morphou through Nicosia to Famagusta not later than 20 August and irrespective of what might be settled at Geneva (No. 57). Nor, despite Dr. Waldheim's readiness to place a 'reinforced' UNFICYP astride a fresh Turkish military advance, could Mr. Callaghan have been reassured by the advice he received from Air Vice-Marshal

F.R.L. Mellersh, Assistant Chief of the Defence Staff, that the most that could be hoped from UNFICYP was 'deterrence' and that 'any question of holding the Turks [was] out of the question'. Mr. Callaghan nevertheless requested that the withdrawal of British forces from Cyprus, including the RAF's Phantoms at Akrotiri, be halted immediately (No. 58). He explained to Mr. Hartman, whom Dr. Kissinger had sent to Geneva, that he had no 'wish to be caught napping twice', and his policy 'was for deterrence not based on bluff'. 'If', he further observed, 'British troops, albeit in blue berets, equipped with anti-tank weapons and heavy artillery, faced the Turks it would be up to the Turks to decide whether to advance or not' (No. 59).

There was a serious flaw in Mr. Callaghan's choice of tactics. As Air Vice-Marshal Mellersh pointed out, UNFICYP was not strong enough even to hinder a large-scale Turkish advance, the additional 5,000 men the force required would mean reducing British force levels in Northern Ireland and withdrawing units from West Germany, and the build-up would probably take at least a fortnight to complete (*ibid.*). It was also far from certain that the UN Security Council would sanction such an UNFICYP deployment. Mr. I. Richard, Britain's Permanent Representative to the UN at New York, found his American colleagues 'distinctly non-committal' on this point. 'There seems', he noted, 'to be a reluctance to take serious issue with the Turks which is similar to their initial reticence in condemning the Greeks' (No. 61). Already, on 6 August, Sir H. Phillips had reported from Ankara that during a recent visit Mr. Hartman had told the Turks that 'unlike some of Turkey's allies they [the Americans] had not switched to support Greece immediately Karamanlis had taken over' (No. 54). Preoccupied by US domestic politics in the wake of President Nixon's resignation, Dr. Kissinger was determined to avoid incurring the hostility of both Greece and Turkey (No. 68). In addition, he was perturbed lest the line proposed by Mr. Callaghan should reduce Mr. Eçevit's room for manoeuvre, and adversely affect his own efforts to move the Turks away from the notion of a single Turkish zone in Cyprus. As Mr. Hartman informed Mr. Callaghan on 11 August, Dr. Kissinger felt that if they 'focused on the military intentions of the Turks it would affect the whole tone of the political discussions'. None of this was to Mr. Callaghan's liking and he did little to disguise his anger. Shortly after midday on 11 August he warned Mr. Hartman that he was 'not prepared to sit around in Geneva forever, particularly if he were not getting backing from Dr. Kissinger', adding that the 'tougher you were with the Turks the more they would listen to you' and that the last time they had backed off was at Nicosia Airport when he had informed Mr. Eçevit that he was 'putting British troops in blue berets but that he was not prepared to see British troops shot up'. If there was no American backing for Britain, he might consider rejecting the Treaty of Guarantee and withdrawing from the SBAs (No. 62).

Mr. Callaghan was also apprehensive about an assertion made by Mr. Günes that the Turkish Government were considering an American proposal for a constitutional settlement in Cyprus based on the adoption of a cantonal system. This, at the very least, seemed to suggest that the Americans were not keeping the British fully informed of their dealings with the Turks. Dr. Kissinger was quick to reaffirm his support for Mr. Callaghan's efforts. Unable to contact Mr. Callaghan himself, he had Mr. Sisco telephone him during the late afternoon of the 11th in order to inform him that a 'strong message' had been sent to Mr. Eçevit, who had 'agreed to hold off' further military action. Mr. Sisco also denied that the Americans had proposed a cantonal solution. Mr. Callaghan nonetheless felt that he had been by-passed, and he made it plain to Mr. Sisco that he was 'not prepared to be dummy in the middle' (No. 63). A subsequent conversation with Mr. Günes left him less pessimistic. There was, he thought, 'just a chance that [they could] reach at least an oral understanding which might open the way to constitutional arrangements acceptable to all the parties' (No. 64), and discussions with Mr. Günes and Mr. Mavros seemed to suggest that, while the Turks were not yet ready to withdraw their forces, Athens and Ankara were prepared to await the outcome of constitutional talks between Mr. Clerides and Mr. Denktash (No. 65). But the fact that Turkish assurances regarding further military action remained conditional, only reinforced Mr. Callaghan in his view that it would 'be much better to stop them by increasing pressure before they move than trying to concert a response while they [were] on the march' (No. 68).

Greek and Turkish Cypriot aspirations were, in any case, so much at odds that the two sides could not even agree a joint press statement setting out the bases of their proposed constitutional talks. Mr. Dentash insisted that the statement include reference to a constitutional revision resulting in the creation of a Turkish federated state covering 34% of the territory of the Republic. This Mr. Clerides rejected: he was prepared only to consider an 'autonomous Turkish community with groupings of villages where possible' (Nos. 69 and 70). A proposal which Mr. Günes put to Mr. Callaghan on the evening of the 12th for a Turkish-Cypriot region in the north of Cyprus, with certain other Turkish cantons delineated within a larger Greek-Cypriot region seemed at first to offer the, admittedly small, prospect of a possible compromise (No. 71). But Mr. Günes then insisted that Turkish forces replace Greek forces in the area within 48 hours and that it be transferred to an autonomous administration. He also stated that he considered the 'Conference was at an end' and that he 'would not negotiate' (No. 72). The next day, Mr. W.T. Rodgers, the Minister of State for Defence, confirmed the substance of Air Vice-Marshal Mellersh's earlier assessment of the military balance in Cyprus: he told the Prime Minister that 'faced with Turkish strength, our own forces whether under UNFICYP control or our own, would have an impossible task if intervention meant fighting' (No. 75). In these circumstances a Greek counterproposal which conceded no more than administrative autonomy to the Turkish Cypriots and some grouping of Turkish villages seemed unlikely to suffice. Mr. Callaghan urged Mr. Clerides and Mr. Mavros to produce proposals which at least conceded the 'principle of geographical separation'—a course which he thought offered the least dangerous solution. 'They had', he added, 'to face the reality that there would be no United States military pressure, that UNFICYP would not oppose the Turkish forces and that, as a result, there was no prospect of external help against Turkish aggression' (No. 73).

During the morning of 13 August Mr. Callaghan persuaded Mr. Clerides and Mr. Mavros to consult their colleagues on the Turkish proposal. He also urged Dr. Kissinger to press Mr. Eçevit to allow the Greek and Greek Cypriot negotiators more time. But Mr. Günes who, Mr. Callaghan protested, had treated him in 'an unforgivable way', steadfastly refused requests for a 36 hour adjournment (No. 74). A meeting of the five heads of delegation which began at 6.30 p.m. on 13 August and continued, with only two breaks, until 2.15 a.m. on the 14th, failed to resolve differences. Mr. Günes maintained that it was not enough for the Conference to agree on principles and delegate detailed discussion to intercommunal machinery in Nicosia. He had, he continued, 'begun to be convinced in Geneva that the threat of diplomatic delaying tactics was looming up, and he did not want the Cyprus drama to drag on as before'. When Mr. Callaghan asked if delegates would return to Geneva on 15 August, he said nothing, and the Conference broke up. Three quarters of an hour later, Turkish forces in Cyprus resumed hostilities, and by 21 August they had occupied approximately 34% of the land area of the island (No. 76). The chances for a diplomatic solution had, as Mr. Callaghan subsequently confessed to Dr. Waldheim, 'dissolved in the face of Turkish intransigence'. Nor did the Secretary of State see any glimmer of hope for diplomatic action for the present (No. 78). Over the telephone, he told Dr. Kissinger that for the time being there would be a 'military solution', there would be a 'great exchange of population', and he concluded 'we'll then just let diplomacy take over when we see the opportunity once more' (No. 77). His immediate concern was to prevent the conflict in Cyprus from developing into a Græco-Turkish war, and to that end he declined Mr. Mavros's request for air cover for the despatch of Greek forces to Cyprus, and advised Dr. Kissinger to consider what might happen if the Turks tried to 'capitalise' on their success (No. 79).

Cyprus: postscript to Geneva

When, following the collapse of the Geneva Conference, British Ministers and officials reassessed their stance on Cyprus they did so on the assumption that talks would recommence in the not too distant future. There were grounds for hoping that Stage III of the Conference might be delayed until about 25 August. As Mr. Goodison reasoned in a draft paper of 16 August, this would allow time in which: (i) to generate international pressure on the Turks; (ii) to bring them to appreciate their difficult position in Cyprus; (iii) to persuade the Greeks and Greek Cypriots, including Archbishop Makarios, to accept the need for bi-regional federation (now regarded in the FCO as the 'best solution' to the Cyprus problem); and (iv) to permit *de facto* changes facilitating a radical separation of the two communities. But Mr. Goodison believed Britain's attendance at Stage III of the talks must depend on the Turks agreeing in advance to negotiate on their territorial demands and to implement relevant parts of the Geneva Declaration. The Greeks and Turks would have to be prepared for 'horse-trading on the size of the Turkish zone' and its reduction in area to something rather smaller than 34% of the Republic. A lasting settlement on this basis would, the FCO hoped, reduce the risk of future Græco-Turkish squabbles, allow Britain to withdraw from its prominent position under the 1960 agreements, and avoid perpetuating UNFICYP, and the British contribution to it, at the existing level (No. 80). Mr. Callaghan was, however, also of the opinion that it was not to Turkey's advantage 'to have no settlement and allow the situation to polarise'. There was, he thought, the danger of the Turks being drawn into ever greater responsibilities in Cyprus which must prove an intolerable burden to them, could drag them into a guerrilla war, and might lead to Soviet interference (No. 81).

It was equally apparent that the longer negotiations were delayed, the more reluctant the Turks might become to make concessions. But, as Sir R. Hooper explained, the Greeks were adamant that they would not negotiate under duress: Mr. Karamanlis and his colleagues could not 'be fooled for a third time and survive as a government'. The Turks must first make troop withdrawals and indicate their readiness to accept for the Turkish Cypriot community substantially less than one third of the Republic. For his part, Mr. Mavros seemed sympathetic towards a Soviet proposal for the summoning under UN auspices of a conference on Cyprus at which Security Council members, Cyprus, Greece and Turkey, would be represented. With a view to narrowing the gap between the Greeks and Turks, Mr. Callaghan considered despatching a Minister of State to Athens, Ankara and Nicosia. However, he wanted first to be sure of Dr. Kissinger's support and, with a view to winning this and discussing short-term tactics and long-term consequences with the Americans, he sent Sir J. Killick and Mr. M.O'D.B. Alexander, his Assistant Private Secretary, to Washington (No. 83). During their meeting with Dr. Kissinger on 27 August they found him less than enthusiastic about committing the United States to a 'major heave' on behalf of further British mediation. The Greek Government had just announced its intention of withdrawing from NATO's integrated command and, evidently still smarting from the personal criticism levelled at him in Greece and elsewhere, Dr. Kissinger was reluctant to appear to share responsibility for a mission which he believed could all too easily fail. 'In the Cyprus dispute', he observed, 'he was not aware that either side was yet ready to make the investment necessary for settlement. Accordingly, an initiative which represented a last final effort was unlikely to succeed.' He suspected that while the Turks might be persuaded to give up some of the territory they had occupied, and to agree to substantial troop withdrawals and a reasonable solution on refugees, these might nonetheless be turned down by the Greeks (No. 84).

Sir H. Phillips shared Dr. Kissinger's belief that the Turks saw time as being on their side (No. 85) and, although Dr. Waldheim thought there was 'evidence ... of a slight narrowing of the gap on both sides' (No. 86), Mr. Callaghan concluded that the time was 'not ripe for a Minister to visit the area'. But he was still worried that events might take a turn for the worse. 'There is', he reminded Mr. Olver, 'a danger of military moves by the Turks on the island, of the declaration of the establishment of an autonomous Turkish Cypriot region in terms which would precipitate strong Greek Cypriot reactions, of an increase in guerilla activities and of further developments in the refugee problem. There is also danger of ill-judged Greek action' (No. 87). Moreover, he was perturbed by the situation in which he found himself. At a Heads of Mission meeting on 10 September he confesed his dislike of 'responsibility without power' and his readiness to move out from the central position on Cyprus before the next round of talks. Despite its SBAs Britain had appeared impotent in handling developments in Cyprus, and the Americans had been unwilling to put effective pressure on the Turks. All, however, he and his officials seemed able to agree on was that Britain should continue to encourage discussions between Mr. Clerides and Mr. Denktash on the problems arising from the crisis. A major British initiative seemed in any case unlikely given the prospect of an autumn General Election (No. 89).

In a personal message to Dr. Kissinger of 11 September Mr. Callaghan emphasised the need for 'effective quiet diplomacy' aimed at encouraging the Clerides/Denktash dialogue. He hoped that Athens and Archbishop Makarios would give 'this tender plant ... a fair wind, and do nothing to put it at risk', and that Ankara would allow Mr. Denktash a 'bit of real negotiating latitude'. But he remained worried that the Turks might take further provocative action, such as the declaration of an independent Turkish Cypriot republic, which would render Mr. Clerides's task impossible (No. 90). There was also, as Mr. M. Perceval of the British High Commission in Nicosia speculated, the possibility that the Turks might resort to further military action in Cyprus ostensibly aimed at freeing Turkish Cypriots trapped in the southern part of the island. Indeed, with some 8,500 Turkish Cypriot refugees at Episkopi in the Western SBA, the British could hardly ignore this problem. On 13 September Mr. Olver suggested to Mr. Clerides, one of whose immediate objectives was to persuade the Turks to withdraw from New Famagusta and to permit the return of its Greek Cypriot inhabitants, that he might attempt to reach an accord with Mr. Denktash which would allow Turkish refugees to go to Turkey in return for Turkish concessions on Greek Cypriot refugees. This, however, Mr. Clerides rejected on the grounds that it would undermine his whole negotiating strategy (No. 91). For his part, Mr. Callaghan doubted if much leverage could be exerted on the Turks over refugees. 'Greek Cypriots', he told Mr. S. Roussos, Greece's new Ambassador in London, 'might find it more important to aim for a withdrawal by the Turkish army. Once there was a settlement there would be a good case for such a withdrawal' (No. 92).

Greek politicians seem not to have had any great interest in achieving a settlement in Cyprus before the holding of their own elections elections, scheduled for 17 November. 'Domestically', noted Mr. F.B. Richards, Britain's new Ambassador in Athens, 'it would be easier for almost any Greek Government too endure a *fait accompli* in Cyprus rather than to endorse an apparently inequitable division of the island by signing an agreement with the Turkish Government' (No. 94). Meanwhile, Greece's future relationship with its NATO allies remained uncertain. Mr. Karamanlis had indicated his intention to remove the 'NATO assigned' status from Greek forces, but as Mr. R.J.T. McLaren, the Deputy Head of Western Organisations Department, explained, this was in practical terms only of marginal significance since the majority of the forces concerned were in peacetime under Greek national command (No. 88). There was still the possibility that the Soviet Union might seek to exploit this situation to its own advantage. The Greeks certainly seemed willing to give the impression of harmony with the Russians in public in order to emphasise their disenchantment with NATO. Mr. J.L. Bullard, the Head of Eastern European and Soviet Department, nonetheless considered it unlikely that the Soviet Government would shift from their policy of cautious cultivation of good relations with both Greece and Turkey, particularly as on 16 October the US Congress had reacted to developments in Cyprus by insisting on the suspension of American military aid to Turkey from 10 December. 'Soviet fear of being excluded from the making of a Cyprus settlement will', Mr. Bullard observed, 'have abated for the time being since no progress is being made in any case. They are not being upstaged, since the stage is empty and dark' (No. 95). Moreover, although when in late October the UN General Assembly debated the Cyprus problem there was strong opposition to a return to the Geneva forum, the Russians had no success in pushing their earlier proposal for an international conference (No. 97).

Mr. Bullard assumed, on the basis of a report from the British High Commission in Nicosia, that Soviet objectives in Cyprus were to prevent partition and to remove the British bases (No. 95). In the autumn of 1974 the latter seemed likely to come about without any Soviet action or pressure. Already in March, shortly after the incoming Labour Government's announcement of a review of current defence commitments and capabilities, the FCO had begun a re-examination of the likely policy implications of a decision to relinquish British military facilities in Cyprus (No. 10). But it was discussion during Stage I of the Geneva talks of the possible demilitarisation of Cyprus which stimulated Mr. Callaghan's interest in the abandonment of the SBAs. A paper of 29 July, prepared by the Defence Policy Staff of the Chiefs of Staff (COS) Committee, emphasised the strategic value of the SBAs to Britain and its allies. In addition, they were judged to exercise a 'stabilising influence' in the island, and without political stability in Cyprus NATO's southern flank could be 'seriously endangered'. The paper, nevertheless, also repeated advice offered earlier by the COS that, in the context of the defence review, 'Cyprus, in common with all other Mediterranean and non-NATO commitments, was not so strategically vital to the UK, despite its importance to the cohesion of NATO's Southern Flank, as to merit inclusion [in the Critical Level of forces judged necessary to maintain confidence in the continuing credibility of Alliance strategy] at the expense of support for the key areas of NATO' (No. 44).

The failure of the Stage II talks at Geneva to establish the basis for a negotiated settlement in Cyprus seemed only to confirm FCO officials in the logic of this course. Sir G. Arthur, DUS responsible for superintending Defence Department noted in a draft paper of 20 August: 'Recent events have shown that from a purely national point of view the SBAs are more a liability than an asset.' Britain's presence in Cyprus had led both Greeks and Turks to expect more vigorous British action than was forthcoming, and Sir G. Arthur observed, so tong as there was tension, the SBAs would be vulnerable for Britain would 'always be caught in the political cross fire'. Moreover, he argued, the military importance of the SBAs to Britain was declining and might soon vanish. The force of Vulcan strike aircraft based there and declared to CENTO could probably be withdrawn after consultation with the Iranian Government, and logistical support for UNFICYP would have to be provided without Britain. Only the need to deny Cyprus to the Soviet Union, and the possible impact a British withdrawal would have on the Anglo-American relationship, seemed therefore to stand in the way of a British withdrawal. With this Mr. Callaghan was largely in agreement. 'I see no future in Cyprus for us', he noted, '[s]o let's not be too long in getting out.' On 9 September the Cabinet's Defence and Oversea Policy Committee agreed that HMG's 'preferred course would be the total withdrawal of [British] forces from Cyprus which should, if possible, be presented in the context of a satisfactory settlement to the Cyprus problem'. But Mr. Callaghan urged that before reaching a final conclusion they must first consult the Americans (No. 82) and, after further consideration of the matter by FCO and MoD officials, Sir J. Hunt, the Cabinet Secretary, visited Washington on 12 November for consultations with Dr. Kissinger. The latter was 'strongly opposed' to the withdrawal of the British presence in Cyprus, particularly in view of the 'relative decline of Western influence' in the eastern Mediterranean (No. 98). And following a personal message from Dr. Kissinger, in which he argued that the elimination of the British SBAs could encourage the Soviet Union and 'damage Western flexibility to act in unpredictable situations', Mr. Callaghan responded on 26 November by assuring Washington that in the circumstances HMG would not proceed with its 'preferred policy'. He added that 'in matters of this sort, we continue to give full weight to the views and interests of the United States wherever these can, even at some cost, be reconciled with our own' (No. 10).

There was in the meantime no progress towards restarting negotiations between Ankara and Athens on Cyprus. In the run-up to a general election on 17 November, the Greek Government was reluctant to accept the principle of a biregional federation, and the collapse of Mr. Eçevit's coalition Government and his replacement by Professor S. Irmak introduced a new element of uncertainty (No. 99). In Sir H. Phillip's opinion Cyprus offered the Turks 'some inconvenience', but was 'not a serious burden'. They would, he observed in a telegram of 21 November, see no reason to give much away, 'especially at a time when Cyprus [was] the only unifying factor among the political parties'. The prospect of Archbishop Makarios's return to Cyprus on 7 December was an additional complication. He was deeply distrusted by the Turks, and Mr. Olver predicted that Mr. Clerides would resign if the Archbishop returned without first 'accepting a realistic negotiating line' (No. 100). Discussions in London with Archbishop Makarios and Mr. Clerides left Mr. Callaghan under the impression that the former was thinking in a much longer perspective than the latter (No. 104). Indeed, British and American officials were perturbed by what they perceived as the Archbishop's 'hankering for a continuance of the present situation' on the grounds that it strengthened his own position, and Mr. Callaghan was not prepared to intervene until the parties were readier to talk (No. 103). During talks in Athens with Mr. Clerides, Archbishop Makarios was persuaded to accept the principle of geographical federation. But as Mr. Bitsios, the new Greek Foreign Minister, indicated to Mr. Callaghan, the Greeks were reluctant to concede more than a cantonal settlement with territorial divisions approximating in size to the respective percentages of population (Nos. 104 and 105).

Intercommunal talks between Mr. Clerides and Mr. Denktash resumed on 14 January 1975 only to be suspended on 13 February following the proclamation of a Turkish Federated State of North Cyprus. This move dampened any lingering hopes for an early settlement of the Cyprus problem. A Joint Intelligence Committee (JIC) paper forecast the continuation of an 'uneasy peace ... on the island, with the Turkish mainland continuing to consolidate its hold on the North of the island and with the various Greek Cypriot factions ... continuing to present a low profile'. Meanwhile, HMG's decision to authorise the transfer to Turkey of some 9,400 Turkish Cypriot refugees from the Western SBA led to violent anti-British demonstrations in Athens and Nicosia, and doubtless contributed to the 'myth, already firmly established in Greek Cypriot minds, that Britain ha[d] aided an abetted Turkey during the crisis'. Mr. Callaghan evidently continued to have misgivings about a situation which left Britain with responsibility, but without power. If faced with Greek Cypriot opposition to Britain remaining in the SBAs, then he was prepared once more to consider withdrawing British forces from Cyprus. For the moment, however, the JIC paper concluded, against 'a reasonably peaceful background, apart from holding the ring and advising moderation on both sides, Britain seem[ed] unlikely to be able significantly to influence events in Cyprus over the next twelve months' (No. 105).

Portugal: responding to revolution

The British Government was hardly better placed to exercise a decisive influence on political developments elsewhere on NATO's southern flank. Almost three months before the *coup* against Archbishop Makarios, Portugal had been shaken by the military toppling of Dr. M.J. de Neves Alves Caetano, the successor to Dr. A. de Oliveira Salazar as Prime Minister in an authoritarian régime whose origins could be traced back to the 1920s. During the morning of 25 April 1974 elements of the Portuguese army seized power in the name of the Armed Forces Movement (AFM) and swept away what Mr. G.E. Clark, First Secretary in the British Embassy in Lisbon, described as '45 years of government by stultification' (No. 106). Mr. Wilson and Mr. Callaghan welcomed the prospect of a democratic Portugal and were quick to recognise the newly-established Junta of National Salvation (JNS) headed by General A.S. Ribeiro de Spínola. In opposition the Labour Party had been particularly critical of Dr. Caetano's rule in Lisbon and his government's repressive policies in Portugal's African territories. Moreover, the sympathy of the Portuguese colonial administration in Mozambique for the White minority government in Rhodesia had impeded British efforts to impose political change upon the rebel colony. Dr. M. Soares, the General Secretary of the Portuguese Socialist Party, was therefore received with considerable enthusiasm when he visited London in May. During a meeting at No. 10 Downing Street Mr. Callaghan expressed HMG's readiness to assist the new government in Lisbon both with administrative reform and in the process of decolonisation (No. 107). But British diplomats in Lisbon were from the first uncertain as to whether the JNS would be capable of contending 'with the forces which they [had] unleashed' (No. 106), especially when the lifting of the rigid political constraints to which most Portuguese had grown accustomed was followed by a wave of demonstrations and industrial unrest which threatened to undermine confidence in the country's economy.

Portugal's interim constitutional arrangements seemed also to offer plenty of scope for institutional in-fighting. Although General Spínola assumed office as President on 15 May and a provisional government, led by Professor Adelino da Palma Carlos and including Communist Ministers, was in place by the 17th, the JNS and AFM continued to exercise a supervisory role. Mr. N.C.C. Trench, Britain's newly-appointed Ambassador in Lisbon, compared the prevailing administrative and political confusion to an ant-heap which had just been broken open: 'Frenzied activity is in progress and ants are scurrying in all directions, but it is not always possible for the observer to discern the pattern that directs their movements, and it is still more difficult to decide what is going on in the sections that have not been exposed to the light of day' (No. 109). Differences over the pace of constitutional reform led in July to the formation of a new and more left-orientated administration, led by Brigadier (subsequently General) Vasco dos Santos Gonçalves, an officer of distinctly Marxist leanings. In the meantime the difficulties encountered by the Lisbon Government in its endeavour to shed its responsibilities in Africa threatened to upset Portugal's fragile political equilibrium. General Spínola, essentially a conservative reformer, was confronted by radicals within the AFM, some of whom had come to identify with the doctrines of the African liberation movements they had once opposed. It was a situation which appeared ripe for exploitation by the Communists and extremist factions of the left. Matters came to a head when on the night of 27/28 September supporters of the left-wing parties, led by the Communists, physically prevented a demonstration in Lisbon in support of the President. Civil war was avoided, but General Spínola resigned, the whole apparatus of government was purged of those not in sympathy with the aims of the left, and the right and centre-right were, in Mr. Trench's words, left 'leaderless and in disarray'. Dr. Soares, who had been Foreign Minister since May, assured Mr. Trench that Portugal's foreign policy remained unchanged. But the Ambassador was less certain. 'So far as NATO is concerned', he opined, 'one is forced to wonder how long the Communist Party, confident in its newly proven power, will continue to acquiesce in Portuguese membership' (No. 110).

The FCO did not consider a Communist takeover in Portugal inevitable. An Office meeting, chaired by the Permanent Under-Secretary (PUS) Sir T. Brimelow, concluded on 25 October that 'the outlook was confused and murky', but that 'it would be wrong and counter-productive to regard Portugal as a lost cause'. On the contrary, Mr. D.C. Thomas, First Secretary in the South West European Department (SWED), thought that, 'within the limits of prudence', they 'should seek to give the Portuguese Government the benefit of the doubt, responding as positively as [they could] to their requests for co-operation and assistance and demonstrating [their] confidence in them, with the aim of thereby of increasing [Britain's] ability to influence their actions'. Mr. Thomas personally favoured a 'positive effort to educate them in [Britain's] assessment of the nature of the Soviet threat' by means of a Ministerial or official visit, efforts to strengthen democratic parties in Portugal, and assistance to the nascent Portuguese trade unions in order to prevent them falling under Communist control (No. 111). It was partly with a view to thus encouraging democracy in Portugal that the Secretary of State visited Lisbon on 6-7 February 1975. But following Mr. Callaghan's return to London, Mr. Trench hastened to caution him against the possibility that he might have derived too favourable an impression from the moderate and reassuring views expressed by the political leaders he had met. 'Portugal', he observed, 'can show a more sombre face, and I would not want you to carry home a conclusion that anxieties about free elections and the nature of the future régime in this country were things of the past' (No. 114). Indeed, following an abortive military *coup* on 11 March, in which General Spínola's associates were implicated, Portugal lurched violently to the left. The AFM established a Supreme Council of the Revolution with wide executive powers; General Vasco Gonçalves, was granted full powers to restructure his Cabinet; and new measures were announced to hasten the socialisation of the economy. The AFM thereby acquired a more permanent basis in the Portuguese political process; the Portuguese Communist Party (PCP) and its allies gained control of key ministries; and the communist-dominated news media intensified its attacks on the West in general and the United States in particlular.

None of this augured well for elections for a Constituent Assembly which were due to be held in the spring, and Dr. Soares, who, though he lost his post as Foreign Minister, remained in the Portuguese Cabinet as Minister without Portfolio, was particularly pessimistic when he discussed matters with Mr. Trench on 13 March. It seemed quite possible that the West would not be able to halt the slide towards a fully-established left-wing military régime. Yet, as Mr. S.J. Barrett, the Head of SWED, pointed out in a minute of 17 March it was not easy for HMG to strike the right balance between necessary reservations about the policy of the Portuguese military leadership and their extreme left-wing allies, and the need not to leave the field wide open for forces opposed to democracy (No. 115). Dr. Soares appears meanwhile to have exploited his links with other European Socialist leaders to alert them of the prospect of Soviet meddling in Portugal (No. 116). At a private meeting of NATO representatives in Brussels on 22 March the West German spokesman even went so far as to suggest that Portugal 'was about to be taken as Czechoslovakia had been after the war'. The US State Department urged NATO allies to agree on parallel *démarches* to the Portuguese Government, expressing their concern about the 'leftist concentration of power' and signs that a 'radical military dictatorship' was being established in Lisbon, and indicating that this could adversely affect Portugal's relationship with its allies. Consideration was also give to the possibility of making direct representations to the Russians (No. 117). This Mr. Callaghan opposed and, on Mr. Trench's advice, he argued against any action which could be regarded as interference in the composition of the Portuguese Government and whose effect might be counterproductive. Rather, Mr. Trench was instructed to inform either Portugal's President or Prime Minister of HMG's interest in the forthcoming elections, and to express the hope that no change would be made which would 'prevent these from being held in a stable and balanced atmosphere' (No. 118).

General F. da Costa Gomes, General Spínola's successor as President, assured Mr. Trench on 24 March that the AFM was determined to hold elections 'in an atmosphere of tranquillity and freedom' and that, once formed, the new Government 'would have no more influence on the elections than the previous one, since political power resided in the Revolutionary-Council' (*ibid.*). In the words of Mr. Barrett, Portugal presented 'the picture of a left-wing military régime working closely with the PCP and its allies while maintaining some of the trappings of democracy' (No. 120). Moreover, British officials could not neglect the possibility of a further rapid deterioration in the political situation in Portugal, which might impact seriously upon relations with its allies. The news that the Portuguese Government was considering a Soviet request for merchant fleet refuelling facilities in Madeira seemed symptomatic of its improving relations with Moscow. In a note of 26 March the MoD's Defence Policy Staff concluded that although the withdrawal of Portuguese forces from NATO would have 'only a limited effect on the military capabilities of the Alliance', it could have a 'major psychological impact' with NATO out of all proportion to Portugal's force contribution. And its effect on US plans for the military reinforcement of the Southern Region 'would aggravate the recent deterioration in the Alliance's posture on the Southern Flank'. Likewise, the Defence Policy Staff reasoned, if the Soviet Union were able to use facilities in Portugal, this would initially threaten NATO's sea lanes in a period of hostilities (No. 119). British diplomats were, nevertheless, uncertain about the extent of Soviet involvement in Portugal. It seemed probable, Mr. Barrett observed in a submission of 1 April, that events in Portugal would 'continue to be home-grown rather than imported from the Soviet Union', though he assumed that the Russians might 'be able to exercise a restraining influence on the PCP's policy and tactics' (No. 120).

One option open to Britain and its principal NATO allies in dealing with this situation was that of seeking to persuade the Russians that Communist subversion in Portugal might result in a setback for *détente* in East-West relations. As the documents in Volume II of this series make clear, the Soviet leadership was anxious to ensure that the then current Conference on Security and Cooperation in Europe (CSCE) should be concluded with a summit level Stage III meeting in the summer of 1975. The West Germans held the view that Stage III might be unattainable if matters worsened in Lisbon. But Mr. Barrett was less certain that the West would have to go that far. He suggested that before Stage III HMG should make the point to the Soviet Union that a Communist takeover in Lisbon or Portugal's departure from NATO 'would be bad for détente', and that at Stage III or after they should be ready to draw it to Moscow's attention that the Soviet Union's policy towards Portugal would be regarded as a 'test of their commitment to détente' (*ibid.*). Others too doubted the wisdom of using a threat to abandon the CSCE to restrain the Russians from real, or supposed, interference in Portugal's domestic affairs. Sir J. Killick, himself a former Ambassador in Moscow, noted on Mr. Barrett's submission: 'CSCE now has in my view a momentum and significance of its own and is not something which can effectively be used as a bargaining counter in this way. I would wish to keep open the option of using the third stage of CSCE as a forum in which we might ventilate developments in Portugal to our advantage.' Britain's chief concern must, he felt, be not only to void appearing to express 'no confidence' in Portugal, but also to avoid the charge of having failed to do all it could. If the Russians were to secure bases in Portugal there was, as Mr. Callaghan indicated, no obvious answer as to what the West should do (No. 121).

The victory of Portugal's moderate left in Constituent Assembly elections on 25 April seemed to suggest that Western observers had less cause for pessimism. The Socialists won nearly 38% of the vote, the Popular Democrats 26%, and the PCP no more than 13%. But a pre-election 'Constitutional Pact' meant that the AFM and the Supreme Council of the Revolution retained their wide-ranging powers. Dr. Kissinger, with whom Mr. Callaghan discussed Portugal on 7 May, remained 'exceptionally gloomy' about the situation there. He thought the country 'was doomed to go Communist', and was particularly concerned about the effect on other countries with large Communist parties, especially France and Italy, if an increasingly neutralist Portugal stayed on in NATO (No. 125). The Communist exclusion of the Socialists from participation in the May Day celebrations in Lisbon, the subsequent closure of the main Socialist newspaper in Lisbon, and the decision of Dr. Soares and his Socialist colleagues to boycott future Cabinet meetings were hardly reassuring (No. 127). Nevertheless, as Mr. H.T. Morgan (AUS) explained to a US diplomat in London, while HMG and its European allies and partners were unhappy about the situation, they 'could think of nothing better to do in practice'. 'Basically', he continued, 'we were hoping to help maintain Portuguese links with the West, and give some support to the moderates in the political parties of the AFM until the military leadership began to come to terms with the facts of life and therefore to be disillusioned with the Communists' (No. 128). In this respect, the British were not wholly at one with the Americans, who seemed at times to favour Portugal's withdrawal from NATO. Other allies were also more openly critical of Portugal than Britain. At a NATO summit in May the British 'took a much more oblique and restrained line about the application of the democratic principle in the area of the southern flank of NATO while the others put much more bluntly the question whether a dictatorship of the Left could remain within the Alliance' (No. 128).

A JIC Report of 26 June highlighted the problems 'an insecure and politically unreliable Portugal' posed for the Alliance. Its expulsion from the Alliance would, the Report concluded, 'be likely to accelerate the unravelling of the alliance, especially on the southern flank'—a prospect which might not seem so remote 'in a post-CSCE atmosphere of détente'. Meanwhile, political developments in Portugal suggested that the AFM was likely to remain in power, but that it might not be able to control the economic and social consequences of the revolution it was trying to bring about (No. 131). On 9 July the AFM Assembly published radical proposals, which in Mr. Trench's words, called for the 'complete purging of the state apparatus, its decentralisation and the creation of a new apparatus on a popular base in the interests of the working masses'. These threatened severely to curtail the functions of the Constituent Assembly and political parties, and soon afterwards Dr. Soares announced that the Socialists were leaving the Government. The Popular Democrats also withdrew from power. There was, Dr. Soares told Mr. Trench, 'an almost total breakdown of governmental authority' (No. 132), and on 22 July he sent a clandestine message to the British Embassy warning that he was expecting a left-wing *coup* within the next few days, and threatening that he was prepared in those circumstances to start a civil war. On the following day he also asked that Mr. Callaghan inform Mr. Brezhnev that a CSCE summit must depend on the Russians desisting from encouraging a Communist takeover (No. 135). Western diplomats assumed that Moscow was financing the Portuguese Communists and that the Soviet Union was therefore in a position to influence both them and elements within the AFM. But as Mr. I.J.M. Sutherland, Britain's Minister in Moscow, pointed out in a telegram of 18 July there was no 'evidence that could be used to prove this incontrovertibly' (No. 134). And in the absence of 'useable evidence' of Soviet interference, Mr. Callaghan believed that 'to hold up Stage III would itself be seen as intervention in Portuguese internal affairs' (No. 135).

Both the British and French Governments were, however, determined to use the CSCE summit at Helsinki to impress on the Russians their concern about the situation in Portugal. In conversation with Mr. Brezhnev, Mr. Wilson stated that the situation there was one 'test of *détente*' (Volume II, No. 138). He also used the summit to impress on President Costa Gomes his concern that the 'freely expressed will of the Portuguese people was being rejected'. The President's response was less than reassuring (No. 136). Nonetheless, the formation of a new Portuguese Government on 8 August in which all the new Ministers were either Communists or supporters of affiliated parties provoked widespread disturbances. The Communists were forced onto the defensive, pressure mounted for the removal of the Prime Minister General Vasco Gonçalves, and by 22 August the FCO was already considering how it could best persuade the European Community (EC) to salvage democracy in Portugal by assisting its ailing economy. 'We are', noted Mr. R.H. Baker, Assistant Head of SED, 'too poor to do much ourselves ... We should therefore be ready to encourage our allies to help. The Germans and the French are the key' (No. 138). But the British were cautious about joining the Americans and other allies in *démarches* to President Costa Gomes in support of General Vasco Gonçalves's opponents. 'We do not wish to omit any action which might promote democracy in Portugal', commented Sir

T. Brimelow, 'But we do not want to take the action proposed by the Americans if its effect is likely to strengthen the Communist hands by an appearance of Western threats.' In the end a *démarche* proved irrelevant since on the evening of 29 August, before Mr. Trench had the opportunity to act in support of his US colleague, General Vasco Gonçalves was replaced as Prime Minister by Admiral J.B. Pinheiro de Azevedo (No. 139).

A prolonged dispute over General Vasco Gonçalves's future role delayed the formation of the sixth provisional Government until 19 September. But the new administration appeared to mark the end of Portugal's drift towards the extreme left, and the distribution of Government portfolios more accurately reflected party support in the Constituent Assembly elections than had previously been the case. Its programme emphasised the importance of democratic freedoms and practices, pluralism in the media and the replacement of unrepresentative local authorities. It, nonetheless, had to face up to the task of tackling Portugal's severe economic problems, wresting power away from the Communists in the trade unions, and restoring discipline in the armed services. Indeed, as Mr. Trench had reported in a despatch of 17 September, although it was generally agreed that the dangers of a 'Communist takeover by stealth' had been averted, there remained the possibility that the Communists would 'try to achieve by force what they [had] failed to achieve by legitimate (or quasi-legitimate) means' (No. 141). The domination of the media by factions and parties of the extreme left, Communist-instigated occupations of farms and foreign-owned properties, and continuing industrial unrest, culminating in mid-November in demonstration by striking construction workers and a thirty-six hour siege of Lisbon's Parliament building, seemed to make this only too apparent. Fortunately for the forces of moderation in Portugal, a left-incited mutiny on 25 November failed to win mass popular support, and the Government was able, with the assistance of loyal forces, to suppress the attempted *coup* (No. 144).

Both the degree of Communist involvement in these events and the extent of Moscow's commitment to revolutionary change in Portugal remained uncertain. Dr. Soares was convinced that the Communist Party was the 'main instigator' of the mutiny: British diplomats were not. They had little doubt that the Communists had been fomenting disaffection in the armed forces and that had the mutiny succeeded, their leadership would have been ready to exploit it. 'But', Mr. Goodison recounted in a letter of 12 January 1976, 'we judge that the Soviet Union would not favour civil war in Portugal, given the damage which this could do to its détente image and to the prospects of other Western Communist Parties, and we therefore believe the Russians will have advised the PCP against fomenting insurrection, as distinct from disaffection' (*ibid.*). An article published four months earlier in *Pravda* by the communist theoretician, Mr. K.I. Zarodov, suggested otherwise. He criticised those Communist parties abroad which were prepared to 'dissolve' themselves in alliance with other parties of the left and argued that the only way socialism was through the hegemony of the proletariat. The article and Mr. Brezhnev's subsequent meeting with Mr. Zarodov were interpreted in the FCO as no more than a reassertion of the authority of Soviet Communist party in a confused political situation (Volume III, No. 81). British officials could not, however, afford to ignore the Soviet Union's proclivity for meddling when the prospects for radical political change elsewhere offered opportunities for advancing the Communist cause in western Europe (No. 140).

Whither Spain

Ever since the fall of Dr. Caetano's régime British officials had found cause to speculate on the possible impact of developments in Portugal upon its neighbour, Spain. Supporters of General Franco's authoritarian rule could hardly derive any satisfaction from the revolutionary changes taking place in Lisbon. As Sir J. Russell, Britain's Ambassador in Madrid, remarked in a telegram of 29 April 1974, they henceforth had to reckon with the spread of the liberal infection. 'The wall', he added, 'is too near for the writing not to be alarming.' Yet, Spain and Portugal were very different countries. In a despatch of 10 December 1974, Sir J. Russell's successor, Mr. C.D. Wiggin, explained that Spain now had a 'vast middle class ... with a lot to lose', the army had not had to 'endure a colonial war of Portuguese proportions', and, at a guess, the bulk of the military could be categorised as 'comparatively moderate reformers'. However, General Franco's ill-health and uncertainty over his future role, the uneven pace of liberal reform, the consequences of the energy crisis and the onset of world economic recession, and the fragmentation of the non-communist left, all threatened to imperil Spain's eventual transition to democracy. To encourage progress in that direction, Mr. Wiggin recommended that the British should be 'more adventurous in [their] contact with Spaniards', keeping in touch with the 'democratic opposition', expanding contacts with '*de facto* oppositionists' within the establishment, and developing 'contacts with the military, particularly the middle and junior officer ranks'. Although it was evident that this latter proposal would meet with some resistance within the Labour movement in Britain, there was a good deal of sympathy for Mr. Wiggin's ideas amongst FCO officials. 'I think', noted Sir J. Killick, 'our experience in Portugal has taught us that there are serious disadvantages in having only a narrow range of "opposition" contacts at a time when fundamental change takes place' (No. 113).

The Americans were also keen to make preparations for the political changes in Spain which must almost inevitably follow General Franco's death or departure from office. Since November they had been engaged in negotiations with Madrid for a renewal of the executive agreement which allowed the US access to military facilities in Spain. The current agreement was due to expire in September 1975, and the Spanish authorities wanted arrangements which would provide Spain with some form of associate membership of NATO. According to Mr. H. Bergold, US Deputy Assistant Secretary of Defense, those concerned with these negotiations in Madrid 'wanted to get Spanish policy on a firmly Atlantic/European course before General Franco went'. Mr. Callaghan was, however, only too well aware of the political difficulties, including Anglo-Spanish differences over Gibraltar, which stood in the way of HMG coming to terms with the present régime in Spain, and he was not prepared to do anything explicit before General Franco's departure. The most he would consider was contingency planning at official level with the Americans in order to prepare for that eventuality (Nos. 123 and 124). During talks with Dr. Kissinger in Washington on 7 May 1975 Mr. Callagahan agreed that Sir P. Ramsbotham and Mr. Sisco might discuss closer relations with Spain in a post-Franco era, but 'on the basis that the point should be got across to the Spanish that there would be all to play for if Franco could be got rid of in the near future'. For the moment, he wished Britain to be active in its contacts with Spain, while excluding military contacts and reserving Ministerial contacts for careful consideration (No. 126).

The British Government was not alone amongst the European allies in resisting US pressure for some explicit linkage between Spain and NATO. At a Ministerial meeting of NATO's Defence Policy Committee on 22-23 May the Danish, Dutch and Norwegian Defence Ministers argued that any hint of association between Spain and NATO would produce a very hostile reaction in their countries (No. 130). The British and US Ambassadors in Madrid nonetheless engaged in discussions on future policies towards Spain, and Mr. Wiggin persisted in urging the FCO to accept the idea of contacts between the British and Spanish armed services. Indeed, in a submission of 14 July Mr. Goodison argued in favour of seeking 'unofficial ways' to build up contacts with the Spanish military. 'Though', he observed, 'the Secretary of State is surely right in saying that they are unlikely to emulate the military in Portugal, they will nevertheless have the last word on many important decisions, particularly the wide range of crucial matters, such as whether the Communists should be allowed to operate as a legal party, that will have a direct bearing on the maintenance of public order.' This continued to meet with a cool response from Ministers. Mr. Hattersley was wholly opposed to the idea, 'partly because in covert operations of this kind the possible gains rarely outweigh penalties of discovery' (No. 133). But developments in Portugal and General Franco's evident frailty seem to have influenced Ministerial thinking, and by 12 August Mr. Hattersley was beginning to wonder if HMG was 'right to stand so aloof from Spain' (No. 136). Even so, the Americans remained far more ready than their European allies to envisage closer ties with Spain, and at a private meeting of NATO Permanent Representatives on 7 November their representative insisted that at Madrid the US 'would urge the necessity of gradual liberalisation' (No. 142).

General Franco's death on 20 November 1975 made progress towards democracy more likely in Spain. This, however, was unlikely to occur overnight and, as Mr. R.A. Hibbert (AUS) argued in a minute of 1 December, there would 'have to be some encouraging signs from Spain before there [could] be encouraging words from Britain'. King Juan Carlos, General Franco's nominated successor, had, as Mr. Hibbert recognised, a 'very hard row to hoe' and was unlikely to achieve anything unless he steered 'a course which, while disappointing everybody, disappoint[ed] nobody more than they [could] bear' (No. 143). Sir J. Killick, who had recently been appointed Britain's Permanent Representative to NATO, was doubtless correct when he surmised that 'developments in Portugal had created a certain disposition in London to move as quickly as possible towards the establishment of working relations with the new Spanish Government' (No. 145). Nevertheless, Mr. Callaghan was remarkably cautious in responding to the gradualist approach of King Juan Carlos's Ministers to the liberalisation of Spain's political institutions. He was evidently uncertain as to where their path of controlled evolutionary change would lead, and he was reluctant to give whole-hearted support to Madrid's efforts to align itself more closely with the other powers of Western Europe. And while the prospect of a democratic Spain suggested that there might be scope for an eventual solution to the long-standing dispute over Gibraltar, British diplomats were not overly optimistic about resolving the issue (Nos. 113, 145 and 1486). During a meeting with Sr. J.M. de Areilza, Spain's new Foreign Minister, on 2 March 1976, Mr. Callaghan warned him with regard to public opinion in Britain that 'it would be wrong to under-estimate the extent of, and how formidable and deep rooted were opposition to a non-democratic Spain' (No. 148). It was perhaps a measure of the extent to which the tensions on NATO's southern flank had eased, that in their dealings with Madrid the British were probably more influenced by Spain's Civil War of the 1930s than Europe's Cold War in the 1970s.

Acknowledgements

In accordance with the Parliamentary announcement cited in the Introduction to the Series, the Editors have had the customary freedom in the selection and arrangement of documents including full access to all classes of FCO documentation. There have, however, in the case of the present volume been a number of exceptional instances when for security reasons it has been necessary to excise certain passages from selected documents. These omissions are indicated with square brackets and appropriate footnote references.

The main source of documentation in this volume has been the records of the FCO held, prior to their transfer to The National Archives, by the former Records and Historical Department. In providing access to these records and for help in locating specific files, I am grateful to Mrs. Heather Yasamee CMG, Assistant Director and Head of the FCO's Information Management Group, and her staff, particularly Ms. Joan McPherson, the former Head of Retrieval Services, and her colleagues at Hanslope Park. I should also like to thank the Histories, Openness and Records Section of the Cabinet Office and the Departmental Records Officer of the Ministry of Defence (MoD) for permission to publish and cite documents in their custody; Mrs. Diane Morrish and Miss Jackie Till for their general and secretarial assistance; and Professor Patrick Salmon, Head of FCO Historians, and my three other colleagues, Dr. Christopher Baxter, Dr. Alastair Noble and Mr. Andrew Plummer-Rodriguez, for their help in completing work on the volume. Special thanks are finally due to Ms. Gill Bennett OBE, formerly the FCO's Chief Historian, who played a key role in ensuring the volume's publication; and to Dr. Kirsty Buckthorp and Dr. Martin Longden, both of whom contributed considerably to the editing of the documents.

KEITH A. HAMILTON

February 2006

CONTENTS

ABBREVIATIONS FOR PRINTED SOURCES

Cmd./Cmnd.	Command Paper (London)
Parl. Debs., 5th ser., H. of C.,	*Parliamentary Debates (Hansard), Fifth Series, House of Commons, Official Report* (London: 1909f.)
Treaty Series	*Treaty Series* (London: HMSO, 1892f)
Volume I	*Documents on British Policy Overseas*, Series III, Volume I, *Britain and the Soviet Union, 1968-1972* (London: TSO, 1997)
Volume II	*Documents on British Policy Overseas*, Series III, Volume II, *The Conference on Security and Cooperation in Europe, 1972-1975* (London: TSO, 1997)
Volume III	*Documents on British Policy Overseas*, Series III, Volume III, *Détente in Europe, 1972-1976* (London: Whitehall History Publishing/Frank Cass, 2001)

ABBREVIATED DESIGNATIONS

AFM/   Armed Forces Movement/
MFA   *Movimento das Forças Armadas*

AKEL   *Anorthotiko Komma Ergazomenou Laou*/Progressive Party of the Working People

ANP   *Acção Nacional Popular*/ National Popular Action

APAG   Atlantic Policy Advisory Group, NATO

APS   Assistant Private Secretary

AUS   Assistant Under-Secretary of State

BBC   British Broadcasting Corporation

CBFNE   Commander British Forces Near East

CBI   Confederation of British Industry

CDE   *Comissão Democrático Eleitoral*/Democratic Electoral Commission

CDS   *Centro Democrático Social*/ Social Democratic Centre

CDS   Chief of the Defence Staff

CENT-LANT   Central Atlantic Command, NATO

CENTO   Central Treaty Organisation

CIA   Central Intelligence Agency

COI   Central Office of Information

COMGIB-MED   Commander, Gibraltar Mediteranean

COPCON   *Commando Operacional do Continente*/Continental Operational Command

COREPER   *Comité des Représentants Permanents*/Committee of Permanent Representatives, EC

COS   Chiefs of Staff

CP   Communist Party

CPRS   Central Policy Review Staff, Cabinet Office

CSCE   Conference on Security and Cooperation in Europe

CYTA   Cyprus Telecommunications Authority

DA   Defence Adviser/Attaché

DPC   Defence Policy Committee, NATO

DSWP   Defence Studies Working Party

DTI   Department of Trade and Industry

DUS   Deputy Under-Secretary of State

EAST-LANT   Eastern Atlantic Command, NATO

EC   European Community/ Communities

EDEK   *Eniea Demokratiki Enosis Kyprou*/Unified Democratic Centre Union of Cyprus

EEC   European Economic Community

EESD   Eastern European and Soviet Department, FCO

EFTA   European Free Trade Association

EIB   European Investment Bank

EID(E)	European Integration Department (External), FCO	GIBMED	Gibraltar Mediterranean Command, NATO
ELDYK	Greek regular contingent in Cyprus	GLP	Gibraltar Labour Party
EOKA	*Ethniki Organosis Kyprion Agoniston*/National Organisation of Cypriot Fighters	GMT	Greenwich Mean Time
EPC	European Political Cooperation	GNP	Gross National Product
ESBA	Eastern Sovereign Base Area (Dhekelia)	GOC	General Officer Commanding
ESEA	*Eniaios Syndesmos Enotikou Agonos*/Committee for the Coordination of the Enosist Struggle	GSP	General Strategic Plan of Supreme Allied Commander Europe
ETA	*Euzkadi ta Askatusuna*/ Basque Homeland and Liberty	HMG	Her Majesty's Government
EUM	Cabinet Ministerial Committee on Europe	HQBFNE	Headquarters, British Forces Near East
FCO	Foreign and Commonwealth Office	IBERLANT	Iberian-Atlantic Command, NATO
FIR	Flight Information Region	ICAO	International Civil Aviation Organisation
FNLA	*Frente Nacional de Libertação de Angola*/National Front for the Liberation of Angola	ICRC	International Committee of the Red Cross
FRAP	*Frente Revolucionario Antifascista y Patriotica*/Antifascist and Patriotic Revolutionary Front	IFT	Immediately Following Telegram
FRD	Financial Relations Department, FCO	ILO	International Labour Organisation
FRELIMO	*Frente Nacional de Libertação de Moçambique*/Mozambique Liberation Front	IMEMO	*Instit Mirovoi Ekonomiki Mezhdunarodnykh Otnoshenii*/ Institute of World Economy and International Relations
FRG	Federal Republic of Germany	IMF	International Monetary Fund
GATT	General Agreement on Tariffs and Trade	IPU	Inter-Parliamentary Union
GDP	General Defence Plan	IRD	Information Research Department, FCO
GGD	Gibraltar and General Department, FCO	ITN	Independent Television News

JIC	Joint Intelligence Committee	MPLA	*Movimento Popular de Libertação de Angola*/Popular Movement for the Liberation of Angola
JNS/JSN	Junta of National Salvation/ *Junta de Salvação Nacional*	MRCA	Multi-Role Combat Aircraft
JTP	Joint Theatre Plan	MRPP	*Movimento Reorganizativo do Partido do Proletariado*/ Movement to Reorganise the Party of the Proletariat
KYP	*Kentriki Ypiresia Pliroforion*/ Greek Central Intelligence Agency	NAC	North Atlantic Council
LUAR	*Liga da União e de Acção Revolucionária*/League of Revolutionary Union and Action	NADGE	NATO Air Defence Ground Environment
MARCON -FOR	Maritime Contingency Force, NATO	NATO	North Atlantic Treaty Organisation
MBFR	Mutual and Balanced Force Reductions [talks]	NCO	Noncommissioned officer
MDP	*Movimento Democrático Popular*/Popular Democratic Movement	NCS	Naval Control of Shipping
MED	Middle East Department, FCO	NENAD	Near East and North Africa Department, FCO
MFA	Ministry of Foreign Affairs	NPG	Nuclear Planning Group, NATO
MIFT	My Immediately Following Telegram	NSP	National Salvation Party
MIPT	My Immediately Preceding Telegram	OAU	Organisation for African Unity
MIRV	Multiple Independently Targetable Reentry Vehicle	ODM	Ministry of Overseas Development
MNC	Major NATO Command	OECD	Organisation for Economic Cooperation and Development
MoD/ MODUK	Ministry of Defence	OPD	Defence and Oversea Policy Committee
MP	Member of Parliament	OSE	*Organización Sindical Española*/ Spanish Trade Union Organisation
MPA	Maritime Patrol Aircraft	PAIGC	*Partido Africano de Independência de Guiné e Cabo Verde*/African Party for the Independence of Guinea and Cape Verde

PAK	*Panellinio Apeleutherotiko Kinima/*Panhellenic Liberation Movement	RN	Royal Navy
PASOK	*Panellinio Socialistiko Kinima/* Panhellenic Socialist Party	SACEUR	Supreme Allied Command Europe
PCD	Protocol and Conference Department, FCO	SACLANT	Supreme Allied Command Atlantic
PCE	*Partido Communista de España/*Communist Party of Spain	SALT	Strategic Arms Limitation Talks
PCP	*Partido Communista Português/*Portuguese Communist Party	SBA	Sovereign Base Area
POL	Petrol, Oil and Lubricants	SED	Southern European Department, FCO
PPD	*Partido Popular Democrático/* Portuguese Popular Democratic Party	SEED	South East European Department, FCO
PQ	Parliamentary Question	Sitrep	Situation Report
PRP BR	*Partido Revolucionário do Proletariado (Brigades Revolucionáries)/*Revolutionary Party of the Proletariat (Revolutionary Brigades)	SPD	*Sozialdemokratische Partei Deutschlands/*Social Democratic Party of Germany
PS	Private Secretary	STANAVF-ORLANT	Standing Naval Force Atlantic, NATO
PSDI	*Partido Socialista Democratico Italiano/*Italian Social Democratic Party	SWED	South West European Department, FCO
PSOE	*Partido Socialista Obrero Español/*Spanish Socialist Workers Party	TCA	Turkish Cypriot Administration
PS/PSP	*Partido Socialista/*Portuguese Socialist Party	TGS	Turkish General Staff
PTR	Police Tactical Reserve	TGWU	Transport and General Workers' Union
PUS	Permanent Under-Secretary of State	TPAO	*Türkiye Petrolleri Anonim Ortakligi/*Turkish Petroleum Corporation
QC	Queen's Counsel	TUC	Trades Union Congress
RAF	Royal Air Force	TUR	Telegram Under Reference
RPP	Republican People's Party	UDI	Unilateral Declaration of Independence

UDSE	*Unión Social Democrática Española/*Spanish Social Democratic Union	UNFICYP	United Nations peacekeeping force in Cyprus
UDP	*União Democrática Popular/* Democratic People's Union	UNGA	United Nations General Assembly
UK	United Kingdom	UNSC	United Nations Security Council
UKDEL	United Kingdom Delegation	USA	United States of America
UKMIS	United Kingdom Mission	USSR	Union of Soviet Socialist Republics
UKREP	United Kingdom Permanent Representative	WED	Western European Department, FCO
UN(O)	United Nations (Organisation)	WOD	Western Organisations Department, FCO
UND	United Nations Department, FCO	WSBA	Western Sovereign Base Area (Akrotiri)
UNEF	United Nations Emergency Force		

CHAPTER SUMMARIES

CHAPTER I

Cyprus: Prelude to Intervention,
24 October 1973—11 July 1974

CHAPTER II

Cyprus: Coup d'État and Intervention,
15 July 1974—15 August 1974

CHAPTER III

Cyprus: Sequel to Geneva
16 August 1974—13 February 1975

CHAPTER IV

Political Change in Portugal and Spain,
1 May 1974—3 April 1975

CHAPTER V

Political Change in Portugal and Spain,
18 April 1975—29 April 1976

FOREIGN AND COMMONWEALTH OFFICE **BRIEFING NOTES**

Cyprus - historical

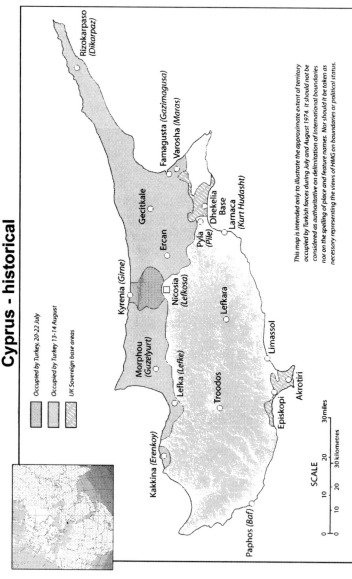

Occupied by Turkey, 20-22 July

Occupied by Turkey 13-14 August

UK Sovereign base areas

Rizokarpaso (Dikarpaz)

Famagusta (Gazimagusa)
Varosha (Maras)

Gecitkale

Ercan

Kyrenia (Girne)

Nicosia (Lefkosa)

Pyla (Pile)
Dhekelia Base
Larnaca (Kurt Hudasht)

Lefkara

Morphou (Guzelyurt)

Lefka (Lefke)

Troodos

Limassol

Kakkina (Erenkoy)

Episkopi
Akrotiri

Paphos (Baf)

SCALE

0   10   20   30miles
0 10   20   30 kilometres

This map is intended only to illustrate the approximate extent of territory occupied by Turkish forces during July and August 1974. It should not be considered as authoritative on delimitation of international boundaries nor on the spelling of place and feature names. Nor should it be taken as necessary representing the views of HMG on boundaries or political status.

Supplied by FCO Maps and Geographical Information Service, tel. (020) 7008 3024

FCO 78 Edition 1 (March 2006)

Users should note that this map has been designed for briefing purposes only and it should not be used for determining the precise location of places or features.
This map should not be considered an authority on the delimitation of international boundaries or on the spelling of place and feature names.
Maps produced for the FCO Library Map Service are not to be taken as necessarily representing the views of the UK government on boundaries or political status. © Crown Copyright 2006

CHAPTER I

Cyprus: Prelude to Intervention
24 October 1973–11 July 1974

No. 1

Mr. S.L.J. Olver[1] *(Nicosia) to Sir A. Douglas-Home*[2]

[*WSC 1/2*]

Confidential   NICOSIA, *24 October 1973*

Summary ...[3]

Sir,

Cyprus: the Enlarged Intercommunal Talks

In his despatch of 27 August, 1971, my predecessor reviewed the course taken by the intercommunal talks during the fourth phase, which ended in deadlock in the late summer of 1971. The prospects for the enlarged intercommunal talks, which began hopefully in June 1972,[4] are now uncertain and deadlock is once again a real possibility. The purpose of this despatch is to analyse the main problems at issue, and to discuss the likely developments in the immediate future. I enclose at Annex A[5] a summary account of the stage now reached in the discussion of each of the major issues at Annex B[5] a chronological record of the enlarged talks.

A measure of progress

2. The enlarged talks have had some success. The presence of the UN Secretary-General's Special Representative in Cyprus and the Greek and

---

[1] British High Commissioner in Nicosia.

[2] Secretary of State for Foreign and Commonwealth Affairs.

[3] Not printed.

[4] Talks aimed at settling intercommunal political and constitutional differences, had begun in June 1968 under the auspices of the United Nations (UN). The Greek and Turkish Cypriot communities were represented respectively by Mr. G.J. Clerides, the President of the Cyprus House of Representatives, and Mr. R. Denktash, the President of the Turkish Cypriot Communal Chamber and, from February 1973, Vice-President of the Cyprus Republic. But four phases of discussions over a three-year period failed to produce agreement. On 8 June 1972 Dr. K. Waldheim, the UN Secretary-General formally inaugurated fresh talks in which the original interlocutors were joined by Mr. M. Dekleris, a Greek, and Prof. O. Aldikaçiti, a Turkish, constitutional adviser, and Sr. B.F. Osorio-Tafall, Dr. Waldheim's Special Representative.

[5] Not printed.

Turkish Constitutional Advisers has been beneficial. Mr. Clerides and Mr. Denktash have felt the need to appear constructive in front of the outsiders. The outsiders themselves have contributed some useful ideas, in particular Mr. Osorio-Tafall's suggestion of a divisible House of Representatives to legislate on matters of communal interest. On a number of questions, advances have been made beyond the point reached in 1971. However, the agreements so far reached will remain provisional until a package deal is achieved: there will be no piecemeal settlement.

A unitary state

3. The talks are intended to find a fresh, mutually acceptable constitution for a sovereign, independent and unitary Republic of Cyprus. However, each side differs in its interpretation of these fundamental terms. The differences spring from the Turkish Cypriots' fear for their physical security and for their continuation as a community, as against the Greek Cypriots' desire for a Greek dominated State which would have complete freedom of action internationally. The Turkish Cypriots insist on full control of their own affairs, and recognition of their status as partners in a bi-communal State. Provided they get the substance of local autonomy, the Turkish side do not much mind what constitutional form it takes. It might be an autonomous local government structure reporting direct to a joint commission at the highest level, such as they requested in 1970; or enhanced powers for the Turkish Cypriot branch of the House of Representatives; or enhanced powers for the Vice-President of the Republic; or a combination of these. There are several permutations, each intended to lead to the same result, and each of which would make minor concessions possible in other areas (*e.g.* the reduction of Turkish representation in the Council of Ministers and Republican Civil Service from 30 to 20 per cent). All this is contrary to the Greek Cypriot concept of a unitary State. As Archbishop Makarios[6] told me when I presented my Letter of Commission, the Greek Cypriot side are prepared to accept, to a certain degree, a form of local government for the Turkish Cypriots, but not such as might lead to the establishment of a cantonal or federal system, which in turn at a later stage could develop into partition. According to the Turkish Cypriots, the 1960 Constitution did in fact create a unitary State:[7]

[6] Mihail Christodoulou Mouskos, Archbishop Makarios III of Cyprus, was the first President of the Republic of Cyprus. During the 1950s he had emerged as spokesman for the Greek Cypriot community and effective leader of the movement for *enosis*—Cyprus's political union with Greece.

[7] Cyprus became an independent sovereign republic following the end of British colonial rule on 26 August 1960. Its Constitution provided for a Greek Cypriot President and a Turkish Cypriot Vice-President elected for a five-year term by the Greek and Turkish communities respectively. The House of Representatives, elected for five years by universal suffrage of each community separately, consisted of thirty-five Greek Cypriot and fifteen Turkish Cypriot members, and certain religious, cultural and social activities were expressly reserved to Communal Chambers elected by the two communities. In practice, the Constitution soon

a State which recognised the existence of two communities, gave them certain autonomous rights in local affairs, (chiefly in religion, education and personal questions such as marriage and divorce) and granted them partnership on agreed terms at Government level. The Turkish Cypriots maintain that anything less than this would mean mere minority status and that it is the fate of minorities always to be at the mercy of the majority. But there seems to have been a steady escalation in their demands, which are now a good deal more far-reaching than the rights assigned to them under the 1960 Constitution.

A sovereign and independent state

4. Archbishop Makarios regards the Treaties of Guarantee and Alliance[8] as invalid, having renounced them unilaterally in 1963 and 1964 respectively. He has said that after a solution of the constitutional problem through the intercommunal talks, the Treaties, which represent the external aspects of the Cyprus problem, will be discussed at a later stage and at another level. He wants the Greek, Turkish and British rights of intervention to be abolished, and the Contingents of the Greek and

---

proved unworkable: irreconcilable differences arose over the ethnic composition of the army and public services, fiscal legislation and the structure of local government. But the thirteen-point proposals put forward by Archbishop Makarios in the autumn of 1963 for its radical revision were rejected by the Turkish Government, and led in December to four days of intercommunal strife. Reference of the Cyprus problem to the UN Security Council (UNSC), was followed by the establishment on 27 March 1964 of a UN peacekeeping force in Cyprus (UNFICYP). Further fighting between Greek and Turkish Cypriots during the summer encouraged the increased geographical separation of the two communities, with the Turkish Cypriots retreating into their own enclaves, and establishing their own government (known from December 1967 as the Turkish Cypriot (Provisional until 1971) Administration (TCA)). The Greek Cypriots continued, in the absence of their Turkish compatriots, to conduct their affairs through the Republic's existing machinery of government.

[8] The Treaty of Guarantee, which came into force with the establishment of the Republic of Cyprus, was concluded between Cyprus, Greece, the United Kingdom (UK) and Turkey. This expressly forbade any activity tending to promote directly or indirectly either *enosis* or partition of the island, and the three guarantor powers in their turn recognised and guaranteed the 'independence, territorial integrity and security of the Republic of Cyprus, and also the provisions of the basic articles of its Constitution'. In the event of any breach in the provisions of the Treaty, Greece, the UK and Turkey undertook 'to consult together, with a view to making representations, or taking the necessary steps to ensure the observance of those provisions'. But Paragraph 2 of Article 4 of the Treaty stipulated that if common or concerted action were to prove impossible, each of the three powers reserved the 'right to take action with the sole aim of re-establishing the state of affairs created by the present Treaty'. See *Treaty Series*, No. 5 (1961), Cmnd. 1253 (London: HMSO).

Meanwhile, the Treaty of Alliance between Cyprus, Greece and Turkey pledged the three powers to cooperate for their common defence, to consult to this end, and to resist any aggression, direct or indirect, against the Republic of Cyprus. A tripartite Headquarters was to be established in the Republic with Greece contributing a contingent of 950 men and Turkey a contingent of 650. These were to be responsible for training the army of the Cyprus Republic. See *United Nations Treaty Series*, Vol. 397 (1961), No. 5712.

Turkish armies to be withdrawn. He wants the guarantees against Enosis (and, incidentally, partition) to be dismantled. Only then in his view, will the Cyprus Republic be truly sovereign and independent. If the Turkish Cypriots insist on continuing guarantees of their minority rights these could be provided by the UN.

5. I shall return below to the question of whether or not the Archbishop really wants union with Greece; but the abolition of the two Treaties would unquestionably remove the legal barriers to 'self determination' which, in the Greek Cypriot language designed for foreign and UN consumption, means Enosis. The Turkish Cypriots, who are morbidly aware of this, insist that there can be no discussion of the Treaties and that the presence of the Turkish mainland Contingent is not negotiable. They maintain that it is only the state of affairs guaranteed by the Treaties which has kept Cyprus independent; otherwise, the island would long ago have been swallowed up by Greece. The Turkish Cypriots say that the Greek Cypriots have every right, if they wish to opt for Enosis; in which case, the Turkish Cypriots would unite with Turkey. This would mean the partition of Cyprus, or 'double Enosis'. As a variant, the Turkish Cypriots sometimes hint that they are considering the proclamation of a Turkish Cypriot Republic. They always maintain, however, that these threats are only a riposte to Greek Cypriot talk of Enosis; that they would prefer an independent Republic (on their own terms naturally); and that partition, for them, is a last resort.

Enosis and partition

6. For more than 20 years Archbishop Makarios has, with few exceptions, spoken of Enosis as a goal which he would like to see achieved in his lifetime. This is a record whose consistency cannot be ignored. However, by putting his terms for Enosis impossibly high, the Archbishop has in practice worked for the continuing independence of the Cyprus Republic. He has done so deliberately. He is determined that Enosis, if it is ever achieved, will be on the terms and at the time of his choice, and in his own best interests. In the meantime, he enjoys being Head of State and is content to rule over a purely Greek community. He summed up his policy characteristically in a letter which he sent in confidence to General Grivas[9] on 4 May 1972, and which Grivas has recently published. 'In

---

[9] Gen. G. Grivas-Dighenis was the military leader of EOKA (*Ethniki Organosis Kyprion Agoniston*/National Organisation of Cypriot Fighters), the Greek Cypriot movement which was engaged during 1955-59 in a guerrilla war against the British with a view to achieving Cyprus's union with Greece. In August 1964 he was appointed Chief of the Cyprus Supreme Military Defence Command, but, following a Turkish ultimatum to Greece on 17 November 1967, he was recalled to Athens (cf. note 12 below). A pronounced critic of Archbishop Makarios and opponent of the intercommunal talks, he returned to Cyprus in September 1971, and set about forming armed groups (EOKA-B) in order to promote *enosis*. In a despatch of 11 March 1974 Mr. Olver commented that it seemed certain that the Greek Government were not displeased by the Archbishop's discomfiture. 'They must', he speculated, 'have hoped that Grivas'

present circumstances the struggle of Cyprus Hellenism is rather defensive. We are defending ourselves against the imposition of an unacceptable solution ... We refuse to accept a solution which would fetter our national future.' In other words, the Archbishop is not prepared to barter away the *status quo*.

7. Enosis is an ancient and honourable ambition. It is understandable that after eight centuries any Greek Cypriot would feel deep guilt if he renounced it permanently, and it is significant that since Independence no leading Greek Cypriot has ever ventured to denounce it publicly and in principle. No single newspaper or party supports Independence in terms. The Turkish Cypriots, for their part, have no wish to become Greek subjects. They might without much difficulty be induced to accept that in a new constitutional settlement no fresh guarantees against Enosis were necessary, provided that the Treaty of Guarantee and Article 185 of the Constitution (which excludes Enosis and partition) remained unchanged. But until the Archbishop and other Greek Cypriot politicians give a lead to their community by ceasing to talk of Enosis and by committing themselves publicly to independence (without the escape hatch of 'self-determination'), the Turkish side will not be prepared to believe in Greek Cypriot and Greek good faith. It is no great exaggeration to say that the intercommunal talks are only about the symptoms of the disease. The real problem remains the political question of Enosis as against independence.

8. It is hard to judge how genuine are the Greek Cypriot fears of partition. Given Turkey's proximity they may be justifiable, but most Greek Cypriots, including the Archbishop, tend to dismiss the possibility of a Turkish invasion. Few Turkish Cypriots would in fact welcome partition, whether it took the form of absorption into Turkey or the declaration of a mini-state. The preparation, execution and consequences of partition would be painful and involve great dislocation of their life. Apart from the movement of population, the community would risk being deprived, at least for a time, of electricity, food supplies, currency and banking facilities. Most educated Turkish Cypriots have no wish to be absorbed into Turkey, whose lower cultural and living standards they despise and the interference of whose representatives they dislike. They would probably welcome an intercommuncal settlement provided it gave them concrete guarantees. Nor would this be contrary to Ankara's interests, since my impression is that the Turkish authorities strategic aim is to ensure that Cyprus shall never come under Greek or other hostile foreign control.

Can the status quo continue?
9. So far as the Greek Cypriots are concerned, there seems no pressing practical reason why the *status quo* should not continue. Archbishop Makarios knows how to wait. I believe that time is not for him; but it is

presence would either force the Archbishop to show more flexibility in the intercommunal talks, or lead to his removal or both' (WSC 1/4).

equally not much against him—at least in the short term—and he knows the problems faced by the Turkish Cypriot community. Internationally the Cyprus Government are occasionally annoyed or embarrassed by the Turkish Cypriots' political pretensions, as during the negotiations for the EEC Association Agreement.[10] Internally, their *amour propre* is hurt from time to time by the activity of the 'Turkish Cypriot Administration'. But the compensations and inevitability of the *status quo* are compelling enough, as a rule, to restrain them from any precipitate action. The economy prospers, although tourism could be dealt a severe blow by any recrudescence of intercommunal fighting. Most Greek Cypriots are not greatly inconvenienced, either personally or financially, by the continuation of the Cyprus problem. Many would resent having to make way for Turkish Cypriot civil servants and to pay some deference to Turkish Cypriot susceptibilities, as would be necessary in the event of an intercommunal settlement.

10. Matters are very different for the Turkish Cypriot community. Although material conditions have eased since 1968, there are signs of war weariness. The hands of the Turkish military and Mr. Denktash's *apparat* lie heavily upon the community. The subsidies from Turkey are barely enough to keep the community afloat, while at the same time embarrassing the Turkish Government; and prices in the Greek Cypriot economy which dominates the Turkish Cypriot economy continue to rise. Few Turkish Cypriots feel any optimism about the future of the community. If there is a settlement, they fear that they will be swallowed up economically by the Greek Cypriots. They may try to secure economic guarantees through the intercommunal talks, but it is impossible to have a guarantee against every eventuality in life. Mr. Denktash sometimes has private doubts even about the readiness of the Turkish Air Force to come to the aid of the community,[11] should Turkey suddenly weaken internally or internationally. If there is no settlement the community will continue its depressing and restricted existence. Either way, the more enterprising young people will continue to emigrate, probably in increasing numbers, if they can still find somewhere to go in Western Europe. Despite all this, there are no signs of desire for an intercommunal settlement at any price. Remembering the events of 1955-59, 1963 and 1967,[12] the Turkish Cypriots will not put

[10] Cyprus concluded an Association Agreement with the European Economic Community (EEC) in December 1972.

[11] During August 1964, when Greek Cypriot forces had been advancing on the Turkish Cypriot-held north-west coast of Cyprus, Turkish air force planes struck at Greek Cypriot positions.

[12] In November 1967 a violent confrontation between Turkish Cypriots and the Cyprus National Guard in the vicinity of Kophinou left twenty-eight dead, most of whom were Turkish Cypriots, and resulted in an international crisis. Turkey alerted its armed forces and issued an ultimatum to Greece threatening war against the Greek mainland and an invasion of Cyprus. The crisis was only defused when Athens agreed to withdraw the 20,000 Greek troops infiltrated clandestinely into the island. On 29 December Turkish Cypriot leaders agreed to

themselves at the mercy of the Greek Cypriots. Some have a vested interest in the institutions of the 'Turkish Cypriot Administration', which they would be reluctant to dismantle. (This is partly what Mr. Denktash means when he says that the 'de facto' situation must be recognised.) The privileges which they are demanding in the intercommunal talks would, if granted, create a complicated, inconvenient and disproportionately expensive administrative machine for the Republic, whose main effect would be to generate continuing inter-communal heat rather than efficiency. But the Turks show no disposition to lower their sights. If anything they are raising them. Although time is against them, the Turkish Cypriots seem to believe that their best course is to sit tight in the hope that something will turn up: perhaps the Greek Cypriot community will tear themselves to pieces or Archbishop Makarios will be removed from power. But even if Makarios went, Mr. Clerides might turn out to be just as tough.

Towards a deadlock?

11. Since the early summer the interlocutors have been gingerly skirmishing around the issue of local government (or local autonomy). Once discussion of this problem has been exhausted, there will be little left to say and the time for political decisions should be at hand. Unless there is a sudden access of trust and goodwill, the Turkish Cypriot side will not concede to the Greek Cypriots the right to control their local government arrangements. Turkey will not force the Turkish Cypriot community into an agreement which might sooner or later lead to the community's loss of identity. As far as one can judge the Greek Government, however great their desire to see an end to the Cyprus problem, would not try to force the Greek Cypriots beyond a certain point: they must surely by now accept that the Archbishop cannot be coerced. The statement made by Mr. Cavalieratos[13] after his meeting with Mr. Bayülken[14] in New York on 2 October, that the intercommunal talks must continue with the aim of finding a solution which will satisfy all the interested parties, suggests that the two 'mother countries' will try to find a way of spinning out the talks. But there must be a limit to this. What will happen if no political decisions can be reached, and the talks cannot be given an artificial lung?

12. In a recent press interview, Archbishop Makarios said that it would not be easy to find an alternative course. The Cyprus Government would probably have recourse to the UN once again. Realistically, he added that although a UN resolution on the Cyprus problem would carry enormous moral weight, it would not solve the problem as there was no practical way of implementing it. But a recourse to the UN would not bring the

---

establish a 'transitional administration' to administer the affairs of the Turkish community 'until the provisions of the 1960 Constitution had been fully implemented'. See notes 7 and 9 above.

[13] Mr. P.A. Cavalieratos was the Greek Alternate Foreign Minister.

[14] Mr. Ü.-H. Bayülken was the Turkish Foreign Minister.

Archbishop much profit. Another resolution on the lines of that passed by the General Assembly on 18 December, 1965, which stressed the right of the Cyprus Republic to enjoy 'full sovereignty and complete independence without any foreign intervention or interference'[15] would be superfluous; and as Turkish diplomacy has been active in the meantime, it is not certain that a new resolution would be passed as overwhelmingly as the last. An important section of the Greek Cypriot Press has been urging the Archbishop to plump for 'self-determination' in his recourse to the UN. This would put the Archbishop's theoretical position close to that of General Grivas. The prospect might tempt the Archbishop: it would help restore his tarnished prestige as a Greek nationalist. But he must know that it would be an empty gesture, which would tend to restrict his freedom of manoeuvre in future and which would embarrass the Greek Government whose co-operation he has said he will seek in determining the course to be followed after a failure of the intercommunal talks.

13. The failure of the talks would not, as matters now stand, greatly prejudice the Archbishop's domestic position. General Grivas would argue that deadlock had proved the bankruptcy of the Archbishop's policy of the 'feasible solution'; but the Grivas movement has been so weakened in recent weeks that it would be unable to exploit this opportunity, as it might have done six months ago.[16] The Archbishop would be able to present the deadlock as a result of his determination not to sacrifice the Greek Cypriot birthright to the Turks. Since he has always been careful to keep a certain distance between himself and the talks, the main loser would be Mr. Clerides. The uncertainty which would follow the failure of the talks would only strengthen the Archbishop's claim that the critical situation required him to soldier on as Head of State.

14. The effect of a deadlock on the Turkish Cypriot community would be more unsettling. Separatist tendencies would be strengthened, and there might be a temptation in some quarters to declare a Turkish Cypriot Republic. If this happened, the Cyprus Government would be bound to react, probably by imposing a blockade on the enclaves, breaking off diplomatic relations with Turkey and requiring all Diplomatic Missions to have no further dealings with the community. This would rapidly lead to international complications, including threats of intervention from Turkey and, possibly, the Soviet Union. In the end, the Cyprus Government would doubtless back down, but a great deal of damage would have been done to

[15] UN General Assembly (UNGA) Resolution 2077 (xx), *UNGA Official Records, 20th session,* Supplement No. 14 (A/6014), pp. 9-10.

[16] See note 9 above. Political differences between Archbishop Makarios and Gen. Grivas had since January erupted in a series of violent incidents, and on 30 March plans were announced to establish a Police Tactical Reserve (PTR). The abduction of the Cyprus Minister of Justice by two armed, masked and uniformed men was followed in August by public protests denouncing Gen. Grivas as a 'criminal'. On 7 October four bombs exploded on a road outside Famagusta along which Archbishop Makarios was intending to travel, and a man arrested there confessed that there had been a plan to assassinate the President.

the Western position. It is to be hoped that if Mr. Denktash were to advocate the declaration of a mini State, the Turkish Government would damp him down. Turkey would have nothing to gain from it; she would not only lose her legal right of intervention in Cyprus under the 1960 Treaties, but would find it more difficult than before to retain her bridgehead in Cyprus, for example by rotating the Turkish mainland Contingent and maintaining links with the Turkish Cypriots. The declaration of a mini State, far from easing Turkey's position, would add to her burden both internationally and in practical terms.

15. I conclude that the most likely consequence of an avowed deadlock would be an increase in intercommunal tension for a time, possibly accompanied by a deterioration in Græco-Turkish bilateral relations and pressure on the Archbishop by sections of his own community to 'do something' about the Turks. There would be a series of pinpricks against the Turks and Western Powers by an irritated Cyprus Government, and we should have to move even faster on our feet than usual in order to maintain decent relations with the Cyprus Government, the Turkish Cypriots and the latter's mainland protectors. I draw some comfort from the calculation that it is not in the interest of any of the parties directly involved to encourage an armed flare-up in Cyprus; but the effect of withdrawing the safety-valve provided by the talks is hard to calculate and eruptions of local intercommunal violence might well recur.

Conclusion

16. The position of the two parties here on the island is essentially simple. The Turkish Cypriots, fearful after their experiences of the last 13 years, want cast iron protection against Greek Cypriot violence and discrimination: given this, they would opt—as Mr. Denktash assured me—for an independent unified Cyprus, in which they must, however, be partners, albeit junior, rather than a mere minority. The Greek Cypriots hanker emotionally after Enosis—though I believe that with the younger generation and some of the wealthier middle-class, the material benefits of independence are beginning to outweigh the cultural attractions of mother Greece. But in any case, Archbishop Makarios and the wiser Greek Cypriot politicians know that Enosis is unattainable given present Græco-Turkish relations. They are willing meanwhile to settle for an independent Cyprus—for an almost indefinite period so long as the door to Enosis is not finally slammed. But it must be a united Cyprus in which—they protest—the Turks will be given their full rights but the Greeks must be in control. And since partition, or anything approaching it, would pre-empt both unification and Enosis, the Greek Cypriots are particularly opposed to any Turkish Cypriot steps towards federalism. It is around this central issue that the argument over local autonomy is raging.

17. Mr. Denktash has often spoken to me of the talks as a vicious circle—and theoretically one can spin round a vicious circle for ever. He himself sees some virtue in spinning out the talks, for fear of removing the

safety-valve, even though the Turkish Cypriot community stands the more obviously to lose from a lengthy prolongation of the *status quo*. As already suggested, this should not suit Archbishop Makarios badly, and there are indications that thought has been given on the Greek side to allowing the present situation to congeal into virtual stalemate—doubtless with suitable 'noises off' such as an approach to the UN. But I have the feeling that the Archbishop hankers after a more active policy than this, and a hint of its direction was given to me recently by the Minister of Foreign Affairs. At the Archbishop's forthcoming visit to Athens—now apparently taken for granted—the main topic for discussion would, according to Mr. Christofides,[17] be how to play the next round in the talks; and one possible formula would be a resumption of the dialogue between Athens and Ankara on the firm understanding that any agreed proposals would then be submitted to an island-wide plebiscite. This proposal has many interesting implications. It offers some confirmation of the rumour, so far denied by both sides, that the Turkish Foreign Minister proposed a resumption of the dialogue to his Greek colleague recently at the UN in New York. Above all, it suggests that, notwithstanding some coolness between the Greek and Cypriot Governments with the appointment of Mr. Markezinis as Greek Premier,[18] the new found co-operation over the Cyprus problem is being maintained. On the Archbishop's part, this seems both confident and skilful: confident, because he risks an adverse public reaction to what would be seen by many as at least a partial relinquishment of the reins; and, skilful, because, with the plebiscite in his hands, he would retain the means of rejecting any unsatisfactory solution and of placing the odium for it fairly on Athens and Ankara. It is possible to argue that this is indeed the Archbishop's main intention in associating with this idea at all. I find that a little too cynical, however, and I should like to think of this as a helpful indication that the Archbishop and the Greek side genuinely want a settlement and are unwilling to opt for a prolonged stalemate.

18. At this delicate stage, it would clearly be unwise for outsiders to interfere—and indeed, I do not regard the talks in their present shape as yet by any means dead. But it is in any case for the parties—the Archbishop, the Greek and Turkish Governments and, perhaps, the UN—to produce an alternative device if the present talks fail. Outside intervention could easily be misunderstood or misrepresented. Nonetheless, there could well come a time when matters hung in the balance and a helpful initiative, perhaps preferably in or through the UN, made the difference between success and failure. We should be alive to this and to the possibility that, with our expertise in this problem, quiet British advice or pressure might be of help. I remain convinced that in the last resort this is a psychological problem. The practical difficulties separating the two

---

[17] Mr. I. Christofides (Christophides) was Foreign Minister of Cyprus.

[18] Mr. S. Markezinis, the former leader of the Greek Progressive Party, was appointed Prime Minister on 1 October. Cf. No. 2, note 14.

sides are by no means insuperable given mutual trust and goodwill. I believe that both parties here realise that time is not working for them: the Turkish Cypriots obviously enough, with doubts about the attitude of future Turkish régimes and with increasing economic and financial difficulties, despite generous Turkish aid; but also the Greek Cypriots, for Archbishop Makarios realises, I think, that a prolongation of the present unstable equilibrium must in the long run risk dragging the whole island down to the level of an impoverished, disillusioned and desperate Turkish Cypriot community: prosperity and peace, even on the miniature scale of Cyprus, are indivisible. This suggests to me that quiet diplomatic pressure towards moderation and a settlement in Nicosia, Athens and Ankara, is for the moment the best contribution that we, and like-minded Governments, can make.[19]

19. I am sending copies of this despatch to Her Majesty's Ambassadors at Ankara, Athens, and Washington, to the British High Commissioner at Ottawa, the UK Permanent Representative to the UN in New York, the Permanent UK Representative to the North Atlantic Council and to the Commander, British Forces Near East.[20]

I have, etc.,

S.L.J. OLVER

[19] Mr. A.C. Goodison, Head of Southern European Department (SED), responded to Mr. Olver in a letter of 6 November: 'We share your views on the possibility of an imminent deadlock and the very limited scope at this juncture for action by Her Majesty's Government. Like you we see a resumption of the earlier dialogue of [*sic*] Cyprus between Greece and Turkey as a possible development.' When in July pressure of business resulted in the division of SED into two separate departments, Mr. Goodison retained responsibility for Cyprus as Head of South East European Department (SEED).

[20] After Cyprus's independence Britain retained, under the Commander British Forces Near East (CBFNE) at Episkopi, military bases in the two Sovereign Base Areas (SBAs) of Akrotiri and Dhekelia. These were provided for in the Treaty Concerning the Establishment of the Republic of Cyprus, which was concluded on 16 August 1960 between Cyprus, Greece, Turkey and the UK. See *Treaty Series* No. 4 (1961), Cmnd. 1252 (London: HMSO).

No. 2

Extract from Sir R. Hooper[1] (Athens) to Sir A. Douglas-Home

[*WSG 1/4*]

Confidential   ATHENS, *6 December 1973*

Summary ...[2]

Sir,

Praxicopematics: or the Fall of Papadopoulos

When tanks and armoured units moved into Athens in the early hours of 25 November, they put an end to six and a half years of control exercised by George Papadopoulos[3] in the name of the 1967 Revolution.[4] The despatch which I now have the honour to submit discusses the events which led up to the fall of Papadopoulos and the manner of his departure. It also offers some very tentative speculations regarding the possible consequences in the short term of these developments ...[5]

12. So one chapter ends and another begins. Papadopoulos has fallen: but he is alive and well and living under guard 'for his own protection' in his seaside house on the road to Sounion, and facing his successors with the delicate problem of what to do with a retired dictator. It is easy now to highlight Papadopoulos's shortcomings and errors. As a leader, he was uninspiring. A poor speaker with no gift for the common touch, he seemed at times consciously set on creating for himself an image which was the antithesis of that cultivated by the professional demagogues whom he detests. He made little effort to use his sweeping powers to reform Greece in accordance with the admittedly rather thin ideology of the revolution.

---

[1] HM Ambassador in Athens.

[2] Not printed.

[3] Col. Papadopoulos was Greek Prime Minister during 1967-73, and President of the Republic of Greece during June-November 1973. He was removed from office when, early on the morning of 25 November, units of the Athens army garrison moved into the capital and effected a *coup d'état*.

[4] A reference to the bloodless *coup d'état* of 21 April 1967 by which Col. Papadopoulos and other middle-ranking Greek officers seized power in Athens. They then claimed that the Greek people must be purged of the habits engendered by a disorderly and corrupt parliamentarianism though a period of 'revolutionary' control exercised by the armed forces.

[5] Paragraphs 2-11 are omitted. They review the political impact of an abortive naval mutiny in May; the subsequent abolition of the monarchy; tentative steps taken by Col. Papadopoulos towards reintroducing civilian rule; reactions to his proposals for restoring parliamentary government; violent clashes between police and political demonstrators in Athens on 4 November; the army's role in subduing student protesters in the Athens Polytechnic on the night of 16/17 November; and the events of 25 November (cf. note 3 above).

For most of his tenure of power, he was content to govern in accordance with Frederick the Great's maxim 'Ruhe ist die erste Bürgerpflicht'.[6] He allowed power to be concentrated into the hands of a tight little clique—himself, his brother, his wife and Rouphogallis[7]—and failed to see the risk he was running by isolating himself from the real foundations of his power, the original revolutionary group and the army. When at last he decided that immobility was no longer possible, he acted too hastily and too late. For all that, Papadopoulos gave Greece six and a half years' stability—of a sort—and quiet in which the country, continuing its postwar economic revival, prospered as never before. His Government scrupulously carried out its NATO obligations. No one would wish to condone its brutalities; and in a country where nothing fails like failure, few, of course, have a good word to say for Papadopoulos at present. But as disillusion with his successors sets in and the memory of his misdeeds fades, people may begin to look back with a certain nostalgia at the era of his rule as one of the few periods of relative calm in the troubled history of modern Greece.

13. Where do we stand now? Behind a Cabinet of mediocrities[8] are the real masters of Greece—Ioannides[9] and his associates. The political basis of their *coup* seems to be 'back to April 1967', the rejection of the corruption (both financial and ideological) of the Papadopoulos régime, and the rejection of the return to the old ways apparently portended by Papadopoulos's manoeuvres in the summer and autumn. The secretive and enigmatic Papadopoulos has been succeeded by the soldierly if somewhat wooden figure of Gizikis.[10] My German colleague compares him to Hindenburg.[11] Others suggest Neguib.[12] Neither analogy is reassuring. The intentions and likely policies of the Government and—perhaps more

---

[6] 'Silence is the first duty of the citizen.'

[7] Col. M. Rouphogallis was Staff Officer, and effective head, of the Greek Central Intelligence Agency (KYP).

[8] In paragraph 10 of this despatch Sir R. Hooper wrote scathingly of the new Greek Government: 'But—Fred Karno's Army as they undoubtedly were and are—they at least presented the appearance of a civilian Cabinet: and the new Prime Minister [Mr. A. Androutsopoulos]—a lawyer who once worked in Chicago and is therefore, needless to say, widely assumed to be the creature of the CIA [US Central Intelligence Agency]—has held various Ministries from 1967 until early this year, and is, if not greatly respected, at any rate fairly well known.'

[9] Brig. D. Ioannides was head of the Greek military police, the moving force behind the *coup* of 25 November, and effective leader of the régime which supplanted that of Col. Papadopoulos.

[10] Gen. P. Gizikis was Col. Papadopoulos's successor as President of the Republic.

[11] As German President, Field-Marshal P. von Hindenburg was responsible for the appointment of Herr A. Hitler as Chancellor in January 1933.

[12] Gen. M. Neguib was one of the leaders of the revolution which deposed King Farouk of Egypt in July 1952. Two years later he was ousted from the Egyptian Presidency by Col. G.A. Nasser.

important—of Ioannides remain obscure. There are already indications of differences on major policy issues between the military leaders of the *coup* and it is too soon to venture on a forecast. But it seems probable that Ioannides will avoid taking any chances on the early introduction of an (as he would see it) unruly and premature democracy. When—and if—democracy comes, it may well approach more closely to the Turkish than to the Western European model. Executive government by second-rate civilians (since no others are likely to co-operate) with Ioannides and Co. keeping tight control from the back room therefore seems the most probable formula for the medium term. But this offers little prospect for a solution of Greece's real difficulties—particularly the economic ones, which with a general recession in prospect and runaway inflation already in full flood in Greece may soon pose problems beyond the capacity of even a much more competent Government backed by a popular mandate.

14. So far as popular sentiment is concerned, the departure of Papadopoulos was greeted by the first real spontaneous and universal outburst of popular feeling I have seen here in two and a half years. The reaction was one of relief and delight. The initial proclamation of the armed forces raised hopes—soon to be damped by Androutsopoulos's frigid policy statement—that Greece was on its way to genuine democracy.[13] But the general euphoria was inspired not so much by enthusiasm for the new Government as by satisfaction at the fall of the old one. To the Opposition, the departure of Papadopoulos was the objective to which they had subordinated all others. It was basically for this reason that they rejected the Markezinis experiment, which, with their co-operation, just might have achieved a peaceful transition to democracy.[14] In doing so, they were in effect opting for a return to full democracy without benefit of Papadopoulos, even if this could only be brought about at the price of a series of *coups*, in preference to the tedious distasteful and devious course of compromise with Papadopoulos. Whether this is what they really wanted is hard to say. But whether or not they get the democracy, they are more than likely to get the *coups*.

---

[13] Mr. Androutsopoulos addressed the nation on radio and television on the evening of 28 November. In Athens telegram No. 426 of 29 November Sir R. Hooper commented that his words would 'disappoint many Greeks including "old politicians" who, following Papadopoulos' fall, had hoped that the way was open to a swift return to political normality'. The speech offered no early prospect of the restoration of the constitutional articles guaranteeing personal liberties, which had been suspended with the declaration of martial law on 17 November, or of early progress toward democratic parliamentary rule.

[14] See No. 1, note 18. As Prime Minister, Mr. Markezinis had sought the support and cooperation of former parliamentary leaders ostensibly with a view to introducing a measure of democracy into Greece's political institutions. In a minute to Mr. C.D. Wiggin (Assistant Under-Secretary of State (AUS)) of 13 November, Mr. Goodison described this move as 'the most encouraging development in Greece for some years'. Mr. Wiggin noted his agreement (WSG 3/548/3).

15. Faced with a deteriorating economic situation and an uncertain political future, public opinion after its initial euphoria is now confused and pessimistic. Greece, it is said is moving nearer the Latin American experience, or back to her own turbulent history of the 'twenties and 'thirties. Shortly before its fall the last Government decided to restrict pleasure motoring by the ingenious device of allowing odd-numbered cars to circulate on one Sunday and even-numbered cars on the next. The crack that was going around Athens last week was that 'it'll be the even-numbered tanks that will be out on the streets next Sunday'. Osbert Lancaster,[15] in his 'Classical Landscape with Figures', dating from the Civil War and still the best guide to modern Greece and its inhabitants, invented the term of 'Praxicopematics' (from praxicopema: a *coup d'état*) for the Greek science of perpetrating *coups*. It may come into fashion again.

16. If so, the outlook is gloomy. If the survival of Governments is to be at the mercy of any handful of determined military conspirators who decide to stage a *coup*, Greece's effectiveness as a NATO ally and her ability to conduct a coherent foreign policy—on Cyprus, on her relations with the European Community, or indeed on anything else—are bound to be called into question. In Brussels, the cast-iron excuse afforded by recent events for postponing a decision on the Community's future relations with Greece may be greeted with relief by hard-pressed Eurocrats; and there can be little doubt that Greece, as of today, is in no state to undertake the responsibilities and obligations of fuller association—let alone membership. But the cost of an unstable Greece to the international balance of forces and to Western interests in South-East Europe may be heavy indeed. To doubts of Greece's political stability must be added similar misgivings about the value of her forces for war. The opponents of the régime have always maintained that political interference by the Papadopoulos régime had destroyed the efficiency and morale of the Greek forces. Up to now they have, I think, been wrong. But there can be little doubt that the massive purges which followed the recent *coup* must have thrown the forces into confusion which will be worse confounded if the process is repeated. Throw in with all this the lack of confidence—in an already shaky world economic conjecture—which prevails in business circles, and you have the makings of a pretty kettle of fish.

17. Finally, what are the implications for British policy? Our objectives are presumably still to preserve Greece as an effective NATO ally; to work for Greek foreign policies, notably over Cyprus which are in conformity with our interests; and to promote our commercial interests here.[16] We

[15] British artist, cartoonist and writer. He served in the British Embassy, Athens, during 1944-46.

[16] These policy objectives were agreed in April at an Office meeting called by Mr. A.H.F. Royle, Parliamentary Under-Secretary of State for Foreign and Commonwealth Affairs.

should also without prejudicing our other objectives, use such influence as we have to promote the return of democracy in Greece.[17]

18. The advent of the new Government has made none of these objectives any easier to achieve. While the new Prime Minister's statement on the Alliance was moderate and his remarks on Cyprus unexceptionable, we may not be able to take Greece's co-operation in NATO or her value to it quite so much for granted as in the past. On Cyprus, too, some of the new military leaders have records of past links with Grivas which are bound to create misgivings, while in the commercial field the discouraging economic climate and restrictive Government policies will force us to work hard to maintain and develop our position. Above all, this is a régime of inexperienced and largely unsophisticated men with some xenophobic tendencies (anti-American feeling has lately reached a disquieting level and is not confined to any particular point of the political compass). The Government do not yet themselves seem to know where they are going. Their chances of surviving the next few months are problematical. But if they do survive, the political, strategic and economic vulnerability of Greece's position may lead them to settle for the same sort of discreet and cautious external policies followed, on the whole, by Papadopoulos. While they find their feet, however, we have to bear in mind the risk that with this Government, even more than with previous ones, moral exhortation from abroad may produce violent and petulant anti-Western reactions, however damaging these may be to Greece's real interests. The new Government is certainly not so far presenting a very attractive face to the outside world. We cannot at this stage be sure that we shall be able to get along with it; but I submit that we and our NATO allies should not be over-hasty in assuming that we cannot. We cannot expect to control the reactions of public opinion and I do not suggest that we should try. But at least until the new régime has made its policies more clear, let us not jeopardise our political strategic and commercial interests in this area by being over-ready with official censure or admonition.

19. I am sending a copy of this despatch to Her Majesty's Representatives in Ankara, Rome, Paris and Bonn, the UK Permanent

---

[17] At a meeting between Mr. Royle and Sir R. Hooper on 20 September it was agreed to include the encouragement of progress towards democracy in Greece as a further policy objective. Mr. Goodison subsequently explained in a letter to Mr. J.B. Denson (Counsellor in HM Embassy, Athens) of 5 October that 'most pressing' amongst the reasons for this change was that 'positive developments in Greece should reduce parliamentary hostility to the Order in Council on completion of negotiations on a Protocol to extend the Greek/EEC Association Agreement to the Community's new members [i.e. Denmark, the Republic of Ireland and the UK]'. Progress towards democracy in Greece should, he added, reduce the constraints which currently prevented full and constructive Anglo-Greek relations, and 'might draw the sting from Scandinavian and Dutch criticism of Greece, and to a lesser extent criticism in Britain, which threatens NATO's fabric' (WSG 3/548/3). Greece's Association Agreement with the EEC had been frozen since the Greek *coup d'état* of 1967, except for its trade provisions which continued to be applied.

Representative, NATO, the UK Permanent Representative to the European Communities, the UK High Commissioner at Nicosia and the Commander British Forces Near East.

I have, etc.,
R.W. HOOPER

No. 3

Letter from Mr. Goodison to Mr. Olver (Nicosia)

[*WSC 1/2*]

Confidential   FCO, *18 January 1974*

Intercommunal Talks[1]

1. Thank you very much for your letter 1/4 of 14 January, with its very useful enclosures of which we have distributed copies as you requested.[2] We shall be studying these with care. It is very useful to have the declared views of Clerides and Denktash on record. It is certainly difficult to see how the two papers could be reconciled.[3] But we are rather encouraged to know that both Clerides and Denktash are showing some flexibility in their thinking about what should be done if the talks reach an impasse.[4]

2. This letter is to record the call upon me by Diamantopoulos, Minister-Counsellor at the Greek Embassy here, on 16 January in so far as it referred to the intercommunal talks (the rest is recorded in our telegram No. 13 of that date).[5] He said that he was speaking to me on instructions in

---

[1] Opening and concluding salutations are omitted from the copy of this document on file.

[2] Enclosed with Mr. Olver's letter were papers by Mr. Clerides and Mr. Denktash presenting their views on the future of local government in Cyprus and an analytical memorandum of 14 January by Mr. D. Beattie, First Secretary in the British High Commission, Nicosia.

[3] *V. ibid.* 'The two papers', Mr. Beattie concluded, 'are in most respects diametrically opposed. Mr. Clerides reserves the lion's share of authority for the State ... In contrast, Mr. Denktash demands the fullest possible local autonomy.'

[4] Both Mr. Denktash and Mr. Clerides were, according to Mr. Olver, ready to envisage an alternative form of intercommunal dialogue through small-scale working meetings to achieve practical solutions in areas of discrimination (e.g. electricity and water). In his letter of 14 January (see note 2 above), Mr. Olver observed that although the prospects for the talks on constitutional questions were 'clearly poor', it was 'still premature to start writing an obituary'.

[5] This and telegram No. 14 to Nicosia of 16 January (WSC 6/548/1) reported Mr. Goodison's conversation with Mr. N. Diamantopoulos about a recent interview given by Archbishop Makarios to the *Irish Times* and subsequent press reports concerning Cyprus Government financial claims for non-SBA facilities used by British troops on the island. Since 1965 HMG had made the discussion of further financial assistance to Cyprus dependent on progress towards an intercommunal settlement and on both communities benefiting from such aid (cf. No. 98, note 15).

order to follow up a conversation between Metaxas, the Head of the Cyprus Department of the Greek Ministry of Foreign Affairs, and John Denson which took place on 11 January.[6] I said that I had not yet received any account of that conversation, which was no doubt coming by bag, given our request to HM Missions abroad to reduce their telegraphing in view of the limitations on our hours of work in London imposed by the fuel crisis.[7] Diamantopoulos immediately, and typically, took fright and offered to go away and come back later when I had seen that report but I soothed him down and urged him to tell me what he had to say.

3. Diamantopoulos said that the Greek Government were very concerned about the intransigence of the Turkish Cypriots. An example of this had been the Turkish alert in the Limassol area which had only been called off after a difficult confrontation (I understand that the alert did not in fact last long and was not particularly significant but I made no comment at this point).[8] There was a tendency on the part of the Turks to create *faits accomplis* on the ground and these must have their effect on the intercommunal talks by increasing a fear of intercommunal violence. He then spoke at considerable length about the intransigence of the Turkish side in the talks. In this situation the Greek Government considered that the well-known policy of HMG of telling both sides that they hoped they would reach agreement, while at the same time we asserted that we would accept any agreement reached between them, was not helpful. It merely encouraged the Turks in their intransigence. The Greek Government hoped therefore that we would speak to the Turkish Government and urge them to press the need for movement and flexibility on the Turkish Cypriot side.[9]

4. I replied that he had described our policy accurately. In contacts with the Foreign Ministers in New York last summer the Secretary of State had spoken in general terms of the importance of reaching agreement and of the need for compromise but had not urged any specific action on either

[6] Mr. Denson reported this conversation with Mr. A. Metaxas in a letter to Mr. Goodison of 16 January. After referring to events at Limassol on 7 January, when Turkish 'freedom fighters' had entered the Turkish quarter of the town and cut off access to it and neighbouring villages, Mr. Metaxas expressed the hope that the British would use their 'influence to prevent such incidents'. He also asked that HMG 'should "show more interest" in the talks'.

[7] A fuel shortage resulting from an over-time ban by British coal miners and the decision by Arab oil exporting states to quadruple the price of oil had led to restrictions on the use of electricity and the introduction, on 1 January, of a three-day working week.

[8] See note 6 above.

[9] In his letter to Mr. Goodison of 16 January (see note 6 above) Mr. Denson noted that the Greeks could not 'seriously imagine we could at this stage (or possibly at any stage) twist Turkish arms'. He speculated whether, despite assurances to the contrary, there were fears in the Foreign Ministry that the new Greek Government could portend a change of policy towards Cyprus, and that this was an attempt to ensure that British support for the talks was maintained.

side.[10] The fact was that the parties concerned were all our friends and we were most reluctant to intervene on one side or the other. In any case, since Metaxas had spoken to John Denson the news had come that we were likely to see a new government in Turkey. We did not yet know exactly what Mr. Eçevit's policy on Cyprus would be.[11] In making recommendations to British Ministers about action in response to what Diamantopoulos had said to me, I should be bound to say that it would be wrong to approach the Turkish Government [on] the lines advocated by the Greeks without having some indication of the new government's policy. Diamantopoulos appeared to accept that this was a reasonable new point. I promised him that when I had received the account of the Metaxas/Denson interview I would report it and his conversation with me and seek instructions, and would then summon him again.

5. At that point Diamantopoulos said he thought it only fair, although it was not in his instructions, to draw my attention to an Athens news agency despatch received from Nicosia that day to the effect that Professor Aldiçaçiti and Mr. Dekleris had made progress on the question of local administration.[12] Although Mr. Clerides had said that outstanding questions had not been settled, Mr. Dekleris had said he wished to stress that the talks had not reached a deadlock. Diamantopoulos thought this was an encouraging report and admitted that it detracted from the effect of the instructions he had received.

6. I have no intention of recommending that we should intervene with the Turkish Government on the lines the Greeks have requested. At the same time, I assured Diamantopoulos that in Sir Horace Phillips's[13] first contacts with the new Turkish Foreign Minister[14] the question of Cyprus was bound to arise and I had no doubt that the Ambassador would, in accordance with our general policy, stress our anxiety to see a successful conclusion to the talks and the need for compromise by all concerned if this was to be reached. If what Metaxas said to John Denson was reflected accurately by Diamantopoulos, then, unless any recipient of this letter telegraphs advising to the contrary, I shall recommend that I be authorised to inform Diamantopoulos that instructions have been sent to Horace Phillips to this effect.[15]

A.C. GOODISON

[10] During 23-28 September 1973 Sir A. Douglas-Home had attended the 28th UN General Assembly in New York.

[11] On 25 January the Turkish caretaker administration of Senator N. Talu was replaced by a coalition of the Republican People's Party (RPP) and the National Salvation Party (NSP), led by Mr. B. Eçevit of the RPP.

[12] See No. 1, note 4.

[13] HM Ambassador in Ankara.

[14] Mr. T. Günes.

[15] In a letter to Mr. Goodison of 4 February Mr. Olver expressed his agreement with the line he proposed to take.

No. 4

Letter from Mr. Olver (Nicosia) to Mr. Goodison

[*WSC 1/2*]

Confidential   NICOSIA, *27 February 1974*

Dear Alan,

Relations between the two Communities in Cyprus

In my letter of 20 February,[1] I promised an analysis of what seems to me a growing separatism on both sides here. Behind a superficially business-as-usual atmosphere, both the Greek and Turkish sides have, I sense, lost interest in the talks. These are still regarded as a useful safety-valve, and I am sure neither side will readily accept the odium of causing them to collapse. But there is no longer, I detect, much real belief on either side—or for that matter on Osorio Tafall's part either—that they can provide any real solution to the Cyprus problem. All concerned are content to play things along quietly, with the constitutional advisers grinding slowly and exceeding small. That the latter are still making helpful noises could be partly professional optimism—but I suspect, on Aldikaçti's part at least, a certain degree of smoke-screen as well.

2. To turn to underlying attitudes. The Archbishop made it clear enough, when I saw him on 18 January, that he was losing faith in any solution through the talks owing to Turkish intransigence; and I reported in my letter of 4 February, his inclination to appeal to the Turkish Cypriot community over the heads of Denktash and the Turkish Cypriot Administration.[2] Attitudes on the Greek Cypriot side have since hardened owing to the row over federalism,[3] and the Archbishop's latest

---

[1] Mr. Olver reported in this letter to Mr. Goodison that the session of talks on 19 February seemed to have 'passed smoothly with a fairly routine examination of the progress made by the two constitutional experts'. But, he added, that the recent 'spate of references to federalism, far from inducing greater flexibility has made the Greek Cypriots even more suspicious of Turkish intentions'.

[2] See No. 3, note 13. In this letter Mr. Olver warned Mr. Goodison that it was most unlikely that the Turkish community would split, 'and efforts by the Archbishop in [that] direction would only be taken by them as further proof of his insincerity'. Mr. Olver thought that if Archbishop Makarios were to move in this direction, HMG might have to contemplate 'something more active than [its] traditional role'.

[3] The recently-published programme of the new Turkish Government affirmed its belief that the 'most appropriate solution' for Cyprus would be found in a 'federal system to maintain the equal sovereignty status of the Turkish community and to ensure peaceful co-operation in every way between the two communities in the State administration'. Sir H. Phillips informed Mr. Goodison in a letter of 3 February that Mr. I. Soysal, the Director-General for Political Affairs in the Turkish Foreign Ministry, had assured him that 'there was no immediate hope or thought that a federation could or indeed should be achieved. There were acceptable solutions which might stop short of this or might diverge to either side of the present path towards local autonomy.' But on 8 February Mr. Diamantopoulos told Mr. Wiggin that if the concept of

statement—to a Belgian journalist on 20 February—was to the effect that 'Turkish Cypriot demands would lead to political and ultimately geographical partition.'

3. A long talk last week with Inhan[4] has given me my clearest insight so far into the Turkish position. To condense an hour and a half's talk into a page or so, it seems to be based on the following points:-

(a) A bi-communal state remains the Turkish objective. But there is no faith in the sort of formulae embodied in the 1960 constitution, which would depend for effective operation on goodwill which does not exist now and which, if it could be conjured out of the air, would not last for more than a year or two.

(b) A federal system—or to call a spade a spade, federation—is therefore the only practical answer to the Turkish need for cast-iron physical and economic safeguards.[5]

(c) Federation can admittedly not work without a geographical base, and in the present state of extreme dispersal of the Turkish population throughout the island it is not immediately practicable. Nonetheless, there already exist in various parts of the island—aside from the Nicosia enclave, Inhan mentioned the north-western enclaves and parts of the central plain—concentrations of Turkish Cypriot population which could be expanded to form Turkish districts. This might conceivably be a gradual process. Some degree of transfer of population might be involved—and Inhan referred to major population transfers in the world as an indication that this need not be ruled out on the tiny scale that would be involved here. Some Turkish families would doubtless be left behind in Greek areas; that would be their look out.

(d) In these Turkish areas there would be a completely self-contained and autonomous Turkish administration from the District Officer downwards, and this in its turn must be responsible to a self-contained central Turkish Administration.

(e) The result would be a federal state of Cyprus, independent, sovereign, perhaps with guarantees for its future given by Turkey and Greece. In

'federalism' were formally introduced into the talks by the Turks, discussion was bound to come to an end (telegram No. 158 to Ankara of 11 February).

[4] Mr. A. Inhan was Deputy Head of Mission at the Turkish Embassy in Nicosia.

[5] On 7 February Mr. E. Barutçu, the Head of the Cyprus and Greek Affairs Department in the Turkish Foreign Ministry, explained to Mr. R.A. Fyjis-Walker, Counsellor in the British Embassy, Ankara, that 'by openly postulating a federal "system" but not "state", the Turks aimed to be in a position where they could rebut Greek Cypriot demands as being "incompatible with a federal system", in the same way as the Greeks always resisted Turkish claims as "incompatible with a unitary state"' (Ankara telegram No. 157 of 8 February). Sir H. Phillips also pointed out in a letter to Mr. Goodison of 15 March that, 'however much they may think of partition as the neatest and most desirable solution', the Turkish Foreign Ministry was still aiming to negotiate a Cyprus settlement which would 'protect the Turks where they are'.

reply to a comment from me, he did not believe that this need amount to partition, nor was he contemplating a total Turkish concentration into any single part of the island.

(f) This could not come about overnight, and the inter-communal talks were of course useful meanwhile. They were even throwing up some helpful ideas on practical administrative points. But they could not, on their present course, lead to a solution: one sticking point inherent in the sort of outline sketched above, emerging already in the talks between the constitutional advisers, was the absolute Turkish insistence on a separate and autonomous Turkish internal security apparatus. There could be no compromise over police or security forces.

4. Inhan has just returned from Ankara. He is a tough but cautious man, and it is inconceivable that the line he took with me should not have been closely rehearsed with Günes. In assessing it, we must doubtless make some allowance for Turkish hopes to frighten us into taking a tough line with the Greek Cypriots, and the Greek Government. But I believe—and such collateral as we have been able to obtain here suggests that this is also the belief in well informed Turkish Cypriot circles—that in essence, behind a front of continued support for the talks, the sort of 'federative system' outlined by Inhan is now the central Turkish objective. Günes' mention of Wales to Horace Phillips would then be a revealing slip rather than a sign of confusion;[6] and the much harder and more separatist remarks which Denktash has made in recent public statements would also fall into place. The obvious assumption would be that Turkish policy over Cyprus was discussed at length between Günes and Denktash when the latter visited Cyprus in January; that the conclusion was then reached that the talks were getting nowhere and that time was not on the Turkish side; and that a hardening of Turkish policy harking back to Inonu's federalism[7] was then decided on. The trouble is that, whatever theoretical plausibility there may be in Inhan's remarks about Turkish areas (paragraph 3(c) above), it is inconceivable that the sort of territorial adjustments involved would be allowed by the Government, or supported by Athens; and any policy on these lines thus contains the seeds of conflict from the outset. Furthermore, though Inhan's denial of any aim for partition may have been sincere, the sort of federal central government envisaged in this Turkish plan would

---

[6] Sir H. Phillips reported in Ankara telegram No. 174 of 13 February that to the 'way of thinking' of Mr. Günes, 'just as say Wales in the United Kingdom and Slovenia in Yugoslavia are much smaller than other units in the whole but have equal rights with these and are not classed as minorities, so must the Turkish Cypriot community be treated (while still remaining in its present locations)'. In his letter to Mr. Goodison of 20 February (see note 1 above) Mr. Olver questioned the value of this analogy. He argued that, apart from the six main towns, where the Turkish community lived in well-defined sectors, the Turks were dispersed all over the island; and a 'closer analogy would be a "federative system" which covered everyone named Jones throughout the United Kingdom'.

[7] Mr. I. Inönü was Turkish President between 1938 and 1950. As Turkish Prime Minister during 1961-63 he supported the idea of federation as a solution to the Cyprus problem.

also be anathema to the Greek side, and in practice something close to partition would be the most likely result.

5. The motives behind all this are speculative. Horace Phillips will be able to comment on how important a factor the traditional outlook of the RPP may be.[8] Growing disillusionment with the talks is undoubtedly a major element: Inhan's impatience with the lack of real progress and what he called 'this comedy' was not concealed. But a further factor, likely to have weighed particularly with Denktash is, I suspect, the belief that time is working against the Turkish Cypriots. Denktash's difficulties over the coming year are likely to grow. Political opposition is expected to sharpen with the increased freedom anticipated here under the Eçevit regime. Denktash has described the promised 20% increase in the subvention[9] from Ankara as insufficient even to keep up with current inflation, and the Turkish Cypriots seem bound to suffer even more severely than the Greek Cypriot community from shortages, rising prices, labour troubles and all the other baneful side effects of inflation which will hit Cyprus this year. It seems possible that Denktash sees his best chance of hanging on as dictator of the Turkish Cypriot community in posing as their tough defender against Greek machinations. Perhaps the best guess is that disillusionment with the talks, party political needs in Ankara and a yearning for tougher action by Denktash have all fed on each other.

6. I do not see in any of this the likelihood of an immediate crisis. The talks can stagger on for some time. Some alternative safety valve might be devised—though no one seems to be giving much thought to this. But I have never subscribed to the belief that the separation of the two communities here was a sound basis for coexistence. I believe on the contrary that the logic of increasing separatism is an eventual confrontation. And a readiness to take risks and to face an eventual showdown seems to me implicit in current attitudes on both sides.

7. One obvious path towards this could be the village elections due this June. I reported the Archbishop's intentions over these briefly in my letter of 4 February. We shall be reporting separately on the complicated internal and intercommunal implications, if they are in fact held and if separate Turkish village elections are held simultaneously. Very briefly, the newly elected Turkish Mukhtars[10] will not be recognised by the Greek Cypriot Administration. From this will follow a whole series of administrative

---

[8] In a letter to Mr. Goodison of 15 March Sir H. Phillips was inclined to play down this factor. 'Cyprus', he noted, 'is a national cause in Turkey: irritation at failure to reach an intercommunal settlement and fear for the well-being of Turkish Cypriots are sufficient cause for a new Turkish Government to look for a different approach that will enable them to outshine their predecessors' efforts.'

[9] During the 1973 intercommunal talks, the Turkish Cypriots proposed that they should have the right to receive financial aid from Turkey. This was agreed on the basis that this aid would be channelled through the Cypriot Ministry for Foreign Affairs and the Central Bank of Cyprus. It was also conditional on this money not leading to economic dislocation.

[10] Village headmen.

consequences which can only lead to an extension of the Turkish Cypriot Administration's activities in the villages and the complete exclusion of such government cooperation and influence as still survive. This could well be the beginning of a long slippery slope encompassing greater dangers. The sort of activities involved in such an extension of the Turkish Administration would be an obvious hostage to fortune. To the Cyprus Government, this would be an illegal extension of an illegal Administration. At present, Turks circulate freely all over the island—in contradistinction to Greeks, who are not allowed to enter Turkish enclaves. The existing Turkish Cypriot Administration could not function effectively without free access to all parts of the Republic. Any further consolidation of the Administration would be totally dependent on such access. The Government could cut this off at the drop of a hat; and in a situation already tipped against them on this score, I fear that little further provocation might be needed to call down checks on Turkish movements on the Greek side here. That would of course rapidly escalate into a comprehensive blockade, with all its attendant dangers. In a battle of this sort confined to the island, the Turkish Cypriots must always lose—and so we should be back in short order to the threat of mainland Turkish intervention.

8. I see very little that we can do in this situation beyond continuing to preach moderation and support for the talks, here and in Athens and Ankara.[11] I still adhere to the view that in substance the gap between the two sides is not wide, given mutual confidence and goodwill. But in the total absence of these, at least between the two leaderships on the island, it seems more than ever clear that the gap will only be closed if pressure can be applied to both sides at a critical moment. This would have, in essence I think, to come from the United Nations. Perhaps the successor to Osorio Tafall—the latter's departure now seems fairly imminent—may produce some new impetus.

Yours ever,
S.J.L. Olver

[11] In telegram No. 159 to Ankara of 11 February Sir A. Douglas-Home left it to Sir H. Phillips's discretion to tell the Turkish Government that HMG had been informed by the Greek Government that if the concept of 'federalism' were introduced into the talks, discussion was bound to come to an end (cf. note 3 above). 'It would', Sir A. Douglas-Home added, 'be a matter of considerable regret if the progress already achieved in the talks should be jeopardised by any misunderstanding over the terms used. In our view what matters most is to continue patient pragmatic examination of specific problems in the talks themselves.'

No. 5

Mr. L.J. Callaghan[1] to Sir R. Hooper (Athens)

No. 49 Telegraphic [WSG 3/548/5]

Immediate. Confidential   FCO, *13 March 1974, 7.50 p.m.*
Repeated for information to Immediate UKDEL NATO,[2] Lisbon, Washington, Priority Nicosia, Ankara, Bonn, Brussels, Ottawa, Rome Oslo, Paris, Luxembourg, The Hague, Copenhagen and Saving to Reykavik.

Greece and NATO

Ministers have decided that the informal visit by HMS Tiger and HMS Charybdis to Athens due to begin on 15 March should not take place. Given the attitude which they took while in opposition to the continuing failure to restore democracy in Greece it would be quite inconsistent to allow a visit of this nature to go forward.

2. You should immediately inform the Greek authorities of this decision at whatever level you judge appropriate. You could point out that HMG laid emphasis in the Queen's speech on their full support of the maintenance of the North Atlantic Alliance. At the same time the Greeks will be fully aware of HMG's concern over the political situation in Greece. In view of the strength of Parliamentary and public feeling here on the subject HMG do not consider it appropriate that this visit should be maintained.

3. You should add that cancellation of the visit will of course arouse press attention. For that reason we will be letting HMG's decision be known at tomorrow's daily News Department press briefing. The announcement is likely to be on the following lines:-

'Certain aspects of the programme of visits by Royal Navy ships abroad are currently under review. The informal visit of HMS Tiger and HMS Charybdis to Athens planned for 15 to 19 March will not now take place.'
You should explain that this low key formulation is designed to avoid the significance of the decision being exaggerated: but the press will of course nevertheless draw the conclusion that the decision has political significance.

4. In making this communication you should try to avoid being drawn into discussion of future policy towards naval visits generally or other aspects of Anglo/Greek relations in which changes might occur. You could

---

[1] As a result of the General Election on 28 February Mr. E. Heath's Conservative Government lost its Parliamentary majority, and on 4 March the Labour leader, Mr. H. Wilson was appointed Prime Minister. Mr. Callaghan succeeded Sir A. Douglas-Home as Secretary of State for Foreign and Commonwealth Affairs.

[2] UK Delegation to NATO.

if necessary point out that HMG naturally expect to have a variety of continuing business to discuss with the Greek Government which they would hope to conduct in a business-like way. Ministers are at the beginning of a detailed review of their policies in a multiplicity of fields both international and domestic. They will wish to give careful and considered examination to Anglo/Greek relations.[3]

5. For your own information we shall be conducting a comprehensive review of sensitive areas in Anglo/Greek relations in other fields as well as naval. Further instructions and guidance will be sent to you as appropriate.

6. UKDEL NATO please pass copy immediate to Killick.[4]

[3] Sir R. Hooper recommended that HMG should avoid being drawn into explanations of the cancellation of the visit. In Athens telegram No. 56 of 14 March he argued that to inform the Greek authorities in the terms proposed might well not only prejudge issues in the proposed review of relations with Greece, but would make it difficult to achieve a business-like relationship with the present Greek régime. Indeed, he predicted that the Greek Government might immediately retaliate against British commercial interests in Greece. But in telegram No. 50 to Athens of 14 March Mr. Goodison insisted that there could be 'no question of concealing basic reason for cancellation and review'.

[4] Sir J. Killick was Deputy Under-Secretary of State (DUS). On 14 March he participated in a reinforced meeting of the North Atlantic Council (NAC) in Brussels. Cf. Volume III, No. 56, note 4.

No. 6

Sir R. Hooper (Athens) to Mr. Callaghan

No. 57 Telegraphic [*WSG 3/548/5*]

Flash. Confidential　　　　　　　　　　　ATHENS, *14 March 1974, 3.30 p.m.*

Following personal for Goodison

I fully accept and agree with HMG's wish to see an early restoration of democracy in Greece and understand that they should wish to exert, and to be seen to exert, their influence to this end. It is difficult to advise from here unless and until I have further information about the policy to be pursued. However, and although I am sure that they are very much in your mind, I feel I must put to you the following considerations.

2. (i) Assuming that the objective is not merely to express our distaste for the present regime, but to work actively to bring about change for the better, we must accept that HMG acting alone or even in conjunction with those of our NATO and EEC partners (e.g. the Dutch and Scandinavians) who think likewise can exercise very little influence in this direction. Only the US Government disposes of sufficient means—strategic, military aid and financial and political

involvement—to make pressure effective.[1] If we act on our own or even in conjunction with the like-minded Western Europeans, we run the risk not only of failing to achieve our objective but of seeing what we are bound to lose commercially and in other ways picked up by others (e.g. the French and Japanese) who are less scrupulous politically. In my view, therefore, the process should begin in Washington.[2] We have a considerable stake in Greece (e.g. defence of SE flank of NATO, Cyprus and £100m. of exports annually) which has to be taken into consideration.

(ii) It is not yet entirely clear to me whether, as assumed above, it is the intention of HMG to work actively for change or whether they wish to revert to something like the policy pursued between 1967 and 1970, i.e. a minimum relationship with the Greek regime as such and the maintenance of a distinction between it and Greece as a NATO ally. If the former assumption is correct, we cannot expect to pursue it while at the same time maintain the kind of businesslike relationship referred to in para 4 of your tel[egram] No. 49.[3] We must be prepared to expect considerably less willingness to cooperate with us both bilaterally and within the framework of NATO. In particular, we should have to accept a lower level of military cooperation in which we are usually the demandeurs. We need not expect public sector contracts, and will be able to do little to protect British interests in the private sector against harassment and obstruction. British subjects in Greece, both resident and tourists, can expect less effective protection. It is possible that as a minor and easily administered pinprick the Greek authorities may delay or even refuse agreement to my successor. I do not wish to sound alarmist and I appreciate that Ministers may decide that the price is worth paying. But I should be failing in my duty to them if I did not indicate the possible size of the bill.

3. I am seeing the Secretary-General of the Ministry of Foreign Affairs this afternoon, and will report further, if necessary.[4]

---

[1] Cf. No. 13.

[2] In a minute to Mr. Wiggin of 18 March Mr. Goodison noted that, according to information reaching Sir R. Hooper, Brig. Ioannides hoped that the Americans would press HMG to refrain from further exasperating the Greek Junta. He had sent a message to the US saying 'that unless the Americans treat[ed] Greece properly as a NATO ally and [met] her needs for defence equipment, the home-porting arrangements for the Sixth Fleet [would] be cancelled'.

[3] No. 5.

[4] During this meeting the Secretary-General, Mr. A.S. Vlachos, told Sir R. Hooper that he thought the Greek Government would be 'extremely resentful both of HMG's decision and of the manner in which it had been taken'. Anglo-Greek relations were, he protested, 'bound to be severely affected and he did not exclude the possibility of a formal protest. This was not the behaviour that Greece expected from an ally.' The next day Mr. L. Migliaressis, the Foreign Ministry's Political Director for Europe and America, informed Sir R. Hooper that the Greek Government wished to 'protest strongly' at the cancellation of the visit which constituted

inadmissible interference in Greece's internal affairs and seriously jeopardised the Atlantic Alliance (Athens telegrams Nos. 58 and 63 of 14 and 15 March). Sir R. Hooper subsequently reported in Athens telegram No. 73 of 19 March that in the first instance retaliation was likely to be in the field of military and naval co-operation, including the non-placement of a frigate contract with a British shipyard.

No. 7

Mr. Callaghan to Sir P. Ramsbotham[1] (Washington)

No. 681 Telegraphic [WSC 3/303/1]

Priority. Confidential   FCO, *25 March 1974, 9 a.m.*

Repeated to Ankara, Athens, and for information to Priority Nicosia, Routine Moscow, UMIS New York

Soviet Policy on Cyprus

1. The Soviet Chargé d'Affaires, Semenov,[2] asked to call on me at short notice on 18 March with what he described as a personal message. In the event, he was received by Mr Hattersley.[3] He did not hand over a piece of paper. He said he had been instructed to inform HMG that Moscow considered it necessary to exchange views on the present situation in Cyprus. President Makarios' Government, as was well known, was making resolute efforts to normalise the situation, to settle the island's problems peacefully in the interests of the Cypriots, both Greeks and Turks, and to consolidate the sovereignty, independence and territorial integrity of the Republic. However, recent reports from Cypriot and foreign sources indicated that the island had become noticeably more complicated as a result of actions hostile to Cypriot independence, primarily actions by extremist circles in Greece. On the island itself there were growing activities against the Government by illegal organisations directed from outside and conducted under the slogan of *enosis*. Nor could one ignore the attempts of certain outside forces to 'solve' the Cyprus problem behind the back of the Cypriot Government and people, against their will and to the detriment of the independence and territorial integrity of the Republic.[4] The consistent and principled position of the Soviet Union was well-known.

[1] HM Ambassador in Washington. During 1969-71 he was British High Commissioner in Nicosia.

[2] Mr. Y.A. Semenov was Minister-Counsellor in the Soviet Embassy in London.

[3] Mr. R. Hattersley was Minister of State for Foreign and Commonwealth Affairs.

[4] Already in February the Soviet press had launched a campaign in support of Cyprus's independence and neutrality and accusing NATO agents of backing an EOKA conspiracy against Archbishop Makarios.

The Soviet Union had spoken resolutely in support of the independence, sovereignty and territorial integrity of Cyprus and for the peaceful solution of the Cyprus question without any foreign intervention in any form. The Soviet position was being brought again to the attention of the United States, Greek and Turkish Governments. Moscow hoped that the British Government, being guided by the well-known decisions of the United Nations Security Council, would help to normalise the situation in Cyprus, which was in close proximity to another region where a highly complicated situation existed. Mr. Semenov then quoted from the Security Council Resolution of 1964[5] and concluded by saying that he had been instructed to seek an exposé of HMG's views.

2. We replied that there was very little difference between Britain and the Soviet Union on the maintenance of the independence and territorial integrity of Cyprus. We agreed that foreign intervention was undesirable. We regarded the activity of the United Nations as helpful. We also recognised that, like us, Greece and Turkey had a special position. We were a little surprised that the Soviet Union should be especially worried at the present time, since the death of Grivas[6] had reduced the risk of guerrilla activity. We were not particularly concerned at the present situation and had faith in the ability of President Makarios to control the situation on the island. Pressed on why this matter had been raised now, Semenov said that his instructions contained no specific references to recent events.

3. We remain puzzled about why the Soviet Union should make this move now.[7] We should be grateful if addressees of this telegram would inform the Government's to which they are accredited of this exchange and seek their views on Russian intentions. We should also welcome the comments of information recipients.[8] At his discretion Mr. Olver may inform the Cyprus Government of the Soviet approach.[9]

---

[5] UNSC Resolution 186 of 4 March 1964 had recommended both the creation of UNFICYP and the appointment of a UN mediator to work with the Governments of Cyprus, Greece, Turkey and the UK in 'promoting a peaceful solution and an agreed settlement ... having in mind the well-being of the people of Cyprus as a whole and the preservation of international peace and security', *Resolutions and Decisions of the Security Council: 1964: Security Council official Records: 19th year* (New York, 1966). Cf. No. 1, note 7.

[6] Gen. Grivas died of a heart attack on 27 January.

[7] In a minute to Mr. Wiggin of 21 March, Mr. Goodison noted: 'The Soviet Embassy last expressed concern to us about developments in Cyprus in April 1970, shortly after an assassination attempt against Archbishop Makarios. We know of no specific reason for the present Soviet concern.'

[8] Similar *démarches* had been made by Soviet diplomats in Ankara, Athens and Washington. Mr. T. Boyatt, the Country Director for Cyprus in the US State Department, thought their explanation was to be found in the close interest the Soviet Union had taken in Cyprus over a number of years, and that the Russians might have attached some credence to 'rumours of a new hard-line Greek head of EOKA' (Washington telegram No. 1081 of 26 March).

By contrast, Sir H. Phillips reported the Turks as feeling that the Russians were acting either: (1) as a result of false information that the Greek and Turkish Governments had agreed

4. We hope Sir R. Hooper will see no objection to action on these lines in Athens, which may serve to reassure the Greek MFA[10] that we shall continue to conduct normal business with them.[11]

on some kind of double enosis which they were about to impose on Cyprus, which Moscow would want to forestall; or (2) 'on an initiative by Makarios who wished to bring pressure on the Greek Government over EOKA which was now firmly in Greek Government hands but which Makarios might also fear was planning his elimination'. Mr. Barutçu thought that in the second case the Russians would have been misled by disinformation: 'The new Greek Government had clearly taken steps to get control of EOKA but he did not believe that they would be so unwise as to use it to eliminate the Archbishop or to try to impose a solution by force. This would mean a direct clash with Turkey.' Alternatively, Mr. Barutçu suspected that Archbishop Makarios might be trying to use the Russians to block any outcome of the intercommunal talks (Ankara telegram No. 323 of 26 March).

[9] In Nicosia telegram No. 70 of 26 March, drafted in response to this telegram, Mr. Olver informed Mr. Callaghan that he had seen Mr. Christofides that morning. While Mr. Christofides exonerated the Greek Ministry of Foreign Affairs, whose support for 'traditional Cyprus policies' he considered 'genuine', he told Mr. Olver that he strongly suspected that other circles in the Greek Government were supporting EOKA. Cf. No. 8.

[10] Ministry of Foreign Affairs.

[11] On 1 April Mr. S. Tetenes, the Greek Foreign Minister, told Sir R. Hooper, HM Ambassador in Athens, that he had denied Soviet suggestions that the Greek Government were supporting and controlling EOKA. He said that with Gen. Grivas's death, 'there was a chance that EOKA might turn away from violent courses and become something more closely resembling a normal political movement'. This, he remarked, would be welcomed by the Greek Government, 'but one private army bred another, and it was unlikely that EOKA would mend its ways if Makarios continued to keep his personal band of thugs (i.e. the Police Tactical Reserve) in being' (letter from Sir R. Hooper to Mr. Goodison of 3 April, WSC 1/2; cf. No. 1, note 16). As, however, Sir R. Hooper pointed out in Athens telegram No. 79 of 27 March, the Greek Foreign Ministry accepted that the military authorities in Athens had links with EOKA supporters in Cyprus of which the Foreign Ministry was not informed and could not control.

No. 8

Letter from Mr. Olver (Nicosia) to Mr. Goodison

[*WSC 1/9*]

Confidential   NICOSIA, *25 March 1974*

Dear Alan,

Greece and EOKA B

In the spring a Cypriot's fancy lightly turns to thoughts of—plots: and spring 1974 is no exception. It is hard to see why the present wave of rumours about sinister doings inside and outside the island should have started. The general scene has been remarkably quiet since Grivas' death.[1] It is perhaps not too cynical to suggest that since nothing appears to be happening most Greek Cypriots have concluded that something must be happening, but that this time the conspiracy is so unusually satanic that (contrary to form) the machinations have been successfully concealed.

2. The rumours started with The Times report on 19 February suggesting that there had been a breakthrough in the intercommunal talks.[2] The left wing press immediately concluded that, since The Times was known to be infallible, the report meant either that a secret agreement had been concluded between Athens and Ankara, or that Cypriot public opinion was being sounded as to the acceptability of a joint formula. Paradoxically, current Turkish insistence on a federal solution, which had clearly helped to delay progress in the intercommunal talks was taken as further evidence that an Athens-Ankara plot had been hatched. The rumours then fed on the following developments:

(*a*) The theft of a small quantity of arms from a National Guard armoury, which first became public knowledge on 12 February. Shortly after The Times report, the pro-Makarios press printed rumours (later denied officially) that arms had been stolen from several camps, which suggested that sections of the National Guard were involved in a wide-ranging conspiracy with EOKA B.[3] At the same time, the indiscreet conduct of some mainland Greek members of the National Guard caused resentment. The General Secretary of AKEL[4] has recently tabled a Parliamentary Question about an incident in which a young recruit was allegedly maltreated by three Sergeants, because he applied to join the Police Tactical Reserve[5] instead of the National Guard, and because when asked who was the Chief of State he had replied 'Archbishop Makarios' instead (presumably) of 'President Gizikis'.

---

[1] See No. 1, note 9. In Nicosia telegram No. 70 (see No. 7, note 9) Mr. Olver wrote that the truce currently being observed by both sides, though fragile, was holding. 'It is', he continued, 'quite incorrect to say that the situation has become more complicated or that there are growing activities against the Government. EOKA's potential for disorganised violence remains; they are not dissolved; but their capacity to influence events diminishes as time passes.'

[2] In this article the Athens correspondent of *The Times* suggested that 'a qualified source' had indicated that 'a breakthrough formula' on Cyprus's future constitution had been agreed between Greek and Turkish negotiators, providing for 'a two-tier local government system at the highest executive level, with legislative channels designed not to violate the unitarian principle' (*The Times*, 19 February 1974, p. 10).

[3] In a letter to Mr. P.D.R. Davies (First Secretary, SED) of 18 February, Mr. Beattie reported that, according to press reports, more than twenty-five weapons, including heavy machine guns, had been stolen from a National Guard Recruit Training Centre at Famagusta.

[4] *Anorthotiko Komma Ergazomenou Laou*/Progressive Party of the Working People, i.e. Cyprus's pro-Moscow communist party.

[5] Cf. No. 1, note 16.

(*b*) The departure of Major Karousos.[6] Shortly after Beattie's letter of 4 March[7] the press, led by Nicos Sampson's[8] 'Makhi', began to allege that he had been forced to leave EOKA B because he was against violence, and that he had been replaced as Commander of EOKA B by a hard-line Greek Commando officer. We have not seen a shred of hard evidence to support either of these allegations, but it is now impossible to shake the credence given to them by most Greek Cypriots. Lyssarides'[9] paper 'Ta Nea' suggested that the new EOKA B Commander was Colonel Papapostolou, the former Commanding Office of the National Guard Commandos who is notorious in Cyprus for his suspected involvement in the attempt on the Archbishop's life and the murder of Georghajis in 1970.[10] When it emerged that Colonel Papapostolou was still peacefully working at his desk in the Football Pools Agency in Athens, Ta Nea brought up the name Colonel Dertilis, formerly Chief of Staff of the Athens Garrison. It has now been established that Dertilis is at his new post in Kavalla, but doubtless Ta Nea will continue to select likely names out of the Greek Army List. There have also been rumours that large numbers of Greek officers and NCOs have arrived secretly in the island to take up posts in the National Guard from which they will help EOKA B stage a coup d'état.

(*c*) The 40-day memorial service for Grivas on 3 March was, like the funeral, attended by the Greek Ambassador and the Commanders of the National Guard and the Greek mainland Contingent. At the service the Vice Chairman of ESEA,[11] Kyriakos Saveriades, made an extremely

---

[6] Maj. G. Karousos, a former Greek army officer, had been widely tipped as Gen. Grivas's successor as leader of EOKA-B. Following the interception of a British yacht off north- western Cyprus on 28 February, Cyprus police alleged that it had been used to take Maj. Karousos clandestinely to Greece.

[7] In this letter Mr. Beattie informed Mr. Davies of speculation in Cyprus about Maj. Karousos's departure. 'Karoussos [*sic*]', he noted, has always been reputed to be a hard and violent man. His departure may therefore be considered a good thing in itself, but we simply do not know enough about EOKA B to assess whether his departure will have reduced the danger of violence.'

[8] Mr. N. Sampson was a journalist, politician and former leader of the EOKA Execution Squad. He founded the daily newspaper, *Makhi* (Combat), and was Progressive Front Member of the House of Representatives for Famagusta.

[9] Dr. V. Lyssarides was medical adviser and confidant of Archbishop Makarios. After founding *Einea Demokratiki Enosis Kyprou* (EDEK)/Unified Democratic Centre Union, a left-wing party, in 1969, he went on to control armed groups used against EOKA B and Gen. Grivas's followers.

[10] On 8 March 1970 President Makarios's helicopter came under fire as he was leaving Nicosia. A week later Mr. P. Georghajis (Yorgadjis), a former Cyprus Minister of the Interior who was thought to be implicated in the assassination attempt, was found murdered in his car outside Nicosia.

[11] *Eniaios Syndesmos Enotikou Agonos*/Committee for the Coordination of the Enosist Struggle, was formed in November 1971 after Gen. Grivas's return to Cyprus. Effectively, the political

anti-Government speech in which he suggested that the presence of the Ambassador and the two officers was a proof of Greek support for the Enosis movement.

(*d*) The failure of EOKA B and the 70 wanted men to respond to the Archbishop's amnesty,[12] which suggests that they are still contemplating mischief.

3.   There has, therefore[,] been an orgy of speculation led by AKEL and Dr. Lyssarides. AKEL happen to be holding their XIIIth Party Congress next month, and are preparing for it with a series of public meetings throughout the island. Their suspicions, freely expressed at these meetings, have therefore gained unusual prominence. In their speeches, the AKEL leadership have alleged that Athens and NATO between them are plotting to impose a federal solution and/or partition on the island. A necessary preliminary to this will be a coup d'état, accompanied by the physical [and/or] political liquidation of the Archbishop. One of our AKEL contacts has suggested that Brigadier Ioannides is planning a double, simultaneous coup in Athens and Nicosia to rid himself of all his internal opponents. This chorus has been taken up by Radio Moscow and *Pravda*, which had not hesitated to affirm that the threads of the conspiracy lead back to the Athens Junta, and NATO Headquarters.[13] Clearly much of this campaign is orchestrated. But our contacts among the left wing have given us the impression that with part of their minds they genuinely believe that something nasty may happen soon, and this conviction is shared by perfectly respectable journalists of the centre. The atmosphere has been sharpened by the anti-Communist campaign at present being waged by the pro-Grivas press. (Incidentally, there is good reason to believe that these

wing of the Grivas movement and therefore opposed to Archbishop Makarios, it claimed to be above party politics.

[12] On 28 January, the day following Gen. Grivas's death, Archbishop Makarios announced the release of 124 supporters of Gen. Grivas, either on trial, convicted or awaiting criminal proceedings. He further extended the amnesty to cover wanted men, provided they abandoned their hide-outs within five days, presented themselves to the competent authorities and handed in their arms. A list of seventy wanted men was published in this connexion (letter from Mr. Beattie to Mr. Davies of 31 January, WSC 1/4).

[13] Mr. Olver observed in Nicosia telegram No. 70 (see note 1 above) that he found recent Soviet moves 'puzzling'. He further explained: 'Against the history of earlier Soviet interventions of this sort, e.g. in 1970, some disinformation could be involved, though it is hard to see what the Russians would expect to gain from this except perhaps credit with Makarios by posing as champions of an independent and unitary Cyprus. They might be trying to remind all concerned of their claim to be a Mediterranean power, in view of their recent loss of influence in Egypt. But the most likely explanation, favoured also by Christofides, is that they have reacted to concern and perhaps some pressure from left-wing circles here—which would have received some corroboration from Government sources. Although this concern is, I believe, unjustified, it could have been strong and genuine enough to prompt the Russian démarche.'

newspapers are helped in various ways by the mainland Greek authorities through financial subsidies or the provision of cheap news print.)

Official Greek and Cypriot Reactions

4. The official Greek reaction to all this has been restrained. As you know, the Greek Foreign Minister in his statement on 16 February expressed support for the intercommunal talks, condemned violence from whatever quarter, and condemned also the theft of the National Guard arms. On 9 March, as reported in Athens telegram No. 4 to Nicosia,[14] Tetenes emphasised that the Greek Ambassador had attended the Grivas memorial service only in order to honour the memory of a National Hero, and that any other interpretation was unacceptable. On 15 March the Greek Ambassador here tried to kill the rumours that the Greek Government have two policies towards Cyprus by emphasising that the Government's policy was expressed only through the Foreign Minister or himself. On 19 March Dekleris denied that a settlement in the intercommunal talks was imminent, and the National Guard stated that there [*sic*] officers and men were strictly confined to their military duties. The Cyprus Government have given the Greek authorities little help in all this. They have merely denied knowledge of any formula for an intercommunal settlement and any knowledge of the identity of the EOKA B Commander; which, of course, leaves both questions open to fertile imaginations. We have had some hints that the Greek Embassy are displeased with this Pilate-like attitude. The only statement helpful to the Greeks which the Cyprus Government have made was about the National Guard arms theft (Beattie's letter 1/10 of 28 February),[15] and this was fairly obviously forced out of the Government by the National Guard Command.

The Greek Ambassador

5. The Greek Embassy have told us that Lagacos[16] was profoundly embarrassed by the manifestations at the Grivas memorial service. They maintain that the 40-day service is almost as important to the Greek Orthodox faithful as the funeral, and that it is natural for those who attended the funeral to attend the service also. Before the funeral, Lagakos

[14] Sir R. Hooper pointed out in this telegram of 12 March that the Greek Foreign Ministry continued to deny any knowledge of Maj. Karousos's whereabouts, and that, contrary to the view expressed by Mr. Beattie (see note 7 above), it was generally thought in Athens that Maj. Karousos represented the moderate faction in EOKA preferring a political to a terrorist role. On balance, however, HM Embassy in Athens did not believe that the Greek Government had intervened in EOKA affairs at this stage. Maj. Karousos had been involved in the December 1967 Royalist counter-coup, and was therefore an 'unlikely agent of the present Government'.

[15] According to this letter, addressed to Mr. Davies, the Cyprus Government had announced that the weapons were missing from a National Guard unit (not from the Recruit Training Centre), and that the National Guard general staff had taken prompt and proper action. Cf. note 3 above.

[16] Mr. E. Lagakos (Lagacos) was Greek Ambassador in Nicosia.

had stressed that he wanted no embarrassing political manifestations and, on the whole, his wishes had been deferred to. It had been thought unnecessary to take similar precautions for the memorial service, but this optimism had been belied. I see no reason to doubt this explanation. More important, Lagakos told me in strict confidence on 20 March that he had returned from Athens on 19 February with instructions to warn EOKA B that the Greek Government wished them not only to remain inactive but to disband. Lagakos did not know whether a new leader had been appointed or, if so, who he was. He had therefore called in Vasiliades[17] and the other ESEA leaders and had made this communication to them. The atmosphere was 'electric'; Lagakos implied by this that the Greek Government's wishes had been rejected. Lagakos said that there was no foundation in rumours of large-scale reinforcements of the National Guard by pro-EOKA Greek officers; both he and General Denisis[18] were very angry about this. The trouble was that some young Greek Officers were inevitably anti-Makarios and right wing in their sympathies. They spoke in an irresponsible way, and what they said was picked up and exaggerated by the left wing press. Lagacos did not expect any immediate outburst of violence from EOKA B, although he thought they were regrouping. In the present comparative lull he regarded it as of the greatest importance that the doves, both here and in Greece, should be encouraged by firm action from the Archbishop against pro-Government illegal groups as well as EOKA. He thought it possible that at any moment a provocative anti-EOKA incident would be engineered which, in its turn, would bring EOKA retaliation and the chain of violence would be resumed. He had stressed this point at recent meetings with the Archbishop who had made vaguely sympathetic noises but no real promise of action.

The Cyprus Government
6. The Government's deep suspicion of the Greek Government remains; I suspect, not so much because of any facts which they may have discovered as because of sheer ignorance of the identity of the present rulers of Greece. The Archbishop, when I saw him early this month, said that he did not doubt the sincerity of the official Greek Government's attitude towards Cyprus, for example over the intercommunal talks, but he believed that there were still important circles close to power in Athens who supported EOKA. He said that he had firm information that a few weeks before Grivas' death Ioannides had been preparing to send a large shipment of arms to Cyprus for EOKA. The Foreign Minister has left me in no doubt that he personally believes rumours that 'circles in Greece', including Ioannides, have been in contact with and backing EOKA since the death of Grivas. He reckoned that EOKA were spending about £1 million per year, and he wondered where money of this kind was coming

[17] Mr. G. Vassiliades (Vasiliades) was President of ESEA.
[18] Gen. G. Denisis was Commander of the Cyprus National Guard.

35

from. Although there can be no doubt about Christofides' pro-Western sentiments, I was disturbed to find that he suspected that the Americans were also involved in support for EOKA, either direct or through pro-EOKA circles in Greece. He remained unshaken by any arguments against this. The Director General of the Foreign Ministry[19] who, unlike his counterpart at the Ministry of the Interior,[20] is sensible and not a mischief maker, has told me that the Government 'know' that EOKA has recently been reinforced by Greek Officers.

The Turks

7. The Turkish Embassy and the Turkish Cypriots are exploiting the rumours for their own propaganda, but they too seem to believe them to the extent that the rumours are feeding their old suspicion that Greece is up to a double game in Cyprus. The Embassy have hinted that if the Greeks mount a coup d'état in Cyprus to take it over, the Turks will be ready to grab their share. Unfortunately, their suspicions may have been strengthened by tactless questioning by members of the American Embassy as to the Turkish attitude in the event of a coup.

Conclusions

8. While one cannot be certain about the real intentions of the régime in Greece, I see no reason to suspect that they are plotting a coup d'état against Archbishop Makarios, and I find the explanations and arguments of my Greek colleague convincing.[21] Violence by EOKA B is a different matter and could occur at any time, particularly if provoked by Lyssarides' supporters or the Police Tactical Reserve (who however have both remained largely inactive since Grivas' death). We know little about EOKA B's capabilities but their record is not impressive. They are unlikely to be able to go beyond the occasional localised attack or ambush (which could, of course, be disastrous if they succeeded in picking off the Archbishop). But although I dismiss as nonsense the present wave of rumours, they must have had a bad effect on the intercommunal talks and the atmosphere of intercommunal relations generally. They will also have further shaken Athens/Nicosia relations, which were fragile enough to begin with. I am sure that the present silly season will pass over, and that those who are now prophesying a coup d'état (either through conviction or malice) will be proved wrong. This would be greatly helped of course, if the sort of relationship which seemed to be emerging between Makarios and

[19] Mr. V. Christodoulos.

[20] Mr. A. Anastassiou.

[21] 'At the same time, and against a background of stagnation in the intercommunal talks', Mr. Olver reasoned in Nicosia telegram No. 70 (see notes 1 and 13 above), 'it is hard to see how Greek interests could be served by promoting internal unrest here. This would only serve to strengthen the left-wing forces whom they fear and to increase Makarios' reliance on these forces, and give the Turks further excuse for intransigence in the talks.'

Papadopoulos could be established afresh with the real centre of power in Athens. Alas this seems unlikely.

Yours ever,

S.J.L. OLVER

No. 9

Letter from Mr. Olver (Nicosia) to Mr. Goodison

[*WSC 1/2*]

Confidential   NICOSIA, *8 April 1974*

Dear Alan,

Intercommunal Talks

In order to catch today's bag, I am having to draft this letter before we learn the outcome of Guyer's efforts.[1] But you ought nonetheless to have the background so far to the breakdown at the meeting on 2 April and to my telegrams No. 76 and 79;[2] and I also enclose copies of statements exchanged over the weekend by Makarios and Denktash.[3] I have had long talks with Clerides, Denktash and Osorio Tafall, and Derek Day[4] had a useful cocktail conversation with Christofides, before he left for Paris for the Memorial Service for President Pompidou.[5]

2. The truth which seems to emerge from the fairly diametrically opposed Greek and Turkish Cypriot versions is that Clerides, acting clearly on direct instructions from the Archbishop, used the pretext of the escalation of Turkey's federalist statements to call a suspension of the talks. At the meeting on 2 April, he put a series of straight questions to Denktash aimed at ferreting out Turkish motives in the light particularly of the latest

---

[1] Sr. R.E Guyer was UN Under-Secretary General for Special Political Affairs. In the light of adverse developments in the intercommunal talks, he was asked by Dr. Waldheim to bring forward a visit planned for May to Nicosia, Ankara and Athens. He left New York for London on 5 April (UKMIS New York telegram No. 339 of 4 April).

[2] In these telegrams of 3 and 5 April Mr. Olver reported that after a three-hour plenary session on 2 April the intercommunal talks had been suspended *sine die*. At Mr. Clerides's request the constitutional experts were also discontinuing their meetings. Mr. Clerides claimed that Mr. Denktash had made it clear that he was now primarily interested in securing 'adequate safeguards for the Turkish community on a federal basis, regardless of whether these fitted within the Greek Cypriot definition of a unitary state'. According to the Turkish version of events, the Greek side had used the federal issue as a pretext to suspend the talks, 'This', Mr. Olver commented, 'may be superficially true: but beneath this lies the usual conflict of motives.'

[3] Not printed.

[4] Counsellor in the British High Commission, Nicosia.

[5] M. G. Pompidou, the President of the French Republic, died on 2 April.

statement on federalism by Eçevit.[6] Denktash gave somewhat evasive replies, claiming broadly that the references by Turkish spokesmen, including Eçevit, to federal solutions were political statements parallel to Makarios' remarks from time to time in support of Enosi[s] and should be so treated: they had no direct reference to the intercommunal talks, which the Turkish side continued to support. A lengthy argument then ensued over the drafting of a communiqué to the press. Tafall put forward a brief anodine draft to the effect that Denktash had explained the Turkish position: this did not effect the agreed basis for the talks which would continue. This was rejected by Clerides. After a long further wrangle over the precise basis for the talks, the meaning of independent and *unitary* state etc., the meeting broke up in disorder with failure to agree on any communiqué and with a statement by Clerides that the talks must therefore be adjourned *sine die*. Decleris [*sic*], who had tended with Tafall to take a middle position in the arguments, then proposed that the two constitutional experts should continue their separate exploration. This was ruled out by Clerides, which produced a furious scene, with Decleris threatening first to disregard the veto and then to report the whole matter to Athens.

3. Denktash, typically, sees in all this a great plot by Makarios. He has claimed publicly that there has been no change in the Turkish position and sticks closely to this even in private. The references to a federal solution were political statements with roots going back to Inönü and the early RPP: they had no direct relevance to the talks and there was no intention that the continuation of the talks should be affected. He denied to me that any sort of geographical federation was in the Turkish mind but admitted that 'functional federalism' was the only formula which they thought likely to give adequate protection to the Turkish Cypriot community. He was convinced that the Greeks had for sometime been looking for an excuse for stalling the talks and that they had seized on federalism for this purpose.

4. The Greek case is that there has, behind the smoke screen of federalist verbiage, been a real hardening of the Turkish position over the last few months. The Cyprus Government has suspected, ever since Denktash presented his paper on Turkish claims to the talks, that the Turks were really working for a federal solution based on an almost wholly separate and autonomous Turkish Cypriot Administration. These suspicions have been steadily reinforced by the various statements by Turkish Government spokesmen.[7] The situation was just tolerable so long

[6] On 27 March, following a lunch given for Mr. Denktash in Ankara, Mr. Eçevit spoke of the Turkish Government's wish for a Cyprus settlement in the 'framework of a single state'. But the Turkish press subsequently reported Mr. Eçevit as having discussed with Mr. Denktash his Government's 'desire to find a peaceful and lasting solution to the Cyprus problem within an independent federative state'. (Ankara telegram No. 335 of 28 March, WSC 3/303/1).

[7] Mr. Davies noted in a minute to Mr. Goodison of 4 April that it was apparent that Mr. Denktash, with Mr. Eçevit's 'tacit support', had shifted his position in the intercommunal talks in a way which he knew would cause a sharp Greek reaction. 'But for all that', he added, 'the

as Turkish federalist claims were phrased—as on the Greek side in relation to Enosis—as the 'desirable but not feasible objective'. The latest statement by Eçevit clearly crossed the boundary. Although we have not seen the full text of Rossides' démarche[8] to the Secretary General, I understand that, after recounting at length the agreed basis for the intercommunal talks with emphasis on the independent, unitary and sovereign state of Cyprus, it reviews the Turkish statements about federalism and concludes that these constitute a real threat to the continuation of the talks: Dr. Waldheim is therefore asked to exert every possible effort to secure the continuation of the talks on the existing agreed basis.

5. As usual in this sort of situation, there is some degree of right on both sides. It is certainly the Greek side that has caused the talks to be suspended. But I discount—and Osorio Tafall agrees here—any idea of an involved Makarios plot to bring the talks to an end. The plain fact is that the Turkish statements on federalism, backed up by Turkish Cypriot actions and statements over the last month or so which have been increasingly separatist and truculent, have both caused the Cyprus Government and the Archbishop genuine anxiety and given them an excellent pretext for calling a halt and involving the UN afresh in an effort to get matters back on the original basis. To this extent, the mere fact that Guyer has flown post haste to Cyprus is a partial victory for Makarios.[9]

6. How serious is all this? In itself, this interlude is, I hope, not too serious; but it is symptomatic of a deeper malaise. Unless the Turks really want the talks to cease and think they can pin the blame in this case on the Greek side which ordered the suspension, a formula for resumption will be found. The Archbishop has confirmed to me that he is willing to accept federalism as a 'desirable' aim on the Turkish side in the same way as he proclaims the desirability of enosis. It is the raising of federalism from 'desirable' to the actual and 'feasible' objective of the talks, which the Government claims to see in Eçevit's latest statement, that Makarios cannot stomach: to allow the talks to carry on with this statement unchallenged would in his view imply acceptance of federalism; instead, it is anathema in any form.

7. But behind this, as I say, is something more serious. I sense—and Tafall agrees with this—that both sides have become increasingly

---

Turks (and the Turkish Cypriots) have at no time made clear precisely what they mean by the term "federalism".'

[8] Mr. Z. Rossides, Cyprus Permanent Representative at the UN in New York, was instructed to protest to Dr. Waldheim about the Mr. Eçevit's statement that Turkey would press for a federal solution to the Cyprus problem, and to urge him or Sr. Guyer to visit Cyprus urgently to try to get the talks restarted on an acceptable basis. (Nicosia telegram No. 76 of 3 April).

[9] When on 5 April Sr. Guyer (see note 1 above), then *en route* for Nicosia, called at the FCO to discuss Cyprus he and Mr. Wiggin agreed 'that the Turks were mainly to blame for the breakdown' of the intercommunal talks. Sr. Guyer took the view that the Turkish Government were pushing Mr. Denktash, rather than the other way round, and said that he proposed to argue that 'they must de-escalate their semantics' (telegram No. 57 to Nicosia of 5 April).

disillusioned with the talks themselves and with their chance of producing an acceptable solution. The original vague skeleton—an improved version of the 1960 constitution, removing some of the obvious friction points (Makarios' thirteen points)[10] and at the same time providing better safeguards for the Turks—looked attractive; but as more and more flesh was put on the bones by the two constitutional experts, it began to look more and more awkward for both sides. The closer they got—and over most issues, including local autonomy but not internal security, they are now very close—the more sharply focussed became the remaining sticking points. An act of faith could have jumped the gap—but neither side is in the mood for that.

8. The result is that both sides have, for different reasons, resigned themselves to getting nothing from the talks. These are still regarded as a mildly useful safety-valve, and there is some reluctance, as you see from the present slanging match between Makarios and Denktash, to be held responsible for calling them off finally. But behind the facade, both sides are settling down for a long haul, both hoping meanwhile to twist the status quo to their advantage. The Greek ploy will be to let time work—as they hope—to their economic advantage: to watch the separatist activities of the Turkish community carefully and if necessary to turn the discrimination screw a little tighter—an embargo here, a travel restriction there; and perhaps, particularly if disruption within the Turkish community offers them real opportunity, to appeal direct to the community over the heads of the leadership. On the Turkish side, the aim will be further consolidation of the 'Turkish Cypriot Administration' into a fully-fledged separate regime.

9. Given continued, and indeed substantially increased, financial aid from Turkey, this is possible—up to a point: and there are signs that Turkey may be willing to go some way along that road—talk of a $50 million development loan, for instance, in addition to the recent 20% increase in the annual subvention. But it is potentially explosive. Geographically, the Turkish community will always be at the mercy of the Greeks: their dispersal into scattered villages; no port or airport; water, electricity and other essential services in Greek hands etc. And it will be always dependent in the last resort therefore on the mainland shield. With every step the Turkish Cypriots take towards further internal independence, they trail their coat. Of ports, for instance, Denktash has said publicly: 'It is unjust that we should have no port: this will have to be remedied.' The most far-reaching and potentially dangerous statement so far was an article in the local Turkish newspaper Bozkurt, reproduced in the official TCA Bulletin thus giving it an official imprimatur despite a subsequent denial by Denktash, which commented on Denktash's recent visit to Ankara. I enclose an extract. As you will see, it looks clearly forward to an independent Turkish Cypriot State, and expressed an impatience which we

[10] See No. 1, note 7.

are finding reflected in official Turkish Cypriot quarters with present slow progress towards this.

10. Makarios repeated to me on Friday[11] that, since neither side wanted violence, the status quo could be maintained for a considerable time in the event of a long stalemate in the talks. This reflects the view that one hears repeated from time to time that the present position suits everyone reasonably well, including ourselves. I have never subscribed to this. Apart from complications over maintaining the UN presence for ever, the intercommunal peace is I believe essentially fragile. Turkish impatience could always, unintentionally no doubt, though the Greeks would not believe that, produce a situation which could escalate into real trouble. Perhaps, like Israel, things have got to get very much worse here before there is any common will towards a solution. This would be sad, for the two sides are really quite close now and have been for some time. All that is needed is a fresh impetus to that act of faith on each side needed to close the gap; but where this will come from at present I fail to see—particularly with strained relations between Ankara and Athens casting their shadow here.[12]

S.J.L. Olver

P.S. Ankara telegram No. 368[13] suggests that, as so often, much will turn on the actual words used. The following is a careful translation of the relevant passage in the Turkish Cypriot Press: 'The Turkish Government,

[11] i.e. 5 April.

[12] The discovery of oil off the island of Thasos intensified an existing dispute between Greece and Turkey over continental shelf rights in the Aegean. Turkey had already granted exploration permits to the state-owned Turkish Petroleum Company (TPAO) and, in the absence of a Greek response to a Turkish offer to negotiate over jurisdiction in the Aegean, decided to proceed with the exploration at 27 points. Then, during a NATO exercise in late March, Turkish aircraft were reported to have been sent on two target runs in the Aegean without Greek or NATO permission. Subsequent reports of alerts and Greek troop reinforcements on the Græco-Turkish frontier were accompanied by a mounting press campaign against Greece in Turkey (Ankara telegram No. 343 of 30 March, and Athens telegram No. 88 of 1 April; WSG 3/318/1).

Sir R. Hooper commented in his letter to Mr. Goodison of 3 April (see No. 7, note 11) that he feared that any personal influence that Mr. Tetenes might have over Greek policy towards Cyprus, would be exerted in favour of a tough line, 'partly because his own inclinations lie in that direction, partly because he thinks it may be a good way of sucking up to the military and hanging on to his job, and perhaps also because he thinks that the best prescription for uniting the nation behind a shaky and unpopular government would be a good old row with the Turks over Cyprus'. But there were, Sir R. Hooper continued, 'still a good many senior soldiers who realise[d] that a direct confrontation with Turkey could end in tears'.

[13] Sir H. Phillips observed in this telegram of 6 April: 'In alleging Turkish "insistence on a federal solution" the Greeks are putting words into the mouths of the Turks. No doubt Denktash for his own ends has been talking louder than the Turkish Government would wish to ... But there is no indication here that the Government is on a new tack.' He added that although it might be 'provocative' of Turkish spokesmen to continue to harp on a 'federative system', this was different from insisting on a 'federal solution'. Cf. note 6 above.

stressed Mr Eçevit, would make every effort to find a peaceful and lasting solution of the Cyprus question within the framework of an independent and federative state.'

SJLO 8 April 1974

No. 10

Minute from Mr. P.D.R. Davies to Mr. Goodison

[*WSC 3/548/3*]

Secret   FCO, *11 April 1974*

Defence Review: policy implications of a decision to relinquish military facilities in Cyprus[1]

The Treaties

1. Legal provision for the relinquishment of the Sovereign Base Areas is contained in an Exchange of Notes annexed to the *Treaty of Establishment,* 1960, ('Appendix P') which states that if 'the Government of the United Kingdom, in view of changes in their military requirements, should at any time decide to divest themselves of the sovereignty or effective control over the Sovereign Base Areas, or any part thereof, it is understood that such sovereignty or control should be transferred to the Republic of Cyprus'.[2] Similar provisions in the Treaty relate to the relinquishment of Retained Sites.

2. But the transfer of the SBAs to the Cyprus Government could well be opposed by the Turks, on political grounds. Since 1963 the Turkish-Cypriots have not participated in central government and administer themselves in largely isolated enclaves. In Turkish eyes, our relinquishment of the SBAs would amount to handing them to the Greek Cypriots (even though the Turks have not hitherto protested about our relinquishment to the Cyprus Government of some of the Retained Sites). The problem would not arise if an intercommunal settlement had been reached by the time it was decided to give up the SBAs and remaining Sites. Otherwise we

---

[1] On 21 March Mr. R. Mason, the Secretary of State for Defence, announced in Parliament a 'review of current defence commitments and capabilities against the resources that, given the economic prospects of the country we can afford to devote to defence' to be completed in 1974. *Parl. Debs., 5th ser., H. of C.,* vol. 870, cols. 153-54. A Steering Committee was subsequently established to make recommendations to the Defence and Oversea Policy Committee of the Cabinet not later than July. Sir T. Brimelow, the Permanent Under-Secretary of State (PUS) was the FCO representative on the Steering Committee, which was to be assisted by the Defence Studies Working Party (DSWP) on which the Office was also represented (circular minute of 19 April from Mr. J.E. Jackson, Head of Defence Department, WSC 2/579/1).

[2] See No. 1, note 20.

should have to find (or persuade the Greek Cypriots to find) some way of meeting possible Turkish objections.

3. Under the *Treaty of Guarantee*, the UK together with Greece and Turkey 'recognise and guarantee the independence, territorial integrity and security' of Cyprus. Our military presence underlines this commitment. But internal security is now 'guaranteed' by the UN Peace-keeping Force. And an external threat to Cyprus would involve the UN and possibly the super powers. (The US intervened in 1967 when Turkey, a signatory of the treaty of Guarantee, was on the point of invading Cyprus.) Thus military withdrawal would make little practical difference to our ability to fulfil our obligations under the Treaty of Guarantee.

Bilateral relations with Cyprus

4. The Cyprus economy is heavily dependent upon foreign exchange expenditure by the SBAs, which currently amounts to about £35 million pa (equal to 10% of Cyprus' GNP and 23% of the total current account receipts in the Cypriot balance of payments). A sudden military withdrawal would be economically and politically damaging to Cyprus. It might be advisable to phase a withdrawal over several years or to offer loans or grants to Cyprus for the transition period.

CENTO[3]

5. The nuclear V-Bomber Force based in Cyprus with its associated medium-range tactical support squadron is declared to CENTO. A withdrawal from Cyprus would entail:

i. relocating the Nuclear Bomber Force to an airfield in another country where it could continue to fulfil its CENTO role.

or

ii. withdrawing the Nuclear Bomber Force from CENTO.

6. Either course of action would require prior consultation with our CENTO ALLIES. (i) above could only be achieved with difficulty; (ii) above might be unwelcome to our CENTO allies, but the V-Bomber is in any case virtually obsolete. And even if these aircraft were replaced by MRCAs,[4] it is surely unconceivable that we would ever contemplate engaging in a nuclear exchange in a purely CENTO context.

NATO

7. None of our Military facilities in Cyprus is declared to NATO. The Cyprus Government would react sharply to any overt NATO use of our facilities. But our military presence in Cyprus indirectly enhances NATO's position in the Eastern Mediterranean both by securing the site from

[3] Central Treaty Organisation. See Volume III, No. 49, note 2.

[4] Multi-Role Combat Aircraft.

Russian penetration, (though given the Cyprus Government's non-aligned stance, it is most unlikely that the Russians would in any circumstances be offered facilities there) and by virtue of the fact that in an extreme case, our forces in Cyprus could be committed to assisting operations on the Southern Flank of NATO. No contingency plans exist for such deployment but the possibility must have occurred to SACEUR[5] and to the NATO Secretary-General, not to mention the Greek and Turkish Governments. The surveillance activities carried out by aircraft based in Cyprus against Russian maritime and air activity in the Eastern Mediterranean area are also of benefit to NATO. The ground radars and air defence fighters in Cyprus provide a valuable extension of NATO's air defence system.[6]

8. It follows that we should inform the NATO Secretary-General and SACEUR of any intention greatly to reduce our military presence in Cyprus. Our NATO allies could not in any way claim that a military withdrawal from Cyprus was contrary to our NATO obligations, but Greece, Turkey and the United States might express concern for other reasons (see paragraphs 3, 5, 12 and 13) ...[7]

The Support of National and Humanitarian Operations in the Eastern Mediterranean

10. The SBAs have assisted the setting up of UNEF.[8] Many contingency plans for the evacuation of British subjects from countries in the area envisage the use of the SBAs. Facilities in the SBAs may be used to assist joint American/British operations to clear the Suez Canal and to assist the monitoring of the disengagement of Egyptian/Israeli forces in Sinai. The SBAs provide logistic support for UNFICYP.

11. We have no treaty obligations to provide resources in Cyprus for any of these activities. There is no obvious reason why the Cyprus Government should not be able to continue to provide such facilities (against repayment) following a British withdrawal.

United Nations Peace-keeping Force in Cyprus (UNFICYP)

12. The UK provides logistic support through the SBAs for the entire Force, including the main communications command communications

---

[5] Supreme Allied Commander, Europe.

[6] A paper prepared by the FCO and attached to a minute from Mr. J.A. Thomson (AUS) to Mr. M.I. Goulding (Private Secretary to Mr. Hattersley) of 6 May examined the political implications of the curtailment of British defence commitments outside of NATO. In addition to the points made by Mr. Davies in this minute, it explained: 'The existence of the SBAs is also of benefit to the Alliance in that it provides a stabilising factor in Cyprus and hence in Greco-Turkish relations, which are continually at risk' (DP 5/3).

[7] A paragraph is here omitted.

[8] The UN Emergency Force (UNEF) in the Middle East was established in November 1956 when, in the aftermath of the Suez Crisis, it was stationed on the Egyptian-Israeli border. It was withdrawn in the spring of 1967, but re-established in October 1973 and charged with supervising the military disengagement process between Egypt and Israel.

network, transport, and two flights of helicopters. The British contingent is the largest in the Force.

13. If it were decided to withdraw the British contingent, logistic support could still be provided by the SBAs to the Force. If we withdrew from the SBAs, alternative logistic support arrangements for UNFICYP would have to be made. The UN would therefore require notice of any intention to give up the SBAs (as of an intention to withdraw our contingent from UNFICYP). If we withdrew from the SBAs we could have less reason to contribute militarily to UNFICYP, (which we regard as in part protecting our installations) but we would still be concerned that the situation in Cyprus should not be allowed to threaten relations between Greece and Turkey.[9]

P.D.R. DAVIES

[9] On 11 April Mr. Goodison noted on this minute: 'Thank you. A helpful survey.'

No. 11

Record of conversation between Mr. Hattersley and Mr. T. Menemencioglu[1] in the Foreign and Commonwealth Office on 24 April 1974 at 11a.m.

[*WST 3/548½*]

Restricted

Present:

Mr. R. Hattersley, MP   HE Mr. T. Menemencioglu
Mr. A.C. Goodison

After an exchange of courtesies, *Mr. Menemencioglu* said that although he had no instructions to do so, he wished to ask Mr. Hattersley about the decision, reported on BBC television on 23 April and in the British newspapers on 24 April, that Her Majesty's Government would be withdrawing its armed forces from Cyprus, following Mr. Judd's[2] tour of the area.[3] He was sure that his Government would wish him to say that HMG should not regard the Cyprus bases merely as a relic of Empire. They had been established by a tripartite Agreement, to which Greece and Turkey were signatories. The situation in Cyprus was not entirely satisfactory but the intercommunal talks had made some progress. There were other questions arising in the region of the Eastern Mediterranean which were making people nervous. A British withdrawal from the bases

[1] The Turkish Ambassador in London.

[2] Mr. F.A. Judd was the Parliamentary Under-Secretary of State for Defence.

[3] Cf. *The Times*, 24 April, p. 1.

could not merely be decided on budgetary considerations. The Turkish Government were sure that HMG would discuss with them and others concerned any such decision.[4]

2. *Mr. Hattersley* said that he had been astonished by the television and press reports. If the account he had received of what the BBC had said was true, then the BBC were quite inaccurate. The Ambassador would be aware that we had decided to institute a review of our defence expenditure. This was only just beginning. It has only just been decided in what terms the review would be held. It was simply wrong to say that we had made any decisions at all. We were not even approaching them. All defence expenditure would be reviewed and he could not predict the results. But there were two or three imperatives. The commitment of HM Government to the Atlantic Alliance was very firm. At the same time, they regarded it as important to save money. But they were also very conscious that the review was related to wider and deeper diplomatic requirements, and the Government entirely accepted that these considerations had to be taken into account. He could not say what decisions would in the end be taken, but they would be fully discussed with those governments concerned. *Mr. Menemencioglu* said that he was very glad to hear this.

3. Mr. Menemencioglu concluded that Turkey also had a new government. They had their hands full with problems of inflation, the budget and an Amnesty Law. *Mr. Hattersley* asked when the Amnesty Law would be passed. *Mr. Menemencioglu* said that the law would certainly be changed in the Senate and it would then have to go back to the Lower House to be passed again, but he thought that this process need take only a week or ten days. *Mr. Hattersley* said that the Ambassador would be aware of our interest in this matter. *Mr. Menemencioglu* said that he did not know what our interest was. *Mr. Hattersley* replied that there was considerable public interest in the case of Timothy Davey,[5] who we hoped would be included in the scope of the Amnesty Law. *Mr. Menemencioglu* said that the boy would certainly be covered by the law and this was not a matter of controversy in Turkey. He had received a large number of letters himself about Timothy Davey. He felt that there was some understanding among the British public of the way in which the Turkish authorities were treating him, that is, with consideration. *Mr. Goodison* confirmed that Timothy Davey was being well looked after.

[4] Cf. No. 10.

[5] In August 1971 Timothy Davey, a British teenager returning from India via Turkey, was arrested in Turkey, charged with conspiracy to sell 26 kilos of hashish, and sentenced to six years and three months' imprisonment. He was released as a result of the amnesty.

No. 12

Sir R. Hooper (Athens) to Mr. Callaghan

No. 119 Telegraphic [WSG 3/318/1]

Priority. Confidential   ATHENS, *15 May 1974, 3.30 p.m.*

Repeated to Priority Ankara, Nicosia, HQBFNE,[1] UKDEL NATO, UKMIS New York, Washington and MODUK[2] (D13 West).

From Counsellor[3]
My tel[egram No.] 115:[4]
Greek/Turkish Relations

1. The 'Observer' report of 12 May that 'the officers ruling Greece' are moving towards armed conflict with Turkey over problems in the Aegean[5] reflects rumours which are current here, reinforced by a bellicose campaign in the press which intensified after Androutsopoulos's statement in Salonika (Tomkys' letter to Cornish of 8 May).[6] Hitherto we have regarded Aegean problems as a further element (in addition to Cyprus, minorities, etc) which embitter Greece's relations with Turkey but have not thought that belligerent Greek statements should be taken at their face value. Now even some politicians of long experience and no love for the régime talk wildly of need for a military showdown and a civilian Minister with very moderate and balanced views has characterised the situation as 'rather dangerous'. Some reassessment is therefore needed.

[1] Headquarters, British Forces Near East.

[2] Ministry of Defence.

[3] Mr. J.B. Denson.

[4] On 8 April UKDEL NATO had expressed HMG's concern about the mounting tension between Greece and Turkey over their rival claims in the Aegean (see No. 9, note 12) to the NATO Secretariat. Dr. J.M.A.H. Luns, the NATO Secretary-General, subsequently informed UKDEL NATO that he had spoken separately to the Greeks and Turks urging conciliation (telegram No. 70 to UKDEL NATO of 5 April; UKDEL NATO telegram No. 165 of 10 April). Athens telegram No. 115 of 14 May reported that the US Embassy in Athens were adopting an 'attitude of studied relaxation' towards the current state of Græco-Turkish relations, and promised an assessment after discussion with the Director responsible in the Greek Foreign Ministry.

[5] This article reported that the Greek government were 'seriously considering going to war to press the claims that the Aegean is a "Greek lake" with Turkey having no rights to the oil now being discovered there'.

[6] In this letter Mr. W.R. Tomkys (First Secretary in the British Embassy, Athens) informed Mr. R.F. Cornish (SED) that in a speech, delivered in Salonika on 8 May, Mr. Androutsopoulos had, while emphasising Greece's belief in peaceful cooperation and the principles of international law, insisted that the Greek people could not be bullied and would protect their legal rights and sovereignty. Mr. Tomkys considered it likely that the speech would be followed by a renewed press campaign.

2. Greek military preparations, such as they are have been reported in DA's[7] telegrams (FOG [No.] 325 of 30 April[8] and FOG [No.] 334 of 13 May).[9] [...][10] This points to precautionary measures rather than to mobilisation for the sort of pre-emptive strike which it is alleged some Greek officers advocate.

3. Director responsible in MFA told me this morning that in the past week there had been three minor incidents involving intrusions into Greek waters by a Turkish gunboat and by a fishing boat and the overflying of Greek territory by Turkish aircraft. Greece had lodged formal protests and the incidents had had no repercussions. Journalists here, drawing on Turkish sources, say that a Turkish fishing boat 18 kilometers off Samothrace was fired at by a Greek gunboat. The Greek authorities have so far refused to comment.

4. As seen from here, a number of factors increase the risk of such minor incidents escalating. Both Greece and Turkey have taken public positions on their rights in the Aegean from which it will be difficult to retreat publicly. The Greeks have emphasized that it is a question of sovereignty; this is inevitably evocative of the comparatively recent 'liberation' of certain Greek islands from Turkish rule. Both sides have allowed or encouraged provocative press campaigns and the earlier efforts of the Foreign Ministry to reduce Greek press attacks on Turkey have not been successful. Almost all Greeks are ready to listen to and accept anti-Turkish propaganda.

5. On the other hand, the régime have no rational interest in a conflict with Turkey which the more sober must realise would inevitably end in disaster for Greece. The press campaign was at first allowed or orchestrated primarily for domestic reasons and the talk of a war with Turkey will have had a unifying effect in the armed forces. The Foreign Ministry have emphasized that the Greek Government is ready to talk to the Turks about any subjects in dispute. Metaxas has told me that a few days ago the Turks handed over a list of the subjects for discussion which, according to prior agreement, excludes Cyprus but at the Turkish instance, includes Aegean problems. The Greeks hope to be ready to send back their list in a few weeks' time. They do not rule out discussion of seabed

---

[7] The British Defence Attaché in Athens, Brig. P.R. Body.

[8] According to this telegram, the British Embassy had evidence that some islands close to the Turkish mainland, notably Samos and Rhodes, had been reinforced in contravention of existing demilitarisation agreements. But Brig. Body also noted that there was neither an alert nor reinforcements along the Græco-Turkish frontier in Thrace, and that he did not believe Gen. Gizikis's recent visit there was intended to arouse any bellicose sentiments.

[9] Brig. Body warned the Ministry of Defence in this telegram that there was increasing evidence the Greeks were making covert preparations to defend their claims by force if necessary. 'Both sides', he observed, 'have now manoeuvred themselves into positions from which it will be difficult to withdraw without loss of face but I remain convinced that all are conscious of the dangers of brinkmanship. Even so the vehemence with which the Greek military spokesmen deny preparing for hostilities makes one suspicious.'

[10] A sentence is here omitted.

questions but do not think this can usefully be done before the Law of the Sea Conference at Caracas or unless certain principles are accepted in advance. Speaking personally Metaxas said that he doubted whether Greek willingness to discuss these matters with the Turks could be made public at present.

6. My assessment therefore is that the principal danger inherent in the situation is of a minor incident escalating to a major clash. This could occur through inadvertence or irresponsibility on the part of the Greek military régime whose decision-making processes are uncertain, and unknown to us. Neither possibility can be ruled out but the first is the more likely.

7. The Head of the Hellenic Armed Services, together with the 3 Chiefs of Staff and a strong contingent of senior officers is [*sic*] attending the Military Committee of NATO this week and there are rumours that there may be a confrontation with Turkish opposite numbers. Anything that could be done in Brussels to avert this would clearly be desirable. In present circumstances we are not in a position to bring influence to bear here. The next meeting of the Greek and Turkish Foreign Ministers is likely to be in Ottawa at the NATO Council.[11]

[11] Foreign Ministers of NATO member-states were due to meet in Ottawa on 18 June to mark the 25th anniversary of the Alliance.

No. 13

Mr. Callaghan to Sir P. Ramsbotham (Washington)

No. 1240 Telegraphic [WSG 3/548/5]

Eclipse. Confidential   FCO, *31 May 1974, 5.15 p.m.*

Repeated for information to Immediate UKDEL NATO, Athens, Nicosia, Ankara.

Following from Wiggin:
Greece

1. You will recall that on 13 May Hartman[1] suggested to Mr. Hattersley in Washington that we and the Americans should try to work out a joint strategy towards Greece.[2] However, Hartman's remarks about Kissinger's

[1] Mr. A. Hartman was Assistant Secretary for European Affairs in the US State Department.

[2] On 13 May, whilst visiting Washington, Mr. Hattersley discussed policy towards Greece with Mr. Hartman. The latter said that the Administration 'reckoned the present regime in Greece about as bad as it could be', but added that it was US policy 'to intervene less in the affairs of other countries', and that Dr. H.A. Kissinger, the US Secretary of State, 'was reluctant to say anything in public about the desirability of a return to democracy in Greece'.

views (para[graph] 9 of the record), his later telephone call (para[graph] 12),[3] and the conversation over lunch with Rush[4] all suggest that Hartman's own views on the Greek problem may not be representative of administrative thinking generally, as does the line Rush took subsequently with the Secretary of State in Washington.

2. Mr. Hattersley would like to try to work out a joint position with the Americans. Subject to your views, he is inclined to think that in the circumstances the best way of proceeding might now be to initiate a routine exchange of views with the State Department at 'working' level, without taking his conversation with Hartman as the point of departure. This might enable us to form a clearer impression of whether Hartman was simply flying a personal kite. We regularly compare notes with the Americans on Greece, as on many other matters. The proximity of the next NATO Ministerial meeting plus current Greek/Turkish tensions[5] give us a natural opening to do so again. (If you thought it helpful you could let Hartman know privately that your approach to the State Department represented our follow-up to his suggestion to Mr. Hattersley.)

3. On substance, you should be guided by the following, making clear that it represents current official level thinking here and should not be regarded as committing Ministers to any particular view or course of action.

4. There is persistent and continuing criticism in this country of the Greek regime. They are arguably more unattractive than their immediate predecessors, and moreover give an impression of general incompetence. It is not unreasonable to fear that under them things in Greece may drift from bad to worse: and that eventually an even more unattractive successor might emerge, which would not necessarily even be 'NATO-orientated'.

5. Ministers are under pressure from various quarters to do more than they have already done to show their disapproval of the Greek regime. For instance, they are being lobbied energetically by a committee headed by

He also revealed that the State Department was considering making contact with some of the Greek 'officers who were becoming disaffected with the new régime, now that it was being run by majors and captains ... [it] was losing support so fast that the facilities enjoyed by the US were being jeopardised'. Americans, Mr. Hartman remarked, believed 'that the Greek regime was now looking for outside disputes which it could exploit in order to strengthen its internal position. The off-shore oil dispute with Turkey [see No. 9, note 12] was one example and Cyprus might be the next.' Mr. Hattersley warmly welcomed Mr. Hartman's suggestion that Britain and the US should work out a joint strategy to deal with the situation (record of conversation between Mr. Hattersley and Mr. Hartman at the State Department on 13 May).

[3] Mr. Hartman had subsequently telephoned to say 'that he had been speaking particularly frankly ... and to ask that what he had said should not be quoted back to other American officials'. *V. ibid.*

[4] Mr. K. Rush was US Deputy Secretary of State. Cf. No. 108.

[5] See note 2 above.

Sir Hugh Greene[6] which has suggested a variety of measures against Greece in NATO going well beyond mere vocal manifestations of displeasure.

6. Officials are inclined to think that the Secretary of State will have to refer to the situation in Greece during the NATO Ministerial meeting in Ottawa.[7] (Recent developments in Portugal will, inter alia, have served to place the spotlight even more on Greece.)[8] They are not, however, inclined to recommend more draconian measures such as attempting to place the Greek question formally on the NATO agenda, or threatening drastic scaling down of NATO military cooperation with Greece, and/or collective suspension of all arms supplies. (These are among possible measures which the Greene Committee have been advocating.) Even if a general consensus in favour of drastic action in NATO could be achieved, officials fear that it would not have the desired effect on the Greek régime's internal policies: might well put in question Greece's continued participation in NATO: and could serve to further heighten tensions in the already tense area of the eastern Mediterranean.

7. Nevertheless, the situation in Greece is undeniably bad for the health and cohesion of the Alliance. Have the Americans any ideas on what effective pressures might be brought to bear on the Greek régime to mend their ways? Is there anything the Americans themselves contemplate doing to that end? (The Greek régime are more likely to listen to the Americans than anybody else: our own ability to influence them in the right direction is unfortunately very limited.) Before submitting to Ministers in advance of the forthcoming Ottawa meeting, we should be grateful for the fullest information the Americans can give us as to how they see the situation in Greece evolving and as to their own intentions.

8. We would also be grateful for their current assessment of the Greek/Turkish dispute.[9] It is undoubtedly potentially dangerous, but as of this moment we find it hard to assess just how dangerous.

[6] Sir H. Greene was Director-General of the British Broadcasting Corporation (BBC) during 1961-69.

[7] See No. 12, note 12.

[8] See Nos. 106 and 107.

[9] See note 2 above. On 24 May the Greek Government made a positive step to reduce tension by telling the Turks that they had had no objection to discussing how to divide the Aegean for purposes of oil exploration. But within a week it became apparent that Turkey was planning to send a survey ship into the disputed area west of Lesvos and that a number of Turkish warships were also moving there, effectively as an escort (letter from Mr. Tomkys to Mr. R.F. Cornish of 29 May; telegram No. 104 to Athens of 30 May; WSG 3/318/1).

No. 14

Sir P. Ramsbotham (Washington) to Mr. Callaghan

No. 1991 Telegraphic [*WSG 3/548/5*]

Priority. Confidential-Eclipse   WASHINGTON, *4 June 1974, 10.52 p.m.*

Repeated for information to Priority UKDEL NATO, Athens, Ankara, and Routine Nicosia

Your telegram No. 1240[1] and tele[phone]con[versation] Wiggin/Sykes:[2] Greece

1. After consulting the dept[artment] by telephone, Minister took action today directly with Hartman (who was supported by his Deputy, Stabler,[3] and by Churchill,[4] Director of Greek Affairs).

2. Hartman did not dissent from the gloomy view we took of the situation in Greece. He said, however, that Dr. Kissinger believed firmly that any change for the better must be left for the Greeks to bring about themselves. He had in consequence shown himself sceptical even over ideas submitted to him by the State Department for conveying to the Greek regime private signals of American anxiety. These would have been based on the deleterious effect which the present situation in Greece was having from the NATO point of view, both politically and in terms of the effectiveness of the Greek armed forces, on the lines which Hartman sketched out to Mr. Hattersley.[5] In addition Hartman attributed part of Dr. Kissinger's reluctance to a simple desire not to add to the problems which the United States had in the Eastern Mediterranean area.[6]

3. Hartman went on to say that Dr. Kissinger was even more strongly of the opinion that public displays of indignation against the Greek regime did not help. He would therefore be opposed to statements being made by Ministers in NATO, more especially at the Ottawa anniversary meeting which was intended to revitalize the alliance. (Hartman noted that so far at least no problem seemed to have arisen with Greece over the text of the alliance declaration.) In the past statements had sometimes been made, with a more or less light touch, by Scandinavian and Dutch Ministers, though usually the Americans (like us) had tried to dissuade them. It would

---

[1] No. 13.

[2] Mr. R.A. Sykes was Minister in the British Embassy in Washington.

[3] Mr. W. Stabler was Senior Deputy Assistant Secretary for European Affairs in the State Department.

[4] Mr. G.T. Churchill.

[5] See No. 13, note 2.

[6] In a letter to Mr. Wiggin of 6 June, Mr. Sykes explained that when he had seen Mr. Hartman there had been 'no shilly-shallying or beating about the bush. Hartman came straight out and gave me Kissinger's views.'

be a more serious affair if one of the major members of the Alliance were to refer to the situation in Greece at a Ministerial meeting. Hartman was sure that Dr. Kissinger would wish to consider the matter with you (or at least have further discussion here) if it should be in your mind to speak in this way. (On present form it looks as if Dr. Kissinger will only break off from accompanying the President to the Middle East in time to get to Ottawa late on 17 June.)

4. Hartman smitd [*sic*] that recent statements by M. Giscard[7] about France's liberal mission raised at least a possibility that the French Foreign Minister might refer to Greece at Ottawa. But the State Department, consider that the French Government will not hold back from their reported arms deal with Greece,[8] particularly in view of the parlous state of the French arms industry: and that this would make the prospect of a French statement at Ottawa unlikely.

5. On the Greek/Turkish dispute (your paragraph 8) Hartman agreed that things had eased slightly for the time being and that the Greek Government appeared to have backed down from a belligerent position (paragraph 3 of Athens telegram No. 141).[9] The Turkish Ambassador here had said to the State Department that both sides were trying to keep things calm.[10] Hartman felt however that the need not to exacerbate tension between Greece and Turkey was another reason for not speaking about the situation in Greece at Ottawa. If the Greeks felt themselves beleaguered in NATO this might only encourage a spirit of belligerence in them. Hartman added that Dr. Kissinger had also shown himself reluctant to see the US involved in the Greek/Turkish dispute, at any rate for the time being. Normal calming action had in fact been taken by the US Embassies in Ankara and Athens on their own initiative. But Dr. Kissinger had failed to respond to a State Dept. message, sent to him while he was in the Middle East, recommending firmer expressions of US anxiety.

[7] M. V. Giscard d'Estaing was elected President of the French Republic on 19 May.

[8] An arms contract had been concluded between the French and Greek governments earlier in the spring for the sale to Greece of 40 Mirage Interceptors, 60 AMX 30 tanks and 4 fast patrol boats (brief on French Arms Sales Policy by Mr. Beattie of 6 September 1974, WRF 10/6).

[9] This telegram of 4 June reported that the latest Greek Government statement declared that the position of the Turkish survey vessel had been established, and that it was being watched for any possible violation of Greek sovereign rights. Paragraph 3 stated: 'As seen from here, the Greek Government, after encouraging public interest and belligerent statements for several months, has now had its bluff called and has backed down, at least so far as the survey vessel is concerned, preferring studiously to ignore the fact that it has been active in the area claimed by the Greeks as their continental shelf. But 2 sides are still on what is potentially a collision course over an issue in which they have taken mutually irreconcilable positions' (WSG 3/318/1).

[10] Mr. Sykes noted in his letter to Mr. Wiggin (see note 6 above) that Mr. Hartman did not appear to have any particularly up-to-date information about the Græco-Turkish dispute. Mr. Hartman thought that 'both sides were anxious to play the issue down, but that given the situation there, tension could arise again at any time'.

No. 15

Letter from Mr. J.R. Leeland[1] (Ankara) to Mrs. G.S. Wright[2]

[*WSC 1/2*]

Restricted   ANKARA, *7 June 1974*

Dear Georgina,

Cyprus

1. William Fullerton[3] and I had a talk yesterday with Bulent Çakim, the Cyprus desk officer in the Ministry of Foreign Affairs. Foreign Minister Günes has recently made the point that the Turks no longer wished to solve their problems with Greece on the basis of a package deal.[4] Çakim explained that the thinking in the MFA[5] was that each matter should now be dealt with on its merits (but in fact, he later suggested a novel modified package—see paras 4 and 8 below).

Intercommunal Talks

2. Çakim said that the Turks were surprised at the tone of the Archbishop's speech at Paphos (reported in Nicosia telegram [No.] 136 to you:)[6] it was disappointing that he had stated that partnership with the Turkish Cypriots was unacceptable; and it was impertinent to suggest that the Turks should be described as privileged minority.

3. The Turkish view (said Çakim) was that there should be two branches of the Cyprus Government that should come together at the top. The Greek Cypriot view seemed to be that there should be a Greek Cypriot Government that should be the sole central authority in the island: this the Turks would resist totally.

4. Çakim said that he expected that the talks would probably start again later this month,[7] and after a few weeks would probably break down again

---

[1] First Secretary, HM Embassy, Ankara.

[2] Mrs. Wright was in SED.

[3] First Secretary and Head of Chancery, HM Embassy, Ankara.

[4] See No. 1, note 4. During the spring of 1970 the Greek Government had tried to break the prevailing deadlock in the intercommunal talks by persuading the Cyprus Government to work out an agreed position on the legislature, executive, judicature, police and local government, which would make possible negotiations with the Turkish Cypriots on a 'package deal'.

[5] Ministry of Foreign Affairs

[6] In this telegram of 3 June Mr. Olver reported a speech, delivered by Archbishop Makarios at Paphos on 2 June, in which the Archbishop had said that, although Greek Cypriots were resuming talks to show a spirit of goodwill, there was 'no more room for any concessions by them'. The 'partitionist plans of the Turkish Cypriots' would, he insisted, encounter firm resistance from Greek Cypriots, who 'would accept neither partnerships nor cantons nor regional self-government nor federation'. Cf. No. 16, note 5.

[7] Mr. Olver reported in Nicosia telegram No. 124 of 20 May that all interested parties had agreed to the resumption of intercommunal talks on the basis of a UN-brokered formula. This referred both to the talks which had started in 1968 and to those reactivated in 1972. As Mr. Olver explained in a letter to Mr. Goodison of 2 May, 'whereas the original talks in 1968

without much chance of resumption. He then went on to give us some purely personal speculation on what might be the ultimate solution of the problem. He suggested that it might just be feasible to exchange two or three of the Greek islands in the Aegean for the Turkish portions of Cyprus. This would help remove problems in the Aegean Sea and also provide opportunities to give Messrs Denktash, Kuçuk[8] and Berberoglu[9] areas of power commensurate with their abilities: but, of course, there would be immense problems involved in the transfer of population; when we queried whether such a transfer would be possible because the people concerned would object, Çakim responded by hinting that he doubted if the idea could at the moment be acceptable to the higher echelons in the Turkish Government and General Staff.

UNFICYP

5. The Turks would probably not oppose a further reduction of the Force. They considered that there was indeed a 'pillow' effect (mentioned in paragraph 2 of Richard Baker's unreferenced letter of 14 May 1974 to Timothy Daunt in New York):[10] but of course it was the Greeks who were unrealistically reluctant to negotiate; the Turks were quite prepared to try to reach an agreement on the intercommunal problem. Reliance was placed by the Turks upon the Turkish Cypriot Fighters, rather than on UNFICYP, for the defence of the Turkish Cypriot community: and, naturally, the Turkish Army was always ready to go to the assistance of their community if the need arose.

National Guard

6. Çakim discounted the rumours of a plot by the National Guard to overthrow Makarios. He said that the stories were put about by the Greeks but in fact all their factions were anxious to promote the possibility of union with Greece: and contrary to appearances that applied also to AKEL and the Lyssarides gang.[11]

---

developed within a framework satisfactory to the Greek side, including the vital reference to a unitary state, the framework for the reopening of the expanded talks in 1972 was kept studiously vague by the Secretary General'. See No. 1, note 4.

[8] Dr. M.F. Küçük (Kutchuk) was Vice-President of the Republic of Cyprus until February 1973. He was also owner of the newspaper *Halkin Sesi* which he used to criticise the TCA.

[9] Mr. M.A. Berberoglu had been a leading Turkish Cypriot member of the Cyprus House of Representatives. He led the Republican Turkish Party.

[10] In this letter Mr. R.H. Baker (Assistant Head of SED) informed Mr. T.L.A. Daunt (First Secretary, UK Mission (UKMIS) to the UN at New York) that he had learnt from the Swedish Embassy that the Americans had expressed the view that UNFICYP, from which personnel of the Austrian, Finnish, Irish and Swedish contingents had been withdrawn in the autumn of 1973 for service in the Middle East, should be further reduced. The Americans stressed the need to bring down the cost of the force. 'They also', according to the Swedes, 'believed that the presence of the Peace Keeping Force might be tending to freeze the existing political differences between the two communities in Cyprus by a "pillow" effect' (WSC 10/6). During 1970-72 UNFICYP's strength was approximately 3,150.

[11] See No. 8, note 9.

Comment

7. Çakim's view on the future of the intercommunal talks is reasonable. It is clear that the Turks are reluctant to make any further concession to the Greek position and there appears to be a hardening of the attitude of Makarios.

8. On the other hand, Çakim's suggestion that there should be an exchange of Greek islands in the Aegean for Turkish areas in Cyprus is very hard to accept.[12] It is perhaps superficially attractive in that it could produce some advantages for the Turks in the present dispute over the division of the undersea bed and territorial waters in the Aegean; and it would remove one of the obstructions to free operation of Turkish aircraft off the Turkish coast (the Lausanne Treaty prohibits Turkish military aircraft from flying over Greek islands).[13] However, it would be necessary for the Turkish General Staff [TGS] to make a careful assessment of the balance of military advantage: traditionally Cyprus has been regarded as 'a pistol pointed at the Anatolian heartland'; and there would also be concern in the TGS that a wholly Greek Cyprus might become communist dominated.[14]

J.R. LEELAND

[12] Sir R. Hooper was perturbed by this personal speculation on Mr. Çakim's part, and thought it would encourage Greek fears that the Turks wanted to use Cyprus as a bargaining counter by which to fulfil their designs on the sovereignty of Lesvos, Chios and other Aegean islands (Athens telegram No. 7 to Ankara of 15 June, WSG 3/318/1). Mr. M.G. MacDonald (Second Secretary, the British High Commission, Nicosia) was similarly concerned. In a letter to Miss R.M. Lowry (SED) of 27 June he dismissed Mr. Çakim's suggestion as 'unlikely to commend itself at this stage to Greece or Turkey or the Turkish Cypriots'. He added: 'The only real beneficiary would be the Archbishop who would have Cyprus all to himself—and even he would then be faced with the decision, *Enosis* to be or not to be.' Mr. Baker subsequently informed Mr. Leeland that SED shared Mr. MacDonald's scepticism (letter to Mr. Leeland of 4 July).

[13] See *Treaty Series* No. 16 (1923), Cmd. 1929.

[14] Mr. Goodison noted on this letter: 'Çakim sounds a thoroughly unreliable young man to me. I shd like more evidence for para 5. Let us write back asking some pointed questions about him.'

No. 16

Letter from Mr. Olver (Nicosia) to Mr. Goodison

[*WSC 1/2*]

Confidential   NICOSIA, *19 June 1974*

Dear Alan,

Intercommunal Talks

1. With the talks sputtering,[1] I have once again been trying to think whether anything might be achieved through some outside initiative, and if so whether we should or could prepare for this in some way now.

2. I would not wish to predict the early demise of the talks. They cling tenaciously to life, and could stagger on for a while yet. But the belief that talking for talking's sake provides a useful safety valve is wearing thin, and the talks hang now mainly on the slender thread of unwillingness on each side to incur responsibility for the final breakdown. The present fact is that both sides have ceased to believe that the talks can produce a solution which would suit them.

3. In this situation, we must, I think, try to return to basic principles and escape from the labyrinth of the talks themselves. Looking back to 1968, one is impressed and depressed by the cyclical nature of events and the extent to which situations in the talks have repeated themselves. Denktash has several times used with me the illustration of a gramophone record grinding round and round. Perhaps the erratic temperature chart of a chronic invalid would be a better simile. Peaks and troughs over the last six years are readily traceable. The latest peak in expectancy of a settlement was last autumn; we are now in a trough; another peak is not altogether to be ruled out. But there is also, I fear, discernable a progressive hardening of under-lying opinion. Solutions which in the early years of the talks might have been well received by the Turkish side would not be acceptable now. Chaglayangil's[2] remark in his press conference before leaving Cyprus recently that the passage of time harmed the talks themselves was, alas, all too penetratingly true. As the two sides have pored over the constitutional details, differences became more clearly defined and hardened, even as progress was seemingly being made. The watershed in this process was probably the exchange in December last year of the documents on Local Government.[3]

---

[1] See No. 9. Intercommunal talks were resumed on 11 June. In a letter to Miss Lowry of 19 June Mr. MacDonald reported that after the second session of the talks on 18 June Mr. Denktash had told reporters that 'the concept of a unitary state as interpreted by the Greek side was not acceptable to the Turkish Cypriots'.

[2] Mr. I.S. Chaglayangil was Chairman of the Foreign Affairs Committee of the Turkish Senate.

[3] See No. 3, notes 2 and 3.

4. What has in essence happened behind all this is, I think, that the Turks have seen in the failure by the Greek Cypriot Administration fully to dismantle the apparatus of discrimination in the aftermath of 1968 and in the Archbishop's continued equivocation over Enosis, a threat against which they had to reinsure with continually increasing premiums: and on the Greek side, an initial willingness to believe that when they talked about a bi-communal state the Turks were genuinely interested in finding a rational formula for a united Government of Cyprus, had gradually given way to a suspicion that a separate Turkish state, in all but name, is the Turkish objective. I think that in the years 1969 to 1972, a great opportunity was lost by the Greek side. An imaginative directive then from Makarios to the Greek Cypriot Administration to end all aspects of administrative discrimination might I believe have won over the Turkish Cypriot community and tipped the scales towards a settlement. That opportunity has gone—for the moment at any rate—and meanwhile, Turkish separatism has markedly hardened. There is some slight evidence for the suggestion that Denktash from the beginning had his sights set on a fully autonomous separate Turkish Cypriot Administration [TCA] and that he has worked patiently over the last six years to achieve this through the consolidation of the TCA. Whether that is true or not, the last year or so has seen steady progress in this direction; it is hard now to believe that this is not Denktash's intention; and the 'open letter' in 'Bozkurt', reported in MacDonald's letter of 10 June to Miss Lowry,[4] which clearly stems from official Turkish sources and speaks defiantly of such measures as an air bridge to counter Greek Cypriot economic encirclement, suggests that Ankara's mind may also be focusing in this direction.

5. Against this background, what, if anything, can be done? Let me first repeat a point that I have stressed before: I do not believe in the prolongation of the status quo as a nice cosy option which would 'suit everyone'. Intercommunal peace might hold for a bit. But the situation would be inherently unstable and dangerous. The Turkish Cypriot community in particular cannot afford to stand still. This has been confirmed by us recently—before the 'Bozkurt' letter—by members of both the Turkish Embassy and the Turkish Cypriot community, in terms which suggest that the subject has been recently discussed in Ankara and that the declaration of a separate Turkish Cypriot State may have been under consideration. But equally, the Archbishop has recently confirmed to me

---

[4] Mr. MacDonald reported in this letter on the publication on 7 June of an unsigned open letter to Mr. Denktash in the Turkish Cypriot newspaper *Bozkurt*. This argued that any hopes of obtaining a result at the conference table had vanished, and that Mr. Denktash must put into effect the measures that he had previously promised if the talks were to reach deadlock. The letter further proposed that the Turkish Cypriots counter Greek Cypriot 'economic and political weapons' by the establishment of an 'air bridge, followed by a passive resistance campaign'. According to Mr. MacDonald, the High Commission suspected that the letter emanated from 'the office of the "Bayraktar" (the serving Turkish officer who controls, clandestinely, all aspects of security in the Turkish Cypriot community)'.

that he does not regard it as safe or feasible to rest on the status quo; and it is significant that, in a conversation on the intercommunal situation early in the New Year, he was already envisaging the possibility that the Turks might declare a separate State and considering possible reactions to this.

6. I do not believe that anything dramatic is likely to happen quickly. Village elections, which at one time I feared might be a potential flash point this summer, have now been postponed till October 1975 which is a relief. But I believe that we may be nearing a point of no return—or rather, no return until there has been another cathartic outburst, and that we ought at least to start considering whether there is any useful initiative which could be launched this summer before things deteriorate further.

7. As usual with Cypriot affairs, the diagnosis is comparatively simple, and a reasonable shot can be made at prognosis; but any prescription likely to be effective seems virtually impossible to find. We have gone through the list of possibles. None seems likely to succeed by itself, and some are doubtful starters to put it mildly. But some combination of these ideas might help, if not actually towards a settlement in the foreseeable future, at least towards putting off the evil day of resumed intercommunal tension and perhaps conflict. The list of possibles, seen from here is:

(a) *Calls for patience, goodwill etc on both sides.* These might be made by Britain; by the United States; by others, the EEC perhaps? and finally of course by the United Nations.

(b) *Intervention by Athens and Ankara.*

(c) *On the view that a major element in the present deadlock is the personal hostility between Makarios and Denktash,* an effort to bring about either a reconciliation between the two or the removal of one or the other—and in practice this would mean the removal of Denktash.

(d) *A major intervention by the UN,* perhaps by Waldheim personally, possible leading to a Security Council Meeting.

(e) *A switch from the internal constitutional problems* which have absorbed the talks hitherto to the question of *guarantees* which has so far been studiously avoided.

Each of these possibles is examined in detail below.

8. *Calls for goodwill*

The climate is unpropitious. The most sinister aspect of the Archbishop's recent Paphos speech reported in my telegram No. 136 was his reference to withdrawing the offers made by the Greek side in the negotiations.[5] This must, I have little doubt, be read as a warning that, in a deadlock, the screws would be turned back—if necessary to the near-blockade conditions of 1964-68; it has been taken so by the Turks, and the talk of air bridges is

[5] See No. 15, note 6. Archbishop Makarios had threatened: 'If the talks failed, the Greek Cypriots would withdraw all offers made so far, and would be ready to face the consequences. They would not give in to pressure, blackmail, intimidation or threats of Turkish intervention, and with this determination would continue their struggle until its happy conclusion.'

their reaction to it. Nonetheless, an occasion could be found for expressing concern to the Archbishop at the present drift and urging on him continued patience and moderation. I could myself do this on instructions, or a higher level message could be sent. The Americans could be urged to make a parallel démarche: the arrival of the new American Ambassador,[6] expected at the end of this month, would be a suitable opportunity. We could try to get others to make similar approaches—the EEC perhaps? Finally, of course, the UN could take up this theme. Weckmann Muñoz[7] is at present expected to take up his appointment on 1 July. He could well bring a suitable message from Waldheim; and in general, I would hope that in the present situation he, and behind him the UN, would be prepared to take a slightly stronger pro-settlement line than we have seen in the closing months of the Osorio Tafall regime. Although unlikely to be decisively effective, an orchestrated series of approaches on these lines to Makarios might achieve something.

9. In his current mood, Makarios would undoubtedly reply that the present situation was produced by intransigent Turkish separatism. Some balancing approach would have therefore to be made to the Turks—and in this asymmetrical situation that would mean primarily in Ankara rather than to Denktash. Here again, conditions are highly unpropitious, with the Eçevit regime pre-occupied with internal or Turco-Greek affairs and entrenched, anyhow, over 'federalism'. But it would be worth trying all the same.

10. *Intervention by Athens and Ankara*

Close agreement between Athens and Ankara on the terms of a solution must remain one of the likeliest ways of reaching a settlement. For the present, however, the prospects of this look particularly remote, first because of the tension between Athens and Ankara themselves and, secondly, because relations between the Archbishop and Athens are at the moment badly strained.[8] A variant of this which has I think never been

---

[6] Mr. R.J. McCloskey, US Ambassador in Cyprus since June 1973, was succeeded by Mr. R. Davies in July 1974. Cf. No. 84, note 5.

[7] Dr. L. Weckmann-Muñoz replaced Sr. Osorio-Tafall as Dr. Waldheim's Special Representative in Cyprus.

[8] Growing EOKA B violence and a Government counter-offensive during the spring and early summer of 1974 and the theft, with the apparent collusion of members of the largely Greek-officered National Guard, of further quantities of arms from a National Guard camp, exacerbated differences between Archbishop Makarios and Athens over the Guard's composition and role. A paper prepared by the British High Commission in Nicosia, 'EOKA B since Grivas', asserted that the Greek Junta doubtless looked on the continued existence of EOKA B, which on 25 April was declared an unlawful organisation, 'as a threat and constraint on the Archbishop, and as a check on the growth of Communist influence in Cyprus, and may well be supporting it for these reasons'. And, in a letter covering this paper and sent to Mr. Goodison on 26 June, Mr. Olver added: 'There is no doubt that Makarios and the Government believe that the Junta is at present solidly behind EOKA "B". Even if this were true—and we have no hard evidence of it—it still seems unlikely that they would join effectively in such a desperate venture. But one can never tell.' Meanwhile, Athens remained reluctant to recall

seriously considered and is very likely a non-starter, but would nonetheless have attractions as seen from here, might be to promote a meeting between Makarios and Eçevit. The rationale would of course be that these two are the main protagonists and that the establishment of a personal relationship of confidence between them would contribute greatly to a settlement. In its implications for Denktash, this would be closely related to the following idea.

11. *Relations between Makarios and Denktash*

I am beginning reluctantly to accept the widely held view that, so long as Makarios and Denktash remain as leaders of the respective communities, the chances of a settlement are slight. If so, progress must depend either on bringing about a reconciliation between them or on removing one or the other. I can think of no way of bringing about reconciliation. The removal of Makarios in the foreseeable future—short of assassination—can I think be ruled out. This leaves Denktash. There have been suggestions from time to time that Ankara was not particularly pleased with the Denktash regime, and I would judge that they would jettison him without hesitation in the framework of some broader solution which was to their interest and which did not imply deserting the Turkish Cypriot community. One might conceivably, I suppose, imagine some such development emerging from a Makarios-Eçevit accord; but that is not very plausible. Short of this, Denktash's position as flag bearer of the embattled community looks reasonably secure.

12. *The United Nations*

To suggest the scope of possible UN action is way outside my competence. It could vary from a somewhat more interventionist role by the Special Representative to a visit to Cyprus by Waldheim or beyond that a full-dress Security Council debate. And the idea that the Government might contemplate referring the question to the UN has been revived by a recent statement from Clerides that, in the event of a breakdown of the talks, it would be necessary to enlighten international opinion on the issues. The complications attending any full-dress Security Council examination of the question are obviously formidable. A serious situation would presumably be needed to promote a meeting at all; there would be great difficulty in reaching agreement on any formula which satisfied all interests; but above all, it would remain unlikely—expect possibly in the field of guarantees, see below—that anything the Security Council could say would have much effect on the parties.[9] Nonetheless, I

officers who failed to comply with Cyprus Government decisions. 'There are', Mr. Beattie commented in a letter to Miss Lowry of 24 June, 'indications that the Greek Government is arguing that in the present state of Græco-Turkish relations the National Guard ought to be strengthened rather than weakened' (WSC 1/9).

[9] Mr. J.O. Moreton, the UK Deputy Permanent Representative to the UN at New York, wrote to Mr. Goodison on 2 July that he thought it almost certainly the case that the Security Council would not adopt a resolution to which either Cyprus or Turkey objected strongly, and that he could not think of 'any formula which would be any good and acceptable to both

should have thought there was a fair chance that the next Mandate renewal meeting in December might generate a much more far-reaching political debate than has been the case hitherto; and that a breakdown in the talks between now and then, which is well on the cards, might produce a Security Council free-for-all for which we should be prepared. Short of that, I would hope that Weckmann Muñoz will arrive briefed with stern messages to the parties from Waldheim and that he will try to do something more than just keep the talks going, which has been Osorio Tafall's major recent pre-occupation.

13. *Guarantees*

The present talks are by definition restricted to examining internal constitutional proposals. Turkish fears are two-pronged. The immediate fear hanging over the Turkish Cypriot community is of discrimination in various forms. But overshadowing this, and of major importance for Ankara in particular, is the fear that whatever constitutional safeguards were devised would eventually be rendered meaningless by Enosis. Enosis—and the preparations for it—are the dark cloud which features in all Denktash's nightmares. The Treaty of Guarantee and the various safeguards in the 1960 Constitution were satisfactory up to a point. But speeches and declarations by Makarios and other Greek spokesmen since 1960 have nibbled away at safeguards, and the Treaty of Guarantee has been the subject of strenuous Greek criticism. Nonetheless, is there any way in which by looking at Guarantees, which we have all so far studiously avoided in the context of the talks, Turkish confidence could be bolstered and a more flexible mood induced in the talks themselves?

14. This would be highly unpopular with Makarios, and doubtless with the Greek Government also, since it inevitably involves a formula of some sort precluding Enosis. Since the Treaty of Guarantee is (despite Turkish support for it for the record) regarded by both sides here as virtually irrelevant, any fresh guarantee would have to be on a wider scale—as a minimum including also the Americans (also likely to be unpopular with Makarios); or preferably, if they could be persuaded to play a more active role, the UN. Here again, the difficulties are clearly very great. But I believe that the main thing is to restore confidence between the two sides, and that a move in this direction of guarantees might be the best way of influencing the Turks.

15. The difficulty would be to put this across to Makarios—and perhaps to Athens. I do not underrate this. It might prove impossible. Presentation would depend a great deal on an estimate of Makarios' real aims. The Turks, and plenty of Greek Cypriots too, believe that Makarios is determined that there shall never be a settlement. I doubt this. Although he would still, I am sure, resist public association with any formula too

Governments'. He concluded: 'A full dress debate on its own would probably do more harm than good ... There is probably little that the Council could do, except in the case of a major crisis (when it might be too late).'

obviously and overtly ruling out Enosis for ever, I think that in his own mind he genuinely accepts the unfeasibility of Enosis and perhaps even prefers the idea of an independent Cyprus. But it must be a genuinely united, single State. He is not going to sign away Enosis only to be faced by a separate Turkish Cypriot State, in effect, the Turkish half of Double Enosis. If we were to try to reach such an accommodation, therefore, as a way of escape from the minutiae of the talks, the bargain would have to be Greek Cypriot acceptance that Enosis really was ruled out, in some form firm enough to satisfy the Turks; balanced by Turkish acceptance of a genuinely unitary though bi-communal Republic of Cyprus. The difficulties of any such bargain are clearly enormous.

16. To sum up, and at the risk, hopefully, of being proved wrong, as in almost all prophecy about Cyprus, I fear that the intercommunal situation over the next few months could develop dangerously. The risk will obviously be higher if relations between Greece and Turkey deteriorate further: we have plenty of evidence already of the evil effect that this is having on both communities here, particularly the Turkish Cypriots. But even without that, this will, I am afraid, be a tense summer and I think that we should be considering now what action we could take to defuse the situation and if possible to improve the prospects for a communal settlement. This letter suggest various directions in which an initiative might be taken to bring home to both sides the need for a genuine fresh effort to bring the talks to success and the dangers of allowing the situation to drift. I do not rate either the likely effectiveness or feasibility of these ideas at all highly. But I believe that we ought to be applying our minds actively to this problem now lest the situation deteriorate seriously later in the year, and I hope that this letter has at least provided food for thought and set up some skittles to be knocked down. It is not easy to make firm recommendations for a situation which is still for the moment hypothetical; but I should favour discussing now with the Americans, perhaps with some of our EEC or NATO friends, but above all with the UN, what concerted action could be taken to bring pressure to bear on the parties in the event of, or preferably prior to, a breakdown of the talks

S.J.L. Olver

No. 17

Letter from Mr. Olver (Nicosia) to Mr. Goodison

[*WSC 1/2*]

Confidential NICOSIA, *11 July 1974*

Dear Alan,

Greek-Cypriot Relations

I had an hour's talk yesterday with Lagacos. He spoke extremely frankly, stressing that he was speaking in this way to me because he felt that, in our special position, we ought to be in full possession of the facts; but he was not talking like this to anyone else, and he particularly asked that his confidence should be respected and that no mention should be made of him as the source of this information. I should be grateful if this confidence could be strictly respected.

2. I enclose a summary record of the talk.[1] He came pretty near—if allowance is made for his personal position—to admitting that the Junta might have been plotting against Makarios. He was clearly himself in a state of shock. He sees his efforts here over the last two years ruined, feels that he can do no further good and is asking to be recalled; and if the Greek Government refuses to do this, he will consider resigning—though he would prefer not to, believing that the duty of professional Greek diplomats is to remain in service in the hope of influencing events for the better.

3. Against this background, I have little doubt that his estimate both of the Greek Government's attitude and of Makarios' position is sincere. On the former, it is to some extent reassuring that Lagacos does not anticipate a last ditch confrontation over the National Guard—though he stressed that the Junta are unpredictable and that he has no real idea of their plans.[2]

---

[1] Not printed. In this enclosed summary Mr. Olver noted that Mr. Lagakos had confirmed that he had brought an invitation from the Greek Government to Archbishop Makarios to visit Athens to discuss the situation in Cyprus without preconditions. The Archbishop had replied that he would be willing to go to Athens at any time, but only after the Greek Government had accepted his demands for the removal of Greek officers from the Cyprus National Guard (cf. No. 16, note 8). In an open letter of 2 July to Gen. Gizikis, Archbishop Makarios accused Athens of conspiring to seize power in Cyprus and to assassinate him, and he requested the immediate withdrawal of 650 Greek officers of the Cyprus National Guard. See G. Clerides, *Cyprus: My Deposition* (3 vols., Nicosia: Alithia, 1989-90), vol. iii, pp. 321-25.

[2] *V. ibid.* Mr. Olver thought that Mr. Lagakos clearly did not consider either passive resistance by the Greek Government or active resistance by the Greek officers in Cyprus to the Archbishop's demands likely options. 'Talk of a coup', Mr. Olver observed, 'we both dismissed: the attempt would fail since the essential support of the National Guard could not be relied on; and even if successful, it would achieve no useful object beyond the removal of Makarios.' Mr. Lagakos agreed 'that the assassination of the Archbishop remained a possibility; he commented

4. As for Lagacos' analysis of Makarios' position and motives,[3] there remains, even after discounting natural Greek bias, a great deal with which we would agree. Lacagos clearly has good sources of information within the Council of Ministers. What he said echoes suggestions that have already reached me that Makarios was playing this hand very much on his own—which means in practice together with his close, left-wing, advisers. Earlier on, when Makarios was protesting to Denisis about the misbehaviour of Greek officers in the National Guard, the selection of officer-cadets and so on, and getting no change from Athens, one could have every sympathy with his position. The fault lay clearly with Athens. In this last round, the emphasis has, I think, shifted. It is now Makarios, out of a mixture of perhaps impatience and fear who is shutting the door. My only comment of substance indeed on Lagacos' analysis would be that I think he makes too little allowance for a, perhaps, genuine fear on Makarios' part of where the Junta's tactics might be leading. It seems particularly unfortunate that Makarios should have foreclosed so rapidly on the Greek Government's invitation to Athens to discuss matters. Lagacos argued with him at length that he had nothing to fear and everything to gain from accepting this invitation—but got no sensible response. Today, the Government spokesman, commenting on press rumours of this invitation, has stated that there was 'no question of President Makarios visiting Athens'. Against this it will be very difficult to re-open the issue—though if I get a chance with Christofides or anyone else worthwhile, I shall suggest that this seems a pity. I do not at this stage see any scope for further involvement on our part than this.

5. The next move is now with Athens. We can only hope it will not be a rash one.

Yours ever,

S.J.L. Olver

that, if they had wished to, EOKA B, and therefore presumably the Junta, could have done this any time in the last six months'. This, Mr. Olver noted, 'is true but does not dispose of the possibility that, driven into a corner as they are now, the Junta might not be tempted to try this'. In the paper enclosed in Mr. Olver's letter to Mr. Goodison of 26 June (see No. 16, note 8), the British High Commission had surmised that EOKA B would be capable of assassinating Archbishop Makarios, but that, while it could attempt a *coup*, its ability to topple the Government and install a new Government remained doubtful.

[3] *V. ibid.* Mr. Lagakos told Mr. Olver that neither he nor, so far as he knew, the Greek Government, had yet seen any proof of Archbishop Makarios's allegations that the Junta were actively involved in the direction and support of EOKA B. He further asserted that the Archbishop was pursuing a highly personal policy, and that he had reason to believe that he was 'relying heavily on assurances from the Russians, who had guaranteed that, in the event of trouble in Cyprus, no "third party" would be allowed to intervene'. With the 'dismembering of the National Guard', Mr. Lagakos foresaw 'a massive increase in the strength and influence of the Police Tactical Reserve with a consequent sharp swing to the left in the balance of forces within Cyprus'.

CHAPTER II

Cyprus: Coup d'État and Intervention 15 July 1974–15 August 1974

No. 18

Mr. Olver (Nicosia) to Mr. Callaghan

No. 180 Telegraphic [WSC 1/10]

Flash. Unclassified   NICOSIA, *15 July 1974, 8.15 a.m.*

Repeated for information to Immediate Athens and CBFNE[4]

My telegram No. 178:[5]
Internal Situation

1. Though information is still incomplete, it looks increasingly like a coup organised by Greek contingent/Greek-officered elements of National Guard.

(*a*) Nicosia airport is sealed and controlled by tanks, presumably from Greek National contingent at Waynes Keep.

(*b*) Tanks are fanning out from Nicosia airport area towards the city and Kykko monastery, which had earlier been turned into barracks for Police Tactical Reserve, has been under tank and mortar attack.

(*c*) The Presidential Palace has been under attack by what look like regular troops since early this morning and is rumoured to have fallen; PTR reinforcements were apparently cut off by Greek troops.

(*d*) Telephones are cut and CYTA[6] is believed to be under control of National Guard.

(*e*) Cyprus Broadcasting Corporation seems similarly to have been taken over and has broadcast announcement that anyone intending to resist National Guard should lay down their arms and surrender. It has just announced the death of Makarios.[7]

---

[4] Commander British Forces Near East.

[5] Mr. Olver reported in this telegram, despatched at 7.05 a.m. (GMT) on 15 July, that the High Commission had just received news of outbreaks of fighting in Nicosia. He believed this to be taking place around the Presidential Palace and the Supreme Court Building.

[6] Cyprus Telecommunications Authority.

[7] Although the Cyprus Broadcasting Corporation continued to affirm that Archbishop Makarios was dead, the Cyprus police network reported that he was alive, and the British High

2. I have no reports so far of casualties among the British community.

Commission learnt that the Bishop of Paphos had asked for UN intervention on behalf of the Archbishop, who was said to be in hiding (Nicosia telegram No. 187 of 15 July).

No. 19

Mr. Callaghan to Sir R. Hooper (Athens)

No. 129 Telegraphic [WSC 1/10]

Flash. Confidential   FCO, *15 July 1974, 1.45 p.m.*

Repeated to Flash Ankara Washington UKDEL NATO UKMIS New York, and for information to Flash Nicosia CBFNE, Cyprus.

1. Athens should deliver by whatever means is quickly possible the following personal message to the Acting Greek Foreign Minister[1] from me. Begins.

'I am gravely concerned by the first reports I have received of events in Cyprus today.[2] Although the situation is not yet entirely clear it is undoubtedly very dangerous with serious implications for the stability of the eastern Mediterranean and for the cohesion of the Atlantic Alliance. I am sure you share my concern that the independence, territorial integrity and security of Cyprus should be maintained. I should be grateful to have urgently your comments on the situation as the Greek Government sees it.' Ends.

2. Athens should also inform the Greek Government that I am sending a message in similar terms to the Turkish Foreign Minister.

3. Ankara should deliver a message in similar terms to the Turkish Foreign Minister and should add orally that, while we understand how gravely the Turks must be concerned about the situation, I hope very much that they will avoid any kind of precipitate action or intervention at this stage. It seems that the fighting is primarily between members of the Greek-Cypriot community. In these circumstances it is clearly essential, if the conflict is not to spread, for the Turkish Government to display exemplary patience.[3]

[1] Mr. C. Kypraios

[2] See No. 18.

[3] When Mr. Fyjis-Walker, then British Chargé d'Affaires in Ankara, delivered this message to Mr. H.E. Isik, Turkey's Defence Minister and Acting Foreign Minister, on 15 July, Mr. Isik stated that he agreed that intervention was 'undesirable but did not affirm that it was unthinkable'. 'Nor', Mr. Fyjis-Walker recorded, 'did he relish any reference, even by way of congratulations to Turkish patience or unilateral restraint ... He gave no sign, and we have detected no others, that the Turks are yet preparing any pre-emptive or offensive action' (Ankara telegram No. 747 of 15 July).

4. Washington should immediately inform the State Department of these messages, together with an oral message from me to Dr. Kissinger that I should be very grateful for his view of the situation, for information on any action which he may contemplate, and for any information about the course of events in Cyprus which he can give us.[4] We are also in touch with the American Embassy here.

5. UKDEL NATO should inform the Secretary-General of the action we are taking and invite him to consider whether he should not himself send messages to the Greeks and the Turks.[5]

6. UKMIS New York should urgently seek the Secretary-General's views on what action, if any, he considers the United Nations might usefully take. They should also suggest to Dr. Waldheim that he should convene an emergency meeting of the contributors to UNFICYP.[6]

---

[4] Sir P. Ramsbotham, HM Ambassador in Washington, informed Mr. Callaghan in Washington telegram No. 2383 of 15 July that he had learned from the State Department that the US Ambassadors in Ankara and Athens and the US Permanent Representative to NATO had been instructed to take similar action to that requested by Mr. Callaghan. 'The State Department', Sir P. Ramsbotham observed, 'have no doubt that the Greek Government are behind the coup, but hope to avoid having to say so publicly.'

[5] Following a call on him by Mr. D.A. Logan, the UK Deputy Permanent Representative to NATO, on 15 July, Dr. Luns sent a message to the Greek and Turkish Foreign Ministers informing them of his growing concern over the consequences of developments in Cyprus and their possible impact on Greek-Turkish relations, the cohesion of the Atlantic Alliance and the security of its southern flank. The NAC discussed the situation on the morning of 16 July (UKDEL NATO telegram No. 365 of 16 July).

[6] Mr. I.S. Richard, the UK Permanent Representative to the UN, put this suggestion to Dr. Waldheim on 15 July, but the UN Secretary-General did not favour UNFICYP contributors meeting at this stage (UKMIS New York telegram No. 777 of 15 July). There was also no US support for this idea: the 'Americans', Sir P. Ramsbotham noted in Washington telegram No. 2383, 'feel that any meeting at the UN would be likely to "internationalise" the situation in an undesirable manner' (see note 4 above).

No. 20

Mr. Callaghan to Sir R. Hooper (Athens)

No. 131 Telegraphic [*WSC 1/10*]

Flash. Confidential   FCO, *16 July 1974, 10.20 a.m.*

Repeated to Flash Nicosia, UKMIS New York, Ankara, Washington, Paris, Immediate Moscow, UKDEL NATO and CBFNE.

Your tel[egram] No. 196:[1]
Cyprus

1. Now that it seems President Makarios is still alive,[2] the situation has of course changed and you should ask to see the acting Foreign Minister again as soon as possible.

2. You should say that in the situation which has now arisen it is more than ever important that the Greek Government should make a statement, along the lines of para[graph] 3 in your tel[egram] under reference,[3] clarifying the attitude of the Greek Government towards the crisis in Cyprus. It seems to me essential that Greece should state unambiguously her intention to observe her international obligations in regard to Cyprus and her determination to observe the independence, territorial integrity and security of the Republic.[4]

[1] In this telegram of 15 July Sir R. Hooper reported that he had delivered Mr. Callaghan's message in No. 19 to Mr. Kypraios, who had replied that the Greek Government were 'not fully informed about the situation' in Cyprus, and that Greek policy remained 'unchanged i.e. that Cyprus should remain an independent unitary and sovereign state, and that a settlement should be sought through a continuation of the intercommunal talks'.

[2] Nicosia telegram No. 202 of 15 July transmitted a pooled despatch from news agency correspondents in Nicosia reporting a broadcast made by Archbishop Makarios, only hours after Mr. Sampson (see No. 8, note 8) had announced over the Cyprus army-controlled radio that he was the Republic's new President. In his broadcast the Archbishop declared that he had been the 'target for the Athens military Junta', but that they had failed. Although Mr. Olver did not hear this broadcast, he confirmed in Nicosia telegram No. 203 of 15 July (despatched at 7.48 p.m., GMT) that the local UNFICYP Commander in Paphos had seen the Archbishop and that Dr. Weckmann-Muñoz, had been invited to call on him the following day.

[3] In paragraph 3 of this telegram (see note 1 above) Sir R. Hooper reported that Mr. Kypraios had indicated his agreement with Sir R. Hooper's personal suggestion that he should include in a statement he would probably be making on 16 July a reference to 'Greece's international obligations in regard to Cyprus and her determination to respect them'. Sir R. Hooper also recommended that the Greek Government should persuade the new régime in Cyprus to make a similar statement.

[4] When Sir R. Hooper delivered this message to Mr. Kypraios on the evening of 16 July, the latter readily agreed that HMG might state publicly that the Greek Government had offered assurances that 'they intended to respect their international obligations in regard to Cyprus' (Athens telegram No. 204 of 16 July).

3. You should go on to say that assuming President Makarios is still alive, he is in the view of HMG the legitimate President of the Republic. It is of paramount importance to secure an early end to the fighting among the Greek inhabitants of Cyprus before other interests become irretrievably involved.

4. We assume that the Greek Government, who have a unique responsibility in the matter, share this view and would wish to do whatever they can to re-establish peace and stability in the island. To this end HMG consider that it would be in the interests of the Greek Government, and would indeed rebound greatly to their credit internationally, if they were to replace at the earliest possible moment the Greek officers of the Cypriot National Guard who, whether correctly or not, are generally held to have been responsible for the attempted coup against President Makarios.[5] Failing action of this kind on the part of the Greek Government, it seems to HMG that the early internationalisation of the crisis is inevitable. This could only result in Greece coming under considerable and unwelcome pressure from the United Nations and elsewhere to take action of this kind.

5. (For Washington)

You should inform the Americans as soon as possible that we share their view that it is right to avoid the internationalisation of the situation in Cyprus.[6] We are therefore taking action in Athens along the lines described above. We hope that the American Ambassador in Athens can be instructed to speak similarly at once.

6. (For Ankara)

You should inform the Turks of the action which we are taking. We leave it to the Turks to judge whether they wish to take similar action themselves or not.[7]

7. (For UKMIS New York)

---

[5] Mr. Kypraios told Sir R. Hooper on 16 July that the rotation of the regular Greek contingent in Cyprus [due to take place on 17 July] would proceed according to plan, and that he had 'urged on all concerned the importance of making certain that there was no reinforcement—or even appearance of reinforcement—of the Greek contingent'. Sir R. Hooper observed in Athens telegram No. 204 (*v. ibid.*): 'All this is not too bad as far as it goes. But as we have learnt from experience, making representations to civilian Ministers is one thing and getting them translated into action by the military is quite another.'

[6] In a telephone conversation with Mr. Callaghan on the afternoon of 16 July Dr. Kissinger said that he was almost in complete agreement with the line being taken by HMG as communicated to him by Sir P. Ramsbotham. He was concerned to 'avoid legitimising the new régime in Cyprus for as long as possible', and to keep other powers from becoming involved in the situation for as long as possible. Dr. Kissinger added that the US Government would under no circumstances support proposals for *enosis* (telegram No. 1538 to Washington of 16 July). Sir P. Ramsbotham reported in Washington telegram No. 2393 of 16 July that American aims with regard to Cyprus remained 'to avoid internationalisation and to prevent the Russians fishing in muddied waters'.

[7] In conversation with the Netherlands Ambassador in London on 16 July Sir J. Killick stated that Britain's 'immediate objective must be to prevail upon Athens to draw back and to restrain the Turks' (telegram No. 92 to The Hague of 16 July).

You should inform the Secretariat of the action we are taking. You should add that we recognise that it may well be that the Security Council will have to discuss the situation in Cyprus. However we hope that it will not be brought into play prematurely and that time will be given for bilateral approaches to the Greek Government to take effect.[8]

You should independently inform Rossides of the action we have taken and of our attitude towards discussion in the Security Council.

8. (For Nicosia)

I recognise that you are not now, and are unlikely to be in the immediate future, in touch with Makarios.[9] Nonetheless if an opportunity occurs for you to inform him of our attitude and of the action we are taking you should do so.

9. (For Paris)

You may inform the Nine[10] of the action we are taking at the meeting which the Presidency has called at 1500z[11] today.

10. (For UKDEL NATO)

You should keep the Secretary General informed.

---

[8] The UN Security Council met on the afternoon of 16 July at the request of Dr. Waldheim and Mr. Z. Rossides, the Cyprus Permanent Representative to the UN, to discuss developments in Cyprus. During the debate Mr. Rossides blamed the *coup* upon Greek officers in Cyprus who were directed from Athens. Mr. E. Megalokonomos, the Greek Deputy Permanent Representative, refuted allegations of Greek interference in Cyprus's internal affairs (UKMIS New York telegram No. 781 of 16 July). Cf. *UNSC Official Records, 29th year, 1779th meeting*, 16 July 1974 (S/PV.1779).

[9] On 16 July Archbishop Makarios was taken by RAF helicopter from the UNFICYP camp at Paphos to the SBA at Akrotiri, from where he was flown to Malta. After spending the night on Malta, he was flown to England on the morning of 17 July by an RAF Comet. On his arrival at Lyneham, he told Mr. D. Ennals, Minister of State at the FCO, that he intended to fly the next day to New York with a view to addressing the UN Security Council (minute of 17 July from Mr. A.J. Coles (Private Secretary to Mr. Ennals) to Mr. A.A. Acland (Private Secretary to Mr. Callaghan)).

[10] The representatives of the Nine member states of the European Community (EC).

[11] i.e. 3 p.m., GMT.

No. 21

Mr. Fyjis-Walker (Ankara) to Mr. Callaghan

No. 754 Telegraphic [WSC 1/10]

Flash. *Confidential*   ANKARA, *16 July 1974, 3.10 p.m.*

Repeated for information to Immediate Athens, Nicosia, UKMIS New York, Washington, Paris, UKDEL NATO, CBFNE and Moscow.

Your tel[egram] No. 131 to Athens:[1]
Cyprus

1. I informed the Director-General for Political Affairs (Soysal) of the action being taken with the Greeks. Soysal was not at first very receptive but became more so as he realised that our action puts pressure on the Greeks without any corresponding call for restraint by the Turks. ('Even-handedness' by the Western Powers has caused some irritation here: the Americans gained some kudos by weighting their representation slightly against Enosis.) But he did not think the Greeks would listen: they were behind the coup, and for instance, if they replaced officers in the National Guard it would only be with more of the same kind. He did not think there would be any point in the Turks taking similar action with the Greeks.

2. Soysal then referred to the Turkish reply to your message (your tel[egram] No. 129 to Athens)[2] due to be delivered to you in London today. Soysal said the essential point was the call for both consultation and concerted action by the UK and Turkey under Article 4 of the Treaty of Guarantee. He drew my attention particularly to paragraph 2 saying that if we could not agree to concerted action, Turkish hands would be legally free to take any unilateral steps they wished.[3] I pressed him hard on any actual lines of action the Turks might wish to see, but he said that could come later. It is not clear which the Turks want more, concerted action or their hands free for unilateral action.

[1] No. 20.

[2] No. 19.

[3] See No. 1, note 8. On 16 July Mr. A. Alacaptan, the Turkish Minister in London called on Mr. Hattersley to deliver a note addressed to Mr. Callaghan from Mr. Isik. This called for consultations with HMG, and suggested that 'the threat directed against the independence of Cyprus could be removed, jointly by Turkey and Her Majesty's Government's forces in Cyprus'. In a minute to Mr. A.A. Acland (Private Secretary to Mr. Callaghan) of 16 July Mr. Goulding noted that Mr. Hattersley thought it clear from what Mr. Alacaptan had said that what the Turks really wanted was 'that we should agree to joint military action to "restore the balance of power" in Cyprus'. Mr. Acland informed the Mr. Alacaptan in a letter of 16 July that Mr. Callaghan would be ready to have talks in London at any time from 17 July.

3. Soysal was unsure whether the situation on the island was improving or not. He thought that pro-Makarios resistance would probably peter out. Nevertheless, if anything, the indications are increasing that Turkish policy is to present a low profile. My D[efence]A[ttaché]'s telegram FOJ 161150z (copied to the Department) recounts the negative evidence, lack of obvious alerts or troop movements and a report from a good source that the military are constrained by instructions from the civilian Government ruling out unilateral military action at the moment.[4]

4. This would fit with what I estimate to be basic Turkish policy, especially under Eçevit, that they will only interven[e] forcefully in the island if they believe a declaration of Enosis to be imminent, or the Turkish Cypriots come under real attack. But if either of these seem likely to happen then the Turkish Government will be determined to intervene with any force necessary for their prevention. The Turks will on no account accept a Greek Cyprus.[5] In any period of tension the Turks take additional precautions to put themselves in a position to intervene if necessary: Soysal confirmed that they are doing this now. But since the basic precautions are virtually permanent (i.e. the intervention force in the Mersin/Iskenderun area) additional overt activity can be comparatively minor.

5. Short of intervention the Turks will feel that they have a range of options. Foremost will be pressure on us to act as a guarantor power, either alone or with them, to rectify, or induce the Greeks to rectify, the situation arising from the coup. Further options will be recourse to the UN, the Americans or other allies. So long as no decision to intervene with force has been taken, the Turks are likely to try a mixture of these options as opportunities offer.

6. In this connection Soysal told me that the Soviet Ambassador is calling on President Korutürk[6] this evening, apparently at the former's request. It is assumed that he is delivering a message from the Soviet Government. I hope to discuss this with Soysal tomorrow: he confirmed that the Turkish Government wish to keep 'within a NATO framework' in dealing with this approach.

---

[4] This telegram, also despatched at 11.50 a.m. on 16 July, concluded that while 'certain predictable and fairly low level precautionary measures' had been taken by Turkey's armed forces, the general military reaction to the situation in Cyprus was 'calm and low key'.

[5] Sir P. Ramsbotham reported in Washington telegram No. 2409 of 17 July that Mr. W.B. Macomber Jr., the US Ambassador in Ankara, had been informed that the Turkish Government had three objectives: (1) the 'restoration of Makarios, or of a successor who "might emerge through the previously established constitutional procedures"'; (2) the withdrawal of the Greek officers in the Cyprus National Guard; and (3) the establishment of a 'secure corridor to the sea' for the Turkish community.

[6] Mr. F. Korutürk was President of Turkey.

No. 22

Minute from Sir J. Killick to Mr. Goodison
[*WSC 1/10*]

Top Secret   FCO, *17 July 1974*

Cyprus

1. The Secretary of State had an office discussion before seeing the Prime Minister this morning taking into account a basis for discussion prepared by Mr. Acland.[1]

2. The Secretary of State said that Mintoff[2] had telephoned to say that Makarios was in bad shape both physically and morally. He had neither clothes nor money. On this it was assumed that the Cyprus High Commission would help but the Secretary of State was anxious to be assured that we would do everything necessary. There might be a longer term problem of finance for the Cyprus High Commission. (SED have asked PCD[3] to look after this angle.) Mintoff said that Makarios only had three bodyguards with him and was anxious to get more of his own staff out of Cyprus. The Secretary of State indicated that he would like to help over this. It was agreed that the new régime would be likely to react badly to physical assistance on our part and that anything done (e.g. by bringing individuals out through the SBAs) would have to be done in secret.

3. An MoD[4] intelligence assessment of the situation was given. The National Guard seemed in complete control of the Greek part of the island and there was no fighting. Our own servicemen had been able to rejoin their families in Limassol. The Turks were in a high state of alert but in a low posture although they could move in a matter of hours. The Greeks were in a slightly higher state of alert than normal but there was no unusual Greek military activity. Although there had been some indications of involvement by the Greek National contingent at an early stage there was no other hard evidence. In reply to the Secretary of State's direct question, the MoD view was expressed that there was no doubt whatever about Greek instigation of the coup.

4. On the operational side the MoD said the Greek National Guard was 10,000 strong with light tanks, artillery and heavy equipment. They could mobilise a further 30,000. Existing British forces in the SBAs could cope with them. In reply to questions however it was explained that this was a defensive assessment. If British forces were to be used offensively, it was

---

[1] Not traced.

[2] Mr. D. Mintoff, the Maltese Prime Minister, met Archbishop Makarios during his overnight stay in Malta. Cf. No. 20, note 9.

[3] Protocol and Conference Department.

[4] Ministry of Defence.

thought the Chiefs of Staff would need reinforcements provided for under present plans—a Brigade Headquarters and two battalions (probably the spearhead battalion from the UK already at 72 hours notice and the Commando embarked in Hermes).[5] In reply to the direct question whether it would be militarily possible to restore Makarios to power, the provisional answer was probably Yes if the only opposition was the National Guard, but the MoD would probably want to put in 'a lot more' as an insurance.

5. Much would depend on the attitude of the population and the extent of a possible internal security problem. This was difficult to assess. EOKA(B) had only 200 armed men at the last count.

6. There was some discussion of the degree of international political support which HMG might enjoy if we embarked on such action. This was generally favourable. The question was raised of the possible need for a UN umbrella. It was pointed out that it would have to be based on the establishment of a clear breach of the Treaty of Guarantee; that it was right to examine the possibility since the Turks might otherwise 'go it alone'; that the return of Makarios would still leave us with an unstable situation, the need for him to make improved constitutional arrangements on the island and a possible demand from him for some kind of continuing military guarantee; the last consideration would affect the Defence Review.[6]

7. The MoD were commissioned to produce an urgent military study before tonight's meeting with Turkish Ministers.[7] For this they would need certain political assumptions and assessments which the FCO would provide. One complication would be how to fit in the evacuation of civilian dependants. The main point the Secretary of State wished to cover was an estimate of how bloody the operation might be. The politician's delight would of course be a bloodless return with flowers. A particular point to clarify would be whether the operation should be based on surprise and how this could be reconciled with the necessary establishment of international support, including the UN umbrella. Certainly the United States would need to be brought in very early and it would be no less crucial to ensure that the Soviet Union did not cause complications.

8. As regards Mr. Acland's questions, it was pointed out that we were faced with a dilemma. Continued support for Makarios in circumstances in which we could not effectively restore him to power would prevent us from establishing the working relations with the régime effectively in control in

---

[5] At a meeting of Mr. Mason with Field-Marshal Sir M. Carver, the Chief of the Defence Staff (CDS), on the afternoon of 16 July it was agreed that it would be 'prudent' for *HMS Hermes*, with 41 Commando, Royal Marines, embarked, not to dock in Malta as planned, on 17 July, but to proceed on towards Cyprus, and where she should thereafter remain within twenty-four hours steaming from Cyprus. Mr. Callaghan subsequently concurred (minute of 16 July from Mr. W.F. Mumford (Private Secretary to Mr. Mason) to the Principal Staff Officer (PSO) to Sir M. Carver).

[6] See No. 10, note 1.

[7] See No. 25.

Cyprus which we would need in order to maintain the SBAs. Makarios outside Cyprus might move closer to the Soviet Union and the latter would be in a position to exploit this situation in the Eastern Mediterranean area. There would also be difficulties for us all in Western Europe in face of what would be regarded as another extension of 'fascism' with consequent demands for the adoption of hostile attitudes both to the régime in Cyprus and the Greek Government. Even if Sampson might continue to avoid enosis and maintain notional Cypriot independence, the balance of things in Cyprus would shift markedly towards Athens. The question would arise how far and how long the Turkish Government could hold off in an internal situation in the Island which would be confused and unstable.

9. At this point the Secretary of State had to leave for a meeting with the Prime Minister before all Mr. Acland's questions could be covered. There was a brief discussion of possible further action *vis-à-vis* the Greek Government today but it was agreed that consideration of this should be suspended until after discussion with Makarios[8] and the Turks, in particular until it was clear what Makarios's intentions were.

JOHN KILLICK

---

[8] Cf. No. 24.

No. 23

Mr. Olver (Nicosia) to Mr. Callaghan

No. 230 Telegraphic [*WSC 1/10*]

Immediate. Confidential   NICOSIA, *17 July 1974, 2.20 p.m.*

Repeated for information to Immediate Athens, Ankara, Washington, Paris, Bonn, UKMIS New York, Moscow, UKDEL NATO, Moscow and HQ BFNE.

I have seen the text of a press statement to be issued this evening about the movements of *HMS Hermes*.[1] The BBC reports that *HMS Devonshire* and *HMS Rhyl* have also been ordered to the eastern Mediterranean and that the NATO powers have issued a statement that they still recognise Makarios as President and calling on Greek mainland officers to leave the island.[2]

---

[1] See No. 22, note 5.

[2] The NAC statement, issued at 12 noon on 17 July, also deplored the outburst of violence on Cyprus and the 'resulting threat to the stability in the area' (UKDEL NATO telegram No. 371 of 17 July).

2. These reports inevitably convey the impression that thought is being given to the possibility of Makarios re-establishing himself in Cyprus as President. I believe that the local repercussions could be extremely dangerous.

3. As I have reported the new régime backed by the National Guard is now in control of virtually the entire island. Opposition has to all intents and purposes died out. The Police Tactical Reserve has surrendered and most of its members are under arrest. I discount the possibility of any local uprising to restore Makarios. The National Guard could without difficulty put down any such attempt.[3]

4. Many Cypriots will be sad that Makarios has gone. Many of them have no respect or affection for the new régime. Nevertheless the régime cannot now be overthrown by any forces within Cyprus. Makarios could only re-establish himself with the military assistance of some foreign power or powers. Many people here dislike the thought that Sampson has been brought to power on the backs of the Greek military: but there is relief at the disappearance of some aspects of Makarios' régime: his restoration by force would be very far from popular and would cause more problems locally than it would solve.

5. Announcements of British military deployment in this area coupled with Makarios' flight via the SBAs[4] will undoubtedly convince some, including probably members of the Government and National Guard, that we plan to intervene militarily on Makarios' behalf. If any such suggestion is allowed to gain currency it would gravely affect the whole future of Anglo-Cypriot relations. It would also have highly dangerous consequences for the large British community and tourist population here.[5]

---

[3] Mr. Olver was personally of the opinion, despite Greek protests to the contrary, that the decision to launch the *coup* was taken in Athens. In Nicosia telegram No. 223 of 17 July he reported on the situation in Cyprus: 'Popular reaction remains bemused and has yet to crystallise. Likely trends are resentment at the inconvenience, damage, danger and loss of life: scepticism at the new régime and dislike of a veiled military dictatorship: relief that the "slide to the left" has been stemmed: for many (but not all) grief at Makarios' departure (mixed with relief at his survival). Greece will not come well out of this: but I should not expect wide-spread popular resistance ... Much will however depend on the régime's ability to maintain law and order, not least among its own supporters: a number of unattractive heavily armed young thugs are roaming the streets.'

[4] See No. 20, note 9.

[5] In Athens telegram No. 209 of 17 July Sir R. Hooper expressed his agreement with the conclusions reached by Mr. Olver in paragraphs 2 and 5. CBFNE also supported Mr. Olver's views. In an exlcusive signal to the Defence Staff, cited by Mr. Olver in Nicosia telegram No. 248 of 18 July (addressed personally to Sir J. Killick), the CBFNE argued that while any damage done to UK relations with the *de facto* Cyprus Government by the rescue of Archbishop Makarios would 'probably not be of a permanent nature', any further rescue attempt of the Archbishop's followers would have a 'most serious effect' on these relations. Mr. Olver added to this: 'In general, I feel at the moment a certain lack of guidance on HMG's aims and intentions. I can understand your preoccupations but should be grateful for anything you can do to fill that gap.' Sir J. Killick replied in telegram No. 160 to Nicosia of 18 July that all that

was being done with regard to the rescue of the Archbishop's supporters was 'to investigate possibilities, and assess their practicability ... no decision [had] been taken and [did] not appear to be called for at present'.

No. 24

Record of conversation between Mr. Callaghan and President Makarios at the Foreign and Commonwealth Office on 17 July 1974 at 5.45 p.m.

[*WSC 1/10*]

Confidential

Present:

The Rt. Hon. James Callaghan MP	Archbishop Makarios[1]
The Rt. Hon. David Ennals MP	HE Mr. Costas Ashiotis MBE[2]
Sir T. Brimelow	
Mr. Wiggin	
Mr. Goodison	
Mr. McNally[3]	
Mr. Alexander[4]	
Mr. Weir[5]	

Archbishop Makarios said that he would be leaving London at 11 a.m. on 18 July. He had asked for postponement of the Security Council meeting until he could be present and he thought that perhaps the morning of 19 July would be most satisfactory. He hoped that HMG would make a strong statement saying that they were not prepared to accept any diplomatic representative of the régime in Cyprus and that the High Commissioner for Nicosia would have no contact with it. *Mr. Callaghan* said that he was listening to what the Archbishop said, but we had business related to the SBA's to discuss with the régime. It was however clear that Archbishop Makarios was the elected and legitimate President of Cyprus and he had

---

[1] See No. 20, note 9.

[2] The Cyprus High Commissioner in London.

[3] Mr. T. McNally was Political Adviser to Mr. Callaghan.

[4] Mr. M.O'D.B. Alexander was Assistant Private Secretary to Mr. Callaghan.

[5] Mr. M.S. Weir was AUS responsible for superintending the FCO's UN Department (UND).

said so in the House of Commons.[6] He considered that this would be the case until there were new elections.[7] *Archbishop Makarios* said it had not been a revolution but an invasion. He did not think anyone could recognise a President nominated by the military government in Athens.[8] The Turks certainly should not do so. The President was not President of the Greek community alone but of the Republic of Cyprus as a whole.

2. *Mr. Callaghan* asked how the Archbishop could recover his powers. *Archbishop Makarios* said this depended upon the Greek Government. If they withdrew their officers from the National Guard and withdrew support from Mr. Sampson, the latter would fall. It was for Britain and Turkey to press the Greeks in every way about their evaluation of the situation and to seek to restore the *status quo* before the coup. *Mr. Callaghan* said that we would certainly declare this to be our aim. The best end was the return of the Archbishop as the legal President, which he was. *Archbishop Makarios* said that if elections were wanted, then they could be arranged under the auspices of the guarantor powers. The Greek Government might be unwilling to permit such restoration for fear that he, the Archbishop, would institute reprisals on his return. A committee, composed of the three guarantor powers and the Government of Cyprus, could be established to supervise the situation and ensure that no misunderstanding of this kind took place.

3. *Mr. Callaghan* asked about the future of the National Guard in these circumstances. *Archbishop Makarios* said he did not want to have any army. The Greeks had said he needed one for fear of Turkish invasion. It was clear that there was greater danger from Greece. *Mr. Ennals* said that the Archbishop had earlier talked of reducing the National Guard to half its present size. Was he now saying it should disappear entirely? *Archbishop Makarios* said that he had proposed cutting it by half because he did not wish to have too many Greek officers nor to humiliate the Greek junta. He had therefore asked that 200 should leave in July, 200 in August, and 100 or 150 should stay in Cyprus as instructors and military advisers.[9] But if the National Guard created difficulties he would not hesitate to abolish it entirely.

[6] On 16 July Mr. Callaghan told the House of Commons 'President Makarios was elected, and is now the elected, leader of the people of Cyprus'. *Parl. Debs.*, 5th ser., *H. of C.*, vol. 877, c. 246.

[7] According to a minute from Mr. Acland to Mr. Goodison of 18 August, Mr. Callaghan also told Archbishop Makarios that HMG had problems about recognition in that one of its criteria 'was exercising effective control over the country'.

[8] Earlier that afternoon Archbishop Makarios told Mr. Wilson: 'It was not enough for the Greek Government to say that they respected the independence of Cyprus. This was not merely a question of refraining from ENOSIS—the fact was Greece had organised the coup' (record of conversation between Mr. Wilson and President Makarios at 2.30 p.m. on Wednesday 17 July at 10 Downing Street).

[9] Cf. No. 17, note 1.

4. *Mr. Callaghan* asked whether Archbishop Makarios had any arrangements to meet Mr. Eçevit. *Archbishop Makarios* said that there were so many Cypriots in London that he had not time for anything other than talking to them. *Mr. Ennals* asked whether the Turks would accept the abolition of the National Guard. *Archbishop Makarios* said they would be happy about this but they would not agree to abolish their own forces. He had in the past proposed abolishing both forces but they had not agreed. *Mr. Callaghan* asked whether there would be understanding in Cyprus for our working closely with the Turks in the current situation. *Archbishop Makarios* replied that we could say that this was being done with his consent.

5. *Mr. Callaghan* informed Archbishop Makarios of the démarches being made by the Nine and of activity by the Secretary General of NATO. Mr. Ashiotis added that the Council of Europe was thinking of holding a special meeting.

6. *Mr. Callaghan* asked Archbishop Makarios about the word 'replace' which we had used with the Greek Government at an early stage about the officers of the National Guard. *Archbishop Makarios* said he did not want them to be replaced but withdrawn.

7. *Mr. Callaghan* said that he would talk to Dr. Kissinger about his meeting with Archbishop Makarios and invite him to put pressure on Greece, and about tactics in the Security Council. *Archbishop Makarios* said that he would only be staying in New York a few days unless it was possible for him to see Dr. Kissinger or President Nixon. He would then be returning to London.

8. *Mr. Callaghan* asked what steps the Archbishop would have to take if he returned to power. The situation could not be exactly the same as it had been. Archbishop Makarios reverted to his proposal for a committee of the four sides. *Mr. Callaghan* asked what relation it would have to an independent sovereign state. It could not supervise elections, which would be insulting. *Archbishop Makarios* said it would be set up by agreement with a sovereign government and its aim would be to avoid any violation of the constitution. It should not be established by the United Nations but by the powers signatory to the Treaty of Guarantee. *Mr. Ennals* said that if the committee were discussed in the Security Council the Soviet Union might be invited to join in. The *Archbishop* said the proposal should not be put to the United Nations, nor should it be aired until after the Security Council discussion was completed, for fear of Soviet intervention.

9. *Mr. Callaghan* asked what the situation would be in Cyprus in a few months' time if Mr. Sampson remained in charge. *Archbishop Makarios* said it would continue to be unstable. No outcome of the talks between the Greeks and the Turks was possible in that case. Even if Mr. Sampson would agree to proposals from Mr. Denktash, his agreement would not have any value. How could Mr. Clerides take instructions from Mr.

Sampson.[10] *Mr. Ashiotis* said that the great majority of the Greek Cypriots were supporters of the Archbishop; there was a minority of opponents. The result would be constant strife. He was sure that the promise of elections put out by the new régime was as unreliable as such promises issued by the military authorities in Greece.

10. *Mr. Callaghan* said that he had heard Mr. Ashiotis broadcast early that morning, complaining that the British Government was not doing enough for the Archbishop. He did not understand why the High Commissioner had felt it necessary to say this. *Mr. Ashiotis* said that he was seeking pressure on the Greeks from the British Government of the kind they had been discussing. He was satisfied that we would do what he had asked. *Mr. Callaghan* said that nothing he had said today was different from what he had said the day before. The objectives of our policy were that the Archbishop should return to Cyprus and that the Archbishop was the legitimate President. *Archbishop Makarios* again asked for a promise not to recognise the new régime. *Mr. Callaghan* said that we had not recognised this régime yet. He had listened to what the Archbishop had said. If we were to recognise the régime it would be done in order to fulfil the objectives which the Archbishop had set out.

11. After further discussions about the Security Council *Mr Weir.* said there was a risk of a challenge to the credentials of the Archbishop and of Mr. Rossides and of a procedural debate. The *Archbishop* said that he would be glad to have an opportunity to have his credentials tested which would give international recognition to his legitimacy.

12. Mr. Goodison said that the Cyprus Ambassador from Cairo had sent a message asking the Archbishop for instructions. The Archbishop said he would bear this in mind.

---

[10] Mr. Olver reported in Nicosia telegram No. 236 of 17 July that Cyprus radio and television had just announced that Mr. Clerides had agreed to continue his role as negotiator in the intercommunal talks.

No. 25

Record of conversation between Mr. Wilson, Mr. Callaghan, Mr.
Mason, Mr. Eçevit, Mr. Isik and Mr. Asiltürk after dinner at No. 10
Downing Street, on Wednesday 17 July 1974[1]

[*WSC 1/13*]

Secret

Present:

Prime Minister	Mr. Bulent Eçevit,
	Prime Minister of the Republic of Turkey
The Rt. Hon. James	Mr. Hasan Isik
Callaghan	Acting Foreign Minister, Minister of Defence
The Rt. Hon. Roy Mason	Mr. Asiltürk, Minister of the Interior
Sir Thomas Brimelow	Ambassador Halûk Bayülken, Special Adviser (former Foreign Minister)
Sir John Killick	HE Turgut Menemencioglu Ambassador to United Kingdom
Mr. Charles Wiggin	Ambassador Orhan Eralp, Turkish Ambassador to NATO
Mr. Arthur Hockaday[2]	Ambassador Ercument Yavuzalp, Director General of the International Security Department, MFA
Mr. Alan Goodison	Minister Ecmel Barutçu, Head of the Cyprus and Greek Affairs Department, MFA
Mr. Joe Haines[3]	General Haydar Saltik, Turkish General Staff
Lord Bridges[4]	General Kemal Yamak, Turkish General Staff
	Mr. A. Alacakaptan, Minister, Turkish Embassy, London

1. *Mr. Eçevit*, beginning the discussion at the dinner table, said that the events in Cyprus amounted to no ordinary *coup d'état* but constituted a violation of international treaties. The Turkish Government appreciated the British decision not to recognise Nikos Sampson. The Turkish Government were not taken in by the offer to continue the inter-communal talks, and

[1] See No. 21, note 3.
[2] DUS responsible for Policy and Programmes in the MoD.
[3] Chief Press Secretary to the Prime Minister.
[4] Private Secretary (Overseas Affairs) to the Prime Minister.

that would not be possible for Turkey, since it would amount to recognition. The dialogue between the communities in Cyprus, already difficult, had come to an end. While he noted the assurances of the Greek Government regarding the international status of Cyprus, and on enosis, the new Government in Cyprus was only a projection of the Government in Athens. In these circumstances Greece would be represented by two governments, one within and one outside NATO. The fact was that the present situation in Cyprus was intolerable: at least before the *coup d'état* some kind of dialogue had been going on between the communities. If the new régime was allowed to take root in Cyprus, it would amount to no more than an extension of the régime in Greece, and both Cypriot communities would suffer. It was impossible to discuss these matters properly with Greece. He had tried to speak to the Prime Minister of Greece for three hours in Brussels, but after that time they had not even been able to reach agreement on calling it a discussion. He was not deceived by the apparent restraint from the use of force against the Turkish communities so far, and regarded the present situation as a form of unnamed Enosis. Pressures on the Turkish community were merely postponed. If it was not feasible to revert to the previous state of affairs, by recalling the Greek officers of the National Guard, it would be impossible for Turkey to refrain from intervention. Intervention would in the last resort result from the humanitarian desire to save Turkish lives and not national reasons. If Sampson's régime were allowed to take root in the island it would be the end of the South Eastern flank of NATO. Immediate and effective practical action was essential in this situation. Turkey wanted a peaceful solution. Britain and Turkey, jointly or separately, should state that they did not recognise the new régime and that the old administration must be restored. If Makarios could not return, the Constitutional provisions should apply. As the two guarantors under the 1960 Treaty, Britain and Turkey and the United States should warn Greece of the violation of the independence of Cyprus which had taken place, and should ask for the withdrawal of Greek forces under effective UN supervision. There should also be international agreement about effective control in the situation thereafter. There should also be sanctions: a more effective Turkish presence on the island was essential, and Turkey wished to bring this about in co-operation with the British Government as the other guarantor, in order to safeguard both communities. The Turkish Government did not wish to exploit the situation in Cyprus, nor did they wish to act alone and create anxieties thereby. The British Government was in a position to help Turkey to achieve this result, and to avoid bloodshed and a confrontation between Greece and Turkey. This could be done by allowing Turkey to send her forces to Cyprus through the British SBAs. He felt that this was an historic moment to use the bases to ensure the independence of Cyprus. Everyone, including the United States and the Soviet Union would welcome such action which would justify the British military presence. He felt that action of this kind, coupled with a joint statement of British and Turkish objectives, would be a relief to the whole population of Cyprus and also to the population of Greece and would facilitate a return to democracy there. It would also restore the condition of NATO in the Eastern Mediterranean. The alternative was unilateral action by Turkey, which he felt would be inevitable later if not sooner—later would be worse and bloodier. If Britain were prepared to accept action on these lines, the Turkish authorities would be careful to avoid any embarrassment, by agreement on the deployment of Turkish forces. The primary concern of Turkey was with the rights of the Turkish community in the Island. Their experience in Cyprus required the Turkish Government to be cautious. The minimum Turkish requirement in the future, whatever the status of Cyprus—independent or 'whatever other arrangement'—would be to secure access to the sea somewhere near Turkey, which would enable his Government to prevent Turks from dying from starvation as had occurred in the past.

2. Mr. Eçevit mentioned a conversation with the United States Ambassador in Ankara earlier that day regarding the Turkish relationship with NATO. Turkey would remain in NATO and meet its commitments. In some respects NATO was even more important than in the past, but co-operation between Turkey and Greece in NATO had lost all sense, since the Greeks were Turkey's only neighbours with whom the Turks had bad relations, and with whom alone they had a military alliance. There were many accumulated bilateral problems, for example the exclusive attitude which Greece had adopted in the Aegean, and the military installations which Greece had erected in the Dodecanese contrary to Treaty provisions, and which were directed against Turkey.[5] If the Turkish proposal was accepted, his Government could compensate for any weakening which would occur as a result of a lack of co-operation with Greece in NATO. But he added that Turkey was prepared to co-operate with Greece, if Britain and the United States could persuade the Greeks to co-operate also: this was his alternative posture.

3. Summing up, Mr Eçevit said that he saw a real opportunity to achieve co-operation between the communities on the island. It was strange that Turkey was 'almost weeping' over the departure of President Makarios. But he saw now a chance to create nationhood on the Island, and without this sense of nationhood an independent state could not be said to exist. It was also a moment for opportunities for a dialogue with President Makarios, an historic opportunity for a peaceful solution and a good future on the Island.

[5] During a meeting with Mr. Callaghan on the afternoon of 18 July Mr. Isik returned to this point. He said that Turkey feared that Greek military measures in the Aegean were directed, not against the common enemy, but against Turkey: 'Greek moves in Cyprus', he added, 'were part of this policy' (record of meeting between Mr. Callaghan and Mr. Isik at the FCO on 18 July at 4.30 p.m.).

4. *Mr. Wilson* said he did not think all the proposals put forward by Mr. Eçevit were on the right road and asked Mr. Callaghan to comment further. *Mr. Callaghan* said he had appreciated the clarity of Mr Eçevit's cool analysis of the situation and the restrained manner in which he had reacted to what had occurred. We agreed that time was important, and that we must avoid the Sampson régime's taking root. We did not disagree with the Turkish analysis of the situation; it had not been an internal *coup*; the officers of the National Guard had been directed, either openly or covertly, from mainland Greece. He agreed that, whether one called it creeping enosis or not, the régime would be much closer to Greece. Further we were agreed on seeking peaceful solutions to the problem. We both had a negative objective: not to recognise the Sampson régime. The British Government were in no hurry to do so. Was there not a positive objective too: to see Archbishop Makarios restored to power. We would sooner see him back in Nicosia than resort to the Constitutional alternative. We had not given up hope that, by some face-saving device, a way could be opened for Makarios to return. We were not sure how this was to be done; perhaps by elections. He had gathered from the Archbishop that he would not be totally adverse to these if he were to return. *Mr. Wilson* interjected that it would be difficult to have elections unless President Makarios, as the legitimate authority, were able to call them himself.

5. *Mr. Callaghan* asked if it was possible to get the Archbishop back by diplomatic action. We should like to do so, but we were not sure that it was possible. The Nine had made a strong démarche in Athens. He himself had spoken three times to Dr. Kissinger asking him to put great pressure on the Greeks to withdraw their officers from the National Guard.[6] Her Majesty's Ambassador in Athens had been summoned to see Brigadier Ioannides on the morning of 18 July. It would be a good thing to put psychological pressure on the Greeks by leaving them in doubt of the content of our discussions. The idea that the Greek forces should be placed under United Nations control was interesting, but it would be better for them to return to Greece. We did not want more troops in the Island, but fewer. *Mr. Menomencioglu* said the proposal had been that the troops should

---

[6] When he spoke to Dr. Kissinger on the telephone at 6.55 p.m. Mr. Callaghan observed that the best outcome would be the return of Archbishop Makarios to office, and that if diplomatic action to this end were to be effective it would be essential for the Americans to be in the forefront. He would try to dissuade the Turks from taking unilateral action. 'As regards the Greeks', he said, 'he intended to keep them in a state of uncertainty about our intentions and felt that this plus substantial pressure from the Americans might force the Greeks to back down. In the first instance this would mean withdrawing the Greek officers of the National Guard.' Mr. Callaghan added that he thought the chances of 'getting Makarios back ... no better than 5 to 1 against', but that six months of 'more or less fascist government [in Cyprus] would result in growing tension, Soviet pressure and possibly clandestine involvement'. Dr. Kissinger agreed with much of what Mr. Callaghan had to say, but observed that he 'did not want to give the Russians an excuse for intervention by going too far in declaring the illegitimacy of the Sampson régime' (telegram No. 2416 to Washington of 18 July, WSC 1/10).

be withdrawn to Greece under United Nations control. *Mr. Callaghan* said we would need to examine closely what the legal basis would be for the use of the SBAs to allow Turkish troops to pass through them. He could not recommend such a course. He had spoken to Dr. Kissinger 10 minutes before, and told him that Mr. Eçevit would be willing to stay longer in London than he had planned. Mr. Sisco[7] or Mr. Ingersoll[8] would fly to London to see Mr. Eçevit on the morning of 18 July. We could have a tripartite discussion. Dr. Kissinger would also be sending his emissary to Athens in the light of the discussions in London. The British proposal was that they should invite the Greek Government to send a delegation to London, whether composed of Ministers or preferably of officers. There would be great advantage in a meeting between British, Turkish and Greek delegations at which the Turkish and British sides could put the Greeks under pressure. *Mr. Wilson* pointed out that tripartite talks were envisaged in the 1960 Treaty.[9] If the Greeks were to refuse to come they would be publicly putting themselves in a very weak position. *Mr. Callaghan* added that Dr. Kissinger had told him that the United States would not acknowledge the new régime. Dr. Kissinger had also said that the Russians had made several approaches to the Americans and had hinted things that were certainly very disagreeable. Dr. Kissinger did not want to rush the deliberations of the Security Council, which would lead to support for Makarios from all quarters and give him a carte blanche even to seek Soviet aid. If we could agree to invite the Greeks to a tripartite meeting this would provide a reason for delaying action in the Security Council. *Mr. Eçevit* reverted to the importance of reassuring the Turkish population of Cyprus by redressing the balance of forces in the Island by the intervention of Turkish troops. He was very sceptical whether diplomatic pressure or even economic sanctions would be effective on Greece. She would still get arms from the arms manufacturers (he understood that Greek forces had been landed in Paphos that very evening). He must consult his colleagues about tripartite talks. He wanted to try all peaceful means, but past experience showed that discussions with the Greek civilians were futile. Nothing would be achieved without real sanctions. *Mr. Wilson* said that the Sovereign Base Areas had been established for the benefit of British forces only. The move suggested would not be advisable. *Mr. Eralp* said that consultation under Article 4 of the Treaty of Guarantee had taken place with Greece through the Turkish Ambassador to Athens, and such consultation with the United Kingdom was taking place that evening. Early action, as distinct from consultation, was now required. *Mr Eçevit* said that action against force must be with force though without bloodshed. *Mr. Callaghan* said that he did not think that we could introduce Turkish troops through the SBA.

[7] Mr. J.J. Sisco was US Assistant Secretary of State for Near Eastern and South Asia Affairs.

[8] Mr. R. Ingersoll was US Deputy Secretary of State.

[9] See No. 1, note 8.

6. *Mr. Eçevit* suggested that the Cyprus question must be seen in a wider context. The Russians wished to play a part because Greece was a NATO Power and they wished to drive a wedge into NATO. *Mr. Wilson* agreed that there was a danger of Soviet intervention, and for this reason it was important to take early action to avoid sterile debate in the United Nations. We should therefore pursue the proposal for tripartite talks. *Mr. Eçevit* said that the Greeks were violators of the Treaty and we should spend half our time arguing about their responsibility for the *coup*. *Mr. Isik* said that the United Kingdom was free to invite the Greeks. *Mr. Wilson* asked whether, if the Turks did not wish to have simultaneous consultations between ourselves, the Greeks and the Turks, would the Turks be willing to come to London again if we found there was progress in our talks with the Greeks? *Mr. Isik* said that they would, but the Greeks must address themselves to the Turks direct if they wished to be in touch with them. The Turkish Ministers repeated that it would be difficult for them to meet the Greeks after the failure of the talks in Brussels; but they were ready to negotiate with Greece if that was what Greece would agree to.

(At this point the two delegations broke off for separate discussions for about 40 minutes.)

7. When the discussion was resumed in the Cabinet Room, *Mr. Eçevit* said that he had just received reports that the National Guard had attacked the Turkish sector killing three Turks, and other reports indicating that action was being taken by the National Guard against the Turkish minority. The Greek Finance Minister had also spoken in an inflammatory way. He recalled that he told the Prime Minister earlier that the Greeks were bound to attack the Turkish sector, as Greek policemen had taken refuge there. His anxieties were thus confirmed even sooner than he had feared.

8. Mr. Eçevit then turned to the suggestions made to him earlier. He noted that the Foreign and Commonwealth Secretary had told Parliament in effect that Greece was an aggressor. He agreed with this view. Therefore Turkey and Greece could not come together. Turkey would not object if the British Government sought to talk to Greece. For their part the Turkish Government had already stated that they would be unable to do so. He would be willing to talk to Mr. Sisco, but the form of such a meeting was important. Tripartite talks between Turkey, Britain and the United States might be variously interpreted by public opinion, and he felt it would be better to meet him at the Turkish Embassy in London. Mr. Eçevit explained that there was some restlessness in Turkey over the fact that there had been no dialogue with the United States: Dr. Kissinger had visited Turkish neighbours but had not been to Ankara. President Nixon had informed him of his intention to visit Turkey, but this had not been fulfilled. Apart from this bilateral reason, he believed it would be right to separate the talks between the guarantor Powers, from discussions between Turkey and the United States.

9. Mr. Eçevit said that it was up to the British Government to decide how to use their bases in Cyprus. So far as he knew there were no provisions restricting the use of the bases. But this was only a detail. The essence of the proposal he had made was to promote co-operation to restore stability. The attacks on the Turkish community in Cyprus he had mentioned meant that his Government would have to act. While Turkey wished for a peaceful solution, they had a duty to protect the Turkish population on the island. They preferred to do this in a bloodless way, and to help relations between the two communities. British participation would have been a factor working to reassure the Greek community. He feared that the British Government might feel a burden on her conscience in future by declining to accept the Turkish proposal: co-operation would have led to a useful result. He recalled that previous interventions, for example those by the United States had merely aggravated the situation and strengthened the position of Greece. The passage of time before action would merely make things more difficult.

10. *Mr. Wilson* said that he thought that he understood the meaning of Mr. Eçevit's remarks. If the situation of the Turkish community on the Island deteriorated, Turkey would feel it necessary to intervene.[10] But he did not think that the SBAs could be used for that kind of intervention. *Mr. Eçevit* replied that he could not insist on the point. The bases were not essential for his purpose. He also informed the Prime Minister that, by taking a great risk, he had decided to postpone the discussion in the Turkish Assembly the following day. But he repeated that access to the sea was essential for the Turkish population, and he hoped that the British Government might be able to find other means of helping Turkey. *Mr. Callaghan* asked what British help in these circumstances would involve. *Mr. Eçevit* meant that he hoped Britain would not put up obstacles and would persuade the United States not to do so. *Mr. Callaghan* said he would consider this suggestion, but he did not think that the British Government could help in any way.[11] He believed that this would constitute a breach of

[10] A briefing paper prepared for Mr. Wilson's meeting with Mr. Eçevit explained: 'Turkish policy towards Cyprus, especially under Eçevit, has been that they will only intervene forcefully on the Island if they believed a declaration of *enosis* to be imminent or if the Turkish Cypriots came under real attack.' And an additional brief added that HMG had 'no knowledge of any unusual concentrations of either Greek or Turkish Forces apart from a reported Turkish naval build up in Marmaris and Mersin' (WST 3/548/2) But in Ankara telegram No. 764 of 17 July Mr. Fyjis-Walker noted that officials in Mr. Eçevit's party were 'mostly sceptical on achieving worthwhile results by political means, especially if, as they saw it, the Americans continue[d] to take a neutral position'. He also reported that it was being said that the Turkish military had been putting pressure on the Government for 'unilateral and forceful intervention' (WSC 1/10).

[11] During their meeting on 18 July (see note 5 above) Mr. Isik told Mr. Callaghan that even if Mr. Clerides were, as Speaker of the Cyprus House of Representatives, to assume power as acting President, 'he might not have effective power and a military presence (which might not be Turkish only but might include for example British forces from the Sovereign Base Areas) would be necessary to protect the Turkish community'. Some increase in the Turkish presence in Cyprus would be a first requirement. But Mr. Callaghan replied that, rather than match the

the Treaty. Was the Turkish Government asking Britain to facilitate a bloodless landing? *Mr. Eçevit* said that the Turks would not necessarily land on the coast. At present they had no access to their population by sea or by air: there was no airstrip under Turkish control. The fact was that there was an essential difference between Greece and Turkey, and Turkey could not be regarded as an equal of Greece in this matter.

11. *Mr. Callaghan* said that he quite understood that, but invited the Turkish Prime Minister to join the British Government in calling for the Greeks to join them in London, or to invite the Greek and British Governments to send representatives to Ankara. *Mr. Eçevit* replied that the Turks felt they had already done their duty in calling for consultations. *Mr. Wilson* said that he understood Mr. Eçevit's remarks as an expression of the Turkish wish that Britain would not blockade an action of the kind contemplated by Turkey, but that they would blockade the Greeks. *Mr. Eçevit* asked if Britain would be ready to do so. *Mr. Callaghan* said it was not impossible. *Mr. Eçevit* said that the Greeks were already reinforcing their forces by air: *Mr. Wilson* said that action against aeroplanes was more difficult.

12. When *Mr. Callaghan* repeated his suggestion that the three Governments should conduct consultations, and that Turkey should put her case to Greece during such talks, *Mr. Eçevit* said that this had already been done, and that no response had been given by the Greek Ambassador to the acting Foreign Minister. The Greek Ambassador had merely replied that his Government had had nothing to do with the events in Cyprus. The Ambassador had not replied to the request put to him for consultations. *Mr. Callaghan* suggested that, even if no fruitful result emerged from such consultations Greece would lose face. *Mr. Eçevit* thought this did not matter to the Greeks. *Mr. Callaghan* then suggested that it would be wrong to confuse the restoration of democracy in Greece with a return to the *status quo ante* in Cyprus. He did not believe that the arrival of more troops in Cyprus would help the latter objective, and suggested that the Turks should help in shouldering responsibility. Then *Mr. Mason* said that it would help to get the three guarantor Powers round the table. If the Greeks came we could pillory them; if they did not come the world would draw the lesson.

13. *Mr. Wilson* asked if the problem for Mr. Eçevit was a political one with his own Parliament: that he could not sit down with the Greeks. *Mr. Eçevit* conceded that this was one factor. He had already taken a risk by talking to Mr. Androutsopoulos in Brussels. He would take another risk of the same kind if he thought it would be worthwhile. But he could not

---

increased Greek military presence in Cyprus with increased Turkish contingents, it would be preferable to reduce forces already there. 'As for the possibility that there might be some Anglo-Turkish arrangement in which the Sovereign Base Areas and British troops within them might be used to protect the Turkish population in the Island, he had', Mr. Callaghan said, 'to warn Mr. Isik that this was quite out of the question.'

consider Greece, an aggressor nation, as a guarantor. *Mr. Isik* said that Turkey might be prepared to consider discussions with Greece, but the Greeks must first be declared as aggressors. *Mr. Eçevit* said it would be 'commendable' for Britain to have bilateral talks with the Greeks. *Mr. Callaghan* said that our motive at the present juncture might be not so much as to convince the Greeks as to pressurise them. Perhaps it would be better to go to the United Nations first? *Mr. Isik* replied that action in the United Nations was a different question from the exercise of responsibility of the guarantors. Britain and Turkey must first condemn Greece in that capacity.[12] *Mr. Eralp* recalled the bitter experience of the London Conference of February 1964.[13] A repetition of that event would be intolerable for Turkey. The Turks wanted the present meeting to issue a joint statement by the two guarantors condemning Greece. *Mr. Wilson* doubted whether this would be the right prelude to the Tripartite Meeting. He still felt that this would be a useful initiative, and understood that the Turkish side would have no objection to an Anglo-Greek meeting. He did not know if the Greek authorities would be prepared to meet the British Government, but he felt that we should try to arrange such a discussion without prior conditions other than unilateral statements on the record. *Mr. Callaghan* suggested that the British offer to Turkey could lie on the table meanwhile. *Mr. Eçevit* conceded that it might help if Britain could talk to the Greeks, but he could not regard them as guarantors. However, he agreed that it might help to bring some pressure to bear on them. *Mr. Callaghan* said that we would not necessarily invite them as guarantors.

14. After further discussion, in which the Turkish representatives suggested that it would be desirable for a joint communiqué to be issued, it was finally agreed that both delegations should make separate statements to

---

[12] On 18 July Mr. Isik asked Mr. Callaghan whether HMG would subscribe to five 'propositions': (1) Would they agree that the situation was 'wholly the fault of the Greek Government'? (2) If so, would HMG ask the Greek Government to 'restore' the situation? (3) Were HMG prepared to press the Greek Government to remove their 'illegal' forces from Cyprus? (4) Would HMG agree that Turkey must have the same 'rights and responsibilities' (e.g. access by sea and air independent of the Greek Cypriots) in Cyprus as Greece? (5) Did HMG favour the 'creation of an organisation which would have a real capability to control all movements of military forces and military equipment in and out of the Island'? He went on to say that if HMG could agree on these five points he would also like them to agree on the 'transitional measures' which would be necessary until they had been implemented. In reply Mr. Callaghan emphasised that the admission of Turkish forces into the SBAs was out of the question, and that putting Turkish forces into Cyprus by whatever means 'would inevitably make more difficult the contacts necessary to achieve Turkey's other objectives'. And while he was broadly in sympathy with the first two points, he maintained that the last three points could not be given effect without consultation with the Greeks and Greek cooperation (see notes 5 and 11 above and No. 28, note 2).

[13] The London Conference of January 1964 was summoned in the aftermath of the upsurge of violence in Cyprus in December 1963 (cf. No. 1, note 7). Attended by representatives of Greece, Turkey, the UK and both Cypriot communities, it failed to make any progress towards abating the crisis. Meanwhile, British forces in the island supervised a limited ceasefire.

the Press. It was also agreed that nothing should be said in response to questions about possible military action, so as to create the maximum possible pressure on the Greek Government.

15. The Turkish Ministers left at about 12.30 a.m.

No. 26

Sir P. Ramsbotham (Washington) to Mr. Callaghan

No. 2414 Telegraphic [*WSC 1/10*]

Confidential   WASHINGTON, *17 July 1974 11.50 p.m.*

Repeated for information to Immediate UKMIS New York.

Your telegram No. 522 to UKMIS New York:[1]
Cyprus

1. I rang Kissinger this evening to explain the purpose behind our draft resolution (which we are discussing now with the State Department).[2] I explained that it was only a preliminary draft, not yet approved by Ministers. I also gave him our latest information about Makarios's objectives for the Security Council meeting and mentioned some of the considerations in UKMIS tel[egram] No. 783[3] about non-aligned pressure for a condemnatory resolution and the chances of pre-empting or avoiding it.

2. Kissinger said he welcomed this opportunity to discuss the problem since it had not been possible in his conversations with you over the open

[1] In this telegram of 17 July Mr. Weir informed Mr. Richard that during his meeting with Mr. Callaghan that evening Archbishop Makarios had made it clear that his main objectives were: (1) to deny international recognition to the new régime in Cyprus; (2) to gain international support for a restoration of the *status quo ante*; and (3) to secure the withdrawal of Greek officers from the National Guard. Cf. No. 24.

[2] Following Mr. Wilson's meeting with Archbishop Makarios, UND drafted a UN Security Council resolution aimed at meeting the Archbishop's main *desiderata*. Its preamble referred to the Security Council's having heard the statement of the 'President of Cyprus' (i.e. Archbishop Makarios), and its substantive text called on the Greek Government 'to state unambiguously their intention to observe their international obligation in regard to Cyprus and, as a contribution to the relaxation of tension in the area, to withdraw from Cyprus its military officers, serving with the National Guard' (telegrams Nos. 520 and 521 of 17 July to UKMIS New York).

[3] Mr. Richard pointed out in this telegram of 17 July that non-aligned pressure for UN action to restore the *status quo* in Cyprus was 'building up'. He thought that the British text would only win Security Council acceptance if Archbishop Makarios indicated clearly that it satisfied him and worked for its adoption, and if one or more permanent members made it known that they would not accept amendments calling for action to restore the *status quo*.

line this afternoon fully to express his views.[4] His main concern was that we should not, by acting precipitately, get embroiled in a civil war and perhaps end up by strengthening the communist position in Cyprus.

3. Kissinger seemed puzzled as to why we were wanting to move so quickly and in such absolute support of Makarios. Was there not a risk of doing Makarios's work for him, without tying his hands in any way? It was also surely a mistake to commit ourselves now to Makarios and thus narrow our options when it was far from certain that Makarios could return to power. Kissinger was also concerned at the line we were taking about the withdrawal of Greek officers in the National Guard. Whatever other role they had been playing they had at least acted as a force against communist infiltration in Cyprus. Kissinger was clearly suspicious that Makarios, returned to power in those circumstances, would not hesitate to regard the Russians as his saviours and allow an already strong Communist Party to gain further strength.[5]

4. Speaking from my own experience in Cyprus, I said I doubted whether the Greek officers in Cyprus effectively played that role. HMG were, of course, acting from their position as guarantors. We also had the Commonwealth connexion to consider. I found it difficult myself to believe that Sam[p]son could survive for long, and Makarios had an astonishing faculty for survival, both physically and politically. He was also Ethnarch and it would be difficult for a new régime to provide a popular substitute.

5. Kissinger said, emphatically that the United States would not accept a Sam[p]son régime. He would like to try and bring in Clerides, if that were possible, but for the reasons he had given, he thought it would be unwise for us to go all-out for Makarios at this stage.

6. As for the possibility of a movement by the Russians and the non-aligned in the Security Council to condemn the Greeks, Kissinger thought we need not worry about this. I expressed surprise but he did not indicate what the American attitude might then be in the Security Council. As to Greece, he would be happy to see the present Government undermined and perhaps collapse through its own internal failings.

---

[4] See No. 25, note 6.

[5] On the evening of 17 July Mr. Stabler told Mr. W.J.A. Wilberforce, Counsellor and Head of Chancery of the British Embassy in Washington, that the Americans had been thinking along the lines of a rather similar draft Security Council resolution to that proposed by the British (see note 2 above), but that they had been careful in public not to commit themselves on the status of Archbishop Makarios, and that they might 'have difficulty with the reference to the President of Cyprus'. He further observed that 'on the assumption that Makarios could be restored only by force from outside Cyprus, the Americans were tempted to wonder whether it might not be possible build on the first of the three Turkish objectives [see No. 21, note 5] and to bring about the replacement of Sam[p]son by a third party who "emerged from the original constitutional arrangements", e.g. Clerides. If such a solution were to be worked out, Makarios's retirement would be the price, and the problem would be how to achieve that' (Washington telegram No. 2415 of 17 July).

7. He asked me to convey his thoughts to you. He had already arranged for Sisco to fly to London tonight to explain some of these considerations[6] and hoped that we could agree to play the hand more slowly. Perhaps the best outcome for the Security Council would be to reach an agreed position on which the Greeks and Turks could negotiate. He hoped that we would take a final decision[7] on action in the Security Council before tomorrow evening and said that he would be in touch with me later tomorrow.[8]

[6] Mr. Sisco arrived in London on the morning of 18 July.

[7] In Washington telegram No. 2417 of 18 July Sir P. Ramsbotham corrected this sentence to read: 'He hoped that we would not (repeat not) take a final decision'.

[8] Sir P. Ramsbotham subsequently informed Mr. Acland in Washington telegram No. 2416 of 17 July that his conversation with Dr. Kissinger had apparently not been recorded in the State Department and that, at the Department's request, he had given to Mr. Sisco a copy of this telegram, omitting the last sentence of paragraph 3 and the second sentence of paragraph 6. Sir P. Ramsbotham added that he feared, 'given Kissinger's idiosyncratic methods of working', he might not record the telephone conversations he had with Mr. Callaghan, and that he would therefore like to receive the gist of these as soon as possible after they had taken place. 'Otherwise', he added, 'improbable though it may seem, I fear there will be a danger of both the State Dept., and this Embassy working in the dark with all the resultant risks of confusion and misunderstanding.'

No. 27

Minute from Sir J. Killick to Mr. Goodison

[*WSC 1/10*]

Secret   FCO, [*18*][1] *July 1974*

Note for the record—Cyprus

I met Mr. Sisco[2] at the airport today and briefed him fully on yesterday's meeting with Makarios and the Turks.[3]

2. He asked for a word with the Secretary of State before meeting the Turks and the Secretary of State came out from Cabinet (which was discussing Cyprus)[4] for a short talk at No. 10.

[1] The typescript of this minute on file was misdated 17 July.

[2] See No. 26, note 6. While in London Mr. Sisco heard that the Greeks had agreed to receive him on 19 July. He planned then to go on to Ankara, and to visit London again on his return journey to Washington (telegram No. 141 to Athens of 18 July).

[3] See Nos. 24 and 25.

[4] At this Cabinet meeting the Prime Minister told his colleagues that he had decided to establish a small group of Ministers to keep the Cyprus situation under review, and to meet at short notice if necessary (Cabinet Conclusions, CC (74) 27th meeting, 18 July). The group included the Prime Minister, the Lord Chancellor, Lord Elwyn Jones, the Home Secretary, Mr.

3. The Secretary of State said he wanted to put across most strongly that American pressure on the Greeks was absolutely vital and must be very hard. He did not feel he had got this across to Kissinger on the telephone.[5] Also, the Greek National Guard officers must be got out or there would be a Turkish landing with the likelihood of a subsequent conflagration. The Greeks might try to join in and although no doubt the Turks would defeat them there would be wider repercussions. He was doubtful whether we would be successful in getting the Greeks to move, but they certainly would not do so so long as there was no effective US pressure.

4. Mr. Sisco said that we needed to gain time and work out options. HMG's efforts were obviously in the direction of getting this process started. They had a special responsibility and interest but if there were ways in which the Americans could help they would do so.

5. It was essential to slow down the UN process. The US had done nothing to 'de-recognise' Makarios and had no intention of recognising Sampson (in the car on the way in he had to me added 'at present') but if the Security Council formally legitimised Makarios there would be a major problem. He did not see how Makarios could be reinstated by political means given the facts of life in Athens. Presumably HMG were not prepared to use force to put him back. The Security Council could do nothing to solve the dilemma presented by the legitimacy of Makarios and the physical control of Sampson. Legitimisation by the Security Council would lead to calls for sanctions etc. and would leave Makarios free to invite the Russians in. We would lose a great measure of control over our own policy to Makarios. He earnestly hoped that Mr. Richard would work in this sense and later added that when the UK and US worked together in this way in the Security Council they could achieve anything.[6]

6. Otherwise our mediatory role would be prejudiced. We needed to work with both Athens and Ankara. He strongly supported British ideas for either meeting the Greeks here for bilateral talks; or, better still, trilateral

R. Jenkins, the Chancellor of the Exchequer, Mr. D. Healey, and Mr. Mason. Field-Marshal Sir M. Carver also attended its only meeting on the afternoon of 20 July (MISC 41 (74), 1st meeting).

[5] See No. 25, note 6.

[6] Dr. Kissinger spoke in similar terms to Sir P. Ramsbotham in a telephone conversation that morning. He told the British Ambassador that 'frankly' he did not like the British draft UN Security Council resolution on Cyprus, and that he hoped there would be no 'excess of zeal' on Britain's part (see No. 26, notes 2 and 3). He thought it would be a mistake to present a resolution which in effect gave unqualified support to Archbishop Makarios and committed the Security Council to a legal position inconsistent with what it could deliver. 'The Americans', Dr. Kissinger stated, 'were not taking any steps to produce a resolution themselves, but they were worried lest we might take what were admittedly only diplomatic steps (which were unlikely to succeed), but which, through the Security Council, might give the Russians a legitimate excuse for interference in Cyprus, which might even lead to their military intervention.' This, Dr. Kissinger insisted, the Americans would resist 'no matter what the legal position might be and would appreciate it "if our friends did not make it more legal than necessary"' (Washington telegram No. 2422 of 18 July).

talks, or if necessary a continuing series of bilateral talks with both separately.[7] This would buy time both in New York and elsewhere.

7. However, there was a need for a viable negotiating package and he wished to pursue this with the Secretary of State after he had met the Turkish delegation.

8. In this connexion, he considered it a mistake to press for the withdrawal of the Greek officers as an isolated step.[8] It might be a[n] 'aftermath' to a constitutional settlement but withdrawal on its own would change the whole balance of the situation in Cyprus. Sampson was not a permanent feature of it but in the existing situation we had to work with him. The package needed must be capable of bridging the gap between Athens and Ankara.[9]

9. The Secretary of State said he disagreed with a good deal of this analysis but accepted that a package solution was required. He would be very happy to have it as a basis for further talks but did not yet see what its shape might be. Pressure on the Greeks to remove the officers was intended to stop the Turks moving. The danger of creeping *Enosis* could lead to the Turkish hawks coming out on top—although probably not too soon.

10. He saw all the dangers to which Mr. Sisco referred. Makarios was not universally popular, but if there could be a prospect of elections as a face-saving device this would be another way of persuading the Turks that all was not lost.

11. HMG had considered the use of force but at the present the decision was negative. Maximum diplomatic pressure should be maintained. One possibility however was a naval blockade designed to prevent reinforcement from Greece and at any rate theoretically the same *vis-à-vis* Turkey. It could control the import of supplies and still keep open the ultimate

---

[7] In telegram No. 141 to Athens (see note 2 above) Mr. Callaghan informed Sir R. Hooper that, in the light of his discussion with Mr. Sisco, he had agreed to invite the Greek Government to send representatives to London for consultations. He had already told the Cabinet that no useful purpose would be served if the Greeks were to send civilian members of their Government since these had no influence (see note 4 above), and he instructed Sir R. Hooper to make clear as best he could that, if the Greek Government accepted the invitation, he hoped they would send people who were 'in a position to take decisions or at least to speak with knowledge of the Greek Government's likely intentions'. Following his meeting with the Greek leaders on 19 July, Mr. Sisco informed Sir R. Hooper that they had agreed to travel to London for talks (Athens telegram No. 231 of 19 July).

[8] See No. 25, note 6, and No. 26, note 1.

[9] In his telephone conversation with Sir P. Ramsbotham on the morning of 18 July (see note 6 above), Dr. Kissinger expressed the hope that, before there was any substantive move in the Security Council, Mr. Callaghan would agree to bring the Greeks and Turks together in London to work out a constitutional solution on the basis of the 1960 Guarantee Treaty. 'Kissinger', Sir P. Ramsbotham noted, 'was clearly troubled that we might be committing ourselves too far without being able to calculate the longer-term consequences.'

possibility of the return of Makarios. If the UN was to be effectively held up, he had got to have something to say in London.[10]

12. Mr. Sisco said that he intended to go to Athens tomorrow (18 July)[11] but the Greeks had not yet accepted his visit. He would be willing to return to London thereafter and the Secretary of State said he would be very grateful for this.

13. Finally, Mr. Sisco said, and the Secretary of State agreed, that he would concentrate with the Turks on convincing them that time was needed, and on persuading them of the merits of the British proposals for consultation among the guarantors.[12]

John Killick

[10] In summing up the Cabinet discussion on 18 July (see notes 4 and 7 above), Mr. Wilson said that military intervention by Britain or the Turks, separately or together, would 'not be desirable'. But he added that if diplomatic pressures on Greece failed, and military action against Cyprus had to be contemplated, 'this should be a United Nations decision and operation'. 'We had', he observed, '... made some precautionary naval dispositions and were studying the possible usefulness of an international blockade to sever communications between Greece and Cyprus.'

[11] This is evidently a mistake and should read 19 July.

[12] Mr. Sisco had talks with Mr. Eçevit in London on the morning and afternoon of 18 June. During the afternoon session Mr. Eçevit presented Mr. Sisco with specific ideas, some of which were, according to the latter, 'tantamount to partition'. These, which Mr. Eçevit urged Mr. Sisco to put to the Greeks, included the establishment of two provisional governments on Cyprus, one for each community, and provision allowing the Turkish community free access to all airports and seaports. Mr. Sisco believed some of these ideas might represent an attempt by Mr. Eçevit, whom he thought inclined towards a peaceful solution, to cope both with a split in his delegation and with pressures from home for a hard line. At Mr. Eçevit's insistence, Mr. Sisco agreed to visit Ankara to inform him about his talks in Athens on 19 July (saving telegram No. 15 to Washington of 19 July). Cf. No. 30.

No. 28

Mr. Callaghan to Mr. Olver (Nicosia)

No. 164 Telegraphic [*WSC 1/10*]

Immediate. Secret   FCO, *18 July 1974, 8 p.m.*

Repeated for information to Immediate UKDEL NATO, UKMIS New York, UKREP Brussels, Dublin, Belgrade, Cairo, Stockholm, Moscow, Helsinki, Ankara, Athens, Bonn, Brussels, Rome, Washington, Oslo, Lisbon, Luxembourg, The Hague, Paris, Copenhagen, Ottawa.

Cyprus

1. I am conscious of the fact that posts most concerned with the Cyprus crisis require guidance about our general objectives and the background to our thinking. What follows is for your own background information, to be kept in mind in discussions with governments and organisations to which you are accredited but not, of course, for indiscriminate dissemination. In a dangerous and fast moving situation, and one on which there is no unanimity of view among the governments most concerned, I cannot yet be too specific.

2. Our recent talks with the Turkish leaders in London were held in response to a request by them for consultations under Article IV of the 1960 agreement on Cyprus.[1] This article provides *inter-alia* for the possibility of unilateral action to restore the constitutional position in Cyprus in the event of failure of the consultations foreseen in the Article. The Turkish Government regard the Greek Government as excluded from such consultations because of their alleged violation of the constitution. In their request for consultation with us, they reserved the right to take unilateral action in the event of the consultations failing to end in agreement. The Turks were interested in bilateral intervention. We urged prudence. We have no evidence that the Turkish Government are planning unilateral military action against Cyprus in the immediate future, and we believe they can be persuaded to abstain from such intervention.[2] However, it would not take much further provocation to make them lose patience. The danger

---

[1] See No. 21, note 3.

[2] Mr. Callaghan warned Mr. Isik, during their conversation on 18 July (see No. 25, notes 5, 11 and 12), that his reaction to the latter's proposals for a joint Anglo-Turkish cooperation on Cyprus 'was based on the hope and expectation that the Turkish Government were not contemplating resort to unilateral action of a military character'. Mr. Isik replied that the last thing the Turkish Government wished to do was to resort to such action. But he repeated that 'the decision to intervene might be forced on the Turkish Government if something could not be done immediately to reverse present trends, and if the situation in Cyprus continued to deteriorate'.

would become especially grave if the Turkish population were subjected to harassment.

3. Our own view is that at present, while doing all we can to restrain the Turks, we should also work by all possible means short of using armed force to bring about the return of President Makarios to Cyprus, possibly to be followed by elections (which he has told us he would be prepared to hold). To those ends we are also working to try to secure the withdrawal, or at least the phasing out of Greek officers in the Cyprus National Guard. We are well aware that it may prove impossible to restore President Makarios at any rate by peaceful means. And we are also aware of the understandable fears expressed that withdrawal of the officers would create dangerous instability in Cyprus leading to further bloodshed possibly involving not only Greek Cypriots but Turkish Cypriots and foreign communities too.[3] (The Americans though opposed to the Sampson régime, are doubtful that the return of Makarios will prove feasible and are worried at the security implications of a withdrawal of the officers.) Nevertheless, it seems to us that the Sampson régime is inherently unstable. And that if some means cannot be found to replace it with a legitimate government there will sooner or later be an even worse explosion which would not necessarily be confined to Cyprus alone. We also have to have regard for the very strong feelings held, in this country, by people of all political persuasions both on the subject of Sampson and on the manner of his coming to power.

4. In addition to our bilateral diplomatic efforts both the EEC[4] and NATO (primarily through Dr. Luns)[5] have been exerting a helpful influence. But the key is perhaps the Americans. I have been urging them very strongly to weigh-in very heavily bilaterally with the Greeks though the result remains to be seen. We must also hope that the United Nations Security Council will succeed in passing a firm resolution backing up this pressure, although there may be an interval between President Makarios

---

[3] Brig. Ioannides told Sir R. Hooper on 18 July that orders had already been signed for the 'replacement', not the 'withdrawal', of Greek officers from the Cyprus National Guard, and that this would happen 'very soon'. Brig. Ioannides made it clear that the Greek Government would not agree to any demand for the withdrawal of their officers from Cyprus, and would 'bitterly resent it if no similar request were made to the Turks' (Athens telegrams Nos. 216 and 218 of 18 July).

[4] On 16 July EC Ambassadors in Paris met at the Quai d'Orsay to draft a joint communiqué 'expressing their disquiet and reaffirming their attachment to the independence of Cyprus and their opposition to external intervention'. It was also agreed that the French Government, on behalf of the Nine, should make representations to Athens and Ankara on the following day 'to make their common position known to the parties concerned' (Paris telegram No. 791 of 16 July, WSC 6/598/1).

[5] When, during a visit by Dr. Luns to the FCO on 19 July, Sir T. Brimelow questioned him on what the consequences of unilateral Turkish action in Cyprus would be for NATO, Dr. Luns said that he 'did not think that it would be necessarily bad' (telegram No. 170 to UKDEL NATO of 19 July, WDN 26/22). Cf. No. 23, note 2.

making his initial speech and the resolution being agreed.[6] It is possible that the weight of world opinion, if nearly unanimously expressed, will cause the Greek Government to make a real effort to lower tensions and to open the way for some face-saving outcome which cannot yet be identified, leading to the restoration of a reputable government.[7]

5. We consider President Makarios still to be the legitimate Head of State of Cyprus. But there can be no certainty that we will be successful in securing the replacement of the Sampson régime and, even if we are, this does not mean that the return of Makarios himself to power will follow, though I believe it probable that he would win any contested election. I have therefore been careful in talking to President Makarios not to commit myself never to recognise the Sampson régime nor to continuing indefinitely to recognise him as the Head of State, although there is no intention of disavowing him.

6. For your own information you should know that British military action is not (is not) at present being contemplated. The political and military dangers of such intervention in the particular circumstances of Cyprus are all too obvious to need elaborating here. You should also know that we do not necessarily rule out the possibility of such intervention in all circumstances for all time. Nevertheless you should be careful to avoid any suggestion that it may be a possibility (except of course in clear-cut circumstances of self-defence).[8]

---

[6] Archbishop Makarios addressed the Security Council on the afternoon of 19 July. In his speech he accused the Greek Government of having 'callously violated the independence of Cyprus'. *UNSC Official Records, 29th year, 1780th meeting*, 19 July 1974 (S/PV.1780). See No. 33, note 2.

[7] In telegram No. 137 to Athens of 17 July Mr. Acland informed Sir R. Hooper that it was Mr. Callaghan's present policy to 'exert maximum diplomatic pressure' on the Greek Government. 'He realises', Mr. Acland continued, 'that it is a long shot but he hopes that the combination of EEC and NATO pressure, with the Americans weighing in heavily if they can be so persuaded, coupled with doubts about our and Turkish intentions, will crack the Greek nerve and at least persuade them to withdraw the National Guard officers.' Sir R. Hooper was therefore instructed not to be 'comforting to Ionnides' if he asked what the Turks were up to.

[8] Cf. No. 22, note 5, and No. 23. By the morning of 18 July *HMS Hermes* was in a position from which its Commando could disembark in Cyprus within twenty-four hours, and *HMS Rhyl* and *HMS Devonshire* would join *HMS Hermes* on 18 and 21 July respectively. Meanwhile, Mr. Richard was instructed in telegram No. 524 to UKMIS New York of 18 July that he might inform Dr. Waldheim that, without considerable prior reinforcement of the SBAs, there could be no certainty that British military intervention would be successful. 'And', the telegram added, 'there could also be no certainty that some other interested powers would not contemplate intervening militarily as well.'

No. 29

Sir E. Tomkins[1] *(Paris) to Sir P. Ramsbotham (Washington)*

No. 9 Telegraphic [*WSC 1/10*]

Immediate. Confidential   PARIS, *19 July 1974, 5.10 p.m.*

Repeated for information to Immediate FCO, Athens, Ankara, Nicosia, UKDEL NATO and UKMIS New York.

From Secretary of State.[2]

Please deliver following message from me to Dr. Kissinger:[3]

Dear Henry,

I am very grateful to you for sending Joe Sisco to London so quickly.[4] We had very useful talks and as I told him I start from the position of wanting to coordinate views with you. If we can work closely together I believe that we can keep this situation under control but you will realise that in some respects we are in a different position from you in that we are a Guarantor of the 1960 Treaty arrangements.

Let me first give you the background to the situation as I see it and then I will try to suggest more specific lines of policy.

Whether or not we will ever get evidence which we can use publicly I have no doubt that Makarios was removed from power either with the connivance of or at the instigation of one of the Guarantor Powers. Inevitably this has brought into question the whole complex of arrangements which were agreed in 1960 and has given the Turks a very

---

[1] British Ambassador in Paris.

[2] On 19 July Mr. Callaghan accompanied the Prime Minister on a visit to Paris. Whilst there, Mr. Callaghan had talks with his French counterpart, M. J. Sauvagnargues, on the proposed renegotiation of Britain's terms of entry into the EC.

[3] Sir P. Ramsbotham arranged for this message to be delivered to the State Department for transmission to Dr. Kissinger, who was then with the US President, Mr. R.M. Nixon, at San Clemente, California. In Washington telegram No. 2434 of 19 July Sir P. Ramsbotham commented: 'We have had indications that Kissinger is still worried that we are rather too committed to Makarios and anxious lest we try to go too fast and too far. As is his habit, he has expressed his anxieties fairly freely to others as well as to us, and they are beginning to creep into the press.' Sir P. Ramsbotham, who was perturbed by press reports of Anglo-US differences over Cyprus, thought that Dr. Kissinger might be seeing the situation 'rather in terms of last autumn's Middle East crisis' and that he appeared to be over anxious about the Russians as the most likely beneficiary of the crisis. That afternoon Dr. Kissinger telephoned Sir P. Ramsbotham to say that there were 'no real differences' between the British and US Governments, and to express his concern about the press starting 'divisive rumours' (Washington telegram No. 2435 of 19 July).

[4] See No. 27.

strong incentive to act unilaterally.[5] I am sure after our conversations with the Turks in London—and I think Joe Sisco will bear this out—that we would be wrong to think that if the Sampson régime consolidates its position in Cyprus and there are no more disturbances for the time being, the situation will settle down and the Turks will become reconciled to it. Even if the Turks do not invade now (and I hope that our efforts and Joe Sisco's will have contributed to holding them back) they will not acquiesce in a new régime in Cyprus which they are convinced is committed to what they call unnamed [*sic*] and I call creeping *Enosis*. While Sampson will no doubt avoid any public declaration of such intent, any practical moves to draw Cyprus closer to Greece or any constraints on the Turkish-Cypriot community will put the Turkish Government under ever increasing pressure to act in the days or weeks ahead. The removal of Makarios as the legitimately elected President is not only a thoroughly undesirable act in itself but has led the Turks to call in question once again the whole relationship between Cyprus and Greece. As you know, the 1960 arrangements have often come under strain and the position of the Turkish community has been precarious. I am sure you will agree that in terms of wider strategy Turkey is at least of as much importance to Western interests as Greece and it is led at present by a much sounder based government than the régime of the Greek colonels in Athens.[6]

I come now to what I think is the policy we should pursue.

(*a*) We should continue to assert the legitimacy of President Makarios without becoming committed to him for all time.

(*b*) We should work for the disappearance of the Sampson régime and the return of arrangements which are at least constitutional and more stable. If it turns out that Makarios is not able himself to act as President there is proper machinery under the Constitution for appointing a

[5] In Ankara telegram No. 777 of 19 July Sir H. Phillips reported that there was a strong feeling amongst Turkish armed forces commanders that if they missed the opportunity to act now the situation in Cyprus would 'consolidate against Turkey' until it was only a matter of time before Athens was in complete control of Cyprus. It was, he added, being said that even 'moderates', including Mr. Eçevit, were 'coming round to the view that, cost Turkey what it may to act on its own, and whatever the Greek retaliation in Thrace or the Aegean coast, better now than later'. Sir H. Phillips feared that by 21 July, after Mr. Sisco's visit to Ankara and the meeting of the Grand National Assembly, 'the armed forces commanders could have won the day and got the green light for action'. He subsequently informed Mr. Olver that, as recent Defence Attaché reports had indicated, there had been a 'substantial build up of Turkish forces on the south coast to a state of full alert', and that 'they must be presumed to be in a state of readiness that would enable them to invade Cyprus at a moment's notice' (Ankara telegram No. 14 to Nicosia of 19 July).

[6] In a telephone conversation with Sir P. Ramsbotham on the evening of 19 July, during which he gave his first reactions to Mr. Callaghan's message, Dr. Kissinger said that he 'basically agreed' with Mr. Callaghan's analysis, and stressed that the US was not working to keep Mr. Sampson in office. That, Dr. Kissinger stated. 'would be the least desirable outcome' (Washington telegram No. 2437 of 19 July).

successor until such a time as new elections are held. Like you I am worried about the danger of increased Soviet involvement in the area. I feel sure myself that a régime which is seen to be an extension of that in Athens will increase this danger rather than reduce it. AKEL may go underground but will get more clandestine Russian support.[7]

(c) We should enter into discussions with the Turks and I hope with the Greeks too about what should be the system [of][8] military arrangements within Cyprus (national contingents and local for[ces]). This is not something which I would have wanted to embark on myself but the intervention of the Greek officers of the National Guard has reawakened the Turks to the importance of this. If they are to be held back from acting unilaterally we may have to work towards a new package which could contain some new security arrangements. We should [have] to start bilaterally but in spite of Turkish reluctance we should aim for a trilateral meeting of the Guarantor Powers eventually.

(d) It may be necessary to think in terms of other modifications to the constitutional arrangements although I have not yet identified those areas where changes might be made.

(e) If we are to get anywhere on the above lines very great pressure must be exerted on the Greeks. The hard fact is that you are better able to achieve this than anyone else. I hope that they will accept our invitation to talks and we will begin the process then but we will need your strong backing.

(f) As regards the United Nations I think that there will have to be a resolution eventually. Provided Makarios and the other parties mainly concerned are able to make their statements I would not object if thereafter there was a time for reflection before any resolution is passed and particularly if you and we are actively engaged in consultations with the Turks and Greeks. As regards the substance of a resolution I am broadly content with the draft put forward by the Non-Aligned.[9] I am

---

[7] Mr. J.A. Dobbs, Minister in the British Embassy in Moscow, argued in Moscow telegram No. 860 of 19 July that the 'overriding Soviet objective' in the Cyprus crisis was to prevent any change in the island's status or the policies of its Government which could lead to an additional NATO presence in the eastern Mediterranean. But, if the Russians were unable to secure the restoration of Archbishop Makarios, he thought they would accept the *coup* as fact and concentrate on pressing the Greek Government to reduce its forces in Cyprus and to guarantee that *enosis* should never become a reality. Their second objective would, he suggested, be to exploit the crisis in any way which would weaken NATO's southern flank and divide the Alliance. He, nevertheless, thought that the Russians would not view a Turkish invasion of Cyprus with any enthusiasm, and that they would be wary of overt meddling in the crisis lest this lead to a closing of ranks in NATO and further complicate East-West relations. Unless new factors emerged, Mr. Dobbs expected the Soviet Government 'to huff and puff as strenuously as usual but in concrete terms to behave with caution ... From their point of view, there is not enough at stake in the Cyprus situation to tempt the Russians to stir the pot very vigorously.'

[8] A word was omitted here in the copy on file.

[9] A draft resolution prepared by the non-permanent members of the UN Security Council called upon all states to respect the sovereignty, independence and territorial integrity of

not keen to weaken the paragraph requesting withdrawal of the foreign military personnel serving in the National Guard but this could perhaps be put in the wider context of improving the system of military security within Cyprus to which I referred above, and of the need for a phased withdrawal. There will no doubt in any case be the usual intensive discussion about the text.[10]

To sum up then, we must work for restraint and a peaceful outcome. To achieve this we will have to provide something both in our bilateral consultations and at the United Nations which will satisfy the Turks and sufficient pressure must be put on the Greek Government to ensure that it moves in the right direction.

I am sorry that this has turned out to be such a long message but I wanted to let you have my thinking.

Since dictating this I have had some disquieting intelligence reports about Turkish movements[11] which makes the need for heavy pressure on the Greeks all the more necessary.

If the Turks do invade it will be a new ball game. Otherwise what I have already said still holds.

All good wishes,
Jim[12]

Cyprus, demanded an immediate end to foreign military intervention in the republic, and requested 'the immediate withdrawal of all the foreign military personnel in excess of those envisaged in international agreements' (UKMIS New York telegrams Nos. 794 and 795 of 19 July).

[10] During his telephone conversation with Sir P. Ramsbotham on the evening of 19 July (see note 6 above) Dr. Kissinger said with regard to these six points: 'On (*a*) the Americans could go along with that, or perhaps keep a step behind. On (*b*) and (*c*) he agreed "more or less". On (*d*) he had no comment. On (*e*) he was ready to put pressure on the Greeks once it was known what we were going to achieve: this was not yet clear. On (*f*) he said that he was not wild about the draft resolution. It should be watered down a little.'

[11] Shortly after this telegram was sent, telegram No. 1553 to Washington of 19 July informed Sir P. Ramsbotham that radar surveillance by Nimrod aircraft indicated that Turkish naval movements were 'compatible with dawn landings on the north coast of Cyprus and near Famagusta' (cf. No. 30).

[12] In his reply to Mr. Callaghan's message, drafted just prior to his learning of the Turkish military intervention in Cyprus (*v. ibid.*) and sent via Sir P. Ramsbotham, for his 'scrap book', Dr. Kissinger again emphasised that it was essential for the US and UK to work closely together in order not to 'set in motion any train of events before we have a precise view of what we want to achieve'. He stated that, while the US Government regarded Archbishop Makarios as the *de jure* Head of State in Cyprus, they wished to 'avoid any particular emphasis on this point' as they searched for a solution, and felt that they 'should not precipitate the downfall of the *de facto* situation in Cyprus until there [was] a viable alternative'. Dr. Kissinger also considered it 'premature to think in terms of other modifications to the constitutional arrangements' for Cyprus, and he noted that, though he accepted that pressure might 'eventually have to be exerted on the Greeks', this could only be usefully done when they had a better idea of what the Turks would accept. Premature action might, he thought, lessen the

103

2. Posts to which this telegram is repeated should not (not) let it be known that I have sent a message in these terms. It is for the information of posts as a further indication of how my thinking on policy is developing.

US's ability to be effective with the Greeks later, and if outside pressure were brought to bear to restore Archbishop Makarios, it would 'only solidify the régime in Athens'. He added, with regard to the debate in the UN Security Council, that he hoped they could avoid any resolution which might 'serve to harden present positions' (Washington telegram No. 2445 of 20 July).

No. 30

Sir H. Phillips (Ankara) to Mr. Callaghan

No. 780 Telegraphic [*WSC 1/10*]

Flash. Confidential ANKARA, *20 July 1974, 3.10 a.m.*

Repeated for information to Flash Nicosia, Athens, Washington, HQBFNE[1] (GOC[2] eyes only).

My tel[egram] No. 779:[3]
Cyprus

1. A Turkish force is going to land in Cyprus imminently—probably within hours of now (0230 hrs GMT 20 July).
2. I have been told this by Sisco, who has just reported it to the State Department. He emerged at 4.30 a.m. local time from his talk with the Prime Minister and the Foreign Minister. He found them almost fatalistically resigned to military intervention. Main reason they gave was that for ten years Turkey had shown patience and acted constitutionally. Looking to the future, the Government had to act now. Once it had done so and had established a bargaining position by developing greater military presence on the island, it would be ready to negotiate—and with anyone.

---

[1] Headquarters, British Forces Near East.

[2] General Officer Commanding.

[3] In this telegram, despatched at 12.01 a.m. (GMT) on 20 July, Sir H. Phillips reported a conversation which he had just had with Mr. Güneş. The Turkish Cabinet were in session preparing for Mr. Sisco's meeting with Mr. Eçevit, and Mr. Güneş left the Cabinet to speak to the Ambassador. He assured Sir H. Phillips that no orders had been given to Turkish ships for a landing on Cyprus. Sir H. Phillips had already warned Mr. Callaghan in Ankara telegram No. 778, despatched at 7.52 p.m. (GMT) on 19 July, that if Mr. Sisco were to arrive in Ankara 'empty-handed', the Turkish Government might decide to resort to force in Cyprus (cf. No. 29, notes 5 and 11).

3. Sisco had tried to reason with the two Ministers on humanitarian grounds and to persuade them to have any decision on military intervention put off for 48 hours to allow some progress towards a political formula. The United States would take a most serious view of it if they did not. After reference back to his colleagues, Eçevit called Sisco in again at 5 a.m. (0200 GMT) and said no delay was possible now. Turkish troops would land in Cyprus (location not revealed). He stressed that if the Greeks did not fire the Turkish troops would not fire: they would stabilise their positions promptly. He asked the Americans to pass this message urgently to Athens.

4. I have just been summoned to the Foreign Minister and will telegraph further on return.[4] Meantime it is vital that the contents of this telegram should not be disclosed to anyone but the addressees, through the High Commissioner in Nicosia will of course want to use the information paragraph 1 (without disclosure of source) as a basis for planning.

---

[4] Sir H. Phillips met with Mr. Günes at 3.30 a.m. (GMT). Mr. Günes then stated that Turkish troops had been ordered to land in Cyprus under Article 4 of the Treaty of Guarantee. Since their last conversation (*v. ibid.*), he said, the concern of all political parties about the situation on Cyprus 'had been brought to a head by the fact that Mr. Sisco had brought no concrete proposals for resolving it. Turkey regretfully had no alternative but to intervene militarily on her own.' Sir H. Phillips expressed his dismay, particularly as there had barely been time to process ideas resulting from the visit of the Turkish Ministers to London (Ankara telegram No. 781 of 20 July). Cf. James Callaghan, *Time and Chance* (London: Collins, 1987), pp. 342-43.

No. 31

Mr. Callaghan to Sir R. Hooper (Athens)

No. 151 Telegraphic [WSC 1/10]

Flash. Confidential   FCO, *20 July 1974, 7 a.m.*

To Flash Ankara, Moscow, UKDEL NATO, UKMIS New York, Paris and repeated for information to Immediate Washington, Nicosia, EEC Posts, NATO Posts, Cairo, Tel Aviv, Beirut and Belgrade.

Cyprus

Faced as we now are by the Turkish invasion,[1] my immediate aims of policy are as follows:

(i) To protect British lives and property in Cyprus:[2]
(ii) To ensure the continued security of the Sovereign Base Areas:[3]
(iii) To put maximum pressure on the Turks to limit the fighting and to bring about a ceasefire at the earliest possible opportunity:[4]
(iv) To get the Turks to issue a statement of intent that they wish to see the return of constitutional rule in Cyprus:
(v) To prevent the Greek Government from escalating the situation or intervening by force and to get them to accept that Sampson and his régime must be removed from the scene. They should make this clear publicly:[5]

---

[1] See No. 30. Turkey's military intervention in Cyprus began at 4 a.m. (GMT), with air sorties, and seaborne and parachute troop landings. Turkish Cypriot fighters were activated, fighting broke out in Nicosia, and Nicosia airport was bombed.

[2] Mr. Olver noted that evening in Nicosia telegram No. 312 that he still had no reports of British casualties. 'The fact that we have escaped so far', he added, 'is due to good luck and the good sense of all concerned. The Airport, the Ledra Palace Hotel and this High Commission have been the centres of fairly violent battles.'

[3] Following reports of intercommunal fighting in Cyprus, especially at Limassol where Greek Cypriots attacked the Turkish quarter, authority was given to CBFNE to send out armed detachments to bring into the SBAs those families still outside the perimeter area who might be at risk. Orders were also given for a second marine Commando to be flown out to Cyprus to protect the SBAs (telegram No. 156 to Athens of 20 July).

[4] At 5.50 a.m. Mr. Callaghan summoned Mr. Menemencioglu to the FCO to complain at having heard 'on the radio and not from his Government news of the Turkish invasion', and to express his regret at the Turkish action. He said that he knew of no attacks on the Turkish community in Cyprus which would have justified armed intervention to protect them; called on the Turkish Government to limit hostilities so far as possible and bring about a ceasefire; and insisted on the need to have that day in London high level representatives of the Greek and Turkish Governments (telegram No. 811 to Ankara of 20 July).

[5] Mr. Callaghan recorded in telegram No. 152 to Athens of 20 July (sent out of sequence at 6.50 a.m. (GMT)) that he had seen Mr. N. Diamantopoulos, the Greek Chargé d'Affaires, informed him of his conversation with Mr. Menemencioglu (*v. ibid.*), and invited the Greek

(vi) To invite immediately the Governments of Greece and Turkey to hold talks in London. The objective of these talks would be to reduce tension and to work towards a return of constitutional rule. My present thinking is that this must mean the removal of Sampson and a return to constitutional procedures.

2. I have talked twice to Kissinger on the telephone. He shares these aims and objectives.[6]

3. I have seen the Turkish Ambassador and expressed my disapproval of their actions and urged policies (iii), (iv) and (vi) on the Turkish Government.[7] HM Ambassador Ankara should take every opportunity to back up these representations.

4. Kissinger is sending Sisco immediately to Athens with the object of urging the Greek Government to abandon Sampson and to send representatives to London for immediate talks. HM Ambassador Athens should back up Sisco in every way possible to achieve this. I have seen the Greek chargé here.[8]

5. I shall also be seeing the Soviet Ambassador very shortly. I will tell him what our objectives are but not (repeat) not the means of achieving the return to constitutional rule.[9] Kissinger agreed that we should set out to the Russians what we think the solution should be but not go into details of the process of getting there. HM Embassy Moscow should make these aims

Government, as guarantors, to send Ministers to London for discussions. These, he stated, might begin bilaterally, with British Ministers talking separately to the Greeks and Turks, and should then become trilateral. Mr. Callaghan also impressed on the Greeks the 'need to desist from any counter action', adding that he looked to them to put right the unconstitutional situation in Cyprus.

[6] According to Washington telegram No. 2443 of 20 July Dr. Kissinger had urged Mr. Callaghan by telephone to convene a meeting in London of the 'Zurich powers' (i.e. the three Cyprus guarantors under the 1960 Treaty). Mr. Nixon subsequently informed the Greek and Turkish Governments that the 'full weight of the US [would] be brought to bear in these talks to ensure the restoration of a just and stable peace in Cyprus' (Washington telegram No. 2444 of 20 July). At his meeting with Cabinet colleagues that afternoon (see No. 27, note 4), Mr. Callaghan re-affirmed that it must be HMG's 'immediate objective to prevent a declaration of war between Greece and Turkey; to bring about a cease-fire in Cyprus; and to get talks started between the United Kingdom, Greece and Turkey'.

[7] See note 4 above.

[8] See note 5 above. At 8 a.m. Mr. Callaghan again summoned Mr. Diamantopoulos to the FCO and read to him a text, subsequently handed to him as a *bout de papier*, in which he emphasised that the Greek Government should neither add to the violations of the constitutional position in Cyprus which had taken place, nor 'make any statement or take any action which would further imperil their relations with Turkey' (telegram No. 155 to Athens of 20 July).

[9] Mr. Callaghan summoned Mr. N.M. Lunkov, the Soviet Ambassador to the FCO at 6.30 a.m. In telegram No. 485 to Moscow of 20 July Mr. Callaghan reported that he had assured Mr. Lunkov that HMG had no prior knowledge of the Turkish Government's plans regarding the invasion, and informed him of what he had previously said to Mr. Menemencioglu and Mr. Diamantopoulos (cf. notes 4 and 5 above).

clear at the appropriate level to the Soviet Government. The Americans will also be taking action.

6. Posts will receive separately brief accounts of my talks with these Ambassadors.

7. UKMIS New York, UKDEL NATO and Paris in the absence of more detailed instructions should be guided by the foregoing and should agree to action by the UN, the NATO Council or the Nine which is consistent with these objectives. UKMIS New York should not (repeat) not however take the lead in proposing action within the Security Council at this stage.

8. Posts to which this telegram is repeated can tell governments to which they are accredited of our general aims but should not speculate on what a return to constitutional procedures might involve.

No. 32

Sir R. Hooper (Athens) to Mr. Callaghan

No. 237 Telegraphic [*WSC 1/10*]

Flash. Confidential   ATHENS, *20 July 1974, 11.15 a.m.*

Repeated for information to Flash Ankara, Nicosia and Immediate UKMIS New York, UKDEL NATO, Paris, Bonn, Washington and Moscow.

Your tel[egram] No. 152:[1]
Cyprus

1. I saw Greek Acting Foreign Minister at 09.15 London time and have just returned.

2. I took him through what you had said to the Greek Chargé d'Affaires[2] and informed him that you had spoken in equally strong terms if not stronger to the Turks. The latter point should help to dispel any idea which might have arisen that we had foreknowledge of their action. I urged that the Greek Government should send representatives to London if possible today for discussions under Article 4 of Treaty of Guarantee on a bilateral and eventually trilateral basis and having during the meeting received your tel[egram] No. 153[3] urged the Greek Government not to do anything to escalate the situation.

---

[1] See No. 31, note 5.

[2] *V. ibid.*

[3] In this telegram, despatched at 8.05 a.m. (GMT) on 20 July, Mr. Callaghan reported that Dr. Kissinger had telephoned him with the news that the Greeks had threatened that, unless Turkish forces withdrew from Cyprus, they would declare both war on Turkey and *enosis* with

3. Kypraios then told me that he had just seen the Turkish Ambassador. He had informed him that the Greek Government had this morning ordered general mobilisation.[4] It had been established as a fact that Turkish forces had attacked the Greek regular contingent (ELDYK) in Cyprus. They demanded the immediate cessation of Turkish military action against Cyprus and a cease-fire. All Turkish troops landed or parachuted into Cyprus to concentrate in the Turkish enclaves by 1400 (presumably Cyprus time) today. The Greek Government were willing to attend talks in London on the basis now proposed but only if there had been a cease-fire. All this does not entirely square with what Hartman told HM Embassy Washington (Washington tel[egram No.] 2447).[5] Americans are at present unable to elucidate this, but we shall enquire further.

4. I said that my Government would be dismayed. If I had understood the Minister correctly, the Greek Government had presented the Turkish Government with a choice between complying with their demands and war. Kypraios at first accepted this—one of the officials present (Ossides) adding 'war on all fronts'. He later tried to back down, saying that he had concluded his message to the Turkish Government by saying that the Greeks were presenting them with an opportunity of settling their differences and stabilising the situation for years to come.

5. I went on to say that the action taken by the Greek Government seemed to me likely to escalate the situation in precisely the way HMG wished to avoid. We were at one with the Greeks in wanting an immediate cease-fire and had indeed told the Turks so. But the Turks were unlikely to accede to this under the sort of threats to which they had been subjected and some room must be left for negotiation. I asked what relative importance the Greeks attached to the cease-fire and the concentration of Turkish forces in the enclaves. Was the latter a condition *sine qua non* to the former?

6. Mr. Kypraios said that Greece did not want to threaten Turkey. But given the disparity of forces, she must do what she could to enable her to

Cyprus. Dr. Kissinger had given Mr. Sisco verbal instructions to warn the Greeks that if they so acted, all US military aid would be 'cut off immediately', and Mr. Callaghan instructed Sir R. Hooper to 'use every means in [his] power to get in touch with the Greek Government at the highest possible level and urge them in the strongest terms on behalf of the British Government that they should not (repeat not) escalate the situation'.

[4] In Athens general mobilisation was ordered at 10 a.m. (GMT) (Athens telegram No. 241 of 20 July). and the Greek army's 10th division moved east towards the Greek/Turkish border in Thrace.

[5] In this telegram, despatched at 9.40 a.m. (GMT) on 20 July, Sir P. Ramsbotham informed Mr. Callaghan that he had been told by Mr. Hartman that Mr. Sisco was on his way to Ankara with a message from Brig. Ioannides outlining Greek terms: an immediate ceasefire, and the immediate withdrawal of Turkish forces from Cyprus. If the latter condition were not met, Greece would declare *enosis* and war on Turkey. No deadline was given for the ultimatum regarding withdrawal, but Mr. Hartman presumed that there must be a 'period of grace' since the message had yet to be delivered to the Turkish Government by Mr. Sisco.

negotiate from a position of strength. Unlike Turkey, she had till now made no warlike preparations. Greek regular troops in Cyprus were already under attack. To that extent, a war situation already prevailed, and it was not of Greece's making. (He has a point—of a sort—here.) In regard to the Greek demands, the cardinal point was of course the cease-fire. But the Greek military also attached great importance to the concentration of Turkish forces. However he did not think they would insist on the operation being completed by 1400 so long as it was carried out within the next 24 or 48 hours.[6]

7. I reiterated that I thought the Greek Government had embarked on an extremely dangerous course. As he knew better than I, the Turks were unlikely to take kindly to being expected to negotiate under duress. They had gravely exacerbated the situation. What we were discussing round the table at the moment might well prove to be the preliminaries to another world war. I begged Mr. Kypraios, who was about to see the Prime Minister, to convey to him the deep anxieties of my Government. I would be asking Mr. Androutsopoulos to receive me so that I might express them in person.

8. I have not yet been able to check with the Americans what Sisco actually said to the Greeks but I got the impression that Sisco either kept in the background or did not utter the threat about military aid referred to in your tel[egram] No. 153.[7] This is however contradicted by your tel[egram No.] 812 to Ankara.[8] Kypraios said that the Greek Government

[6] Sir R. Hooper later reported in Athens telegram No. 244 of 20 July that the Greek Foreign Ministry had informed other Western Ambassadors that no time limit was to be set for the concentration of Turkish forces in the Turkish enclaves, nor was a condition to be made on how long they should stay there.

[7] See note 4 above. That afternoon Mr. H.J. Tasca, the US Ambassador in Athens, told Sir R. Hooper that in an early morning meeting with senior Greek generals he and Mr. Sisco had found Brig. Ioannides 'extremely hawkish'. They had initially been reluctant to use the threat of cutting off American military aid to Greece, fearing that it might prove counter-productive. But, after their first meeting with Mr. Kypraios they had changed their minds and, following clearance from the White House and State Department, they used a second meeting with the acting Foreign Minister to make the threat 'in courteous but unequivocal terms' (Athens telegram No. 242 of 20 July).

[8] In this telegram, sent at 9.50 a.m. on 20 July, Mr. Callaghan reported he had learned from a further telephone conversation with Dr. Kissinger that Mr. Sisco believed he could restrain the Greeks and persuade them to agree to a ceasefire if the Turks were prepared 'to withdraw their forces into their enclaves in Cyprus'. According to Dr. Kissinger, the Greeks would then be ready to send someone to London immediately. Mr. Callaghan fully endorsed these ideas, and he instructed Sir H. Phillips to urge the Turkish Government to accept an arrangement along these lines. He also suggested that it would be useful if the Turks were to make a statement that their objectives in Cyprus were limited. But Mr. Günes, whom Sir H. Phillips saw later that day, insisted that if Turkish troops withdrew to the Turkish Cypriot enclaves they would be left vulnerable, and that 'talks now in London could only be negotiation from weakness'. He was not very hopeful about his colleagues either agreeing to a declaration on Turkey's limited objectives, or accepting Mr. Callaghan's invitation to London (Ankara telegram No. 793 of 20 July).

did not want *Enosis* 'though if the Cypriot people themselves wanted it, that would be a different matter'. He had no repeat no knowledge of a proposal for partition (Ankara tel[egram] No. 12 to Athens).[9]

9. I am trying to see the Prime Minister (he is proving very difficult) and will report further as necessary.

[9] Sir H. Phillips informed Sir R. Hooper in this telegram of 20 July that it had been reported in Ankara that that morning the Greek Government had 'offered (or suggested) the partition of Cyprus'.

No. 33

Mr. Callaghan to Sir R. Hooper (Athens)

No. 162 Telegraphic [*WSC 1/10*]

Flash. Confidential   FCO, *21 July 1974, 6.02 p.m.*

Repeated for information to Immediate Nicosia, Washington, UKMIS New York, UKDEL NATO, Paris, Moscow and Vienna.

My tel[egram] No. 1556 to Washington:[1]
Cyprus

1. Since all your communications systems are over-loaded the purpose of this telegram is to bring you up to date in the briefest terms of events at this end since my telegram under reference was sent.

2. In the course of the afternoon I have talked three times to Kissinger, twice to Eçevit and once to Kypraios.

3. My impressions are as follows:

(*a*) Both Greece and Turkey say that they accept Resolution 353.[2]

[1] In this telegram, sent at 1.59 p.m. (GMT) on 21 July, Mr. Callaghan informed Sir P. Ramsbotham of telephone conversations he had in the previous 90 minutes with Mr. Eçevit, Dr. Kissinger and Dr. B. Kreisky, the Austrian Federal Chancellor.

[2] UNSC Resolution 353 was adopted on 20 July. It called, in Paragraph 1, upon all states to respect the 'sovereignty, independence and territorial integrity' of Cyprus; appealed for a ceasefire; demanded an immediate end to foreign military intervention in 'contravention of operative Paragraph 1'; requested, in Paragraph 4, the withdrawal without delay from the Republic of foreign military personnel present 'otherwise than under the authority of international agreements', including those whose recall President Makarios had requested in his letter to Gen. Gizikis of 2 July (see No. 17, note 1); and called, in Paragraph 5, on Greece, Turkey and the UK to enter into negotiations without delay 'for the restoration of peace in the area and constitutional government in Cyprus' (UKMIS New York telegram No. 806 of 20 July).. Mr. Richard subsequently noted in UKMIS New York telegram No. 808 of 20 July that there had been 'some pressure for a demand for Turkish withdrawal and considerable pressure for getting Makarios in on any negotiations', and that the UK Mission had resisted

(b) Greece. The Greeks will not attend talks until a cease-fire has been achieved.[3] Our own and US reports indicate that the Greek Government is very shaky and that there may be some change in the near future. I judge that any Greek régime is likely to be under enormous pressure to step up its military action against Turkey unless a cease-fire is achieved tonight.[4]

(c) Turkey. Eçevit agrees to the principle of a cease-fire. And would be prepared to announce this tonight, but wants a meeting early tomorrow in order to discuss the modalities of it. This may be a delaying tactic and there is a strong risk that discussion of the 'modalities' will be prolonged and difficult.[5]

4. In the absence of an immediate agreement on a cease-fire we are exploring whether it would be possible to hold a meeting at 0800 tomorrow 22 July in Vienna with the Greeks and the Turks. Eçevit accepts this and wants me to be present. Kreisky told me earlier in the day that he could make arrangements. If this can be agreed I would envisage an announcement from London stating the agreement of the Governments of Turkey and Greece and urging all concerned meanwhile to put into effect immediately operative Paragraph 2 of Security Council Resolution 353.[6]

amendments to Paragraph 4 'which would clearly have covered the Turkish invasion force', and to Paragraph 5 which would have involved President Makarios or the Cyprus Government in the projected tripartite talks. 'The package', Mr. Richard added, 'was eventually approved by Makarios and the way opened for unanimous adoption of the Resolution.' Cf. *UNSC Official Records, 29th year, 1781st meeting*, 20 July 1974 (S/PV.1781).

[3] In Athens telegram No. 256, despatched at midday (GMT) on 21 July, Sir R. Hooper noted that the Greeks had made it abundantly clear that they would not send a representative to London unless there were a ceasefire and Turkish forces in Cyprus withdrew to the Turkish enclaves. Meanwhile, Mr. Sisco returned from Ankara to resume his talks with the Greek leaders and, at 1.07 p.m. (GMT) Sir R. Hooper reported in Athens telegram No. 257 that Mr. Sisco had told him that a ceasefire in Cyprus had been arranged and 'barring last-minute hitches, [was] likely to be announced within the next half-hour'.

[4] In his report to Dr. Kissinger, copied to Mr. Callaghan in Washington telegram No. 2454 of 21 July, Mr. Sisco stated that while the Greek Government accepted the ceasefire as provided for in Resolution 353, Mr. Androutsopoulos was predicting a change of government within the next twenty-four hours, and had implied that this would be 'very bad indeed and that [neither] he nor the Foreign Minister would serve in whatever new Government [was] announced'. For this reason, Mr. Androutsopoulos declared, no Greek Government could yet take a decision to go to London for talks on 23 July.

[5] Mr. Callaghan reported in telegram No. 1556 to Washington (see note 1 above) that Mr. Eçevit had left him under the impression that he would be urging his colleagues to accept a ceasefire. Mr. Eçevit also informed Mr. Callaghan that in the present circumstances he thought London too far from Turkey for a tripartite meeting, and Mr. Callaghan concluded that Vienna was 'probably the best option'.

[6] Paragraph 2 of Resolution 353 called upon all parties to the present fighting, as a first step, to cease all firing and to exercise the utmost restraint and to refrain from any action which might further aggravate the situation.

5. At the time of despatch, this plan depends on Greek acceptance which may well not be forthcoming. Kissinger is far from optimistic but he and Sisco are having a try. If they fail the only alternative course is to put more pressure on Eçevit for an immediate cease-fire without prior discussions about modalities.[7]

---

[7] Mr. Callaghan informed Sir R. Hooper in telegram No. 165 to Athens of 21 July that during his telephone conversation with Mr. Kypraios that afternoon he had been left with the definite impression that if there were no ceasefire that day the Greeks might 'do something really reckless tomorrow'.

No. 34

Mr. Callaghan to Mr. Dobbs (Moscow)

No. 489 Telegraphic [*WSC 1/10*]

Immediate. Confidential.   FCO, *21 July 1973, 10.39 p.m.*

Repeated for information to Priority Washington, Athens, Ankara, UKMIS New York, UKDEL NATO, Paris.

My tel[egram] No. 485:[1]
Cyprus

1. On my instuctions and on my behalf Killick invited the Soviet Ambassador to call at 20.45 this evening. He explained that I was anxious as far as possible to keep the Soviet Government informed of developments. In a very fast moving situation, I could not do this myself at the time. Killick told Lunkov that I had spent nearly all day on the telephone, repeatedly to Kissinger, several times to the Turkish Prime Minister and also once to the Greek Foreign Minister. It appeared that both Greece and Turkey said that they accepted Resolution 353.[2] The problem was how to bring about a cease-fire so that the talks among the three Governments which Resolution 353 called for could take place. One possibility suggested by the Turkish Government was that a cease-fire should be agreed in principle, but that talks might open before it took effect. I had made it clear that I was available at any time to open talks and, if this could facilitate things, could envisage the talks taking place elsewhere than in London. But at the time of this conversation we were

---

[1] See No. 31, note 9.
[2] See No. 33, note 2.

still awaiting a report of Mr. Sisco on his latest exchanges with the Greek Government which were still going on.

2. Killick explained that we had hoped by now to be able to give the Soviet Embassy some firm news. It was impossible to forecast how things might develop and we would do our best to be in touch with them again. Meanwhile we hoped that the Soviet Government would use its influence for the implementation of Resolution 353 and would be interested in any comment the Soviet leadership might have to make on what I had said to Lunkov yesterday (my tel[egram] No. under reference).

3. In reply, Lunkov referred only to the Soviet Government's statement published this morning (your tel[egram] No. 866)[3] and to Brezhnev's[4] speech in Warsaw. He singled out in particular Soviet advocacy of the independence and sovereignty of the state of Cyprus and opposition to *Enosis*: (omitting the alleged intention of making it a NATO base) the restoration of the legal Government of Cyprus led by Makarios: and the cessation of outside interference particularly the removal of all Greek military personnel.

4. He also wished to draw my attention to the Soviet denial of any Soviet military alert measures.[5]

5. Killick thanked him for the assurance of the Soviet Government's wish to avoid any external interference and said he would report to me.

6. See MIFT.[6]

---

[3] This telegram reported a Soviet Government statement published in *Pravda* of 21 July which condemned the Greek 'militarists' for 'continuing their aggressive actions against the independent Cypriot state', and stated that certain NATO countries had 'practically started on the road towards helping the putschists'. Mr. Dobbs subsequently commented on this statement that its most notable feature was 'the complete absence of any criticism of the Turkish landings [factually reported elsewhere] or hint of support for a ceasefire'. After noting that the Soviet Foreign Minister, Mr. A.A. Gromyko, had seen the Turkish Ambassador on 19 and 20 July, he observed: 'It is beginning to look as if the Russians may have connived at the landings in the calculation that they were difficult to prevent anyway, that the first task was to overthrow any régime closely connected with Greece and that the possible danger of a Cyprus linked to NATO through Turkey could be dealt with later' (Moscow telegram No. 868 of 21 July).

[4] Mr. L.I. Brezhnev was General Secretary of the Central Committee of the Communist Party of the Soviet Union (CPSU).

[5] During their meeting on the morning of 20 July Mr. Callaghan and Mr. Lunkov had listened to the BBC radio news which carried reports from Washington that seven Soviet air divisions were in a state of alert. This was denied in *Pravda* of 21 July which announced, on the authority of 'competent organs', that Soviet armed forces were 'in a normal everyday state' (Moscow telegram No. 867 of 21 July).

[6] My Immediately Following Telegram. In telegram No. 490 to Moscow of 21 July Sir J. Killick reported that he had further remarked to Mr. Lunkov on a personal basis that the Ambassador had not mentioned the allegation in the Soviet Government's statement alleging that NATO members had failed to support Archbishop Makarios and had 'practically started on the road towards helping the putschists'. Sir J. Killick also observed that he had taken pleasure in informing Mr. Lunkov that HMG had been glad to accede to the Soviet request to include 41 Russian tourists in British evacuation arrangements—assistance which would not have been possible without British forces in the SBAs.

No. 35

Sir R. Hooper (Athens) to Mr. Callaghan

No. 266 Telegraphic [WSC 1/10]

Flash. Confidential ATHENS, 21 *July 1974, 11.00 p.m.*

Repeated for information to Flash Ankara, and to Immediate Nicosia, Washington, UKMIS New York, UKDEL NATO, Paris, Moscow and Vienna.

My tel[egram] No. 262:[1]
Cyprus

1. Sisco, who was less optimistic than he was earlier today, seems to be at a loss how to proceed, and it is clear that if Eçevit remains obdurate there is not much else to be done but to put more pressure on him (your tel[egram] No. 162)[2]. Unfortunately so long as the Turkish forces continue to maintain or improve their position he has everything to gain and very little to lose by stalling, while the Greeks would face a very serious problem with their own military and with Greek public opinion were they to agree to attend talks while fighting is still going on, as would be the case if Eçevit's present formula were accepted.

2. The Greek Government is in fact between the devil and the deep blue sea and all the indications are that, as you say in your tel[egram] No 162,[2] its internal position is very shaky. If there is no cease-fire and the Turks continue on the offensive, pressure from the military to go [to] the aid of the Greek Cypriots may become irresistible; and if the moderates try to resist it, the military will sweep them away. If there is a cease fire, this may

---

[1] In this telegram of 21 July Sir R. Hooper reported that when he had called on Mr. Sisco at 5.40 p.m. (GMT), Mr. Sisco had said that 'it was clear the Turks were stalling'. In a talk with Dr. Kissinger, Mr. Eçevit had accepted a ceasefire 'in principle' and agreed that the Greeks and Turks should send representatives to work out details 'somewhere in Europe'. But while, on his return to Athens, Mr. Sisco had found Mr. Kypraios and Mr. Androutsopoulos 'tempted' by this offer, the latter had doubted if he could obtain the agreement of the Greek military leadership. Mr. Sisco added that the Turks had so far failed to carry out their commitment to the US 'which was that, if the Greeks would accept the UN Resolution, the Turks would convene a meeting of the Council of Ministers and thereafter announce their acceptance of the ceasefire'. The Americans, he explained, had also threatened the Turks with a stoppage of arms supplies if they did not reach an accommodation. He did not think supporting action from Britain in Athens would be useful: the Greeks, he observed, now regarded the US as their 'only friend' and were 'terrified he would leave'. Cf. No. 33, note 3.

[2] No. 33. In Ankara telegram No. 804, despatched at 10.28 p.m. (GMT) on 21 July, Sir H. Phillips reported that the Turkish Cabinet had just concluded its meeting without any announcement.

strengthen the hand of the moderates against the military hawks. A cease-fire on terms reasonably acceptable to Greece, where public opinion, though more reluctant to resort to war than are some of the military, is nevertheless determined not to allow Cyprus to fall to the Turks, might indeed not only strengthen the moderates, but seriously weaken the chauvinist military whose gamble would be seen to have failed. It might also pave the way not only for a settlement in Cyprus but for a more liberal régime in Greece. But the military extremists no doubt realise this, and might well pre-empt this possibility by repudiating any cease-fire the government might agree to throwing out the moderates and going to war regardless.[3]

3. The prospect is unattractive whichever way one looks at it. There seems to be no alternative to continuing to bring pressure to bear on Eçevit, trying to bring home that the longer he stalls the harder it will be to hold the Greeks back and the less likely it becomes that the end product of the crisis will be a Greek Government with which the Turks can live in the long term. So far as the Greeks are concerned, I do not think we can expect them to accept talks while fighting continues or that any government which did so could survive for long. We can only try to restrain them as best we can and, when and if the Turks, by agreeing wholeheartedly to a cease-fire, make it possible for the Greeks to attend a meeting, go to the limit to see that the Greek military do not try to overthrow it. But, thanks to Mr. Eçevit, time is running out on us and the prospects of a meeting in Vienna this morning seem to be vanishing.

---

[3] The British Defence Attaché in Athens had reported in telegram No. FOG 368, desptached at 12.21 p.m (GMT) on 21 July, that according to his US colleagues the Greek military authorities were satisfied that the Greek national contingent and the National Guard could contain Turkish incursions in Cyprus for several days, but felt they would have to intervene if the situation deteriorated rapidly. The US Military Attaché considered the Greek military deployment on the Turkish frontier complete, and that the Greeks would declare war at dawn on 22 July. Greek forces had also been concentrated in Crete evidently with the object of reinforcing Cyprus. Meanwhile, at 2 p.m. on 21 July Mr. Logan telephoned Mr. Wiggin from Brussels to say that a senior Greek officer at NATO had said that all Greek officers would be withdrawn from the Alliance forthwith. He had, however, given no formal notification of Greece's withdrawal from NATO (Cyprus: timetable of events, 20/21 July).

No. 36

Mr. Callaghan to Sir E. Tomkins (Paris)

No. 353 Telegraphic [*WSC 1/10*]

Flash. Confidential   FCO, 21 *July 1974, 11.09 p.m.*

Repeated to Flash UKDEL NATO, and for information to Flash Washington, Athens, Ankara, and to other EEC posts, and Immediate Nicosia, UKMIS New York, Moscow and Vienna

My tel[egram] No. 162 to Athens:[1]
Cyprus

1. The efforts to bring about a meeting to discuss a cease-fire seem temporarily at least to have failed. The Greeks will not enter into talks with the Turks until there is a cease-fire and the Turks will not agree to a cease-fire until there have been talks about modalities.

2. Kissinger and I have now agreed that the best hope in the immediate future is for maximum pressure to be brought on the Turks and the Greeks by way of formal notes from the members of the NATO Alliance and the EEC demanding that they accept the cease-fire as laid down in Security Council Resolution 353. 1400 hours GMT should be set as the time as a means of increasing the pressure. General Goodpaster[2] should also weigh in on the military net.

3. My immediate following telegram contains suggested text of démarche.[3] It has not been agreed with the Americans though they are aware of its broad outlines. I have talked to Sauvagnagues who is in full agreement. Sir E. Tomkins should support him in getting the earliest possible agreement of the Nine. This should be done during the night and the note delivered immediately it is agreed by the Ambassador of each country individually. Kissinger will be sending instructions to Rumsfeld[4] in NATO which Mr. Logan should urgently and strongly back up. If the Americans have not acted Mr. Logan should take the initiative himself.

4. Kissinger has just told me that he has spoken extremely toughly to Eçevit who is prepared to recommend to his Cabinet acceptance of the cease-fire as proposed. Sisco is working on Greeks. He still hopes that these American recommendations can be urgently backed up as proposed above.

---

[1] No. 33.

[2] Supreme Allied Commander, Europe (NATO).

[3] The text of the suggested note contained in telegram No. 354 to Paris of 21 July urged the Greek and Turkish Governments 'in the strongest possible terms' that they should implement Paragraph 2 of Security Council Resolution 353, and agree that a ceasefire should come into effect by 2 p.m. (GMT) on 22 July.

[4] Mr. D.H. Rumsfeld was US Permanent Representative to NATO, Brussels.

5. I have recommended to Dr. Kissinger that the text of the note should not be released until after the deadline has passed and that the fact notes are being delivered should be played down, although not concealed, until then.[5]

---

[5] At midnight (GMT) on 21 July Dr. Kissinger telephoned Mr. Callaghan to say that the Turks had accepted that a ceasefire should come into operation at 2 p.m. (GMT) on 22 July. It was nevertheless agreed that the exercise of coordinating and delivering the notes should go ahead in order to maintain pressure on both parties (telegram No. 355 to Paris of 22 July). Sir R. Hooper subsequently reported in Athens telegram No. 268, despatched at 3 a.m. (GMT) on 22 July, that Mr. Sisco had informed him that the Greek and Turkish Governments had agreed to a ceasefire as provided for by Security Council Resolution 353 and that this would be confirmed by both Governments at 7 a.m. (GMT). Mr. Sisco and Mr. Tasca later revealed that one of their main difficulties had been in being sure that they were dealing with an authoritative Greek Government. But in the end they had not found it necessary to 'avail themselves of the discretion given them to threaten that if in the event of a refusal the US would reconsider the whole of her relationships in this area' (Athens telegram No. 271 of 22 July).

No. 37

Extract from Conclusions of a Meeting of the Cabinet held at 10 Downing Street on 22 July 1974 at 12 noon

CC(74) 28 [WSC 1/10]

Secret

Cyprus

The Cabinet had before them a Note by the Secretary of the Cabinet[1] (C(74) 77) covering a report by officials on the situation in Cyprus.[2]

The Foreign and Commonwealth Secretary said that the Greek and Turkish Governments had agreed to a ceasefire in Cyprus, to come into effect that afternoon. They had also agreed to hold discussions with us, as the three Governments guaranteeing the 1960 Treaty. He hoped that these discussions could begin within the next two days; they would probably take place in either Vienna or Geneva.[3] The Turks must be disappointed at the

---

[1] Sir J. Hunt.

[2] This report summarised military and diplomatic developments since the Turkish intervention in Cyprus.

[3] Early on the morning of 22 July Mr. Callaghan instructed the British Ambassadors at Ankara and Athens to propose the opening of tripartite talks in Vienna at 10 a.m. (GMT) on 23 July. The Greeks were doubtful about attending talks on 23 July, and were inclined to favour Geneva as a venue. And while Mr. Günes accepted the British invitation in principle, he initially wanted the talks postponed for a day or two. Only on the afternoon of 22 July did the

meagre success of their armed intervention. They would not of course admit this publicly; and they could claim that by establishing several thousand of their troops on the island they could ensure that Cyprus would return to constitutional government, and they were in a better position to protect the Turkish Cypriots.[4] It remained to be seen whether the return of President Makarios would be acceptable to the Greek and Turkish Governments or, indeed, to the Cypriots themselves. If he did not return, the requirements of the constitution would be met by the appointment in his place of Mr. Clerides, Speaker of the House of Representatives, pending new elections. Throughout the past few days he had been in frequent touch with the United States Secretary of State, Dr. Kissinger, and with the Greek and Turkish Governments. Initially the United States Government had been preoccupied by the wish to prevent Greece from leaving the North Atlantic Treaty Organisation and their anxiety to retain the facilities in Greek ports which were important to the American Sixth Fleet. The Americans had been rather slow to appreciate the prime importance of the situation in Cyprus itself. But once the Turkish attack had taken place they had worked hard, in full consultation with us, to avoid war between Greece and Turkey. Indeed it was the dependence of both countries on American aid which gave the Americans, and them alone, the leverage to insist upon a ceasefire.

The Prime Minister, summing up a brief discussion, said that our Armed Services had achieved an outstanding success in bringing the Service families and so many British and foreign residents and tourists into the safety of the Sovereign Base Areas. There had been some public criticism that a warning had not been given to British tourists to leave Cyprus as soon as there was speculation about a possible Turkish invasion. We had been right not to do this: if we had advised British subjects to leave earlier this would have made little practical difference and would have confirmed the Greek Government and their supporters in Cyprus in their suspicion that we were in collusion with the Turks: the danger of Greek-Cypriot violence against our people would then have been much increased. The ceasefire was an important achievement, and although the Americans had been immediately responsible, it was also a success for our own efforts.

Turks agree to meet at Geneva on 23 July (telegram No. 829 to Ankara of 22 July; Ankara telegrams Nos. 810 and 815 of 22 July, WSC 1/11).

[4] The report circulated by Sir J. Hunt (see note 2 above) explained that the Turks had 'badly misjudged both the potential extent of the National Guard resistance and the ability of outlying Turkish Cypriot enclaves to hold out until relieved'. They had not attempted to secure the deep-water port of Famagusta, and their failure to gain control of Nicosia airport had evidently prevented the rapid build-up essential for a successful operation. 'If', the report concluded, 'the conflict continues the Turks would probably be able gradually to gain the initiative if they succeeded in reinforcing quickly, but there is no question now of a quick victory, and the Greek Cypriots will be able to use captured Turkish-Cypriot enclaves as a bargaining counter when the situation turns against them.' Meanwhile, heavy fighting had continued throughout 21 July in most areas, particularly in Kyrenia and Nicosia.

The Cabinet –

Took note, with approval, of the Prime Minister's summing up of their discussion.

No. 38

Note by Mr. Acland

[*WSC 1/10*]

Confidential   FCO, *22 July 1974*

Note for the Record

The Secretary of State talked to Dr. Kissinger at 4.30 p.m. on 22 July from the House of Commons.

1. The following points were discussed:

(*a*) Kissinger said that the Americans understood that a *coup* had taken place in Greece under General Davos.[1] He doubted if the Greeks would be ready to attend a meeting tomorrow. He suggested Thursday[2] and agreed with the Secretary of State that Wednesday afternoon was the right time to aim for. The Secretary of State asked Kissinger to put all pressure on the Greeks to agree.

(*b*) Kissinger said that Sisco would be returning to Washington. He would send Buffum[3] to be in London first thing on Wednesday morning. He would be fully briefed on Kissinger's own views and could go on to Geneva if necessary.

(*c*) Kissinger said that the Americans were in touch with Waldheim about increasing the UN force in Cyprus. He hoped that the UK would support this move. The Secretary of State said that we would although it would probably involve supplying more troops ourselves. (The Secretary of State subsequently asked me to put this to No. 10 and the Ministry of Defence.)

---

[1] General I. Davos, the Commander of the third Army Corps, stationed in northern Greece, had issued an ultimatum demanding a return to civilian rule.

[2] i.e. 25 July. The Turks had been prepared to postpone the opening of talks until the afternoon of 24 July, and, following Greek protests that they were not yet ready, and telephone conversations which Mr. Callaghan had with Mr. Eçevit and Dr. Kissinger, it was agreed that the talks would be delayed for a further 24 hours (telegrams Nos. 834 and 844 to Ankara of 22 and 23 July, WSC 1/11).

[3] Mr. W.B. Buffum was US Assistant Secretary of State for International Organisations Affairs.

(*d*) Kissinger said that he was seeing Makarios that afternoon. He would play it cool and would be non-committal though he would be friendly. The Secretary of State advised Kissinger to move delicately with this question. He should not get himself isolated in not supporting Makarios. Kissinger said that he merely did not want to enter into any final commitments. The Secretary of State said that we would keep Makarios informed of the plans for the talks and Denktash and Clerides too.

(*e*) The Secretary of State said it was very important to get rid of Sampson quickly. Kissinger said that he could count on American support for this.

2. Dr. Kissinger subsequently telephoned again at 17.00. He said that the Americans certainly did not want Sampson as the final outcome but before they turned on him they wanted to see what the general package looked like. He would keep Makarios in play but not go overboard for him. The Secretary of State said that perhaps Clerides was the right man to aim for on a temporary basis but there would have to be elections subsequently and Makarios would have to be able to run in them. Getting rid of Sampson seemed to be the first point in any package. Sampson could not remain for long. Dr. Kissinger said that he would not oppose the holding of elections. He thought that he supported the Secretary of State on procedure and probably on the outcome. The Secretary of State said he expected support for both.[4]

3. Dr. Kissinger said that although the process had been very painful the present situation was probably a net gain for the West.

A.A. Acland

[4] At 6.15 p.m. Mr. Callaghan telephoned Dr. Kissinger again. He informed Dr. Kissinger that he was unable to contact Mr. Eçevit on the telephone, and asked Dr. Kissinger to tell Mr. Eçevit, if he could reach him, that in response to a Turkish appeal for UN reinforcements to deal with inter-communal strife Britain would be offering two companies of Coldstream Guards and two squadrons of armoured cars. Mr. Callaghan also said that there 'was talk of the Turkish Air Force bombing a UNFICYP camp'. This Mr. Callagahan considered 'intolerable', and he urged Dr. Kissinger to warn Mr. Eçevit 'in general terms that if this happened we (the British) "would stop them"' (note by Mr. Acland of 22 July).

No. 39

Sir R. Hooper (Athens) to Mr. Callaghan

FOG No. 376 Telegraphic [WSG 1/8]

Immediate. Confidential   ATHENS, *23 July 1974, 7.30 p.m.*

Repeated for information to DA[1] Ankara, DA Nicosia.

From DA. MoDUK[2] for D13 West FCO for SED. Sitrep 8[3]

First. General. Champagne flows in Athens since announcement at 1600 hrs that military Junta would hand over to political administration. Gen. Davos Commander C Corps attended meeting convened by President Gizikis this afternoon and is reputed to have guaranteed the support of the army in the north to a new Government. It is significant that General Angelis former C-in-C armed forces and subsequently Vice President to Papadopoulos is alleged to have attended this meeting.[4]

He is firm supporter of NATO.

Second. Army Greeks continue to reinforce Greek-Turkish border. Reported by Shawcross newly appointed Times correspondent on border.

Third. Hellenic Navy. Remains at sea. Ferries *Adonis* and *Cyclades* have been painted with red cross markings presumably to evacuate casualties from Cyprus.

Fourth. HAF.[5] Olympic airways have been flying troops to Rhodes.

[1] Defence Attaché or, in missions in Commonwealth countries, Defence Adviser.

[2] Ministry of Defence.

[3] Situation Report No. 8.

[4] Shortly after midday Sir R. Hooper had reported in Athens telegram No. 289 that there were widespread reports that the Greek Government was about to fall and that Gen. Gizikis, was 'holding a meeting with "old" politicians to try to form a new government'. It later emerged that as a result of this meeting Mr. C. Karamanlis, a former Prime Minister, had been invited to return from his self-imposed exile in Paris to form a government. He was sworn in as Prime Minister during the early hours of 24 July.

[5] Hellenic Air Force.

No. 40

Mr. Callaghan to British Representatives Overseas

Guidance No. 96 Telegraphic [WSC 1/10]

Confidential   FCO, 25 July 1974, 4 p.m.

My tel[egram] Guidance No. 93:[1]
Cyprus

We regret that the forecasts in paragraph one of our guidance telegram under reference were so quickly and amply fulfilled.[2] We now attempt a fresh start in a completely new situation.

2. Instructions for use.

Paragraphs 3-9 are for your background guidance. The remainder may be used freely as necessary.

3. Following the Turkish military intervention, all efforts were devoted to the cessation of the fighting and the protection and evacuation of British and other civilians. Diplomatic activity, including an incessant stream of personal telephone conversations between the Secretary of State and Dr. Kissinger, and the Turkish and Greek Governments, was frenetic. So were the activities of Mr. Sisco, Dr. Kissinger's representative in the area. All this culminated in the early hours of 22 July in Greek and Turkish acceptance of the ceasefire called for in Security Council Resolution No. 353. The Resolution now constitutes the basis for further action.

4. The ceasefire was slow to take effect and has appeared fragile. During 24 July, the gravest threat to its continuation centred upon Nicosia airport where the United Nations force had assumed control but which appeared subject to threat of Turkish attack, HMG took prompt and effective steps to reinforce UNFICYP from British forces in the island.[3] We also deployed from UK a force of Phantom aircraft which will remain under UK, not UNFICYP, control. The Turkish Foreign Minister has now assured the

---

[1] This telegram of 20 July reviewed developments in Cyprus since the overthrow of Archbishop Makarios. It pointed out that there was 'strong circumstantial evidence to suggest that the régime in Athens were closely involved in the execution, if not the planning, of the coup'.

[2] *V. ibid.* The first sentence of this paragraph stated: 'In the current very fast moving situation this guidance may, at least on details, be out of date by the time you receive it.'

[3] During a telephone conversation with Mr. Eçevit at midday on 23 July Mr. Callaghan said that ninety minutes earlier the UN Commander in Cyprus had reported that Turkish forces were attacking Nicosia airport in battalion strength in violation of the ceasefire. Mr. Eçevit claimed that neither he nor the Chief of the Turkish General Staff had any information regarding this (record of telephone conversation between Mr. Callaghan and Mr. Eçevit on 23 July at 12.45 p.m.). Such reports had seemed likely to upset efforts to persuade the Greek Government to send representatives to Geneva. As Mr. Wiggin warned Mr. Acland in a minute of 24 July, the Greeks were in a 'very jittery state' and believed that violations of the ceasefire were continuing (WSC 1/11).

UN Secretary-General that Turkey had no intention of trying to take possession of the airport 'by force, the threat of force or other coercive means'. Nevertheless, we are far from assuming that the ceasefire will hold, and there is room for considerable doubt about the Turkish Government's information about and control of Turkish military activity.

5. The Secretary of State, once the Greek and Turkish Governments had publicly announced their acceptance of the ceasefire, immediately made a specific proposal for the tripartite negotiations called for in Paragraph 5 of Resolution 353. (The three Governments are of course the guarantors under the 1960 Treaty.) But before this could be agreed, there were welcome developments in both Cyprus and Greece, with the disappearance of Sampson[4] and the change of government in Athens. HMG unreservedly welcome both.

6. As a result the opening of the tripartite talks in Geneva was inevitably somewhat delayed, but all three Foreign Ministers with their delegations are proceeding to Geneva today (25 July).[5]

7. Despite the favourable changes in the situation in both Athens and Nicosia, the problems confronting the Geneva meeting are formidable. Its prime objective must be to reinforce the ceasefire and to ensure, in terms of Paragraph 7 of Resolution 353, that peaceful conditions are restored as soon as possible. As part of this objective, it will undoubtedly be necessary to make a start on discussion of the restoration of constitutional government in Cyprus and thus to offer Turkey in particular an incentive to maintain the ceasefire. Since the Foreign Ministers will expect to meet only for two or three days in this round, while there will no doubt be a first exchange of views, the chief practical result is expected to be agreement on the establishment of continuing machinery at working level. The Foreign Ministers' Conference is by definition tripartite, but it will no doubt be necessary for the continuing machinery to make provision for the participation of Cypriot representatives including both communities.[6] A representative of the UN Secretary-General will probably participate as an observer in the Foreign Ministers' meeting.[7] The Americans will also be

---

[4] On 23 July Mr. Sampson resigned, and Mr. Clerides assumed the Presidency of Cyprus.

[5] During a telephone conversation with Mr. Callaghan at 4 p.m. (GMT) on 24 July Mr. G. Mavros, the newly-appointed Greek Foreign Minister, confirmed that he and his colleagues would be arriving in Geneva on the following afternoon (telegram No. 851 to Ankara of 24 July, WSC 1/11). The talks were scheduled to begin in the Palais des Nations, Geneva on 25 July.

[6] At a meeting held in Mr. Callaghan's office on 23 July to discuss Conference modalities it was agreed that Stage I of the two-day Conference would probably concentrate on four items: (1) the opening session to allow Greeks and Turks 'to get their grievances off their chests'; (2) measures to make a ceasefire stick; (3) an agenda for the longer term Stage II; and (4) participation in Stage II ('Preparations for a Cyprus Conference', unsigned minute of 23 July, WSC 1/11).

[7] Sr. Guyer was appointed UN observer at the talks.

represented in Geneva, but it remains to be decided whether and how they should be formally associated with the Conference.[8]

8. It is impossible until the Greek and Turkish governments have stated their positions in Geneva, and probably until Cypriot representatives have also become involved, to make any forecast of the form that restoration of constitutional government may take. The Treaty of 1960 must obviously be the starting point.[9] One crucial element will be future internal security arrangements and in particular the future of the National Guard.

9. You will be aware that Clerides has replaced Sampson as 'President' of Cyprus. This could lead to a difficult situation arising between Makarios and Clerides. It is not wholly clear at present whether Clerides sees himself in an acting role until such time as Makarios can return to Cyprus, or whether he regards himself as having replaced Makarios. However, he seems definitely to be leaning heavily towards the latter. The relevant provisions of the Cyprus constitution are complex. But it is probably fair to state that, in the former case, Clerides would be acting constitutionally, certainly if he could claim Makarios' approval: whereas in the latter he would be acting unconstitutionally.

10. Line to take.

We wish to volunteer as little comment as possible on the constitutional problem at present. You should not take the initiative in raising it. If it is raised with you and you have to reply you should base yourself as necessary on the following points.

(*a*) We continue to recognise Archbishop Makarios as the lawfully elected President of Cyprus.[10]

(*b*) The Cyprus Constitution provides that in certain circumstances the President of the House of Representatives (i.e. Mr. Clerides) may exercise Presidential powers.

(*c*) (If pressed) in a confused and evolving situation we cannot comment on the precise relationship between Archbishop Makarios and Mr. Clerides at present.

[8] Mr. Buffum was appointed US observer at the talks.

[9] In a paper of 22 July, 'British Objectives in a Cyprus Conference', drafted at Sir J. Killick's request, Mr. J. Cable, AUS and Head of Planning Staff, contended that although the 1960 Treaty provided the British *locus standi* and the basis for the Conference, it would be important to prevent conformity with it being regarded as the 'framework for discussions and the touchstone for any proposals put forward'. Mr. Cable maintained that, whatever the original merits of the Treaty arrangements, they had now collapsed, and that HMG should make it clear that 'the touchstone for choosing the immediate measures required to alleviate the present crisis should be practicability and acceptability' (WSC 1/11).

[10] Participants in Mr. Callaghan's office meeting of 23 July were of the opinion: 'Makarios held the key since, unlike Turkish Cypriots, he was not susceptible to outside control. Even a chastened Makarios was likely to be the main obstacle to a long term settlement. The Americans seemed likely to ditch him in favour of Clerides' (see note 6 above).

(*d*) Our High Commission in Cyprus are, of course, maintaining necessary contacts with the authorities there to enable them to carry out their duties.

11. As regards the general situation, you should emphasise, with due recognition of the helpful role played by Dr. Kissinger and Mr. Sisco, that the Secretary of State has throughout made and continues to make unremitting efforts in the discharge of HMG's role as guarantor of the status of Cyprus under the Treaty both to restore and maintain peaceful conditions on the island and to facilitate the return to constitutional government. In all this, HMG have no desire nor indeed power to impose solutions, which must, to be durable, rest upon the consent and agreement of the parties concerned.[11] While they have throughout urged restraint and the Secretary of State has expressed regret that the diplomatic possibilities were not exhausted at the time of the Turkish invasion, the important thing now is to look to the future and to do everything possible to fulfil, through the continued discharge of HMG's role as guarantor, the provisions of Resolution 353.

12. On any suggestion that HMG ought to have restored President Makarios by force, you should quote the Secretary of State's remark in an ITN interview on 19 July: 'It wouldn't be very sensible to put him back by using force if it was against the will of the people.'

---

[11] Mr. Cable argued in his paper of 22 July (see note 9 above) that it should be Britain's long term objective to 'eliminate liabilities and responsibilities disproportionate to our resources and of which we might have to bear the burden unaided'. In the case of Cyprus this would mean progressively reducing 'those British responsibilities not shared with our allies and partners'.

No. 41

Mr. D.H.T. Hildyard[1] *(UKMIS Geneva) to FCO*

No. 722 Telegraphic [*WSC 1/11*]

Immediate. Confidential　　　　　　　GENEVA, *26 July 1974, 11.45 p.m.*

Repeated for information to Immediate Athens, Ankara, Washington, UKMIS New York, Nicosia, CBFNE Bonn, Moscow, Paris.

Conference on Cyprus:
Second Day

Following from Secretary of State.[2]

1. This has not been an easy day but it has ended on a more optimistic note than had earlier seemed possible.

2. We began with a brief tripartite meeting but the remainder of the day's business was transacted in a series of bilateral discussions between this delegation and the two others. At the end of the proceedings, late this evening, Mavros[3] and Günes had a brief talks *tête-à-tête*. The back-drop to our negotiations has been provided by a steady flow of reports, reaching Geneva through various channels, suggesting continued expansion by the Turks of the zone between Nicosia and the north coast which their troops are occupying.[4]

---

[1] UK Permanent Representative to the UN and other International Organisations in Geneva.

[2] In UKMIS Geneva telegram No. 707 of 25 July Mr. Callaghan reported to Mr. Ennals on his discussions during his first day in Geneva. He observed that his tripartite meeting with the Greek and Turkish Foreign Ministers that evening had been 'heavy going. (I much prefer [Labour Party] National Executive Committee.)', and that they had discussed 'interminably' a simple declaration: the Turks insisted on reference to the Treaty of Guarantee and the Greeks were determined to stand on Resolution 353 only. Mr. Callaghan added that judging by that night's performance he was not very optimistic. 'I still', he confessed, 'find it hard to fathom Turkish motives and objectives.'

[3] On 25 July Mr. Callaghan had found Mr. Mavros 'very excitable' and thought it would 'not take much to make him walk out if things [went] badly' (*v. ibid.*).

[4] The FCO replied to an enquiry from Mr. Callaghan as to whether the Royal Navy or the US 6th Fleet could readily stop Turkish reinforcements reaching Cyprus (UKMIS Geneva telegram No. 709 of 25 July), that British air and naval forces at present in the area were sufficient to prevent an attempt by Turkish ships to land reinforcements in defiance of an embargo if the Turks aimed at achieving this without the use of force. If the Turks were prepared to use all the forces at their command, British forces could not guarantee that they could prevent every Turkish ship landing reinforcements: but they could present a 'very considerable deterrent'. Telegram No. 311 to UKMIS Geneva of 26 July further explained: 'Prevention of Turkish reinforcement might precipitate the use of considerable force and could only be achieved by a larger naval presence and increased air force to assure local air superiority.'

3. My objective throughout has been to bring home to the Turks that they would have to concede something and to the Greeks that they would have to accept less than they hoped for if the Conference was to continue. At my first meeting with Günes, I told him clearly that the Turks would have to accept a standstill and the creation of a buffer zone surrounding their troops. They had occupied territory since the ceasefire which they had been unable to gain before it and the world would settle for nothing less than a standstill now. Moreover, if they did not give this much to the Greeks, the Karamanlis Government, which the Turks recognised as being the best they could hope for, would fall. I attempted to persuade Mavros on the other hand that he could no[t] hope to get the Turks to accept immediate withdrawal to the ceasefire positions of 22 July and that he should be prepared to work for a standstill as an interim measure.[5]

4. Günes was initially unyielding, refusing to contemplate the imposition of any restrictions on the Turks' freedom of action under the Treaty of Guarantee: and making difficulties about the presence of UNFICYP in any buffer zone affecting regular Turkish forces on the grounds that if the Turks wished to prevent e.g. a Greek declaration of *Enosis* they would have to fight their way past UN troops.[6] Mavros insisted on the impossibility of recognising Turkish gains since the July 22 ceasefire, explaining privately that to do so, given the weakness of the new Greek Government's position at home, would inevitably result in their fall.

5. After a break in the late afternoon, during which Günes consulted his Government, the Turks reappeared with outlines of a text for a declaration by the three Governments. This covers the modalities of the ceasefire but also raised in stark terms a number of constitutional issues. It gives the Greeks nothing on withdrawal.[7] Nonetheless the ceasefire section represents

---

[5] In conversation with Sr. Guyer on 25 July Mr. Callaghan said that he thought the delegates should spend a couple of days trying to make a provisional ceasefire work, and be careful to describe the arrangements made as temporary. They should meet again, possibly in a fortnight, to see whether the 1960 Constitution should be put into force again or amended, and with a view to removing troops from the island (record of conversation between Mr. Callaghan and Sr. Guyer at the Residence of the British Ambassador to the UN in Geneva on 25 July at 3.30 p.m.).

[6] At a tripartite meeting with the Greek and Turkish Foreign Ministers on the morning of 26 July Mr. Callaghan suggested that they should arrange 'careful monitoring and supervision by UNFICYP of the resupply of troops and troop movements' (record of meeting between Mr. Callaghan, Mr. Mavros and Mr. Günes held at the Palais des Nations, Geneva, on 26 July at 10.50 a.m., WSC 1/13). Meanwhile, Sir R. Hooper urged Mr. Callaghan, in Athens telegram No. 2 to UKMIS Geneva of 26 July, to 'try to find some way of lowering the "threshold" at which the Turks [would] begin to apprehend confrontation with us, with the US, and perhaps more importantly the UN to a point at which Turkish encroachments cease'.

[7] Mr. Günes complained to Mr. Callaghan that he had had to spend a great deal of money on a long telephone call to persuade his colleagues in Ankara to offer as much as they had, and he maintained that, given the danger that Turkey's coalition Government might collapse, there was little room for negotiation. 'I told him', Mr. Callaghan noted in a message to the Prime Minister, 'that the cost of his telephone call was cheaper than a war which could well be the

a distinct advance on the line being taken by Günes earlier in the day. He said he had been surprised by the moderation of the instructions he had received from Ankara. It accepts, for instance, a role for UNFICYP in the buffer zone. A lot of work will be needed to make this text acceptable to the Greeks but when I presented it to Mavros this evening he at least agreed to consider it. As a package it will be quite unacceptable to him but there are elements in it on which we may be able to build. I am working on these.[8]

6. The principal achievement of the day has been that Mavros has been dissuaded from leaving the Conference and returning to Athens as he has regularly threatened to do. It is not impossible that provided the overnight news from Cyprus is not too bad, we may be able to agree on a text before we leave.

7. (For Athens). This answers your tel[egram] No. 3 to me.[9]

---

alternative if Mavros had to go back to Athens with no face saving arrangement at all' (UKMIS Geneva telegram No. 723 of 26 July). During a subsequent talk with Mr. Callaghan, Mr. Günes remarked, with regard to a possible change of government in Ankara: 'It might be preferable therefore to have war with Greece because the alternative would be Turkey detached from the West' (record of *tête-à-tête* conversation between Mr. Callaghan and Mr. Günes on 26 July at the Palais des Nations at 9.30 p.m., WSC 1/13).

[8] When on the evening of 26 July Mr. Callaghan put the latest Turkish proposals to Mr. Mavros, the latter replied that, while he was prepared to consider the Turkish ideas, he could not accept the paper as a 'package deal'. Mr. Callaghan said that 'it was clear that all three sides looked forward to the ultimate demilitarisation of the Island and he himself would be willing to call into question the British bases there if this would contribute to such a solution' (record of conversation between Mr. Callaghan and Mr. Mavros at the Palais des Nations, Geneva, on 26 July at 10.30 p.m., WSC 1/13).

[9] Athens telegram No. 3 to UKMIS Geneva of 26 July requested information on further developments in the Geneva negotiations.

No. 42

Note by Mr. Goodison
[*WSC 1/13*]

Secret   GENEVA, *27 July 1974*

The Work of the Drafting Committee[1]

1. The principal points raised were:

(*a*) *The Treaty of Guarantee.* The Turks continue to be anxious to insert references to the Treaty of Guarantee, which they regard as having given legal cover for the despatch of troops to the Island and for any future military activity they may wish to undertake.[2] The Greeks (and indeed ourselves) consider that the invocation of the Treaty by the Turks in these circumstances means that they are entirely reserving their freedom of action and negating any promises about the limitation of this. But it is a sticking point for the Turks. All we can do is to try to modify the form of their reservation on this point. The best we can hope for is probably a formal oral (not written) statement by the Turks, and we should press for this.

(*b*) *The status quo ante.* The Turks demanded that all Turkish enclaves should be restored to what they were before the fighting began, with the Turkish Freedom Fighters fully operational, all Greeks forbidden to enter them, and UNFICYP protecting them. They decline to consider any improvement in the *status quo ante* before a constitutional settlement is reached.

(*c*) *UNFICYP.* The Turks deny that UNFICYP has the right to oppose the forces of a Guarantor Power or to control its activities. They are willing to accord UNFICYP a limited role only.

(*d*) *The status of the Turkish community.* Many of the Turkish amendments are intended to increase the powers of the Vice-President, and to secure Greek and British recognition of the (illegal and so far unrecognised) Turkish Cypriot Administration. This would prejudice subsequent discussion of the constitutional position as a whole and must be unacceptable to us at this stage.

---

[1] This meeting of Conference's Drafting Committee was intended to prepare a draft tripartite declaration on Cyprus for submission to Ministers. It was attended by Mr. Wiggin, Mr. Goodison and Mr. J.R. Freeland (Legal Counsellor) for the UK; Mr. M.A. Kirça (Turkey's Permanent Representative in Geneva), Mr. E. Yavuzalp and Mr. Barutçu for Turkey; and Mr. D.S. Bitsios (Under-Secretary of State in the Greek Foreign Ministry), Mr. I.A. Tzounis (Tsounis) (Director-General of Political Affairs in the Greek Foreign Ministry) and Prof. E. Crispis for Greece.

[2] Cf. No. 1, note 8.

(*e*) *Turkish military aims.* The Turkish Ambassador to the United Nations at Geneva has said that what is vital to Turkey in this negotiation is:

i. That Turkish troops should not withdraw from their present lines;
ii. That the Cyprus National Guard be withdrawn from areas formerly under the control of the Turkish Freedom Fighters;
iii. That Turkish troops should be able to return fire against them.

(*f*) *Asymmetry between Turkish and Greek Cypriot positions.* The Turks want free movement for the Turkish Cypriots (which they claim is essential for the Turkish Cypriots' livelihood) but want to restrict Greek movement in the old Turkish enclaves and the newly occupied Turkish zone. This position is not compatible with the 1960 Constitution which the Turks claim to be restoring, Also it is illogical, since many Greek Cypriots depend for their livelihood on access to areas now within the Turkish zone. It should be possible to expose the weakness of their position on this.

(*g*) *Arms importation.* The Turks don't want any restriction on arms importation—since they say it cannot be enforced or monitored.

(*h*) *Map.* The Greeks consider that a map should be attached to the Declaration. All three delegations have promised to obtain information about their view of the current position of the Turkish forces and to seek consent to an overflight of Turkish positions by an UNFICYP helicopter. The Turks may not consent to this. It will remain very difficult to establish co-ordinates and to draw a line, particularly since the date and time to which it should refer has not yet been fixed.

2. All these but the last are Turkish points. Since the Turks now have a substantial force in the Republic they have a dominating position and feel themselves able to refuse concessions. Our aim is to secure a really effective cease-fire, since without this war between Greece and Turkey may well ensue, and we have no alternative but to side with the Greeks.

3. All this ignores the political will to reach agreement enunciated by the Greek and Turkish Foreign Ministers at their private meeting on 27 July.[3] It is clear that the Turks at least gave no instructions to their officials to make concessions which would achieve that agreement. Only a further Ministerial Meeting to examine the detailed texts produced by officials can show whether in fact the two sides are prepared to make the necessary concessions to preserve peace.

[3] Not printed. At a meeting of Mr. Callaghan, Mr. Mavros and Mr. Günes, Mr. Mavros conceded that 'he could not settle all the problems now', to which Mr. Günes replied that 'having reached the age of 50 he felt that he had spent too much of his life talking about Cyprus. Never again in his life did he wish to discuss it. He was an optimist and he felt that it should be possible to get it out of the way' (record of a meeting at the Palais des Nations, Geneva, at 10.30 a.m. on 27 July).

4. The Secretary of State may consider the best tactics at that meeting to express sympathy for the Greek point of view, while conceding some minor points of substance to the Turks. He will wish to bear in mind that the Greeks need a cease-fire more than the Turks; it is the latter therefore who most need manoeuvring into an agreement.

5. With a break of an hour for dinner the session lasted 14 hours. I recommend that the Ministerial Meeting be kept shorter than this.[4]

---

[4] Cf. No. 45.

No. 43

Mr. Olver (Nicosia) to Mr. Callaghan

No. 451 Telegraphic [WSC 1/10]

Priority. Confidential   NICOSIA, *27 July 1974, 5.45 p.m.*

Repeated for information to Priority UKMIS New York, UKMIS Geneva, Athens, Ankara, HQBFNE.

My telegram No. 446:[1]
Cyprus Settlement

1. The following are the main political points raised.

(*a*) Denktash confirmed that the Turkish aim was an independent Cyprus with autonomy for each community's canton within a federal structure. They did not want partition: this would inevitably lead to double *enosis*. They were determined on the other hand to put an effective end to Turkish fears of discrimination. They hoped that, given time, cooperation between the communities would grow. The present opportunity would be used to make sure that the Turkish Cypriot community was able to stand up for itself and could no longer be disregarded or bullied. Denktash expected that the broad principles would be quickly settled in Geneva and that there would then be a fairly brisk negotiation between him and Clerides here over the detailed administrative and constitutional arrangements. He fully agreed that the prospects of reaching this sort of agreement with anyone but Clerides were slight and he accepted the force of my plea to do everything he

---

[1] In Nicosia telegram No. 446 of 27 July Mr. Olver informed Mr. Callaghan that he would be seeing Mr. Clerides and Mr. Denktash that morning. Mr. Olver noted that Mr. Clerides was 'apparently still willing to embark on negotiations with the Turks on the basis of the present territorial situation', but Mr. Olver judged any further perceptible Turkish 'adjustment' would render this impossible.

could to help keep Clerides in power—though he feared this would amount to very little.[2]

(*b*) Clerides took a remarkably similar view of the intercommunal situation. There were in his view two possibilities: partition or a federal solution. The former would lead to double *enosis*. The latter would start off with two autonomous cantons, but the island would remain independent and in the course of time cooperation between the two would grow. Clerides said that it was only realistic to realise that the situation had now fundamentally changed. He had often warned Makarios to be prepared to give more autonomy to the Turks—in vain. He, Clerides, would be willing to negotiate with Denktash a federal solution based on broadly the present territorial division. (He did not explicitly renounce the claim that the Turks should revert to the situation as at the original cease-fire, but this was implicit in what he said.) Clerides thought he would have the support of the great majority of the Greek Cypriot population in this and the main National Guard leaders had already signified their assent to it.

(*c*) Clerides repeated several times the view that the prospects for a peaceful and positive intercommunal future in Cyprus were potentially better now than before the upheaval: the sort of solution which might now emerge was, he thought, realistic and should prove stable. But it all hinged on there being no further breaches of the cease fire and on the maintenance of a sharp negotiating momentum. The fact that he had succeeded Sampson had given rise to hopes of peace and an intercommunal settlement. He must be able to show results in this direction. Otherwise his position, already delicate, would become precarious.

(*d*) On his internal position, Clerides said that he was gradually consolidating his hold over the extreme right wing and was developing excellent relations with the National Guard. They now supported him and obeyed his orders. He had been under pressure to replace the Minister of the Interior (Pantelis Dimitriou) by an ex-EOKA National Guard officer: he had flatly refused and threatened to resign, and this hurdle was now passed. But his situation remained very delicate and he needed all the support he could get.[3]

---

[2] Mr. Olver observed in his telegram No. 446 (*v. ibid*): 'Clerides is much the best and the strongest leader that we can expect to see here in the foreseeable future. Although it is not easy to forecast prospects of reaching a sensible political settlement, they look immeasurably greater under him than under any other prospective President, including Makarios. I hope therefore that the need to help Clerides retain power can also be borne predominantly in mind.'

[3] Of Mr. Clerides's political future, Mr. Olver wrote in his telegram No. 446 (*v. ibid.*): 'Although it remains true that Clerides has the support of majority political opinion from both right and left wings, his position is nonetheless very delicate. The threat comes from extreme right wing EOKA elements, not yet under any real political control and all heavily armed.'

(e) On the constitutional position, Clerides said he had to be careful not to call himself acting President, which would infuriate his right wing support, not [*sic.*] to claim any permanence for his appointment, which would alienate the left. He considered it essential that he should remain in office through the coming period of inter-communal negotiation and reconstruction which he of all Cypriots was best qualified to handle. Thereafter, the question of a permanent appointment could be considered. (He has stated publicly that elections for the Presidency should then be held.) Clerides had advised Makarios that it would be better in the present troubled situation for Makarios to avoid making statements or trying to take any active part in the island's affairs: and he claimed that Makarios had accepted this advice. He had also disuaded Makarios from going to Geneva: Makarios would he thought settle for a bit in London. He thought that any attempt by Makarios to return to the island now or in the near future would lead to civil war: in the longer term, things might change.[4]

[4] In his telegram No. 446 (*v. ibid.*) Mr. Olver advised Mr. Callaghan 'whatever our constitutional view, I hope that we can, in order to avoid undermining Clerides, refrain as far as possible from widely publicised statements supporting the return of Makarios to Cyprus'.

No. 44

Note by the Defence Policy Staff of the Chiefs of Staff Committee

DP Note 210/74 [DP 13/441/1]

Secret   CABINET OFFICE, *29 July 1974*

The Strategic Importance of Cyprus and Implications of Demilitarisation

Introduction

1. While at the Geneva Conference on Cyprus the Secretary of State for Foreign and Commonwealth Affairs has telegraphed that he was increasingly interested in the idea of total demilitarisation of the island and that this might involve the abandonment of the Sovereign Base Areas (SBAs). He agreed with the US representative that both countries should make an assessment of the strategic value of Cyprus and of the implications of demilitarisation.[1]

[1] During their talks on 26 July (see No. 41) Mr. Callaghan asked Mr. Günes whether demilitarisation in which all troops were withdrawn from Cyprus with UN forces using one of the SBAs was a possibility. Mr. Günes replied that he was certainly in favour of demilitarisation on the 'condition' that the island 'should not fall into the hands of the Soviet Union' (record of a *tête-à-tête* conversation between Mr. Callaghan and Mr. Günes on 26 July, WSC 1/13). The next day Mr. Callaghan told Mr. Buffum that so long as the SBAs existed they gave the Russians an excuse to claim that demilitarisation was a fraud, and that he was inclined to think

Aim

2. To summarise the strategic importance of Cyprus, including the SBAs, to the UK and to assess the military implications of total demilitarisation.

Strategic Importance

3. The COS[2] examined the importance to the UK of military facilities in Cyprus in March 1971 and this was subsequently re-affirmed in October 1973. ...[3] The more important points covered in these studies were:

... [4]

(*b*) *Air Reconnaissance and Maritime Support.* Akrotiri airfield provides an excellent base for the conduct of air reconnaissance and maritime support operations in the Eastern Mediterranean.

(*c*) *Air Defence.* Ground radars and air defence fighters in Cyprus provide a valuable extension of the NATO air defence system.

(*d*) *Southern Flank of NATO.* The UK's position in Cyprus is important to the cohesion of NATO's vulnerable Southern Flank and there is good reason to suppose that the UK would be able to use the defence facilities in Cyprus, including the Vulcan force which is targeted in conjunction with SACEUR's GSP,[5] without serious interference, in the event of hostilities with the Warsaw Pact.

(*e*) *Soviet Denial.* UK military presence in Cyprus denies a strategically valuable site to Soviet penetration.

(*f*) *CENTO.*[6] The facilities in Cyprus make possible an effective declaration of UK air forces to CENTO (these are the only forces declared to CENTO). This UK support for CENTO also benefits NATO in bolstering the Southern Flank.

(*g*) *Staging Post.* RAF Akrotiri is a secure and important staging post on the military route to the Middle and Far East.

(*h*) *Training.* There are valuable training facilities and rights in Cyprus for all three Services.

(*j*) *Support for the UN.* The provision of UK force contributions and logistic support for UNFICYP is an effective way of actively supporting the UN.

(*k*) *Internal.* The UK military presence in Cyprus provides an important element in the maintenance of stability in the island. Such stability in turn facilitates the use of the bases.

---

that the strategic value of the SBAs was less than formerly (UKMIS Geneva telegram No. 726 of 27 July). In a letter to Mr. Hockaday of 29 July Sir G. Arthur, DUS responsible for superintending the FCO's Defence Department, requested this assessment on Mr. Callaghan's behalf.

[2] Chiefs of Staff.

[3] A sentence is here omitted.

[4] A sub-paragraph is here omitted.

[5] Supreme Allied Commander Europe's General Strategic Plan.

[6] Central Treaty Organisation.

Defence Review

4. In the Defence Review[7] the Chiefs of Staff, in formulating the Critical Level, assessed this as the minimum level of forces which, in their judgement, the UK needs to contribute to NATO to preserve the confidence of allies in the continuing credibility of NATO strategy. Under this concept it was assessed that Cyprus, in common with all other Mediterranean and non-NATO commitments, was not so strategically vital to the UK, despite its importance to the cohesion of NATO's Southern Flank, as to merit inclusion at the expense of support for the key areas of NATO.

5. The Steering Committee,[8] however, recognised that it might be decided that the UK must retain some presence in Cyprus ...,[9] especially as withdrawal from either or both of the SBAs would be likely to lead to severe tension between Greece, Turkey and Cyprus. In this case they stated that a detailed study of force levels would be required. ...[10]

Demilitarisation

6. *Concept.* No definition has yet been provided of demilitarisation in the context of Cyprus but it is assumed that the basis would certainly be the withdrawal from the island of the Greek and Turkish National Forces, the disbandment of the Cypriot National Guard[11] and the Turkish Freedom Fighters; and possibly, also, under total demilitarisation, the disbandment of UNFICYP and the withdrawal of all UK forces from the island including the SBAs. It has been suggested that law and order would be maintained by the police supported by a lightly armed local gendarmerie of about 4,000 men. Unless other arrangements for the logistic support of UNFICYP were made, the Force could not continue to operate in its present form if the UK forces were withdrawn from the SBAs.

7. *Timescale.* It is considered that demilitarisation could only be achieved in a phased programme, which would involve detailed and protracted negotiations. Even if the principle were to be accepted in the near future the actual withdrawals could only take place if and when peace and stability were established on the island. As far as the UK is concerned, final withdrawal from RAF Akrotiri would probably have to be timed to fit in with the plans for commitments further East, including the option to reinforce Hong Kong.

[7] See No. 10, note 1.

[8] *V. ibid.*

[9] Words are here omitted.

[10] A sentence is here omitted. The Steering Committee's draft report to Ministers, submitted on 9 July, pointed out that Britain's position in Cyprus was 'important to the cohesion of NATO's southern flank' (DP 5/3).

[11] The current strength of the Cyprus National Guard was estimated at about 10,000 men.

8. *Prospects for Stability*. In general the SBAs are welcomed by both communities because of the economic contribution they make to the island and their stabilising influence. On the other hand, the SBAs exist, *de facto* if not *de jure*, by courtesy of the Cypriot people who could quickly render them untenable if they wished. Because of the large number of illegal or unregistered firearms, the history of inter-communal bitterness and recent strife, the prospects for stability even with an effective police force, backed by an armed gendarmerie, are poor. The British High Commissioner's assessment of the present state of the Cypriot police is that they are completely demoralised.

9. *Guarantees of Security*. If the Republic of Cyprus were eventually to be totally demilitarised it would be necessary to seek guarantees from, at least, the US and the USSR. These would probably only be acceptable under UN auspices and thus other nations, including the UK, could be involved in future peace keeping operations in the Republic.

10. *Future of Military Facilities*. There could, in fact, be advantages in UK forces leaving under a guarantee of total demilitarisation of the island rather than through a unilateral withdrawal under the Defence Review. The former should ensure the denial of military facilities on the island to the Russians ...[12] Against this has to be balanced the fact that demilitarisation might eventually create the right atmosphere for a take-over by AKEL (the Cyprus Communist Party) and thus to an increase of Russian influence and Soviet access to the airfields, ports and intelligence facilities.

11. *US Interests*. ...[13] The US has ...[14] used the facilities on the island for a number of purposes connected with the Arab-Israeli conflict, in particular air reconnaissance and the clearance of the Suez Canal. The US observer in Geneva has stated that Cyprus might be an important ancillary base in any future Middle East conflict. Thus any consideration of total demilitarisation will need to be undertaken in close consultation with the US.

Conclusions

12. We conclude that:

(*a*) *Strategic Importance*. The events of the last fortnight have not altered the strategic importance of Cyprus to the UK, nor the judgement that the retention of military facilities there cannot be justified at the expense of the Critical Level. However, they have re-emphasised the necessity of finding some permanent solution to the political stability of the island if the Southern Flank of NATO is not to be seriously endangered.[15]

[12] A clause is here omitted.

[13] A sentence is here omitted.

[14] A word is here omitted.

[15] When this note was discussed by the COS Committee on 30 July, Air Chief Marshal Sir A. Humphrey, the Chief of the Air Staff, stated that he thought the study had seriously

(b) Demilitarisation

(1) Total demilitarisation could meet the Chiefs of Staff requirement, in order to meet the Critical Level, to withdraw forces from Cyprus; with the possible attendant advantage of guarantees for the Island's security by the UN and the super powers.

(2) Demilitarisation in any form would be a long, complicated, contentious and most difficult process, still carrying with it the risk of a sudden requirement for military reinforcement/intervention to restore peace. If the UK still occupied the SBAs, the UK would inevitably be involved in such operations.

Recommendations

13. We recommend that on the basis of this paper, and in the light of the Chiefs of Staff discussion, the Secretary of State should be briefed for the OPD[16] meeting on Wednesday 31 July[17] that the Chiefs of Staff consider that:

(a) There could be advantages in the demilitarisation of Cyprus, especially if it enabled the UK to withdraw from the island in the longer term with the least military and political penalties.

(b) Demilitarisation is likely to prove a most complex subject, which requires detailed study in conjunction with the US before any definite proposals can be formulated.

(c) It will be difficult to complete such a study in advance of a decision on Cyprus in the context of the Defence Review.

A.S. MORTON
Rear Admiral
Assistant Chief of the
Defence Staff (Policy)

---

underestimated the strategic importance of Cyprus to the Western Alliance and the practical problems of initiating and enforcing demilitarisation. He considered that the assumption that Cyprus had little effect on the strategic military balance was unfounded since its value would increase with the re-opening of the Suez Canal (COS, 22nd. mtg., 30 July).

[16] The Cabinet's Defence and Oversea Policy Committee.

[17] The Defence and Oversea Policy Committee met on the morning of 1 August to discuss progress with the Defence Review (OPD(74) 13th mtg., DP 5/3).

No. 45

Mr. Hildyard (UKMIS Geneva) to FCO

No. 748 Telegraphic [WSC 1/11]

Flash. Confidential   GENEVA, *29 July 1974, 7.10 a.m.*

Repeated for information to Flash Athens, Ankara, CBFNE, Washington, UKMIS New York, and to Immediate UKDEL NATO Paris, Moscow.

Following from Secretary of State.
My telegram No. 743:[1]
Cyprus

1. The Ministerial meeting, with advisers present, began at 1600 Geneva time on 28 July and went on through the entire night without a break, apart from a few short recesses for consultations. I took the other Ministers through the draft which officials had prepared and every passage in square brackets was exhaustively discussed. Concessions were made at various points, mainly by the Greeks, though with some minor changes on the part of the Turks.[2] At about 0430 we reached a text which seemed fairly satisfactory. It was hard work getting Mavros and Günes this far and there were times when it looked as though the talks would break down completely.[3]

[1] In this telegram of 28 July Mr. Callaghan reported that during a meeting with Mr. Günes and Mr. Mavros that morning the 'going was sticky, with Günes noticeably less co-operative' than on 27 July. None of the disputed points had been resolved, and Mr. Callaghan had had to persuade Mr. Mavros, who threatened to return to Athens for consultations, to stay in Geneva for another meeting that afternoon. Mr. Callaghan thought the prospects 'fairly gloomy' and suggested, via Mr. Buffum, that Dr. Kissinger apply pressure. 'I intend', he added, 'to keep noses to the grindstone and to go through the whole of the draft with the hope of producing at least a text which each Minister can take back to his capital *ad referendum*.'

[2] One of the main sources of disagreement was Mr. Mavros's wish that paragraph 4 of the draft tripartite Declaration should affirm their intention 'to proceed to the withdrawal without delay from the Republic of Cyprus of foreign military personnel other than those permanently stationed there under the authority of international Agreements'. But Mr. Günes insisted that Turkish forces would be withdrawn only when a 'final solution' had been found to the Cyprus problem, and that they must look for a 'broad formula which involved no commitment'. Mr. Callaghan, although sympathetic to Greek demands for a withdrawal of foreign forces, felt they could not expect the Turks to 'leave immediately', and sought to promote a compromise formula which would refer to withdrawal both 'with the least possible delay' and 'after consideration of constitutional problems' (record of meeting between Mr. Callaghan, Mr. Mavros and Mr. Günes at the Palais des Nations, Geneva, on 28 July at 4.30 p.m., WSC 1/13).

[3] Mr. Mavros reminded his colleagues that the Soviet Union had requested a meeting of the UN Security Council, and that it was calling for immediate implementation of Security Council Resolution 353. He would, he said, 'have to fly to New York the next day'. Mr. Callaghan pointed out that if they could not reach an agreement the UN would not be able to do so. 'A

2. Günes then delivered a bombshell by saying that he had to refer the whole text to Ankara and get final authority for it, although he had telephoned Eçevit several times during the night. I then saw him privately. He told me that the Turkish Government was in real difficulties with its generals. He admitted that the army was hardly under control and that violations of the cease-fire were continuing to take place in Cyprus. It was essential that any text agreed here should not be rejected by the military. When Eçevit had told him at an earlier point during the evening that he could not accept a paragraph which Günes had already approved he had not dared to tell us that he wanted to go back on it.

3. I then produced a formula more favourable to the Turkish point of view in the paragraph relating to withdrawal. Günes promised to consult his Government and meanwhile I sold the new text to Mavros.[4]

4. The next news was that there might be some two hours delay before we had final word from the Turkish Cabinet. I got through on the telephone to Eçevit and, far from raising merely the one point which I thought might be outstanding, he said that there were six or seven issues in the Greek attitude which he found unsatisfactory or unacceptable. I was pretty rough with Eçevit, telling him that it seemed clear that he did not want an agreement at all. He then limited his demand to the request that the entire paragraph referring to Turkish withdrawal should be omitted.[5]

5. I am now trying yet again to find a text acceptable to Mavros and the Turks but we cannot go on like this for much longer.

Soviet intervention would not', he added, 'be helpful. There was a prospect of war between Greece and Turkey. They had to make up their minds what they wanted to happen' (*v. ibid.*). On 29 July Mr. V. Safronchuk, the Soviet Acting Permanent Representative to the UN, submitted a draft resolution to the Security Council calling for the despatch to Cyprus of a special mission to verify the implementation of Resolution 353. See *UN Yearbook* (1974), pp. 270-71.

[4] This (paragraph 4) stated: 'In the context of their decision urgently to seek a solution designed to ensure the security of all the people of Cyprus, the Foreign Ministers declared their aim that all military personnel in the Republic of Cyprus other than those permanently stationed there under the authority of international agreements and those whose presence is authorised by the United Nations should be withdrawn with the least possible delay consistent with finding a just and equitable solution to the Cyprus problem. The three Foreign Ministers agreed on the desirability of elaborating measures which would lead to the reduction of the numbers of armed forces and the amounts of armaments, munitions and war material in the Republic of Cyprus and that consideration should also be given to the possibility of its eventual demilitarisation' (chronology of the events of 29 July at the Palais des Nations, Geneva, Annex A, WSC 1/13).

[5] During this telephone conversation, which took place at 7 a.m. (Geneva time), Mr. Eçevit told Mr. Callaghan that he was not satisfied with the current text of the draft Declaration 'in so far as it related to: the position of the Vice-President; withdrawal; Nicosia airport; recognition of the Turkish Cypriot Administration; and Greek maltreatment of Turkish villagers' (*v. ibid.*).

No. 46

Mr. Hildyard (UKMIS Geneva) to FCO

No. 757 Telegraphic [WSC 1/11]

Flash. Confidential   GENEVA, *29 July 1974, 9.08 p.m.*

Repeated for information to Flash UKMIS New York, Athens, Ankara, Nicosia, Immediate UKDEL NATO, Washington, Paris, Bonn, Moscow

Following from Secretary of State
My tel[egram] No. 748:[1]
Cyprus

1. This telegram summarises events from about 0700 hours to 2130 hours today, a period during which there were no trilateral meetings.

2. My first attempt at yet another formula on withdrawal acceptable to both Turks and Greeks was acceptable to the former but not to the latter. At about the same time we were also informed that the Turks had had second thoughts about another aspect of the then current draft Declaration in that they wished to delete a quotation from the Treaty of Guarantee relating to the basic articles of the constitution.[2] The Greeks reacted very badly to this too.

3. At about 1400 hours I had a long private session with Günes out of which evolved a new formula on withdrawal, largely of his making, which I thought might well be acceptable to the Greeks. He made clear he was putting it forward on a 'personal' basis and undertook to seek Ankara's approval with utmost urgency.[3]

---

[1] No. 45.

[2] During the trilateral Ministerial meeting on 28-29 July (*v. ibid.*) Mr. Günes had sought the agreement of Mr. Callaghan and Mr. Mavros to the insertion in the draft Declaration of a sentence reserving Turkish rights under the 1960 Treaty of Guarantee. Mr. Callaghan had thought it 'reasonable' to insert something of this kind at the end of the Declaration, but Mr. Mavros argued that since there were divergent interpretations of the significance of Article 4 of the Treaty (the Greeks maintaining that it gave no government the right to land troops on the island), there should be a separate statement to the effect that each delegation reserved its opinion on the meaning of the Treaty. Agreement was eventually reached on the text of a separate statement proposed by Mr. Callaghan and to be signed by each delegation. This made it clear that the adherence of the three Governments to the Declaration 'in no way prejudiced their views on the interpretation or application of the 1960 Treaty of Guarantee or their rights and obligations under that Treaty' (record of meeting between Mr. Callaghan, Mr. Mavros and Mr. Günes at the Palais des Nations, Geneva, on 28 July at 4.30 p.m., WSC 1/13).

[3] This stated: 'The three Foreign Ministers agree to implement Resolution 353 in its entirety and within the shortest possible time, as the situation improves in the Republic of Cyprus and as a just and lasting solution is found to the problem of Cyprus permitting the re-establishment of peace and security in the Republic of Cyprus' (UKMIS Geneva telegram No. 756 of 29 July).

4. After a fair lapse of time the Turkish delegation gave us Ankara's 'revised' version of the Günes/Callaghan formula. The English texts of the original and revise are in MIFT. It will be clear from cursory comparison that, while the original might be acceptable to the Greeks in their present circumstances, the 'revised' would be totally unacceptable.[4]

5. With time marching on I decided for reasons mentioned later in this telegram that we would have to force the pace. I saw Mavros and showed him both texts explaining their status and emphasising that I was doing so unofficially. He immediately confirmed that, whereas he was prepared to accept the original, the revise was totally unacceptable. He said that he would be giving a press Conference at 5 pm local time at which he would announce failure and his immediate departure. (Earlier in the day I had discouraged him from going to Brussels for a NATO Council meeting).

6. I told Mavros that Greeks, Turks and British in Geneva alike were far too tired by then to take hasty decisions. I said that I [was] fully prepared to make the question of the rival texts on withdrawal a breaking point and to face the Turks with a specific time limit. But we all needed a night's sleep and also time to mobilise such support as we could to encourage the Turks to think again. Things could not go on as they were and I proposed to tell Günes that, as far as HMG was concerned, I had to deliver a diplomatic ultimatum on timing to him. Either the Turkish Government reverted to the original formula on withdrawal by 0930 hours tomorrow local time or I left and made my reasons for leaving publicly clear. Mavros agreed with these tactics and said that he would cancel his press conference and take the line in response to enquiries that the Geneva talks were still in being.

7. I saw Günes again immediately afterwards and laid it on the line. My main message to him was that, while I accepted his personal good faith and integrity, I could not continue to negotiate in present circumstances with what might be described as a highly random telephone wire. I duly delivered my 'ultimatum' and explained the timing thereof, and told him in terms that if the end result was a disaster for NATO and Anglo/Turkish relations, and perhaps many other things, the world would judge where the blame lay. I added that the Security Council would be meeting again tonight. We had no wish to see the problem transferred from Geneva to New York, but equally we could not control events in New York. The Turks would have to defend themselves there as best they could. Günes reacted to all this with a certain dignity and restraint. His basic defence,

---

[4] According to UKMIS Geneva telegram No. 756 (*v. ibid.*), which was evidently numbered out of sequence and sent 22 minutes after the above telegram, the revised Turkish formula stated: 'The three Foreign Ministers agreed that, after the establishment of complete security on the Island and the mutual confidence between the parties concerned within the framework of a lasting and equitable status acceptable to all, consideration should be given to the possibility of elaborating measures which would lead to the timely and phased reduction of the numbers of armed forces and the amount of armaments, munitions and material.'

which I readily accepted, was that he had made it clear to me that the formula on withdrawal which we had agreed was strictly *ad referendum* and he could not guarantee Ankara's approval.

8. Even Turks can be unusually frank in the middle of the night or when on the edge of exhaustion. From a variety of conversations at varying levels I have come to the conclusion that the Turkish delegation here is, and feels itself to be, a cypher. Officials in my party have privately been advised by the Turks that the only way we can hope to reach 'agreement' in Geneva is to get rough and put the maximum pressure on Ankara. At this point, some of our Turkish sources said that the problem is not merely 'the military' but the eccentricities of Eçevit himself and his parliamentary problems.[5]

9. We have kept the Americans fully informed and I have given them the texts in MIFT (I have also put Guyer in the picture).[6] I have asked the Americans to exert maximum pressure on Ankara before the deadline. One senior Turkish official while undertaking to report faithfully and urgently what I had said to Günes urged that I should myself telephone Eçevit again. But I decided this might be counter productive.

10. If we can get over the withdrawal hurdle we will still be left with the constitutional one. But I believe that should prove soluble, subject to all the usual provisos about this extremely difficult negotiation.

11. At the time of despatch there are indications that the Turks have discretion now to produce a tolerable formula for the Declaration. But difficulties have also arisen over the delineation of the standstill lines and the extensions of the buffer zones.

[5] After a meeting with Mr. Mavros at 4.30 p.m., Mr. Callaghan learnt from Mr. P.J. Goulden (First Secretary, Planning Staff) of a message from Mr. Kirça. The latter recognised that the latest Turkish version of Paragraph 4 was unacceptable to the Greeks and that it 'would lead to very unfortunate conclusions being drawn about Turkey's long-term intentions'. He therefore urged 'that pressure should be applied not on Mr. Günes, who was "shattered"', but on Mr. Eçevit. If HMG 'threatened to cause difficulties in the Security Council—and if Dr. Kissinger reinforced these threats—Mr. Eçevit', he thought, 'would probably cave in and revert to the Günes-Callaghan version' (chronology of the events of 29 July, WSC 1/13).

[6] In UKMIS Geneva telegram No. 14 of 29 July to UKMIS New York Mr. Callaghan informed Mr. Richard that that they had 'nearly come to the show down' in Geneva, and that if the Turks were to 'sabotage' efforts to reach an agreed solution, HMG might 'well want to turn the heat on them in the Security Council and elsewhere'. Mr. Callaghan thus thought it all the more desirable that Mr. Richard should try to avoid the adoption of any resolution until the outcome was clear in Geneva.

No. 47

Mr. Hildyard (UKMIS Geneva) to FCO

No. 760 Telegraphic [WSC 1/11]

Immediate. Confidential   GENEVA, *30 July 1974, 10.25 a.m.*

Repeated for information to Immediate Washington, Ankara, Athens, Nicosia, CBFNE, UKMIS New York, UKDEL NATO, Paris, Bonn, Moscow

Following from Secretary of State.
My telegram No. 2 to Washington (now repeated to other posts):[1]
Cyprus

1. Sisco and Eagleburger telephoned to Acland again at 02.00 local time to say that Kissinger had talked to Eçevit at length. After a lot of argument Eçevit had agreed to a formula which reaffirmed the desire to implement the Security Council's call for a cease-fire and peace and the establishment of constitutional government in Cyprus through negotiation. Sisco said that the Americans immediately realised that this selective quoting of Security Council Resolution 353 and without any reference to withdrawal would be unacceptable to the Greeks. For a further 30 minutes Kissinger had argued with Eçevit to get an improvement of the text and also to give more flexibility to the Turkish delegation in Geneva. Eçevit finally agreed to the following formulation but was not prepared to put it forward himself.

'The three Foreign Ministers reaffirming that Security Council Resolution 353 should be implemented, agree that within the framework of a just and lasting solution acceptable to all the parties concerned and as peace, security and mutual confidence are established on the island, measures should be elaborated which will lead to the timely and phased reduction of the number of armed forces and the amounts of armaments, munitions and other war material in the Republic of Cyprus.'

---

[1] In this telegram of 30 July Mr. Acland, who had accompanied Mr. Callaghan to Geneva, informed Sir P. Ramsbotham that during a telephone conversation with Mr. L. Eagleburger (US Under-Secretary of State) he had explained, with regard to the proposed texts of Paragraph 4 (see No. 46, notes 3 and 4) of the Declaration, that the Greeks would require reference to withdrawal of forces from Cyprus 'with the least possible delay'. Mr. Callaghan, who had also spoken to Mr. Sisco, had said that he would prefer any new American formulation 'to come from the Turks as their suggestion since so many proposals put forward by [the UK delegation in Geneva] and accepted by the Turkish delegation in Geneva [had] subsequently been turned down in Ankara'.

Sisco asked whether I would be prepared to put forward this text myself.

2. I then spoke to Sisco myself. I said that I thought I could sell it to the Greeks although it would be greatly improved if some indication of the time scale (for example 'with the shortest possible delay' were inserted after the reaffirmation that Resolution 353 should be implemented). I agreed that I would put it forward provided there was no doubt whatsoever that if it were accepted by the Greeks it would then be acceptable to the Turks. Sisco said that he would get Eçevit's agreement and would only ring me back if there were any difficulty. I also told Sisco that the Turks were being very difficult over UNFICYP and over cooperation with the UN in general and on the military, not [*sic*] here had asked for a wholly unrealistic withdrawal (10 miles had been their initial figure) by the National Guards from the positions occupied by the Turkish armed forces. I asked Sisco to urge greater realism and cooperation on the Turks.

3. We heard no more from the Americans but at 0845 Kirça (the Turkish Permanent Representative in Geneva who had been much involved in the negotiations) telephoned to say that he had received information from Ankara that following consultations in capitals during the night (he specifically mentioned Kissinger's involvement) he should give us a text for discussion this morning. He then read out to Acland the American formula set out above (paragraph 1) but including the words 'in the shortest possible time' after 'should be implemented'. The Turkish delegation have since given us this text in writing. The addition is of course helpful from the Greek point of view.

4. I am putting it to Mavros and will urge his acceptance of it.

No. 48

Mr. Hildyard (UKMIS Geneva) to FCO

No. 761 Telegraphic [*WSC 1/11*]

Immediate. Confidential   GENEVA, *30 July 1974, 12.03 p.m.*

Repeated for information to Immediate UKMIS New York, Athens, Ankara, Nicosia, UKDEL NATO, Paris, Bonn, Moscow

My telegram No. 757:[1]
Cyprus

Following from Secretary of State.

1. During the evening of 29 July Ambassador Kirça of Turkey called on Wiggin. He said he was instructed to lodge a formal protest by the Turkish

[1] No. 46.

Government that the British Government should have seen fit to issue an ultimatum merely because a text elaborated by the Turkish Foreign Minister on a strictly provisional *ad referendum* basis should subsequently have been amended by the Turkish Government in Ankara. The Turks had behaved with complete correctness and goodwill throughout, and there were no grounds for threatening them with ultimata.

2. Kirça then handed Wiggin yet another formula on the withdrawal question saying that he was not doing so on a take-it-or-leave-it basis. The Turkish Government would be prepared to consider suggestions for improvement. He added that when Wiggin had made any comments he wished on the Turkish protest and had studied the draft formula he himself would have some further comments to make on a personal basis.

3. Wiggin said that he would categorise what I had said to Günes as a negotiating deadline rather than as an ultimatum. The practical fact of the matter was that we could not go on sitting here forever going round in circles. The Ambassador would know where we felt the blame lay at present. As for the latest Turkish text it seemed to him to be a variant of its immediate Turkish predecessor. As such he was sure it would be totally unacceptable to the Greek Government and that we ourselves would not be able to support it.

4. From then on Kirça spoke 'personally'. He made clear that both the protest and the latest formula were part of a face-saving device. He said that Günes would be prepared to settle for a text which in substance was much nearer the text he and I had worked out together (text in my telegram No. 758)[2] provided there were some differences of language. Wiggin asked how one could be certain that any such text would be acceptable to Ankara even assuming it was acceptable to the Greeks. Kirça claimed that this time it would be acceptable in Ankara, if that assessment proved false he expected Günes would tender his resignation. Wiggin said that on that basis he was prepared to recommend to me that I should not insist on the text a [*sic*] provided that before the deadline the Turks had produced another text which was reasonable and likely to gain acceptance. (Wiggin made clear that we were not prepared to produce another one ourselves.) He would make this recommendation on the understanding that, if the new Turkish text was unacceptable or if Ankara went back on it, that would be finally that. Kirça accepted this.

5. Kirça then expressed the hope that we would continue to [do] all we could to bring pressure to bear on Ankara. But he warned that in any direct communication we might have with Eçevit we should not be too brutal. He knew Eçevit well. The man was a mixture of good and bad and at the moment he was in a strange frame of mind. It would be better to make the tone soft however firm the substance.

[2] Not traced. This is probably a reference to the text included in UKMIS Geneva telegram No. 756 of 29 July. *V. ibid.*, note 3.

6. Wiggin thought it very unlikely that I would wish to get in direct touch with Eçevit again overnight. Our position was clear and there was really no more to be said at present. However, we had been keeping the Americans fully in the picture and they were completely up to date on the situation in general and the withdrawal text problem in particular. What they might do about it was not for him to say.

7. Wiggin told Kirça that, just before their meeting, news had reached him from our military advisers who had been meeting with their Greek and Turkish colleagues that the Turks had gone back on their agreement that an UNFICYP helicopter with Greek, Turkish and British officers aboard should carry out a survey as soon as agreement was reached in order that buffer zones could be worked out in detail. He understood moreover that the Turks were insisting that the buffer zones should be 10 kilometres wide all in Greek-held territory possibly with some special provisions made for Nicosia itself. If this sort of thing went on he did not see how we were ever going to be able to reach agreement. Kirça sadly nodded assent.

8. Kirça was urged to let me have a new text on withdrawal as soon as possible and not later than 0900.

No. 49

Chronology of Events of 30 July, 1974 at the Palais des Nations Geneva[1]

[*WSC 1/13*]

Secret

0015-0845
An account of the numerous telephone calls between Geneva, Washington and Ankara is given in Documents No 32-35.[2]
0945

---

[1] This chronology is of uncertain provenance. Along with other chronologies, it appears to have been compiled soon after the conclusion of the Geneva Conferences on the basis of telegrams and other records. It was subsequently included in a volume of printed documents, entitled *The Geneva Conferences on Cyprus, July-August 1974*, which forms part of an internal Departmental Series of SED correspondence (DS (L) 625, WSC 1/13). The original typescript of the document has not been traced.

[2] This is a reference to documents included in *The Geneva Conferences on Cyprus* (*v. ibid.*). Document Nos. 32-34 are: Washington telegram No. 1 to UKMIS Geneva of 29 July; UKMIS Geneva telegram No. 2 to Washington of 30 July; and a note by Mr. Acland of 30 July. None of these is printed here. Document No. 35 is printed at No. 47.

The Secretary of State called on Mr. Mavros and said that he had had a disagreeable session with Mr. Günes the night before. He had issued an ultimatum that a satisfactory draft of paragraph 4 should be produced by this morning.[3] He had asked the Americans to intervene in Ankara. The result had been the Turkish offer of a draft of this paragraph which he thought Greece would find satisfactory (see Document No 35).[4] This formula was then discussed and Mr. Callaghan explained that he did not think it was negotiable. *Mr. Bitsios* asked what 'as' and 'within the framework' meant. *Mr. Wiggin* replied that it did not mean that there would be no Turkish withdrawal without a lasting solution already having been realised. It meant that the Turks would be willing to withdraw gradually in parallel with the implementation of a lasting solution. *Mr. Callaghan* said that you have to have a framework to begin with. It was not the end of the process. *Mr. Mavros* said that we would in fact amend the Security Council resolution by accepting that the Turkish withdrawal would not be immediate. *Mr. Callaghan* said that we faced a situation where the Turks asserted that Resolution 353 did not apply. We had to face the fact that we should not achieve withdrawal until we achieved something like a just and lasting solution. Mr. Callaghan added that the Turks had refused to accept an amendment which he had proposed to paragraph 1 ('in fulfilment of Resolution 353') and that on paragraph 5 the Turks continued to insist on the deletion of the words 'and also the state of affairs established by the basic articles of its Constitution').[5] The Greeks reacted badly to this deletion and the British side argued that the words still in paragraph 5(*b*) 'the re-establishment of constitutional Government in Cyprus' had the same significance as the deleted phrase. *Mr. Tsounis* said that the Greeks wished to insert in paragraph 3(*d*) 'within the shortest time possible'[6] and that they wished to include in paragraph 2 after the word UNFICYP 'and not to exceed under any circumstances one kilometre in width'.[7] A lengthy discussion of Turkish proposals for the size of the buffer

[3] Cf. Nos. 46 and 48.

[4] No. 47.

[5] Paragraph 5 of the proposed Declaration was intended to establish the basis for the negotiations called for in Resolution 353 for the restoration of peace and the reestablishment of constitutional government in Cyprus. The draft which emerged from the experts' meeting (see No. 41) referred to the respect of the guarantor powers for the maintenance of the independence, territorial integrity and security of Cyprus and 'also the state of affairs established by the Basic Articles of its Constitution'. In a meeting with Mr. Callaghan on the morning of 29 July Mr. Günes requested the deletion of any reference to the 1960 Constitution (chronology of the events of 29 July at the Palais des Nations, Geneva, WSC 1/13).

[6] Paragraph 3(*d*) of the Declaration provided for the exchange or release of military personnel and civilians detained as a result of the recent hostilities, under the supervision of the International Committee of the Red Cross.

[7] This would seem to refer not to paragraph 2, which made no mention of UNFICYP, but to paragraph 3(*a*) which provided for the establishment of a 'security zone' of sizes to be

zone followed and it was agreed that this would be discussed separately on a tripartite basis. *Mr. Callaghan* proposed, and *Mr. Mavros* agreed, that the next meeting would be held from 8 August in Geneva, should last three days, and should begin without representatives of the Greek and Turkish Cypriots who should attend at a later stage. The procedures would be established at the first meeting, which might involve the setting up of committees. *Mr. Mavros* agreed and said that no meetings on the topic of Cyprus could be held in London or Zurich, given their associations with the 1959 negotiations.[8] It was also agreed that Mr. Mavros would advise President Makarios not to come to Geneva and not to ask for an appointment with Mr. Callaghan in London, but to await an invitation to call.

1035

Mr. Günes called on Mr. Callaghan who informed him that the Greek side accepted the new draft of paragraph 4. They were not however happy with the deletion which the Turks had proposed in paragraph 5. *Mr. Günes* said that if this proposal had resulted in the Greeks losing their illusions about Turkish intentions, then the solution to the Cyprus problem which was indicated by the Turkish proposal, would be facilitated. There was then some discussion of the position taken up by the Turks in the Military Experts Committee[9] and it was agreed to have a special meeting on this subject. *Mr. Callaghan* stressed that this was a major issue.

1145

Mr. Mavros called on Mr. Callaghan who gave him an account of his last talk with Mr. Günes.

1215

At a tripartite Meeting with officials present, the three Ministers agreed on the text of the Declaration apart from the question of buffer zones and demarcation, which were left for a further Meeting. (See Document No. 36).[10] As regards civilian prisoners, raised by Mr. Günes Mr. Mavros spoke as recorded in UKMIS Geneva Telegram No. 3. (See Document No. 37).[11]

established by representatives of Greece, Turkey and the UK 'in consultation with UNFICYP', at the limit of the areas under Turkish occupation.

[8] The tripartite (UK, Greece and Turkey) discussions leading towards Cyprus's independence from British colonial rule produced the Zurich Agreement and the Lancaster House settlement in February 1959.

[9] At a military experts' meeting the Turks were initially reluctant to accept British and Greek proposals that UNFICYP helicopters should survey the line of the Turkish advance in Cyprus (note on a meeting of military experts held at the Palais des Nations, Geneva on the evening of 27 July). But on 29 July Mr. Günes told Mr. Callaghan that his Government agreed to UNFICYP helicopter reconnaissance (chronology of the events of 29 July at the Palais des Nations, Geneva).

[10] Not printed. This record of a meeting of Mr. Callaghan, Mr. Günes and Mr. Mavros at 12.15 p.m. on 30 July registered their agreement that the second stage of the Conference should begin on 8 August, and that they should be joined by representatives of the two Cypriot communities on 10 August. After expressing his appreciation to Mr. Günes and Mr. Mavros for

1515

The three Ministers met with official advisers and military experts present. *Mr. Callaghan* proposed that the Turkish and Greek commanders in Cyprus with British and UNFICYP officers should meet to establish the demarcation line of the area controlled by Turkish forces. They should begin by comparing their maps of the respective positions. *Mr. Günes* agreed, and said that if there were any differences between the maps, they should be corrected by means of aerial reconnaissance. *Mr. Callaghan* said it was a matter of urgency. There was a danger of incidents if the line was fixed at a leisurely pace. *Mr. Günes* said he would instruct the Turkish officers to co-operate in this work at once. The helicopter reconnaissance should however, for security reasons, be carried out only by departing from the nearest possible place to the area in dispute and following an established route. He hoped that the British Government would make a helicopter available for it. The survey should be carried out by representatives of the three Guarantor Powers rather than by UNFICYP, who should be informed of the results of their work. After discussion, it was agreed that a British helicopter would be used, drawing a large Union Jack to ensure its identification, that an UNFICYP officer should be present and that the Greek officer would be present as a representative of the mainland Government and not as a representative of the Cyprus National Guard. Discussions then turned to the size of the proposed buffer zone. Mr. Günes said that there would be no question of evacuating the city of Nicosia. The same rules could not apply as in the countryside. All that was required was to fix a line in order to make a new Green Line. As regards the airport, he would not go into detail. He had submitted a document on this subject which was to be discussed in Stage II of the Conference and the matter should be left till then. As for the remainder of the zone, a distinction should be made between one from which everyone was to be evacuated, when a wide zone would be impossible, and a buffer zone from which only armed forces would be removed. He did not favour the first alternative. A 10 kilometre zone would prevent mutual artillery fire. Normal life within the zone should continue. The villages should be administered as they had been and should only contain police forces. They should contain neither Turkish nor Greek army forces, nor the Turkish freedom fighters, nor Cyprus National Guard, nor EOKA B. In Turkish villages there should be Turkish police; in Greek villages Greek police; in mixed villages UNFICYP; the number of police permitted should be proportionate to the population and they should be armed only with side-arms. The fields should be cultivated, if necessary under UNFICYP supervision. There was an interest in keeping the zone wide in order to preserve Turkish and

their efforts, Mr. Callaghan 'offered an apology for what might have appeared as roughness on his part in the pursuit of agreement'. Mr. Günes 'indicated acceptance'.

[11] Not printed. UKMIS Geneva telegram No. 3 to Ankara of 30 July documented Mr. Mavros's assurance to Mr. Günes that Turkish prisoners would be liberated within days.

Greek rights and avoid the danger of incidents. *Mr. Mavros* said that at 221400Z [2 p.m. (GMT) on 22 July] the Turkish armed forces controlled 300 square kilometres of Cyprus. At 291800Z [6 p.m. (GMT) on 29 July] they controlled 400 square kilometres of Cyprus. A 10 kilometre buffer zone would add 600 square kilometres, including 33 Greek villages and one Turkish village. The most fertile area of the Island was involved, and he was sure that the Greek villagers would be unwilling to remain in such a zone. The population would be left at the mercy of gangsters and bandits and a sense of insecurity would reign. Such a proposal was impossible. They had to inspire confidence. If it were true that Greek Cypriot artillery were prepared to fire on the Turks then the Foreign Ministers were wasting their time. If he were to accept the Turkish proposal the area in question would die. He asked his colleagues to consult their Governments; there was no negotiating margin left for him. He attached the utmost importance to co-operation between Greece and Turkey. But there was no point in delaying his departure if this point could not be resolved. Mr. Günes had said that he had no objection to the supervision of cultivation by UNFICYP. But what size would it have to be to provide such a service on a 24 hour basis to 34 villages? *Mr. Callaghan* said this was a practical question. They were agreed on the principle of separation; they were agreed on effective cease-fire; they were agreed that they did not want any dead villages. The area proposed by the Turks as a buffer zone was a large area compared with that occupied by the Turkish forces. UNFICYP however was to reach a size of 4,328 by 4 August, nearly twice its previous strength. But he believed that trouble was more likely from trigger-happy possessors of small arms than those commanding artillery; he did not think it necessary to fix a buffer zone designed to frustrate the activities of the latter. If UNFICYP were not to be permitted to have fixed posts in the buffer zone, UNFICYP's task would be more difficult, and this argued for a smaller zone. The arguments for a large zone might be militarily justified but the Foreign Ministers must give them a civilian dimension; they must take risks not acceptable to the military, who were always too careful. The political argument was that a large buffer zone was bound to increase the civilians' fears. The smaller the zone the less the uncertainty. There was a danger that in a large zone further undesirable elements might creep in. They needed to consider the matter in a broader dimension. *Mr. Günes* said that he was not demanding a zone protected against Greek artillery, but they should recognise that they were all Mediterraneans, and hence hot-headed people. UNFICYP had not done their job badly for the past 10 years; in a demilitarised area policed by them, peace should be preserved better than elsewhere in the Island. The alternatives were a security zone of a completely different character (that is to say, one completely evacuated), or none at all. *Mr. Mavros* intervened to report Turkish attacks on various objectives in Cyprus. He would like Mr. Günes to ask the Turkish general what was happening. He proposed a recess meanwhile. *Mr. Günes* promised to do so. The National Guard however appeared to wish to attack the Turkish Army. The only remedy for this state of affairs was rapid signature of the Declaration. He was against a recess. *Mr. Callaghan* agreed. On the main question, it seemed to him that something was required to prevent people straying from one area to another. Perhaps they should accept the principle of a buffer zone but agree to discuss its details at their meeting in a week's time. *Mr. Günes* accepted the idea of a temporary agreement. He said he hoped no-one would be mad enough to extend the area they occupied after signature of the Declaration. In a week's time they would have more confidence in one another. If he reduced his demand to 8 kilometres the Greeks would not be satisfied. He was ready to continue the discussion now or to defer it for a week. *Mr. Mavros* said this was an easy way out. He did not see how the situation would be improved if the discussion were deferred a week. *Mr. Günes* asked Mr. Mavros to state what kind of zone he had in mind. *Mr. Mavros* said he was prepared to accept an evacuated zone not exceeding 500 metres provided that there were no large number of residents to be removed from the zone. Greek language broadcasts from Paris had stated that Turkish troops were advancing in all sectors to anticipate an agreement in Geneva. He did not believe this was so; but the tension in Athens could be imagined. *Mr Günes* said that the Declaration provided for the ascertainment of the limits of Turkish occupation. Mr. Mavros should tell his people that his signature of the Declaration had halted the Turkish advance. At that moment, the distance between the opposing forces was generally more than 500 metres. He was ready to make concessions, say to 5 kilometres, but he did not want to embark on bargaining. *Mr. Callaghan* said that there were unfathomed depths to the situation which had not yet been plumbed. Evacuation of a buffer zone had no appeal for him. He preferred fixed posts for UNFICYP to enable them to control entry. He did not think they had sufficient information to enable them to regulate the matter that day. In a week's time they would be better informed, and on this point he agreed with Mr. Günes. He suggested that in the last sentence of paragraph 3 (*a*) the words 'This zone' should be replaced by 'Pending the determination of the size of the security zones, the existing zone'.[12] It would be reasonable to inform the public that they must find out where the line was before they determined how big it should be. *Mr. Mavros* said that he wished to correct a misunderstanding. It was not his concern to mislead public opinion. He wanted Mr. Günes to look him in the eyes and say whether he feared that Mr. Mavros would order the Greek artillery to fire. He did not object to discussing this next week. But the difference between a Turkish demand for a zone 16, 10 or 5 kilometres wide and a Greek zone of 500 metres was no topic with which to begin their next round of discussions. The lines in Nicosia should be notified as a joint working document to the three Powers on 31 July. *Mr. Günes* said the idea evoked

---

[12] Cf. note 9, above. This sentence provided for the non-entry of forces other than those of UNFICYP into the security zone.

by Mr. Mavros was far from him. From a practical point of view, to halt the forces without a buffer zone would cause problems. There was a difference of character between an extremely small evacuated zone, 100-1,000 metres wide and the 10 kilometre zone he advocated. Mr. Callaghan's proposal for United Nations control of line-crossing was a different proposition. If there were to be sentries with United Nations patrols as well a difficult situation might be created. It was inconceivable that there should be no agreement between them simply because of the security zone. But there could be no solution in the face of Greek insistence on a 1 kilometre zone. There must be a real security zone and not a tenuous line. *Mr. Callaghan* said that they were not going to reach agreement on this subject. They must either consider it next week or look at the longer term repercussions of disagreement. He believed that an evacuated area would lead in the direction of partition, which everyone had repudiated. If they were to defer discussion of the topic they could not define the limits of the discussion now. Meanwhile the details of the line must be communicated to them by the next night. *Mr. Günes* repeated that he thought no agreement possible, now or later, on the basis of an inhabited zone no bigger than 1-2 kilometres wide. It was not a matter of difference of scale but of concept. *Mr. Mavros* said that on the northern frontier of Greece they had a 1,000 kilometre frontier without a buffer zone and without incidents. How was it imaginable then that they could not live in Cyprus without a buffer zone? If Turkey was worried about artillery he was prepared to accept that Greek Cypriot artillery be withdrawn beyond its maximum range. *Mr. Günes* said that no agreement would be possible next week without a buffer zone; and he would not be able to agree to any mission for UNFICYP. *Mr. Callaghan* said he was not willing to discuss the matter for another two hours. He must leave for London. *Mr. Mavros* asked what would happen if they could not reach agreement next week. *Mr. Günes* said he could not descend below 5 kilometres then or later. If this was not acceptable the negotiations were terminated. *Mr. Mavros* said that he was willing to leave the matter for a week. But he did not accept this adjournment on any particular basis. The matter remained absolutely open. He was not facing the general of a victorious army. *Mr. Günes* said he was willing to leave it till next week. He had not formally proposed a 5 kilometre zone for fear they would think he was bargaining, but he had hoped such a width would prove satisfactory. *Mr. Mavros* said it was not possible to draw lines as if in *baklawa*. It was agreed that officials should now prepare the English and French texts for signature and that Mr. Callaghan should communicate them to the Secretary-General of the United Nations on behalf of the three Ministers. The meeting closed about 6.45 p.m.

Officials then, with considerable difficulty, established the English and French texts of what had been agreed, Mr. Callaghan offered champagne to the other delegations and the Declaration and Statement were signed after 10 p.m.[13]

[13] See *Cyprus. Declaration and Statement by the Foreign Ministers of Greece, Turkey and the United Kingdom of Great Britain and Northern Ireland, Geneva, 30 July 1974*, Cmnd. 5712 (London: HMSO, 1974).

No. 50

Mr. Richard (UKMIS New York) to Mr. Callaghan

No. 924 Telegraphic [*WSC 2/522/2*]

Routine. Confidential   UKMIS New York, *2 August 1974, 1 a.m.*

Repeated for information to Routine Ankara, Athens, Nicosia, Moscow, Paris, Washington, UKDEL NATO, CBFNE, Saving Baghdad, Canberra, Jakarta, Lima, Nairobi, San José, Vienna, Yaoundé.

My tel[egram] No. 920 (not to all):[1]
Cyprus

1. In the comparative lull after the latest round in the Security Council on Cyprus, you may find it of use to have a tentative assessment of the UN angle with my guesses on the problems we are likely to face here in the next round.

2. I assume that (*a*) we will continue to want the broad approbation of the Council for action over Cyprus with which HMG are associated and (*b*) UNFICYP will remain, if not absolutely indispensable, highly desirable for discharging the task assigned in the Geneva Declaration and more generally.[2]

3. The Russians clearly pose the major problem.[3] For the next month they enjoy the advantage of the Presidency of the Council. With a

[1] In this telegram of 1 August Mr. Richard reported that the UN Security Council had adopted Resolution 355 which took note of a statement by Dr. Waldheim of 31 July informing the Council of the Geneva Declaration, and requested him to take appropriate action. The USSR and Byelorussian SSR abstained from voting. See *UN Yearbook* (1974), p. 273.

[2] Paragraph 3 of the Geneva Declaration of 30 July pronounced on (*a*) the formation of an as yet undetermined security zone at the limits of the areas occupied by the Turkish armed forces, to be entered only by UNFICYP; (*b*) the evacuation of Turkish enclaves by Greek or Greek Cypriot forces, which would then be protected by UNFICYP; and (*c*) UNFICYP's role in policing mixed villages. See No. 49, note 13.

[3] Cf. Nos. 29, note 7, and 45, note 3. On 29 July Mr. Lunkov delivered to Mr. Hattersley an oral message from the Soviet Government which blamed the situation in Cyprus on 'those NATO circles which, in order to achieve their strategic aims, [were] ready, no more and no

Secretary-General who scares easily, they could disrupt UNFICYP at almost any time.

4. Subject to correction by Sir T. Garvey, I would regard the Russian performance yesterday and today as a somewhat ill-tempered demonstration that the USSR cannot safely be ignored by those more closely involved in the Cyprus crisis. The veto may have been excessive and due more to Malik's disposition than anything else but there does seem to have been an underlying political purpose, designed to establish that we ignore them at our peril.[4] Although the Russians will doubtless take any opportunity to make trouble, I still feel that the tentative assessment in my tel[egram] No. 858[5] remains valid: they will not seriously upset the apple cart and thus risk a major clash with the United States so long as they are not forced into the position of being invited to acquiesce in a decision blatantly contrary to their theology on peacekeeping, or unless they genuinely believe that the continued existence of Cyprus as an independent non-NATO country is at serious risk.[6] If this is right, they may e.g. raise the matter of equitable geographical representation in UNFICYP but not press it to extremes unless provoked.

less, to trample on the territorial integrity and sovereignty of Cyprus'. Mr. Lunkov added that while what the British had been saying on Cyprus was 'not bad on the whole', their statements had 'not always corresponded with British actions' (telegrams Nos. 511 and 512 to Moscow of 29 July, WSC 2/1). Such language caused a good deal of irritation in London, and on 2 August Sir T. Garvey, the British Ambassador in Moscow, complained to Mr. V.P. Suslov, head of the Second European Department of the Soviet Foreign Ministry, that the line the Russians were adopting 'was not merely disobliging, it was counter-productive, and [the] Soviet Government would do well to drop it' (Moscow telegram No. 941 of 2 August).

[4] Late on the evening of 31 July Mr. Y.A. Malik, the Soviet Permanent Representative to the UN, had dramatically vetoed the original draft of Security Council Resolution 355 (see note 1 above). Mr. Malik, whose advisers were according to Mr. Richard 'clearly aghast at his performance', emphasised that his veto was cast on 'procedural grounds', and that he 'would not be steam-rollered without instructions'. However, Mr. Callaghan was reluctant to 'utter a strong public condemnation of this deplorable Soviet performance' until Soviet motives and intentions had been more fully assessed (UKMIS New York telegrams No. 913 of 31 July and No. 915 of 1 August; telegram No. 584 to UKMIS New York of 1 August).

[5] In this telegram of 25 July Mr. Richard suggested that the Russians could treat any alteration in the composition of UNFICYP, such as would result from the UN accepting an Australian offer to supply 600 troops, 'as ground for raising the equitable geographical representation issue'. But Soviet conduct in the Security Council, particularly on 24 July, had, Mr. Richard noted, 'so far been circumspect' and their Acting Permanent Representative had indicated informally to his Australian colleague that 'they would not make trouble' (WSC 10/22).

[6] Sir T. Garvey discounted the idea that the Soviet veto was a 'calculated piece of theatre (Russians make muddles like the rest of us) designed to stop us ignoring them'. He reasoned that the Soviet aim in Cyprus was the restoration of the pre-*coup status quo*, and that while they appeared ready to build on the Geneva Declaration, they might 'be expected to be troublesome about any developments on the ground smelling of *de facto* partition and any permanent military occupation; and to get nasty if the game [showed] signs of going against them' (Moscow telegram No. 944 of 3 August).

5. The Russians seem to have put their money at the UN on Makarios and are likely to continue to work for the return of Makarios or a political associate favourable to the left. But here too they seem from New York to be unlikely to go to extremes.

6. A further problem is posed by the attitude of the non-aligned. With a few exceptions, such as Yugoslavia, who are not Council members, they are now less vocal in their support of Makarios. But they were nevertheless determined not to be associated with the Geneva Declaration and clearly felt very strongly over preserving the independence and territorial integrity of Cyprus, and also over the principle of Cyprus's representatives being free to determine the future of the island. And they will be tempted to fall for the line that the UN, not Geneva, is the appropriate forum for negotiation. Most of them are profoundly ignorant about the historical, military and political realities in Cyprus. They are worried about the role UNFICYP may now be expected to play, the danger that it may meet armed opposition and the risk of its helping to consolidate Turkish occupation of part of Cyprus. They have been brought, with increasing reluctance, through Resolution 353 and on to 355. But it will be difficult to keep them with us.

7. If the foregoing analysis is broadly correct, problems could well arise from the implementation of UNFICYP's role over paragraph 3(*a*) (*b*) and (*c*) of the Geneva Declaration.[7] There would seem to be great scope here for disagreement, particularly over security zones, protection of enclaves and policing of mixed villages, not to mention Nicosia airport. The Secretary-General is therefore right to emphasise the overriding importance of real cooperation from the parties: at the moment this applies particularly to the Turks. A connected problem, particularly relevant to para[graph] 3(*c*) of the Declaration, may be posed by manpower. Will UNFICYP be able to do all that is expected of it with some 5,000 men? The Russians might tolerate some further reinforcements by existing contributors but any question of fresh contingents would raise the composition issue.

8. If further tasks are assigned to UNFICYP at the resumed negotiations there are thus obvious risks and I could not guarantee that we would be able to get the proposals through the Security Council without having to pay what might be an unacceptable price.

9. Waldheim has already raised the question of finance (para[graph] 1 of my tel[egram] No. 907).[8] It seems bound to be raised again and raised soon

---

[7] See note 2 above.

[8] Mr. Richard reported in UKMIS New York telegram No. 907 of 31 July that, when pressed, Dr. Waldheim declined to follow Mr. Callaghan's advice that he should simply apprise the Security Council of the Geneva Declaration, and say that he intended to take the action it envisaged for the UN in accordance with the request from the Greek, Turkish and UK Foreign Ministers. Dr. Waldheim said that he regarded his mandate as limited, that he intended to put it squarely to the Council that new tasks were intended for UNFICYP, and to make it clear that the financial basis required changing. Mr. Richard and his US colleague then persuaded Dr. Waldheim that at that stage he should not raise the subjects of finance, UNFICYP

if substantial contributions are not forthcoming. Again, the mandate could be put at issue. The US Mission have told Waldheim that they are trying to help (no details). You may wish to consider whether we can, particularly by persuading others to contribute.[9] A French contribution would be particularly welcome, as others might follow a French lead. I understand that the French Government no longer has objections on principle but only budgetary difficulties (who has not?) you may wish to thank M. Sauvagnargues personally for the great help which the French mission here gave us over Resolutions 353 and 355: perhaps the question of finance could be raised at the same time.

10. It will be important too, now that we have got him the authority he wanted, to stiffen Waldheim to resist Soviet pressures. This would be easier if help could be given over his very real financial problem. The content of his report to the Council under Resolution 355 will be very important. The next Soviet thrust is likely to be geared to it. This may not be for a week or so, unless in the meantime the cease fire fails to hold.

11. When the Geneva negotiations are resumed, you may wish to bear in mind the attitude of the non-aligned here (para]graph] 6 above). At least the appearance of very close Cypriot association with any future negotiation will be particularly important and, if Makarios is not there, it might help if his reasons were made public: if he could be persuaded to give the proceedings and the Greek Cypriot representatives his apostolic blessing, so much the better. Meanwhile, there is an educational job to be done. I am doing my best here but it might also pay dividends, since consideration of Cyprus by the Council seems likely to continue over the next few months, to try to educate selected governments. Judging by performances here, Kenya should be a priority target.[10]

---

withdrawal from Turkish areas, or the details of UNFICYP's role in implementing the Geneva Declaration.

[9] In telegram No. 579 to UKMIS New York of 31 July Mr. Callaghan instructed Mr. Richard to oppose any attempt to revise UNFICYP's mandate, or any proposal to increase the number of troop contributors 'that could let in East Europeans primarily on the grounds that consideration of such basic questions would inevitably take time and that [they were] faced with an emergency in which immediate action [was] essential'.

[10] During the UN Security Council debate on 31 July on the original draft of Resolution 355 Mr. C.G. Maina, Kenya's Permanent Representative to the UN, condemned, in what Mr. Richard described as a 'singularly unhelpful speech', Greek and Turkish 'aggression' in Cyprus. He went on to say that Cyprus should have taken part in the Geneva negotiations, that the Security Council's intentions were being 'frustrated by manoeuvres to suppress Cyprus's independence', and that the Geneva Declaration was inconsistent with Resolution 353 (UKMIS New York telegram No. 916 of 31 July).

No. 51

Minute from Sir J. Killick to Mr. Goulding

[*WSC 3/303/1*]

Confidential   FCO, *2 August 1974*

Cyprus: the Soviet Attitude

1. The recent APAG[1] paper on the future of détente said: 'The world stands to gain immeasurably if the Soviet Union could be brought to conduct its foreign relations as a responsible state rather than as a faction in a global war'. It seems to me that Soviet behaviour during the Cyprus crisis has oscillated somewhere between these two extremes, perhaps closer to the second than to the first.

Soviet Objectives

2. Soviet aims in Cyprus were well analysed by Mr. Dobbs in Moscow telegram No. 860.[2] The Russians were quite content with Cyprus as it was a month ago: non-aligned, rather shaky, and with ample possibilities for Soviet activities through Makarios, through AKEL and no doubt through covert channels as well. (I still wonder what on earth 41 Soviet 'tourists' were doing in Cyprus. I doubt if they were deserving railway-workers on holiday.) Everything that has happened during July has made matters worse from the Soviet point of view. The original *coup* removed the figurehead on whom the whole situation (so satisfactory to the Soviet Union) rested. It also carried the risk of *Enosis* and the incorporation of Cyprus into the NATO strategic system. The Turkish invasion removed the dangers of *Enosis* (which is why the Russians smiled on it at first) but soon introduced a new spectre: that of partition and perhaps double *Enosis*, or at least a greatly increased Turkish presence on the island, which with the change of Government in Athens, opened the prospect of a less independent and non-aligned Cyprus, more under the influence of, and in closer relations with, two NATO powers. Moreover, Sampson, whom everybody wanted to see out, was replaced by Clerides, a much more credible substitute for Makarios. The change of government in Athens simultaneously removed an embarrassing mole from NATO's cheek and opened the door to a round of successful diplomacy from which the Soviet Union was excluded. The activity lay in London and Geneva, and the credit went to Britain, the United States, Greece and Turkey—in fact to everybody except the Soviet Union itself, and its favoured Cypriot leader, Makarios.

[1] NATO's Atlantic Policy Advisory Group.

[2] See No. 29, note 7.

Soviet Tactics

3. During these three weeks the Russians have found themselves unable to bring to bear their regular levers of power. The special relationship with Washington was useless, because Dr. Kissinger's objectives were clearly the opposite of theirs. (The Russians must know that he opposed the return of Makarios from the start, and they may suspect the CIA of having engineered the *coup*.) France, the traditional Soviet Trojan horse in Western Europe, has remained loyal to the position of the Nine under a fusillade of personal messages from Brezhnev to Giscard. Non-aligned opinion was divided and slow to mobilise. The General Assembly was not in session, and the Security Council was only on the fringe of events.

4. In the circumstances, it is depressing but not surprising that Soviet behaviour has been opportunist, unscrupulous and unhelpful.[3] They emphatically did not like the spectacle of a major crisis developing in an area of keen political and strategic interest to the Soviet Union. Still less did they like seeing this crisis being handled through channels in which the Soviet Union played no part whatever. This situation of powerless concern brought out all the worst in Soviet diplomacy. They gave no credit where credit is due (and have not even so far uttered a word of thanks to us for evacuating their tourists).[4] They lashed out wildly at the traditional Aunt Sally, NATO. They demanded instant access to the Prime Minister, while keeping our Chargé d'Affaires waiting six hours before he was received by a Head of Department in the Foreign Ministry. They showered the world with statements and messages which boiled down to very little except that the Soviet Union was frustrated and upset. Their problems were magnified by the fact that throughout the crisis the Soviet bureaucracy was reacting to a rapidly moving situation, and not dictating events but responding to them: this is what the Soviet machine is worst at. And Brezhnev himself was away in Poland for two or three vital days over the weekend of 21 July.[5]

5. Matters might have continued in this style if Waldheim had not decided that he needed specific endorsement from the Security Council for follow-up to the Declaration of Geneva. For the first time, this put the Russians in the position of being able to influence the course of events, negatively if not positively. It is no surprise that Malik used the veto to prevent the ball being snatched out of Soviet hands before Moscow had time to decide what to do with it.

6. They seem at no stage to have seriously contemplated military intervention. Despite some limited alert measures in the Soviet Union

---

[3] Cf. Volume III, No. 67.

[4] Mr. Hattersley sidelined this sentence and noted: 'Not so. RH.'

[5] In a minute to Mr. Acland, also of 2 August, Sir J. Killick recalled: 'Mr Dobbs, an experienced observer, suggests incidentally that the ineffectiveness throughout of the Soviet MFA may well result from a distinct shift in the conduct of foreign policy to Brezhnev and his personal staff.'

(which they have publicly denied) and some troop movements into Romania/Bulgaria whose scope and significance are obscure, their naval movements in the Mediterranean were discreet.

Future Soviet Intentions

7. Moscow telegram telegram No. 860 is still valid. The main Soviet aim at the moment must be to continue to find some means of controlling events, or at least influencing them significantly. To this end they will seize any opportunities which may occur, either in the United Nations or elsewhere. Their Presidency of the Security Council gives them an advantage which they will exploit to the full, short of actually breaking the rules. When the Geneva Conference reconvenes, they will certainly hope to have more of a presence than a single representative whom nobody consults. They will try to rally non-aligned opinion to their support. Their general objective will be to restore, to the extent that this is still possible, the situation as it was a month ago, i.e. a unitary and non-aligned Cyprus having only weak links with members of NATO and no connexion with NATO itself. This negative aim (to keep NATO out) will be more important to them than the positive one of promoting trouble on NATO's southern flank. This is another case where the Soviet Union emerges more as a '*status quo* power' than as a promoter of instability. Above all, the Russians will wish to maintain undamaged their special relationship with the United States. This means that so long as America is willing to remain on the sidelines of the crisis, there is a good chance that the Soviet Union will do the same.

8. The above was drafted before I saw Sir T. Garvey's telegram No. 935,[6] which makes many of the same points.

JOHN KILLICK

---

[6] In this telegram of 1 August Sir T. Garvey, who had just returned to Moscow, stated that he believed the Soviet Government's main apprehension was that the current Cyprus crisis might be exploited to convert a non-aligned Cyprus under Archbishop Makarios into 'an off-shore island partly or wholly under NATO control'. He thought that the Geneva Declaration would, if fully-implemented, meet many of their requirements, but that they might want 'to hold up the game until they [had] time to weigh the risks ... and until blocking mechanisms [could] be built in designed to safeguard their interests'. The latter, Sir T. Garvey suggested, might include a demand for an East European contingent in UNFICYP.

No. 52

Mr. Olver (Nicosia) to Mr. Callaghan

No. 627 Telegraphic [WSC 1/13]

Priority. Confidential   NICOSIA, *5 August 1974, 3.40 p.m.*

Repeated for information to Priority Athens, Ankara, Washington, Moscow, UKMIS New York, UKDEL NATO, CBFNE

The Second Geneva Conference

1. In the hope that Geneva 2 will take place as planned, it may be helpful to you to have some back-ground thoughts as seen from here.
2. With the good progress made today over demarcation of the cease-fire line,[1] the danger of an unprovoked resumption of Turkish hostilities has receded. But we are aware from many comments, from Denktash downwards, that the area taken by the Turks falls far short of their hopes and plans. In this situation, a real communal pretext such as a serious attack on a Turkish community in Greek-held Cyprus would be a heaven-sent pretext. For this reason it is essential that the intercommunal temperature should be kept down.
3. From that point of view, it is important to keep up the momentum. Any long lapse or interregnum could lead to a dangerous increase in intercommunal tension which on each side remains only just beneath the surface. Meanwhile, far more publicity, local and world-wide, needs to be given to the helpful UN, ICRC[2] etc, efforts to produce a return to normality and to giving the lie to atrocity stories. Perhaps we could help in this. A long stalemate in Geneva would be particularly dangerous from this point of view. If the main constitutional discussions were making no progress, it would be important to devise and spotlight alternative fields in which progress of some sort could be seen to be made.
4. A transfer of the Greek Cypriot population out of the Kyrenia area is going on steadily. This is undoubtedly considered Turkish policy and people are being told that they will never come back. This is tragic, and we must obviously do what we can to contest these forced evictions. In the long run, however, a Kyrenia province largely populated by Turkish Cypriots, with the rest of the island mainly Greek Cypriot, might be communally more stable than the present situation, provided that relations

---

[1] A team comprising British, Greek and Turkish representatives, assisted by an UNFICYP representative, met for the first time on 2 August with a view to verifying the demarcation of the ceasefire line. The main difficulty was over the north-western area where the discrepancy between the original Greek and Turkish lines was at its widest, the Greek line being drawn east of Karavas and the Turkish line approximately half way between Lapithos and Vasilia (Nicosia telegram No. 688 of 8 August).

[2] International Committee of the Red Cross.

between the two areas were firmly controlled. A properly supervised programme of voluntary transfer, once things settled down, would not necessarily be a bad thing. So long as it was seen as a possible prelude to partition, it would be strenuously opposed by the Greeks. But with effective guarantees against partition, and after a cooling off period, cooperation between the two communities to this end would not be inconceivable.

5. A fully federal solution is clearly the least that the Turks will accept. Many Turks here, including Denktash, openly bemoan the slowness of their generals in not grabbing more land. Efforts at constitutional cheese-paring could therefore be dangerous. But there will be many on the Greek Cypriot side, and perhaps also in Greece, who will be thinking along the old constitutional lines of local autonomy, etc. Clerides is not amongst these. He realistically accepts the need for some far more drastic solution. But there is a considerable educational job to be done among both right and left wing here, and particularly among Makarios' supporters, in which he will need all the help we can give him. It will be particularly important for Makarios not to intervene unhelpfully.[3]

6. Partition is I think anathema all round—to the Turks, to most Greeks, and above all to the Russians.[4] It would inevitably lead to double *enosis*, and would sow the seeds of future intercommunal trouble here and tension between Greece and Turkey. We should do all we can to avoid it and work for a genuinely independent, non-aligned Cyprus: non-aligned in Cypriot terms will continue to mean fundamentally pro-British and pro-Western unless we play our cards disastrously.

7. Independence and the avoidance of partition will be closely bound up with the emergence of a genuine federal government superimposed above the two, Greek and Turkish, provincial Governments. With current Turkish pretentions to their own separate Kyrenian state, this may not be easy—but it will be essential.[5]

---

[3] During a meeting with Mr. Callaghan on 1 August Archbishop Makarios made it clear that his aim was to stay out of current events and to keep his options open. The Archbishop said that he proposed to give Mr. Clerides no advice, and implied that, for the present at least, he would refrain from public statements which could be taken as 'interference' or which could embarrass the Greek Government. He did not, in any event, intend to visit Geneva. In telegram No. 408 to Nicosia of 5 August Mr. Callaghan reported that he thought this attitude had its 'good and bad points': the Archbishop was 'not trying to circumscribe Clerides' freedom of action'; but he evidently meant to wait and see the result, to accept it or denounce it. 'I fear', Mr. Callaghan noted, 'it is the latter course which he may have in mind' (WSC 1/14).

[4] Cf. No. 50, note 6.

[5] Sir H. Phillips thought that this assessment of Turkish-Cypriot ideas was an 'accurate reflection of the view' in Ankara. 'If', he observed, 'it goes too far for Greece and involves a breakdown at Geneva the Turks will not mind. If the Greeks walk out the Turks will portray themselves as the righteous party. And freed of the constraint of negotiations they will simply continue to consolidate their position on the island—justifying any continued military activity by the Greek refusal to sit down and talk' (Ankara telegram No. 936 of 6 August).

8. A fresh look will need to be taken at the whole question of guarantees—against both *enosis* and any future Turkish intervention. The latter may well in these new circumstances be the more important (it has been conveniently forgotten that the *coup* here did no more for Greek-held Cyprus than produce the situation that has obtained in Turkish Cyprus for some years). We shall doubtless wish to get rid of the Treaty of Guarantee: since neither British nor Greek military action under the Treaty can be imagined, its chief effect is to provide the pretext for Turkish intervention. But to avoid future tensions over *enosis*, some effective guarantee of continued independence will be needed, perhaps under the UN umbrella: perhaps pointing to some guaranteed neutral status such as Austria, (without of course its Soviet connections). The removal of all foreign troops would form part of this pattern.

No. 53

Steering Brief for the United Kingdom Delegation to Stage II of the Geneva Talks on Cyprus

[*WSC 1/13*]

Confidential   FCO, *7 August 1974*

Introduction

1. Stage II is being held on 8-9 August, with Mr. Clerides and Mr. Denktash, joining for 10 and 11 August. Thereafter talks are expected to continue, with or without a recess, at official level.[1] Talks between the Secretary of State and the Foreign Ministers of Greece and Turkey will take place in accordance with paragraph 5 of the Geneva Declaration of 30 July 1974 and Security Council Resolution No. 353. (Copies attached.)[2]

2. Two problems, which will have to be resolved in the light of events, are:

(i) whether the Secretary of State will wish to be involved in the subsequent ministerial meetings which will probably be necessary;[3]

---

[1] In guidance telegram No. 103 of 7 August Mr. Callaghan emphasised that it was 'particularly important to avoid the impression that long term questions concerning the island [were] being decided behind the backs of the Cypriots'.

[2] Not printed.

[3] Already in a minute of 23 July to Mr. M. Elliott (Private Secretary to the PUS), Mr. Cable had cautioned Sir T. Brimelow against the Cyprus crisis being allowed to 'pre-empt a greater degree of Ministerial attention than the importance of the subject for British national interests deserve[d]'. He thought that, while it offered opportunities for British Ministers to play a leading and exciting role on the world stage, it could involve Britain in 'expensive and nationally unrewarding commitments' and 'divert Ministerial attention from the more pressing

(ii) whether the constitutional talks should continue in Geneva (as in the case of the official talks on political and military problems) or in Nicosia. The participation of Mr. Clerides may dictate Nicosia, though there is a greater danger of impasse there.

British Objectives
3. Immediate objectives are:

(i) to achieve as much progress as possible towards making the ceasefire and buffer zone arrangements stick;
(ii) to give an impetus, and if possible guidelines, to the constitutional negotiations;
(iii) to establish a satisfactory machinery for the continuation of discussions at official level and for periodic ministerial involvement.

4. For the longer term, we should also bear in mind the following objectives:

(i) to permit the gradual disengagement of HMG from the prominent position accorded to them in the 1960 agreements and the Geneva Declaration;
(ii) to avoid perpetuating the work of UNFICYP—and Britain's contribution to it—at its present level;
(iii) to keep open our options on the Sovereign Base Areas.

Tactics
5. There is a strong case for pursuing in Stage II the reverse of the tactics we used in Stage I. With five delegations participating and the threat of war receding, the danger is that other delegations will dig in for a very long session. This could enmesh us in negotiations until 1975 or even beyond. We will in any case have less scope in Stage II to coerce other delegations or to bridge the gaps between them by skilful drafting. This suggests that, instead of letting the others define their positions and then seeking a compromise between them, we should take the initiative with an opening statement designed to lay down the agenda for Stage II and to suggest guidelines on the most pressing issues.[4]
6. During the tripartite discussions on Thursday and Friday,[5] we should focus on:

problems, particularly economic and domestic, on which [Britain's] national survival (to which Cyprus [was] irrelevant) depend[ed]'. Sir T. Brimelow noted his agreement (RS 14/1).

[4] In a personal message to Dr. Kissinger, transmitted in telegram No. 1643 to Washington of 6 August, Mr. Callaghan confessed with regard to the forthcoming Geneva talks: 'At the moment I don't have much feel on how to play the second round. I think I shall need to see the whites of their eyes before I shoot. If you have any thoughts I hope you will let me know.'

[5] i.e. 8 and 9 August.

(i) securing Greek and Turkish agreement on short-term measures for the restoration of peace (the 11 items considered in Brief No. 2);[6]

(ii) a discussion of the general principles to be followed in the constitutional talks (Brief No. 3). [7]

7. During the five-sided discussions on Saturday and Sunday we should concentrate on:

(i) securing Greek-Cypriot and Turkish-Cypriot cooperation for the peace-keeping measures agreed trilaterally;

(ii) agreement to the machinery for constitutional discussions (paragraphs 12-14 of Brief No. 3).

(iii) agreement on the framework for the constitutional discussions, possibly in the form of a joint declaration. Ideally this declaration should neither commit HMG nor imply that HMG are dissociating themselves from it. A suitable formula might run on the following lines:

'[the five parties], recognising the need for amendment to the 1960 Constitution, agreed that talks should take place between representatives of the Turkish and Greek Governments and of the Turkish and Greek Cypriot communities on a clear understanding that all four participants renounce ENOSIS, double ENOSIS or partition as the basis for a settlement to the problems of Cyprus'.

8. It will be necessary to put strong pressure on the other four parties from the beginning, in order to prevent them from returning to their traditional bad habits. Arguments in favour of urgency, which we might deploy, include:

(i) the risk of increasing Soviet interference;

(ii) the threat to the economy of the Island;

(iii) growing international criticism of Turkish military occupation;[8]

---

[6] Not printed. This brief suggested an agenda of ten subsidiary items: (1) the demarcation of the Turkish controlled areas; (2) prisoners; (3) the Kyrenia/Nicosia buffer zone; (4) evacuation of Turkish enclaves occupied by Greek Cypriots; (5) protection of other Turkish villages; (6) violations machinery; (7) foreign forces; (8) indigenous forces; (9) rehabilitation of isolated villages; (10) Nicosia airport; plus item (11), not to be tabled at the outset, the role of UNFICYP.

[7] Not printed. Brief No. 3 envisaged constitutional talks, involving Mr. Clerides and Mr. Denktash, taking place in Nicosia, but with participants being given a mandate to report to Geneva whenever they reached an *impasse*. It further recommended that, if possible, neither British officials nor Ministers should attend the detailed constitutional negotiations after Stage II of the Geneva Ministerial talks. 'But', the brief concluded, 'as and when the participants in the Constitutional talks report to the main Conference in Geneva, whether at Ministerial or official level we will necessarily become involved even if we have been able to avoid direct day-to-day participation.'

[8] Commenting in guidance telegram No. 103 (see note 1 above) on the fragility of the situation in Cyprus, Mr. Callaghan observed: 'Much depends on Turkish political intentions and on the behaviour of Turkish forces in the field. We hope that the Turks will be constrained by a combination of international pressure from the UN and Geneva, and by the realisation

(iv) criticism from the UN about the delay in implementing Resolution 353; risk of a special session of the General Assembly;
(v) the importance of keeping the Clerides, Karamanlis and Eçevit governments in power;[9]
(vi) the desirability of enabling UNFICYP to justify its performance to the other contributors.

Background

9. The recent history of the Cyprus problem shows that there is movement only after a violent upheaval. The best chance for reaching a constitutional settlement is to do it quickly before the problem again congeals. The Greek Cypriots and Archbishop Makarios in particular are beginning to recover their nerve, argue legalistically and actively present their case to the Soviet Union and the Third World. The large Turkish military presence in Cyprus should, however, concentrate Greek Cypriot minds on realities which they have ignored since 1960. While it may take time for the details of a new constitution to be worked out, it is important that Athens and Ankara should now exercise maximum pressure on the Cypriot communities to accept the general principles of a new constitutional order.

10. It is doubtful whether Cyprus is viable as an independent state, politically or economically. There is no popular attachment to the Republic. In the 1950s the Greek Cypriots fought us for union with Greece not for independence which the majority have tended to regard as an unsatisfactory compromise, if not a betrayal. The Turkish Cypriots, who probably have no great enthusiasm for Turkey, would have preferred Cyprus to remain a British colony: in their minds, the Republic is associated with Greek Cypriot domination. Cyprus's main sources of income are agriculture (frequently afflicted by drought): tourism (badly hit by this year's fighting, and the occupation of Kyrenia by the Turks): expenditure by the British force (which may well be reduced after the Defence Review): the £12 million annual subsidy from Turkey (most of which used to find its way into Greek Cypriot hands, but which will do so no longer): mining (now in decline): some light industry: and the relatively small amount spent by UNFICYP. Despite these negative features, all

---

that, in the long-term at least, occupation of part of Cyprus by them would become increasingly uncomfortable. There are faint signs that political sobriety may be beginning to reduce the intemperance of the Turkish military. But the Turkish Government, despite its new-found popularity, may still lack real authority to make the concessions needed to keep the Greek Government talking and to impose sufficient restraints on the Turkish forces in Cyprus.'

[9] In guidance telegram No. 103 (*v. ibid.*) Mr. Callaghan affirmed that he wanted 'to save the Greek Government from humiliation which could result in a return to overt military rule in Greece and a renewed danger of war with Turkey'. He likewise wished to ensure that Mr. Clerides, the 'most moderate and broad-minded of the Greek Cypriot politicians', should not have to return from Geneva empty-handed, or with the Greek-Cypriot position further undermined, since that would increase the danger of reprisals by EOKA-B.

parties are formally committed to respect the independence, security and territorial integrity of the Republic, and we shall have to abide by this. If the negotiations fail Cyprus may face partition between Greek Cypriots and Turkish Cypriots; annexation of part of the island by Turkey; partition between Greece and Turkey; or less probably, total annexation by Greece or Turkey. These possibilities can be used as powerful incentives to the Greek Cypriots to reach agreement on a constitutional settlement.

11. It is possible to argue that HMG's basic objectives could in the right circumstances, be secured by any of the variants of double ENOSIS. But this could not be achieved satisfactorily in the foreseeable future. There would be severe international criticism if we connived at the extinction—and incorporation into the area covered by the Atlantic Alliance—of a sovereign state which is a member of the United Nations and the Commonwealth. The Russians would work hard to wreck such an outcome. Furthermore the internal situation is not yet right for the consolidation of the two communities in wholly separate enclaves nor are there natural boundaries which might provide a stable frontier.

12. For the immediate future, therefore, the only feasible course seems to be to work with Athens and Ankara to promote a bi-communal system, with a greater degree of Turkish Cypriot autonomy than foreseen in the 1960 Constitution and less intermingling of populations.[10] This would enable Stage II to continue within the framework of Resolution 353. It would also leave open the option of Cyprus remaining a unitary State or, if communal tension and external pressure remain intolerable, of moving towards progressively greater separation of the two communities.

13. Separate briefs are attached on:

(i) the restoration of peace in the area (Brief No. 2);[11]
(ii) the re-establishment of constitutional Government in Cyprus (Brief No. 3);[12]

[10] In a minute to Sir J. Killick of 7 August Mr. Cable suggested with regard to the Cyprus talks, a 'shift of emphasis in basic strategy away from constitutional arrangements towards settling the situation on the ground' (e.g. the demarcation of a ceasefire line and its supervision, agreement on the non-reinforcement of Cyprus, and the organisation of the physical separation of the two communities). He added: 'I suggest we need to avoid the Sunningdale syndrome [the unsuccessful attempt to achieve a new constitutional settlement in Northern Ireland]. A Constitution is only the icing; it will melt if we try to apply it before baking the cake, as it did in Ulster.'

[11] See note 6 above. Brief No. 2 defined HMG's specific objectives with regard to the restoration of peace as: (i) to make the cease-fire stick; (ii) to set up machinery for dealing with cease-fire violations which would remove the need, or excuse, for unilateral action, except by UNFICYP; (iii) to establish measures for the control and limitation of forces and weapons in the Republic and to initiate moves for the withdrawal of foreign forces other than those stationed there under the Treaty of Alliance, with a view to the eventual demilitarisation of the Republic; (iv) to agree humanitarian measures for those whose freedom of movement, security or livelihood had been affected by the crisis; and (v) to 'achieve a satisfactory temporary arrangement for the operation of Nicosia Airport'.

(iii) confidence-building measures (Brief No. 4).[13]

[12] See note 7 above. It would not, according to this brief, 'be feasible at Ministerial level to enter into detailed negotiations about amendments to the Constitution'. But the brief included amongst HMG's short-term objectives the acceptance by Greek and Turkish Cypriots of guidelines, and agreement on machinery for the continuation of discussions at official level and for periodic Ministerial involvement. 'We should', the brief stated, 'try to avoid becoming a guarantor of any new constitution ... The Treaty of Guarantee has more often than not been a burden to us; it binds us to uphold the state of affairs established by the basic Articles of the Constitution which in practice we have been unable to enforce.'

[13] Not printed. This outlined a number of measures which the UK delegates might propose with a view to increasing confidence between the Greek and Turkish-Cypriot communities.

No. 54

Record of a conversation between Mr. Callaghan and Mr. A. Hartman[1] at the FCO on 8 August 1974 at 10.30 a.m.

[*WSC 3/304/2*]

Confidential

Present:

The Rt. Hon. James Callaghan, MP	Mr. A. Hartman
Mr. R. Hattersley, MP	The Hon. Earl D. Sohm[2]
Dr. J. Cunningham, MP[3]	Mr. R.B. Oakley[4]
Sir John Killick	Mr. A.G. James[5]
Mr. T.F. Brenchley[6]	Mr. C.E. Dillery[7]
Mr. C.D. Wiggin	
Mr. M.S. Weir	
Mr. A.C. Goodison	
Mr. P.J. Goulden	
Mr. M.C.S. Weston[8]	

[1] US Deputy Assistant Secretary of State for European Affairs. In a personal message transmitted in Washington telegram No. 2599 of 3 August Dr. Kissinger had suggested to Mr. Callaghan that Mr. Hartman, whom he was sending on a fact-finding mission to Athens, Ankara and Nicosia, should visit London on his return (WSC 1/13).

[2] Minister in the US Embassy in London.

[3] Parliamentary Private Secretary to Mr. Callaghan.

[4] Political Officer in the US Embassy in Beirut.

[5] Counsellor in the US Embassy in London.

[6] Mr. Brenchley was AUS.

[7] Political/Military Affairs Officer in the US Embassy in London.

[8] First Secretary and Assistant Head of SEED.

Mr. Callaghan said that he had originally not thought that it would be necessary to have anyone of the seniority of Mr. Buffum or Mr. Hartman[9] in Geneva for the second round of the talks. He had, however, changed his mind and it would be very helpful to have Mr. Hartman there. The Russians would, of course, be there too. He intended to make a point of seeing Mr. Minin[10] in order to avoid Soviet complaints. They had the potential to make mischief in Geneva. *Mr. Hartman* agreed. He would also be seeing Mr. Minin. The Soviets had the potential to make mischief in the Security Council too.

2. *Mr. Callaghan* said that what worried him was that despite the agreement which had been signed in Geneva the Turks were not just mopping up. They were clearly pushing west. *Mr. Hartman* agreed that the Turks were pushing west. He noted that they had not tried to push further east. Part of the explanation was that they were probably only just now occupying territory which they had led Ankara to believe was already held. It had been made clear to him in Ankara that the intention was to occupy the whole of the Pentadakhtylos range. He did not think that the Turks intended to go further. He had been told in Athens that although Mr. Mavros would have to make statements about the need to return to the 30 July line, the Greeks would not make a big issue of this. They would, however, be deeply concerned if the fighting was still going on. The key issue was to keep Mr. Mavros at the table and prevent him from going to the Security Council. Even if the fighting had stopped by the time the second round at Geneva started, it would certainly be necessary to begin with a discussion of the implementation of the Declaration. But there would be no progress until there could be a more general exchange about how each side saw the future. Mr. Eçevit accepted this. So too did Mr. Karamanlis. Unfortunately Mr. Mavros did not. He could not see further than the ceasefire. He must be shown that by focusing on the short-term issues he was in fact increasing the political pressures on him. It was only when the process had really started that he would have the political strength to take the tough decisions that would be necessary.

3. *Mr. Callaghan* wondered if he should take part in the talks at all if the fighting was continuing. *Mr. Hartman* said that the important thing was to keep the process going. As long as there was talking, there was hope. The UK role should be that of a patient referee. A general exchange of view would be useful. After that, it might be possible to lay down the framework for continuing the process at a lower level. *Mr. Wiggin* said that the problem was that the Greeks would not sit down at all if the Turks were still advancing. While he agreed that the Greeks would probably not insist on a return to the 30 July line, the Turks must be persuaded that enough

[9] On 7 August Dr. Kissinger's office had telephoned the FCO to suggest that Mr. Hartman should go to Geneva for the beginning of Stage II of the Cyprus talks. Mr. Callaghan had welcomed the idea (telegram No. 1659 to Washington of 7 August, WSC 1/13).

[10] Mr. V.I. Minin was the Soviet Special Observer at the Geneva Conferences.

was enough. *Mr. Hartman* said that the Turks would clearly complain that there had been no progress on the things which interested them in the Declaration. Mr. Averoff[11] had, however, told him in Athens that now that there was a new Commander of the National Guard he would be able to get a start made on the things which interested the Turks simply by lifting the telephone. (He himself was somewhat sceptical of this since there seemed to be significant groups of officerless National Guard at large.) As he saw it, the aim should be to have one group of senior officials sit down and discuss the implementation of the Declaration while another group discussed constitutional issues. Apart from *enosis* and partition, nothing should be ruled out. Mr. Clerides had told him that he was ready to discuss a 'cantonal' system and had accepted that the idea of a 'unitary' State was out. He clearly could not accept the continuation of the large Turkish military presence for long but he had said that he would be prepared to discuss the possibility of larger forces remaining than had been agreed earlier.

4. Mr. Hartman said that in the longer term the only solution was for the Turks and Greeks to accept the need for better relations with each other. The aim of the Conference should be to develop this sort of attitude. *Mr. Callaghan* agreed but said that the Greeks could not be humiliated by sitting down to talk while fighting was going on. *Mr. Hartman* said that Mr. Mavros was by no means typical of the Greek leadership. Mr. Karamanlis and Mr. Averoff were much less concerned with short-term problems. They were prepared to admit that the situation had been caused by the mistake of the previous Greek Government and understood that better relations with Turkey were the only answer. He thought Mr. Eçevit was beginning to feel the same but, like the Israelis in 1967, the Turks had to be brought down to earth. This could not, however, be done if the Geneva talks broke down and the matter was taken to the United Nations where the Soviets would see that the situation was kept on the boil.[12]

5. *Mr. Callaghan* asked Mr. Hartman whether it would be better to have the further talks in Nicosia rather than in Geneva. *Mr. Hartman* replied that it was important to preserve the Geneva framework. It would probably be necessary to have further talks in Nicosia since Mr. Clerides could not be abroad for too long since his position was weak and he needed support from Athens. Perhaps this would be forthcoming now there was a new Commander of the National Guard. The fact was that there were 'new

[11] Mr. E. Averoff-Tossizza was Greek Minister of National Defence.

[12] In Ankara telegram No. 936 of 6 August Sir H. Phillips reported that Mr. Eçevit had been 'unyielding' in his talks with Mr. Hartman, and that his solution to the Cyprus problem was a Turkish autonomous federated zone (or zones) amounting to 30 per cent of the island. 'Rightly or wrongly', Sir H. Phillips observed, 'the Turks see themselves as holding the winning cards in Cyprus. They will not be dictated to by anyone, will not yield on anything unless on reciprocity, and will compromise only so far as the security achieved by their military superiority is not put at risk.'

realities' in Cyprus. It was now generally recognised that there were two communities. It was also clear that no one wanted Archbishop Makarios back. *Mr. Callaghan* agreed that the talks would probably have to be in Nicosia though he wondered if this would mean a loss of momentum. *Mr. Hartman* suggested that there should be periodic meetings of the three Guarantor Powers to review the situation. Perhaps the three Foreign Ministers could meet in New York when they were there for the General Assembly, possibly having held a short meeting before that. *Mr. Callaghan* agreed that it would be useful to have a meeting of the guarantors at the end of August or beginning of September in order to give the impression of continued activity when the General Assembly started.

6. *Mr. Hartman* said that he had noticed that the new realities had not been appreciated by UNFICYP. UN representatives in Cyprus tended to be very legalistic and were only focusing on demarcation and to some extent on the problems of Nicosia airport. The United States had made the point to Mr. Urquhart[13] in New York that it was necessary to deal with the Turkish enclaves also. *Mr. Callaghan* said that we had the same impression and had made much the same point to the UN.

7. *Sir John Killick* raised the possibility of a small token withdrawal by the Turks. When *Mr. Hartman* said that the Greeks did not seem so concerned about this, *Mr. Callaghan* suggested that the Russians and the non-aligned were, however, concerned. He had to think of his own position domestically and at the UN. *Mr. Hartman* said that one could get 80 votes for almost anything in the UN but the fact was that the members of the UN were not willing to take responsibility. If the three Guarantor Powers tried to find an equitable and just solution, they ought to be prepared to take a little head from the UN.

8. *Mr. Callaghan* said that he remained uncertain about Turkish intentions with regard to their troops. He had spoken to Mr. Günes of the parallel of Northern Ireland. *Mr. Hartman* said that the Turks felt they had been forced to act in order to protect their people. *Mr. Callaghan* said that 25,000 troops were hardly necessary for this. With this number, they could take over the whole island. *Mr. Hartman* said that Archbishop Makarios had told him that he would prefer the Turks to do this rather than that there should be a bad agreement. *Mr. Callaghan* said that he would not put his hand to a bad agreement. *Mr. Hartman* said that it was not necessary for the Secretary of State to put his hand to anything except encouraging the parties to find more common ground. When *Mr. Callaghan* suggested that this would mean there would have to be some Turkish withdrawal, *Mr. Hartman* said that this was the only lever the Turks had. They had to be brought to see that withdrawal was in their long-term interest. He agreed that it would be difficult to keep Mr. Mavros at the table, but it must be

---

[13] Mr. B.E. Urquhart was UN Under-Secretary General for Special Political Affairs.

remembered that the other Greek leaders had more patience than Mr. Mavros.[14]

9. In conclusion, *Mr. Callaghan* said that he had welcomed the opportunity to exchange views with Mr. Hartman and looked forward to talking to him further on the aircraft.[15]

---

[14] In Washington telegram No. 2638 of 8 August Sir P. Ramsbotham reported that the US Government's policy towards Cyprus was 'to avoid action which might cause any of the parties to feel isolated'. They were, he added, by no means unsympathetic to the Greek Government's position, but doubted whether continual approaches to the Turkish Government would be effective and believed that public reproaches over Turkish action 'would be positively counter-productive'.

[15] Language attributed to Mr. Hartman during his visit to Ankara was, however, the cause of some concern in the FCO. Sir H. Phillips reported in his telegram No. 936 (see note 13 above) that Mr. Hartman had told the Turks that 'unlike some of Turkey's allies they [the Americans] had not switched to support Greece immediately Karamanlis had taken over'. As Mr. Wiggin noted in a minute to Mr. Acland of 7 August this implied that the British having started 'pro-Turkish' suddenly switched to being 'pro-Greek'. 'This', he added, 'is not only a gross and unfair oversimplification; it is a line which could undermine our honest broker role in Geneva II; it is all too likely that we will find ourselves having to side with the Greeks rather than the Turks more often than not in order to keep the negotiations going; it will not help us to keep them going if the Americans keep suggesting to the Turks that we are "pro-Greek".'

No. 55

Miss A.M. Warburton[1] *(UKMIS Geneva) to FCO*

No. 794 Telegraphic [*WSC 1/13*]

Immediate. Confidential   GENEVA, *8 August 1974, 10.30 p.m.*

Repeated for information to Immediate Nicosia, Ankara, Athens, UKMIS New York, UKDEL NATO, Paris, Washington, Moscow and Bonn

Following from Secretary of State:[2]
Cyprus

1. I began with a brief press conference at 15.45 local time, in which I expressed my disappointment that the terms of the Geneva Declaration had not been fully carried out. I hoped to see words matched by deeds. My primary concern was the future of the people of Cyprus. I was not here as a judge attaching blame to any party.

---

[1] Counsellor and Head of Chancery at UKMIS Geneva.

[2] Mr. Callaghan arrived in Geneva in the early afternoon of 8 August.

2. I next saw Guyer. He was anxious to assure me that despite allegations to the contrary, UNFICYP were fully carrying out their part in implementing the Geneva Declaration. He was concerned at Turkish protests against UNFICYP activity in the zones controlled by their armed forces.[3] I promised to try to get him admitted to the tripartite meetings as an observer.

3. A meeting with Mavros followed at which he concentrated on Turkish violations of the ceasefire. Until these stopped he was unwilling to permit an exchange of prisoners. Unless he obtained an immediate Turkish assurance that their armed forces would advance no further and indeed should go back to the line as at 22.00 hours on 30 July he would be obliged to leave Geneva and appeal to the United Nations, where he believed the Turks would be isolated. I did not attempt to dissuade him at this point from recourse to the Security Council, but assured him that I was sympathetic to his complaint of Turkish violations and said I was not prepared to see the Greek Government humiliated. I cast doubt however on the likely success of any recourse to the United Nations in securing Turkish withdrawal or compliance with the ceasefire. Mavros was in an emotional mood and not really responding to argument.

4. My meeting with Günes was not dissimilar. But his preoccupation was the failure of the Greek Cypriot National Guard to evacuate Turkish villages as provided for under paragraph 3(*b*) of the Geneva Declaration.[4] I pressed him hard on Turkish compliance with the ceasefire, and he admitted to me that Turkish troops had advanced west of Kyrenia, while asserting somewhat feebly that they were only returning fire directed against them by Greek forces. He asserted that he could not give way to blackmail promoted by a Greek press campaign. He was unwilling to give any assurances about observance of the ceasefire in the absence of evacuation from Turkish villages, and insisted that the Declaration must be implemented as a whole. I took the opportunity to tell him that I considered the number of Turkish troops in the Kyrenia enclave far in excess of those needed to protect the Turkish Cypriot community and that I hoped to see some withdrawals at an early date,[5] while understanding

[3] Sr. Guyer also informed Mr. Callaghan that the news from Cyprus was 'very bad' and that he had just received reports of heavy fighting on the Green Line (record of meeting between Mr. Callaghan and Sr. Guyer at the Palais des Nations, Geneva on 8 August at 4 p.m.). Cf. No. 52, note 1.

[4] According to Mr. Günes, '37 Turkish Cypriot villages had been abandoned by their inhabitants. 80 had been occupied, and 60 were under threat of occupation. 81,000 people (two-thirds of the entire Turkish Cypriot population) were defenceless' (record of a conversation between Mr. Callaghan and Mr. Günes at the Palais des Nations, Geneva, on 8 August 1974 at 5.15 p.m.).

[5] During his conversation with Mr. Günes, Mr. Callaghan stated: 'There were already, he was told, 25,000 Turkish troops in the Island, together with tanks, ground-to-air missiles and other weapons; yet they would be unable to protect the Turkish Cypriot community unless they occupied the whole Island, which Turkey had said was not her intention' (*v. ibid.*).

that he would wish to see progress on the constitutional issue before these took place.[6]

5. After a silent session in the council for the benefit of photographers, the tripartite meeting began at 19.00 hours. Mavros immediately proposed that Guyer be admitted as an observer. I supported him warmly and to our surprise Günes agreed. I then set out the balance sheet of failures and successes in implementing the Geneva Declaration and urged its implementation in full. I argued that if this meeting were to fail, the Cypriot communities had nothing to look forward to. Lengthy exchanges between Mavros and Günes confirmed their obsessions with, respectively, observance of the ceasefire and standstill called for in the Declaration of 30 July on the one hand and the evacuation of Turkish villages on the other. To get the meeting to focus on constructive work I proposed that officials should produce reports on the implementation of paragraphs, 2, 3(b) and 3(d) of the Declaration[7] in time for a Ministerial meeting at 18.00 hours local time tomorrow, at which we should discuss any points of difference arising from their reports, and Nicosia airport. This was agreed after some argument. I also suggested we should begin to discuss constitutional issues. Mavros declined to do so in the absence of Clerides and Denktash. Günes indicated that he would make a statement on this subject.

6. Given the firm positions of Mavros and Günes on the issues which they have at heart I am fairly well satisfied at having prevented this first meeting from breaking up in disorder. Much of what they said was designed for subsequent publication, but at least they managed to say it without anyone walking out, and we are to meet again tomorrow. I did not hope for much more.

[6] Mr. Callaghan also warned Mr. Günes that if the Conference failed, the Cyprus problem would go to the United Nations where it would be exploited by the Soviet Government 'whose interest was to weaken Greece, Turkey and NATO' (*v. ibid.*).

[7] Paragraph 2 called on all forces to desist from all offensive or hostile actions; paragraph 3(b) called for the immediate evacuation of all Turkish enclaves occupied by Greek or Greek Cypriot forces; and paragraph 3(d) provided for the release or exchange of military personnel and civilians detained as a result of the hostilities. A Working Group composed of British, Greek and Turkish officials, met, along with a UN representative, on 9 August to review the implementation of paragraph 3(b). In a minute of 10 August Mr. Freeland reported on its proceedings to Mr. Goodison: 'The general attitude of the Turkish representative was to bridle at attempts to discuss anything other than immediate evacuation; intermittently to bang the table and make as if to walk out; and on several occasions to question the need for any report to the Ministers.' By contrast, he noted, that the Greek line was that 'the first task of the Working Group was to examine the list presented by the Turks and check its accuracy'.

No. 56

Record of a conversation between Mr. Callaghan and Dr. Waldheim in the Palais des Nations, Geneva, on 9 August 1974 at 12 noon

[*WSC 1/13*]

Secret

Present:

The Rt. Hon. James Callaghan MP	Dr. Waldheim
Mr. Brenchley	Mr. Guyer
Mr. Acland	Mr. Weckmann-Muñoz
Mr. P. Goulden	

Mr. Callaghan said that he was unhappy that the Conference seemed to be developing to the exclusive benefit of the Turks. *Dr. Waldheim* commented that the Greeks were in a depressed and even desperate state of mind. Mr. Mavros had confided that he was considering trying to send troops to Cyprus by convoy under assurances from the United Kingdom, United States and USSR, organised by the United Nations, that the convoy would not be attacked by Turkey. Mr. Mavros was also considering the possibility of activating the Security Council or calling for a Special Session of the General Assembly. He seemed to realise that a troop convoy would be unrealistic and that a special session of the General Assembly could not be set up in less than a month—especially with the Islamic grouping controlling the membership of the non-aligned group and five seats in the Security Council. There was an element of wishful thinking in much of Mr. Mavros' conversation.

UNFICYP

2. *Dr. Waldheim* asked for advice about UNFICYP's position in the Turkish controlled area. Mr. Eçevit had written to him on 6 August that UNFICYP had no judicial right to take action in an area controlled by a Guarantor Power; it should therefore withdraw from the Kyrenia/Nicosia enclave and transfer its humanitarian activities there to the ICRC. Dr. Waldheim himself was reluctant to agree. The ICRC had asked the United Nations to continue to organise convoys in the Kyrenia/Nicosia area. It would be difficult for UNFICYP to withdraw from this area without leaving the Island altogether. Dr. Waldheim was haunted by memories of U Thant's disastrous decision to withdraw UNEF forces from Sinai in 1967.[1] Unfortunately the UNFICYP mandate was out of date. It had been

---

[1] On 19 May 1967 U Thant, the then UN Secretary-General, complied with demands from President Nasser of Egypt for the withdrawal of UNEF from Sinai in accordance with the terms

drawn up to avert inter-communal trouble, not to deal with the existence of a Guarantor Power on the Island.[2] Resolution 355[3] had, by a compromise, given Security Council backing for an enlarged UNFICYP role, but the United Nations' position in Kyrenia/Nicosia was undignified.

3. *Mr. Callaghan* commented that UNFICYP had a clear role in the Turkish controlled area: to defend the Greek Cypriots at Bellapais, etc., who still numbered several thousand. UNFICYP had a *locus standi* under paragraph 3(*c*) of the Geneva Declaration, which made it responsible for security in mixed villages throughout the Island. But it would be risky to rely on this alone since the Turks could later clear the mixed villages of Greek Cypriots. [4] It would be better to base UNFICYP firmly on the 1964 mandate and to take a strong line against withdrawal. *Dr. Waldheim* agreed that he would do so. Meanwhile he would give a dignified refusal to Mr. Eçevit and Mr. Günes.

Turkish enclaves

4. *Mr. Callaghan* pointed out that the Turkish Government based their position on the continued occupation of Turkish villages, contrary to paragraph 3(*b*) of the Geneva Declaration. They claimed that these villages were starved, attacked and short of water. *Mr. Weckmann* strongly dissented. The situation had been restored in most Turkish Cypriot areas. UNFICYP were looking after Turkish Cypriot villages which had surrendered or had been surrounded (and from which Turkish Cypriots were not allowed to depart). The problem areas were limited to Paphos, Limassol and Larnaca. *Mr. Callaghan* commented that the Turks complained that the United Nations was less active in looking after Turkish villages than in resisting the Turkish advance on Nicosia Airport. *Dr. Waldheim* replied that the two situations were very different. At Nicosia Airport, the United Nations had secured an agreement among the local commanders and possessed, thanks to Her Majesty's Government, sufficient strength to resist the Turks. This was not so *vis-à-vis* the National Guard or the Turkish mainland forces in other parts of the Island. *Mr. Callaghan* urged Dr. Waldheim to publicise any information which helped to correct the obsessive fears of the Turkish Government that Turkish Cypriot villages were in danger of annihilation.

---

on which it had entered Egypt in 1956 (see No. 10, note 8). This was widely perceived as having facilitated the outbreak on 5 June of hostilities between Israel and its Arab neighbours.

[2] UNSC Resolution 186 of 4 March 1964 recommended the creation of a UN Peace-Keeping Force in Cyprus: according to Paragraph 5, 'the function of the Force should be, in the interest of preserving peace and security, to use its best efforts to prevent a recurrence of fighting and as necessary, to contribute to the maintenance and restoration of law and order and a return to normal conditions'. *UNSC Official Records: Resolutions and Decisions, 19th year* (1964), p. 2.

[3] See No. 50, note 1.

[4] *V. ibid.*, note 2.

United States Attitudes

5. *Dr. Waldheim* mentioned that it was United States fears about the Soviet Union which prevented him from seeking a mandate for UNFICYP from the Security Council. The United States seemed, from reports about Dr. Kissinger's letter to Mr. Eçevit, to be exercising very little pressure on the Turks. *Mr. Callaghan* said that signs were beginning to emerge of divergence between the British and American positions.[5] He suggested that he and Dr. Waldheim urge on Mr. Hartman the need both to support UNFICYP and to urge restraint on the Turkish Government. *Dr. Waldheim* agreed.

Turkish mainland forces

6. Mr. Callaghan said that he felt strongly that 30,000 Turkish troops were out of all proportion to Turkey's legitimate objectives under the Treaty of Guarantee. He asked whether Dr. Waldheim intended to do anything about the 'timely and phased reduction' foreseen in the Geneva Declaration. The Russians were already giving strong emphasis to the withdrawal of both Greek and Turkish troops. Dr. Waldheim commented that the United Nations could exert moral pressure and that strong political pressure would build up in the Security Council and later in the General Assembly. He agreed however with Mr. Weckmann's assessment that the Turks would not withdraw forces until they had secured their constitutional objectives.

[5] Cf. No. 54, notes 14 and 15.

No. 57

Record of a conversation between Mr. Callaghan and Mr. Günes in the Palais des Nations, Geneva, on 9 August 1974 at 6 p.m.

[*WSC 1/13*]

Secret

Present:

The Rt. Hon. James Callaghan MP   HE Mr. Günes
Mr. Brenchley
Mr. Carter[1]
Mr. Acland

Mr. Günes said that it was 'indispensable' for Turkey to reach agreement very quickly about certain principles for a final solution on the Cyprus problem. The general outline of the Turkish proposal was already known: they thought that the only solution was to create within a united republic of Cyprus, whose territorial integrity he fully respected, two (and only two) administrative autonomous regions.[2] From the Turkish point of view, prolongation of the Conference, with referral of questions to expert groups, would be no better than an immediate failure. He thought however that it might be better for the principle he had outlined to be put forward by Denktash rather than himself. He was not suggesting discussion of constitutional detail nor of the boundaries of the proposed regions, all he wanted now was acceptance of the broad principle.

2. *Mr. Callaghan* asked Mr. Günes (*a*) whether he envisaged that the proposed autonomous Turkish region should be the same as the military occupied zone (*b*) if not, whether it would include areas such as Famagusta (*c*) given the creation of the two autonomous zones, what would be the functions of the Central Government?

3. *Mr. Günes* replied that the Turkish military occupied zone covered only one twenty-fifth of the territory of Cyprus and would be insufficient for a Turkish Cypriot administrative region; the boundary would have to be drawn in the light of considerations such as population and land ownership. The Turkish region could only be in the north of the Island,

---

[1] Mr. P.L. Carter was AUS and interpreter to Mr. Callaghan.

[2] In Nicosia telegram No. 723 of 10 August Mr. Olver commented on this proposal that 'leaving aside the question whether the Turks [could] in any case be persuaded to accept substantially less than this solution, two clearly demarcated autonomous regions of Cyprus, in each of which the Greek or Turkish Cypriot population respectively was in substantial majority, under a central government on the lines suggested by Günes would as seen from here be the solution most likely to lead to stability'. And while he admitted that a population transfer would be 'a painful business', he argued that without it two separate autonomous regions would be 'almost as bad. Either would lead almost inevitably to a future Ulster.'

but he would say nothing precise about Famagusta. As for the Central Government, it would have responsibility for such matters as international relations, currency, Federal Courts, central taxation etc.: there would be a legislative assembly to deal with matters concerning the whole population, with a President and Vice-President but there should be no provision by which Government could be paralysed by a veto. He emphasised however that these ideas were personal and very provisional. While the Central Government looked after subjects affecting the totality of the population, communal points should be decentralised; this would reduce friction.

4. *Mr. Callaghan* pointed out that we must have regard to political realities; Makarios was playing a waiting game, and if he thought a Federal solution was going too far, he would step in to denounce the break up of the unitary State. If Clerides were pushed too hard the way would be opened for Makarios' return, with all the consequences which that would entail.[3]

5. *Mr. Günes* said that Makarios would not agree to the principle he was proposing. But then no solution to which Makarios would agree was acceptable to the Turkish Government.

6. *Mr. Callaghan* asked Mr. Günes what the Turkish Government's policy would be if the principle he had outlined were not accepted but received no clear reply. He then outlined his own thinking:

(*a*) too many Turkish troops were in Cyprus for the small area they occupied; there would therefore always be a temptation for them (especially if the Conference failed) to make further advances, although he accepted Mr. Günes' statement that this was not the present policy of the Turkish Government;

(*b*) Cyprus was an independent, non-aligned Commonwealth country and it was for the community leaders to solve their constitutional problems, seeking (if they wished) guidance from Ankara and Athens respectively; we had taken part in Constitution making in 1960 only as part of the decolonisation process and our responsibility in this respect was finished; but

(*c*) we had other responsibilities as a Guarantor Power.

7. If the Conference failed Mr. Callaghan saw two possibilities (*a*) the Greeks might want to send their own troops into Cyprus,[4] and it would be difficult to counter the argument that they were doing it as a Guarantor Power to protect Greek Cypriot interests in view of the presence of excessive numbers of Turkish troops and (*b*) Turkish forces might unilaterally expand their occupied zone and Mr. Callaghan made it clear

---

[3] Mr. Olver also observed with regard to Mr. Günes's proposal: 'Under a firm lead from Athens, whom he could use as a scapegoat, I believe Clerides might be willing to try something on these lines: but only if he were sure that Makarios would not stab him in the back with calls to his own supporters to disown this traitor to the Cyprus cause' (*v. ibid.*).

[4] Cf. No. 56.

that the British Government would take a very serious view indeed of such action.

8. It was desirable to ensure that the Turkish community were given real powers and functions which they could genuinely exercise and fulfil; but since this would be difficult for the Greeks to accept, Mr. Günes should say at the same time as putting forward his demand for new powers for the Turkish Cypriots that he intended to phase out Turkish troops and, as an earnest sign of good intentions, announce that some withdrawals would begin at once. This would give the Conference some basis for discussion and perhaps even agreement. It would then be necessary to ask Clerides and Denktash to resume discussion on this new basis and report to the Conference in three to four weeks. Such an accommodation should be acceptable to Greek public opinion and give Turkish Cypriots the promise of an acceptable future.

9. *Mr. Günes* said he was ready to reduce Turkish forces but on condition that he had a better idea of the future status of the communities within the Island, and this meant that the principle of autonomous regions must be agreed by the Conference and the community leaders and its application started.[5] He hoped Mr. Callaghan and Mr. Hartman, to whom he had also spoken, could help in this regard with Clerides and other interested parties. In response to a question he confirmed that he would be happy that Mr. Callaghan should discuss the idea with Clerides later this evening.[6]

10. *Mr. Callaghan* made three final points. (*a*) He would not advocate the principle of regionalisation to Clerides; he would only discuss it with him. (*b*) If Mr Günes felt it essential to have a quick result then he must make a concrete move concerning withdrawal of forces; he would not get acceptance of his principle in return for vague assurances. (*c*) Mr. Callaghan accepted the role which Mr. Günes asked him to undertake only on the basis of the personal assurance given to him earlier by Mr. Günes—which he accepted—that the Turkish Government had no intention of enlarging the Turkish occupied zone.[7]

[5] Mr. Callaghan subsequently outlined Mr. Günes's position to Mr. Mavros, who, he reported, 'surprisingly seemed quite receptive provided he could sell the idea to Makarios'. Indeed, Mr. Callaghan was left under the impression 'that Mavros wanted to get rid of the Cyprus problem at almost any price provided Greek face could be saved' (UKMIS Geneva telegram No. 801 of 10 August).

[6] When during dinner with Mr. Clerides on 9 August, Mr. Callaghan put to him Mr. Günes's ideas, Mr. Clerides replied that any sizeable autonomous region must inevitably contain a large Greek Cypriot majority, and that the creation of such a region with a Turkish Cypriot majority would involve massive transfers of population. 'He would not', he said, 'contemplate this and even if he were prepared to, he could not sell it to the people of Cyprus.' Mr. Clerides was, however, 'inclined to accept an administrative federal system which would give autonomy to a series of Turkish-Cypriot enclaves which would be linked together under a Turkish-Cypriot Administration' (*v. ibid.*).

[7] Later that evening Mr. Callaghan was informed in telegram No. 356 to UKMIS Geneva of 9 August of a recently received report of a Turkish military plan to implement the second phase of Turkey's operations in Cyprus not later than 20 August and irrespective of the results of the

Geneva Conference. This would involve the Turks extending their occupation from east of Morphou, through Nicosia, to the port of Famagusta. A further third-phase advance might then be attempted if no satisfactory agreement were reached at Geneva. According to a special assessment by Joint Intelligence Committee (JIC) staff (JIC(A)(74)(SA)91), the plan made military sense and was in conformity with what had been known about Turkish planning prior to the intervention. If accomplished, it would also leave the Turks with roughly the 30% of Cyprus to which Mr. Eçevit had referred. Nevertheless, while the JIC thought such a plan existed, and while they could not exclude the possibility of its implementation, they concluded that it was more likely to be a contingency plan which might be executed if the Turks failed to achieve demonstrable progress towards their goals at Geneva.

No. 58

Miss Warburton (UKMIS Geneva) to FCO

No. 807 Telegraphic [WSC 1/13]

Immediate. Confidential   GENEVA, *10 August 1974, 1 p.m.*

Repeated for information to Immediate UKMIS New York, Washington, UKDEL NATO, Athens, Ankara, Nicosia, Moscow, Paris and Bonn

Following from Secretary of State:

1. In the light of my conversations with Günes and Denktash[1] I arranged for the UN Secretary General to come for a private talk with me at UKMIS this morning.

2. I warned him that there was evidence (which I did not specify) that if the conference did not produce an agreement satisfactory to the Turks they might take military action to extend their occupation zone in breach of the ceasefire.[2] This would be a most serious step and one which would have implications for the UK as a guarantor power.

---

[1] See No. 57. During a meeting with Mr. Callaghan on the morning of 10 August Mr. Denktash explained that he had 'sold' to Mr. Günes the plan for regional autonomy based on geographical separation, rather than the 'functional federalism based on the existing Turkish enclaves' which he had previously been discussing with Mr. Clerides. He also said 'that if there were no agreement in principle on regional autonomy the Turkish Army could well move to Famagusta'. After pointing to the serious repercussions that might result from such action, Mr. Callaghan warned Mr. Denktash that as a Guarantor Power he was 'not satisfied that there was no danger to the independence, territorial integrity and security of Cyprus from the Turkish side', and that, while he could still see some prospect of settling the Cyprus problem at least for some years, he saw no chance of settling it if the Turkish army advanced (UKMIS Geneva telegram No. 808 of 10 August).

[2] See No. 57, note 7. Mr. Vlachos informed Sir R. Hooper on the evening of 10 August that Greek military intelligence had concluded from reports from Turkey that the Turks were planning to resume hostilities in Cyprus on a large scale, and that they were expecting an

3. The UN would be immediately involved from a military point of view as a Turkish advance across the ceasefire line would be through areas patrolled by UNFICYP. What instructions would he give to UNFICYP in such circumstances?

4. Dr. Waldheim said that UNFICYP's original mandate did not extend to action against the force of a UN member state. Nor were they in sufficient numbers or strongly enough armed to stand against the Turkish army. Nevertheless he had the clear impression that the Turks were reluctant to get into a position of actually fighting UNFICYP. The Nicosia airport incident had proved that. If UNFICYP were reinforced rapidly enough at the critical moment to look like a credible deterrent force and if they stood fast he thought that the Turks might back away.[3]

5. I said that this was very much on the lines of my own thinking. At Nicosia airport we had been able to provide British reinforcements to UNFICYP sufficiently rapidly. If it looked as though a Turkish advance was imminent we could do so again.[4] Could I then look to the reinforced UNFICYP to stand astride of the Turkish advance? Waldheim declared his readiness to co-operate fully on that basis.

6. We discussed time scales. I said that Turkish action might occur as early as the week beginning 19 August. He replied that in the light of his own conversation with Denktash he would not rule out the possibility of even earlier action, i.e. next week. In such an emergency he would need to operate either from New York or possibly Geneva. He was due to go to Bucharest at the end of next week and had planned to spend a few days meanwhile in Salzburg. He thought it best not to disturb these plans in a way likely to excite attention. He could be reached in Salzburg at any time and could be in Geneva in an hour. Alternatively, if the situation seemed to warrant his return to New York, it would be natural for him to route himself via London. I said that the latter might be particularly convenient as I would have to return to London myself to consult my colleagues. We left it that Brenchley, who was the other person present at our

---

attack on National Guard positions at dawn on 11 August. However, Mr. Vlachos thought there was an 'element of bluff' in all this (Athens telegram No. 427 of 10 August).

[3] See No. 40.

[4] In UKMIS Geneva telegram 806 of 10 August Air Vice-Marshal F.R.L. Mellersh, Assistant Chief of the Defence Staff (Operations) and a member of the UK delegation at Geneva, reported to Air Marshal Sir P. Le Cheminant, the Vice Chief of the Defence Staff, Mr. Callaghan's concern at the 'hard-line attitude' adopted by the Turks at Geneva and the strong indications that Turkish forces might soon attempt a major break out from the area then under their control. He had, in response to a request from Mr. Callaghan for advice on what UNFICYP 'suitably reinforced' could do by 'interposing itself', emphasised that 'deterrence was all we could hope for and that any question of holding the Turks [was] out of the question with the estimated Turkish force levels and in the face of Turkish air [*sic*]'. Mr. Callaghan had also asked that the Phantoms, due for withdrawal on 12 August, be kept at Akrotiri (cf. No. 40) and that the withdrawal of other British forces be halted immediately (WSC 1/10). See No. 59, note 7.

conversation, would keep in touch with the UN staff in Geneva about his movements, but that Waldheim would not inform them of the real inwardness of his doing so.

7. Waldheim subsequently spoke to Brenchley privately in the UN building. He said he had been reflecting on his conversation with me and had looked through the UN resolutions. He had complete prerogative to deploy UNFICYP where he thought fit, but it was clear that he would have to report at once to the Security Council if an emergency such as that contemplated arose. He did not think this would be an impediment. His guess was that the Soviet Union would dislike Turkish army action and would not oppose his use of UNFICYP. They might not positively support him but would perhaps abstain again. Likewise the Chinese would probably again absent themselves.

8. He gave Brenchley details of the present deployment of UNFICYP, with British to the West of the Turkish occupation zone, Finns to the east of it and Swedes in Famagusta. The numbers were at present tiny. Brenchley pointed out that the demarcation exercise for the ceasefire line was now completed and this gave a starting point for discussion of the buffer zones. If they could be fixed it would be natural for UNFICYP to deploy stronger forces to them. Waldheim said that this would be a great help.

9. I was impressed by Waldheim's staunchness. My strong impression is that he does not wish to expose himself to criticism such as that met by U Thant in 1967 over his withdrawal of UN forces in Sinai.[5]

---

[5] See No. 56, note 1.

No. 59

Record of a meeting between Mr. Callaghan and Mr. Hartman at the Hotel la Réserve,[1] Geneva, on 10 August 1974 at 2.30 p.m.

[*WSC 1/13*]

Secret

Present:

The Rt. Hon. James Callaghan MP   Mr. Hartman
Mr. Brenchley   Mr. Oakley
Mr. Acland
Miss Fort[2]

Mr. Callaghan, referring to the Turkish refusal to meet because of the dispute about name cards, said that if no signals were received from the Turkish side soon he would ask Mr. Günes and Mr. Mavros to come and have a talk with him.[3] He quoted Mr. Attlee's[4] saying that you should never walk out of a meeting because if you did you had only got to walk back. He would pick it up again when Mr. Günes had cooled down. He said that he had had meetings with Mr. Denktash, Mr. Clerides and Mr. Mavros. Mr. Clerides and Mr. Mavros had admitted that the strength of the National Guard was larger than had been thought and could be raised to 35,000 with mobilisation. He understood that there were arms which could be deployed which had never been used yet. Mr. Callaghan said that he had asked Mr. Denktash that morning what would happen if the talks broke down. Mr. Denktash had said that the Turkish Government did not send their troops to Cyprus to play football. Mr. Callaghan said that Mr. Denktash's remarks had done nothing to allay his suspicions. It was

---

[1] During the second stage of the Geneva Conference Mr. and Mrs. Callaghan were accommodated at the Hotel la Réserve in Geneva.

[2] Miss M. Fort was Second Secretary in the FCO.

[3] In a note of 10 August Miss Warburton recorded that there had been a number of exchanges on name cards and seating arrangements for the Stage II talks, with the Turks steadily insisting that place cards for the Cypriot representatives should read 'Turkish Cypriot Community' and 'Greek Cypriot Community', and the Greeks at first demanding that they should be seated behind cards reading 'Republic of Cyprus'. For his part, Mr. Clerides, although prepared to have no name card at all, wanted a reference to 'Cyprus' in some form or other if name cards appeared. When no agreement was reached on place cards on the morning of 10 August Mr. Günes and Mr. Denktash left the Conference venue in the Palais des Nations. At about 1.15 p.m. the Turkish delegation informed the British that they would accept place cards reading 'Greek Community of Cyprus' and 'Turkish Community of Cyprus'. As Mr. Callaghan subsequently reported in UKMIS Geneva telegram No. 811 of 10 August, the 'meeting "à cinq" with the Cypriot Communities at last started at 17.00 with no photographs, no place cards, and no prejudice to the positions of the parties'.

[4] Mr. C.R. Attlee was Prime Minister during 1945-51.

probable that Mr. Günes had been working on his Cabinet to maintain the ceasefire but that the coalition partners and the army had been working against it. Mr. Günes appeared to be striving hard for acceptance of the general principle of separation in Geneva.

2. Mr. Callaghan said that the United Kingdom evaluation of Turkish intentions was somewhat confused. *Mr. Hartman* said that the United States assessment was not clear either. *Mr. Callaghan* said that his main concern was that a similar situation to that before the Turkish invasion would not arise again. Then Mr. Eçevit had come to London to ask for the use of the Sovereign Base Areas.[5] Her Majesty's Government had refused but then had done nothing because he and the Prime Minister had lost 24 hours in having to go to Paris for a meeting. But Mr. Callaghan did not wish to be caught napping twice. He was therefore taking precautions and had postponed the return of the Phantoms and the further withdrawal of British troops.[6] He had asked for an assessment of what reinforcements would be needed to stand between the Turks and any advance they chose to make.[7] He had also indicated his position on the Phantoms and the troop withdrawal to the British Press. He had talked to Dr. Waldheim about the position in general terms. Dr. Waldheim had said that the best basis for preventing military action by the United Kingdom was a United Nations mandate. Mr. Callaghan made it clear that he was speaking personally for the moment but that he had alerted the Prime Minister. Mr. Callaghan said that he was not prepared to allow the Turks to break the cease-fire Agreement because the consequences would be too grave and would bring about unimaginable happenings on the Island. As for the Greek Government there was a danger of increasing tension between them or of the Greek Government being driven from office. His policy was for deterrence not based on bluff.[8]

---

[5] See No. 25.

[6] See No. 58, note 4.

[7] Air Vice-Marshal Mellersh advised Mr. Callaghan in a paper of 10 August that the Turkish army was 'looking for an excuse to continue operations'. He estimated that, although there were sufficient UN troops on Cyprus to supervise a demilitarised zone around the present Turkish mainland forces and to monitor minor breaches of the ceasefire, UNFICYP was 'not strong enough even to hinder' a large-scale Turkish military advance. Moreover, he believed that there could be no question of Britain offering the extra 5,000 men UNFICYP would require without reducing force levels in Northern Ireland and withdrawing units from Germany. 'The build-up', he noted, 'would take … up to a fortnight and I would not be surprised if the Chiefs of Staff would wish to include air defences in the face of the considerable threat from the Turkish Air Forces' (WSC 1/10).

[8] In Geneva telegram No. 2 to Paris of 10 August, Mr. Callaghan instructed Sir E. Tomkins to inform M. Sauvagnargues of his fear that in a few days decisive deterrent action might be required to prevent the Turks seeking by force of arms substantially to extend the area they occupied in Cyprus. Mr. Callaghan hoped that in such a case he would have the 'full support of the Nine [EC member states]'. It would, he thought, 'be timely', if M. Sauvagnargues could, either for France alone or as current EC President, 'put the Turkish Government on notice that he expects them now to solve the Cyprus problem by diplomatic and not by military means'.

3. *Mr. Hartman* said that President Ford's[9] initial message to President Korotürk had referred to the Cyprus situation and had said that it was undesirable to humiliate the Greeks. Mr. Eçevit had told the American Ambassador in Ankara that he shared the view that Karamanlis should not be humiliated. Mr. Eçevit had said that Mr. Karamanlis could agree to principles now that would be politically distasteful since he could still blame the Colonels for the moment. Mr. Eçevit was prepared for the implementation of those proposals not to be hurried. The proposals which Eçevit wanted accepting were for separation and autonomy within each delineated area. The American Ambassador in Ankara thought that these were non-negotiable demands rather than an initial negotiating position. Eçevit had said that he would do his best on the implementation of the cease-fire.

4. Mr. Hartman said that he had told Washington that Mr. Mavros appeared to be relaxed and that Mavros would have no difficulty with these ideas if Makarios could accept them. Mr. Clerides had said that it would mean the end of him on the Island and had asked for Greek support. Mr. Günes had said that the principles gave a framework within which they could work but with them there would be long inter-communal talks reaching nowhere.

5. Mr. Hartman asked for Mr. Callaghan's views about how much give there was in the Turkish position. *Mr. Callaghan* said that he thought there was none and he gave as an example Turkish intransigence over the name cards. Mr. Denktash had told him that he had promoted the regionalisation plan in Ankara.

6. Mr. Callaghan said that it was his firm view that now was the time to stand up to the Turks and make them realise that we were earnest but that United Kingdom and United States policies must be co-ordinated. He was sure that Dr. Waldheim, if prompted by the United Kingdom, would seek further assistance to reinforce UNFICYP. If British troops, albeit in blue berets, equipped with anti-tank weapons and heavy artillery, faced the Turks it would be up to the Turks to decide whether to advance or not. Mr. Callaghan asked Mr. Hartman to ask Washington for their comments on his plan. *Mr. Hartman* undertook to do so.

7. Mr. Hartman said that if there was any give in the Turkish position then negotiations could be successful but that there was a danger that the Turks were looking for an excuse to break off the talks. *Mr. Callaghan* said that he thought the Turks were still undecided. For the moment it appeared they were not seeking a *casus belli* but trying to get what they wanted through diplomatic pressure. He thought there was a possibility for rational compromise on Clerides' plan for functional federalism with no geographical boundary. Clerides could not agree to dividing the Island on a line but he was also convinced that if the Turks could not compromise they would march. Mr. Callaghan said that he was not willing to pressurise

[9] Mr. G. Ford succeeded Mr. Nixon as US President on 9 August.

Mr. Mavros or Mr. Clerides into a humiliation which he would share. *Mr. Hartman* said that problem was that for the moment the Greek and Turkish Cypriots were talking past each other about their most extreme positions. It was necessary to get them talking to each other. Mr. Callaghan agreed.

8. Reverting to the question of Turkish military intentions, Mr. Hartman said that he thought that Mr. Callaghan should not get into the position of not considering other avenues. *Mr. Callaghan* said that he would of course leave an escape route for the Turks but he would be grateful for United States views on what route could be left. He said it was important that they should not delay to the extent that there was no time to take any countering action. It should not be allowed to get to the point where the Turks thought they could push and push and for example take Famagusta without receiving any adverse response.

9. *Mr. Hartman* thought that he would recommend that Dr. Kissinger send a message to Mr. Eçevit asking what Eçevit's remark 'other means' meant; painting a picture of the consequences of further military action; and drawing a distinction for him between the situation now and that obtaining formerly. He would recommend giving as examples of the differing situation that: there was no odious régime in Athens, no illegal régime in Cyprus, the Turkish Cypriots were protected, and formerly there had been no United Nations Resolution. Dr. Kissinger was very conscious that the Turks felt that, whenever there was a choice between Greece and Turkey, the West chose the Greeks.[10]

10. *Mr. Callaghan* agreed that the Turks were feeling isolated but he thought that they also had a great admiration for Israel and might be tempted to follow the Israeli example after the Six Day War.[11] He hoped that the Turks could be made to realise the consequences of any further military action. *Mr. Hartman* said that the Turks might find themselves bogged down in a guerilla war with world public opinion against them, cut off from the West and with only the Soviet Union to go to. He thought that Dr. Kissinger would be prepared to advance these arguments which should appeal to Eçevit's intelligence. *Mr. Callaghan* said that he did not agree with the assumption that in this case arguments would appeal to rational people. *Mr. Hartman* said that he must assume that the Turks must have considered these arguments even if they had rejected them. *Mr. Callaghan* asked Mr. Hartman to convey his views to Dr. Kissinger and say that Mr. Callaghan thought it was necessary to give some prudent

[10] In UKMIS Geneva telegram No. 809 of 10 August, in which he reported this conversation, Mr. Callaghan noted that, in response to his query as to whether HMG would have US political support in deterring the Turks, Mr. Hartman was 'fairly non-committal', and that the proposal might have fallen outside his terms of reference.

[11] Since the Arab-Israeli War of June 1967 (cf. No. 56, note 1) Israeli forces had remained in occupation of the Sinai peninsula, Syria's Golan Heights, the Gaza strip, the old city of Jerusalem and the remainder of Palestine formerly administered by Jordan.

forethought to Turkish military intentions so that the United Kingdom and United States attitude was decided before a response was needed.

No. 60

Miss Warburton (UKMIS Geneva) to FCO

No. 813 Telegraphic [*WSC 1/13*]

Immediate. Confidential GENEVA, *10 August 1974*[1]

Repeated for information to Immediate Athens, Ankara, Nicosia, Washington, UKMIS New York, UKDEL NATO, Paris, Moscow, Bonn.

Following from Secretary of State. My tel[egram No.] 811:[2]
Cyprus: Meeting of the five parties

1. At the meeting of the three Foreign Ministers and Clerides and Denktash,[3] I suggested that although there were important matters about the implementation of the Declaration and others not covered by it still to be discussed, we should nevertheless devote ourselves to constitutional questions. It took half an hour for my colleagues to agree, while they made points for the record about the implementation of the Declaration.

2. Then followed a pair of oratorical performances by Clerides and Denktash, with occasional interventions by the Ministers when they paused for breath. The history of Cyprus for the past 20 years was covered exhaustively and no grievance was left unaired. On substance, Clerides asserted that the meaning of the Declaration was clear. There could be no question of anything but a reversion to the 1960 Constitution in full, and he was willing to put this into effect. Thereafter, he would be willing to discuss with Denktash possible amendments to the Constitution, but this was not the business of the Guarantor Powers. I said that, as far as the UK

---

[1] This is the date of drafting. The telegram was despatched at 9 a.m. on 11 August.

[2] See No. 59, note 3. In this telegram Mr. Callaghan provided a 'partial round-up' of developments that day. He noted that since Mr. Denktash's views and Dr. Waldheim's assessment had tended to confirm his own apprehensions that they 'could be faced by a fairly early move by the Turkish Army to extend their existing zone of occupation', he had 'set in hand the preparation of some contingency plans'. Mr. Callaghan also reported that he had learned that morning from Mr. Mavros and Mr. Clerides that they expected the Turks to demand 30 per cent of the island and to insist on large population transfers. Mr. Clerides had said that he could 'accept functional federation but not geographical separation', and Mr. Mavros had asserted 'that if the Turks moved forward again the Greeks would have to send a division to Cyprus by convoy'.

[3] The meeting, which began at 5.20 p.m. in the Palais des Nations, was attended by Mr. Callaghan, Mr. Mavros, Mr. Günes, Mr. Clerides, Mr. Denktash and Sr. Guyer.

was concerned, I agreed. Clerides asserted that if Turkey did not support a return to the 1960 Constitution, she could not defend her armed intervention as being in accordance with the Treaty of Guarantee. Günes and Denktash attempted to bury this in a flow of words. They contended that the 1960 Constitution was no longer valid as a starting point. Denktash argued for a geographical basis for the two autonomous administrations as the only means of security for the Turkish community. Clerides replied that this could only lead eventually to partition and double enosis. All parties asserted that this was not their aim and that they were determined to sustain an independent Cyprus.

3. It was eventually agreed that Clerides and Denktash would discuss this question further alone tomorrow and come back to the three Ministers in the evening. Meanwhile we shall meet at 10.30 with a limited number of officials to discuss outstanding matters other than the Constitution. We shall begin with paragraph 3(d) of the Declaration.[4]

4. I was struck by several references by Günes to the uselessness of continuing our discussion unless his wishes could be met. Whether this is a manner of speech or has a more sinister significance I would prefer to leave as an open question for the time being. The next 24 hours should make his intentions clear.

---

[4] This provided for the exchange or release of military personnel and civilians detained as a result of the hostilities.

No. 61

Mr. Richard (UKMIS New York) to Mr. Callaghan

No. 971 Telegraphic [WSC 2/522/2]

Immediate. Secret   NEW YORK, *11 August 1974, 7 a.m.*

Repeated for information to Immediate Ankara, Athens, Bonn, Moscow, Nicosia, Washington, UKMIS Geneva (for Secretary of State) and UKDEL NATO.

UKMIS Geneva tel[egrams] Nos. 806-809.[1]

I have discussed in general terms with Urquhart (please protect) the current situation and in particular the line which Waldheim took with you (UKMIS Geneva tel[egram] No. 807). He is by no means as confident as Waldheim that your proposals can be accomplished within the existing UNFICYP mandate and without prior reference to the Security Council. I am sure this is the advice he will give to the Secretary-General.

---

[1] See No. 58, and No. 59, note 10.

2. My assessment is as follows:

American and Russian attitudes will be of major importance at the UN, as well as in influencing the parties directly. You will doubtless have been informed of US intentions by Hartman, but I should emphasise that, so far they have been distinctly non-committal here. There seems to be a reluctance to take serious issue with the Turks which is similar to their initial reticence in condemning the Greeks.[2] Although we managed to push the Russians into stating that they called for withdrawal of the Turkish invasion force, their position is still unclear. Waldheim's assessment that they would abstain in the circumstances he foresees (para[graph] 7 of UKMIS Geneva tel[egram] No. 807) may be right (and I am myself inclined to take that view also) but I could not advise to rely upon it. This is particularly so if far-reaching proposals on UNFICYP, e.g. major reinforcement by Britain, were involved.[3] The Russians may indeed be broadly neutral but their natural propensity for stirring up trouble is hardly likely to desert them totally at this stage of the game. Certainly we could not rely on their acquiescence (let alone their approval) if they were to see advantage in the situation.

3. The attitude of the non-aligned in the Council has throughout been somewhat ambivalent. My feeling is that, in most circumstances, Iraq and Indonesia at least would be reluctant to adopt an overtly anti-Turkish posture. Once the non-aligned were split, there is no knowing how any vote would go: many would be tempted to abstain, and the pressures on them would depend e.g. on such factors as whether or not they could be induced to accept that this was in reality a situation in which Cyprus was trying to control its own destiny and was being frustrated by the invading Turks.

4. Resolution 355 clearly gives Waldheim authority to cooperate in establishing a security zone under UNFICYP control around the Turkish-controlled area. Once this was established with UNFICYP *in situ*, the position in the event of a Turkish threat to push forward into Greek Cypriot-controlled areas would indeed be analogous to the position over Nicosia airport on 23-24 July.[4] But, until they were in position it clearly would not be.

5. As I understand it, the present situation is that the bulk of UNFICYP remains deployed throughout the Greek Cypriot-controlled part of Cyprus and with some 150 troops in the Turkish-controlled area. There is light

---

[2] Cf. No. 27.

[3] Prior to reinforcement, the British contribution to UNFICYP had consisted of half an infantry battalion and one armoured reconnaissance squadron, plus logistic support units. Since the onset of the crisis this had been increased to a level of one infantry battalion, one armoured reconnaissance regiment and logistic support units (letter from Miss S. Fletcher (MoD) to Mr. D. Doble (Defence Department, FCO) of 13 August (DP 13/441/2).

[4] See No. 40.

patrolling/observation of the demarcation line but no static O.P.s[5] and no fixed UNFICYP positions. In order to carry out the sort of operation Waldheim discussed with you (UKMIS Geneva tel[egram] No. 807) a substantial part of the force would have to be ordered to redeploy into the area of the demarcation line (with any reinforcement it might get) with specific orders that it should maintain positions across the prospective line of march of the Turkish army. Except under para[graph] 3(*a*) of the Geneva Declaration (i.e. the establishment of the security zone) as endorsed indirectly by Resolution 355, there would appear to be no Council mandate for such action. Although Waldheim implied that he would nonetheless give the necessary orders there must be some doubt as to whether he would in fact do so if it came to the crunch. The weight of Secretariat advice from here would undoubtedly be against this without specific fresh authority from the Council and I could not guarantee that such authority would be forthcoming, at least until it was too late (para[graph] 3 above). Moreover I am not clear what Waldheim means when he talks of informing the Council. If in advance of the deployment, there could well be problems. If afterwards, Council approval would depend on whether or not the operation had been successful.

6. Waldheim is indeed admirably staunch on occasion, as he was over Nicosia airport. But he can also be unpredictable (my tel[egrams] Nos. 906 and 907).[6] I think it might not be wholly wise to rely totally on the line he took with you today.

7. Reluctantly, I think it necessary to make the point that at least so long as UNFICYP is not deployed as necessary, I could not guarantee, in the event that you decide to take military measures as a Guarantor Power (para[graph] 7 of UKMIS Geneva tel[egram] No. 807), your being able to do so under UN auspices (para[graph] 3 of UKMIS Geneva tel[egram] No. 806).[7]

8. Having sounded the above warning note, I must say that, if the UN were now to stand by and allow the Turks to expand massively out of their present positions, it would be difficult thereafter to place much credence on their peace-keeping commitments.[8] Ideally we need some UN forces to be

---

[5] Observation Posts.

[6] See No. 50, note 8. In UKMIS New York telegram No. 906 of 30 July Mr. Richard reported that his attempts to secure a meeting of the UN Security Council that night to consider the Geneva Declaration had foundered on Dr. Waldheim's unwillingness, in the face of Soviet opposition to authorising action of any sort, 'to commend the agreement or actively seek endorsement for action by UNFICYP under it'.

[7] See note 1 above. In paragraph 3 of this telegram Air Vice-Marshal Mellersh noted that he would emphasise to Mr. Callaghan that there were 'problems of the availability and movement of any British reinforcement of UNFICYP and the threats which might develop to SBAs even though action would be under UN auspices'.

[8] In UKMIS Geneva telegram No. 21 of 11 August to UKMIS New York Mr. Callaghan observed that when he had spoken to Dr. Waldheim he had found him clearly much influenced by this point. 'He', Mr. Callaghan recalled, 'also had the 1967 Sinai parallel [see No. 56, note 1]

placed in such a strategic position that their presence amounts to an obvious military and political deterrent to the Turks. If they can be so positioned before matters come to a head, then the prior approval of the Council may not be necessary, though that means Waldheim issuing the necessary orders on his own authority.

9. If then the deterrent is successful, there will not in my view be any great difficulty with the Council. If the deterrent is not successful, then the absence of prior approval is hardly likely to be noticed in the new situation which will have arisen. The doubt arises if there is to be major reinforcement and if Waldheim then feels he has to go to the Council for prior approval. If he does, we will have to prove that there is imminent danger and that may be difficult too.

in mind. These seemed to be the two factors underlying his, I agree, surprising degree of staunchness. Nevertheless, I take your point that he can be unpredictable' (WSC 1/13).

No. 62

Record of a meeting between Mr. Callaghan and Mr. Hartman at UKMIS Geneva on 11 August 1974 at 12noon

[*WSC 1/13*]

Secret

Present:

The Rt. Hon. James Callaghan MP	Mr. Hartman
Mr. Brenchley	Mr. Oakley
Mr. Acland	
Mr. Goodison	
Miss Fort	

1. *Mr. Callaghan* said that he had seen Mr. Mavros and Mr. Clerides that morning and that Mr. Mavros had given him a list of Turkish Cypriot villages that the Greek side were prepared to evacuate at once. They amounted to some 20 per cent of the Turkish Cypriot population at present under the control of the National Guard. In the first phase they would be isolated villages and not the enclaves. [1] Mr. Callaghan was having

[1] According to Mr. Mavros's list, the priority for evacuation of enclaves was: six villages in the Limassol region; the Turkish Cypriot quarter in Paphos; and the Turkish Cypriot quarter in Larnaca (UKMIS Geneva telegrams Nos. 4 and 5 to Ankara of 11 August). Mr. Callaghan later recorded in UKMIS Geneva telegram No. 817 of 11 August that the Greeks had handed over all the villages listed and that they had released sixteen Turkish officers to UNFICYP. Meanwhile, Mr. Mavros suggested to Mr. Callaghan that the Conference should make proposals on amendments to the 1960 Constitution, and that officials should work on this and

difficulty in finding Mr. Günes to tell him of this proposal. He thought it essential that it should be transmitted to the Turkish Government while their Council of Ministers was still taking place. It was odd that Mr. Günes had not only adjourned the meeting of the three Foreign Ministers but that he had disappeared. *Mr. Hartman* said that he had seen Mr. Günes that morning at 09.00 when he had simply said that he did not want a formal meeting of Foreign Ministers until after the Turkish Council of Ministers Meeting had finished.[2]

2. *Mr. Callaghan* said that, as Mr. Hartman would be aware, HMG had carried out the initial military steps of which he had informed him the previous day and that he had made them public.[3] He had asked Mr. Hartman to call on him in order to hear Dr. Kissinger's reaction to Mr. Callaghan's view of the threat of Turkish military expansion and of his proposal to attempt to deter Turkish activities by re-inforcing British troops under UN auspices in Cyprus. *Mr. Hartman* said that Dr. Kissinger was not happy with HMG's approach. When Mr. Hartman had informed Dr. Kissinger of the British assessment he had talked to Eçevit on the telephone and sent him a message urging the Turks to continue the talks, and to refrain from military action.[4] Dr. Kissinger had received assurances from Mr. Eçevit with which he was content. Dr. Kissinger thought that the line proposed by Mr. Callaghan would have the effect in Turkey of bringing domestic pressures to bear on Mr. Eçevit to take a harder line. These pressures would work against Dr. Kissinger's efforts to convince Mr. Eçevit of the limits to which Turkey could go and of the extent of Mr. Clerides's and Mr. Mavros's opposition. Dr. Kissinger would like the political discussions to be kept going. He thought there was a real possibility of moving the Turks off their idea of a single Turkish zone in Cyprus. The Turks should be allowed to back down from their extreme position by the negotiation of a diplomatic framework, which should include a timetable and programme for the next meeting of the Geneva Conference. Dr.

report back to the Foreign Ministers in three weeks' time (record of a conversation between Mr. Callaghan, Mr. Mavros and Mr. Clerides at the Palais des Nations, Geneva, on 11 August at 11 a.m.).

[2] Mr. Callaghan reported in UKMIS Geneva telegram No. 817 (*v. ibid*) that Mr. Günes had asked that there should be no plenary session that day since he was awaiting instructions from Ankara. He also noted that he had been told by Mr. Kirça that the Turkish Council of Ministers were in session for most of that day, discussing 'American "proposals" for a constitutional settlement on the basis of a cantonal system not involving two regions only'. Cf. No. 63.

[3] See No. 59. On 11 August Mr. Callaghan issued a statement to the British press in which he was quoted as having said that British forces were ready to open fire, and in the event of Turkish expansion, had been ordered to take necessary action to protect British troops in UNFICYP (Ankara telegram No. 13 to UKMIS Geneva of 12 August).

[4] According to UKMIS Geneva telegram No. 817 (see notes 1 and 2 above) Dr. Kissinger's letter to Mr. Eçevit 'had spoken "in the friendliest possible way" of the serious consequences of military action'.

Kissinger would react very strongly against another public announcement of British military activities. It would have an adverse effect on his tactics with Mr. Eçevit.

3. Mr. Hartman said that, in his conversation with Mr. Clerides, he had asked him what was the limit he could go to. Mr. Clerides had said that he could consider complete Turkish autonomy under a central Turkish Administration with complete jurisdiction over the areas they controlled in groupings of villages; but not the proposal for a single Turkish zone. His condition was that there must be some prospect of eventual withdrawal of Turkish forces. Mr. Hartman thought that discussion should start to be easier since Mr. Clerides was not insisting on a unitary State. He was even prepared to consider a totally new Constitution even though it might be produced by amending the 1960 Constitution.

4. Mr. Hartman, in his meeting with Mr. Günes, had pointed out to him that the Greeks were trying to control the National Guard and were not operating against the enclaves. Mr. Günes had said that his position would not be clear until after the Cabinet Meeting in Ankara. It was very difficult for the Turkish side to agree on several zones or cantons. They had no way of ensuring that this proposal did not once more dissolve in fruitless and lengthy inter-communal talks once the pressure was off. He had dismissed Mr. Clerides's readiness to abandon the concept of a unitary State. There was *de facto* separation in whole areas. He thought that it was impossible simply to put the two communities together and expect them to talk. The Guarantor Powers should not wash their hands of the problem. The Greek and Turkish Governments should be represented at the constitutional talks even if Her Majesty's Government were not prepared to be there. Mr. Clerides had taken a similar line, but had said that he would want a British observer and a British legal expert present. Mr. Hartman said that Mr. Günes had left him with the impression that he and others in Ankara were trying to seek authority for more flexibility in their approach to the concept of separate administration.

5. *Mr. Callaghan* said that he thought that Dr. Kissinger was not facing up to the real problem on the military side. He asked Mr. Hartman to find out from Dr. Kissinger what the United States reaction would be if the Turks used force to enlarge their bridgehead. *Mr. Hartman* said that Dr. Kissinger would not get boxed in on this question. He would privately paint a picture for Mr. Eçevit so that Mr. Eçevit himself would come to the intellectual conclusion of the grave consequences for himself, his party and his country. *Mr. Callaghan* said that that was one line of presentation but that he hoped that Dr. Kissinger was facing the question of how he would react in the face of Turkish military expansion, even if he were not prepared to tell him. *Mr. Hartman* said that Dr. Kissinger was afraid that even to focus on this eventuality would influence events to move on to a military plane. If the focus moved from the diplomatic negotiations then they could not advance. *Mr. Callaghan* said that they were both guessing about Turkish intentions. He felt that the worst interpretation possible

should be put on them. He thought that they had sufficient pointers in this direction for Her Majesty's Government to prepare contingency plans. *Mr. Hartman* said that nothing they said precluded Dr. Kissinger from planning. It was natural for him to do so. But Dr. Kissinger was convinced that Mr. Eçevit understood that any further action on their part would have serious consequences. If they focused on the military intentions of the Turks it would affect the whole tone of the political discussions.

6. *Mr. Callaghan* said that two interpretations could be put on Mr. Günes's conduct—he could be clearing the decks before military action or it could merely be his unfortunate tone. *Mr. Hartman* thought the Turks had made their hardest pitch for their most desired position and that we would now have to see if there was any receding from that in further discussion. *Mr. Callaghan* said that he was prepared to assume some irrationality on the Turkish part. *Mr. Hartman* said that it was fine to make that assumption in the back of his mind but that if it deflected the focus of his intention he would get in a dead-end. *Mr. Callaghan* pointed out that it was Mr. Günes who was preventing the Ministers from meeting. He was not prepared to sit around in Geneva forever, particularly if he were not getting backing from Dr. Kissinger. *Mr. Hartman* said that Dr. Kissinger's efforts were designed to make the Turks see the limit of their possibilities. Mr. Günes should get instructions from home allowing him to be more flexible. He counselled patience on Mr. Callaghan's part. *Mr. Callaghan* said that on the previous occasion in Geneva Mr. Günes had agreed on proposals which were subsequently overruled from home. Now he was waiting for moves from the other side. Mr. Callaghan was anxious to put the evacuation plan to Mr. Günes in order to demonstrate that there was movement on the Greek side. But Mr. Günes would have to show himself a bit more accommodating to us. *Mr. Hartman* again urged Mr. Callaghan to be prepared to listen and wait. *Mr. Callaghan* said that he was prepared to listen. He had shown no impatience in the meetings, but he also had a responsibility to take military precautions. The tougher you were with the Turks the more they would listen to you. He thought that Dr. Kissinger was mistaken about this. The last time the Turks had backed off was at Nicosia airport when he had said to Eçevit that he was putting British troops in blue berets but that he was not prepared to see British troops shot up. He believed that the Americans were not yet handling the Turks in a way which would have an effect. He wished to work with the United States on this and would not make an announcement today about his intention to order in more Phantoms and further British troops at once. He would wait to see what came out of the Turkish Council of Ministers but thereafter he would see if he wished to make any publicity for the reinforcement. *Mr. Hartman* urged him to inform Dr. Kissinger beforehand if he intended to make such an announcement.

7. *Mr. Callaghan* agreed to do so and stressed his strong desire to work with the United States, but he reserved his position on British policy. He said that there were 12,000 British dependants in Cyprus and that he

would have to make a decision on whether to move them into the SBAs, an operation which would take some time. He was not concerned with his position at the bar of history but if he did not take a decision to move in the families for their own protection he would have a great responsibility to bear if they were put in danger. Dr. Kissinger was concerned with the broader issues of the south-east flank of NATO and of the United States' relations with Turkey and Greece but Mr. Callaghan had these other problems of the security of British citizens. *Mr. Hartman* said that Dr. Kissinger was not just concerned with questions of NATO strategy. His main concern was how to convince the Turks not to follow the Israeli example in 1967.[5] He had the same objective as Mr. Callaghan but had reached a different assessment of how it could be achieved. He wished to put private pressure on Eçevit, as in his letter, describing the possible consequences to Mr. Eçevit and telling him of the inability of the United States to support such moves.[6] *Mr. Callaghan* said that he was sure that Dr. Kissinger was right to make this effort but that HMG had to take other precautions. From a short-sighted view, it might be the best thing for British interests for HMG to reject the Treaty of Guarantee and withdraw from the SBAs.[7] If there was no American backing for Britain, he might consider this, but he would want to know what the American position was and would talk to Dr. Kissinger on the telephone before taking any decisive steps.

[5] See No. 59, note 11.
[6] See note 4 above.
[7] Cf. No. 44.

No. 63

Record of a telephone conversation between Mr. Callaghan and Mr. Sisco on 11 August 1974 at 5.20 p.m.

[*WSC 1/13*]

Secret

Mr. Sisco explained that Dr. Kissinger had been trying to contact Mr. Callaghan but, while the call was going through, had been called to the White House. Dr. Kissinger had been led to believe that Mr. Callaghan was concerned about the possibility of the Turkish Army moving forward on 11 August. This could have been [the] result of confusion in American minds arising from the previous night's reports from Athens. Dr. Kissinger had sent a strong message to Mr. Eçevit who had 'agreed to hold off'.[1] Dr. Kissinger also understood that Mr. Callaghan was apprehensive about

[1] Cf. No. 64, note 2.

United States proposals to the Turks. There had been no United States proposals, though the Americans had asked the Turks whether they were considering the possibility of cantonal rather than a geographically separate solution. Mr. Sisco emphasised that any proposals about Cyprus should be framed together by the British and United States Governments.[2]

2. *Mr. Callaghan* accepted Mr. Sisco's reassurances but said that he would have liked to have been better informed about American conversations with the Turks. He was not prepared to be a dummy in the middle though he would be happy to continue to work with Dr. Kissinger through Mr. Hartman.

3. Mr. Callaghan said that he had not received any firm reply from Mr. Hartman about whether the United States Government were prepared to concert with Her Majesty's Government on a plan of action in the event of the Turkish forces moving forward again in Cyprus. He was working hard along the diplomatic path in order to keep things going. But we should keep in mind the darker possibilities. *Mr. Sisco* undertook to think about these and let Mr. Callaghan have a reply.

[2] See No. 62, note 2. In UKMIS Geneva telegram No. 817 (see No. 62, note 1) Mr. Callaghan observed with reference to Mr. Sisco's explanation: 'I welcomed this assurance. It seems nevertheless that Kissinger must have put forward some ideas.'

No. 64

Record of a conversation between Mr. Callaghan and Mr. Günes in the Palais des Nations, Geneva, on 11 August 1974 at 5.45 p.m.

[*Callaghan Private Office Papers*]

Confidential

Present:

The Rt. Hon. James Callaghan MP	Mr. Günes
Mr. Carter	Private Secretary[1]
Mr. Goulden	

1. *Mr. Callaghan* said that he regretted the way in which the British and Turkish positions appeared to have drifted apart in the last two days. Mr. Günes would understand his anxiety on receiving reports which suggested that the Geneva Declaration might be under threat. His fear was not that Mr. Günes would renege on his assurances but that forces in Turkey would compel the Turkish Government to adopt another course. This risk put Ministers under greater obligation to find an appropriate solution. But Mr. Callaghan could not propound a solution which, according to Mr. Clerides,

[1] Mr. O. Akbel.

would lead either to war in the island or the overthrow of the Clerides Government. A war in Cyprus might well end in Turkish victory but would be followed by 25 years of EOKA-type activity. It would not be feasible to base discussions on proposals which were not acceptable to both communities on the island. What was needed was an approach which met the Turkish Cypriots' quest for security without involving the betrayal of the Greek Cypriots. A cantonal model might satisfy these conditions but it would take some time to get the Greek Cypriots to swallow it. Mr. Callaghan was ready to concentrate on finding an agreed framework for the future of Cyprus, leaving aside for the moment the less central problems arising from the Geneva Declaration. But he would wish to associate Mr. Denktash and Mr. Clerides in this work.

2. *Mr. Günes* repeated that the Turkish Government had no intention of extending its zone by military measures without compelling reason. They would not take military action on the pretext that Greece refused to implement the Geneva Declaration. They wanted the Conference to succeed and were prepared to consider several alternatives. He expected to receive soon from Ankara authority to discuss a cantonal as well as a geographically separate solution. He thought that Mr. Clerides and Mr. Denktash, who were compelled in the end to find a *modus vivendi*, would accept one or the other, even though they might not at present be able to say so publicly. He proposed that the Conference should try to agree on general directives which might be left to the Cypriot communities to implement in detail within a fixed time limit.

3. Mr. Günes stressed however that he could not afford to let the Conference become bogged down in legalistic debate and expert committees. If this happened it would be better to admit failure and seek a solution by other—not necessarily military—means. Turkey was at a crossroads and needed an early settlement on Cyprus to avoid internal trouble and the risk of unravelling all her foreign relations. The relationship between Turkey and Greece was intrinsically more important than Cyprus. But Cyprus was the sole preoccupation of Turkish public opinion.

4. Mr. Günes then outlined the main pros and cons of a cantonal and a geographically separate model for Cyprus. He personally preferred the latter since it was clearer, simpler and less likely to lead to intercommunal fighting in the future. He emphasised that he did not see the creation of two geographically separate administrations as a stepping stone to double *enosis*. Turkey did not want to see a Greek base in Cyprus which might permit Greek airplanes to penetrate much more deeply than at present into Turkish territory. Mr. Günes was convinced that the Greek and Turkish Cypriots, although emotionally attached to the mainland, were more attached to their own system, with its less onerous taxes and military obligations. His objective assessment, therefore, was that neither

community in the island would wish to proceed from a dualist federation to double *enosis*. [2]

5. *Mr. Callaghan* said that he did not want to commit himself on the merits of the two models, but would like to hear more about them at dinner with Mr. Mavros and Mr. Günes that evening.[3]

6. Mr. Callaghan and Mr. Günes then visited Mr. Mavros to outline their conversation. It was agreed that the three Ministers should try to reach an informal agreement on the broad outline of a solution, which Mr. Clerides and Mr. Denktash should then discuss in detail with a view to reporting back to the Conference in about three weeks.[4]

---

[2] Later that evening, following a meeting with Mr. Günes and Mr. Mavros at which they agreed to discuss over dinner a cantonal solution to the Cyprus problem, Mr. Callaghan noted in UKMIS Geneva telegram No. 817 (see No. 62, notes 1 and 2): 'It seems that the Turks have decided against the military option for the time being. According to Sisco [cf. No. 63], Eçevit told Kissinger earlier today that the Turks would "hold off"—though this of course suggests that the idea of military action is not far from their thoughts. I do not think we need for the moment pursue the precautionary measures which have been under discussion. Our discussion at dinner will be crucial. I think there is just a chance that we can reach at least an oral understanding which might open the way to constitutional arrangements acceptable to all the parties. The Greeks have made substantial gestures towards the fulfilment of the Declaration. They still need a concession from the Turks in the military field, either in the form of withdrawal from areas they claim or of a token reduction of troops in Cyprus. If the Turks are seriously interested in [*sic*] the latter at least should not be impossible for them.'

[3] Cf. No. 65.

[4] *V. ibid.* Paragraph 6 of this document was omitted from the printed copy reproduced in WSC 1/13.

No. 65

Summary record of a discussion between Mr. Callaghan, Mr. Günes and Mr. Mavros at dinner at the Hotel la Réserve, Geneva, on 11 August 1974 at 9 p.m.[1]

[*WSC 1/13*]

Confidential

Present:

The Rt. Hon. James Callaghan MP	Mr. Günes
Mr. Carter	Mr. Mavros

1. There was a good deal of historical propaganda, to which Mr. Günes and Mr. Mavros reverted throughout the dinner. On a Cyprus settlement, *Mr. Günes* said that he must have some guarantees that there were going to be changes. *Mr. Mavros* said that the Greeks must have time to consider these changes. Mr. Clerides and Mr. Denktash got on well together. A solution must be achieved and perhaps they were the best placed to achieve one. *Mr. Callaghan* suggested that the Conference should end with no statement by the three Foreign Ministers, but with one from Mr. Clerides and Mr. Denktash. This might say that they had agreed that over the next weeks they would discuss alone, without any observer, what changes would be necessary to ensure the security of the population of the Island within the framework of a united Cyprus; it would say that substantial changes were needed; they would meet the Foreign Ministers again in three weeks' time to inform them of the progress they had made. This meeting need not necessarily take place in Geneva. *Mr. Mavros* agreed. *Mr. Günes* said that this would not offer the guarantee he sought. In the past, whenever such discussions had been initiated, the urgency had died away from them fast. *Mr. Callaghan* said that there could be no such guarantee; a solution could not be forced on the Cypriots. Mr. Günes would have to rely on the goodwill and good faith of Mr. Clerides and Mr. Denktash; he no doubt wanted to go back to Turkey and be able to report that the Conference had been very successful; the formula which been put forward did not explicitly say that there was any alternative to a bi-regional federation. *Mr. Günes* said that the only possible solution was the erection of two autonomous regions. *Mr. Callaghan* warned him that Cyprus was not the prisoner of the Turkish Army; the Turkish Army was the prisoner of Cyprus. *Mr. Günes* admitted that the expense of keeping the army in Cyprus was high. He did not demur when *Mr. Callaghan* said that Mr.

---

[1] This record was based on notes taken from an oral account given by Mr. Callaghan after the dinner.

Denktash had told him that he had persuaded the Turkish Government to espouse bi-regional federation as a policy. *Mr. Mavros* was eloquent on the importance of Cyprus ceasing to be a 'place d'armes'. He reminded Mr. Günes that he had the guarantee inherent in the fact that Turkey could always invade Cyprus again if she thought it necessary. He proposed that Mr. Callaghan should talk to Mr. Clerides and Mr. Denktash about his proposal, and this was agreed. It was also agreed that Mr. Clerides was not amenable to instructions from the Foreign Ministers. *Mr. Callaghan* said that the clearer they were in their own minds about the intended outcome of the Clerides/Denktash talks, the vaguer the statement could be.

2. *Mr. Günes* said that perhaps Turkey alone of the three Foreign Ministers should also issue a statement saying that there would be a withdrawal of Turkish forces in a comparatively short time, parallel with the implementation of the proposals formulated by Mr. Clerides and Mr. Denktash. The agreement would begin to be applied very quickly and then they would begin to withdraw their forces. *Mr. Callaghan* said that he was unsure about the timing of such a statement. If the Foreign Ministers were to receive the report from Mr. Clerides and Mr. Denktash on 2 September, it might be best for Mr. Günes to make the statement then, conditional on the implementation of the report. *Mr. Mavros* did not press for earlier action.

No. 66

Record of a meeting between British and US officials at Geneva on 12 August 1974 at 10.30 a.m.

[*WSC 1/13*]

Secret

Present:

Mr. A.C. Goodison   Mr. Hartman
Mr. M.O'D.B. Alexander

Mr. Hartman said that Mr. Callaghan had requested further details of United States thinking.[1] Dr. Kissinger had sent Mr. Eçevit a message opposing unilateral Turkish action and advocating political action; he had included the cantonal idea as an example of political flexibility; this idea had been mentioned to Mr. Callaghan by Mr. Hartman on the aeroplane to Geneva on 8 August. Mr. Eçevit had replied that he was thinking of putting proposals forward in Geneva which would include the cantonal proposal. Dr. Kissinger had replied urging flexibility. Mr. Eçevit had said

---

[1] See No. 62.

that Turkey would take no military action pending the conclusion of discussion in Geneva.[2] Dr. Kissinger wished to stress that any proposal put forward by Turkey was a Turkish and not a United States proposal. It was not beyond the Turks to allege that they were acting on American instructions; this might involve the United States more than they wished to be involved. Dr. Kissinger had also instructed Mr. Hartman to say that the United States Government supported British efforts to solve the crisis by diplomatic means; that they had told the Turks that they could expect no support in the Security Council from the United States if they made a military move; indeed, that if they made such a move, the United States would mount a major diplomatic effort, with the United Kingdom, to halt them. But the United States could not themselves consider taking military action, particularly so soon after the inauguration of President Ford, nor did they consider that the threats of military action were helpful or appropriate in these circumstances. The United States Government considered that talk of military action distracted concentration from the political options. Of the points he had made, that regarding the Security Council was the most important; the United States would mount an all-out effort, as it had done to stop the Turkish invasion of Cyprus.[3]

[2] Sir H. Phillips informed Mr. Callaghan in Ankara telegram No. 11 to UKMIS Geneva, despatched on the evening of 11 August, that, although Mr. Macomber had earlier found Mr. Eçevit 'unyielding on the principle of delineation along a line virtually cutting the island in two', Mr. Eçevit had later appeared ready to consider a combination of delineation and cantonisation. 'The important thing', Sir H. Phillips noted, 'is that the Turks are showing signs of being less inflexible on ways and means of achieving their objective. (Though Dr. Kissinger apparently does not relish Eçevit's inclination to refer to "the American plan".)'

[3] In his telegram No. 11 to UKMIS Geneva (*v. ibid.*) Sir H. Phillips reported that the Americans found the Turks 'obsessed by a feeling of isolation and of abandonment by friends and allies notwithstanding the rights of their case'. He added that the British attitude to Turkey was 'arousing some resentment' in Ankara, and that he hoped 'a more flexible Turkish approach to the negotiations might help to improve the atmosphere'.

No. 67

Sir R. Hooper (Athens) to Mr. Callaghan

No. 430 [WSC 1/13]

Immediate. Confidential   ATHENS, *12 August 1974, 11.15 a.m.*

Repeated for information to Immediate UKMIS Geneva, Ankara, Nicosia, CBFNE, Washington, UKMIS New York and UKDEL NATO.

Ankara tel[egram] No. 8 to UKMIS Geneva:[1]
Turkish intentions in Cyprus

1. In his telegram under reference Sir H. Phillips has given an able and sympathetic analysis of current Turkish attitudes. This is both timely and necessary now that Turkey is in danger of forfeiting the international sympathy which was handed to her on a plate by the follies perpetrated by the previous Greek Government.

2. It has to be accepted that any solution in Cyprus based on 'power sharing' is a dead duck, and has been so for years. Neither side has seriously tried to work the 1960 Constitution. Both sides are to blame—in what proportions it would be futile to argue now, though the Greek Cypriots, aided and abetted by successive Greek Governments, 'democratic' or otherwise, must bear their full share of responsibility. It has also to be accepted that the Turks have decided that they can no longer acquiesce in the situation described in Sir H. Phillips' para[graph] 2[2] and that the previous Greek Government offered them a golden opportunity to put their decision into effect. In these circumstances, the Turkish military are prepared to go to the brink of disaster and possibly beyond in order to

---

[1] In this telegram of 11 August Sir H. Phillips reported that he had gathered from what the US Ambassador in Ankara had told him that Mr. Eçevit felt that the UK was 'swinging in favour of Greece', and that the Turks were 'therefore looking for American understanding of their case'. Sir H. Phillips believed that Britain should also look at Turkish behaviour 'with understanding'. He remarked that 'what hardens the Turks is the seeming refusal of Clerides if not Mavros to recognise that Greek dominance in Cyprus is gone for good. So long as there is any danger of an attempt to re-assert it the Turkish armed forces will persuade the Government that they must go on consolidating and if necessary expanding'. He concluded: 'We should not underestimate their determination, their toughness, and their value to us as democratic allies. Nor, I hope, will we forget that they do have what is basically a righteous cause in Cyprus—however much we may deprecate aspects of their behaviour there which, as they see it, are designed simply to ensure that they do not lose the initiative they have won.'

[2] Sir H. Phillips explained in this paragraph of his telegram (*v. ibid.*) that Turkey was determined 'never again' to have the 'Turks in Cyprus treated as second-class citizens under the Greek yoke', and 'to be powerless to counter the danger to Turkey that a Cyprus dominated by a hostile Athens could mean'.

secure the objectives set out in Sir H. Phillips' para[graph] 3,[3] which they consider to be the only basis on which the position of the Turkish community and Turkey herself in Cyprus can be permanently safeguarded. They are prepared to do this regardless of the odium Turkey may incur internationally and of the possible effects on their relations with Greece and on the latter's internal stability. In this, they have not been deterred to any significant extent either by any military threat that Greece can pose or by the attempts which have been made internationally to impose restraint on Turkey.

3. The Turkish attitude is understandable, however much one may deplore it. But it can be doubted whether the course of action on which the Turks seem to be set is likely to achieve the results which they seem to expect. I cannot of course speak in regard to Clerides, though it is possible that within the limited options open to him, he is less intransigent than we may think. The Greeks, for their part, have certainly come a long way (and at considerable risk to their own internal position) towards accepting an effective degree of local autonomy in Cyprus, though what they may be able to concede may not be in all respects what the Turks want. The prospects of the Turks obtaining by negotiation a great deal of what they are aiming at are therefore perhaps better than they may at present believe. On the other hand, if they attempt to obtain by force what they may think it impossible to achieve at the Conference table, any resulting settlement cannot be permanent. They probably have the military capacity to impose their demands in the short term. But is unrealistic to suppose that in such circumstances there could be a sovereign independent Cyprus under a central Government representing both communities. The result is more likely to be a *de facto* partition of the kind the Turks say they do not want. The danger of a further explosion would always be present. It would be necessary to maintain indefinitely a large international peace-keeping force in Cyprus; while the adverse economic and political consequences for the island itself of such a state of affairs needs no emphasis.

4. It can of course be argued that Turkish dignity and security are involved: but similar considerations apply on the Greek side also, and what may be regarded as an honourable solution in Ankara may not necessarily appear so in Athens. If the Turks decide to throw in their hand at Geneva and enlarge their area of occupation in Cyprus by force, the consequence may well be war between Greece and Turkey—a war from which, the Greeks may well not be deterred by the virtual certainty of defeat. Internationally, the consequences are incalculable—at least they would make the eastern flank of NATO totally vulnerable and the credibility of the alliance as a whole very doubtful. The Russians could be able to assert

[3] According to paragraph 3 of Sir H. Phillips's telegram (*v. ibid.*) the Turkish Government had three principles 'not open to negotiation': '(*a*) a sovereign independent Cyprus under a central government, (*b*) within this, geographic delineation of the two communities, (*c*) absolute autonomy for these'.

themselves in the eastern Mediterranean as never before. This, in the long term, would be a far greater threat to Turkish security than a Cyprus dominated by a Greece which, though it might be hostile, is nevertheless only one third the size of Turkey.

5. War between Greece and Turkey would bring about, if not the fall of the Karamanlis Government, at least the revival of military influence over it to a point at which it would be unable to continue on its present course of restoring democracy. Any hope of rebuilding Greek-Turkish relations and *a fortiori* of a rational settlement of Greek-Turkish problems would disappear. If, as seems likely in a straight fight, Greece were to sustain a defeat comparable to that of 1922,[4] it is conceivable that from the ensuing political collapse, there would eventually emerge a left wing government, neutralist or Soviet-orientated, which would be even less to Turkish tastes than what they have got now.

6. There is of course an element of bluff and blackmail in what both the Greeks and the Greek Cypriots say to us about the fragility of their respective governments and the consequences which might ensue from their fall. But the danger is nevertheless a real one, and if the Turks in fact intend to try to impose a solution by force, they will bear a very heavy responsibility.

---

[4] The Græco-Turkish War of 1920-22 followed the Greek military occupation of Izmir (Smyrna) in May 1920 and the challenge posed by the followers of Mustapha Kemal Pasha (Atatürk) to the efforts of the victorious Allies to impose their terms on a defeated Ottoman Empire. Further advances by Greek forces into Asia Minor culminated in their catastrophic defeat in September 1922. The subsequent Treaty of Lausanne (1923) deprived Greece of territorial gains resulting from the Treaty of Sèvres (August 1920).

No. 68

Miss Warburton (UKMIS Geneva) to Sir P. Ramsbotham (Washington)

No. 4 Telegraphic [*Callaghan Private Office Papers*]

Flash. Secret   GENEVA, *12 August 1974, 11.56 a.m.*

Repeated for information to Immediate FCO (for Sir J. Killick)

Personal for Ambassador from Secretary of State.
Your telegram No. 2666 to FCO:[1]
Lunch with Kissinger

1. I would like you to get across to Dr. Kissinger my strong wish for complete frankness and trust between us in the handling of the Cyprus problem not only as regards the broad strategy but also on day to day tactics. In the last 48 hours this mutual confidence has been somewhat impaired.

2. There may be some genuine differences of assessment between myself and Dr. Kissinger about the attitudes and policy of the Turkish Government at present. My view is that the approach to the Turks must proceed on parallel lines namely on the diplomatic and the military level. I do not forget that four hours before they landed on 20 July our Ambassador in Ankara was assured that no orders had been given for landing. Nor do I forget their firm intention to take over Nicosia airport from which they were finally diverted in part at least because I told Eçevit that I would not stand by and see the 16/5th Lancers slaughtered.[2] Although I have been here in contact with Günes for a total of 11 days now, it is still not possible for me to fathom his real intentions. Every assurance about no further military advance is hedged about in some way.

3. The Americans here have professed concern about what they see as the introduction by us of a new military dimension into the situation the day before yesterday,[3] but they must not forget that the military dimension is constantly hanging over our heads in the form of the Turkish army. I sense that Kissinger may feel he should have been consulted before we announced the halting of troop withdrawals from Cyprus. On reflection I wish I had done so. However, Hartman here was told what we proposed almost as soon as the decision had been taken. Kissinger should also know

---

[1] In this telegram of 11 August Sir P. Ramsbotham informed Mr. Callaghan that he was lunching with Dr. Kissinger on 12 August, and that Dr. Kissinger would no doubt wish, *inter alia*, to discuss Cyprus (WSC 3/304/2).

[2] The 16/5th Lancers were part of UNFICYP.

[3] See No. 58, note 4.

that I have for the moment suspended action on the proposal to send the reinforcements which was under discussion yesterday.

4. As regards Kissinger's letter to Eçevit[4] you should stress that I am grateful for his intervention and for securing from Eçevit an undertaking to 'hold off' on military action in Cyprus.

5. On the other hand I would have expected to learn from the Americans direct rather than through the Turks here that Kissinger's letter contained thoughts on the island's constitutional arrangements. Whether or not Sisco is right in claiming that the letter contained no 'proposals' is, I suspect, largely a matter of semantics: it is evident that Eçevit was invited to consider the cantonal approach.[5] This is now being referred to by the Turks as the 'American Plan'. The Americans here have transmitted to Washington my request for a sight of Kissinger's letter but so far there has been no response. I do not want you to press the request any further but you should make the point, in whatever terms you see fit, that if we and the Americans are to work together on this I must know exactly what is in Kissinger's mind.[6]

6. Please make sure that this temporary difference in emphasis between myself and Kissinger is seen in its proper context. It is a minor disagreement within the family and like all family quarrels we shall turn fiercely on any outsider who tries to butt in. I spoke to Sisco on the telephone yesterday and told him that I did not propose to be the 'dummy in the middle'.[7] I hope he has got the message. You should make it clear to Kissinger that my concern is to ensure that cooperation, to which I attach the highest importance, continues to be as close and as cordial as ever.

7. You should also see the account in MIFT[8] of a conversation between Hartman and the Private Secretary. Once again the Turkish assurance

---

[4] See No. 63.

[5] See No. 62, note 2.

[6] Sir P. Ramsbotham's lunch with Dr. Kissinger was unfortunately interrupted for a long period by a summons from President Ford to help prepare his speech to the joint session of Congress. But Sir P. Ramsbotham saw Dr. Kissinger again later in the afternoon of 12 August and they managed to complete their discussion on the basis of this telegram. In response, Dr. Kissinger explained that he had been totally preoccupied during the past week with the change of Presidency, and that during 6-10 August he had been 'virtually out of touch with the Cyprus problem'. He had, he said, thought it right, besides warning Mr. Eçevit against a military move, to also offer him a way out by encouraging him to put forward his own proposal at Geneva. Dr. Kissinger had not, he insisted, put forward a proposal of his own, and he promised to send Mr. Callaghan a copy of his letter to Mr. Eçevit. 'He was', he observed, 'determined to avoid the United States incurring the hostility of both Greek and Turkish Governments, as this could only weaken NATO. He would be frank in saying that he perhaps cared less about events in Cyprus itself' (Washington telegram No. 4 to UKMIS Geneva of 12 August, WSC 3/304/2).

[7] See No. 63.

[8] Not traced. In UKMIS Geneva telegram No. 819 of 12 August, despatched at 12.08 p.m., Mr. Callaghan reported that a member of his staff had learned from Mr. Hartman that earlier that day Dr. Kissinger had either telephoned or sent a message to Mr. Eçevit urging on him 'the need for flexibility at the negotiating table and restraint in the island'. Dr. Kissinger had

about military action appears to be conditional. It reinforces my view that it will be much better to stop them by increasing pressure before they move than trying to concert a response while they are on the march.

8. We will try to get you an account of what has transpired this morning before your lunch. Hartman is fully in the picture.[9]

also emphasised to Mr. Eçevit that there were no US 'proposals' for tackling the Cyprus problem, and that all the Americans had done was to tell the Turks what they meant by 'flexibility' and given them examples of what flexibility might imply. Mr. Hartman added that: (1) Dr. Kissinger continued to support Mr. Callaghan's efforts to solve the Cyprus problem diplomatically; (2) Dr. Kissinger had made it clear to the Turks that the US would not support them in the UN Security Council if they took military action; (3) if the Turks took military action there would be a major US diplomatic effort in NATO and bilaterally to stop them; (4) the US could not consider military action against the Turks; (5) Dr. Kissinger did not consider threats of military action helpful in the present circumstances, since such gestures tended to create problems for Mr. Eçevit with 'extremists' in Turkey. Mr. Hartman was informed that Mr. Callaghan was not contemplating any further military action at the moment and that all new action on reinforcements had been suspended since 11 August (WSC 3/304/2).

[9] During his meeting with Dr. Kissinger, Sir P. Ramsbotham urged him to telephone Mr. Callaghan at once. Cf. No. 72, note 3.

No. 69

Miss Warburton (UKMIS Geneva) to FCO

No. 820 Telegraphic [WSC 1/13]

Flash. Confidential   GENEVA, *12 August 1974, 2 p.m.*

Repeated for information to Flash Washington, Immediate Athens, Ankara, Nicosia, UKMIS New York, UKDEL NATO, Paris and Bonn.

Following from Secretary of State: Cyprus

1. I saw Clerides this morning, who had already seen Mavros. I gave him a draft statement (text in MIFT).[1] He found this generally suitable apart from the passage relating to the autonomous administrations within a

[1] UKMIS Geneva telegram No. 821 of 12 August included the draft text of an 'agreed press statement' in which Mr. Clerides and Mr. Denktash would record that they were 'agreed that a fundamental revision of the system of Government of the Republic of Cyprus [was] necessary to ensure conditions' in which the two communities could 'live together' in 'peace, with mutual trust and in full confidence that the security of each is safeguarded'. It further stated that they were agreed that this revision should result in the establishment of a 'system based on the existence of two autonomous administrations within suitable boundaries, united under a central government', and that 'such changes should take place within the framework of a sovereign, independent and integral Republic of Cyprus'. They were to hold discussions in Nicosia in order to elaborate the envisaged changes, and to inform the Guarantor Powers of the changes agreed.

suitable boundary. He said the word 'boundaries' was impossible for him and preferred 'based on two national communities which shall enjoy autonomy'.[2] I urged him to talk to Denktash.

2. I next saw the latter, who told me he had been depressed to hear that Günes seemed now ready to agree to a cantonal system rather than two regions only. (It seems that Günes did not go as far at dinner as his instructions permitted.) Denktash did not comment on my draft but said he would first wish to consult his Turkish Cypriot colleagues and the Turks. He believed that he and Clerides could settle the matter between themselves provided the latter was firmly backed by the Greek Government. He agreed to meet Clerides this afternoon in my room. I would leave them alone but would be available for consultations if they sent for me. (Clerides has subsequently agreed to this procedure.)

3. Denktash was also concerned about the situation of 60,000 Turks who had been displaced from their homes and whose harvest and animals had been taken away. He did not know how he was going to feed them.

4. I put to Mavros the point that he must give Clerides support. He said that the Greek Government certainly intended to do so, with a statement by Karamanlis. They had been in touch with Makarios by telephone who had raised no objection to the procedure proposed. Mavros was anxious that while the talks continue between the Cypriot leaders the three Foreign Ministers should meet to discuss matters other than the Constitution. Günes has declined to do so for the time being.

5. My view is that the responsibility for determining the Constitution of Cyprus in the future must be placed firmly on the Cypriot leaders. This flows naturally from the fact that Cyprus is an independent state and will help to avoid difficulties with the Soviet Union or the non-aligned. It means that no new responsibilities are placed on the United Kingdom.[3] In the short term a statement on the lines of that in MIFT may well prove easier to negotiate here than one to be signed by the three Guarantor Powers. I shall of course work for endorsement by Günes and Mavros of

---

[2] Mr. Callaghan told Mr. Clerides that he thought that 'unless the boundaries were referred to in the statement, the Turkish side would not accept it'. He also undertook that if Mr. Denktash and Mr. Clerides could reach agreement on the draft, 'then he would put pressure on the Turkish Government over Turkish withdrawal' (record of a meeting between Mr. Callaghan and Mr. Clerides in the Palais des Nations, Geneva, on 12 August at 10.30 a.m.).

[3] Mr. Cable explained what he perceived to be Britain's basic dilemma over Cyprus in a minute to Mr. M.C.S. Weston of 12 August: 'we want to get off this hook ourselves, but we do not want our withdrawal to deteriorate into war. Nor do we want to let the Russians in by involving the United Nations further. Unless we can find friendly and reliable partners to share our burdens and responsibilities, there is a risk that, for purely historical reasons, we shall become deeply and expensively involved in a problem which is no longer directly relevant to specific British interests.' In an attached paper he reasoned that the EEC would be the appropriate regional organisation to cope with the problem. Mr. Cable thought this would also emphasise Britain's readiness to accept the idea of European political cooperation and 'give this added importance and a new dimension' (RS 14/1).

anything that Clerides and Denktash can agree. I am not yet clear in what way this might be done—unilateral press statements may be best.

No. 70

Record of a conversation between Mr. Callaghan and Mr. Clerides at the Palais des Nations, Geneva, on 12 August 1974 at 4.40 p.m.

[WSC 1/13]

Secret

Present:

The Rt. Hon. James Callaghan MP[1]	HE Mr. Clerides
Mr. Goulden	HE Mr. Denktash

Mr. Denktash acknowledged that the British draft attempted to provide a framework for constitutional talks which met the difficulties of both sides.[2] But he feared that, without a firmer and more precise framework, discussions in Nicosia would get nowhere. Already Turkish Cypriot opinion was complaining that the Geneva talks were being used as a stalling device while the Greek Cypriots laid mines and erected fortifications around the Turkish enclave.

2. *Mr. Clerides* said that he was glad to have Turkish Cypriot views presented forthrightly as in Mr. Denktash's draft.[3] There was no question of any Greek Cypriot being able to agree to such a draft in 15 days or even 15 years. The geographical limits proposed were inconceivable. *Mr. Denktash* commented that the details were 'completely negotiable', it was the principle that mattered.

3. *Mr. Clerides* said that he had told Mr. Denktash that he was prepared to consider an autonomous Turkish Cypriot community with groupings of

---

[1] Mr. Callaghan later reported in UKMIS Geneva telegram No. 824 of 12 August that he had joined Mr. Clerides and Mr. Denktash twenty minutes after they had begun their meeting.

[2] See No. 69, note 1.

[3] Not printed. Mr. Denktash's draft declaration differed from the British draft (*v. ibid*) insofar as it referred to 'the existence in practice' of 'two autonomous administrations', and to a constitutional revision which 'should result in the establishment of a federal system of Government based on the following fundamental elements': the Republic should be an 'independent bi-national State'; it should be composed of 'two federated States with full control and autonomy within their respective geographical boundaries'; in determining the competence of the Federal Government, account should be taken of the bi-national nature of the state; and the area of the Turkish Cypriot federated State should 'cover 34 per cent of the territory of the Republic falling north of a general line starting from the Limnitis-Lefka area in the west and running towards the east, passing through the Turkish controlled part of Nicosia, including the Turkish part of Famagusta and ending at the port of Famagusta'.

villages where possible; he would, for example, be willing to treat the 12 villages in the Chatos area as an autonomous group. Where the Turkish villages could not be grouped together, he would accept the same degree of autonomy, including police matters, administered from a central authority in Nicosia. *Mr. Denktash* said that this would not offer adequate security. 103 Turkish villages, including several large ones, had been overrun in the recent fighting. For the future, something more secure was required.

4. In reply to questions from Mr. Callaghan, Mr. Denktash confirmed that 'bi-national' in paragraph 3(*a*) of his draft could be amended to 'bi-communal'. He explained that he had asked for an administrative zone comprising 34 per cent of Cyprus because, according to the latest figures, the Turkish Cypriots owned 34 per cent of the land. This figure was however negotiable. *Mr. Callaghan* commented that it would be unreasonable for the Turks to have an administrative zone comprising 34 per cent of the Island. Presumably other criteria could be borne in mind, such as the 80/18 population ratio. *Mr. Denktash* concurred. *Mr. Clerides* said that he could not agree to link the size of an administrative zone with the size of each community's agricultural holdings. But in any case he could not accept the principle of drawing a single line across Cyprus even in a document which might not be published.

5. *Mr. Callaghan* asked how many people would have to move to create two homogeneous administrative zones. *Mr. Clerides* estimated a figure in excess of 100,000. *Mr. Denktash* pointed out that there were already 44,000 Turkish refugees in Cyprus, 23,000 from 1963 and 20,000 from 1974. He doubted whether many of these would return to their homes. *Mr. Clerides* said that he thought they would. There were over 60,000 Turks living contentedly under Greek Cypriot administration.

6. *Mr. Callaghan* said that he had a feeling in favour of some measure of geographical separation. Was this principle wholly unacceptable to the Greek Cypriots? *Mr. Clerides* said that he could not accept the principle of two separate States federated at the top. He could however contemplate a system in which villages were grouped together under different communal administrations.[4]

7. *Mr. Callaghan* asked why Mr. Denktash preferred geographical separation to a cantonal solution. *Mr. Denktash* said that the former had two advantages: in a Turkish administrative zone, Turks would have guaranteed access to utilities and medical services; and they could, if necessary, defend themselves. *Mr. Clerides* commented that Mr. Denktash seemed to contemplate a boundary rather than an administrative line. *Mr. Callaghan* said that a geographically separate Turkish administration would

---

[4] Mr. Olver warned Mr. Callaghan in Nicosia telegram No. 19 to UKMIS Geneva of 12 August that he could not see how the Greek Cypriots could possibly afford to cede any more territory outright either by negotiation or force. 'The National Guard', he wrote, 'would fight bitterly. Notwithstanding the risks of Turkish air strikes, there would be an extreme danger of renewed National Guard action against Turkish communities in Greek-held Cyprus.'

not help any Turkish Cypriots who remained outside it. *Mr. Denktash* replied that their protection would be guaranteed by the Turkish contingent. *Mr. Callaghan* replied that he had hoped recent events might encourage both parties to consider reducing their contingent and military forces. *Mr. Callaghan* said that there appeared to be a fundamental difference between Mr. Clerides' concept of administrative federation and Mr. Denktash's ideas about a defensible geographic boundary. *Mr. Clerides* agreed. The parties were too far apart to agree on any principles. *Mr. Callaghan* noted that this was so only if the Turkish Cypriots insisted on a single line. He understood however that a more flexible cantonal model was also under consideration. He could see the advantages of several large, geographically separate Turkish Administrations. Such an arrangement would offer greater security to Turkish Cypriot farmers in other parts of the Island. He wondered fatalistically whether Cyprus might have to go through a period of misery and chaos. But, although Cyprus today was the prisoner of the Turkish Army, tomorrow the Army would be the prisoner of Cyprus. We needed a security system for the Turkish Cypriots which did not depend on the Turkish Army.

8. In summing up Mr. Callaghan said that he agreed that the Turkish Cypriots needed to be given a greater sense of security. This would include some geographical separation but need not imply a single line. There was a need for a different system for policing the Island. But it was also necessary to reduce the numbers not only of the Turkish armed forces but also of the National Guard, etc.

9. *Mr. Clerides* commented that, if a solution were found, the National Guard would be dissolved, as would the Turkish Cypriot fighters. He would be content to see them hand their weapons over to an international force, possibly to the Guarantor Powers. He was prepared to consider a mixed police system, including a state police force comprising Turks and Greeks in proportion to the population and two separate communal police forces.

10. It was agreed to resume at 7 p.m.

No. 71

Record of a conversation between Mr. Callaghan and Mr. Günes at the Palais des Nations, Geneva, on 12 August 1974 at 6.30 p.m.

[*WSC 1/13*]

Secret

Present:

The Rt. Hon. James Callaghan MP	HE Mr. Günes
Mr. Carter	Mr. Akbel
Miss Fort	

Mr. Callaghan told Mr. Günes that he had seen Mr. Clerides and Mr. Denktash together and that Mr. Denktash had given him a copy of Mr. Denktash's statement on the constitutional arrangements.[1] There had been a certain amount of cross-talk between them but Mr. Clerides found the line covering 34 per cent of the Republic across the whole of the Island totally unacceptable. Mr. Callaghan did not see any prospect of Clerides even saying privately, and certainly not publicly, that he could agree to it. Mr. Callaghan said we could not know what would happen in three weeks' time but he thought that the most we would be able to get Mr. Clerides to agree to was a cantonal arrangement. The proposed draft statement that Mr. Callaghan had presented this morning left this issue open, not because he wished to avoid it but in order to allow time for more understanding between the parties. He further proposed that the words 'suitable boundaries' be replaced by 'operating within conveniently appropriate areas'. He undertook to pass this on to Mr. Clerides. There was no point in urging a single geographical zone on him but he would be prepared to advocate a cantonal solution.

2. *Mr. Günes* said that he had spoken to Mr. Denktash, that he had understood Mr. Callaghan's feeling about a cantonal solution and that it had been studied by the Government in Ankara, and agreed by the Turkish Cabinet, that the best solution for the two communities would be to divide the Administration into two main regions, but that in the Greek Cypriot region certain other Turkish cantons should be delineated. He had prepared in agreement with his Government, a draft statement covering the proposal.[2] It was very important for him to reach a conclusion. If the

---

[1] See No 70, note 3.

[2] Not printed. According to this paper the principal Turkish Cypriot district would be limited by a line running west to east including Panagra-Myrtou-Somatos-Skylloura-Yerolakkos-the Turkish controlled sector of Nicosia—Moka-Angastina-Yenagra-Maratha-Styllos 'Fresh Water Lake'—the Turkish part of Famagusta and, in the north-east by a line excluding Galounia, but including Komi Kebir, Ayios Evstathios and excluding Gastria. There would also be Turkish districts in Lefka, Polis, Paphos, Larnaca and Karpassos.

Conference went on much longer under the present conditions there would be problems not only between Greece and Turkey but among all the allies. He said that if the Conference could not agree it was better to leave the problem as it was. He thought it was essential that the Conference should take a decision on his proposal that evening. He had taken up Mr. Callaghan's idea of cantons, which he knew was shared in other milieux. He had not tried his draft on Mr. Clerides or on anyone else. It was final on certain points. It also had points which were open to discussion between the two communal leaders. *Mr. Callaghan* asked about Famagusta. *Mr. Günes* said that the town would have Greek and Turkish quarters and the port of Famagusta could have a Federal Port Authority. His proposal was a guarantee of the future structure of the Island, and should be instituted without delay so that the atmosphere in Cyprus did not get any worse. Otherwise the problem would have to be discussed in some place other than Geneva. *Mr. Callaghan* asked him what other place he was thinking of. *Mr. Günes* said he did not know. He said that he and Mr. Callaghan had other problems. They were busy Foreign Ministers who could not afford to devote all their time to Cyprus.

3. *Mr. Callaghan* asked how this plan would be announced and by whom. *Mr. Günes* said it should be announced tomorrow morning by the leaders of the communities and the Guarantor Powers should simply say that they had taken note of the agreement and should then proceed to arrive at a peaceful settlement of all other questions.

4. *Mr. Callaghan* thanked Mr. Günes for his efforts and said that he thought that it was a serious attempt to solve the problem, but that he would guess that Mr. Clerides would say that it was impossible for him to accept it tonight. If Mr. Clerides accepted it in Geneva he would be overthrown on his return to Cyprus. *Mr. Günes* said that if it were not solved this evening, he would be overthrown. But Mr. Clerides would never put this forward in his country unless he were forced to do so. Mr. Günes did not know if Mr. Denktash would be able to stay within his limits but sometimes a surgical operation was necessary and it would prove to be of benefit to all. At certain times in political life certain things had to be done, even if there were the danger of being overthrown. Mr. Clerides must have been aware of the risks he was running, even in coming to Geneva. It was better that Cyprus remained a serious crisis than that relations between allies deteriorated. The Cyprus problem had not yet crystallised but it was beginning to gather too much weight in world affairs. The Soviet Union was trying to put out feelers for a General Assembly from which very undesirable consequences would come. He did not want the Security Council or the United Nations to take up positions.

5. *Mr. Callaghan* asked if Mr. Günes would give him his genuine opinion of what effect his proposals would have in Greece and if he thought the Karamanlis Government would fall. He said that this would be dangerous since Mr. Mavros had told him that either a Right wing or a Left wing takeover would result in Greece being taken out of NATO. *Mr. Günes*

opined that the Greek Government would not be overthrown. If the Greek Junta had thought it could have taken effective action against Turkey at the time of the invasion, it would have done so, but Greece was not armed sufficiently and they would find more reasonable procedures. Neither a Right wing nor a Left wing Government could have restored the situation in Cyprus. *Mr. Callaghan* said that they could however take them out of NATO. *Mr. Günes* said that he did not think that the allies had to choose between Turkey and Greece. The situation in Turkey was not all that different. The atmosphere was very tense in Turkey. It was no longer possible to let the Conference drag on for another few days. He suggested that they should see if they could not agree.

6. *Mr. Callaghan* said that he would like time to think about Mr. Günes' proposals and that he had better put off his meeting with Mr. Denktash and with Mr. Clerides. *Mr. Günes* suggested that they should meet officially *à cinq* with a few senior advisers. They were all experienced politicians and they must all be ready to study matters and accept their responsibilities. He agreed that the proposal had risks for the Greek Government but he thought that it was a minor risk. The boundaries and the size of the other cantons were open to negotiation. *Mr. Callaghan* pointed out that the proposal only dealt with questions of geographical limits and that it did not deal with the functions of an Administration. *Mr. Günes* said that he was prepared to discuss this. Since they were agreed on the independence, sovereignty and integrity of Cyprus, he thought that they should however allow the Central Government to work out the technical details of Administration. *Mr. Callaghan* said that it was not a wholly technical question since it was important what powers each side had. *Mr. Günes* said that he thought that there should be a federal legislation for the whole State, federal foreign policy, a central Defence Ministry, a national currency, a national roads system, national postal and telephone communications and a federal police force, as well as communal police forces, but he did not want to prejudge the last issue. *Mr. Callaghan* asked if he envisaged getting rid of national contingents. *Mr. Günes* said he had not given any thought to it but he had not excluded it either. His proposal would allow each community a system of security which would not necessitate Turkish or Greek contingents on the Island. *Mr. Callaghan* asked Mr. Günes if he could have time to consider the proposal and agreed that they might want to have a five-power meeting later that evening.

7. (During this conversation Mr. Günes handed to Mr. Callaghan a map of Cyprus, printed in the United Kingdom, on which the geographical effect of his draft had been illustrated by rough lines in blue pencil. He left the map with Mr. Callaghan but next day at his request, it was returned to him.)

No. 72

Record of a conversation between Mr. Callaghan and Mr. Günes at the Palais des Nations, Geneva on 12 August 1974 at 10.40 p.m.

[*WSC 1/13*]

Secret

Present:

The Rt. Hon. James Callaghan MP	HE Mr. Günes
Mr. Carter	another member of
Mr. Alexander	the Turkish delegation[1]

Mr. Callaghan explained that while Mr. Clerides was anxious to put forward further proposals he could not do so that evening.[2] Mr. Mavros was reluctant to attend a meeting without Mr. Clerides. While Mr. Callaghan was perfectly ready to have a meeting that evening it seemed that a meeting in the morning was the only possibility. *Mr. Günes* said that he was reluctant to go under the impression of giving an ultimatum. If he insisted on a meeting that evening it was because he was up against an absolute time limit and if there could not be a meeting he would have to consider that the conference was at an end. (At this point Mr. Callaghan left the meeting briefly to take a telephone call from Dr. Kissinger.)[3]

2. Mr. Günes continued that since he considered the Conference at an end, he could not receive any counter proposals from Mr. Clerides. However, he had no plan to leave Geneva immediately and if Messrs.

---

[1] Unidentified.

[2] Mr. Callaghan conveyed the substance of Mr. Günes's proposals to Mr. Clerides earlier that evening. He told Mr. Clerides that if the talks were to break down he should ensure that he was left in a public position of appearing ready to agree to reasonable proposals, and of being willing to continue the talks for a reasonable period of time. 'Mr. Clerides', he advised, 'should produce a reasonable document, acceding to some of the British proposals and to some of Mr. Denktash's proposals.' Mr. Callaghan added that 'the further Mr. Clerides could go towards a cantonal system, the more difficult would be the position of the Turks' (record of a conversation between Mr. Callaghan and Mr. Clerides at the Palais des Nations, Geneva, on 12 August at 7.35 p.m.).

[3] During the ensuing telephone conversation Dr. Kissinger informed Mr. Callaghan that he had spoken to Mr. Eçevit, who had told him that he realised the Greeks would want to make counter-proposals, and that the meeting should be resumed on 13 August. According to Dr. Kissinger, Mr. Eçevit had also revealed that if the Greek National Guard were willing to withdraw from the Turkish line, 'the Turks would not advance into the space created'. Dr. Kissinger mentioned that he liked the idea, put to him earlier that day by Mr. Clerides, that Mr. Callaghan should visit Ankara if this seemed necessary to keep the talks going. Mr. Callaghan said he would consider this further (summary record of telephone conversation between Mr. Callaghan and Dr. Kissinger on 12 August at 10.45 p.m.).

Mavros and Clerides could accept the essentials of the Turkish plan, he would still be available to receive this information. The essentials were:

(*a*) That the main region in the North should be accepted along the lines set out on the map left earlier in the evening with Mr. Callaghan.[4]

(*b*) That this area should be evacuated by Greek forces and occupied by Turkish forces within 48 hours and turned over to autonomous Administration at the same time.

(*c*) That the five other Turkish districts should be instituted.

All the other elements in the Turkish proposal were open to negotiation, and discussions could begin once the main outlines were agreed. Inability to accept any counter proposals was based partly on their view that the Conference had already ended and partly on the fact that Mr. Günes was not in a position to make any concessions on the basic points.[5]

3. *Mr. Callaghan* recapitulated the course of the Conference and the many occasions on which the Turks had been responsible for delay. He could not accept that the Conference should be terminated so abruptly. *Mr. Günes* repeated that he did not want to appear unreasonable and was willing to offer Mr. Mavros and Mr. Clerides time for reflection but he could not negotiate concessions on the three points nor accept counter proposals. He was prepared to receive his colleagues' reactions any time during the course of the following day. *Mr. Callaghan* asked whether Mr. Günes could consider acceptance of the principle of separate regions but no more at this stage. *Mr. Günes* said that there had to be a concrete example of what this meant. He did not think a meeting would help since it would result in polemics and tension. *Mr. Callaghan* asked how and when the Turkish proposals had been put to the Greeks and Greek Cypriots. *Mr. Günes* said that they had been taken round to his colleagues at 10.30 that evening (*i.e.* 30 minutes prior to this part of the conversation). *Mr. Callaghan* said that this was no way to do business and that Mr. Günes owed it to his colleagues to inform them formally of the Turkish proposals. (At this point

---

[4] See No. 71.

[5] Shortly after his meeting with Mr. Clerides (see note 2 above), Mr. Callaghan informed Mr. Denktash of Mr. Günes's proposals. Mr. Denktash 'was not happy' with these, adding that he had 'hoped that a cantonal solution might offer a diplomatic way out of the impasse'. But he explained that the Turkish community could not insist on anything which the Turkish Government would not back, and that conversations with Ankara during the day had revealed a feeling that delay would lead to a gradual mobilisation of world opinion against Turkey. 'The Turks', he observed, 'were maddened by Greek claims that the Turkish armed forces had been stopped and hemmed in. They were willing, if necessary, to shoot their way through UNFICYP lines' (record of a conversation between Mr. Callaghan and Mr. Denktash at the Palais des Nations on 12 August at 8 p.m.). In UKMIS Geneva telegram No. 824, despatched at 9 p.m. on 12 August, Mr. Callaghan recalled that Mr. Dentash had also told him that Mr. Günes was 'under instructions to "finish" the talks here tonight'. Mr. Callaghan thought the implication of Mr. Denktash's remarks was the Turks 'might be thinking of attacking at dawn'.

the meeting was interrupted and Mr. Günes took a telephone call from Ankara, evidently from Mr. Eçevit).

Mr. Günes resumed by agreeing that there should be a meeting the following morning.[6] He owed it to Mr. Callaghan and his other colleagues as a matter of courtesy. For practical purposes he considered the Conference was at an end but not formally. He would make his presentation, he would listen to questions but he would not negotiate. The meeting might begin at 10.00 and, in order that Mr. Mavros and Mr. Clerides might have time for reflection it might be resumed at 18.00. He would then expect either acceptance or rejection of the Turkish outline. *Mr. Callaghan* agreed to the meetings but said that he hoped Mr. Günes did not underrate the difficulties Mr. Clerides would have in accepting the Turkish proposal so quickly. If he were given three weeks the answer might be given.[7] *Mr. Günes* said that his theory was different and that he described his theory as being one of realism.[8]

---

[6] See note 3 above.

[7] In a minute to Mr. Brenchley of 13 August, headed 'A pessimistic view', Mr. Goodison questioned the value of gaining time for further Greek Cypriot consideration of the Turkish proposals. Time might, he reasoned, allow Dr. Kissinger to press the parties into a settlement and the Greek Government to consolidate its power in order to take the risks an agreement would involve. But he thought it would also permit massacres in Cyprus, mass expulsions from occupied territory, mass movements of panic-stricken refugees, and preparations for war in Greece and regrouping for war in Turkey. 'Thus', he concluded, 'we need an agreement, not a diplomatic conjuring trick, now. I do not believe we can secure this' (WSC 1/11).

[8] Following this meeting, Mr. Callaghan reported in UKMIS Geneva telegram No. 825 of 12 August that the Turks were still insisting on an answer to their proposals on 13 August and that the positions of the two sides remained very far apart. 'We shall', he concluded, 'almost certainly need to orchestrate further pressure tomorrow'.

No. 73

Miss Warburton (UKMIS Geneva) to FCO

No. 826 Telegraphic [*WSC 1/13*]

Flash. Confidential   GENEVA, *13 August 1974, 12.15 p.m.*

Repeated for information to Flash Ankara, Washington, Athens, Nicosia, CBFNE, Paris, UKMIS New York, Immediate UKDEL NATO, other EC Posts, Moscow and UKREP Brussels.

Following from Secretary of State.

1. At 10 a.m. this morning Clerides handed Denktash a counter-proposal which, while it conceded administrative autonomy and some grouping of Turkish villages, excluded the possibility of a geographical zone or of population movements. I told Clerides and Mavros that this would not, in

my judgement, satisfy the Turks. They had to face the reality that there would be no United States military pressure, that UNFICYP would not oppose the Turkish forces and that, as a result, there was no prospect of external help against Turkish aggression. I urged them to produce a counter-proposal which at least conceded the principle of geographical separation.[1] Clerides said that he could not do so from Geneva: Greek Cypriot opinion was not ready and Makarios, with whom he spoke yesterday, would certainly disavow it.[2] They agreed to fly to Athens and Nicosia to discuss the principle with their colleagues and to return tomorrow night with a clear answer.[3]

2. I conveyed this to Günes. His reaction was that whilst there was no Turkish ultimatum, the time limit for consideration ran out at 22.00 hours tonight: (this kind of statement is typical of the Günes method of discussion) that the Turkish Government would probably not agree to extend the time limit: and that he must insist on a prior declaration that Clerides accepted both the principle of a geographical zone and the need to draw it in broad terms in the next two days.[4] He indicated that some of the details were still

[1] Mr. Callaghan added 'that he was coming to the personal view that the least dangerous solution was to allow the Turks to concentrate in a single zone within a Federal State'. He also told Mr. Clerides and Mr. Mavros that, while he understood the Greek feeling that it would be better to lose territory by military aggression than to suffer diplomatic humiliation, 'Greek Cypriots would be worse off if they lost their possessions by force than if they made diplomatic concessions. He hoped that Mr. Denktash would be able to negotiate more sensibly—and with less fear—if the detailed constitutional talks could be transferred to Nicosia' (record of a conversation between Mr. Callaghan, Mr. Clerides and Mr. Mavros at the Palais des Nations, Geneva, on 13 August at 10 a.m.).

[2] According to the record of this conversation (*v. ibid.*) Mr. Clerides informed Mr. Callaghan that 'neither he nor Archbishop Makarios could accept a federation on a geographical basis. The proposed Turkish zone would contain a Greek Cypriot majority or would require the movement of about 90,000 Greek Cypriots to the south. It also included millions of pounds worth of investments and tourist potential.'

[3] In Athens telegram No. 434 of 13 August Sir R. Hooper informed the FCO and UKMIS Geneva that that morning Mr. Vlachos had put to him, as a personal suggestion, the idea that if the British and US Governments were to put forward as their own proposal the idea of territorial autonomy the Greek Government and the Clerides Administration might be prepared to talk percentages with a view to arriving at an acceptable compromise. But Mr. Vlachos also insisted that it 'would be necessary for British forces to bar the Turks way to their main objectives (i.e. Famagusta and Kokkina)'. Mr. Brenchley subsequently advised Sir R. Hooper in UKMIS Geneva telegram No. 2 to Athens of 13 August that 'it was not in the Secretary of State's mind for British troops to be used as suggested'.

[4] Mr. Callaghan proposed to Mr. Günes a recess until the evening of 14 August in order to give Mr. Clerides and Mr. Mavros an opportunity to work out with their colleagues a clear answer to the Turkish proposals. But Mr. Günes insisted that Mr. Eçevit wanted the problem settled that night, and that Mr. Clerides must, before leaving Geneva, agree both to a geographical zone and its demarcation in the next two days (record of a conversation between Mr. Callaghan, Mr. Denktash and Mr. Günes at the Palais des Nations, Geneva, on 13 August at 11 a.m.).

negotiable: he mentioned an area of 30-34 per cent for the Turkish zone. But he could not accept the idea of three weeks of negotiation in Nicosia.[5]

3. At the end I asked him to put to Eçevit my judgement that, if the Greeks and Greek Cypriots were given 48 hours, they would work hard on their respective Governments and would possibly return prepared to discuss the broad shape of a single Turkish Cypriot geographical zone.[6]

4. I have spoken to Kissinger who at once promised to put maximum pressure on Eçevit to agree to a 36 hour recess without any prior declaration by Clerides. (I have since heard, via Eagleburger that Kissinger has told Eçevit, that if he cannot give the Greek Cypriots 36 hours, the Americans will have to 'oppose' the Turks. Eagleburger was not sure what this formula meant.)[7]

5. Meanwhile I have Günes's agreement that, irrespective of the reply from Ankara we should have formal session *à cinq* later this afternoon.[8]

---

[5] *V. ibid.* Mr. Günes told Mr. Callaghan that he 'needed an early decision on the practical details of a geographical zone'. But, he maintained that, while it was 'essential to establish the broad boundaries', he was not suggesting that the Conference should draw detailed demarcation lines.

[6] Mr. Günes doubted whether Mr. Clerides would be able to convince Archbishop Makarios of the need for a settlement based on the notion of a geographical separation of the two Cypriot communities, but Mr. Callaghan argued that 'with agreement in Nicosia and Athens, Mr. Clerides could begin to out-flank Archbishop Makarios' (*v. ibid*).

[7] See No. 74.

[8] See No. 76.

No. 74

Record of a telephone conversation between Mr. Callaghan and Dr. Kissinger on 13 August, 1974 at 12.15 p.m.

[*WSC 1/13*]

Secret

Mr. Callaghan said that he had been working hard to alter the Greek position but it was essential that Dr. Kissinger should speak to Mr. Eçevit. He had persuaded Mr. Mavros and Mr. Clerides to agree that they should consult their colleagues in Athens and Nicosia on the proposal that there should be one zone only of Turkish Cypriot Administration and one of Greek Cypriot Administration. They would return to Geneva the next evening with the results of their consultations. It was his impression that they would recommend such a solution to their problems. The Turkish Foreign Minister, however, who had treated Mr. Callaghan in an unforgivable way, had refused to give them the opportunity to do this unless Mr. Clerides was willing to state in advance of his departure that he accepted the principle of a single geographical zone. This was intolerable behaviour. The Greeks had after all got to have time to discuss this proposal with Archbishop Makarios and secure acquiescence. Mr. Günes had said that he would put Mr. Callaghan's proposal to his Prime Minister with a negative recommendation. In response to a question, Mr. Callaghan said that it was hardly possible to say that Mr. Mavros and Mr. Clerides would attempt to convince their colleagues. In his judgement, they would advocate a single Turkish Cypriot administrative zone and they would return with a positive decision; but it would be for a Turkish Cypriot zone less than 34 per cent of the territory of the Republic, which was what the Turkish side was at present demanding. He hoped that Dr. Kissinger would be willing to press Mr. Eçevit to give them time to secure this. Dr. Kissinger replied that he agreed it would be intolerable for the Turks to maintain a deadline of this kind, and he would press Mr. Eçevit to raise it.[1]

---

[1] On instructions from Dr. Kissinger, the US Ambassador in Ankara urged Mr. Eçevit to agree to a 36-hour adjournment to the talks in Geneva. Mr. Eçevit at first refused, but later that afternoon, following a US Government announcement deploring any resort to further military operations while all possibilities of diplomatic negotiation were not exhausted, he agreed to reconsider the matter with his colleagues. Sir H. Phillips reported that Mr. Macomber thought that if there could be any progress at all, however slight, at Mr. Callaghan's current meeting, 'Eçevit might just manage to agree to an adjournment' (Ankara telegrams Nos. 17-19 of 13 August).

No. 75

Note from Mr. W. T. Rodgers[1] to Mr. H. Wilson

[DP 13/44½]

Secret   MoD, *13 August 1974*

Prime Minister

1. In the light of the JIC assessments (JIC(A)(74)(SA) 91[2] and 92)[3] and the Foreign Secretary's personal telegram to you last Saturday[4] and of

---

[1] Minister of State for Defence.

[2] See No. 57, note 7.

[3] This JIC Special Assessment of 11 August focussed on Turkish intentions in Cyprus. It concluded that there was a 'serious risk' that the Turks would break off the Geneva talks and attempt to seize more territory on Cyprus, and that if they decided to do this the UK could expect little or no advance warning.

[4] In this message, sent to Mr. Wilson in UKMIS Geneva telegram No. 805 of 10 August, Mr. Callaghan referred to the JIC Special Assessment contained in telegram No. 356 to UKMIS Geneva (see note 2 above). 'My conversations with Günes and Denktash', Mr. Callaghan observed, 'strengthen my view that we may well see the intentions outlined in that

subsequent events, I asked the Acting Chief of Defence Staff[5] for an appreciation of what could be achieved by the further reinforcement of Cyprus. I thought you might find it helpful to have his report which is attached.[6] I would draw your attention particularly to paragraphs 3, 4, & 7.[7]

2. As I see it, the question is whether if the Turks move we can so reinforce UNFICYP as to enable them to interpose in such a way as to prevent the Turkish advance; or alternatively to have sufficient forces on the ground to go it alone with the same purpose in mind.

3. The report concludes that we cannot and advises on military grounds against further reinforcement of UNFICYP. CBFNE might have other specialist requirements which it would be right to meet.

4. It is not for me to consider whether the Secretary General of the UN will feel free to authorise the reinforcement of UNFICYP and to use it effectively, although the indications are that he will not. But, faced with Turkish strength, our own forces whether under UNFICYP control or our own, would have an impossible task if intervention meant fighting. If on the other hand UNFICYP can restrain the Turks without fighting, i.e. by political pressure, its present size suffices.[8] The situation would of course be

report carried out unless there is acceptance of the broad principles of autonomous regional separation along the lines proposed by Eçevit and Günes.' He added that his present view was that he and the Prime Minister would need to meet urgently either in London or elsewhere with some of their colleagues (Callaghan Private Office Papers).

[5] Air Chief Marshal Sir A. Humphrey.

[6] Not printed. In this report of 13 August Sir A. Humphrey pointed out that once 40 Commando was complete in Cyprus on 15 August, CBFNE would have available in the SBAs four major units and two Armoured Reconnaissance Squadrons, a force sufficient to evacuate British service dependants from dormitory towns. Thereafter, CBFNE could, if required, reinforce UNFICYP with a Brigade Headquarters and two major units, still leaving himself sufficient to secure the SBAs against anything except a direct attack. But, he noted, unless it were decided to evacuate families well before a Turkish attack started, this reinforcement could not be provided until at least six hours after the Turkish operation had begun or at best was imminent.

[7] These paragraphs asserted that: even if time allowed, it was not at all clear what the British reinforcement of UNFICYP could achieve given the much larger Turkish forces, currently estimated at 32,500 men with artillery, air support and some tanks; that no parallel could be drawn with the recently successful UNFICYP deterrence of a Turkish attack developing on Nicosia airport, since the Turks had then been confused and surprised at being faced with UN forces backed by the UK at a time when there was still effective Greek resistance at their beach head; and that neither the reinforcement of UNFICYP by the introduction of artillery nor the use of Phantoms in an anti-armour role would be anything like sufficient to redress the balance of forces in Cyprus.

[8] The JIC Special Assessment of 11 August (see note 3 above) noted: 'Attempts are being made to mobilise UNFICYP to resist a further Turkish advance, but although Waldheim is so far proving admirably robust, it is clear that there will be difficulties. The UN does not have sufficient forces in the area physically to stop the Turks, who in their present mood will not necessarily shrink from brushing UN forces aside. There may also be constitutional difficulties

both more complicated and more dangerous if the Greek [Cypriot] National Guard were actively engaged in fighting or additional Greek mainland forces were landed.

5. There are also the longer term consequences to be considered of war with a NATO ally and the dangers of getting bogged-down for a long period, bearing in mind especially our Northern Ireland commitment.[9]

7. My conclusion is that we can plan to do no more than look after our own families, defend if necessary the SBAs, act ad hoc on a humanitarian basis and be in a position to help UNFICYP after the completion of the Turkish move if asked.

8. I am copying this to the Foreign and Commonwealth Secretary and to Sir John Hunt.

WILLIAM RODGERS

which could prevent timely UN intervention and which could give the Russians further opportunities for mischief making and could cause trouble with the non-aligned.'

[9] In his report Sir A. Humphrey argued that the only thing which might cause the Turks to pause was the political risk that if they fought UNFICYP, 'there would be a powerful and unpredictable reaction from the UN'. But if the Turks were sensitive to that kind of risk, he thought the actual size of UNFICYP would be 'largely irrelevant'. By making additional British forces available to UNFICYP, HMG would meanwhile 'run on to the horns of a dilemma': 'Either', he observed, 'we could be exposing them unnecessarily to a highly dangerous military situation if the UNFICYP deterrent were to fail; or, in the event that it succeeded, we could find ourselves indefinitely committed to force levels in Cyprus which we could only maintain at the direct expense of Northern Ireland and at as yet incalculable cost in terms of roulement and length of unaccompanied service.'

No. 76

Record of a meeting between Mr. Callaghan, Mr. Günes, Mr. Mavros, Mr. Clerides and Mr. Denktash at the Palais des Nations, Geneva, on 13 August 1974 at 6.40 p.m.

[*WSC 1/13*]

Secret

Present:

British Delegation:	*Greek Cypriot Community:*
The Rt. Hon. James Callaghan MP	HE Mr. Clerides
Mr. Brenchley	
Mr. Goodison	
Greek Delegation:	*Turkish Cypriot Community:*
HE Mr. George Mavros	HE Mr. Denktash
Mr. Bitsios	
Mr. Tzounis	
Turkish Delegation:	*United Nations*
HE Mr. Turan Günes	Mr. Guyer
Mr. Bilge[1]	Mr. Weckmann-Muñoz
Mr. Kirça	and others

Mr. Callaghan observed that the Meeting ought to have begun at 10 a.m. He had no other comments for the moment.

2. *Mr. Günes* said that the previous day, after Mr. Denktash had submitted his proposals about the future constitutional structure of the Island and had discussed them with Mr. Clerides, he had formed the impression that the proposals were not acceptable to Mr. Clerides, nor, possibly, to Mr. Mavros. He had therefore persuaded Mr. Denktash to agree to some changes in his preliminary proposals, and he had himself submitted a document to Mr. Callaghan.[2] He had explained which points in this document were negotiable and which were not. Mr. Günes considered the adoption of his proposals by the Turkish Cypriots as a major concession by them. He had wanted a meeting yesterday evening to finish the Conference, and to declare either a positive result or a failure. He had however explained his proposals officially only to Mr. Callaghan, and had sent copies to Mr. Clerides and Mr. Mavros since he had been unable to meet them. He had expected an answer that evening, but Mr.

---

[1] Mr. A.S. Bilge was Turkey's Ambassador to Switzerland.

[2] See No. 71.

Callaghan had pointed out that he could not expect an immediate answer to documents submitted only at 11 p.m.

3. Mr. Günes said that he was ready to express his position orally to his colleagues if they thought that his proposal deserved study and attention on their part. He was also ready to discuss and negotiate on any parts that were negotiable. He concluded by asking Mr. Mavros to confirm or deny a report on Athens radio that the National Guard had ceased evacuation of the Turkish Cypriot enclaves. He observed that so far not many enclaves had been evacuated despite the Geneva Declaration of 30 July.[3]

4. *Mr. Callaghan* referred to a serious situation which was developing in the Nicosia area. 330 British subjects who were visiting Turkish Cypriot relations had been stranded there. On 10 and 11 August arrangements for their evacuation had been agreed with the Turkish Cypriot and Greek Cypriot authorities, but the Turkish military authorities had refused clearance. The Turkish Ambassador had yesterday promised to take up the matter with Ankara, but despite a personal reminder no reply had yet been received from him. The co-operation of the Turkish military authorities was needed for the conveyance of these British subjects to Kyrenia and their departure from the Island. The Turkish Government alone was responsible for the failure so far of these evacuation arrangements.

5. *Mr. Günes* said that this was the first he had heard of the matter. He would issue the necessary instructions. *Mr. Callaghan* said that Mr. Barutcu had been informed of the matter some time ago, but there had been no reply. *Mr. Günes* promised that his officials would contact Ankara urgently and get instructions.

6. *Mr. Mavros* said that the evacuation of the first batch of Turkish Cypriot enclaves had been completed on 12 August. National Guard authorities had begun to free the prisoners of war. Some urgent matters connected with evacuation and the release of prisoners had arisen yesterday; he had asked for a Ministerial Meeting about them but Mr. Günes had refused to discuss them. The Turkish authorities had not released any prisoners. There was also a most urgent problem concerning Greek Cypriots living in the Turkish occupied area; this too should have been discussed yesterday. It was because of the Turkish Government's failure to show a spirit of reciprocity that the evacuation of the second batch of enclaves had not begun.

7. *Mr. Günes* noted that the Athens Radio report was accurate. As for the exchange of prisoners, a plan had been agreed, for which, however, the help of the ICRC would be required. The Greek Cypriots in the occupied zone were neither prisoners of war nor internees, but simply persons who happened to be in the zone. He was surprised that Mr. Mavros had tried to link evacuation (which was provided for by an article of the Geneva Declaration) with a matter which was not touched on in the Declaration.

---

[3] See No. 49, note 13.

8. *Mr. Callaghan* said that on 6 August he had sent personal messages to Mr. Günes and Mr. Mavros proposing practical measures for the repair of Nicosia Airport. The British Government were prepared to do the work themselves. Mr. Mavros had agreed, but Mr. Callaghan had not fully understood Mr. Günes' reply. The matter should have been discussed yesterday, but was not.

9. *Mr. Günes* replied that he had agreed that the airport should be repaired, and the three Guarantor Powers should contribute to the work. *Mr. Callaghan* replied that although Mr. Günes' proposal would have needed detailed discussion, the British side would have been ready. But, although Ministers had been in Geneva for six days, the subject had not been discussed, and meanwhile the people of Cyprus were suffering because the airport was not functioning.

10. *Mr. Günes* suggested that the Meeting should consider his constitutional proposals. *Mr. Clerides* interposed that thousands of Greek Cypriots have been driven out of the areas occupied by the Turkish armed forces. Women and children had been sent over to the Greek side, separated from their husbands who were still detained by the Turks. He sympathised with Mr. Günes' concern about evacuation of Turkish Cypriot villages by the National Guard; he hoped that Mr Günes would show similar sympathy for the 28,000 Greek Cypriots expelled from the occupied area, and requested that those who were still detained should be released.

11. *Mr. Günes* said that these people had not been driven out of their homes; they had 'emigrated'. There were thousands of Turkish Cypriots who had been forced to seek refuge in the Sovereign Base Areas; they also constituted an humanitarian problem. However, he could not understand why a legal obligation stemming from the Geneva Declaration should be linked to another problem which had not been mentioned in the Declaration. The evacuation of the enclaves was not only a humanitarian question but an aspect of the restoration of the two autonomous Administrations mentioned in the Geneva Declaration.

12. *Mr. Mavros* said that the question of the prisoners had been discussed during Stage I of the talks. Immediately after the Turkish invasion of 20 July there had been 3,000 Greek Cypriot refugees. By 30 July the number had increased to 15,000, as a result of the Turkish violations of the ceasefire line. Since 30 July, the number had risen to 25,000 because of violations of the confrontation line agreed on 30 July. In addition, some 5,000 prisoners of war were missing, bringing the total number of Greek Cypriot refugees to about 30,000.

13. *Mr. Günes* said that he was surprised to find Mr. Mavros considering as internees the 5,000 Greek Cypriots who were left in the occupied zone. At the same time, Mr. Mavros appeared to assume that those who had left the zone should be free to re-enter it; there was a contradiction here. There was also a Turkish Cypriot refugee problem. Since 1963 25,000 Turkish Cypriots (20 per cent of the community) had been refugees, but no one had worried about them. The proportion of refugees in the Greek

Cypriot community was much smaller. *Mr. Mavros* said that the Greek Cypriot refugees were refugees because of violations of the ceasefire. Those in the enclaves were another problem.

14. *Mr. Callaghan* observed that if there was to be a list of omissions, he should record that Ministers had been due to meet at 10.30 a.m. to discuss the buffer zone, but had not done so. In addition, the Turkish Delegation had failed to discuss prisoners and Nicosia Airport. If the Conference failed, as seemed likely, he wondered how the continuing human problems would be tackled.

15. *Mr. Clerides* proposed an adjournment of discussion of the constitutional issues for 48 hours, during which discussion of the other issues might continue. He had in any case intended to ask for an adjournment since he needed time to consider the proposals submitted by Mr. Denktash and Mr. Günes. In response to questions by Mr. Callaghan, Mr. Clerides confirmed that he would be ready to discuss the constitutional issues after 48 hours, and that he and Mr. Mavros would temporarily leave Geneva to consult their colleagues. During their absence, the discussion of human problems could be conducted at official level. *Mr. Mavros* said that he would have to be away for 24 or 36 hours. In his absence, Mr. Bitsios would continue discussion of the humanitarian problems.

16. *Mr. Günes* could not agree to the proposed procedure. He wanted to know on what grounds the Conference would be adjourned. It had been stated clearly in the Geneva Declaration that constitutional problems would be discussed with the participation of the representatives of the Greek Cypriot and Turkish Cypriot communities, and therefore the Greek and Greek Cypriots side ought to have arrived ready to accept or reject proposals. The views of the Turkish Government had previously been well known in their general outlines, and therefore his proposals could not have been unexpected. He was not sure whether Mr. Callaghan's proposals for discussion of the humanitarian problems afforded substance for debate. There were other fora and organisations, including the United Nations and ICRC, for this kind of subject. If his colleagues were ready to discuss his constitutional proposals, he was ready to explain his views.

17. *Mr. Callaghan* said that he would be glad to hear any views for a solution, subject to the British reservation that a Constitution could not be imposed on the Sovereign State of Cyprus. There had been no Ministerial Meeting all day on Sunday 11 August because Mr. Günes had said that his Cabinet was meeting and he had no instructions. Surely it was reasonable for Mr. Clerides, in his turn, to be allowed to consult his colleagues.

18. *Mr. Günes* said that the purpose of the Turkish Cabinet Meeting had been to find a compromise which in fact represented a major change in the Turkish position. He did not know what Mr. Clerides' position was. In his first statement he had doubted the competence of the Conference to consider constitutional problems. Nor did he know the position of Mr. Mavros and the Greek Government.

19. *Mr. Callaghan* said that after Ministers had sat in Geneva for four days. Mr. Günes had submitted his constitutional proposals at 10.30 p.m. and demanded a reply the same night. At his own request, Mr. Günes had then postponed his deadline by 24 hours. If he had submitted his proposals earlier, matters would have been different; as it was, it was only reasonable that the Greek Cypriots should have time to consider them.

20. *Mr. Clerides* said that the Republic of Cyprus was an independent and Sovereign State, and that no one had the right to impose a constitutional solution on her. But he would not object if the purpose of the present discussions was to help find a solution. He had, however a number of questions about Mr. Günes's proposals. For example, what would happen to the Greek population in the area to be occupied by the Turkish Cypriots? Would they have the right to vote for an Administration in which they would not be represented? What compensation would they receive if they chose to 'emigrate?' *Mr. Mavros* said that it was obvious that certain matters would need thorough study in Athens, Ankara and Nicosia. If he had known in advance that four days would be lost, he and Mr. Clerides could have left Geneva to consult their respective Governments. After 20 years of permanent crisis, they were asking only for 24 hours and 48 hours respectively for consultations.

21. *Mr. Günes* said that he was not asking his colleagues to endorse his proposals but to discuss them. *Mr. Callaghan* said that if the Turkish Government were ready to allow an adjournment, Mr. Clerides and Mr. Mavros would benefit from a statement of views by Mr. Günes and Mr. Denktash.

22. *Mr. Mavros* said that the Greek Government would in no circumstances be prepared to dictate a Constitution to the Sovereign State of Cyprus. In this respect his Government's position was identical with that of the British Government. He would listen to Mr. Günes but would not say tonight which points he accepted or refused. He needed 24 hours to consult his Government. The situation was critical; if one party refused an adjournment, its motives would be clear.

23. *Mr. Günes*, after reiterating many of his previous points, said that if he had asked for meetings to be postponed, it was only because the Turkish Government had felt obliged, in its relations with its allies, to be more accommodating. Cyprus was a Sovereign State, but the Guarantor Powers were obliged by the Treaty of Guarantee to give their approval to any change in the Constitution. Why should Mr. Clerides and Mr. Denktash not agree on a draft Constitution. And the five parties then meet to agree the results? The solution found in Geneva should be accepted by the two communities in Cyprus. However, he saw no point in expanding his views if his colleagues had none of their own to put to him. His colleagues had no ideas with the exception of Mr. Clerides, who was only proposing a return to the 1960 Constitution.

24. *Mr. Denktash* said sarcastically that the Greek Cypriots were trying to get to love their sovereignty after 11 years of trying to destroy it for the

sake of *enosis*. It was not contrary to the concept of independence if the Cyprus communities co-operated with the Guarantor Powers, especially since it was the Guarantor Powers who had to pay the bill in the event of any disturbance in Cyprus. During the intercommunal talks, it had been a fact that both he and Mr. Clerides had acted in close co-operation with Ankara and Athens and had stressed to their communities that the line followed by them was endorsed by their respective national centres.

25. Mr. Denktash said that the Guarantor Powers were supposed to be helping Cyprus and that it was wrong to say that they could put forward no solution. Mr. Günes' proposal was not an attempt to impose a solution. The Turkish Government had watered down his own proposal and had urged reason, diplomacy and statesmanship on him in the hope of a speedy solution. In 1968 he had been prepared to talk in the hope of a quick solution because of the many human problems of refugees and displaced Government employees.[4] He had decided to talk then and had not stopped to bargain because the security of his community and the discrimination practised against it was uppermost in his mind, but now he saw no solution for the security of his community except on a geographical basis.

26. He said that no one was trying to take away the independence of the Island. He thought that in 20 years time Cyprus would be a sort of Switzerland with *enosis* forgotten and permanent happiness for the people. The proposed surgical operation was a little harsh for the time being but it would bring about real communal happiness. No one was taking away the independence or sovereignty of Cyprus and no one was doing harm to the Greek community, but, unless a solution were found, there would be harm for Greek and Turk alike. In 1968 all the urgency had been on the Turkish Cypriot side. Now there was urgency on both sides. Mr. Clerides had as big a problem as the Turkish Cypriot community had. While Mr. Mavros was only counting the increase in refugee people on the Greek side, the Turkish Cypriot community would have 40-45,000 refugees. These factors and human realities must force any responsible leader, among them he included Mr. Clerides, to settle the question very quickly in order to avert the further catastrophic event looming ahead of them, instead of arguing about whether the Guarantor Powers could discuss their problems.

27. He said that because both sides resented the idea that one of them alone should take the Island, the 1959 Agreement for communal autonomy and independence should have succeeded but that the majority community had not liked sovereignty and independence and had been encouraged to dissent by Athens. They were now on the verge of the ruin of both communities. He hoped that the Guarantor Powers would pull them back from the verge. If two peoples were to co-exist the first thing they needed was respect but there was no respect where there was fear. The Turkish Cypriot community were afraid of the Greeks. He said that they should not refuse the help now granted to them by the Guarantor Powers on the

[4] See No. 1, notes 4, 7 and 12.

grounds that their sovereignty did not allow it. Without Turkey's help he could not do anything and Mr. Clerides knew that without Greece neither could he, but they could both also draw benefit from their double parenthood.

28. Mr. Denktash said that Mr. Clerides did not want to discuss the Turkish proposal but Turkey was in an urgent mood for the reasons they all knew and therefore they should look at this proposal. They could not shut their eyes to the realities or to the human aspects to which Mr. Callaghan referred. They had never had a unitary State. It was torn in two but they must act quickly before catastrophe overtook them. They had asked Greece and Turkey to be their guarantors in order to help them against extremists but the reverse had happened. If they were to change the position they must try to do it in Geneva. There were enough dead heroes already in Cyprus. The troubles that had lasted from 1955-1974 meant that a whole generation had grown up hating each other. Since Turkey would not allow *enosis*, Cyprus was destined to be an independent country. It could be a happy country if it could be accepted that Turkey would intervene if necessary. He appealed for those who knew each other to help each other to both a new way and a new life. If they went the old way there would be a Conference every few years and more people would die.

29. *Mr. Callaghan* said that he had been very moved by what Mr. Denktash had said. There was a common humanity which bound them all and Mr. Denktash had made a more powerful case than any of them. He felt a large measure of agreement with what Mr. Denktash had said. Despite Mr. Denktash's plea not to lose themselves in legal byways, his reason for participating in the present Conference was based on respect for Resolution 353 which called on the United Kingdom, Greece and Turkey to enter into negotiations on the Constitution, until the United Nations Mandate was withdrawn or until they had reported their failure to make recommendations on the constitutional problem.

30. It was important to establish a legitimate basis for their constitutional advice.

31. Mr. Callaghan pointed out that Turkey had said they had taken action under Article IV of the Treaty of Guarantee. That Article called on the Guarantor Powers to consult together before taking action. Turkey had asked the United Kingdom on the day after the Sampson *coup* for discussions and he had replied to their message within one hour of receiving it and had met the Turkish Prime Minister in London. Mr. Callaghan had then asked the previous Greek Government to come to London on Monday 22 July for consultations. In the meanwhile Turkey had taken action before those consultations were completed. But Turkey must know that under Article IV the Powers were obliged to consult and concert their action if possible. If Turkey continued on this course they would have to defend their action against disapproval from the whole world. The United Kingdom did not consider that the Treaty of

Guarantee would allow a complete departure from the 1960 Constitution and no legislation passed in London, Ankara or Athens could change that. Today the Island was the prisoner of the army, tomorrow the army would be the prisoner of the Island.

32. Mr. Callaghan said that they did also however have responsibility under the Treaty and in common humanity. Mr. Denktash had reminded them that both communities were staring in the face of ruin. Moreover, Cyprus was facing the gravest difficulties in its internal affairs and economy. The problem must be solved by agreement not by threat of force. He said that on reflection he was more inclined to favour Mr. Denktash's solution than Mr. Günes's. He was prepared to give both proposals serious consideration but not to come to a final conclusion to meet a deadline that night. He would state his conclusions when he had had time to study the matter. He had not yet heard the case put in full by Mr. Günes. When he heard it explained he would then like to take Mr. Günes's and Mr. Denktash's proposals away to consider them. If he could not decide on this question that night then it was even more unreasonable to expect Mr. Clerides to accept it. Mr. Clerides had asked for 36 hours to look at a problem that had been in the making for a couple of hundred years. Three out of the five representatives present were ready to agree to adjourn for 36 hours. The diplomatic processes had not been exhausted and would not be until Mr. Clerides had had time to consult his colleagues. A military solution would not do. Mr. Callaghan proposed that the meeting adjourn for an hour.

33. *Mr. Clerides* said that he deplored the situation which had created conflict between the two communities. That conflict was derived from the fact that in Zurich three wise men had worked out a Constitution. It had caused resentment because it was not a Constitution of the people's own choosing. It had created a number of psychological problems and there was a will to change it and to make it workable. It was better to have 36 hours for consultation than to walk away having accepted a solution because 30,000 Turkish troops had landed and because a statement had been made that they should either accept the Turkish solution or submit to Turkish arms. People had not been proud of their sovereignty in the past. They had felt that certain Treaty obligations were a limitation of that sovereignty. Mistakes had been made by the leadership of both communities. There had been a lack of understanding between them. The Turkish side had extracted their last pound of flesh and the Greek side had been mistaken in not understanding the problems of a minority community.

34. He said that if they were going to learn from the mistakes of the past a new arrangement must be accepted by both sides or otherwise they would have to fight for generations. He had given his own proposal to Mr. Denktash and to Mr. Callaghan. He was not saying that it must be accepted or that he himself would accept or reject Mr. Denktash's or Mr. Günes's proposals. All he needed was time to consult with his colleagues.

His acceptance would have no value if it were not possible for him to deliver. *Mr. Callaghan* asked if Mr. Clerides would be prepared to accept an hour's adjournment. *Mr. Clerides* said that he had an aircraft standing by all day and that for him every hour counted.

35. *Mr. Günes* said that at the time of the *coup* in Cyprus the Turkish Government had consulted the United Kingdom but had not consulted the Greek Government because there had been no point in consulting the Greek Government because they had organised the *coup*. Even Mr. Rossides had said so. He hoped that the Conference would end positively tonight. He posed the hypothetical question that if he had had no proposal would his colleagues have asked for time to consult. It was obvious they were unprepared. If his colleagues could say to him that certain things in his proposal were unacceptable then he would consider their views and see if he could or could not change it and perhaps he would be able to amend it. But if they had different views on time limits just as they might have on substance then they were not agreed and the Conference had failed. He would be happy to answer his colleagues' questions but he asked if his colleagues could say that they accepted this part of it or that or, if they were not in a position to take a public stand, could they say they were in favour of it. He agreed on an hour's adjournment.

36. *Mr. Mavros* pointed out that Mr. Günes had said that some of the points in his proposal were not negotiable. He asked what Mr. Günes would say if Mr. Mavros said that he would give him an answer on the next day? Was it an ultimatum or not? He had heard on the radio that unless they had decided on the Turkish proposal by 10 p.m. tonight the Turkish Army would advance. *Mr. Günes* said that it was true that Ankara wanted a solution found today but he was not aware that the army would advance if not. There was no ultimatum, a Government could ask its friends for a decision within a time limit but that was not an ultimatum since everyone was free to accept or refuse his proposals. *Mr. Callaghan* again proposed an hour's adjournment. It was so agreed at 21.00.

[The plenary resumed at 22.15]

37. *Mr. Günes* circulated a memorandum.[5] Introducing the two Turkish proposals he said that he could accept either. The important and non-negotiable elements were: geographical separation and federation within a single state. No system based on other principles would be viable or likely to bring security. Once the principles were accepted, there were two fundamental questions to be resolved:

[5] Not printed. This proposed two alternatives: (1) the plan presented by the Turkish delegation on 12 August (see No. 71); and (2) Turkish Cypriot autonomy to the north of a general line, including the Turkish part of Famagusta and the Turkish-controlled sector of Nicosia, and then continuing westwards so that the zone would be equal to about 34 per cent of the territory of the Republic of Cyprus. This zone was to be evacuated by elements of the Greek armed forces, the Greek Cypriot National Guard and irregular Greek forces, and the public services and the maintenance there of order and security were immediately to become the responsibility of the Turkish Cypriot Administration.

(i) the competence of the communal and federal Administrations. This would require elaborate study. Ministers should agree on the principles and leave the details to specialists in constitutional law;

(ii) size and location. He recognised that Ministers could not set up as topographers, but they should establish the rough outlines of the communal zones. Mr. Denktash had proposed a Constitution based on two regions. This had the advantage of being less complicated and more secure. But he could appreciate the fear that the existence of two separate nations in Cyprus might tend towards *enosis*. He did not share these views since each of the two communal Administrations would be able to prevent the other from declaring *enosis*—by being able to follow suit. However, recognising these views, he was prepared to consider a more complicated model based on several cantons. These would not, as in Switzerland, be separate administrations: each part of the Turkish zone would come under a single communal administration. This model represented a major Turkish concession.

38. Mr. Günes said that it was not enough for the Conference to agree on principles and to delegate the detailed discussion to the intercommunal machinery in Nicosia. The Conference must take precise decisions which would not permit the Greek or Turkish Cypriots to renege or to interpret the guidelines in a selective way. Without such precision the two communities could, as in the past, be the victims of political accident and changes in personnel.

39. Mr. Günes claimed that his proposals were not novel. They had for some time been considered between Greece and Turkey. Documents to this effect could probably be found in Athens and Ankara. Everyone had known, before the Conference, what Turkey's proposals would be. They had been discussed for six months in the intercommunal talks. What was needed was not time for reflection but an urgent decision. The Conference had been beating about the bush since 8 August. His doubts about Greek sincerity had been reinforced on learning that the Greek Government had publicly reaffirmed its recognition of 'Monsignor Makarios'. Mr. Günes proposed, therefore, that the Conference should decide during this session on both the principle of geographical separation and the size of the communal zones. The latter was negotiable; he had mentioned 34 per cent but the figure could be smaller or larger.

40. *Mr. Clerides* denied that the Turkish plan had been known in advance. The intercommunal talks had been about functional, not geographical, autonomy. It was known that Mr. Eçevit favoured federation; but he had repeatedly stated that he did not want geographical separation. Mr. Clerides said that the non-negotiable parts of the Turkish proposals revealed that Turkey was trying to impose a solution. It was impossible to offer an immediate answer when the Turkish proposals did not give any clue as to the powers to be retained by the Central Government. He could

not, therefore, accept or reject the proposals but must insist on 48 hours to consider them.

41. *Mr. Mavros* said that the failure of the 1960 Constitution had been due to its hurried drafting. The Turkish demand for an immediate answer smelt of an ultimatum. He clarified that, while the Turkish [*sic*] Government recognised Archbishop Makarios as the legitimate President of Cyprus, his return to Cyprus could be decided only by the Cypriot people.

42. *Mr. Günes*, responding to Mr. Mavros' claim that he had been wasting the time of the Conference, said that there had been plenty of action in the corridors. He quoted a very recent American Press statement as evidence of intense diplomatic activity. 'The avenues of diplomacy are not exhausted and a resort to force would be unjustified.' As to the powers of the Federal State, it would clearly not have an army; equally clearly there would be a single Foreign Ministry and diplomatic representation. The weakness of the Cyprus Constitution was not due to hurried drafting; it had taken 22 months to prepare. And even if the Conference agreed on the principles, it would take a long time to produce a new Constitution.

43. Mr. Günes said that the request for a two-day recess was, in his view, a delaying tactic. A state of acute crisis had been reached. It would be better to take advantage of this and to seek a solution than to use prophylactic methods which would allow the Cyprus disease to break out again in a few years' time.

44. *Mr. Mavros* and *Mr. Clerides* repeated their insistence on consulting their Governments. *Mr. Clerides* was surprised that Mr. Günes had circulated his plan for the solution to the Cyprus problem to Dr. Kissinger, the NATO allies and the EEC members, but had not given a copy to Mr. Clerides. Cyprus was not a colonial State. *Mr. Callaghan* commented that Mr. Clerides need not be upset. He understood that the United States and the Nine were at that moment urging the Turkish Government to accede to Mr. Clerides' request.[6] The question was not whether Mr. Günes could agree to their departure for their capitals; but whether he would agree to a meeting on their return.

---

[6] Cf. No. 74, note 1. Discussions were already underway on the drafting of joint démarches for delivery by France (the current holder of the EC Presidency) on behalf of the nine EC member-states. Just prior to this meeting, Mr. Callaghan had telegraphed to Paris his view that for 'presentational purposes' these démarches should be made in both Athens and Ankara. 'But', he insisted, 'their main force will obviously have to be directed to deterring the Turks.' While he thought the Greeks would only resort to military measures after a Turkish advance in Cyprus, his considered opinion was 'that there would be a very great risk of a Turkish attack as soon as was militarily feasible after the Conference had broken up possibly at dawn on the following day'. Meanwhile, he felt that the 'most effective line' that Sir H. Phillips could take in Ankara would be that 'irrespective of the merits of the case, unilateral military action by Turkey at this stage would deprive Turkey of any diplomatic or economic support and put at risk her mutually beneficial relationship with Western Europe' (UKMIS Geneva telegram No. 5 to Paris of 13 August, WSC 6/598/1).

45. *Mr. Denktash* said that Mr. Clerides had complained that NATO and the EEC had been informed of the situation. Even though Cyprus was not a colony they had the right to be informed in the effort to keep the peace. Cyprus had for too long been upsetting the peace in the area for them to appeal to the gallery at this stage. He hoped that God would give them wisdom to settle their urgent problem with great speed. Mr. Günes' plan was worth considering. Mr. Denktash rehearsed events since 1955 and said that the Turkish community had always been prepared in the past to come to a settlement with some protection of their rights but that experience had taught them that only a geographical base could give them true protection. Constitutions were not god-sent documents. They needed better protection. The Turkish Foreign Minister had put forward a watered-down version of his own plan. He admitted he was not very happy with it and was glad that the pendulum had swung round to a single zone for the Turkish community.

46. *Mr. Clerides* said that he too could give his version of events since 1960. They had both found the 1960 Constitution unworkable and requiring amendment. Mr. Denktash had alleged that it needed amendment in order to provide for the protection of his community but from the Greek Cypriot point of view, the rights given to the minority under the Constitution in certain ways impeded Central Government. Mr. Clerides said they were agreed that there was a need for autonomy or for a certain degree of autonomy for the protection of both communities. There was common ground between them both for the amendment of the 1960 Constitution and for the bi-communal nature of the State of Cyprus. He questioned how they could best provide for the safety of the Turkish community and of the Greek community. Mr. Denktash had said that the line would not be a defined frontier but an administrative line. He asked why it was necessary therefore to shift populations around. Would it not be possible to have groupings of villages, which would provide adequate protection? The Denktash and Günes proposals would mean that they would have the problem of refugees in both zones. He asked what would be the status of Greek Cypriots in places behind the Turkish line and if they would have political rights. If they had, they would be in the majority in the Turkish zone and would control the government of it. He needed time to consider the proposals put forward and he might make counter-proposals, but he was not prepared to say if he would accept Mr. Günes' proposals in principle now because without further consideration when the points he had raised were discussed, he would be at a definite disadvantage.

47. *Mr. Callaghan* asked Mr. Clerides if, with an adjournment for 48 hours, would he be able to answer the question on cantons, functions and administration. *Mr. Clerides* said that he would be able to give a definite answer in 48 hours to Mr. Denktash's and Mr. Günes' proposals and on the other questions.

48. *Mr. Günes* said that too much thought had been given to the secondary question of the presence of the Turkish armed forces. The intervention of the Turkish armed forces had prevented *enosis* and had enabled them to talk and to make progress, since Mr. Clerides was now prepared, whereas he had not been before the Turkish intervention, to amend the 1960 Constitution. The Turkish armed forces were not a threat and they should therefore not be brought into the discussion but Mr. Mavros had now asked them to remove the Turkish armed forces. Mr. Günes said he did not want to impose a solution through the offices of NATO or the EEC but it had merely been his duty to inform them of the problem. Their attitude had not been what Mr. Callaghan had said it was—a warning against using force before diplomatic measures were exhausted.

49. Mr. Günes said that he had asked if Mr. Clerides and Mr. Mavros were ready to accept two or more regions in which there were two autonomous Administrations—but their reply had been negative. *Mr. Callaghan* pointed out that their reply was that they needed more time for consideration. *Mr. Günes* said that Cyprus was not a colony but a State in flux. He asked who could guarantee that in the next 24 or 48 hours there would not be a change of Government in Mr. Mavros' or Mr. Clerides' capitals. He was very surprised that the solution he had proposed had not been studied by them both. He could not understand how they could take a decision on this in 24 hours' time if they had not already taken some political decisions. If there were no guarantee for him that in 24 hours he would have a satisfactory answer on this problem he could not see any hope of his being able to postpone discussion for 24 hours.

50. *Mr. Callaghan* said that Mr. Günes had told him that he was not seeking a solution under threat. But if Cyprus were plunged into bloodshed it would be very difficult for Mr. Günes to prove that he knew what the answer would have been in 36-48 hours. Mr. Clerides had said that he was prepared to consider these proposals. Mr. Callaghan was also prepared to consider them, but, without accepting them in principle at once, to discuss them with his Prime Minister the next morning and to return to Geneva. He was concerned that they were throwing away a lot with no other solution in sight. He confessed that he did not know where they should go from here. Turkish enclaves were surrounded by Greek National Guards and the Turkish Army was on the Island. Even if the Turkish zone were extended by another 20-50 kms there would still be a problem to be solved. He confirmed his undertaking to return in 36 hours and he thought that Mr. Clerides and Mr. Mavros would also.[7]

---

[7] Mr. Callaghan had already drafted a letter, dated 13 August, which he had intended to send by hand to Mr. Karamanlis if the Turks agreed to a 36 hour adjournment. In this he acknowledged that the 1960 Constitution had 'not withstood the test of time', and he went on to say that he had concluded 'with regret' that if the two communities in Cyprus were to flourish 'there must be two autonomous administrations in Cyprus concentrated in two well

51. *Mr. Günes* said that he had never intended to take a stand without making concessions. He had made concessions. They had taken time to tackle the problem. Without insisting too much, he had tried a compromise when Mr. Denktash had spoken to him of his plan but he must have an immediate solution here and now as he was losing hope. If they could not agree despite all their efforts there might be other means to follow because the Geneva Conference had failed. He said that he was too well-acquainted with the Cypriot problem, that too many words had been spent on it. That was why he had proposed something original.

52. Mr. Günes said that the Cyprus situation was a tragic one but, when he had proposed a happy outcome for it, he was told it was not in keeping with the Cyprus drama. He was told that the others must have consultations, but they had all been consulting in Geneva. They were all close to telephones. He did not see what could be done in Nicosia, Athens or Ankara that could not be done in Geneva. He said that it might be difficult for his colleagues to say yes now because of public opinion in Cyprus. But there was also the factor of public opinion in Turkey.

53. He did not want to be among the collection of naïve politicians who had pronounced success on Cyprus and had then been proved wrong. The Conference must have the courage to take the bull by the horns. It was not in 24 hours that public opinion would allow them to make statements that they could not make now. All they could do was to consult their political friends, enemies and rivals; but it was their enemies that were a worry. There was nothing to guarantee that they would accept within 24 hours. Diplomatic means, as far as the Geneva Conference was concerned, were exhausted. He hoped that there were other means.

54. *Mr. Clerides* said that the reason he wanted to go to Cyprus was not to gauge public opinion but to consider with his advisers the serious considerations with which he was faced. He had received the Günes proposals at 11.30 p.m. on 12 August. At 9.30 a.m. on 13 August he had asked for an adjournment and he had waited around all day for the Turkish Council of Ministers to decide on his request. It was unfair to pressurise him to accept something as serious as this without consultation with his advisers and further to imply that if he did not accept the Turkish Army would march. If the Turkish Army marched the Greek Cypriot people would fight. Mr. Clerides said he had not rejected Mr. Günes' or Mr. Denktash's proposals but he refused to be cornered in this way.

55. *Mr. Mavros* said that they had been asked to take a decision under pressure of an ultimatum. A deadline had been fixed in the manner of a

defined geographical regions'. He added that he could not see how, given the events of the last fourteen years and the determination of the Turkish Cypriots to have their own administration, this could be avoided. The two regions would, he insisted, have to be united in a federal system. If Mr. Karamanlis reached the same conclusion, he could, Mr. Callaghan noted, count on his support and that of HMG for decisions taken in this sense (undated minute from Mr. Alexander to SEED covering the text of Mr. Callaghan's draft letter).

victorious commander on a battlefield. Dr. Kissinger said that diplomacy was not exhausted but Mr. Günes said it was. Mr. Mavros asked what was left to them. If diplomatic ways could not work then military action would be forced on them. He had been asked to discuss at gun point a matter, not in the Security Council Resolution, not covered in the Treaty of Guarantee, and with the request of the representative of the Republic of Cyprus for 48 hours' adjournment ignored. He posed a question to Mr. Denktash but he said he did not expect an answer since Mr. Denktash would be too embarrassed to give one. The question was: did Mr. Denktash really believe that Mr. Clerides was ready to commit his people here, right now, without consultation? He said that they could not continue discussions under these circumstances. He thought it was necessary to give an immediate report to the United Nations Secretary-General on what had been happening here.

56. *Mr. Günes* said that they did not speak at gun point here. If they were looking for ways to get guns to rust by diplomatic means, one day those guns would blow up. He ran through the Geneva Declaration point by point and said it had not been complied with. Even with the texts as clear as they were it was obvious that they were not going to be carried out. How then could they be carried out in 48 hours? He was not critical of Mr. Mavros and of Mr. Clerides but he no longer had confidence in the Government of Greece. Their request for postponement was merely procrastination until circumstances were in their favour. Mr. Günes asked for a statement from Mr. Clerides and Mr. Mavros agreeing in principle to geographical separation.

57. *Mr. Mavros* refuted Mr. Günes' points about the Geneva Declaration. He agreed that Greek forces had not been withdrawn from Cyprus but asked how they could without reciprocity. The cease-fire had been violated more than 100 times by the Turkish armed forces. 11,000 people had become refugees since the day the Geneva Declaration had been signed. The Greek side had liberated prisoners without receiving any reciprocal gesture from the Turks. The Turkish armed forces had doubled since the day of the Geneva Declaration. The Greek Delegation would board the plane for Athens within the next few hours. There was no one who could stop them but they were ready to come back within 48 hours. *Mr. Callaghan* proposed a 15 minute adjournment and it was so agreed.

[After some 20 minutes, the session began again at 1.40 a.m. on 14 August, 1974.]

58. *Mr. Denktash*, in reply to Mr. Mavros said that it was up to Mr. Clerides to decide whether or not he needed consultations with his colleagues. However, he asked whether Mr. Clerides conceded that the Turkish Cypriot community was in need of protective measures, and that these might be ensured by a geographical formula. Mr. Clerides was not being asked to agree to a detailed solution, but to a general framework. The idea that Turkey was adopting a threatening attitude appeared to be

gaining ground in the Conference room; however, when half of the Turkish Cypriot community was dominated by the National Guard and EOKA B, the community did not feel free from coercion. Mr. Denktash said that both he and Mr. Clerides must take a courageous step to break the vicious circle. Their personal continuance in public life was not important if they made a real contribution to a solution which would be recognised by later generations. When Turkish Cypriot villages had been attacked, Mr. Denktash had advised the inhabitants not to fight and to surrender their arms to UNFICYP. He might later be accused of cowardice, but not of sacrificing human life to no purpose.

59. *Mr. Günes* said that he would repeat his proposals once more and ask his colleagues whether they could accept them.

(*a*) Did they agree that the Island should be given a constitutional sector [*sic*] based on regionalism? and

(*b*) Did they agree to a region extending from the Turkish sector of Famagusta to the Turkish sector of Nicosia, continuing westwards on a line to be determined later, on the basis that the total area under Turkish Cypriot Administration in the form of zones and cantons was to cover about 34 per cent of the area of Cyprus?

(This zone should be determined by demarcation lines and should be transferred to the control of the Turkish Cypriot Administration within a reasonable period of time. The security zone should be established within three or four days and extend outwards from the zone at present occupied by the Turkish armed forces.)

60. Mr. Günes said that for this evening he would set aside the rest of his proposals and ask Mr. Mavros and Mr. Clerides whether they could accept those which he had just outlined. If there were no reply, there would be no point in continuing the Conference. If the Conference did not reach a solution, he hoped that it would not end in recriminations.

61. *Mr. Clerides* said that he would be prepared to consider both proposals carefully and with an open mind, and to give a reply in 48 hours.

62. *Mr. Günes* understood Mr. Clerides to mean that he was not able to accept his proposals at the moment, but that he did not exclude the possibility of considering them.

63. *Mr. Callaghan* said that Mr. Clerides had made himself quite clear. If he had agreed to consider the proposals with 'an open mind', that meant that he had no fixed prejudice against them.

64. *Mr. Mavros* said that his position was clear. The Guarantor Powers had no right to impose any particular constitutional structure on Cyprus. The Greek Government, however, would not object to anything that might be agreed between the two Communities.

65. *Mr. Callaghan* asked whether Mr. Günes was ready to return to Geneva on Thursday morning (15 August). *Mr. Günes* replied that he

considered the answers given by Mr. Clerides and Mr. Mavros to be negative.

66. *Mr. Callaghan* said that he could not agree; Mr. Clerides' answer had not been negative.

67. *Mr. Günes* said that even before the talks Mr. Clerides had told the Press that he had an open mind, but his basic attitude had not changed. The work of the Conference was finished.

68. *Mr. Clerides* said that from the beginning he had had an open mind. He had received Mr. Günes' proposals very late. He regretted that Mr. Günes had not come to the table with an open mind, in that he had described some of his proposals as not negotiable. Did Mr. Günes declare the Conference as having failed, simply because Mr. Clerides had asked for 48 hours to consider his proposals with an open mind?

69. *Mr. Günes* said that the Conference had not failed because Mr. Clerides had asked for another 48 hours, but because he had pursued dilatory tactics throughout.

70. *Mr. Clerides* said that he had asked for only one adjournment, whereas Mr. Günes had repeatedly asked for adjournments, and obtained them, so that his Cabinet might deliberate. He had received Mr. Günes proposals at 11 p.m. the previous day. At 9 a.m. he had requested an adjournment, and had waited until 6 p.m. before he knew whether or not an adjournment would be granted. If there had been delaying tactics, they had been used by Mr. Günes, not by himself. Mr. Clerides then put two questions to the representatives of the other two Guarantor Powers:

(*a*) what view did they take of Mr. Günes' conclusions that the Conference had ended; and

(*b*) what position would they take should the Turkish Army advance further in Cyprus?

71. On (*a*), *Mr. Callaghan* said that the British Government, together with the other Governments of the European Community, did not believe that all diplomatic possibilities had been exhausted. The Nine had made representations in Ankara; they believed that the negotiations should continue, and that was also the view of the United States Secretary of State.[8] It was unreasonable to deny a request for an adjournment of 36 hours. On (*b*) the United Kingdom had always put troops at the disposal of the United Nations in circumstances like those of the present. Britain had also made a substantial contribution to UNFICYP. This particular question would be considered in due course when the participants reported to the Security Council.

72. *Mr. Mavros* said that the Conference faced a threat of military action, if indeed military action had not already begun. If he was right, evidence would shortly be available to prove that the Conference had been conducted under the threat of military action. He agreed with Mr.

[8] See note 5 above.

Callaghan and Dr. Kissinger that the diplomatic means of settling this dispute had not been exhausted. The participants should now report to the Security Council. It was dangerous to believe that the future of Cyprus could be settled by military action; this could only be done round the negotiating table, where discussions could be conducted freely and without the threat of force. If the Conference ended in failure, the responsibility would not be that of the Greek Government.

73. *Mr. Callaghan* read from a telegram (which he had just received) the text of the démarche made by the French Ambassadors in Athens and Nicosia [*sic*] on behalf of the Nine.[9]

74. *Mr. Günes* said these were his final words. The Cyprus problems had been discussed for the last 20 years under two threats directed against Turkey: delaying tactics in the diplomatic field, and the threat of armed force against the Turkish Cypriot community. When the Turkish Army landed in Cyprus, it was not confronted by 1,200 Greek Cypriot soldiers, as might have been expected from the constitutional provisions for the Cyprus Army. It was wrong to say that the Conference was being held under the threat of Turkish bayonets; in Cyprus there was an army directed not only against the Turkish Cypriot community, but also against Turkey. The danger of further Turkish military operations in Cyprus had existed ever since the landing of the Turkish armed forces; but Turkey had accepted the cease-fire from the outset, and had herself asked for the Geneva Conference to be held as soon as possible. Unfortunately, he had begun to be convinced in Geneva that the threat of diplomatic delaying tactics was looming up, and he did not want the Cyprus drama to drag on as before. No one could say that the Turkish Government had tried to solve the problem by force; they had after all engaged in consultations under the Treaty of Guarantee.

75. *Mr. Clerides* admitted that when the Turkish armed forces landed in Cyprus they had found that they were received by the National Guard. They had also found, as was evident from successive reports by the United Nations Secretary-General, a Turkish Cypriot Army 12,000 strong, trained, staffed and equipped by Turkey. This was not a constitutional army. *Mr. Denktash* said that the Turkish Cypriots had only reacted to moves by the Greek Cypriots. They had replied to the *enosis* movement with an anti-*enosis* movement. They had replied to the establishment of the National Guard by the establishment of the Turkish Cypriot Fighters.

76. In response to questions by Mr. Callaghan, *Mr. Clerides* and *Mr. Mavros* said that they were prepared to return to Geneva on Thursday

---

[9] Paris telegram No. 6 to UKMIS Geneva of 13 August contained the draft text of a démarche which it had been agreed the French Ambassadors in Athens and Ankara should make on behalf of the nine EC member-states. This addressed a solemn appeal to Greece and Turkey to continue the negotiations, and drew their attention to the responsibilities which would be incurred 'in the eyes of the Community by whoever engaged a military action risking opening a conflict with incalculable consequences' (WSC 6/598/1).

morning. *Mr. Callaghan* confirmed that he also was prepared to do so. *Mr. Denktash* said that he was bound to the Turkish Government; he would come if the Turkish Foreign Minister would do so. *Mr. Günes* said nothing. The Conference broke up at 2.25 a.m.[10]

[10] At 3 a.m. (GMT), following the breakdown of the Geneva talks, Turkish forces resumed hostilities in Cyprus. According to Nicosia telegram No. 752, despatched at 3.15 a.m. on 14 August, 'Fighter bombers went into action east of Nicosia and firing broke out on the demarcation line' (WSC 1/10). Turkish forces subsequently advanced from their Kyrenia base westward and south-eastward, heavily bombing Nicosia and its airport. At midday on 16 August Mr. Eçevit announced that Turkish forces would ceasefire at 4 p.m. By 21 August they had occupied approximately 34% of the land area of Cyprus up to a line extending south-eastwards from one mile west of Karovastasi to Nicosia and then, after bordering the British SBA at Dhekelia, on to the western coast of the island at Ayios Mennon (Ankara telegram No. 1002 of 16 August; telegram No. 501 to Nicosia of 21 August; WSC 1/10).

No. 77

Record of a telephone conversation between Mr. Callaghan and Dr. Kissinger on 14 August 1974 at 1.45 p.m.[1]

[WSC 3/304/2]

Confidential

Foreign Secretary
Hello. Henry?

Dr. Kissinger
Good morning. How are you?

Foreign Secretary
It's late night for you isn't it?

Dr. Kissinger
No, no it's early in the morning.

Foreign Secretary
Early in the morning.

Dr. Kissinger
Yes, that's right.

[1] Mr. Callaghan spoke to Dr. Kissinger on the telephone in 10 Downing Street.

Foreign Secretary
Oh, I see. I was suggesting to Harold[2] that he might like to have a word with the President perhaps a bit later today, just to exchange views ...

Dr. Kissinger
I think that's a good idea.

Foreign Secretary
All right, I will get him to do that then.[3]

Dr. Kissinger
Let me talk to the President for a minute about this.

Foreign Secretary
Yes.

Dr. Kissinger
He thinks that's an excellent idea.

Foreign Secretary
Right.

Dr. Kissinger
Jim, what is your view on where we stand?

Foreign Secretary
Well, I was just thinking—I think in military terms, obviously the Turks will carry on until they have got this line that they have figured out on the map, and cynically, let's hope they get it quickly.[4]

Dr. Kissinger
I agree.

Foreign Secretary
They will then stop, and there will be no political solution. We shall have a continuation of guerrilla warfare between EOKA B and the Turks. They will eventually pull their army back because they won't be able to afford to keep it there. Now, in the meantime, NATO will be just that much weakened, and I think you ought to make a fresh assessment of the south east corner of NATO, because neither of them are of very much use to us at the moment.

---

[2] Mr. H. Wilson.

[3] See note 6 below.

[4] See No. 76, note 10.

Dr. Kissinger
Well do you think, Jim—we were talking here about ways to move this negotiation—if you think it has any chance.

Foreign Secretary
Not in the slightest.

Dr. Kissinger
Do you think a NATO ministerial would be a good framework, or would be a possible framework to get them started again?

Foreign Secretary
Henry, I don't want to be negative because it's not my approach, but I really don't. I think NATO would get itself embroiled in it with even more dire consequences for its future without being able to solve it because at the moment no Greek Cypriot can sit down with a Turkish Cypriot, or with a Turk. And by rushing into this, the Turks have made a settlement impossible. My own very strong view is that if I reproach myself with one thing it is that I didn't put more pressure on the Greeks earlier than I did.

Dr. Kissinger
I quite agree.

Foreign Secretary
To try to get them to give way. I think if we'd had this thirty-six hours without military action—if the Turks hadn't rushed into military action—we could have got it. But now, Henry, I don't think there's the slightest chance of them moving.

Dr. Kissinger
… and frankly I didn't recommend it myself, so we were all wrong.

Foreign Secretary
Well, that's right. Well, if we want to excuse ourselves, Günes didn't put his plans forward until 10.30 on Monday night and then wanted a meeting that night in order to settle it.[5] So none of us really knew what we were finally up against, even though we'd read it in the newspapers. However, that is no good looking back. But as to the future …

Dr. Kissinger
You don't think there would be any sense, Mavros has been eager to come over here—would there be any sense in doing that?

---

[5] See No. 72.

Foreign Secretary
Well, yes there would because I think Greece needs massaging now. You've got to be careful that you don't give them more of an appearance of doing something without doing anything. Because they'll turn on you very, very quickly, as they've begun to turn on us a bit.

Dr. Kissinger
The Greeks?

Foreign Secretary
The Greeks will, yes. Because they want some action, you see and they are not going to get any action. You're not going to act, we're not going to act unilaterally and the UN is going to get out of the way.

Dr. Kissinger
OK. Why don't we let the thing sit then for a day and see how it looks tomorrow morning.

Foreign Secretary
I would. I don't think it will look much better tomorrow morning except we may know more how far the Turks have got, and where they are going to stop. But in terms of diplomatic action, Henry, we haven't got a chance here unless something breaks that I can't foresee for some weeks. That's my feeling as of today.

Dr. Kissinger
We will not do anything without consultation with you.

Foreign Secretary
No Sir, very good. And likewise the same. Let me just put it in a nutshell.

Dr. Kissinger
We won't do anything today.

Foreign Secretary
All right.

Dr. Kissinger
Let me put the President on. He wanted to say hello to you.

Foreign Secretary
That's very kind of you, yes.

President of the United States
Good morning Mr. Minister.

Foreign Secretary
Mr. President, Sir, may I offer my respectful congratulations.

President
Well, thank you very much and I want you to know that we appreciate what you have been trying to do in a very difficult situation.

Foreign Secretary
Well, that's very kind of you. You know that Henry and I—well I have a great respect for him, and I hope we've got a great friendship together and Mr. President, I just want to say this to you, Sir, that in the end, when the chips are down it's only the United States who can really pull the chestnuts out of the fire, and there are times when not even you can do that. This was one of them.

President
I fully appreciate that, but we have to have good friends and allies like Great Britain to work with and for that reason we are darn grateful for all that you have been trying to do.

Foreign Secretary
Well, thank you Sir, very much, I look forward to meeting you I must say in the near future, and may I wish you the very best of good luck. You've got a hell of a job but it's a wonderful challenge too, and we'll all be rooting for you and hoping for great success for the United States.

President
Thank you very much and give the Prime Minister my very best.

Foreign Secretary
Yes, I will Sir. Shall he call you later?

President
Yes, I would like to have him do so, Sir.

Foreign Secretary
All right, I'll do that Mr. President. Could I have just one more word with Henry?

President
Yes, Henry is right here.

Foreign Secretary
Henry, if I can put the position in a nutshell, I think it comes to this: that the Turks have got a good case. In my view this can now only be

resolved by the creation of a zone. A zone in which they will have autonomy within a federal republic. This could be got by negotiation but in the temper of today, no one can begin to get anything like this. And so you have a military solution for the time being, in which they will police their own boundary. You'll have a great exchange of population with the Greeks moving out and we'll then just let diplomacy take over when we see the opportunity once more, to see if we can get a peaceful solution in the island. Now as regards Greece and Turkey, it is Greece who will need massaging because the Turks are too jingoistic, indeed too close to Hitler for my liking. All right?

Dr. Kissinger
I completely agree with you Jim. And the tragedy is that it could have worked out that way through diplomacy ...

Foreign Secretary
I believe you. Well, goodbye old man and all the best to you with your preoccupations.

Dr. Kissinger
Thank you Jim. You've been ...

Foreign Secretary
Thank you goodbye.[6]

---

[6] This telephone conversation was followed by a short meeting on certain military aspects of Cyprus at which were present Mr. Wilson, Mr. Callaghan, Mr. Rodgers, Sir A. Humphrey, Mr. Hockaday and Sir J. Killick. According to a minute of 14 August from Sir J. Killick to Mr. Goodison, Mr. Callaghan said 'that it was clear the US would do nothing militarily. The UK could not act unilaterally. The UN he thought would keep their heads down. He was sure the Turks were very concerned not to embarrass us and would leave the SBAs alone.' Mr. Wilson summed up the outcome of the meeting by saying that there was 'clearly no purpose in further reinforcements' in the SBAs. 'There could', he concluded, 'be no question of British military intervention which would mean war with Turkey. The UN could have no conceivable capability to intervene militarily and we should not envisage any further substantial contributions of forces to UNFICYP.' In a subsequent telephone conversation with President Ford, the Prime Minister observed with regard to Cyprus that it was going to be 'a long diplomatic haul now' (record of a telephone conversation between Mr. Wilson and President Ford on 14 August at 5 p.m.).

No. 78

Record of a meeting between Mr. Callaghan and Dr. Waldheim in the FCO on 14 August 1974 at 3.30 p.m.

[*WSC 2/522/2*]

Confidential

Present:

The Rt. Hon. James Callaghan MP	Dr. K. Waldheim
Sir John Killick, KCMG	Herr Prohaska[1]
Mr. T.F. Brenchley	
Miss M. Fort	

1. *Mr. Callaghan* said that the chances for a diplomatic solution had dissolved in the face of Turkish intransigence. He sincerely believed that if the Turks had not been determined to attack it would have been possible to get Mr. Denktash and Mr. Clerides after consultations to agree in Geneva to a federal solution with two zones. The Turks had ruined that prospect. He had been very firm with Mr. Günes when the latter had claimed that Turkey had rights to invade as a guarantor power. Mr. Callaghan had made it clear that no guarantor had the right to compel a constitutional solution by force. The United Kingdom did not intend to take unilateral action which would make matters worse in this dreadful embroglio. He did not think that the United Nations had the capacity to stop the invading Turkish Army.

2. *Dr. Waldheim* said that only a Resolution under Chapter VII language would give him a mandate to separate the two communities.[2] The UNFICYP troops could use their weapons only in self-defence but failing the establishment of clear buffer zones and with only light weapons they had no chance to fight a regular army. *Mr. Callaghan* said that it would only have been possible if they could have stationed troops across the line of advance as a deterrent but there were limitations of will in the UN as an organisation. *Dr. Waldheim* said that it would have been feasible with a new Resolution but they had not got one. It was open to question whether all the Permanent Members of the Security Council were ready to accept Chapter VII Language. *Mr. Callaghan* said that there was a very mixed bunch on the Security Council and that it would not be easy.[3]

---

[1] Dr. A. Prohaska was Head of the Office of the UN Secretary-General.

[2] Chapter VII of the UN Charter covers action with respect to threats to the peace, breaches of the peace, and acts of aggression.

[3] During a subsequent conversation with Dr. Waldheim, Mr. Wilson commented that HMG's view was that 'the Russians could afford to sit and watch the present events which were leading to the collapse of the eastern flank of N.A.T.O.'. But, he added that it was also their view that 'neither Britain nor the United Nations should enter into military conflict with

3. *Dr. Waldheim* said that he was not happy with the situation where the public was getting the impression that the UN were not effective. But they could not defend the island with only 4,000 lightly armed soldiers.

4. *Mr. Callaghan* said that he had just talked to Dr. Kissinger and President Ford. They did not know what to do and had asked Mr. Callaghan for advice and for his views. But he too felt devoid of ideas for the present. He thought that the Greeks might not sit down and talk with the Turks for a long time and he therefore saw no glimmer of hope for diplomatic action for the present. Dr. Kissinger had asked him if NATO should take action but Mr. Callaghan had said no.[4]

5. *Mr. Brenchley* said that there were radio reports that the Turks were over-running the island in a line from Kyrenia to Larnaka. Only when they had achieved their objectives would they say that they were ready to return to the conference table, but by that time the Greeks might refuse. *Mr. Callaghan* said that equally he was not very willing to go quickly to the conference table in the face of a victorious Turkish army dictating terms. He explained some of Mr. Günes' delaying and dead-line tactics. He asked Dr. Waldheim if he had any idea of where the negotiations should go next.

6. *Dr. Waldheim* said that the Turks would be happy to negotiate when they had enough territory. He was afraid that there would be much bloodshed and heavy fighting between the National Guard and the Turkish Army and around the Turkish enclaves. His problem was what to do with UNFICYP. The present mandate would not solve the current problem. He felt that he should try to give new clear instructions to UNFICYP and he had already arranged the transfer of the Swedes to Famagusta, although they were only a couple of hundred in strength. *Mr. Callaghan* said that UNFICYP's role should be to protect the Greek Cypriots in the Turkish zone and the Turkish Cypriots in the Greek zone. *Dr. Waldheim* explained that the Turks wanted UNFICYP to leave the Turkish controlled area. *Mr. Callaghan* said that after the latest Turkish move it was imperative that they should stay. There was a danger of real panic among the Greek Cypriots and the Greeks were in the great majority in the proposed Turkish zone. Of course the Turks hoped the Greek Cypriots would leave the Turkish zone, but now UNFICYP had as big a problem in the Turkish zone as formerly in the Greek zone. *Dr. Waldheim* said that Mr. Eçevit had told him that UNIFCYP had no right to be there, and that the ICRC could look after it. *Mr. Callaghan* emphasised that in his view UNFICYP would have no basis for their presence in the Greek zone if they withdrew from the Turkish zone.

7. *Mr. Callaghan* asked if it would be easier for UNFICYP to have a new mandate. *Dr. Waldheim* said that they did not have too much difficulty at present but a new revised mandate would make their task more feasible.

Turkey' (record of a conversation between Mr. Wilson and Dr. Waldheim at 10 Downing Street on 14 August at 4 p.m.).

[4] See No. 77.

Mr. Callaghan thought that the Turks would say that they would look after the Greeks in a new Turkish zone. *Dr. Waldheim* said that the Security Council would not go along with that, but with a new mandate he could keep UNFICYP in the area. *Mr. Callaghan* asked how many troops UNFICYP would need. *Dr. Waldheim* said that now he would have to make an appeal to the troop contributing countries. Mr. Günes wanted an Islamic contingent. Dr. Waldheim had until now declined in case nations other than the present contributors became involved, but perhaps Iran would be an acceptable contributor. Mr. Günes had suggested Libya, Algeria or Pakistan. *Mr. Callaghan* said that if anything he would prefer Iran, or as a second choice Algeria, but not Libya. *Dr. Waldheim* said that Algeria would be easier for him as it was non-aligned. *Mr. Callaghan* explained that the United Kingdom would find it difficult to contribute more troops. They already comprised 35-40 per cent of UNFICYP and he did not want it to look too lopsided.

8. *Dr. Waldheim* raised the question of Nicosia airport. He had just received a report from Prem Chand[5] via New York. Prem Chand thought that Britain and UNFICYP should control the airport together. Dr. Waldheim had no objection so long as it was presented as a UN controlled area even though with a strong British contingent. Mr. Eçevit had assured him that he would not give the order to attack UNFICYP. He asked Mr. Callaghan what they should do if the Turkish Army attacked the airport. *Mr. Callaghan* said that he understood that the Turks had already attacked Greek installations at the airport. He did not know what his recommendation would be about the airport. He would have to consider it with the Ministry of Defence. *Dr. Waldheim* said that at present UNFICYP were under strict instructions to defend the airport. He was satisfied that the agreement on a local basis was satisfactory for the present but Mr. Günes had criticised him for not handing the airport over to the Turks. In the new situation he thought the Turks would try to take the airport. *Mr. Callaghan* said that he was in favour of holding it but that he would consult the Ministry of Defence and would let Dr. Waldheim know in a message that night or the next morning.

9. *Dr. Waldheim* asked if the United Kingdom were going to request a new meeting of the Security Council. He thought that the non-implementation of the Security Council Resolutions should be raised. If by tomorrow morning the Turks did not stop advancing a Security Council meeting should be called. The Russians were not happy with the situation but Ambassador Malik was cooperating and had called the Security Council very promptly for the latest meeting. *Mr. Callaghan* said that he had ensured that the Russians in Geneva were given regular briefings, partly with this in mind. He thought there should be another Security Council meeting to keep the pressure up on Turkey. *Dr. Waldheim* thought that psychologically it was a good thing and suggested that the next Resolution

[5] Gen. Prem Chand was Commanding Officer, UNFICYP.

should perhaps condemn the fact that Turkish Forces had not complied with the Security Council Resolutions.[6] *Mr. Callaghan* said that he thought that the Americans realised now that they had acted too late and a United States official that morning had told him 'We did not give the backing you needed'. He was satisfied that the Americans were fully conscious of the position but previously they had been distracted by the human tragedy in Washington. He had spoken to President Ford that morning and had said to him that in the last resort only the United States could pull the chestnuts out of the fire.[7] He thought that President Ford realised that.

10. *Dr. Waldheim* confirmed that it was a very good idea for the Secretary of State to be prepared to go to New York to address the Security Council.

---

[6] On instructions from Mr. Callaghan, Mr. Richard asked for an urgent meeting of the Security Council, and this was fixed for 6 a.m. (GMT) on 14 August. Following consultations with other Missions, he tabled a draft resolution which, after amendment, was adopted as Resolution 357 at 8.30 a.m. This (1) reaffirmed Resolution 353 in all its provisions; (2) called upon all parties concerned to implement those provisions without delay; (3) demanded that all parties to the present fighting cease firing and military action forthwith; and (4) called for the resumption of negotiations without delay, the restoration of peace in the area and constitutional government in Cyprus. The Council was to remain seized of the situation and 'on instant call to meet as necessary' to consider what effective measures might be required if the ceasefire were not respected (UKMIS New York telegrams Nos. 989 and 990 of 14 August). See *UNSC Official Records: Resolutions and Decisions, 29th year* (1974), p. 8.

[7] See No. 77.

No. 79

Mr. Callaghan to Sir P. Ramsbotham (Washington)

No. 1713 Telegraphic [WSC 1/10]

Immediate. Secret   FCO, *15 August 1974, 6.10 p.m.*

Repeated for information to Athens, Ankara, Nicosia, UKDEL NATO.

Cyprus

1. I had a further telephone conversation at 14.40Z[1] with Dr. Kissinger about various aspects of the present situation.

2. We began with the request from Mavros for air cover for a possible Greek convoy from Crete to Cyprus (Athens tel[egram] No. 450 refers).[2] I

---

[1] 2.40 p.m. GMT. Mr. Callaghan had previously discussed Cyprus with Dr. Kissinger on the telephone at 10.30 p.m. on 14 August (telegram No. 263 to Athens of 14 August).

[2] In this telegram of 14 August Sir R. Hooper reported that Mr. Mavros wished to know what HMG's reaction would be to a proposal to despatch a Greek division, then assembling in Crete, to Cyprus, not with the object of engaging in active hostilities against the Turks, but in order to 'hold a demarcation line'. He also wanted to know whether HMG would be prepared

told Kissinger that I had now instructed HM Ambassador at Athens to tell Mavros that, for a number of reasons, HMG could not agree to his request. This had been made easier by Makarios telling me this morning that he saw no point in the reinforcement envisaged by Mavros.[3] Kissinger confirmed that he had no similar request from the Greeks and that he agreed with my decision.

3. I told Kissinger that following my conversation with Dr. Luns earlier today, I had decided not to pursue the idea of a Ministerial meeting of the North Atlantic Council early next week. Kissinger agreed and added that he felt there should be no new diplomatic initiative until the situation in Cyprus was clearer. I added that I had attempted to persuade Dr. Luns, who was in a very legalistic frame of mind, from going to Athens to pursue the question of Greece's relations with NATO. I feared that if he did so he would get the wrong answers.[4] Kissinger was sure that this was right.

4. Rather surprisingly, Kissinger said that Mavros had not yet replied to the invitation to visit Washington. I told him that we had seen a news flash more than an hour earlier reporting that Mavros had announced he was too busy to visit the US now. Kissinger said he would await formal notification although the press report were [*sic*] no doubt correct.

5. I told Kissinger that I was hoping to have a few days away from the Office in the immediate future and that I did not intend to hurry back if attempts were made to re-convene the Geneva Conference early next week. My inclination was to ask a junior Minister to go for the opening session and to come in myself at a later stage in the proceedings. Kissinger felt strongly that this was the right approach and said that it would inhibit efforts to create further show-downs in the opening phase of the Conference.

6. Finally, we discussed briefly the longer term situation. I expressed my concern about Turkey's intentions in the rest of the Aegean, e.g. on the

to provide air cover for the convoy after it had passed beyond the effective range of the Greek air force: 'Britain could, he [Mr. Mavros] said, take this action jointly with Greece (i.e. under the Treaty of Guarantee or possibly under UN auspices).'

[3] Mr. Callaghan informed Sir R. Hooper in telegram No. 267 to Athens of 15 August that he had given 'Mavros no encouragement in Geneva to think that we would provide air cover for a Greek convoy', and he advised the Greek Government 'most strongly' against sending more troops to Cyprus at this stage. He reasoned that such military action would 'make war between Greece and Turkey inevitable', aggravate the situation in Cyprus, lead possibly to Turkish attacks elsewhere in the Aegean, and increase the risk of double *enosis*. Cf. No. 80, note 6.

[4] Immediately following the second Turkish invasion of Cyprus on 14 August, the Greek Government informed Dr. Luns that they wished to withdraw from the Alliance's integrated defence organisation. When Dr. Luns called at the FCO on the morning of 15 August Mr. Callaghan advised him 'not to stand on punctilio with the Greeks at a time when they were obviously very sore'. He added: 'they probably felt a need to take public measures to demonstrate that they were not passive in the face of their NATO partners' alleged failure to come to their aid over Cyprus' (telegram No. 194 to UKDEL NATO of 15 August, WSG 2/579/2).

question of the continental shelf. Had the Americans thought what they would do in the event of Turkey trying to capitalise outside Cyprus on its present success? Kissinger said that he would have to 'crack down' on the Turks in those circumstances. He would certainly look at the military supply situation.[5] I told him that I was not sure that we could wait until the Turks acted. If for instance they created a situation where the *de facto* partition of the island resulted in *enosis*, whether double or otherwise, the consequences could only be unfortunate.[6] Among other things Makarios would become [a] Greek politician. An alliance between Makarios and Papandreou[7] would result in a neutralist government in Greece. Kissinger said he would ask his staff to do a study of the issues I had raised.

[5] Dr. Kissinger told Sir P. Ramsbotham on 17 August that he had sent messages that day to the Greek and Turkish Prime Ministers. He had assured Mr. Karamanlis of the US Government's understanding of his difficulties and its willingness to help in finding a 'reasonable solution', but had also urged him 'not to press for what was no longer realistic'. Meanwhile, he had warned Mr. Eçevit that the Turks would have to give up some of the territory they had taken in Cyprus (Washington telegram No. 2733 of 17 August, WSC 1/16).

[6] In Ankara telegram No. 989 of 15 August Sir H. Phillips reported that Mr. Eçevit had assured Mr. Macomber that Turkish forces would not secure more than one third of Cyprus; that eastward of Nicosia they would not advance south of a line running generally from the capital to Famagusta; and that to the west of Nicosia they would not advance 'south of what Turkey originally had in mind as the basic line'.

[7] Mr. A.G. Papandreou was a member of the Greek Government until the Colonels' coup in 1967, when he was imprisoned for several months. He was founder and chair of PAK (*Panellinio Apeleutherotiko Kinima*/Panhellenic Liberation Movement) during 1968-74. Cf. No. 102, note 5.

CHAPTER III

Cyprus: Sequel to Geneva
16 August 1974–13 February 1975

No. 80

Draft Paper by Mr. Goodison[1]
[*WSC 1/10*]

Confidential   FCO, *16 August 1974*

Cyprus: Policy after Stage II

Our main priority is to obtain a lasting settlement in Cyprus which will:

(i) reduce the risk of future Greco/Turkish squabbles;

(ii) allow us to withdraw from our prominent position under the 1960 agreements and the Geneva Declaration;

(iii) avoid perpetuating UNFICYP—and our contribution to it—at its present level.

2. We believe that a bi-regional federation in Cyprus, on lines advocated by Mr. Denktash, but involving an area under Turkish Cypriot administration rather smaller than 34 per cent of the Republic, offers the best solution.[2] To achieve this, the Turkish military advance should cease at the Attila line.[3] Thereafter, a few days may be needed for the Turks to accept that they must be ready for real negotiation and for the Greeks and Greek Cypriots to get used to the new situation and to return without too much loss of dignity to the conference table. This suggests that we should

---

[1] Mr. Goodison explained in a covering minute to Sir J. Killick and Mr. Acland of 16 August that on his return from Geneva he had prepared this draft paper with a view to defining British policy. But in a note of 17 August Mr. Goodison indicated that Mr. Callaghan had directed that the paper should not be circulated within the FCO or to overseas posts. 'He', Mr. Goodison added, 'has approved the broad outlines as guidance for ourselves. There are however many nuances he would wish to amend.'

[2] In a minute to Sir J. Killick of 16 August, headed 'Cyprus: a geographical solution', Mr. Goodison maintained; 'It is important that we should avoid any suggestion that in favouring the geographical separation of the two communities as the most viable solution of the Cyprus problem, we are working for the partition of the Island.' Partition had a 'bad name internationally' and, he reasoned, was contrary to the UK's obligations. He therefore recommended that HMG should use the term 'biregional federation', reserving the term 'cantonal federation' for Mr. Günes's proposal involving more than one area for each community.

[3] A notional line extending from Morphou in the west to Famagusta in the east and incorporating the northern sector of Nicosia.

not go to the conference table until we are sure of the basic ingredients of a settlement in terms of the broad policies and attitudes of the parties.

3. We also want to limit the damage to NATO, the scope for Soviet intervention and the harm to our own relations with Turkey. In Cyprus itself, we want to avoid the risk of Turkish forces being drawn into fighting beyond the Attila line, of Dhekelia becoming involved, or of guerilla fighting on a large scale. These objectives may push us in the direction of an early Stage III, especially if Dr. Kissinger puts pressure on us to return to Geneva soon.[4] But, if we have the chance, we should delay a Stage III conference until about 25 August in the hope of:

(i)   generating international pressure on the Turks;

(ii) bringing the Turks to appreciate their difficult position in Cyprus (including the financial strains their military action will impose);

(iii) getting the Greeks and Greek Cypriots—including Makarios—to accept the need for a bi-regional federation;

(iv) permitting *de facto* changes which will facilitate a radical separation of the two communities in Cyprus (that is, population movements and consolidation of the Turkish zone).

4. With this policy in mind, action may be needed over the next week in four respects:

(i)   *Discouraging the Greeks* from action likely to make Stage III even more difficult (in particular military action against Turkey). This suggests a policy of sympathy towards Greece (personal messages, etc.), plus strong urging from ourselves, the Americans and the Nine to keep Greece within the reach of the conference table.[5]

(ii) *Building up Mr. Clerides.* The chances of a radical settlement in Cyprus depend on having Clerides rather than Makarios at Stage III. The Secretary of State has already embarrassed Makarios by moving him

---

[4] Cf. No. 79. The Turks were, according to notes recording a briefing by Sir J. Killick on the morning of 16 August, 'expressing readiness to return to the conference table and talking of going to Geneva as early as 17 or 19 August, but the likelihood of early Greek or Greek Cypriot willingness to resume talks seemed small'.

[5] In a personal message to Mr. Karamanlis, transmitted in telegram No. 274 to Athens of 16 August, Mr. Wilson stressed that he thought the despatch of a Greek division to Cyprus would be a 'most unwise course'. After urging Mr. Karamanlis to work in parallel for a negotiated settlement, he added: 'As I see it, the best way of bringing the Turkish Government to a more realistic frame of mind is to avoid any action likely to prolong the fighting: to continue to attract the support of international opinion; and to make clear that a Turkish Cypriot region within a federal state of Cyprus can be legitimised only with the agreement of our two Governments and the Greek Cypriots.'

towards stating his terms before we resume in Geneva;[6] this line could perhaps be developed to Clerides' benefit. But there is not much we can do about this. The danger of a declaration of *enosis* was greatest on 14 August and we should take no preventive action against this unless we have some indication that it is contemplated. We do not want to suggest that ideas of this kind are current, given the assurances of the Greeks and Greek Cypriots at Geneva. We must also encourage the Greeks to continue to help Clerides by removing undesirable Greek influences from Cyprus. We must do what we can to discourage reprisals against the Turkish Cypriot community outside the Turkish zone.

(iii) *Maintaining our position as honest broker.* We should not take any action to strengthen Turkish belief that we are wholly *parti pris* (e.g., by sponsoring UN resolutions or publishing a White Paper). We should stick to the Secretary of State's line that the Turks have a case even though their methods are regrettable.

(iv) *Constraining the Turks.* It would suit our strategy if the Turkish armed forces ended up with 25/30 per cent rather than 40 per cent of the island. But they cannot be negotiated with in their present self-confident mood.[7] We should therefore do what we can to make them more amenable by Stage III. One particularly difficult problem will be the possible enforced transfer of Greek Cypriots from the Turkish occupied zone. In one sense this could facilitate the bi-regional federal solution; on the other hand it would increase the danger of reprisals against Turkish Cypriots. It is difficult to see that HMG could or should do anything to influence this either way. It would no doubt be a matter for the Security Council.

5. The main forms of pressure on the Turks are:

To delay over attendance at Stage III. As soon as their military advance stops, the Turks will want a quick conference.[8] We aim to make our

---

[6] Sir J. Killick said in his morning briefing (see note 4 above) that Archbishop Makarios had, in talks with Mr. Wilson and Mr. Callaghan, stated the he was 'opposed to the despatch of Greek forces to Cyprus'. With regard to political settlement, the Archbishop had said that he 'was in favour of the resumption of talks and [he] gave some indication of moving towards acceptance of two administrative zones'.

[7] Brig. H.H.M. Marston, the British Defence Attaché in Ankara, reported in a telegram of 17 August: 'Turks are exultant after military victory and absolutely convinced of own rectitude. They will be extremely difficult to deal with in any terms except own. Criticism is anathema and Britain is being attacked vituperatively in press ... We are held to be anti-Turkish and by our attitudes and statements we are responsible for much of the present world criticism of Turkey.'

[8] Sir H. Phillips reported in Ankara telegram No. 1006 of 16 August that Mr. Eçevit had told him that afternoon that after the end of Turkish military operations that evening his Government would be ready to resume negotiations at any time. 'At one point', Sir H. Phillips noted, 'Eçevit said that if the Greeks did not agree to resume negotiations the position would

attendance at Stage III conditional on Turkish agreement in advance to negotiate on their territorial demands; to implement relevant parts of the Geneva Declaration; and to make practical arrangements not covered by the Declaration, e.g. on Nicosia Airport.[9]

NATO. Although a useful political framework in which Greece and Turkey can keep in touch, any definite action by the Alliance can only alienate one or the other to no good purpose. NATO should not be obliged to take sides.[10] We have discouraged the Secretary General from overmuch activity.

The UN. The best forum for multilateral action in the short term, because the pressure on Turkey will be less obviously from the West. Criticism in the UN will show the Turks that they have little support even in the Third World, but it should not be allowed to become too shrill. Security Council activities will make it harder for the Russians to sit on the fence and tempt them into undesirable opportunist activities. Ideally, we want a resolution which does not permit the Turks to justify their military presence by reference to the Treaty of Guarantee.[11] Pressure on the Turks will build up as we approach the General Assembly (17 September).

Nine. A strong collective line would be good for the Nine even though it would probably have little effect in the short term. Bilateral pressure (especially German military aid) are likely to be more vigorously applied if done under the umbrella of the Nine. Pressure should be directed to moderating the Turkish negotiating position. The French are anxious to give the Greeks comfort and it is no bad thing to use the Nine for this purpose.

---

inevitably crystallise into two separate areas without the bond of central government' (WSC 1/16).

[9] Mr. Callaghan informed Sir H. Phillips in telegram No. 989 to Ankara of 16 August 'we are working on the assumption that a certain amount of foot-dragging on our part—despite the risks this will involve in the island—is likely to help the Greeks to accept a diplomatic defeat and to persuade the Turks to accept reductions in the 30-34% of territory they were demanding at Geneva'.

[10] At an informal meeting in Brussels on 21 August of the political Counsellors of the thirteen NATO delegations other than Greece and Turkey, it was generally agreed not to press the Greeks into any decision which might give practical effect to their intention of withdrawing their military forces from the Alliance. The order to withdraw had not yet been given (UKDEL NATO telegram No. 447 of 21 August, WSC 1/16). Cf. No. 79, note 4.

[11] On 16 August the Security Council adopted as Resolution 360, a French-sponsored draft resolution, recording the Council's 'formal disapproval of the unilateral military actions undertaken against the Republic of Cyprus', and urging 'the parties to resume without delay, in an atmosphere of constructive co-operation, the negotiations called for in Resolution 353 (1974) whose outcome should not be impeded or prejudged by the acquisition of advantages resulting from military operations' (UKMIS New York telegram No. 1018 of 16 August, WSC 2/522/2).

Possible Courses of Events

6. If this policy is successful, we would probably return to Geneva after 25 August, perhaps with a delegation headed by a Minister of State. We would hope to have prepared the Greeks and Turks for horse-trading on the size of the Turkish zone—involving some trimming of Turkey's opening bid (possibly to, say, 25 per cent, though we do not want to become impaled on percentages). This would have to be agreed on the map at Geneva III. We would then have a framework for detailed intercommunal talks in Nicosia within precise time limits. The other necessary ingredient for the framework would be an agreement on the competence of the federal and communal administrations.

7. In addition, the conference would have to address itself to the implementation of relevant parts of the Geneva Declaration and other politico/military matters.

8. There are, however, other less convenient possibilities to be borne in mind:

(i) *The extension of guerilla warfare.* Attacks on the Turkish enclaves and guerilla resistance within the Turkish zone might raise the risk of the Turkish forces advancing even further. This might oblige us to consider an earlier return to Geneva and a more active UNFICYP role than we now envisage.

(ii) *Trouble within Greece.* Karamanlis may fail to hold his position. This would increase the risk of war between Greece and Turkey or of Greek reprisals against the West. This too might force us back earlier to Geneva, partly under American pressure. In this situation there could be something to be said for by-passing Mavros and Günes and seeking to bring Eçevit and Karamanlis to the conference table. But this would depend on the willingness of the Prime Minister to be present.

(iii) *The overthrow or death of Clerides.* The only other Greek Cypriot with the authority to make the necessary concessions in Geneva II[I] would be Archbishop Makarios. But his presence would reduce the chances of an early agreement—even though it would be useful to have him embroiled in the compromise. This possibility suggests that we should keep Makarios informed and continue to try to get him to declare his position. Public acceptance by Makarios that Geneva III should be conducted on the basis of the Denktash proposals would, in itself, help to protect the position and life of Clerides. But this Makarios is most unlikely to give.

(iv) *Intransigence.* The Turks might refuse to accept our minimum demands for flexibility at the conference table. The Greeks and Greek Cypriots might refuse to sit down with the Turks. The Greek Cypriots might refuse to accept the principle of a bi-regional federation. All or some might refuse to go to Geneva unless the Secretary of State were to be present himself. We should in all these cases seek to postpone renewed talks: but international pressure for their resumption would be likely to increase quickly.[12]

[12] Mr. Callaghan explained in telegram No. 1729 to Washington of 17 August that he accepted that it was for HMG to convene further talks. Otherwise, he feared negotiations 'in other and possibly less desirable fora [would] be mooted'. He was not, however, prepared to embark on a fresh negotiating round without some assurance that the parties were willing to consider concessions in the absence of which success was inconceivable, and he felt that if he were to get anywhere with the Greeks and the Turks he would have to be able to say that he believed Mr. Clerides would accept a biregional federation in principle whatever his reservations in detail (WSC 1/16).

No. 81

Mr. Callaghan to Sir H. Phillips (Ankara)

No. 1004 Telegraphic [*WSC 1/16*]

Flash. Confidential   FCO, *20 August 1974, 2.00 p.m.*

Repeated for information to Flash Washington, Immediate Athens, Dhekelia, UKDEL NATO, UKMIS New York, Moscow, Bonn, Paris, UKMIS Geneva.

Cyprus Negotiations

MIFT contains a personal message from me to Eçevit.[1] You should seek an appointment with him as soon as possible and, after delivering the message, speak on the following lines.

2. I have noted Isik's statement that the Turks might prefer to negotiate about the future of Cyprus without a British presence.[2] I want to make it clear that we have no desire to interfere in or impede direct negotiations between Greece and Turkey or between the two communities in Cyprus. If Eçevit believes that Karamanlis is willing to meet him bilaterally, and that a meeting of the five parties would reduce their chances of success, then I would not pursue proposals for an early meeting in Geneva. I am taking soundings simultaneously in Athens on similar lines. But if the other parties

[1] In this message, transmitted on 20 August, Mr. Callaghan welcomed assurances offered by Mr. Eçevit to Sir H. Phillips on 16 August that his Government were ready to resume negotiations on Cyprus at any time (see No. 80, note 8). But Mr. Callaghan added that he believed that, if a settlement were to be negotiated successfully, it would be important for the Turkish Government 'to reiterate its willingness to accept that there should be a phased withdrawal of Turkish troops, along with all other foreign forces, from the republic and that the area they at present control should be reduced to some extent'.

[2] Sir H. Phillips noted in Ankara telegram No. 1025 of 19 August that the statement attributed to Mr. Isik 'was less categorical than as reported by the BBC and *The Sunday Telegraph* and should not be assumed to be a consider[ed] Government opinion yet'.

would like a meeting of the Five, then I would be willing to propose one on 26 August, in Geneva, provided I have some assurance that the parties are willing to negotiate and to make such concessions as will give some prospect of achieving a lasting settlement.

3. You should make it clear to Eçevit that I do not believe that it is to the advantage of the Turks to have no settlement and allow the situation to polarise. There would be danger, as I made clear to Günes in Geneva, of their being drawn further and further into responsibilities in Cyprus which could only prove an intolerable burden for them, militarily, financially and administratively. The dangers of guerilla warfare are great. The dangers for Turkey's international reputation are also great. It will be difficult to contain interference from the Soviet Union unless a settlement can be achieved in the near future.[3]

4. At the same time, I believe such a settlement can best be achieved on the basis of the bi-regional federation which we favour and which is attainable if the Turks are willing to make some concessions. As I made clear at Geneva, it is my belief that an arrangement on these lines holds the best hope for the future and I believe it may be acceptable both to the Greek Cypriots and the Greek Government. There are, however, a number of points on which I need some assurance of Turkish willingness to negotiate if I am to be sure that negotiations have a chance of success. You should then specify the points in para[graph] 3 of my tel[egram No.] 19 to Dhekelia, omitting the passage in brackets, and add the point that there should be no forcible expulsion of Cypriots from either region.[4] It is also

---

[3] But in a minute to Sir John Killick of 19 August Mr. Goodison listed as advantages the Turks would derive from refraining from further negotiations: (1) they need make 'no concessions whatsoever'; (2) they retained absolute control over the area they occupied; (3) they would be free to take any further military steps they liked; and (4) external pressures on them to reduce the number of their forces in Cyprus would lessen. At the same time they would still bear the international odium from which they currently suffered, and 'in the absence of any constitutional settlement, foreign governments [would] continue to treat the Greek Cypriots as constituting the Government of Cyprus'. On 20 August Sir J. Killick annotated his agreement. 'In essence', he wrote, 'the advantages for the Turks are all short-term, and the disadvantages long-term ... For the Greeks, the problem seems to me to be one of timing. They need a negotiated settlement, but must avoid humiliation, and perhaps see that the longer they wait, the less high price they may have to pay as the disadvantages begin to tell on the Turks.'

[4] Mr. Callaghan reasoned in this telegram of 18 August that if Mr. Clerides could achieve the consent of the Greek Cypriot community to a biregional federation, he would try to ensure that the Turks accepted in advance of any talks an early reduction in their force numbers in Cyprus, and seek agreement from them that the area they presently occupied might be reduced in the course of the negotiations. But he added in parenthesis that he had 'little hope that any substantial reduction [would] be possible'. On 19 August Mr. Clerides told Mr. Olver that, subject to Greek participation in negotiations, he would 'be willing to accept the basic idea of a federation based on two autonomous zones coupled with a central government of an independent Cyprus'. This, however, he insisted would be conditional on: (1) Turkish willingness to discuss substantial withdrawals from their present demarcation line; (2) a marked reduction of the total area held by the Turks (he was ready to consider 18-20% of the land area); (3) no

important at an early stage to arrange for the protection of Turkish Cypriots in the Greek Cypriot administered region and *vice versa* and to discuss the role of UNFICYP in this regard. I attach particular importance to the phased withdrawal of troops from the republic, perhaps in the framework of a long-term arrangement for its demilitarisation on lines briefly discussed at the first Geneva Conference.[5] You should add that I am encouraged by Dr. Kissinger's latest statement (Washington tel[egram] No. 2750) to believe that the Turkish Government share this general approach.[6]

5. If Eçevit repeats the line in para[graph] 2 of your tel[egram No.] 1006,[7] you should suggest that the total area at present controlled by Turkish troops seems disproportionate to the Turkish population of the island and that it is obvious that arrangements must be made to ensure that both regions are administratively, socially and economically viable.

6. The delimitation of the regions will clearly necessitate detailed talks, whether between officials of the Five or between representatives of the two communities will have to be for the conference to decide. My own tentative view is that if there is to be a meeting of the Five at Geneva, the Ministers might withdraw after a couple of days in which they would have established the broad lines of a settlement and affirmed their political will for a settlement.

forced exchange of population; and (4) a total, though phased, withdrawal of Turkish forces (Dhekelia telegram No. 36 of 19 August).

[5] See No. 44, note 1.

[6] This telegram of 19 August reported a press statement of Dr. Kissinger in which he stated that: (1) the US insisted on a strict maintenance of the ceasefire; (2) the imperative and urgent need to begin negotiations; (3) the US's continuing support for efforts to bring parties to the negotiating table; (4) that the Turks would have to display flexibility and that Mr. Eçevit had assured him that Turkey considered the demarcation line to be 'negotiable' and would carry out the provisions of the Geneva agreement calling for phased troop reductions; and (5) that while the US greatly valued its traditional friendship with Greece, it would 'not be pressured by threat of withdrawal from the Alliance, which Greece joined in its own interest, or by anti-American demonstrations' (WSC 3/304/2).

[7] See No. 80, note 8. Sir H. Phillips reported in this telegram of 16 August that Mr. Eçevit had made it clear to him with regard to the current demarcation line that 'there would be no major variation of this as established' with Lefka as the western point.

No. 82

Draft Paper by Sir G. Arthur
[*WSC 10/14*]

Top Secret   FCO, *20 August 1974*

The Sovereign Base Areas in Cyprus[1]

Cost

1. The identifiable cost of maintaining the SBAs, given the level of forces stationed in them before the recent crisis, is about £58 million a year. This is higher than the savings set out in previous Defence Review studies (£38 million), since the latter assumed that some of the forces previously stationed in Cyprus would be redeployed and not disbanded. Annex A[2] gives a breakdown of the costs and a brief statement of the function of the various elements in the forces.

Political Considerations

2. Recent events have shown that from a purely national point of view the SBAs are more a liability than an asset. We could occupy them in political comfort only so long as intercommunal strife in Cyprus and hostility between Greece and Turkey could be kept under control. The logic of our position was false, and it was revealed as such as soon as the precarious balance in the island was disturbed by the Greek-instigated coup. The Turks expected us to intervene, or failing that, to ease their intervention. Later on, the Greeks expected us to deter, and if necessary, to oppose Turkish expansion in the island. We did neither, though to all appearances we were best placed, since we alone commanded bases in Cyprus, to do both. Even if we had been prepared to act, we would have been inhibited by the need to get into the SBAs some 11,000 Service dependants living outside—in itself an action with political implications. So all we could to was sit and watch; to secure the SBAs themselves; to evacuate British subjects (once we had taken care of Service dependents) and nationals of third countries; to provide a haven for refugees from both communities; and to support a United Nations force that was bound to be ineffective in the face of Turkish intervention. But for the SBAs, many

---

[1] See Nos. 10 and 44. This paper was one of a number commissioned by the Defence Review Steering Committee Sub-Committee, and was due for consideration by the Sub-Committee on 22 August. In a covering minute to Sir J. Killick of 20 August Sir G. Arthur explained that it had been agreed in the FCO, but had not yet been seen by other Whitehall Departments. 'It may', he observed, 'come in for some rough handling at the Sub-Committee, some of whose members will not like its forthright style and conclusions. However, I think the Ministry of Defence members will agree with the general proposition that the SBAs are more a liability than an asset, though there are a lot of people in the Ministry of Defence who take the opposite view.'

[2] Not printed.

more innocent civilians would have been killed, it is true; but we shall get little thanks for that, and we shall be fortunate if we find an issue from our difficulties without damage to our relations with Greece or Turkey or both.

3. It may be some time before the affairs of Cyprus are settled once more. Even if a settlement is reached soon, it will be fragile, and the hostility between Greeks and Turks, both in the island and outside, is not likely to die down for a long time. So long as there is tension, the SBAs will be vulnerable, for we shall always be caught in political cross fire. There may be a new and continuing anti-British feeling in both Cypriot communities. And if, as seems probable, the division between the Greek and Turkish regions passes near Famagusta, the Dhekelia SBA will be particularly exposed.

4. In the Eastern Mediterranean as a whole our possession of the SBAs has sometimes brought political disadvantage. RAF[3] aircraft flying from Cyprus, however innocently, lent colour to the 'Big Lie' of 1967;[4] and during the Arab-Israel war of 1973 we only escaped the imputation of involvement by suspending all but the most innocuous flying activity from the bases and most military training on the island. In better times the SBAs have been useful, for example in connection with the clearance of the Suez Canal. But it is generally in our national interest to keep out of conflicts in that part of the world. The possession of a local military base makes this disinvolvement more difficult.

5. It seems therefore that if we consider our narrow national interests alone, we shall conclude that we should be better out of Cyprus. It may be that we could turn a decision to withdraw to advantage in the negotiation of a settlement (e.g. as an incentive to the withdrawal of others or to demilitarisation), but the likelihood is marginal and the timing is problematical. However, we may need to come to a decision before the negotiation of a settlement is far advanced; and if we wait till a settlement has been reached, we may find it difficult to withdraw for fear of disturbing the new balance.[5]

6. If we consider our wider interests, however, we may find strong political arguments against withdrawal. It is difficult to weigh these at the present time: we can only say that they are related to a possible need to

[3] Royal Air Force.

[4] This 'Big Lie' was the accusation made by President Nasser, in a telephone conversation with King Hussain of Jordan on 6 June 1967 that British and US carrier-based aircraft were assisting the Israelis in their hostilities with Egypt.

[5] In a letter to the Prime Minister of 8 August, Mr. Healey asserted that he was under the impression that the Defence and Oversea Policy Committee had concluded on 1 August (cf. note 1 above that HMG should make public before the end of September its decision in principle to wind up Britain's military commitments outside of NATO. This he considered essential in order to maintain Cabinet and Labour party unity on public spending. He added that he thought Mr. Callaghan 'might find it useful to keep the planned rundown of [British] forces in Cyprus as one of his objectives in the ongoing negotiations with Greece and Turkey' (DP 5/3).

deny Cyprus to the Soviet Union. But there is one argument we can already state with some precision: we know that the Americans wish us to stay in Cyprus for political reasons.[6] [...][7] we may well come under considerable pressure from them. We should certainly not take a decision to withdraw without thorough consultation with the Americans. We should also consult NATO in view of the effect our withdrawal might have on the Southern flank.[8]

7. The SBAs are also essential for the provision of logistic support to UNFICYP. While alternative means of providing such support could if necessary be found, they would certainly be more expensive and less convenient. The UN Secretariat would have to be given the maximum possible warning of our intention to withdraw from the SBAs.

8. We also note that the very fact of our withdrawal, especially from Akrotiri, may create a serious problem. Nicosia airport is likely to be a contentious point in any settlement, for it is on the likely boundary between the regions and may have to be shared. But if we withdraw, Akrotiri will fall to the Greek Cypriot region; and unless it was demilitarised it would give the Greeks an immense advantage in future hostilities. The Turks might even demand the inclusion of Dhekelia in the Turkish Cypriot region. But these and other related problems are points for a negotiation whose course we cannot foresee. For the purpose of the Defence Review we shall assume that apart from the arguments in paragraph 6 above, there is no political objection to withdrawal.

Military Considerations

9. The principal military functions of one or both of the SBAs have been:

(*a*) They are an important staging post on the route to South East Asia and the Far East.

(*b*) They provide some support for our effort in Oman.

(*c*) They provide a base for a force of Vulcan strike aircraft [...],[9] which constitutes our only remaining force declaration to CENTO.[10]

---

[6] During the COS Committee meeting on 30 July (see No. 44, note 15) it was agreed: 'There were dangers that attempts to demilitarize Cyprus could lead to an increase of Soviet influence in the Island; moreover, any attempt to bring demilitarisation about too quickly would carry with it a serious danger to the Island's internal stability.'

[7] A clause is here omitted.

[8] In a minute to Mr. A.H. Campbell (DUS) of 19 August, Mr. P.R.H. Wright, Head of Middle East Department, added to the list of political arguments against withdrawal that it 'would be seen by the Gulf States, including Saudi Arabia and Iran, as a further diminution of UK's status as a world power' (WSC 10/24).

[9] A phrase is here omitted.

[10] Mr. P.R.H. Wright observed (see note 8 above) that apart from 'some practical difficulties which a withdrawal might bring for the supply and servicing of [British] Forces in Oman and the Liaison Team in Kuwait, the only substantive effect of a withdrawal on [his] Department's sphere of interest would be the loss of the Vulcan Bombers declared to CENTO'.

(*d*) They provide support for UNFICYP (see para 7). Indeed in the recent crisis UNFICYP could probably not have been kept in being without them. They are also of considerable value to UNEF.[11]

10. It may be said of these functions that:

(*a*) If we withdraw from Singapore and cease to provide a reinforcement capability for Hong Kong (both of which seem likely), we shall not need a staging post in Cyprus.[12]

(*b*) We could support our modest effort in Oman, for as long as may be necessary, from the United Kingdom.

(*c*) We do not need to declare forces to CENTO any longer. Our chief aim in doing so has been to maintain our credit with the Shah. His confidence has grown in recent years and his interests now centre on the Persian Gulf and the Indian Ocean. We shall have to consult him about the withdrawal of the Vulcan force, but he is not likely to object seriously.

(*d*) Support for UNFICYP (and UNEF) could be arranged without us, as it has been for UN forces elsewhere. We should however beware of the facile notion of 'handing over the SBAs to the UN'. If that idea has meaning (which is doubtful), it would probably involve a Soviet presence in Cyprus. Under the 1960 exchange of notes, the Republic of Cyprus has the reversion.[13]

11. It seems, therefore, that the military importance to us of the SBAs has declined, is still declining, and may soon vanish. They may in any case be difficult to maintain in future at the level of the past. Forces of that size can only be kept in Cyprus if they are 'accompanied'. It would be expensive to provide accommodation for dependants inside the SBAs, and it will be at best inhibiting, and at worst dangerous, to allow them to reside outside again.[14]

---

[11] See No. 10, note 8.

[12] *The Statement on Defence Estimates 1975* (Cmnd. 5976) asserted that, while the UK would maintain its existing consultative commitments towards Malaysia and Singapore, it would, with the exception of a small residual contribution to the Integrated Air Defence System, withdraw its forces from the region by April 1976. Meanwhile, reductions were to be made in British servicemen and locally-enlisted personnel in Hong Kong.

[13] But in a minute to Sir G. Arthur of 20 August Mr. Campbell pointed out that if the UN were to take over the SBAs this was unlikely to involve a Soviet presence, since the Security Council would have to agree on the composition of any UN force and the permanent members would in practice have a veto over the introduction of Soviet or East European troops. 'For the present', he observed, 'I doubt whether it is worth examining this idea any further and at this stage of consideration it is perhaps enough simply to say that we are not in a position to hand over the SBAs to the UN (because of the agreement of 1960) and that any logistic or other facilities which the UN might require in Cyprus would have to be granted to them by the Government of Cyprus' (DP 13/441/2). See No. 10.

[14] Mr. Callaghan agreed with the 'general approach of this paper and with the conclusions'. On the bases, he commented: 'we should now prepare plans for closing them down. I see no

[...].[15]

future in Cyprus for us. Politically whatever we patch up in Geneva III (if indeed it ever takes place) will be unlikely to last if the Greeks sometime later insist on revenge. Then we should be embarrassed once more. So let's not be too long about getting out.' He did not anticipate 'much difficulty' from the Cabinet, but asked 'at what stage should we begin to talk to the U.S. because our major interest is not a U.K. interest any more, but a general interest in preventing the Island from being used for anti-Western purposes?' (minute of 23 August from Mr. Alexander to Sir G. Arthur). The paper was submitted to Ministers on 5 September, and the Defence and Oversea Policy Committee agreed on 9 September that HMG's 'preferred course would be the total withdrawal of [British] forces from Cyprus which should, if possible, be presented in the context of a satisfactory settlement to the Cyprus problem'. But Mr. Callaghan argued that before reaching a final decision it would be necessary to discuss this matter with the Americans, and it was agreed that, since they might raise overriding objections to a total withdrawal, officials should 'continue to study the possibilities of a partial withdrawal, including giving up the Eastern SBA' (OPD(74) 14th mtg., DP 5/3).

[15] The five following paragraphs are here omitted.

No. 83

Sir R. Hooper (Athens) to Mr. Callaghan

No. 499 Telegraphic [*WSC 1/16*]

Flash. Confidential   ATHENS, *26 August 1974, 10.25 a.m.*

Repeated for information to Flash Washington (for Sir J. Killick), Immediate Ankara, Nicosia, UKMIS New York, UKDEL NATO, Paris, Bonn, Moscow, CBFNE.

Your tel[egram] No. 300:[1]
Cyprus

1. You will by now have seen my tel[egram] No. 498 which gives some general indication of how we have been thinking here.[2]
2. On the specific proposal in your TUR,[3] Mavros and to some extent Karamanlis are in an emotional state, and others in the background are

[1] In this telegram of 25 August Mr. Callaghan informed Sir R. Hooper that he had asked Dr. Kissinger if he would receive Sir J. Killick and Mr. Alexander 'to discuss in depth the short term tactics on Cyprus in the light of the long term consequences of failure to achieve a settlement'. Mr. Callaghan was considering sending a Minister of State to Nicosia, Ankara and Athens to attempt to narrow the gap between them, but, he noted, this would depend on his securing Dr. Kissinger's support. 'I am not sure', Mr. Callaghan added, 'that Dr. Kissinger, in his present attitude, is taking sufficient account of the longer-term consequences of failure.'

[2] Sir R. Hooper complained in this telegram of 25 August that the Greeks had not treated the British 'particularly civilly' in their efforts to restart the dialogue (see note 5 below).

[3] Telegram Under Reference.

even more so. They are probably, in the last resort and under very strong pressure from as many quarters as possible, willing to discuss a settlement on the basis outlined in para[graph] 3 of your tel[egram] No. 280.[4] But

(*a*) they are adamant that they cannot negotiate under duress;

(*b*) they argue that they have been had for mugs twice by the Turks at Geneva. They cannot be fooled a third time and survive as a government, and they no longer have any confidence in Turkish assurances;[5]

(*c*) they regard the sort of concessions the Turks appear prepared to make (Ankara tel[egram] No. 1043)[6] as totally insufficient, if not illusory. I have repeatedly pressed them to indicate what they would regard as a sufficient earnest of Turkish good will to bring them to the conference table. For obvious practical reasons they have so far been unwilling to do more than reiterate their insistence on withdrawal from Famagusta and to the 9 August line—a position so unrealistic as to amount to a flat refusal to talk;

(*d*) nevertheless, though I may be wrong, I think that if the Turks are prepared to go as far as I suggested in paragraph 3(1) of my tel[egram] No. 498 last sentence,[7] or to adopt a realistic attitude on the points set

---

[4] In this telegram of 20 August Mr. Callaghan proposed that the Greeks join in early negotiations over Cyprus (arguing that delay would 'inevitably reduce the prospects of securing concessions from the Turks'), and restated his view (in paragraph 3) that a settlement might eventually be achieved on the basis of a bi-regional federation.

[5] Mr. Mavros rejected any early return to a Geneva-type negotiation. And, despite the assurance offered by Sir R. Hooper to Mr. Karamanlis on 21 August that HMG had no intention of attempting to force Greece 'to endorse a humiliating *fait accompli*', Mr. Mavros asserted in a memorandum, handed to the Ambassador by Mr. Bitsios on 24 August, that Greece would not participate in any negotiation 'under the pressure of "faits accomplis"'. Mr. Bitsios added 'that the Greek Government's formal pre-requisite for a return to Geneva remained the Turkish withdrawal from Famagusta and to the line of 9 August' (Athens telegrams No. 481 of 21 August and Nos. 493 and 496 of 24 August).

[6] In this telegram of 21 August Sir H. Phillips reported that Mr. Eçevit had told him that morning that his Government: (1) considered 'the demarcation of the autonomous regions to be negotiable within reasonable bounds', though he added that this would not change the 'general basis' of the Turkish Cypriot claim to about one third of the island; and (2) confirmed its readiness to comply with the Geneva Declaration in the matter of the phased reduction of troops. Mr. Eçevit said there should be 'no forcible expulsion of Cypriots from either region'. But he also remarked that his Government was thinking of a 'large-scale voluntary movement of Turks from the enclaves into the Turkish-controlled region', and that those Greek Cypriots who left 'would not be invited to return'.

[7] See note 2 above. 'In essence', Sir R. Hooper observed in this sentence, 'the problem is one of getting the Turks to come far enough to meet the Greeks—e.g. by way of a withdrawal of troops which would significantly reduce the disparity of strength, and territorial concessions which would bring the area now under Turkish occupation to something more consistent with the Turkish population of the island—to make a meeting possible.'

out by Clerides (paragraphs 3 and 4 of Nicosia tel[egram] No. 834 to you),[8] and if we and the Americans could give some sort of guarantee that the Turks would deliver, then there is some hope that the Greeks (and, it seems, the Greek Cypriots) would agree to a discussion. Their international position might indeed be weakened were they to refuse.

3. All this, however, is contingent on our and the Americans (plus any support we can get) being able and willing to put pressure on the Turks going well beyond anything the Americans or indeed we ourselves, have so far been willing to contemplate. If Dr. Kissinger is prepared to pay this sort of price, well and good. But unless he is, and unless the pressure succeeds in producing the sort of package that the Greeks could be pushed into accepting as a basis for discussion, I fear we shall get nowhere. The Greeks have already rebuffed us over our approach to Karamanlis. Unless we can go to them with something concrete (which presupposes having got the Turks sewn up first) they are likely to do so again; and in Mavros' present mood I would not put it past him to refuse to see a British Minister at all.

4. I do not of course underrate the potential long term consequences of a continued deadlock, though an all out war between Greece and Turkey is perhaps a fairly remote contingency at present. We have not too much time to play with. But what we have would, I believe, be usefully employed in allowing doubts about the merits of the Russian proposal[9]—to build up; letting the Greeks simmer down; and allowing the thought to gain ground in their minds that they may not after all have been all that clever in accepting it even in principle.[10] (I agree with Clerides' assessment of their attitude. This is very much Mavros' personal baby.) At the same time I

---

[8] In paragraph 3 of this telegram of 25 August Mr. Olver reported three key points put to him that afternoon by Mr. Clerides regarding the proposed negotiations: (1) the Turks must show a readiness for really meaningful adjustment of the area occupied; (2) it must be clear that they were talking not just about a reduction of Turkish forces, which was a meaningless phase, but about a phased total withdrawal; and (3) whatever the people on either side of the line finally decided to do, they must first be allowed back to their homes. Mr. Clerides suggested in paragraph 4 that a Turkish offer immediately to allow the return of displaced Greek Cypriots to the new town of Famagusta (Varosha) 'would at a stroke fulfil one of Karamanlis' conditions, help lighten the refugee problem and produce an immensely improved general climate'. Cf. No. 87, notes 3 and 4.

[9] On 23 August the Soviet press published a Government proposal for convening, within the framework of the UN, an international conference on Cyprus at which Security Council members, Cyprus, Greece and Turkey would be represented. Sir T. Garvey thought the statement 'timed to put a spoke in the wheel of [Mr. Callaghan's] efforts to get parties back to Geneva' (Moscow telegrams Nos. 1036 and 1045 of 23 August). And although Mr. Malik was unable to provide him with any details of what the Soviet initiative would amount to in practice, Mr. Richard considered it 'consistent with their [the Russians'] long term aim to reduce NATO's role in Cyprus and the eastern Mediterranean, to eliminate the SBAs, to end the Treaty of Guarantee, and to ensure a non-aligned, independent Cyprus' (UKMIS New York telegram No. 1041 of 24 August).

[10] In Athens telegram No. 498 (see notes 2 and 7 above) Sir R. Hooper noted that Mr. Karamanlis had been 'making sympathetic noises to the Soviets about their proposal'.

think we have to make it clear to Dr. Kissinger that unless we are both prepared to go to the limit in exerting pressure to secure from the Turks the far reaching concessions that will be necessary, the whole exercise will fall flat on its face and had much better not be attempted.[11]

[11] Mr. Callaghan wrote to Mr. Sykes in telegram No. 1749 to Washington of 22 August that he would be grateful if Dr. Kissinger would consider a further effort to persuade the Turks to make some gesture, such as withdrawing troops from Cyprus. He admitted that, since it seemed they were building up troops there, this might be 'little more than window-dressing', but he could think of nothing that would do more 'to "save Greek honour" and make it easier for the Greeks to come to Geneva'.

No. 84

Record of a meeting between Dr. Kissinger and Sir J. Killick held in the Department of State, Washington, on 27 August 1974 at 11.40 a.m.[1]

[*WSC 3/304/2*]

Secret

Present:

Dr. Kissinger
Mr. Ingersoll
Lt.-General Scowcroft[2]
Mr. Eagleburger
Mr. Buffum
Mr. Kubisch[4]
Mr. Crawford[5]
Mr. Stabler

Sir J. Killick
Mr. Sykes
Mr. Alexander
Mr. Cornish[3]

1. *Sir John Killick*, after thanking Dr. Kissinger for receiving him, and extending the Secretary of State's good wishes, said that Mr. Callaghan was deliberately maintaining a low profile at the moment while diplomatic soundings continued. However, he had been thinking ahead, with some misgiving. He wanted to exchange views in some depth, which was

[1] See No. 83, note 1.

[2] Lt.-Gen. B. Scowcroft was Deputy Assistant to the US President for National Security Affairs.

[3] Mr. J.E. Cornish was First Secretary at the British Embassy in Washington.

[4] Mr. J.B. Kubisch had just been appointed US Ambassador to Greece.

[5] Mr. W.R. Crawford Jr. was US Ambassador designate to Cyprus. He succeeded Mr. R. Davies, who was fatally wounded when on 19 August shots were fired through the window of the US Embassy in Nicosia during a violent anti-American demonstration.

impossible by telephone or through messages. (*Dr. Kissinger* interjected, jocularly, that the great diplomatic feat had already been achieved of casting him as the villain of our negotiations.[6] Defending his performance during the crisis, he made it clear that he considered US policy to have been correct and added that it would have been exactly the same even if there had been no Presidential transition.)

2. *Sir John Killick* went on to recall that Mr. Sisco had asked us at the beginning of the crisis in mid-July whether we could envisage a package solution for Cyprus.[7] At that point we had said it was too early to do so. Now, on paper, the elements were much clearer. In essence a realistic settlement would involve a bi-regional federal Cyprus. *Dr. Kissinger* agreed that this was the only basis on which a settlement could ever be reached. The question, however, was whether the United Kingdom, the United States or the Turks should be responsible for extracting it. *Sir John Killick* went on to say that, whatever view we took of Turkish actions, another element of the solution was likely to be an exchange of population. This would have the advantage of facilitating a self-policing solution with no need for outside forces, including UNFICYP. This applied no less to the British guarantor role; all parties were disenchanted with us in one way or another for not having used our military force on the island on their behalf. *Dr. Kissinger* interjected that he did not think that the Turks were unhappy on this score.

3. *Sir John Killick* said that such a solution was, however, still merely a theoretical one. Practically, the prospects for the negotiation of such a solution were not good. It could not be imposed. *Dr. Kissinger* asked whether any Greek government could accept such a solution. *Sir John Killick* agreed that it was difficult. Mr. Karamanlis did not have a united Government on the Cyprus issue. *Dr. Kissinger* commented that, now that the Greeks had leaked to the press the terms of his latest communications to Mr. Karamanlis, it was even less easy to communicate with Athens.

4. *Sir John Killick* said that the Turks would never agree to withdraw to the line they held on 9 August. Mr. Clerides had, however, put forward proposals on the three main issues in more reasonable terms. There would have to be a meaningful adjustment of the Turkish-held area, more generous than their offer so far; there would have to be not merely a reduction but a commitment to phased total withdrawal of Turkish troops; and there should be no forced transfer of populations, even though people might decide to leave after they had been allowed to go back to their homes. *Dr. Kissinger* said that it was crazy of the Turks to have made public their readiness to reduce their area to 28% of the island; such a concession should have been kept for the negotiations. *Mr. Cornish* said that Professor Ülman had told us in London that the figure of 28% related to Turkish-

[6] See note 16 below.

[7] See No. 27.

owned land, and that additional land would be needed for security purposes: the details would have to be worked out in negotiations.[8]

5. *Dr. Kissinger* agreed that a settlement on these lines should be realisable. However, the Greek position was difficult, and they were now publicly threatening US bases in Greece. He asked General Scowcroft to have prepared in 48 hours a study of the effects of United States withdrawal from their bases in Greece. *Sir John Killick* suggested if something better could be extracted from the Turks on these issues there would be some hope of 'bringing the Greek Government to realise that it can rely on the friendly support of all of us, but must take an active part in negotiations', to quote from Dr. Kissinger's message to Mr. Callaghan.[9] Only American influence could achieve this, and the problem of anti-American feeling in Greece could be eased as a result of successful American diplomatic action. He wondered, incidentally, whether the Soviet Union was also prepared to bring pressure on Turkey.[10] *Dr. Kissinger* said that the Soviet Union had not held any manoeuvres in the area of Turkish frontiers and had not moved troops into Bulgaria. They had done just enough to stimulate the left wing in Greece, but not enough to have any effect in Ankara.[11] Mr. Dobrynin[12] asked him every three days to agree to joint United States/Soviet guarantees for a Cyprus solution. Mr. Dobrynin had evidently expected a negative American reaction, which he had received. Dr. Kissinger had now asked him for a written explanation of Soviet ideas on how to arrive at the settlement to which the proposed

---

[8] On 25 August Prof. H. Ülman, Mr. Eçevit's foreign affairs adviser, referred publicly in London to the Turkish need for 28% of Cyprus. Sir H. Phillips thought this might be a hopeful sign of greater Turkish flexibility. But in a conversation with Mr. Ennals, Prof. Ülman insisted that the Turks wanted 28% plus 'something for the security of the area' (Ankara telegram No. 1065 of 26 August; telegram No. 1771 to Washington of 27 August; WSC 1/16).

[9] Washington telegram No. 2801 of 24 August contained the text of a message from Dr. Kissinger to Mr. Callaghan. In this Dr. Kissinger offered his support for Mr. Callaghan's suggestion that the Geneva Conference be reconvened to discuss a bi-regional federal system in Cyprus. He also expressed the view that a 'long period of stalemate would only be an advantage to the Soviets'; that the only hope the Greeks had for improving the present situation was return to the negotiating table'; and that a prolonged stalemate would diminish British and US capability of exercising a positive influence on the Turks (Callaghan Papers).

[10] In his message to Mr. Callaghan (*v. ibid.*) Dr. Kissinger described the latest Soviet move (see No. 83, note 9) as 'decidedly unhelpful'. He added: 'Should this proposal be accepted, the Soviet Union will have succeeded in gaining a voice in an area in which up to now it has had little influence. This in turn would undermine further our basic security interests in the eastern Mediterranean.'

[11] Sir T. Garvey thought the Soviet leadership had, as opportunity offered, pursued several specific interests: support, so long as it seemed feasible, of a non-federal, non-aligned Cyprus Republic; consolidation of their position in the eastern Mediterranean; and a reduction of Greece's and Turkey's links with NATO. The Russians, he added, recognised that Turkey was a 'much tougher nut to crack' and that pressure on Turkey was likely to be counterproductive (Moscow telegram No. 1050, of 26 August, WSC 1/16).

[12] Mr. A.F. Dobrynin was Soviet Ambassador in Washington.

guarantee should apply. If Mr. Dobrynin responded to this and suggested a bi-zonal solution, this would be of interest to the Greek Government. Dr. Kissinger emphasised that the United States would in no circumstances become a joint guarantor with the Soviet Union, and would strongly oppose a Soviet unilateral guarantee. He was not in any case sure how serious the Soviet proposal was: he described it as 'one of Gromyko's legalistic phobias'.[13] *Sir John Killick* asked whether we could be kept fully informed of these exchanges.

6. *Sir John Killick* turned to the effects of continuation of the present situation. He thought he detected an important difference between us here. Dr. Kissinger's latest message to Mr. Callaghan had spoken of the undesirability of a long period of stalemate. Did this mean that in the American view a short period of stalemate was inevitable or even desirable? In our view, time was not on our side and even a short stalemate could have harmful consequences. If things did not move forward, they would move back.

7. *Dr. Kissinger* said that time was, in particular, not on the side of the Greeks. Although United States-Greek relations had to be allowed to simmer down, he would welcome British efforts to move forward as soon as possible. *Sir John Killick* agreed, and pointed to the dangers inherent in the present situation, not least because of the Turkish Cypriots held by the Greeks in the southern part of the island. We were very grateful to Dr. Kissinger for persuading Mr. Eçevit not to mount his helicopter rescue operation. This showed how decisive American influence could be. *Dr. Kissinger* commented that it did not follow that, if the Turks did something else undesirable, the Americans had not tried (and failed) to oppose them.

8. *Sir John Killick* said that a further danger was an outbreak of guerrilla warfare on the island. *Dr. Kissinger* commented that one could not successfully fight a guerrilla war against the Turks, who were without Anglo-Saxon scruples.

9. After *Sir John Killick* had referred to the further possible dangers of Turkish consolidation in the north of the island being reinforced by settlers from the mainland and also of further Greek military moves, *Dr. Kissinger* said that he agreed that some movement in the present situation was

---

[13] Mr. Sykes had earlier reported, with regard to the American handling of Cyprus and the Soviet proposal for a conference (see note 10 above) that it had to be admitted that Dr. Kissinger did 'not seem to have any particular idea of how to proceed next, other than to do his best to thwart the Soviet initiative'. He was also reasonably sure that Dr. Kissinger would oppose an idea tentatively put forward by Sir R. Hooper for using a Soviet-type meeting in order to probe the Soviet proposals so as to see whether the Russians had any positive contribution to make or whether they could be 'exposed as mischief-makers'. 'While I am sure Kissinger has no illusions about the Russians', Mr. Sykes concluded, 'I think he would be reluctant, for wider reasons (Middle East, SALT, and the whole corpus of his détente policy) to see them pushed too publicly into the dock' (Washington telegram No. 2802 of 25 August, WSC 1/16). On 30 August Mr. Dobrynin told Mr. Stabler that the Soviet Government 'now had no wish for any form of joint US/Soviet action' (Washington telegram No. 2851 of 30 August).

needed. He asked whether it would be impossible to partition the island with one part going to Greece and another part to Turkey, provided that the United States did not appear to have arranged it. *Sir John Killick* said that we did not exclude this happening, but it was the worst outcome for the Soviet Union.

10. Sir John Killick then turned to another problem of timing which he felt bound to mention as a matter of fact. It was being speculated in London that a British general election might be announced shortly and might be held at the beginning of October.[14] In such circumstances Mr. Callaghan might be available for consultation but would clearly not be able to go to Geneva. He would be fully taken up with the election campaign. Quite apart from this problem, there was also a limit to the length of time during which British Ministers were prepared to be seen to be available for negotiations which did not take place, while being unable to stop the Turks from unilateral acts which worsened the prospects and which were contrary to Security Council Resolutions which Britain had supported. Responsibility without power was an unpalatable situation which left HMG open to adverse criticism. *Dr. Kissinger* said that he was not arguing against a British initiative. He supported the British wish to have the ball in play.

11. *Sir John Killick* said that Mr. Callaghan had not yet taken a decision on what to do next. He wished first to have a full report on Dr. Kissinger's thinking. He wished to continue to play a responsible role, but further Turkish provocative action would put a severe strain on his readiness to continue to help. Our assessment, shared by all our Heads of Mission in the area, was that the short-term risks were considerable, but that the key to progress lay in Ankara. Mr. Callaghan was considering the idea that Mr. Hattersley, the Minister of State, should visit the area in order to undertake shuttle diplomacy between the three capitals. Mr. Hattersley's first task would be to see what he could extract from the Turkish Government, although it might tactically be wiser if he visited Nicosia beforehand. After Ankara he might go to Athens, and then fly backwards and forwards as necessary. However, Mr. Callaghan would not wish to go ahead with this proposal unless he was sure that Dr. Kissinger not only fully supported it as an idea, but was also ready to help assure its success by undertaking a major heave with the Turkish government. Without such an American effort the emissary, and indeed Mr. Callaghan and HMG would be put in an unacceptably exposed position. The British Government, perhaps supported by the Nine and other members of NATO, would of course bring pressure as necessary on the Greek Government, with which the US might understandably feel it was not at present well-placed.

12. In this connection, Sir John Killick referred to the concern Dr. Kissinger had expressed in his latest message about European support of

---

[14] The Prime Minister announced on 18 September the holding of a General Election on 10 October. Mr. Wilson's Labour Government was subsequently returned to power with a majority of three in the House of Commons.

Mr. Karamanlis. Sir John Killick assured Dr. Kissinger that we would never go along with a polarisation of the kind Dr. Kissinger feared.[15] *Dr. Kissinger* replied that up to a point the efforts of the Europeans in Athens were helpful, though it would be very dangerous if they tried to exploit anti-American feeling. There was also a danger that by stiffening the backs of the Greek Government we would lead them to be less flexible than was necessary. More generally, Greece could only find its way back into NATO by becoming less anti-American. *Sir John Killick* acknowledged this but pointed to the need to support Mr. Karamanlis in his difficult position. His survival was important for the future of democracy in Greece. *Dr. Kissinger* said he totally supported this, but expressed his concern that anti-American feeling in Greece was not a result of the present Cyprus situation but sprang from the increasing preponderance of the left wing. The army was itself becoming more radical and no longer acted as a counterweight to the left. Mr. Karamanlis could fall if he signed any foreseeable agreement over Cyprus, since he would be attacked by nationalists on both the right and the left who would say he had sold out Greek national honour. It was particularly important that the anti-American element in Greek policy should not be encouraged to grow.[16] He had therefore been concerned to see an intelligence report that the French had suggested to the Greeks that France should replace the United States' presence in Greece. Dr. Kissinger asked whether NATO had any meaning in this sort of crisis. If not, the Americans would have to ask themselves a number of serious questions.

13. Turning to the Soviet proposal for an international conference, *Sir John Killick* said that he thought that it contained the seeds of its own destruction. Even the Greek Government had replied to it by asking a number of awkward questions. Nor did we think that there was a particular risk that Western pressure on Turkey would drive them into the arms of the Soviet Union. *Dr. Kissinger* said that there were two dangerous directions in which Turkey could move, towards the Soviet Union or

---

[15] In his message (see notes 9 and 10 above) Dr. Kissinger had stated his concern that European efforts to support Mr. Karamanlis's Government might be misconstrued in Athens 'as evidence of European support for Greece as a counter-weight to American support for Turkey', which might result in a further polarisation of the situation and the strengthening of the extreme left in Greece. Mr. Sykes had already expressed his concern over 'Kissinger's suspicions of the Nine' in Washington telegram No. 2802 (see note 13 above). He had not been able to establish what precisely was on Dr. Kissinger's mind, but he thought that it 'might be connected with reports that France [had] been offering aid to Greece'.

[16] In a letter to Sir J. Killick of 29 August, covering the draft record of this meeting, Mr. Sykes observed that Dr. Kissinger's attitude towards the Greek Government seemed to contain a 'personal element' and might 'perhaps be more susceptible to variation with the passage of time'. 'I think', he continued, 'it is quite understandable that he should have been upset by attacks on "Kissinger the murderer", by the rough treatment he has been receiving from the Greek Americans and particularly their Congressmen here, and by the grossly unfair way in which he has been blamed for the death of Rodger Davies [see note 5 above]'.

towards Qaddafi-type nationalism.[17] Turkey was unlikely to move towards the Soviet Union as a direct result of the present crisis. But he saw some possibility of movement in the second direction in two or three years' time if the Turks were subjected to humiliating treatment by the West. There was a danger that we might lay the seeds for this now. *Sir John Killick* commented that he saw little likelihood of the Turks being humiliated in their present strong position. *Dr. Kissinger* agreed, and said that even if maximum pressure was put on the Turks they would be left with a much stronger position than they had held before 15 July.[18]

14. Dr. Kissinger then spoke about the last round of negotiations in Geneva. He said that he had not been in sufficiently close touch with the progress of the negotiations to be able to understand why no proposals had been put on the table. The only way to have held back the Turks would have been to flood them with proposals which they could not have ignored. Pressure should have been put on the Greeks to make concessions, since, however wrong and maddening the Turks were, it should have been possible to get them to accept less at the negotiating table than they would have been able to grab by force. Expressions of outrage at Turkish behaviour only stiffened the backs of the Greeks and gave the Turks more excuse for attack.[19]

15. Dr. Kissinger went on to say that his first concern was that he was very reluctant to let the United States take up a position in which they had to back one side without knowing its tactics. Last time round, the US had been sufficiently involved to carry some responsibility, but not sufficiently to have control. He was reluctant to risk this again. He did not think that in the last resort anything could in fact have stopped the Turks. But Mr. Eçevit had told him that he was willing to hold his hand for 48 hours if agreement could be reached on a security zone 5 to 8 kilometres deep. Dr. Kissinger had simply not known what had happened to this proposal.

16. Dr. Kissinger emphasised that there would have to be substantial Greek concessions if a solution was to be reached. The Greeks would improve on their present position, but the Turks would still be left with a position better than that they held on 9 August.

17. *Sir John Killick* said that we were not sure whether our initiative would succeed, but we felt bound to consider making an attempt. *Dr. Kissinger*

[17] Col. Muammar al-Qaddafi had, since 1969, established a radical Arab nationalist régime in Libya. It had nationalised foreign property in Libya and offered support to Muslim revolutionaries abroad.

[18] Mr. Sykes commented on the US approach to Turkey that although Dr. Kissinger was 'prepared to spend a substantial amount of America's capital, he [would] do so only at a moment when he was reasonably sure that he [would] not spend it in vain' (see note 15 above).

[19] Dr. Kissinger returned to this theme in a conversation with Sir P. Ramsbotham on 8 September. 'Hard', he observed, 'as it might have seemed at that time, as indeed it might seem now, it was the Greeks who should have been pressed to declare what concessions they could offer: with that, something might have been achieved' (Washington telegram No. 2923 of 9 September).

agreed, but said that his second worry derived from the fact that considerable US pressure on Turkey would be needed. If the British initiative failed, it would be said that the reason was that the United States had not pushed hard enough in Ankara. Thus the United States, not the United Kingdom, would be left holding the baby.

18. Dr. Kissinger said that he was not blaming anyone for what happened at Geneva. On Sunday 11 August he had tried in his telephone conversation with Mr. Eçevit to generate negotiations which might have gained another 36 hours. At the end of that time the Turks would still have attacked, since Mr. Mavros would not have offered the Turks a large enough zone. But the end position would have been more favourable.

19. *Mr. Alexander* said that although Anglo-American communication in Geneva during the negotiations had been very good, the negotiations themselves had been very messy. In retrospect, it might have been better if we had put forward our proposals on 11 August. But the preceding day had been spent arguing about irrelevancies such as place cards. On 11 August itself the Turkish Cabinet had been in session, and there was no meeting at which proposals could have been put to the Turks. It had also been important to stay on speaking terms with the Greeks. If we had endorsed the regional solution too early, Mr. Mavros might have left the negotiations and returned to Athens. *Dr. Kissinger* agreed that the negotiations could not have succeeded. He explained that his cantonal proposal was aimed at making it easier at a later stage to move to a bi-zonal solution. Dr. Kissinger added that his own experience led him to believe that a mediator had to be seen to be less eager than the parties themselves. It was best if the latter were generating the pressure for progress. If the mediator himself was under time pressure his task was very difficult.

20. For these reasons Dr. Kissinger thought that there were two chances in three that the proposed British initiative would fail. He did not want the United States to be landed with responsibility for a failure. If the United Kingdom were to carry through its initiative on its own, he would give it his blessing. But if United States pressure was an essential factor, there might easily be trouble. Only the United States could bring sufficient pressure on Turkey, so if sufficient Turkish concessions were not achieved the conclusion would be drawn that the United States were incompetent or that they had deliberately held back. A successful initiative would depend on the right timing. The right sort of negotiations supported at the right moment by a tremendous heave could be successful. But Dr. Kissinger asked whether a British junior minister was in the best position to carry this out. *Mr. Stabler* agreed: the Turks had nothing to lose by staying where they were. *Sir John Killick* emphasised that we would not go forward with our initiative unless we were sure that the Americans would undertake a major heave in its support. *Dr. Kissinger* asked whether this meant a threat to cut off military aid. *Sir John Killick* said it was for the US to judge how to use its leverage in Ankara. He had not envisaged going so far. But a major effort at persuasion, involving perhaps a message from President Ford

supporting our initiative, would be necessary. The aim would be to obtain Turkish concessions on the size of the Turkish region, total phased military withdrawal, and a strong indication that Greek Cypriots would not be forced out of the Turkish Cypriot region. A statement of the Turkish position on these points could then be taken to Athens.

21. *Dr. Kissinger* said that the United States Ambassador in Ankara would support us, and he would not wholly exclude a message from the President to Mr. Eçevit, though it was important to conserve such messages for the time when they were really needed. But he was still concerned that the United States would be left to take the blame if the initiative failed because the United Kingdom was under pressure of time. His experience of mediation had been that it usually took months to set up a basis on which shuttle diplomacy could be effective. This had not been possible for the Syrian-Israeli negotiations, and as a result they had almost failed. In the case of the Egyptian-Israeli negotiations, however, there had been many meetings before he had gone to Egypt, and both sides had pleaded with him for greater speed. In the Syrian case he had only achieved results after successfully slowing down the process.[20] In the Cyprus dispute he was not aware that either side was yet ready to make the investment necessary for settlement. Accordingly, an initiative which represented a last final effort was unlikely to succeed. If it failed the British Government would be tempted publicly to condemn the Turks for thwarting our efforts. The United States might have to join in these condemnations, and this would ruin later attempts for successful mediation by the United States.

22. Moreover, Dr. Kissinger said, even if the Turks made substantial concessions, for instance by reducing their area by 25% which he thought highly unlikely, there was still the problem that the Greek Government might not accept it.

23. *Mr. Alexander* said that Dr. Kissinger might be worried that the forthcoming elections would put the British Government under time pressure. But Mr. Callaghan would certainly ensure that negotiations which started now would not fail because of domestic British considerations. *Dr. Kissinger* said that he was not worried by this. If the Turks could be brought to make a reasonable proposal, it would be better from all points of view not to try to conclude the negotiations before the elections. His fear was that the negotiations might fail, and the United States would be blamed, not by Mr. Callaghan, in whom he had great confidence, but by the Greeks. And how much time would Mr. Hattersley have? If he left at the end of the week, it would still take at least a week before he could make any progress. The Turks would not yield to the first onslaught, if indeed they would yield to British pressure at all. It would be a considerable diplomatic achievement to bring about a stalemate and avoid breakdown. *Sir John Killick* said that we would not want to blame anyone. Our desire

---

[20] See H.A. Kissinger, *Years of Upheaval* (London: Weidenfeld & Nicolson and Michael Joseph, 1982), pp. 799-853 and 935-78.

was not to lay ourselves open to charges of impotence in a situation in which we had responsibility without power. We had no wish to be put in this position once again. However, there was no means of preventing the press from drawing conclusions of its own about whose fault failure was.

24. *Mr. Alexander* accepted that there were two chances in three of the initiative failing. But how long could we wait without the situation deteriorating still further? *Dr. Kissinger* said that he expected that there would have to be United States pressure on the Turks on a number of points. He agreed with us on the optimum solution. But the Turks did not react well to public pressure. He was ready to spend a substantial part of American capital with the Turks, and he agreed that Turkey would not turn to the Soviet Union just because they had to accept two-thirds of what they had conquered. The question was whether this was the right time to make the effort. One difficulty was that the United States, as a matter of strong principle, did not wish to be seen to be acting under pressure. The United States would not help the Greeks until they had stopped kicking the Americans around. It had taken the Arabs six years to learn a similar lesson.

25. Dr Kissinger added that there were strong arguments against cutting off American military aid to Turkey. In particular, once it was cut off it was very hard to judge when to resume it, particularly because of Congressional complications. In the meantime there would be an irrevocable effect on the direction of Turkish policy. *Sir John Killick* asked whether Congress was likely to force Dr. Kissinger's hand on this. *Dr. Kissinger* said that this was a possibility. He did not want to make it more likely by helping to bring about a situation in which, when Congress resumed in the second week of September, the Turks had once again been shown to have taken up a very tough position.

26. Summing up this part of the discussion, Dr. Kissinger said that he agreed that the United Kingdom should take an initiative. The United States would give major support, but he had a 'gut feeling' that the time was not yet ripe. *Mr. Stabler* added that the Turks did not yet see time as working against them. Nor were they particularly concerned by world opinion building up. *Dr. Kissinger* agreed. In the General Assembly the Greeks would be lucky to achieve a simple majority in their favour: they would not achieve a two-thirds majority. The Muslim countries in particular were behind Turkey, and Greece was not in a strong position. It would be possible to achieve a two-thirds majority for a very generalised resolution, but not on one giving Greece what they wanted on specific points. *Mr. Buffum* commented that we were perhaps not aware of the extent of Dr. Kissinger's previous efforts to persuade Mr. Eçevit to be more flexible. It was not clear to him what more could be done. *Dr. Kissinger* explained that he had written to Mr. Eçevit asking for greater flexibility, and suggesting in particular that the Turks should give up half of Famagusta. Mr. Eçevit had replied that he was not willing to do this. *Sir*

John Killick said that there seemed to be a gap in our knowledge here, and Dr. Kissinger agreed to let us have details.

27. *Mr. Sykes* asked whether there was not a danger that in the face of continued Turkish inflexibility the Greeks might not do something quite irrational, for example in Thrace.

28. *Dr. Kissinger* returned to the problem of the timing of the British initiative. An announcement of British elections would not make it easier for a British mediator to wait long enough for a breakthrough. Instead, he would almost inevitably have to insist on deadlines and take sides when they were not kept. A low-key attempt to look for flexibility without involving much expenditure of prestige could be useful, and the United States could back it quite seriously. But a do-or-die effort would be likely to have the wrong consequences, with Turkey or the United States taking the blame and Congress cutting off military aid to Turkey. The Turks would then face the whole year without military aid, and they would have to look for it elsewhere.

29. Dr. Kissinger said that he accepted that the British elections would not be a factor if the negotiations went well, so there would be no pressure to conclude the negotiations until after the elections were over. But if the negotiations failed there would, he thought, be undesirable British domestic repercussions. Moreover, Mr. Hattersley would feel himself under pressure to produce quick results, and it would be difficult for those with whom he was negotiating not to feel that he was under time pressure. *Mr. Alexander* emphasised that Cyprus would not be a big electoral issue in the United Kingdom, and *Sir John Killick* emphasised that he had mentioned the possibility of an election only as a matter of fact.

30. *Dr. Kissinger* asked whether Sir John Killick could stay for another day. In the meantime he would like to talk to the President. *Sir John Killick* agreed.

31. *Mr. Alexander* asked how, in Dr. Kissinger's view, the prospects for negotiations would improve with the lapse of time. Dr. Kissinger replied that the Greeks would have to learn not to kick the United States around. The United States was willing to help the Greeks but only without pressure from them. Moreover, the Greek Government might in time come increasingly to wish for a negotiated settlement, whereas now they might prefer an imposed settlement which they did not have to accept. The United States had made a number of efforts to get on to better terms with Mr. Karamanlis, both through private communications and public statements. Every time the Greek reply had been to kick the United States in the teeth by totally misrepresenting what they had said. Nor had they given any indication of how the United States could act in the Greek interest. Mr. Mavros continued to say that there must be a return to the line of 9 August. He had also leaked Dr. Kissinger's latest letter to the press. Until the Greeks were willing to make their position clear there was no room for United States action. The United States would back a Greek attempt to reduce the present Turkish area by a third, though the Turks

would probably not give up as much. A solution to the refugee problem would probably not be very difficult, but the question of troop withdrawal was a tough one. But Dr. Kissinger had no feel for what concessions the Greek Government might make. However, he thought that the Greeks might be moving in the right direction and becoming less insolent. It was possible that after two weeks the timing might be much better. At the right moment the US would certainly be prepared to expend the credit it had with the Turks.

32. On the internal Greek situation, Dr. Kissinger said that the political structure was such that the United States would be under attack even if there had been no Cyprus problem. The left wing had nearly succeeded in 1967, and the Greek army had now been destroyed as a counterweight and was also becoming more radical. Mr. Karamanlis was on a narrow ledge. He was trying to take over the Right Wing of Mr. Papandreou's supporters. Once he succeeded, he might be more reasonable.

33. Dr. Kissinger then summarised his position. He agreed with the concept of a British mediatory effort with American support; with the solution we had in mind, which he described as the only realistic one; and with the need for the mediation effort to start in Ankara. He was, however, not clear what would happen when British mediation ran into difficulties. He thought that the proposed date for the start of the effort was slightly premature, given the difficulty of US communications to the Greek Government and American ignorance of what the Greeks really wanted. He had looked again at the telegrams reporting Mr. Hartman's talks with Mr. Karamanlis before the second round in Geneva, and was still able to form no conception of what Mr. Karamanlis had wanted. Dr. Kissinger was also worried about the British elections. He thought, however, that in two weeks the position might be better. Even so, both the Turks and the Greeks would be very obstinate, and there would be a stalemate. To keep the negotiations going through 4 weeks of stalemate would be a massive achievement, but the United Kingdom could not let talks go on for so long without laying herself open to accusations of impotence. Dr. Kissinger added that the Turks might agree to substantial troop withdrawal and to a reasonable solution on refugees. This might, nevertheless, be turned down in Athens. Finally, he said that he would think further about what had been said and talk to the President at length before giving his answer on the following day.[21]

---

[21] After this meeting Sir J. Killick telephoned Mr. Callaghan to discuss its outcome. Mr. Callaghan said that he too had concluded that it was too early to send a Minister of State to Ankara, and he authorised Sir J. Killick to assure Dr. Kissinger that domestic pressure was not an issue in regard to the formulation of British policy towards Cyprus (Washington telegram No. 2820 of 27 August, WSC 1/16). Cf. Volume III, No. 68.

No. 85

Sir H. Phillips (Ankara) to Mr. Callaghan

No. 1074 Telegraphic [*WSC 1/16*]

Flash. Confidential   ANKARA, *27 August 1974, 2.33 p.m*

Repeated for Information to Flash Washington (for Killick), Immediate Athens, Nicosia, UKMIS New York, UKDEL NATO, Paris, Bonn, Moscow, CBFNE.

Athens tel[egram] No. 499:[1]
Cyprus

1. As you know from my telegrams, the Turks will be extremely hard to budge. Nevertheless it might be just worth trying to sell them a variant of the terms suggested in Nicosia tel[egram] No. 834[2] and Athens tel[egram] No. 498[3] as possibly acceptable to the Greeks and Greek Cypriots for a return to negotiations.

2. The basic elements might be in an announcement by the Turks that:

(*a*) they are prepared to work out a just bi-regional federation:

(*b*) they reaffirm the aim of timely and phased reduction of the number of armed forces in the island:

(*c*) the Turkish Cypriots have a right to a 'fair' proportion of the island—fair in relation to the productive capacity and area necessary to maintain Turkish Cypriot viability:

(*d*) whatever political settlement is finally reached, all Cypriots have the immediate right of return to their own homes for domestic purposes.[4]

3. I take it that to have any effect on the Greek side the announcement would have to come firmly and unequivocally from Eçevit himself. Getting him to do this and to include all four points would not be easy. It would

---

[1] No. 83.

[2] *V. ibid.*, note 8.

[3] *V. ibid.*, notes 2, 7 and 10.

[4] Mr. Olver doubted whether this 'package ... would be enough as it [stood] to swing Clerides'. An advance on paragraph 2(*d*) would, he thought, have a 'powerful effect', but he did not think that HMG should delude themselves that the Greek Cypriots would 'be taken in by mere presentational gimmicks'. 'They have', he observed, 'had far too long an experience of negotiating with the Turks (and of course *vice-versa*) and are in far too cynical a mood to be lulled by vague promises.' On details in paragraph 2, Mr. Olver argued that: 2(*b*) contained what 'could prove a tiresome confusion ... between "phased reduction" and "phased withdrawal"'; 2(*c*) would require more precision; and 2(*d*) was 'the most important single issue' (Nicosia telegram No. 859 of 29 August).

need the combined persuasion of ourselves and Dr. Kissinger: but if the latter was prepared to put his full weight behind it it might not be impossible.

4. The various elements would have to be presented to Eçevit as in practice not meaning much derogation from the present Turkish position. For example, a 'fair' proportion of the island would be vague enough not to involve necessarily much more of a reduction in the present Turkish area than is now envisaged (from what the Prime Minister told me last night I suspect that although he disavowed Professor Ülman's reference to 28% (para 7 of my tel[egram] No. 1065)[5] the Professor may have let slip what Eçevit actually has in reserve as a bargaining point). And the return of Greek Cypriots to their homes would not preclude a later voluntary exchange of population.[6] Eçevit would have to be persuaded to overcome any hesitation over these elements by accepting that they were designed more for flexibility offered by their wording (and consequently the likelihood of being acceptable to the Greeks) than for their content as concessions much beyond what is already conceded in principle.

5. Admittedly not many good reasons can be adduced for the Turks accommodating the Greeks in this way. But the longer-terms considerations affecting us all might become more important for the Turks as well: the need to avoid Soviet interference;[7] the dangers of the UN General Assembly getting its hands on the problem; the isolation or encirclement of Turkey by questionable if not unfriendly communist and Arab countries, and now a Greece possibly moving towards enosis and/or wooed by the communists.

6. If there is anything in the foregoing suggestions that might give some hope for a new approach, how to put them to Eçevit would then have to be considered. This might be done in a message from yourself or Dr. Kissinger; if from you, to be brought by a Minister if it is decided that one

---

[5] See No. 84, note 8. Sir H. Phillips pointed out in this telegram that the Turks saw time as being on their side. They were not, he thought, likely to declare war unless Greece attacked the mainland or Turkish forces in Cyprus, and in that case, or possibly in the event of the Greeks proclaiming *enosis*, they might occupy the whole of the island. But even without war or *enosis*, if the Greeks continued to refuse negotiations, the Turks, he predicted, would ostentatiously consolidate and build up the northern part of Cyprus, and that could reach in all but name a state of partition. 'We should', Sir H. Phillips added, 'not underestimate their determination (*a*) never again to be subjugated to the Greeks in Cyprus, and (*b*) not to be deflected by outside opinion from whatever action they regard as necessary to ensure this.'

[6] In Nicosia telegram 859 (see note 4 above) Mr. Olver suggested that Mr. Clerides's admission that the great majority of Greek Cypriots would not wish to live under Turkish rule might offer scope for compromise between Mr. Denktash's insistence that there should be no Greek Cypriot majority in the north, and Greek Cypriot demands to be allowed to return to their homes.

[7] On the evening of 27 August the Turkish Foreign Ministry issued a statement turning down the Soviet conference proposal (Ankara telegram No. 1082 of 28 August). See No. 83, note 9.

should come, since the Turks might regard as nugatory a purely exploratory visit with no new initiative.

No. 86

Mr. Callaghan to Mr. Richard (UKMIS New York)
No. 657 Telegraphic [*WSC 2/522/2*]

Immediate. Confidential   FCO, *28 August 1974, 5.15 p.m*

Repeated for information to Immediate Nicosia, Athens, Ankara, Washington, Moscow, Bonn, Paris, UKDEL NATO, CBFNE.

Nicosia tel[egram] No. 846:[1]
Cyprus: Secretary General's Visit

1. In talks with Mr. Ennals yesterday, Waldheim reviewed his exchanges in Ankara, Athens and Nicosia.[2] Much of the ground is covered by telegram under reference.

2. Waldheim reported that, in response to Karamanlis's demand for Turkish concessions before any resumption of negotiations, Eçevit presented the following points. The reduction of Turkish forces could begin as soon as Turkish Cypriots who so wished were allowed to move into the Turkish-held zone, with the implication that these reductions could start before major negotiations. The Turks regard the demarcation line as negotiable, and would consider a reduction of their zone to 30 per cent of the island, but only as part of a negotiated settlement. The return of Greek refugees to the Turkish zone would also have to be deferred until a settlement, and would be affected by consideration of security and 'living space'.

3. There was evidence, in Waldheim's view, of a slight narrowing of the gap on both sides. Karamanlis in his second meeting with him had made

[1] In this telegram of 27 August Mr. Olver reported on the recent meetings of Mr. Clerides and Mr. Denktash with Dr. Waldheim, who was then on a fact-finding mission to Cyprus, Greece and Turkey. He further noted that Moscow's proposal for a UN Conference on Cyprus 'could be regarded as virtually dead', since Mr. Denktash had 'dismissed it out of hand' and Mr. Clerides regarded it as 'a mischievous distraction'.

[2] Mr. Ennals and Mr. Hattersley met with Dr. Waldheim at Heathrow Airport on his return from Cyprus on 27 August and discussed: (1) prospects for a resumption of negotiations; (2) UNFICYP; and (3) humanitarian problems in Cyprus. Dr. Waldheim stated that Mr. Karamanlis 'had made emphatically clear the impossibility of a resumption of the Geneva Conference without significant concessions from the Turks in order to assist him in facing his domestic public opinion' (record of a meeting between Mr. Ennals, Mr. Hattersley and Dr. Waldheim at Heathrow Airport, London, on 27 August at 3.15 p.m.)

no reference to the line of 9 August, and Eçevit had clearly stated Turkey's willingness to negotiate a withdrawal to 30 per cent of the island.[3]

4. On UNFICYP, the Turks were hostile and negative. They suggested that the force in their zone should be confined to camps except for Turkish-supervised missions to investigate particular incidents. Waldheim intends to put these demands to a confidential meeting of troop-contributing states in New York in the next three days, before referring them to the Security Council. Waldheim seemed to agree with our view that a buffer-zone would appear to be sanctioning the demarcation line. We spoke also of this possibility of 'a new mandate' for UNFICYP.[4]

5. Waldheim did not think that talks in Nicosia between Clerides and Denktash could be a substitute for a Conference on the Geneva model (not necessarily at Geneva) which he saw as the eventual forum for a settlement. However, they could help to prepare the ground, and give an impression of action in the interim, which would be important to satisfy the general assembly. The Greeks had welcomed the proposal and he intended to send Eçevit a message through Olcay[5] today proposing that the talks be pursued, with Weckmann as Chairman and Greek and Turkish diplomatic observers. We said that we would support such a proposal. There was no need for a British observer if the UN provided a Chairman.

6. We agree with the view expressed in para[graph] 3 of telegram under reference that Denktash is not free enough to contribute much to these intercommunal talks, but they would be valuable at least as a stop-gap, and possibly as something on which more could in due course be built.[6]

---

[3] At the meeting with Mr. Ennals and Mr. Hattersley (*v. ibid.*), Dr. Waldheim explained that Mr. Eçevit 'regarded the demarcation line as negotiable, but any reduction of Turkish-held territory would have to form part of a negotiated settlement'.

[4] Mr. Olver observed in Nicosia telegram No. 846 (see note 1 above) that Dr. Waldheim had 'predictably got nowhere with Denktash who said that this was solely a matter for the Turkish military authorities'. Dr. Weckmann-Muñoz told Mr. Olver, with regard to the existing UN mandate, that anxiety centred on the role to be played by UNFICYP in policing the buffer zone 'which must presumably be set up between the two autonomous regions once political negotiation over the line had been completed'.

[5] Mr. O. Olcay was Turkish Permanent Representative to the UN at New York.

[6] Mr. Olver noted in paragraph 3 of his telegram (see notes 1 and 5 above): 'As a safety valve and for the purpose of filling the vacuum with at least some talking somewhere, the Clerides-Denktash meetings are clearly valuable, though they will inevitably suffer from the extent to which Denktash's hands are still tied by the Turkish military. But I do not share Waldheim's optimism that these local talks can easily or profitably be converted into full-scale political discussions or provide any substitute for Geneva.'

No. 87

Mr. Callaghan to Mr. Olver (Nicosia)

No. 559 Telegraphic [*WSC 3/548/3*]

Immediate. Confidential. FCO, *29 August 1974, 6.50 p.m.*

Repeated for information to Immediate Athens, Ankara, Washington, Priority UKMIS New York, UKDEL NATO, UKMIS Geneva, Moscow, Paris, Bonn and CBFNE.

Washington tel[egram] No. 2820: (not to all):[1]
Cyprus

1. In the light of Killick's exchange of views with Dr. Kissinger, I have concluded that the time is not ripe for a Minister to visit the area.[2] I have therefore been considering what our strategy on the Cyprus question should be over the next week or two.

2. I consider that there is still plenty of scope for exploratory diplomacy, (as distinct from a major initiative to get back to the conference table), designed to establish in more detail what the real position of the parties now is and, if possible, to bring them closer. We have only just completed the first round of diplomatic contacts to this end. The second round began with Mr. Ennals's conversation with Professor Ülman, reported in my tel[egram] No. 1771 to Washington.[3] I should be grateful if, as opportunity offers, Sir H. Phillips would attempt to establish the Turkish reaction to this conversation and in particular to the proposal that, in advance of negotiations, the Turks should evacuate the new city of Famagusta, a proposal which has fast become, it seems, the main Greek prerequisite, perhaps superseding the return to the 9 August line.[4] At the same time, the Mavros memorandum cannot represent the real thinking of the Greek

---

[1] See No. 84, note 21.

[2] See No. 83, note 1, and No. 84.

[3] See No. 84, note 8. According to this telegram, when, during his conversation with Prof. Ülman and his colleague Senator H. Inan on 27 August, Mr. Ennals asked the Turks to consider a gesture such as withdrawing from the largely Greek Cypriot new city of Famagusta in advance of a conference, they simply 'took note'. They also repeated that Turkey 'had no desire to force communities to move'. But Prof. Ülman added to an assurance that Greek Cypriots presently in the SBAs would be allowed to return to their homes in the Turkish-occupied area the qualification 'when there is an agreed solution'.

[4] During a general discussion of Cyprus with Mr. Menemencioglu on 30 August Sir T. Brimelow suggested that a Turkish withdrawal from the Greek city of Famagusta 'would not involve any agreement to a general movement of population but could be regarded as a sizeable gesture of goodwill'. In a subsequent telephone conversation with the Turkish Ambassador, Sir T. Brimelow stressed that 'it was a limited but sizeable gesture since 30,000 Greeks would be involved' (telegram No. 1061 to Ankara of 30 August, WSC 1/10).

Government and there is still much to be done in Athens to establish what this is.[5] I believe that you have now sufficient information about my thinking to pursue these enquiries without more specific instructions, and I should be grateful if Sir R. Hooper would continue to do so. In all this, I am concerned primarily to explore, and to avoid commitment to any course of action which cannot effectively be followed through.

3. Meanwhile, it would be helpful to me to be able to discuss the whole problem with you, and I shall soon be making proposals for an office meeting, to be attended by Mr. Olver, Sir H. Phillips, Sir R. Hooper and Mr. Brooks Richards,[6] in a week or so's time.

4. I have not excluded the idea of despatching an emissary, not necessarily a Minister, to the area in due course and this would be one of the topics to be discussed at the meeting.

5. I remain concerned that time may not be on our side. There is a danger of military moves by the Turks on the island,[7] of the declaration of the establishment of an autonomous Turkish Cypriot region in terms which would precipitate strong Greek Cypriot reactions, of an increase in guerilla activities, and of further developments in the refugee problem. There is also danger of ill-judged Greek action. We cannot control such developments, but the Americans have told us that they are putting some pressures on Turkey to contain the situation.[8]

6. On the other hand, political pressures are slowly being built up on the parties in favour of negotiation. The Western European countries are naturally pursuing their bilateral relations with Greece and Turkey and cannot fail to be advocating negotiations, and I welcome this. Meanwhile, the General Assembly is approaching, at which both Greeks and Turks will be exposed to international pressures of various kinds and at which there is some possibility of the Greek and Turkish Foreign Ministers meeting bilaterally. Such a meeting is also to be welcomed. These pressures should reduce to some extent the danger of their becoming fixed in mutually incompatible postures. It will be your task to monitor the development of their thinking and to influence it in such a way that it does not become ossified.

7. As for a Geneva-type conference, my position remains that I see no advantage in promoting one until I am reasonably satisfied that the conditions for successful negotiations are present. I accept that HMG must continue to play a leading mediatory role on the Cyprus question until a

[5] See No. 83, note 5.

[6] Mr. F. Brooks Richards was British Ambassador in Saigon. On 11 September 1974 he succeeded Sir R. Hooper as British Ambassador to Greece.

[7] Mr. Olver reported in Nicosia telegram No. 855 of 28 August that on 27 August Turkish forces had cut the main road between Nicosia and Larnaca, and that since then Turkish infantry and tanks had 'stampeded' the population of Athna village into Athna Forest refugee camp inside the neighbouring SBA (WSC 1/10).

[8] Cf. No. 84.

settlement or a more stable status quo has been established. But I do not intend to go back to the Conference table until there is a real prospect of a successful conclusion.

8. Washington should ask the State Department to inform Dr. Kissinger of these views.[9]

[9] On 30 August Mr. Stabler repeated to Mr. Sykes Dr. Kissinger's admission that 'he had very little "feel" for the Greek Government's real views and intentions'. Dr. Kissinger was therefore considering the despatch of a 'low-profile emissary' to Mr. Karamanlis to obtain some 'feel' for his views. But Mr. Stabler stressed that no firm decision had yet been taken about this (Washington telegram No. 2851 of 30 August, WSC 3/304/2).

No. 88

Minute from R.J.T. McLaren[1] to Mr. H.T. Morgan[2]

[*WSG 2/579/2*]

Confidential   FCO, *5 September 1974*

Greek Withdrawal from NATO[3]

1. Mr. Karamanlis has sent a message to the Prime Minister (copy attached) explaining the reasons for the Greek military withdrawal from NATO.[4] Similar messages have been sent to all other Allied Heads of Government (less Turkey) and to the NATO Secretary General, Dr. Luns. The Greeks have made public the facts that such messages have been sent and the gist of their contents. The Prime Minister will no doubt wish to reply in due course.

2. Mr. Karamanlis' letter contains a rehearsal of familiar, and in many respects tendentious, complaints about the Allies' failure to prevent the Turkish invasion of Cyprus and subsequent military advances. It does not however shed much new light on Greek intentions with regard to NATO. On this latter point the relevant passages in the letter read:

'My Government have therefore decided that they must assume themselves the protection of the independence of Greece and place again the Greek land, sea and air forces heretofore assigned to the integrated Allied military organisation under national command ...

[1] Deputy Head of Western Organisations Department (WOD).

[2] AUS responsible for superintending SEED and SWED.

[3] See No. 79, note 4.

[4] Not printed. This circular letter of 28 August, addressed also to other allied Governments, was transmitted to the FCO in Athens telegram No. 510 of 29 August. In it Mr. Karamanlis complained that NATO had 'reacted with surprising apathy, strangely limiting itself to the role of a mere bystander' when a member of the Alliance 'attacked an independent country' and made imminent the threat of conflict between two member states.

Greece shall recover forthwith, over her entire territory, airspace and territorial waters full exercise of sovereignty which was heretofore limited on account of her participation in NATO and as a result of the permanent presence on Greek soil of foreign military installations and facilities or of the regular use of Greek airspace and territorial waters by foreign military aircraft and naval vessels. Greece is ready to examine with her Allies the practical measures called for by the implementation of these decisions.'

3. The only aspect of Greece's military relationship with NATO on which Mr. Karamanlis' letter indicates a clear decision—the removal of 'NATO assigned' status from Greek forces—is in practical terms the least significant: the majority of the forces concerned are in peacetime under Greek national command anyway. Their transfer to SACEUR's operational control would only occur in circumstances of severe East/West tension, involving the threat of a Warsaw Pact attack on Greek territory. In other respects Mr. Karamanlis' letter prompts more questions than it answers. We do not know, for example:

(*a*) whether overflights of Greek airspace by Allied military aircraft will still be permitted;[5]
(*b*) whether Greece will wish to participate in some way in the NATO Command structure;
(*c*) whether the NADGE[6] (air defence radar) installations in Greece will be maintained as part of the Allied chain of such installations;
(*d*) whether the various NATO communications networks which pass through Greek territory will need to be re-routed;
(*e*) whether the various NATO training facilities in Greece (e.g. the missile firing and aerial bombing ranges in Crete) will be discontinued;
(*f*) whether Greece will expect to continue to receive NATO infrastructure funds.

Until these and other questions have been clarified it will be difficult to make a full assessment of the consequences of the Greek withdrawal for the Alliance as a whole. In the meantime I attach a copy of a preliminary assessment prepared by the Defence Policy Staff in the Ministry of Defence.[7]

4. Nor is it entirely clear what the Greek Government intend to do about their bilateral arrangements with the Americans. Athens tel[egram] No. 511 reports a conversation between the Greek Minister of Defence and HM Ambassador in which Mr. Averoff said that a decision had been taken to close all US installations and to cease granting facilities. Most of these

---

[5] Sir R. Hooper reported on 6 September that 'previous clearance of all overflights is now required' (Athens telegram No. 530 of 6 September).

[6] NATO Air Defence Ground Environment.

[7] Not printed.

facilities exist under bilateral rather than NATO arrangements, and the Greeks appear to have taken little action as yet to implement their decision. The extent to which they do implement it is likely to depend on their assessment of US attitudes.[8]

5. Our longer term aim must be to maintain the Greek commitment to the Alliance and to minimise any damage to the Alliance's defensive capability as a result of changes in the Greek military relationship with NATO. The Greek decision to withdraw militarily from NATO seems to have been prompted in large part by domestic political considerations, but it was no doubt also conceived as a means of exerting pressure on individual Allies, particularly the Americans, to be more active in support of the Greek cause in the future. It is unlikely that the Greeks have, even now, thought through fully the implications of their decision or have precise ideas on how it is to be put into effect.

6. As the immediate shock of the Turkish invasion of Cyprus subsides, and as moves towards the resumption of negotiations or at any rate the achievement of a more stable *status quo* develop, the Greeks may begin to take a more realistic and less emotional view of their relationship with NATO. This suggests that our best course in the immediate future would be to refrain from demanding greater precision from the Greeks about their intentions, and to avoid detailed discussion with them of the various issues concerned. As far as possible we would deal with the Greeks in the Alliance on a 'business as usual' basis, leaving the onus on them to seek specific changes in existing arrangements.

7. We know that the Americans agree with this general approach (the concluding paragraph of a State Department telegram of instructions to the US delegation at NATO reads:

'It should be up to the Greek Government to take the initiative to alter its relationships with its Allies; we must avoid even the suggestion of making the Greek Government take undesirable decisions because of perceived pressure by her NATO Allies. Finally it will be in our interest to extend as long as possible discussions with Greece on its future NATO role in order to give time for tempers to cool and to avoid prematurely closing doors to Greek participation.')

We also understand that the Americans are likely to propose informal discussions in NATO about how the Allies might respond if and when the Greeks demand detailed negotiations. We see merit in this idea. We

[8] Mr. Averoff told Sir R. Hooper on 30 August that this decision would be implemented 'gradually and by negotiation', adding that 'the decision was irreversible unless the American attitude which had caused it to be taken changed, i.e., Greece received more support from the US against Turkey'. Sir R. Hooper noted that Mr. Averoff was 'not clear' about what effect the Greek decision would have upon Anglo-Greek bilateral military relations, though Sir R. Hooper suspected that the Greeks would like to see these continue (Athens telegram No. 511 of 30 August).

envisage that the Allies' response would be a judicious mixture of the stick and the carrot. In many instances it might be possible to devise cosmetic or face-saving changes to current procedures which the Greeks could represent as Allied concessions to Greek 'sovereignty'; in others it might be more appropriate to remind the Greeks of what they would stand to lose—for example the benefits of common NATO infrastructure funding, possible claims for compensation for existing NATO funded projects and access to military courses and training facilities—if they were to press their demands too far.

8. These considerations suggest that the Prime Minister's reply to Mr. Karamanlis should be brief, unprovocative and unhurried. Other members of the Alliance are likely to share this view.[9] It is clearly desirable that all the replies should be more or less on the same lines and an informal meeting of Permanent Representatives to NATO would be the best means of concerting them. There has already been one such meeting at which a preliminary exchange of views took place (UKDEL NATO tel[egram] No. 453).[10]

9. I submit a draft telegram of instructions to Sir E. Peck on the above lines together with a draft letter to No 10 Downing Street.[11]

10. South East European Department and the Ministry of Defence concur.

R.J.T. McLaren

---

[9] Mr. C.C.C. Tickell, Head of Western Organisations Department, minuted Mr. McLaren on 12 September that the US Embassy had urged HMG to delay its response to Mr. Karamanlis's circular letter. He noted that the matter 'had been debated at the highest level in Washington', and the US Government 'had concluded that the interests of the Alliance would be best served if no reply were sent, at least in the immediate future'.

[10] In this telegram of 30 August Sir E. Peck, the UK Permanent Representative to the North Atlantic Council (NAC), reported on an informal meeting with the Permanent Representatives of Belgium, France, West Germany and the USA, summoned by Sig. C.P. Pansa, the NATO Acting Secretary-General, to discuss Mr. Karamanlis's message. During the ensuing discussion Sir E. Peck agreed with his American colleague, Mr. Rumsfeld, that the allies should be in no hurry to respond, though he thought some sort of reply might become necessary if the Greeks decided to publish their intentions.

[11] Not printed.

No. 89

Record of a meeting held at the Foreign and Commonwealth Office on 10 September 1974 at 3.00 p.m.[1]

[*WSC 3/548/3*]

Confidential

Present:

The Rt. Hon. James Callaghan MP	Mr. Brooks Richards CMG
The Rt. Hon. David Ennals MP	Mr. T.F. Brenchley CMG
Mr. Roy Hattersley MP	Mr. J.O. Moreton CMG MC[2]
Sir Thomas Brimelow KCMG OBE	Mr. A.C. Goodison
Sir John Killick KCMG	Miss E.M. Booker OBE[3]
Sir Robin Hooper KCMG DSO DFC	Mr. A.A. Acland
Sir Horace Phillips KCMG	Mr. P.J. Weston[4]
Mr. S.J.L. Olver CMG MBE	Mr. M.C.S. Weston

1. *Mr. Callaghan* said that he saw no particular interest in Britain remaining in the forefront of the search for a settlement in Cyprus. He accepted that we had certain obligations but we should move out of the centre of the stage as soon as we could do so honourably. Dr. Kissinger thought Mr. Callaghan should continue to take the lead in the next round of talks. However, he did not like responsibility without power and for his own part he would not mind moving out from a central position before the next round.[5]

---

[1] This Heads of Mission meeting was summoned on 30 August to review the situation in Cyprus and decide HMG's next moves (telegram No. 569 to Nicosia of 30 August). A preliminary session was also attended by Mr. Ennals, Mr. Hattersley and, for part of the time, Mr. Callaghan (record of a meeting held at the FCO on 10 September at 11 a.m.).

[2] UK Deputy Permanent Representative to the UN. Mr. Moreton was substitute for Mr. Richard who wished to remain in New York for a possible Security Council debate on Cyprus.

[3] Deputy Head of News Department.

[4] Assistant Private Secretary to the Secretary of State.

[5] At the morning session (see note 1 above) Sir J. Killick described Mr. Callaghan's thinking as it had developed during the Cyprus crisis. 'The principal impressions had', he stated, 'been our military impotence, despite the existence of the bases, the American unwillingness displayed since the time of Mr. Sisco's mission to put effective pressure on the Turks, the flouting of the Geneva I Declaration by the Turks, and the fact that Geneva II had failed to deter the Turks from further action.' Sir J. Killick added: Mr. Callaghan 'must now consider carefully before embarking on anything like Geneva III. There were more risks than advantages in prospect. A prudent policy was necessitated by the situation in which we had responsibility without power ... The prospect of a General Election in any case meant that it would be inconvenient to embark on active diplomacy during the next couple of months ... Ideally our objective was a political settlement which would not require any continuing British guarantee.'

2. *Sir Horace Phillips* said that if we intended to disengage, he would like to make two points. First, we were a Guarantor Power. The Turks would be against any move we made to disengage. Secondly, did dis-engagement mean giving up the SBAs? If we were to leave the Dhekelia SBA, the Turks would take the view that it should be handed over to them. *Mr. Callaghan* said that in accordance with the Treaty obligations, we should have to hand over the SBAs to the Republic of Cyprus.[6]

3. After some discussion about Turkish behaviour at Geneva II, *Sir Thomas Brimelow* said that it was clear that the Greeks did not want to enter into negotiations at present. He believed that the talks between Clerides and Denktash provided the best immediate hope. We should give a steer in this direction and speak to the Greeks and Turks to this effect.[7] *Mr Olver* said that there were signs that the Turkish Government were now prepared to use Denktash.[8] He was less sure about how much freedom of manoeuvre Clerides had. *Mr. Callaghan* asked what the Turkish attitude was over Famagusta. *Sir Horace Philips* said that they were prepared to allow all except able-bodied men to return there. *Mr. Callaghan* wondered whether this would make possible a deal involving the return of Greek Cypriots to Famagusta and the departure of Turkish Cypriots in the Western SBA. *Sir Robin Hooper* said that the Greeks wanted control of Famagusta[9] but *Sir Horace Phillips* commented that they would not get it. The only concessions the Turks were likely to make were at the Western end of the line.[10]

4. *Mr. Callaghan* asked whether the present division of the Island was viable. *Mr. Olver* said that a division based on the present line was not viable. The answer to whether any Greek region was viable really

---

[6] See Nos. 44 and 82.

[7] In a minute to Mr. Acland of 6 September, covering the agenda to this meeting, Mr. Goodison stressed that consideration must be given to what might happen if there were no agreed Cyprus settlement. He further observed: 'The likely course of events still seems to be the collapse of the Cyprus Government and an uncontrolled slide into double *enosis*, very possibly followed by Turkish military moves to occupy the whole of the Republic. Is there anything we can do to prepare ourselves for that?'

[8] Cf. No. 86, note 6.

[9] See No. 87, note 4. When, on 2 September Sir R. Hooper asked Mr. Mavros what the Greek Government would regard as a 'reasonable basis' for discussions with the Turks, Mr. Mavros replied that while Greece accepted that there must be a 'regional solution' in Cyprus, the Turks should withdraw from the new town of Famagusta and allow the Greek Cypriot inhabitants to return there. He also insisted that: (1) the territory to remain permanently under Turkish-Cypriot control should be 'substantially less' than that presently occupied by Turkish forces; (2) refugees should be allowed to return; (3) there should be no exchanges of population, whether *de facto* or *de jure*; and (4) all foreign troops should be withdrawn from Cyprus, other than those in the SBAs (Athens telegram No. 519 of 2 September, WSC 1/16).

[10] During the morning session (see notes 1 and 4 above) Sir H. Phillips affirmed 'that the Turks were unwilling to make any concessions before negotiation, virtually regardless of any pressure that might be exerted on them. The Turkish economy and Turkish military strength had hardly been affected by the Cyprus military operation. The Turks would be ready, if necessary, to let the present solution crystallise without a settlement.'

depended on what the Turks wanted. They did not need anything like the present area unless they wished to reduce the Greeks to a position of economic inferiority.

5. Mr. Olver said that he had detected some slight signs that there was common ground between the two sides on the transfer of population. The Turks wanted to move their people from the south to the north. The Greek Cypriots wanted their people to be able to go back to their homes, not so much to settle in them as to see if there was anything they could salvage and perhaps to sell them. He thought it was just possible that some agreement might be reached between Clerides and Denktash on this.[11] It might be possible to deal with the problem of the Turks in the Western SBA on a similar basis. *Sir Thomas Brimelow* agreed and suggested that on the latter the details should be worked out by Clerides and Denktash. It would however be necessary to work on both Athens and Ankara. *Sir Horace Phillips* also agreed, though he felt that there was a difference between this case and others since we had sovereignty over the Western SBA. Following further discussion, it was agreed that *Sir Thomas Brimelow* should speak to the Turkish and Greek Ambassadors. Mr. Olver would follow up on his return with Clerides and Denktash.

6. *Mr. Callaghan* suggested that Makarios was forcing himself more and more into the picture. *Mr. Olver* said that Makarios was becoming more extreme. Clerides was more worried about him than about EOKA. After Sir John Killick had read a summary of Makarios's press conference in Geneva,[12] *Mr. Callaghan* commented that Makarios had moved backwards. He had earlier seemed prepared to envisage a geographical solution. *Mr. Olver* said that Clerides believed that Makarios might return as the head of a government of national salvation, pledged to offer eternal resistance to the Turks. *Sir John Killick* suggested that we would split ourselves from Makarios by backing a bi-regional federation in a UN resolution of the kind Lord Caradon was pressing for.[13] *Sir Thomas Brimelow* said that we

[11] At the morning session (*v. ibid.*) Mr. Olver stated that Mr. Clerides accepted a 'bi-regional federation', but that he could not accept the present proportions: 'Before he could take the same position in public he needed cover from Athens and from Makarios. He had come a long way to getting it from Karamanlis, but he had been undercut by Mavros and more particularly by Makarios' recent public statement ruling out a regional solution.'

[12] During a press conference in Geneva on 8 September Archbishop Makarios stated that he intended to return to Cyprus 'in the very near future'. He added, with regard to conditions for the resumption of negotiations on the island's future, that 'one prerequisite was that Turkey should agree to some 200,000 uprooted Greek Cypriots returning to their homes'. *The Times*, 9 September 1974, p. 6h.

[13] Lord Caradon, the Governor of Cyprus during 1957-60, was Chairman of the newly-formed Association of the Friends of Cyprus, a group which Mr. Goodison later described as 'in practice primarily friends of Greek Cyprus' (minute from Mr. Goodison to Mr. Morgan of 6 November, WSC 1/16). During meetings with Mr. Callaghan and Sir J. Killick in early September, Lord Caradon had argued in favour of a British initiative in the Security Council, comprising a comprehensive proposal for a Cyprus settlement, which would restore the UN's authority (telegram No. 700 to UKMIS New York of 13 September, WSC 18/10).

should encourage Clerides and Denktash to make as much progress as possible before Makarios returned since there would be little chance of progress thereafter. *Sir John Killick* wondered if Makarios would ask for Greek military reinforcements if he returned to Cyprus. *Mr. Olver* thought this was unlikely. He would probably concentrate on building up political support in the UN, for example. *Sir Thomas Brimelow* commented that this would tempt the Turks to occupy the whole island. *Mr. Olver* said that Clerides had told him that many Cypriots would not mind this since they believed that it would force the Greeks to declare war.

7. *Sir Horace Phillips* again suggested that thought should be given to where the balance of our interest lay, in Athens or Ankara. He did not suggest that we should come out in support of one side to such an extent that we alienated the other but Turkey was clearly the better ally against the USSR. *Mr. Callaghan* suggested that in this Sir Horace Phillips appeared to agree with Dr. Kissinger. *Sir John Killick* commented that this would not be right for us. Kissinger had accepted that there was little danger of losing the Turks to the Russians. Our interest surely lay in keeping Greece in the Western camp.[14] *Mr. Callaghan* said that when he was in Washington he hoped to thrash out the whole question with Dr. Kissinger and try to reach agreement on the solution to the problem. *Sir Thomas Brimelow* said that the problem was to decide what the basis for such an agreement should be. He believed that we should try to keep in the background as much as possible. *Mr. Callaghan* agreed. But what was the answer? *Sir Horace Phillips* said that Clerides/Denktash talks provided the best hope. *Mr. Ennals* also agreed. He recalled that the UN Secretary General had been in favour of such talks.[15]

8. *Sir Robin Hooper* said that it was becoming more and more apparent that the Greeks were going to get the dirty end of the stick. We should not become identified with any major sell out.[16] This argued in favour of us withdrawing from the centre of the stage and leaving Clerides and Denktash to get on with their talks, though they had been talking without much result since 1960. *Mr. Callaghan* remarked that this would strengthen the Turkish view that time was on their side. *Sir Horace Phillips* and *Sir Robin Hooper* agreed that it was.

9. *Sir John Killick* suggested that we should aim to persuade Dr. Kissinger that encouraging Clerides and Denktash to pursue their talks was the correct policy. We should also try to persuade him to ensure that the Turks did nothing to spoil these talks.

10. *Mr. Callaghan* asked what the Greeks wanted from the Turks to make the acceptance of a difficult outcome more palatable. *Sir Robin Hooper* said that, as an opening bid, they wanted withdrawal from Famagusta, an area based more closely on Turkish population and substantial withdrawal of

[14] Cf. No. 84.

[15] See No. 86.

[16] Sir R. Hooper had argued during the earlier session (see notes 1, 4, 10 and 11 above) that there 'was a danger that the Greeks might look for a scapegoat and settle on us'.

Turkish troops.[17] *Sir Horace Phillips* said that the Turks would never give up Famagusta though they would allow selected Greek Cypriots to return. On area, they were certainly prepared to negotiate and on withdrawal, they had accepted the formula of 'timely reduction' in the Geneva declaration. *Mr. Ennals* suggested that we should encourage Eçevit to let Denktash out on a longer string. In view of what Mr. Olver had said, perhaps we should encourage the Greeks to do the same with Clerides. *Sir Thomas Brimelow* thought that the Greeks would ally themselves with Makarios and cause the maximum amount of trouble in the UN. Eventually they would probably try to restore Makarios in place of Clerides. *Sir Horace Phillips* said that the Turks were certainly against the internationalisation of the problem. *Sir Thomas Brimelow* said that the continuation of the Clerides/Denktash talks was probably the best defence against internationalisation. *Sir John Killick* commented that what ever view we took of the chances of Clerides and Denktash succeeding, support for their talks was the one totally defensible line. *Mr. Olver* said that as far as the Greek Cypriots were concerned, the problem was Makarios. We could do nothing about him but perhaps the Greeks could.[18] *Sir Robin Hooper* said that no Greek politician had ever been able to do anything about Makarios. *Sir John Killick* agreed but suggested it should be part of our aim to persuade Athens to try to do so.

11. *Mr. Callaghan* wondered what we should do if the Turks declared an independent Turkish Cypriot Republic as they had threatened.[19] *Sir Thomas Brimelow* suggested that we should take the line that such a declaration was incompatible with the 1960 Treaty. *Mr. Callaghan* wondered whether we should tell Dr. Kissinger in advance the line that we would take. *Mr. Goodison* suggested that, if we do so, we should make clear that, following

[17] During the morning session (*v. ibid.*) Sir R. Hooper said that the Greek Government were 'interested in the idea of a package deal with Turkey, involving agreement on the Aegean, minority problems, etc.'. He further observed 'Mavros talked of "quiet diplomacy", which in practice meant waiting for something to turn up. Many Greeks were flirting with the idea of a turn to the left, but a real move was not likely in the immediate future.'

[18] Mr. Olver had said during the morning session (see notes 1, 4, 10, 11, 15 and 16 above) that 'Clerides' position was weak and he was constantly looking over his shoulder, not so much to the right at Eoka-B, as to the left at Makarios and Mavros'. In a conversation with Mr. Olver on 6 September Mr. Clerides had predicted that, if negotiations were delayed further and the Turkish zone was consolidated into something approaching an autonomous republic, there would either be 'lunatic efforts at guerilla activity' and interfactional strife on the Greek side, or a government of national unity opposed to federation or partition and headed by Archbishop Makarios who would 'return in triumph to lead this sort of national resistance against the Turks' (minute by Mr. Olver of 6 September, WSC 1/16).

[19] Mr. Denktash was quoted in the Nicosia press of 27 August as having threatened: (1) to set up an independent Turkish Republic of Cyprus if Greece put the Cyprus problem to the UN General Assembly; and (2) to extend Turkish boundaries, possibly taking the whole island, if Greek Cypriots launched a guerrilla war (Nicosia telegram No. 848 of 27 August (WSC 1/16).

the Geneva declaration, we recognised the existence in practice of an independent Turkish Cypriot administration.[20]

12. *Mr. Callaghan* wondered what we should be doing at the UN. *Mr. Moreton* said that he did not think there was any particular problem at the UN. The line we intended to take was helpful since we were supporting the idea of talks between Cypriots. *Mr. Callaghan* also wondered what should be said to Lord Caradon. *Sir John Killick* suggested that we should again explain to him that we do not agree with his objections to a bi-regional federation or with his proposal that we should produce an equivalent to Resolution 242.[21] The latter would serve only to reinforce UK responsibility. *Mr. Callaghan* agreed with this line and suggested that Mr. Ennals should speak to Lord Caradon accordingly.

12. [*sic*] Mr. Callaghan suggested that, on his return to Cyprus, Mr. Olver should speak to Mr. Clerides and Denktash and encourage them to go on with their talks.[22] *Sir Thomas Brimelow* agreed and added that *Mr. Olver* should emphasise the importance we attached to these talks.

13. [*sic*] Mr. Callaghan said that the possibility of sending an emissary was on the agenda. It was clear from the discussion that there was no call for this at present.[23]

---

[20] In telegram No. 679 to Nicosia of 13 September Mr. Callaghan noted that he had concluded from reports of Turkish intentions that if the Greek side were to declare *enosis* or made it clear they would never negotiate, the 'Turks might set up an independent Turkish Cypriot Republic, which could then vote itself into the Turkish Republic, rather than proceed to simple annexation' (WSC 1/10). The next day, Mr. Olver reported that he had been assured by Mr. Denktash that morning that there was no intention of declaring an autonomous Turkish republic in the near future. It had, Mr. Denktash, admitted, been his idea, 'as a way of putting pressure on the Greeks to negotiate: but Ankara had restrained him and it had in any case not worked' (Nicosia telegram No. 984 of 14 September, WSC 2/522/2).

[21] UNSC Resolution 242, adopted in November 1967, concerned the Middle East, principally Israel. It emphasised 'the inadmissibility of the acquisition of territory by war' and called for a 'just and lasting peace' in the region through the 'withdrawal of Israeli armed forces from territories occupied in the recent conflict'.

[22] On 6 September Mr. Clerides and Mr. Denktash met in the Ledra Palace UN conference area, Nicosia, to discuss a number of humanitarian matters, including the exchange of prisoners. They agreed to hold regular weekly meetings and, during a subsequent private conversation, they also agreed that they should try to find some common grounds between their two positions on political and constitutional issues. (Nicosia telegrams Nos. 918 and 942 of 7 and 10 September, WSC 1/19).

[23] In a minute to Mr. Callaghan of 4 September, Mr. Ennals insisted that HMG still had a moral obligation to continue with the diplomatic effort to narrow the gap between Ankara and Athens in order to bring about, if possible, a resumption of the Geneva Conference, and he proposed that he (Mr. Ennals) should visit Cyprus in the following week to look at humanitarian problems and to discuss prospects for a resumption of meetings between Mr. Clerides and Mr. Denktash. According to Mr. Ennals, Mr. Hattersley agreed. But, in a subsequent minute to Mr. Goulding of 6 September, Mr. Goodison expressed doubts about this course. He feared that it would encourage false hopes of a 'spectacular contribution' by HMG to the international relief effort, and that it might discourage the UN from assuming responsibility for refugees in the SBAs. In any case, Mr. Goodison thought that there was not

14. [*sic*] The meeting concluded with discussion of the line to be taken with the press.[24]

much 'exploratory work to be done in Cyprus' since Mr. Clerides and Mr. Denktash, to the extent that they had independent policies, appeared to want to see negotiations started.

[24] On 11 September Sir T. Brimelow, used separate meetings with Mr. S. Roussos, the new Greek Ambassador in London, and Mr. Menemencioglu, to convey to them the conclusions of the Heads of Mission meeting. A speaking note, copies of which he handed to both Ambassadors, pointed out that HMG attached particular importance to the talks taking place between Mr. Clerides and Mr. Denktash (records of meetings between Sir T. Brimelow and the Greek and Turkish Ambassadors on 11 September).

No. 90

Mr. Callaghan to Sir P. Ramsbotham (Washington)

No. 1884 Telegraphic [WSC 3/304/2]

Immediate. Confidential   FCO, *11 September 1974, 6.35 p.m.*

Repeated for information to Immediate Athens, Ankara, Nicosia, UKMIS New York and Priority Paris, Bonn, Moscow, UKDEL NATO, UKMIS Geneva, UKREP Brussels.

Your tel[egram] No. 2924 (not to all).[1]

1. Thank you for this valuable account of Kissinger's thinking, which was fully taken into account at the Heads of Mission meeting on 10 September.[2] Please now deliver the following message from me to Kissinger (which other posts should treat as for their background information on the results of the meeting).

---

[1] Sir P. Ramsbotham reported in this telegram of 9 September that when, on the previous day, he had called on Dr. Kissinger to discuss the Cyprus situation, the latter had said that he agreed with Mr. Callaghan that: (1) the 'time was not ripe to expend prestige in a major effort to get negotiations re-started'; (2) it was necessary first to establish the positions of the parties and what they were prepared to concede and 'allow time for political pressures to develop from various quarters in the direction of negotiations'; and (3) they 'could not afford too much time' because the situation could become 'rigid'. Dr. Kissinger also insisted that it was for the Greeks to give the first indication of what they were prepared to concede, and that, as regards the Turks, the US 'would be ready to make a big heave at the right time and when the right sort of negotiations were in sight'. This, however, would not include the cutting off of military aid since that would further complicate the situation with Congress and, 'once cut, US aid could not under Congressional procedures, be easily restored for a long time'. Meanwhile, Mr. Stabler was despatched to Ankara to warn Mr. Eçevit that Turkey risked having US aid cut off because of the 'misuse of military equipment provided for NATO purposes' and Turkey's failure effectively to control poppy production (Ankara telegram No. 1183 of 13 September, WST 3/304/1). Cf. 84, note 19.

[2] See No. 89.

Begins:

Dear Henry,

It was good to talk to you on the telephone on 9 September,[3] and I want to say again how grateful I was for the full account of your thinking on Cyprus which you gave Peter Ramsbotham before our heads of mission meeting on 10 September. I can say at once that our discussions reinforced my feeling that we are very close in our assessments. Neither the Turks nor the Greeks are yet in a position, for their different reasons, to make the necessary moves without which a return to a Geneva-type conference would be anything but fruitless or harmful. In Cyprus itself, time is not on our side, and I was disturbed to be told that Clerides is taking the line that he now perceives the threat to his own position as coming less from EOKA than from a broad spectrum of 'national salvation' type, ranging from AKEL and Lyssarides right through even to EOKA (if they can get in on the act), with Makarios at its head and under the simple slogan of eternal struggle against the Turks. But there must always be an element of risk in the situation.

2. When the Prime Minister and I talked to Makarios on 15 August, he said nothing that absolutely ruled out a biregional federal solution.[4] But, to judge from his recent statements, and from what he said to me today, when we had another exchange of views, his position has hardened unhelpfully.[5]

3. It emerged from our Heads of Mission meeting that quiet diplomacy must continue to be the order of the day, the only encouraging feature being the continued development of the dialogue between Clerides and Denktash.[6] It is a small miracle that it has survived the charges and

[3] No record of this telephone conversation has been traced in FCO files.

[4] In telegram No. 11 to Dhekelia of 16 August Mr. Callaghan reported Archbishop Makarios as having told him and Mr. Wilson on 15 August that he 'did not want to commit himself to a particular solution' of the Cyprus problem. Mr. Callaghan 'formed the impression' from this conversation that Archbishop Makarios 'was not violently opposed to a federal and zonal solution' (WSC 1/14).

[5] During a meeting he had with Mr. Callaghan that morning Archbishop Makarios insisted that, while he could accept Greek and Turkish Cypriot autonomy, this had to be 'on the basis of ethnic criteria not on a geographical basis'. He said that he was not happy with the proposed solution of a geographical federation since he could not envisage this being possible without a complete transfer of population, and he thought it would 'lead inevitably to double *enosis*' (draft record of a conversation between Mr. Callaghan and Archbishop Makarios held at the FCO at 10 a.m. on 11 September, Callaghan Papers).

[6] See No. 89, note 22. Mr. Clerides informed Mr. Olver on 13 September that he had proposed to Mr. Denktash that the Turks should agree to withdraw 'from the Morphou area in the west, the south-east bulge and New Famagusta', that the area thus liberated should become a buffer zone under UN control to which the Greek-Cypriot population should be allowed to return. 'This', Mr. Olver noted, 'would enable Clerides publicly to accept negotiations (which he still envisaged within the Geneva framework) on the basis of geographical federation and would also get Karamanlis off the hook' (Nicosia telegram No. 982 of 14 September, WSC 1/19).

counter-charges of atrocities etc. Of course one cannot put great faith in it: it is still at the stage of small beginnings, and by no means certain that it can extend so as to begin to get to grips with the basic issues of constitutional settlement. Our original idea was that this could only happen after there had been a measure of broad agreement on principles at a five-sided meeting. But if the dialogue can be encouraged and fostered, it seems to us to open the only hope of progress, however modest, in the immediately foreseeable future. It also has the great merit of being entirely defensible as a desirable vehicle, worthy of our support (Cypriots getting together to solve their own problems) against all criticism at the UN and from elsewhere, and perhaps sufficient to carry us through the General Assembly without other undesirable initiatives. I see no point in looking further ahead for the moment, though I look forward to some discussion of the longer-range implications and possibilities when we meet.

4. However, if this tender plant is even to survive, I believe some effective quiet diplomacy is needed. For one thing, Makarios and Athens must be willing to give it a fair wind, and do nothing to put it at risk, and we shall be prepared to do what we can to ensure this. On the other side two things are required from Ankara. First, a willingness to allow Denktash a bit of real negotiating latitude, so that some effective progress can be registered even without the direct Turkish seal of approval. (I am not sure that Denktash even wants the scope of the talks widened and it may be more a matter of persuading Ankara to thrust it on him.) Second, and perhaps crucially, to persuade the Turks that this approach is in their material interest, and not just a holding device, with the main object of ensuring that further provocative Turkish action on the island does not bring the talks to an abrupt halt by making it impossible for Clerides to continue. I hope ill-advised Turkish military action is now unlikely, but I am particularly worried about reports of the intended declaration of an 'independent Turkish Cypriot Republic' on 16 September or thereabouts.[7] I am sure none of us can prevent the continued remorseless establishment of a Turkish Cypriot Administration, but it must surely be in the Turkish interest to go about this in the least ostentatious and challenging way. If you agree with all this, would you be willing to use your influence in Ankara accordingly?

5. Meanwhile, we are fully conscious of the difficulty and threat presented by the refugee problem, particularly in terms of the temptation constantly before the Turks of mounting a rescue operation. We ourselves are confronted by the special difficulty of the refugees in the SBAs (for the most part Greek Cypriot in the Eastern SBA, mainly from Famagusta, and Turkish Cypriot in the Western SBA, mainly from the Limassol area). As you are no doubt aware, Denktash has specifically requested our help over the latter, and although we do not discount the humanitarian aspect, the political implications of simply agreeing amount in the last analysis to

[7] See No. 89, notes 19 and 20.

facilitating the population of the Turkish-controlled zone with Turkish Cypriots. So we are working hard to evolve some kind of evenhanded package which would include ideally a Turkish move to permit the return of Greek Cypriots to new Famagusta. Peter Ramsbotham will be able to give you the details of this, and a progress report. This is a situation which must be defused somehow, and any help you can give will be most welcome.

6. For the rest, it follows that any idea of emissaries to the area remains on ice for the time being. But I am very glad that you are sending somebody to Athens.[8] Our Ambassador there tells me that there are signs of Greek resentment, in their search for a scapegoat, passing to us from you. I hope this is more consolation to you than it is to me![9] (You might, incidentally, like to glance at an article on US-Greek relations in *The Economist* of 7 September. I wish I could claim the credit for it: I shall no doubt get the blame in Athens!).[10] However, this will not deter me from going along in a positive spirit with impending moves to bring Greece back into the Council of Europe and to revive Greek association with the EEC, which seem to me desirable and necessary on their merits.[11] I shall of course continue to be concerned that such developments do not take on a flavour which is unhelpful to you.

7. I am glad that we are both relaxed about other initiatives such as those by the Yugoslavs, Romanians[12] and Pakistanis, and even at the UN

[8] Dr. Kissinger told Sir P. Ramsbotham on 8 September (see note 1 above) that he had decided to send 'as a private emissary to Karamanlis, Bill Tyler, former US Ambassador to the Netherlands and now Director of Dumbarton Oaks Research Library (Byzantine Studies)'.

[9] In his conversation with Dr. Kissinger on 8 September (*v. ibid.*) Sir P. Ramsbotham mentioned Mr. Callaghan's concern at hearing that Dr. Kissinger had been upset by reports of criticisms of his efforts emanating from British Ministers and the British press. Dr. Kissinger had, according to Sir P. Ramsbotham, admitted that it irritated him 'that he should be the one to be the most criticised in the world press for the failure of the Geneva talks, when he had fallen over backwards both to support us whenever we had asked for American action, and to avoid diminishing your [Mr. Callaghan's] central role' (Washington telegram No. 2923 of 9 September).

[10] This article argued that there was no credible evidence with which to support Greek assertions that the Americans had organised the whole Cyprus crisis for their own purposes. *The Economist*, 7 September 1974, pp. 16-17.

[11] Relations between Greece and the EEC, as governed by Greece's Association Agreement, were suspended following the Colonels' *coup* of 1967, and two years later Greece was also obliged to withdraw from the Council of Europe.

[12] A paper of 3 September drafted by Eastern European and Soviet Department (EESD), 'Cyprus, Greece and Turkey: Balkan Reactions', argued that the Yugoslavs had sought to promote the idea of a six-power (the five permanent members of the UN Security Council and one non-aligned state) guarantee of Cyprus, less because they wanted to 'cut a fine figure on the world stage as leaders of the non-aligned movement', and more because they feared the Russians would use the crisis to extend their influence in the Balkans, possibly by installing their forces in Bulgaria. It was assumed that the Romanians, who had offered their services as mediators in the dispute, were simlarly apprehensive (WSC 2/1).

by the non-aligned.[13] I agree that some of these do not excite much enthusiasm but I do not see that they can effectively do harm, and they do serve to keep up a certain pressure in the right direction. I think we must approach the General Assembly in the same general spirit. Incidentally Makarios told me that he would be visiting Yugoslavia and Algeria and hopes to address the General Assembly. He wants to 'internationalise' the problem, whilst agreeing with me that the UN is not going to solve it.[14]

8. I will do my best to keep in touch over the period ahead, and we shall of course remain ready to resume a Geneva-type role if and when the right conditions can be established. I shall be very glad of your views and to know whether we are in broad agreement on the next steps.

9. All good wishes, especially in your difficult Middle East dealings.[15]

Yours ever,
Jim.

Ends.

[13] Since 14 August the Pakistani President, Mr. Z.A. Bhutto, had been seeking to bring the Greek and Turkish Governments together in order to resolve their differences over Cyprus. Subsequent Pakistani efforts to persuade the Turks to withdraw from the Greek Cypriot areas of Famagusta and permit the return of Greek Cypriot refugees to the north of the island as part of an overall settlement on a federal basis seemed to offer some hope for a successful settlement (record of conversation between Pakistan Foreign Secretary, Mr. Agha Shahi, and HM Ambassador, Islamabad, on 7 September, FSP 2/5).

[14] See note 4 above.

[15] Dr. Kissinger embarked on a fresh round of shuttle diplomacy, aimed at promoting agreement between Israel and its Arab neighbours, during 9-15 October. See H.A. Kissinger, *Years of Renewal* (New York: Simon and Schuster, 1999), pp. 381-82.

No. 91

Mr. Callaghan to Sir H. Phillips (Ankara)

No. 1129 Telegraphic [WSC 19/1]

Immediate. Confidential   FCO, *12 September 1974, 12 p.m.*

Repeated for information to Immediate Athens, Nicosia, Washington and Priority UKMIS New York, UKDEL NATO, Bonn, Moscow, Paris, UKDEL Strasbourg, CBFNE.

Cyprus: Turkish Ambassador's call on PUS: MIPT.[1]

Herewith text of speaking note given by PUS to Turkish Ambassador on 11 September:

1. Mr. Denktash has raised with our High Commissioner in Cyprus the question of the Turkish Cypriot refugees at present in the Western Sovereign Base Area. His suggestion is that they should be evacuated to Turkey in a Turkish ship. Transport from the shore to the ship would be by Turkish landing craft. The plan seems thereafter to involve the transfer of many of them to the Turkish-controlled area of Cyprus.

2. We are deeply concerned by the whole problem of the refugees in Cyprus. As regards the Turkish Cypriot refugees in the Western Sovereign Base Area we shall be glad to see them moved to somewhere where they can be properly accommodated. We should like this to be arranged as soon as possible, and certainly before the onset of winter.

3. We have however been advised by our representatives in Nicosia and Athens that the acceptance by us of the proposal made by Mr. Denktash (which has already been reported in the press) would be interpreted as a first step towards a general transfer of population, to which Mr. Clerides and the Greek Government are opposed. It appears therefore that the

---

[1] My Immediately Preceding Telegram. As a result of the fighting in Cyprus there were by September some 7,600 Turkish Cypriot refugees at Episkopi in the Western Sovereign Base Area (WSBA). They were reluctant to return to their homes in the south of the island, and Sir H. Phillips reported in Ankara telegram No. 1104 of 4 September that the Turkish Foreign Ministry had enquired as to whether they might be transferred to a Turkish ship for transportation to mainland Turkey, or, as Sir H. Phillips surmised, possibly for disembarkation at Kyrenia. Mr. Denktash made a similar proposal to Mr. Olver (Nicosia telegram No. 933 of 9 September). Telegram No. 1128 to Ankara of 12 September recorded a meeting between Sir T. Brimelow and Mr. Menemencioglu on 11 September during which the former stated that HMG hoped that Mr. Clerides and Mr. Denktash could talk about the refugee and other problems 'in an exploratory way and in confidence without either side losing face'. In handing a copy of this speaking note to Mr. Menemencioglu, Sir T. Brimelow asked him to treat it as an oral representation.

acceptance of Mr. Denktash's proposals would involve Her Majesty's Government in serious difficulties with the Greek Government as well as with the Greek Cypriot community and its leaders.

4. The Turkish Government are aware of the present reluctance of the Greek Government to resume negotiations. Her Majesty's Government would like to see negotiations resumed: but they are convinced that a precondition for the resumption of negotiations is to reduce the gap which at present exists between the views of the parties to the negotiations. If Her Majesty's Government were to accept Mr. Denktash's proposal, the effect would be to widen this gap rather than narrow it.

5. We think that the best possibility of progress, which we are anxious to achieve, would be to place Mr. Denktash's proposal in a broader context. We think it ought to be balanced against some progress in the resettlement of Greek Cypriot refugees. We also think that the persons best qualified to discuss the modalities of such an arrangement are Mr. Clerides and Mr. Denktash. Our general view hitherto has been that the best solution for the problem of the refugees would be to create conditions in which they could return to their homes, but we appreciate that this raises delicate issues regarding guarantees of security and we have no wish, by advancing our own views, to complicate the discussions which we should like to see started between Mr. Denktash and Mr. Clerides.[2] If such talks take place, and they lead to the conclusion that the safe return of the refugees to their homes and their settlement in their homes in conditions of security cannot be guaranteed, we should be prepared at that point to seek the agreement of Mr. Clerides and the Greek Government to our accepting Mr. Denktash's proposal in the form in which it had been put to us. If such agreement has not been given by the time a comparable or greater number of Greek Cypriot refugees have been resettled (preferably in the Greek part of Famagusta, though we should be prepared to consider alternative proposals) we should at that point be prepared to give effect to Mr. Denktash's proposal without further ado.[3]

[2] Mr. Menemencioglu insisted, however, that Mr. Eçevit considered it important for all items to be settled at formal negotiations for otherwise it would be much more difficult for the Turks to make concessions (*v. ibid*). Moreover, when on 13 September Mr. Olver put it to Mr. Clerides that he should try to reach an accord with Mr. Denktash, whereby the British would permit the Turkish Cypriot refugees to go to Turkey in return for Turkish concessions on Greek Cypriot refugees, Mr. Clerides rejected this approach since it would undermine both the basis on which he was tackling the refugee problem with Mr. Denktash and his whole negotiating strategy (cf. No. 90, note 6). The next day Mr. Denktash, who was equally unenthusiastic about the British proposal, indicated to Mr. Olver that it impinged on the broader question of a return of the Greek Cypriot refugees to parts of the Turkish-occupied area of the island (Nicosia telegram No. 982 of 14 September).

[3] In a note, delivered by Mr. Menemencioglu to Mr. Ennals on 16 September, the Turkish Government expressed its deep regret at the position taken by HMG on the Turkish Cypriot refugees. 'A refusal to recognise their right to free departure would', the note claimed, 'change their status of refugees to a position of hostages.' This was rebutted by Mr. Ennals, who argued that the 'premature removal' of the refugees to Turkey must make more remote the chances of

a settlement emerging from the Denktash/Clerides talks' (telegrams Nos. 1146 and 1147 to Nicosia of 16 September).

No. 92

Letter from Mr. M. Perceval[1] (Nicosia) to Mr. M.C.S. Weston

[*WSC 1/10*]

Confidential   NICOSIA, *12 September 1974*

Dear Weston,

Turkish Military Intentions

1. This is an exercise in making bricks from straws in the wind. As our bag service is returning to near normal, there is some chance that not all of what follows will be overtaken, or for that matter, disproved by events before the letter reaches you.

2. We are in an uneasy period, not without menace of renewed Turkish military action. There was much apprehension at the end of last week that the tanks might roll on Larnaca, and even farther afield, coinciding with the wave of propaganda about Greek Cypriot atrocities.[2] Mr. Eçevit's assurances to the US Ambassador, leaked later to the press, brought the temperature down somewhat,[3] but it can soon rise again, especially as the Turks switch their propaganda efforts from dead Turks to live Turks in the shape of their communities in the south of the island demanding rescue. It takes only an outbreak of pointless shooting across the Green Line in Nicosia, such as we had last Thursday night, to send Greek Cypriot cars flooding out towards the hills again, for they suspect, as do we, that the Turks may take advantage of the slightest military opposition, as the pretext to stage 'Phase Three', as the much rumoured rescue operation has been baptised.

3. Not that there is in fact any National Guard activity to provide a pretext. The Guard is essentially passive at the moment; it has been defeated in the field, has no illusions that another round would give a different result, knows that Greece has chosen not to fight in (or indeed for) Cyprus, and as General Karayannis[4] told the Defence Adviser,[5] aims only

---

[1] Mr. M. Perceval was First Secretary in the British High Commission, Nicosia.

[2] On 3 and 5 September the FCO received warnings from the Greek Embassy in London that Athens had information that the Turks were planning military action against Larnaca (telegram No. 617 to Nicosia of 5 September).

[3] According to Washington telegram No. 2911 of 6 September, Mr. Eçevit had assured Mr. Macomber that, contrary to rumours, there was no Turkish plan to make a foray into Larnaca.

[4] Lt.-Gen. G. Karayannis was formerly Commander of the Cyprus National Guard.

to regroup to create a viable force 'from the ashes' and to squash EOKA
B. It follows that such important ceasefire violations as there have been,
have been Turkish.[6] They have swept and searched villages between their
lines and the ESBA[7] in what must be an attempt to squeeze the inhabitants
out completely, using the convenient excuse of possible guerrilla
activity—of which, to date, there has been none, though the Turks may yet
provoke it.

4. In the north-west, Turkish Cypriot forces have been moving east from
their enclaves to link up with the mainland forces, bringing Limnitis into
the bag, and no doubt the same thing will soon happen with Kokkina
(—and who knows, some villages even beyond that). On Monday night,
shooting in the Pyroi-Athienou area caused some nervousness, as of course,
the Turkish armour and infantry there would be the ones used for any
thrust on Larnaca. For this, they could certainly keep the element of
tactical surprise, and their tanks could be in Larnaca in one or two hours.
Snatch and rescue for the Turkish detainees and communities in Limassol
and Paphos are feasible as sea-helicopter operations, though likely to be
costly in lives and equipment, and difficult of extraction, unless armour
were sent to establish corridors.

5. A variant on the multiple snatch scenario, would be a single operation
against Larnaca, liberating a group of some 700 Turkish Cypriots, and
hopefully, intimidating the Greeks into releasing the other Turkish Cypriot
groups all over the South. However, such a move could also mean the
Turks staying in Larnaca, because

(*a*) they are not overly good at withdrawing from supposed bargaining
counters,
(*b*) it would give them a shorter line to defend than the present Nicosia-
Famagusta one, and
(*c*) it would give then a lien on Dhekelia if in the future HMG decided
to relinquish the SBA's.
(*d*) it would also give them the island's sole oil refinery.

6. The disadvantages of a multiple or single 'rescue' operation include
the very real danger of condemning the bulk of the 40,000 or so Turkish
Cypriots scattered in towns and villages all over the south, to savage
reprisals by EOKA B or dislocated National Guard units, people in short,
who had little more to lose and might prefer a holocaust. It was, after all,
the Turkish offensive of 14 August which condemned the unfortunate
inhabitants of Maratha and other atrocity sites. However, it has long been

[5] Col. J.J.G. Hunter.

[6] In Nicosia telegram No. 881 of 2 September Mr. Olver reported that ever since 16 August
there had 'been a steady stream of violations of the cease-fire by Turkish troops'. He added:
'None of us here is in any doubt that these actions are totally unprovoked and militarily
unjustified breaches of the cease fire.'

[7] Eastern Sovereign Base Area (Dhekelia).

our impression that the primary Turkish objective in Cyprus is strategic, in which case, these communities in the south might be regarded as expendable though an excellent excuse for military or political moves. A military operation by the Turks which provoked such a response, would start a process whereby they could end up by occupying the whole island. The political odium would be considerable, but they might risk this if strategic reasons indicated that they should go ahead, or perhaps, if they fell victim to their own propaganda and were forced forward by internal political pressure.

7. It is worth pointing out that a pounce on Larnaca, alone or as part of a broader operation, would inevitably trap very large numbers of Greek Cypriot refugees behind the Turkish lines (and no doubt, in the ESBA). There would be no time to empty the sack of the Greek population as happened with the (deliberately?) ponderous advance on Famagusta last month. This would upset the demographic concept of a Turkish populated Turkish zone which Denktash has clearly signalled with his threat to bar the return to the north of young Greek Cypriot males, which is tantamount to barring breadwinners as a class. On the other hand, it would give the Turks a massive group of hostages to use in bargaining for the release north of the Turkish Cypriots in Greek-controlled areas. Freedom of movement for Greeks in the ESBA could even be traded off against that for the Turks in the WSBA. However, while such ideas may exist on drawing boards, their chances of being carried out without severe consequences for unfortunate civilians on both sides, seem slight.

8. Objectively, it would seem that time, like strength is on the Turkish side in Cyprus. Why therefore take another bloody gamble, when negotiation should eventually give a better result? The question is presumably whether the Turks view matters in the same light. Have they set themselves some timetable from which they are too inflexible to depart? Will they set artificial deadlines for the release of what we might describe as 'Sudeten Turks' (though heaven knows, the Turkish Cypriot community has suffered enough in the last 11 years at the hands of the Greeks without being used as a pawn now by the mainland Turks) and stick to them? We have no firm evidence, and the people in Denktash's 'Autonomous Administration' cannot give us any, as they are without voice or authority, and can say and do only as they are programmed.

9. The one thing that is clear, is that so long as there are Turkish Cypriots in Greek-controlled areas, the situation here will remain tense. While statements in Ankara by politicians about unilateral measures to save these communities may contain an element of bluff in order to put pressure on the Greek Cypriots, these threats are as likely to be counter-productive as productive, and could lead the Turks into doing exactly what they have threatened to do. And only strong American pressure at the crucial moment is going to stop that.

Yours ever,

M. PERCEVAL

No. 93

Record of meeting between Mr. Callaghan and Mr. Roussos at the Foreign and Commonwealth Office on 18 September 1974 at 3.15 p.m.

[*WSG 3/548/3*]

Confidential

Present:

The Rt. Hon. James Callaghan MP   HE Mr. Stavros H. Roussos
Mr. P.J. Weston
Mr. R.F. Cornish[1]

1. Mr. Callaghan welcomed Mr. Roussos as a representative of the new democratic Greece. Our policy was one of full support for Greece. The Council of Ministers on 17 September had welcomed a meeting of the Association Council at any time.[2] The British Government welcomed both the prospect of a new association in the EEC context and early progress in the Council of Europe. There might be some in Europe who would want further evidence of democracy in Greece, for example, elections, but we were prepared to move now. Mr. Roussos said that this would strengthen the Greek Government's position. Her relationship with Europe was a political matter, not a legalistic or technical one. The Chief Legal Adviser to the Council of Europe saw no reason to delay over Greece's readmission.[3]

2. Mr. Roussos said that he had been directed by Mr. Mavros to report to HMG on Mr. Mavros's recent visit to France, Germany and Belgium and on his latest thinking on Cyprus.[4] Mr. Mavros now accepted that a federal form of government in Cyprus was inevitable. It was important that the central power should have full authority to act as such. Turkey seemed to envisage a very loose federal link which would be no more than a cover-up for partition. Mr. Mavros thought it important that the separate

---

[1] Currently First Secretary in SEED.

[2] See No. 90, note 11. On 17 September the EC Council of Ministers agreed that they were ready to attend a Greek Association Council meeting at any time, and that they were prepared to offer: (1) the unfreezing of the Greece/EEC Association Agreement; (2) to sign an additional protocol extending the Association Agreement to the EC's new members (i.e. the UK, the Republic of Ireland and Denmark); (3) to negotiate an interim protocol; and (4) to unfreeze financial aid to Greece (SEED briefing paper of 18 September, WSG 2/579/2).

[3] *V. ibid.* The Foreign Ministers of the nine EC member states agreed on 16 September to support Greece's readmission to the Council of Europe.

[4] Mr. Roussos had recently met Mr. Mavros in Brussels.

administrations should exercise authority over territories commensurate with the size of the Greek and Turkish Cypriot populations. This was a matter not only of geography but also of economics, since Turkey now occupied 70-75% of Cyprus' total resources. Mr. Mavros attached importance to the human aspects of the Cyprus problem, and was particularly anxious that refugees should not be deprived of the possibility of returning to their homes. The resettlement in the North of Turks from other parts of the Island and from outside created a problem. Mr. Mavros also attached importance to the demilitarisation of Cyprus though in this he did not include the SBAs.

3. Mr. Mavros realised that HMG had reservations about discussing Cyprus in the UN. He hoped HMG understood that the Cypriots wanted to mobilise world opinion and wanted to use the UN as a safety valve. But the Greek Government would not press for an early debate in New York.[5]

4. *Mr. Callaghan* said he regarded a UN debate on Cyprus as inevitable but he hoped that the Cypriots would realise that it would not produce a solution and would not necessarily change the situation on the ground. The longer the situation was left, the more it would harden, and the less likely it would be that a federal solution acceptable to Greek Cypriots could be achieved. Presumably Cyprus would be an election issue in Greece. The Greek Government might be well advised to press ahead on Cyprus so that they could present firm arrangements to the Greek people before the elections. Britain was ready to return to a Conference, but only when there was some prospect of agreement. It seemed to him essential for the Greeks to work for a geographical solution involving a federal arrangement and some kind of boundary which could be negotiated. On the question of Turkish Cypriots in the Western SBA, he said this would be much easier to resolve if the Turks were to allow Greek Cypriots back to Famagusta.

5. *Mr. Roussos* said that HMG's position on Turkish refugees in the WSBA was wise.[6] The Turks had taken a similar attitude a few weeks ago when they had said that all matters must be resolved in the framework of a general settlement. It would be a grave injustice if the Turkish refugees were allowed to move to the North.

6. *Mr. Callaghan* emphasised that we could not stop them if they wanted to move overland. They were not hostages and were free to go. The only question which HMG were considering was the Turkish request to send ships to bring them to Turkey.[7] We had told everyone that this question

---

[5] Sir T. Brimelow had explained to Mr. Roussos on 11 September (see No. 89, note 24) that HMG 'did not think that the UN could solve the problem'. There would, he continued, 'be added complications if the problem was internationalised by discussion at the UN ... it might just create Turkish obstinacy'.

[6] During his meeting with Mr. Roussos on 11 September (*v. ibid.*) Sir T. Brimelow said that it was HMG's opinion that the humanitarian problem should be discussed 'as a whole' and the question of Turkish Cypriot refugees in the WSBA 'should not be discussed in isolation'.

[7] See No. 91.

should be settled by Clerides and Denktash, and for that reason had given no firm reply to the Turkish request. But the refugees could not stay in the bases for ever.[8] It was important to realise that Greek Cypriots were bound to suffer more in any settlement. There would be no equality of sacrifice. The sooner the settlement, the better for Greek Cypriots. In answer to a question, Mr. Callaghan said that he thought a Turkish area of 40% was much too large. It should be somewhere between 17% and 40%. The longer the settlement was delayed, the larger the Turkish area would be.

7. *Mr. Roussos* then said that the Turks were capitalising on every aspect of the Cyprus situation. They made political capital out of the refugees and out of Nicosia airport. Greece would be glad to see Britain repairing the airport but the preliminary conditions laid down by the Turks would prejudge the status of the airport. He hoped that the Americans would be prepared to exercise firm pressure on Turkey.

8. *Mr. Callaghan* said that criticism[s] of American actions were largely unjustified. They had been trying. The Turks were stubborn and even with the maximum American pressure they would have gone ahead with the invasion. Dr. Kissinger had in effect managed to preserve his credit with the Turks.[9]

9. Turning to Mr. Mavros's European visit, *Mr. Roussos* said Mr. Mavros had hoped that France and Germany would guarantee a loan to Greece from international institutions or from the oil producing countries. The Greek deficit would be US $400 million this year and they expected the same in 1975. Her reserves were only US $1000 million. The French were trying to get the Community to help but the Nine would have to conform to the lowest common denominator and Community action might not be very effective. The Germans had expressed concern over Greece's military withdrawal from NATO.[10] They had said that the EEC and NATO were two complementary organisations. They were also worried by the wave of anti-US feeling in Greece.

---

[8] As Mr. M.C.S. Weston pointed out in a submission of 19 September, that the pressures on the UK to release the refugees would grow, and it was already clear that a decision could not be delayed much longer since, quite apart from the cost (then running at £10,000—£15,000 per week), HMG increasingly lay itself open to the charge of denying the refugees their basic human rights (WSC 19/1).

[9] Cf. Nos. 84 and 88.

[10] According to SEED's briefing paper (see notes 2 and 3 above), while Mr. Mavros had made it clear in public that Greece would 'continue to boycott the military side of NATO even if a satisfactory solution was found to the Cyprus question', in private he had recently been less dogmatic. He had given the impression to the Belgian Permanent Representative to the NAC that as a result of his talks in Belgium, Germany and elsewhere, he was much less determined to press on with the withdrawal from the integrated defence organisation. No recommendations appeared yet to have been made by the Greek Chiefs of Staff regarding withdrawal, and no move had been made towards starting negotiations with the Americans for the closure of US military bases.

10. *Mr. Callaghan* said that he understood the reasons for Greece's decision over NATO and would not press the Greek Government on it except to express the hope that it would not be permanent. Reverting to Cyprus, he suggested that the Greek Government should consider under what conditions they would be prepared to return to the conference table; and that Mr. Mavros might do well to come to New York with some ideas in mind.[11] If the Greek Government, Archbishop Makarios and Mr. Clerides were able to stomach a genuine federal solution, he would regard this as a realistic approach and would do all he could to make such an arrangement work. He saw no case for double *enosis* or for partition. He had been concerned when Archbishop Makarios had told him that he was not happy about a geographical settlement. We all had to accept things which we were not happy about.[12]

11. Greece and the Greek Cypriots should now put forward some ideas on the nature of a federal state. If Archbishop Makarios was able to agree to them this would represent a good start. In answer to a question Mr. Callaghan said that he thought it was unrealistic to expect the Turks to accept a direct ratio between the size of the Turkish area and size of the Turkish Cypriot population. When asked if he thought the Turks would allow Greek Cypriot refugees to return to their homes he said this would have to be explored. The Turks would want a majority of Turkish people in their area. He guessed that if there was a good atmosphere Greek Cypriots would be allowed to return to the North and wind up their affairs over a few years. But he imagined that over time there might well be pressure for them to move.

12. One way or another Turkish Cypriots would find their way to the North and Greek Cypriots to the rest of the Island. There was much to be said to putting forward proposals rather than letting the matter settle. In answer to Mr. Roussos' remark that if the Turks were to get their way on refugees, they would have less incentive to go for a political settlement, Mr. Callaghan said he doubted that much leverage could be exerted on the Turks over refugees. Greek Cypriots might find it more important to aim for a withdrawal by the Turkish army. Once there was a settlement there would be a good case for such a withdrawal.

13. The British Government could put forward proposals for a settlement but we thought it better if these emerged from talks between Clerides and Denktash since a lasting solution would come best from within the Island. *Mr. Roussos* reaffirmed that the Greek Government wanted a settlement,

[11] Both Mr. Callaghan and Mr. Mavros were planning to attend the UN General Assembly at New York. During their meeting there on 23 September Mr. Mavros said that it was not possible to return to Geneva in the present circumstances and that the Greek Government considered the talks between Mr. Clerides and Mr. Dentash the 'best forum for negotiation' (record of a conversation between Mr. Callaghan and Mr. Mavros at the UN, New York, on 23 September at 4 p.m.).

[12] See No. 89.

but on honourable terms. When asked who should put forward firm proposals, he suggested that Mr. Callaghan and Mr. Mavros should discuss this in New York,[13] and observed that Dr. Kissinger would also be there.

[13] See note 11 above. During their conversation in New York, Mr. Mavros informed Mr. Callaghan that the Greek Government would agree to the division of Cyprus into two zones if the Cyprus Government did. The most important factor from the Greek point of view was, he insisted, how much territory the Turks would demand: 'they should not get much more than their percentage of the population justified'.

No. 94

Letter from Mr. Richards (Athens) to Mr. Goodison
[*WSG 1/5*]

Secret   ATHENS, *3 October 1974*

Dear Alan,

Greece, Cyprus and Turkey: Political Calculations

The date for the Greek election has now, as you know, been announced as 17 November.

2. The Greek Government is, I believe, under no illusion that a satisfactory settlement of the Cyprus problem can be achieved before the election. Indeed, the range within which any settlement could be achieved is not wide and a settlement, if it comes, will depend in broad terms upon Greek acceptance of a Turkish *fait accompli*. For Karamanlis and Mavros, therefore, the period before their election is one in which they need to be seen to be active in promoting the cause of the Greek Cypriots, but they do not in fact have any political interest in achieving a conclusion to the negotiating period before mid-November (this contrasts to some extent with the argument put by the Secretary of State to Mr Roussos on 18 September;[1] naturally our own interest in progress is less dominated by Greek electoral considerations than is that of Karamanlis and Mavros).

3. This manoeuvre is difficult but by no means impossible to achieve. They are, I should say, under considerable political pressure not to give away anything tangible in this period since that would afford a ready target for their critics and perhaps also a rallying point for hostility within the Armed Services. There is, however, relatively little sign of marked public mass pressure for early progress in Cyprus. This is in contrast with the very considerable and deep feeling of renewed hostility toward Turkey, a hostility which will certainly make government more difficult in the longer

[1] See No. 93.

run but which does not present immediate problems. There are also positive factors in the conciliatory tone adopted by Günes, both in his conversation with the Greek Ambassador in Ankara and also in Brussels. In the Foreign Ministry at least, the possibility of a satisfactory package being achieved was last week regarded as likely[2] and this was reflected to some extent outside, where there were expectations (shared by Mario Modiano[3] for example) that Dr. Kissinger was at last prepared to commit himself to working for an acceptable solution.

4. On the negative side, as seen from here, must be put the gravely weakened position of Clerides and the prospect of the deeper involvement of Makarios.[4] I share the Secretary of State's doubts about the ability of Karamanlis to control the Archbishop and his concern less Makarios wreck any possibility of constructive negotiations, but Karamanlis has been generally as forthcoming as could be hoped with Tassos Papadopoulos[5] this week and was categoric in his statement that Makarios cannot return to Cyprus while the crisis continues. One must add to this the consideration that the return of the Archbishop would put a renewed strain upon relations between Athens and Nicosia and re-open the whole question of

---

[2] In Nicosia telegram No. 1030 of 22 September Mr. Olver reported that Dr. Weckmann-Muñoz, who had been assisting in the Clerides-Denktash talks, claimed to have had a 'positive' response from Mr. Denktash and both the Greek and Turkish Embassies in Nicosia to soundings he had made for a solution based on a seven-point framework. This included: a preliminary agreement on the nature and powers of federal and local governments; a voluntary withdrawal of the Turkish army to an agreed demarcation line; a partial return of Greek Cypriot refugees to their homes; an inflow of Turkish Cypriots into the occupied area; and the participation of Greek and Turkish diplomats in talks in preparation for a five-party conference or other type of international meeting on Cyprus (WSC 1/19).

[3] The Athens correspondent of *The Times*.

[4] Mr. Olver reported in Nicosia telegram No. 1045 of 26 September that that morning he had found Mr. Clerides 'extremely depressed'. Mr. Clerides confirmed a statement already broadcast by the BBC that he expected Archbishop Makarios to return to Cyprus after the UN General Assembly debate, adding that he had made it clear to Mr. Karamanlis that this would cause internal trouble and 'reduce, if not extinguish, the chances of progress in his talks with Denktash or any negotiated settlement'. The Archbishop's return would, he said, inevitably result in his own resignation from not only the acting Presidency but from politics altogether (WSC 1/19). Mr. Callaghan, who had already urged Archbishop Makarios to refrain from public statements damaging to the Clerides-Denktash talks, subsequently suggested to Sir P. Ramsbotham that either the State Department or Dr. Kissinger might seek to influence him (telegram No. 2013 to Washington of 27 September, WSC 1/14).

[5] Deputy President of the Cyprus House of Representatives. In Nicosia telegram No. 1057 of 28 September Mr. Olver forecast that either Archbishop Makarios's return to Cyprus, or, in his continued absence, Mr. Papadopoulos's succession to Mr. Clerides as Acting President, seemed 'likely to be disastrous'. According to Mr. Olver, Cyprus Ministers regarded the likely inter-factional consequences of the Archbishop's return as serious, and Mr. Denktash had made it clear that 'though the Turks [were] willing to show flexibility to Clerides, they [would] not deal with Makarios—still less with Tassos Papadopoulos' (WSC 1/14).

the Greek officers and control of the National Guard.[6] This is fraught not only with implications for a settlement in Cyprus but also for Karamanlis' relations with the Greek Armed Forces here.

5. If it is accepted that the Greek Government wish to travel hopefully but not to arrive before 17 November, then their longer term objectives are less certain. Domestically it would be easier for almost any Greek Government to endure a *fait accompli* in Cyprus rather than to endorse an apparently inequitable division of the island by signing an agreement with the Turkish Government. On the other hand, as Mavros has from the start shown himself to be aware, the problem is inextricably tied up with a series of other problems between the two mainland countries, of which the Aegean, the continental shelf and the minorities in Thrace and in Turkey are the most obvious. A responsible Greek Government cannot but be aware that the Aegean problem is singularly intractable and that, if no settlement in Cyprus is agreed by Greece, then Turkish probing in the Aegean may well be resumed. Already they will have noted reports in the Greek press that further concessions have been let by the Turkish Government in the Aegean in areas claimed by Greece. And without an agreed settlement over Cyprus the omens for the Greek and Turkish minorities in Istanbul and Thrace must be poor. On the other hand, Greek agreement in Cyprus to a bi-regional solution, as postulated by Turkey, could provide a basis for the sort of global treatment of the two countries' problems that George Mavros and Bitsios have seemed to envisage.

6. To sum up, the Greek Government does not want a settlement before the elections. I do, however, believe that its more responsible members realise the need sooner or later to achieve a negotiated settlement and not merely to tolerate a *fait accompli*. This is partly because of the need to go on to negotiate the other Greek/Turkish problems, but partly also because they no doubt fear that the alternative may not be a continuance of the present *status quo* but that of the Turks assuming control of the island as a whole. This links up with my comments in a separate letter by this bag on Karamanlis' relations with the Armed Forces at this juncture.[7] With the possible return of Makarios and with the prospect of no negotiated

---

[6] In an address to the UN General Assembly on 1 October Archbishop Makarios stressed that any negotiations on the Cyprus problem would have to take place in a wider international conference than that at Geneva, and that negotiations could not begin whilst Cypriot territory remained under foreign occupation. He maintained that no argument could justify Turkey's demand for geographical federation, and insisted that it was 'imperative that the Turkish troops and indeed all foreign troops [were] withdrawn from Cyprus' (UKMIS New York telegram No. 1227 of 1 October, WSC 2/522/2). Cf. *UNGA Official Records, 29th session, Plenary Meetings*, vol. i, pp. 339-42.

[7] In a letter to Mr. Goodison of 2 October Mr. Richards noted with regard to the prospect of an election that while Mr. Karamanlis had 'the strength of public opposition to the junta to support him', he was 'handicapped by the fact that seemingly inevitable failure to resolve the Cyprus problem in a manner honourable and favourable for Greece [would] tend to consolidate army opinion against him'.

settlement for somewhile in Cyprus, Karamanlis' relations with the army will be put under strain and, in the worst case, the Aegean dispute may be revived. In that case it would be far harder for any Greek Government to decline conflict than has been the case in Cyprus, and to do so would be to run the further risks of a *coup* here.

Yours ever,
F.B. RICHARDS

No. 95

Minute from Mr. J.L. Bullard[1] to Sir. J. Killick

[*WSC 3/303/1*]

Confidential   FCO, *30 October 1974*

Soviet Policy on Cyprus

1. You and the PUS may like to see the replies from Moscow, Athens, Ankara and Nicosia to my letter telling them of his wish that we should keep a very careful eye on Soviet policy on Cyprus.[2]

2. The PUS was concerned that the Russians might possibly decide to throw their full weight behind the Greek and/or the Greek-Cypriot position, with the result that (to take an extreme illustration) we might wake up one morning to read the news of a Greco-Soviet Treaty of Friendship. There seems to be general agreement that this line of development is unlikely.[3]

3. We concluded in August (in 'Communist Policy and Tactics') that 'until the situation in Cyprus and Greece crystallises it is likely that the

---

[1] Head of Eastern European and Soviet Department (EESD).

[2] On 20 September Mr. Bullard wrote to Mr. B.G. Cartledge, Counsellor and Head of Chancery in the British Embassy in Moscow, to inform him that Sir T. Brimelow had asked EESD to 'keep a very careful eye on Soviet policy on Cyprus'. Mr. Bullard was personally of the opinion that 'the Russians were likely to continue to avoid a clear-cut commitment to either side', but he noted that there was an increased risk that 'international attitudes may polarise on Cyprus as they did between 1956 and 1973 over the Middle East'. He thought it unlikely either that the Greeks or the Turks would wish to draw close to the Soviet Union, or that the 'Soviet Union would be willing to drift into a more or less total non-relationship with Turkey as they eventually did with Israel' (ENS 2/1). Replies to Mr. Bullard's letter are not printed.

[3] But Mr. Richards pointed out in his reply of 9 October, addressed to Sir J. Killick, that in some groups within the Greek army 'notably the middle rank followers of the junta—views on external relations seem[ed] to have become so anti-American and anti-Western as to overlay fear of Communism'.

Russians will continue to avoid a clear-cut commitment to either side'.[4] I suggest that this remains true. There is no immediate prospect of a resolution of Cyprus's political problems; the world is awaiting the outcome of the Greek elections on 17 November; and in Turkey the dissolution of Mr. Eçevit's coalition has made the political future much less clear than it was.[5] Soviet objectives in Cyprus (as described by Mr. Day) are to prevent partition and to remove the British bases.[6] The first involves Soviet relations with Greece and Turkey (see below) more than with the Cyprus Government. The second is unlikely to be promoted by direct Soviet action or pressure. Events seem to be moving in that direction in any case.[7] The return of President Makarios to Cyprus would be a bonus for Soviet interests, but again it cannot be promoted by direct Soviet involvement. As Mr. Day points out, the Archbishop's return could also bring other problems.[8]

4. Nor would it appear to be in Soviet interests in the foreseeable circumstances to shift from their present policy of cautious cultivation of good relations with both Greece and Turkey towards outright support for Greece. I agree with Mr. Cartledge that the strategic importance of Turkey is the prime consideration in Soviet minds. If anything, this has become more important as a result of the Cyprus crisis, and the Russians will not be willing to sacrifice their careful and persistent effort over many years towards better relations with Turkey.[9] The Russians are of course aware of

[4] Not printed. *Communist Policy and Tactics* was a monthly review of current developments in the Communist world, prepared by the FCO for circulation within the British diplomatic service.

[5] On 18 September the Turkish Government collapsed when the NSP withdrew from its coalition with Mr. Eçevit's RPP. Mr. Eçevit remained in office in a caretaker capacity and, following an unsuccessful attempt to form a new Government, was appointed Prime Minister-designate on 10 October.

[6] Mr. D.M. Day, the Counsellor in the British High Commission, Nicosia, suggested these two objectives in a letter to Mr. Bullard of 2 October describing a conversation he had had on 30 September with the Counsellor of the Soviet Embassy in Nicosia.

[7] Sir T. Garvey doubted if the extrusion of the British from the SBAs was a 'major current motivation' for the Russians. In a letter to Sir J. Killick of 23 October, he wrote: 'They have heard about the Defence Review. They probably reckon that the SBAs will drop into Cyprus's lap before very long. But they need to know who on the Cypriot side will be there to catch them. Meanwhile, they probably see the UK presence as a stabilising, and not very troublesome, element in what is otherwise a rather distorted situation.'

[8] In his letter to Mr. Bullard (see note 6 above) Mr. Day had reported that the Counsellor of the Soviet Embassy had conceded that the early return of Archbishop Makarios to Cyprus might lead to 'fresh divisions' within the Greek Cypriot community. Mr. Day thought that this might indicate that the Russians feared that a consequence of the Archbishop's return could be a 'further consolidation of Turkish control over the north and thus be one step further towards partition'.

[9] In a letter to Mr. Bullard of 25 September Mr. Cartledge observed: 'I feel reasonably certain that the Russians regard their relations with Ankara as being a far more important and delicate issue both in the short and longer term than consolidating a new relationship with the

the new possibilities for advancement in Greece but these will only bear fruit as a result of slow and careful investment. The Russians will certainly be aware of the political hostility towards Communism which remains in Greece (described by Mr. Richards in his letter).[10] At the same time they are aware that pressures for political changes favourable to Soviet interests are being generated domestically in Greece, and need not be bought by Soviet concessions.

5. I believe that in their usual style the Russians will continue to ride both horses as long as it is possible to do so. Only determined and sustained Turkish hostility, which is very unlikely to occur, could force the Russians off their present posture into a one-sided commitment to Greece. In any case, the Russians are not doing too badly with their present policy. Soviet fear of being excluded from the making of a Cyprus settlement will have abated for the time being since no progress is being made in any case. They are not being upstaged, since the stage is empty and dark. This may change as the US deadline of 10 December approaches.[11] But the Russians will continue to try to avoid making their position on Cyprus any more precise (which could only lead to disagreement with either Athens or Ankara). Their generalised, insubstantial and propagandist line on Cyprus has a certain appeal for the non-aligned and even for Greece and Turkey. As a result they are able, in bilateral discussions with both countries, to point to wide areas of common ground and to receive occasional praise from both for the constructiveness of their attitude.[12]

Greeks ... They will of course wish to ride both horses for so long as they can, and they have so far contrived to do so without falling off. But the geographical proximity of Turkey, and in particular its control of the Dardanelles, is the essential strategic point which will be uppermost in Soviet minds. ... the Soviets have as much to lose as the Turks from a deterioration in Soviet/Turkish relations.' Mr. Cartledge, nevertheless, expected that if and when the prospect of Archbishop Makarios re-establishing his personal authority became a 'real possibility', the Russians would be 'prepared to apply a little firmer pressure than hitherto in Ankara' (ENS 2/1).

[10] Mr. Richards explained in his letter to Sir J. Killick (see note 3 above) that the views of Greek army officers from the rank of major upwards appeared 'still very largely to be coloured by the nationalist and anti-Communist sentiments generated by the civil wars of the late 1940s'.

[11] On 19 and 24 September first the US Senate, and then the House of Representatives, passed resolutions calling for the suspension of American military aid to Turkey. These were the prelude to a clash between Congress and the Administration, during which Dr. Kissinger's diplomacy was subjected to considerable criticism. Finally, on 16 October, following their failure to overturn a Presidential veto, both Houses passed a new continuing resolution on foreign aid which allowed President Ford to defer the suspension of military aid to Turkey until 10 December, on condition that no arms provided by the US to Turkey were sent to Cyprus (Washington telegrams Nos. 3369 and 3407 of 16 and 18 October, WST 3/304/1). Cf. No. 90, note 1.

[12] Sir T. Garvey did not think the Russians had a 'master-plan'. 'Hence', he observed in his letter to Sir J. Killick of 23 October, 'their time-wasting gimmicks ... While waiting for something to turn up they do what they can to maintain their support on the ground (AKEL) and to keep the Archbishop dusted off for possible re-entry' (see note 7 above).

6. The available evidence (including some from unusual sources) on Greek and Turkish attitudes to the Soviet Union suggests that, although they are willing in bilateral discussions to emphasise the common ground for atmospheric reasons, they are both fully aware of the points of differences, and wary of Soviet intentions. Greek behaviour suggests that they are willing to give an impression of harmony with the USSR in public in order to emphasise their disenchantment with NATO. In private, however, they are ready to complain to the Russians and to argue robustly with them about the Soviet record. The possibility that Mavros may split away from Karamanlis as the election campaign proceeds (with Mavros taking a more pro-Soviet line) will not be lost on the Russians, and there is some evidence that the Russians have begun to encourage divisions between them already.

7. As Mr. Fyjis-Walker says in his letter, the Turks are taking care to avoid unnecessary complications with the Russians.[13] But, as we have seen over the Soviet proposal for an international conference and over the question of 'foreign' troops, the Turks are willing to stand up to the Russians for their vital interests. We may therefore see Turkish concessions to the Russians over small matters unrelated to Cyprus in order to keep general relations harmonious. There are indications that the Turks are taking a harder line over ship visits by NATO navies to Turkish Black Sea ports, and there is the story (on which I have minuted separately) that the Turks may authorise Soviet trains to cross Turkey carrying arms supplies for Syria and Iraq.

8. My conclusion is that Soviet policy on Cyprus continues much as before, keeping good relations with both Greece and Turkey and avoiding commitment to any specific solutions to the problems of Cyprus.

9. Our article in 'Communist Policy and Tactics' has come in for some criticism from posts. I am glad that it was read with such attention, as a result of my letter, even if not for its own sake at the time. I acknowledge the validity of the comments although I do not think Mr. Richards' points were ignored in the article to the degree suggested in his letter.[14]

---

[13] Mr. Fyjis-Walker pointed out in a letter to Mr. Bullard of 22 October that when the Russians discovered that the Turks were unmoved by exhortations to remove all foreign troops from Cyprus or to agree to an international conference, they had seemed 'to have been careful immediately to back pedal and to push nothing unacceptable to the Turks'. He also explained: 'A cardinal point of Turkish policy has undoubtedly been to avoid unnecessary complications with their neighbours so long as this did not mean knuckling under to them: and so far the Russians have humoured them.'

[14] In his letter (see notes 3 and 10 above) Mr. Richards observed that *Communist Policy and Tactics* had left him 'with a feeling that, partly because the analysis proceeded on a country by country basis, the picture of Soviet Union in a series of inhibiting quandaries may to some extent be misleading when the region is regarded as a whole'. Mr. Richards argued that *Communist Policy and Tactics* left 'a misleading and over-complacent' impression that recent events in Cyprus had 'made matters worse from the Soviet point of view in the area as a whole', when the disintegration of NATO cooperation in the region, US unpopularity in Greece, US/Turkish strains, and the restoration of the Greek Communist Party to legal activity were 'major gains'.

10. I will thank the 4 posts in due course.[15]

J.L. BULLARD

[15] On 1 November Sir J. Killick noted on this minute that, although the Soviet interpretation of *détente* did not debar the Russians from fomenting trouble in the Western world, sooner or later the Americans must be expected to make it clear to them that trouble-making throughout the Mediterranean area would prejudice their overall relationship. 'Both the Cyprus situation itself, and the complex of other situations in Southern Europe, necessitate', he reasoned, 'a significant degree of caution and probably lead to a good deal of indecision on the Soviet side. I believe that an important element in this must be Soviet reluctance to become landed with the sort of open-ended economic commitments which successful Soviet support of Communist take-overs in all these countries would inevitably bring.' Sir T. Brimelow added on 5 November: 'On the whole bleakly reassuring, Many thanks.'

No. 96

Letter from Mr. Goodison to Mr. Day (Nicosia)

[*WSC 1/16*]

Confidential   FCO, *1 November 1974*

British Responsibility for the Cyprus Crisis

1. In your letter of 21 October you reported the Foreign Minister and others' view that HMG had failed in their responsibilities under the Treaty of Guarantee.[1] In his letter of 24 October about a recent visit of Greek journalists to the UK (a letter not copied elsewhere) Brooks Richards reported that not only Karamanlis, whose exchanges on this topic with him and with Robin Hooper have been recorded in telegrams, but substantial numbers of Greek officials and others take the same view in conversation with our people in Athens.[2] Nor are we immune here; the Cyprus High

[1] Mr. Day reported in this letter on conversations he had recently had with Mr. Christofides and Mr. N. Pattichis, the Cyprus Minister of Communications and Works. Both expressed their serious disappointment at HMG's failure to fulfil what they regarded as its obligations under the Treaty of Guarantee. 'There is', Mr. Day reflected, 'strong feeling here, not merely confined to members of the Government, that the British should have "done something" and that our long association with Cyprus reinforced by the Treaty of Guarantee placed special and unique responsibility upon us.'

[2] In this letter of 24 October Mr. Richards pointed out that while Mr. Mavros had been 'well-disposed' towards Mr. Callaghan and the British team at Geneva, 'it would be a mistake to conclude that there [had] been no continuing disposition [in Athens] to criticise British policy about the eventual outcome of the crisis'. He explained that after the break up of Geneva II 'the Greeks were not slow to say that we had failed in our responsibilities as a guarantor power'. It would, he concluded, 'be unwise to dismiss this as a passing phase of emotional pique: I fear that as a result of our alleged failure as a guarantor power and the stories about military collusion with the Turks, unfounded as these were, our position as a major Western friend of Greece has slipped'.

318

Commissioner played the same record to me on 23 October and I recently spent much of an otherwise agreeable Dutch dinner party refuting similar arguments from an Englishwoman who knows Cyprus well. They both took the view that it had been our job to overthrow Sampson by force.

2. Meanwhile, the Turks tell me that it is our fault if we do not like what has happened. Had we accepted Eçevit's magnanimous proposal at No. 10 Downing Street all would have been well.[3] I told their Minister Counsellor on 24 October that even if I could have foreseen the future my advice to the Prime Minister would have been the same.

3. I entirely endorse your line, particularly the point that we would have put at risk the lives not only of British service families but also of tourists in Cyprus and in Greece. No one will admit that we could not have foreseen that Sampson and the Greek junta would fall so easily. Robin Hooper made the point effectively (Athens tel[egram] No. 520).[4] But the bull point, which you know well, and which I do not make to foreigners for fear of making us look foolish, is that we did not in fact have any troops to spare from internal security duties in the SBAs for any kind of offensive action even if we had wished to contemplate it. There was little point therefore in discussing whether we should or should not use troops.[5]

4. Another line, which can be used with Greeks and not with Turks, is that if it is their view that Articles 2, 4 and 103 of the UN Charter[6] override the Turkish claim, that Article 4 of the Treaty of Guarantee justifies the use of force in Cyprus,[7] then the Charter must also prevent HMG from using force. Or, more generally, that if the Treaty does not authorize the use of force by Turkey then it does not authorize the use of force by us. Furthermore they might be reminded that Archbishop

---

[3] See No. 25.

[4] In this telegram of 2 September Sir R. Hooper recorded that when, that day, he had paid a farewell call on Mr. Karamanlis, the latter had complained that 'although Britain had had the right, the duty and the means to intervene in Cyprus, she had failed to do so'. Sir R. Hooper replied that neither he nor HMG could accept these criticisms and that the means at Britain's disposal for discharging its duties under the Treaty of Guarantee were 'far less extensive than appeared to be generally assumed'. He added that an intervention in the early stages of the Cyprus crisis could only have been against the *coup d'état* for which Mr. Karamanlis's predecessors had been largely responsible, and he asked what Mr. Karamanlis imagined the reaction to this would have been in Greece?

[5] See No. 75.

[6] Article 2 of the UN Charter specifies that all members should 'refrain in their international relations from the threat and use of force against the territorial integrity or political independence of any state, or in any other manner inconsistent with the Purposes of the United Nations'; and Article 4 makes membership dependent on states accepting the obligations contained in the Charter and their ability and will to fulfil these obligations. Article 103 states that in the event of a conflict between the obligations of UN members under the Charter and their obligations under any other international agreement, their obligations under the Charter should prevail.

[7] See No. 1, note 8.

Makarios denounced the Treaty of Guarantee as invalid over ten years ago. His supporters cannot invoke it to criticize us now.

5. But the fact is surely that people who are in a mess usually seek an external scapegoat and it is more agreeable to blame the British than themselves for it. Rational argument cannot stop them from seeking to put the responsibility on our shoulders in order to remove it from their own. In most cases, their motivation is probably unconscious. In the case of the Archbishop it will not be, and in Ashiotis at any rate, if not in Christophides and Pattichis, I hear the Master's voice. While we should not hesitate to reply to such criticisms as forcibly as we can, my view is that for a long time to come we shall have to be used to hearing them.

6. If I am right, then although we should not lose sight of our unpopularity, we should not allow it to influence our policies. In the conversation quoted in Paragraph 2 above, the Turkish Minister Counsellor said 'on a purely personal basis' that no one in Turkey could understand why we valued a settlement in Cyprus more highly than the friendship of the Turkish people—for this was how they interpreted our refusal to allow the Turkish Cypriots in the WSBA to leave. I would know that we were universally loathed for our cruelty. I replied that if that was the attitude of the Turkish Government I could not understand how they rated the temporary difficulties of 8-9,000 Turkish Cypriots as more important than securing the long term future of 100,000. He said he was speaking more of public opinion and the press. I answered that at the height of the Timothy Davey affair,[8] both in Turkey and here, public opinion and the press had been inflamed against one another, yet I thought both there and here this had been forgotten. I hoped this would prove an equally passing phase.

7. I went on to say that if HMG were to play a useful part in achieving a settlement I thought we must be not only impartial but frank and truthful about our views. I would adhere to that policy. I had in mind a dictum of the Secretary of State, who said to me after a talk with Archbishop Makarios this summer: 'That is a very wicked man: I have only one rule in dealing with wicked men; I always speak the truth'. I do not think this is a bad rule in dealing with all the parties to the Cyprus dispute. But I am straying from my theme.

8. I am writing separately about the views you quote on the form of settlement.[9]

A.C. GOODISON

[8] See No. 11, note 5.

[9] Mr. Goodison wrote in this letter to Mr. Day, also of 1 November, that in general he avoided advocating in any detail the form of a final settlement on the grounds that this was for the communities to decide. 'I stick', he noted, 'to the formula that in our view a biregional federation holds the best promise of a durable solution and go no further.'

No. 97

Mr. Richard (UKMIS New York) to Mr. Callaghan

Saving No. 182 Telegraphic [WSC 2/522/2]

Confidential   NEW YORK, *4 November 1974*

Repeated for information to Saving Ankara, Athens, Nicosia, Paris, Washington, CBFNE.

My immediately preceding Saving telegram:[1]
UN General Assembly: Plenary: Agenda Item 110: Cyprus

1. Both the debate on Cyprus and the efforts by the non-aligned coordinating committee[2] to work out a compromise draft resolution proceeded sluggishly all week. On 31 October the committee had drawn up another text for the draft which gave the Greek Cypriots most of what they wanted on withdrawal of troops and the immediate return of refugees to their homes. In discussing this draft with members of the committee, Gunesh [Mr. Günes] took the line that, if it was tabled, he would instruct his delegation to vote against it and would return at once to Ankara (cf. his performance at Geneva). The committee then thought again and, during 1 November, produced the draft which was eventually adopted, knowing that it would not be opposed by Turkey. Guyana, which had consistently taken the Greek Cypriot side in the non-aligned coordinating committee, refused to co-sponsor. The non-aligned having tabled their draft, Kyprianou[3] attempted to secure additional preambular paragraphs, mentioning the support of Greece and Turkey for Cyprus's sovereignty, independence and

---

[1] UKMIS New York Saving telegram No. 181 of 4 November reported that on 1 November, after five days of debate on the Cyprus question, the UN General Assembly had adopted Resolution 3212. This (1) called on all states to respect the sovereignty, independence, territorial integrity and non-alignment of Cyprus and 'to refrain from all acts and interventions directed against it'; (2) urged the speedy withdrawal of all foreign armed forces from the Republic and 'the cessation of all foreign interference'; (3) considered that the constitutional system of Cyprus concerned Greek Cypriot and Turkish Cypriot communities; (4) commended the contacts and negotiations taking place on an equal footing between the two communities and called for their continuation 'with a view to reaching freely a mutually acceptable political settlement, based on their fundamental and legitimate rights'; (5) considered that all refugees should return to their homes in safety; (6) expressed the hope that, if necessary, further negotiations could take place within the framework of the UN; (7) asked the Secretary-General to continue to provide UN humanitarian assistance to all parts of the population of Cyprus; and (8) called upon all parties to cooperate fully with UNFICYP, which might be strengthened if necessary (UKMIS New York telegram No. 1526 of 2 November). See *UNGA Official Records, 29th session*, Supplement No. 31 (A/9631), p. 3.

[2] This committee, elected by the non-aligned states, consisted of representatives of Guyana, India and Yugoslavia.

[3] Mr. S. Kyprianou was Cyprus delegate to the UN General Assembly.

territorial integrity and also incorporating preambular paragraph 6 of his own draft (A/L 738).[4] The sponsors wisely refused to consider any amendment whatever and decided to push the resolution through on 1 November, since they feared that further attempts at amendment and additional dispute would develop if there was any delay over voting.

2. The Greek Cypriots over-played their hand to some extent. The Turkish Cypriot case was presented with considerable skill in the Special Political Committee (my tel[egram] No. 166 saving of 27 October).[5] Not only the recital of what the Turkish Cypriots had had to put up with but the exposure of the Greek Cypriot attachment to independence and non-alignment probably had some effect. On the other hand, the sentiment of the Assembly was clearly against the indefinite maintenance of a large body of Turkish troops in Cyprus and in favour of a speedy resolution of the refugee problem, without their being made part of the haggle over a political settlement. The outcome may therefore have been to impress upon the Greek Cypriots that they could not expect the international community to secure for them any of the conditions which they sought to impose as a preliminary to negotiation; but the Turks may also have been impressed by the sense of disapproval of the scale of their military operations and the evident desire that they now behave with magnanimity, particularly over the resettlement of refugees and the reduction of their military presence.

3. Although the East Europeans and Cuba dutifully supported the Russian proposals over an international conference,[6] these proposals were studiously ignored by all other contributors to the debate. Not even the Greek Cypriot representatives bothered with them. The Russian explanation of vote indicates that they will keep on trying but they cannot have been encouraged by the course or outcome of this debate.[7]

4. In the latter stages of the debate, the Turkish delegation and the Turkish Cypriot representatives had been dropping broad hints about the likelihood of substantial Turkish concessions in Cyprus before the Greek

---

[4] This preambular paragraph noted the Cyprus Government's opposition to the annexation of the Republic, or any part of it, by any other state, 'or to the merger of the Republic or any part of it with any other State, or to its partition or division in any form'. *UNGA Official Records, 29th session*, Annexes, Agenda Item 10.

[5] This is evidently a reference to UKMIS New York telegram No. 166 of 29 October, which reported on the morning session of the Assembly's Special Political Committee. Mr. V.A. Chelik, representing the Turkish Cypriot Community, had then argued that 'Makarios and the perpetrators of the 15 July coup differed only over timing and modalities: both aimed at *enosis*', and that *coup* had 'swept away whatever elements of legality remained in Cyprus, putting the whole population and the stability of the region in jeopardy'.

[6] See No. 83, note 9.

[7] Mr. Richard reported in UKMIS New York Saving telegram No. 181 (see note 1 above) that the Soviet delegate, Mr. V.L. Issraelyan, had said, after the passage of Resolution 3212, that 'effective steps' were still required to secure the future of Cyprus, and that an 'international conference under the aegis of the UN remained the best way'.

elections.[8] The Turkish Mission profess ignorance of the details of any Turkish move but the implication was that it might include both a withdrawal which would allow a significant number of refugees to be resettled and reduction in the number of Turkish troops in Cyprus. No hints were given as to whether the Greek part of Famagusta would be included in the area from which the Turks would withdraw.

5. I hope you will agree that the outcome of the debate was reasonably satisfactory. Our own interests in Cyprus were never seriously threatened and have been adequately safeguarded. The negotiating process may have been assisted: there was widespread support for the Clerides/Denktash talks.[9] While any wider negotiation is seen as taking place in a UN framework and there was strong opposition to any return to the Geneva forum, the Russians got nowhere in pushing their proposal for a major international conference. Some pressure may have been exerted on the Turks and the Greek Cypriots may have been made aware of the need for greater realism in negotiating. In short, the debate and resolution may do some good and are unlikely to do any harm; this was as much as we dared to hope for when the discussion started.

[8] *V. ibid.* Mr. Günes told the General Assembly that once the Greeks had accepted that the 'recognition of strict equality between the two communities was the *sine qua non* of "peaceful and harmonious co-existence and collaboration among citizens of the federal Cypriot State"', the 'delimitation of the federal zones, the withdrawal of Turkish forces and other questions would be resolved in negotiation amongst Turkey, Greece and the representatives of the Turkish and Greek communities'.

[9] Mr. Denktash seemed to hold out the prospect of some progress in the talks when on 14 October he indicated to Mr. Clerides that the Turks were thinking of a withdrawal of forces in the Larnaca and Famagusta districts, and that they might be prepared to move back in the area of Pyroi. This may, as Mr. Clerides surmised, have been intended to strengthen Mr. Clerides's position. But Mr. Day thought it inconceivable that Mr. Denktash would have dropped these hints without some authority from Ankara, and unlikely that the Turks would be prepared to make such a significant gesture unless they were able to obtain something in return, such as Mr. Clerides's public acceptance of a bi-regional federation (Nicosia telegram No. 1142 of 16 October, WSC 1/19).

No. 98

Record of a meeting held at the Foreign and Commonwealth Office on 8 November 1974 at 3.15 p.m.

[*WSC 10/14*]

Secret

Present:

Sir Thomas Brimelow	Sir John Hunt,[1] Cabinet Office
Sir John Killick	Mr. H.F.T. Smith,[2] Cabinet
Mr. J.A. Thomson[3]	Office
Mr. H.T. Morgan[4]	Mr. A.P. Hockaday, MoD
Mr. J.E. Cable	Cdr. B.C. Perowne, MoD
Mr. J.E. Jackson	
Mr. A.C. Goodison	
Mr. M. Elliott	
Mr. M.C.S. Weston	

1. The meeting was held to discuss the agenda at Annex A.[5] The draft paper (agenda item (*a*)) is at Annex B.[6]

2. *Sir J. Hunt* said that Ministers had decided that our preferred course was to withdraw from both SBAs. They recognised that this might not be possible and their decision was provisional, since some members of the Cabinet were against withdrawal. Ministers felt, however, that even if we could not withdraw totally, we should make substantial reductions. Withdrawal was a course to be worked towards, but not something about which Ministers would wish to make a statement. It was not intended that anything should be said about withdrawal from Cyprus in the statement to be made to Parliament on the Defence Review on 3 December. *Mr. Hockaday* said that, as he understood it, the most that would be said on 3 December was that withdrawal from the SBAs might take place as part of a general Cyprus settlement and that meanwhile there would be some

---

[1] Secretary to the Cabinet.

[2] Deputy Secretary to the Cabinet. See No. 140, note 9.

[3] AUS superintending Defence Department.

[4] AUS superintending SEED from September.

[5] Not printed. The agenda listed ten items relating to what Ministers intended with regard to the SBAs, how any decision should be presented to the Americans and other parties, and the modalities of withdrawal.

[6] Not printed. After recalling the agreement reached in the Cabinet's Defence and Oversea Policy Committee at its meeting on 9 September (see No. 82, note 14), this FCO draft paper examined various options for disposing of the SBAs. It argued that a decision to withdraw 'would give us a card of potential value in promoting a settlement'.

reductions. He assumed, however, that something would be said to the Americans about our preferred course. The MoD would not dissent from the view expressed in the paper that withdrawal was a good card with which to promote a settlement. But the timing of playing it would require careful consideration. *Sir J. Killick* said that we had previously understood that a reference to withdrawal from Cyprus would be included in the statement on the Defence Review. The paper was therefore intended to make a virtue of a necessity.[7] In his view, the earlier we played the card, the better.

3. After Sir J. Hunt had confirmed that there would be no mention of withdrawal from the SBAs in the statement on 3 December, *Sir Thomas Brimelow* said that the starting point for the FCO in drafting the paper had been Mr. Callaghan's wish to withdraw. The aim of the paper was to decide how best withdrawal could be presented. *Mr. Hockaday* said that the MoD were content with the paper, as revised. In the light of what Sir J. Hunt had said, the first sentence of paragraph 20[8] would need revision. He was also doubtful about the statement in the last sentence of paragraph 19 that giving both the bases to the Greek Cypriots would be least likely to lead to further difficulties in the longer term.[9] *Sir J. Killick* said that if we found that we could not withdraw, it was essential that we should make clear that UK forces in the SBAs were not available for use in Cyprus itself. *Sir J. Hunt* thought that it should be made clear in the course of the negotiations on a settlement that the SBAs were available. Perhaps more thought should be given to the economic facts (paragraph 9 of the draft paper).[10] *Sir T. Brimelow* suggested that the speaking note should be made rather more provisional. He suggested a number of amendments with this aim in view. (These are incorporated in the revised draft speaking note at Annex C.)[11] The speaking note should perhaps be regarded more as a negotiating draft than as an actual speaking note.

[7] In a letter to Mr. Hockaday of 5 November, covering copies of the draft paper, the draft agenda and a speaking note, Sir J. Killick observed 'in general political terms, the aim of demilitarisation provides the best rationale for our decision to withdraw by raising it from the straight calculation of national interest (which it is) to a defensible international act' (RS 14/1).

[8] This stated: 'The talks envisaged in this paper would be extremely difficult, since they would be taking place after it had become publicly known that we were proposing to withdraw.'

[9] Paragraph 19 considered the options and implications of withdrawal from either or both SBAs. It foresaw difficulties in handing over the ESBA to the Turkish Cypriots because of the large area in the vicinity of Cape Greco which would then accrue to them.

[10] This pointed out that the loss of spending power resulting from a British withdrawal 'would be a grave blow to the economy of the island, more particularly to the area remaining under Greek Cypriot control'.

[11] Not printed. This draft speaking note, prepared for discussions with the Americans, affirmed that the British believed that 'agreement on the demilitarisation of the whole of Cyprus would be an important factor in any lasting settlement', and that in this context and in that of the current Defence Review, HMG had decided to relinquish the SBAs.

4. *Sir J. Hunt* said that he intended to take the following line with the Americans:

(*a*) Retention of the SBAs is expensive.

(*b*) It was never intended that the troops in the SBAs should be used in Cyprus. In the recent crisis, the troops had, however, been a liability.

(*c*) A decision had been taken to reduce the RAF element next spring.

(*d*) Our preferred course was to get out. If this card was played at the right time, we believed that it could help in achieving a peace settlement.

(*e*) In any case we should wish to reduce our presence and concentrate it. [...]¹² How did the Americans see it?

In answer to questions, he would add that no mention of Cyprus would be made in the statement to Parliament on 3 December.

5. *Sir J. Hunt* wondered how his discussion with the Americans should be followed up. *Sir T. Brimelow* suggested that there should be separate Anglo/US consultations on Cyprus, preferably in London. In answer to questions, *Sir J. Hunt* said that, if there was a leak, he would propose to go no further than the general line agreed for the whole Defence Review, saying that the subjects discussed in Washington were ones of common UK/US interest. As for speaking to the Germans, he would propose to take the same line [...].¹³ In speaking to NATO, we should present the straightforward military facts about the Defence Review and say nothing about the SBAs, except about the withdrawal of the Vulcans. If the Americans raised great objections, the problem would have to be considered by Ministers again. He suggested that we should also make clear to NATO that we were flexible about withdrawal from the SBAs. *Mr. Thomson* and *Mr. Goodison* both suggested that it would be unwise to reveal our hand in this way. *Sir T. Brimelow* suggested that we should only say that we were ready to consider what steps would best contribute to a lasting solution. *Sir J. Hunt* accepted this and said that he would say to the Americans that we had no intention of telling NATO yet that we were ready to get out.

6. There was a brief discussion of the remaining items on the agenda. In the course of this, *Mr. Hockaday* said that the Chief of Staff was doubtful about the concept of demilitarisation. *Sir J. Killick* explained that the concept had been introduced largely to justify withdrawal. The Chief of Staff's point was well taken. It was agreed that the possibility of a "fighting" or "operational" withdrawal should be considered. However, if Akrotiri was available, the Service personnel and the remaining families could, if necessary, be got out of Cyprus within 48 hours.

7. It was agreed that there was no need to consult Heads of Mission at this stage. They should, however, be informed of the results of Sir J. Hunt's

---

¹² A sentence is here omitted.

¹³ A phrase is here omitted.

visit to Washington.[14] It was also agreed that it would probably be necessary at some stage to set up an interdepartmental committee to deal with the problems arising from the rundown of the SBAs. *Mr. Hockaday* suggested that this might be based on the committee which had been set up to deal with Appendix R problems.[15]

8. *Mr. Jackson* said that the FCO had been asked for their views on the proposal to halve the number of aircraft in Cyprus by 1 February 1975. *Sir T. Brimelow* suggested that we should delay giving the FCO's formal views until Sir J. Hunt returned from Washington.

[14] On 14 November Sir J. Hunt reported to the Defence and Oversea Policy Committee on his consultations with Dr. Kissinger and Dr. J.R. Schlesinger, the US Secretary of Defense, in Washington on 12 November on the implications of the Defence Review. During these consultations Dr. Kissinger expressed his concern about the situation in the eastern Mediterranean and the 'relative decline of Western influence there': he would, he stated, 'therefore be strongly opposed to the withdrawal of the British presence in Cyprus, a development which he did not believe would assist in achieving a satisfactory political settlement in the island'. The same objections, Dr. Kissinger said, did not apply to a reduction in the size of British forces on the island provided Britain retained the SBAs (minutes, OPD(74) 17th mtg.).

[15] This is a reference to the interdepartmental committee dealing with problems arising from Appendix R to the British White Paper on Cyprus (Cmnd. 1093) of 1960. Appendix R, which came into effect through the Exchange of Notes appended to the Treaty of Establishment (see No. 1, note 20), provided for British financial assistance to Cyprus after independence. The situation was due for review every five years and in 1965, in the wake of intercommunal strife, the UK decided to suspend further aid (cf. No. 3, note 5). However, in August 1973 the Cyprus Government presented HMG with claims for £76.6 million for the use by British forces of various sites, services and facilities during the previous eight years. While Conservative Ministers were ready to discuss the resumption of financial assistance, on condition that both Cypriot communities benefited, the incoming Labour Government insisted that there could be no substantive negotiations on aid pending the outcome of the Defence Review (minute from Mr. Goodison to Mr. Wiggin of 8 July, WSC 6/548/1).

No. 99

Mr. Callaghan to Mr. Richards (Athens)

No. 388 Telegraphic [*WSC 3/304/2*]

Immediate. Secret FCO, *15 November 1974, 7.10 p.m.*

Repeated for information to Priority Ankara, Nicosia and Washington.

Your tel[egram No.] 639:[1]
Cyprus

1. Please seek an interview with Bitsios before the new Greek Government is formed, and convey to him orally the following from me.

2. I am very grateful to Bitsios for his account of his talk with Kissinger[2] and of his meeting with Günes in New York. I greatly appreciate his taking me into his confidence. Although there is a hiatus in negotiations over the future of Cyprus (apart from the Clerides/Denktash talks). I think it useful and important that we should continue to keep in touch and explore the possibility of extending the common ground between the parties.

3. While wider negotiations are in abeyance, the main way forward must be the Clerides/Denktash talks and I am very glad that Mr. Karamanlis has given them the support which they deserve. I hope that Clerides and Denktash will be able to make some advance in their private talks on the political issues. It is a pity that Dr. Kissinger's visit to Ankara did not come off.[3] In the internal political situation prevailing in Turkey, it may not prove possible to hold fruitful discussions with the Turks for some time yet, but I hope that Dr. Kissinger's ideas on Turkish concessions were in principle welcome to the Greeks.

---

[1] In this telegram of 8 November Mr. Richards reported a meeting with Mr. Bitsios, Mr. Mavros's successor as Greek Foreign Minister. Mr. Bitsios had recently been in Rome for the UN World Food Conference, and he informed Mr. Richards of a conversation he had had there with Dr. Kissinger on 5 November (WSC 1/16). Dr. Kissinger had been planning to visit Ankara in order, he informed Mr. Callaghan, 'to obtain some modest gestures and strong backing for [the] Clerides-Denktash talks' (Washington telegram No. 3638 of 8 November).

[2] *V. ibid.* According to Mr. Bitsios, the concessions Dr. Kissinger was prepared to try to extract from the Turks included a pull-back in the Famagusta area. But in response to Dr. Kissinger's request for 'explicit Greek acceptance of the principle of a federation on a geographical basis', Mr. Bitsios had said that it was 'quite impossible for him as Foreign Minister of a caretaker Government and on the eve of the Greek election to make the concession'. Mr. Bitsios nevertheless told Mr. Richards that he knew Mr. Callaghan believed that the only basis for a solution was a geographical federation, and that 'he knew this himself' (Athens telegram No. 640 of 8 November, WSC 1/16).

[3] Dr. Kissinger's planned visit to Ankara was cancelled following the refusal, on 7 November, of the NSP to sanction proposals Mr. Eçevit had intended to put to Dr. Kissinger, and the failure of Mr. Eçevit to reform his administration. On 17 November Prof. S. Irmak was appointed Turkish Prime Minister. Cf. No. 95, note 5.

4. I am personally convinced that the Turks will not settle for anything less than a biregional geographical federation. It is too late now to go back to earlier ideas of a cantonal solution,[4] or even the line proposed by Güneş at the second Geneva meeting. They might have satisfied Turkish aspirations in the past, but the fact is now that, unless a settlement is achieved, the Turks will not move out of Cyprus. I understand completely the difficulties for the Greek Government of any public or explicit acceptance of the principle of a biregional geographical federation.[5] However, I consider it unlikely that the Turks will be prepared to enter into negotiations for a settlement without acceptance of this principle. Once this principle is accepted, however, I believe that they would be willing to discuss the reduction of the area they at present hold. It may not be necessary for the Greek side to accept the principle in public or explicitly before the negotiations, as long as they are willing to give private assurances to the Turks. As a seasoned practitioner in the conduct of negotiations, Mr. Bitsios will, I am sure, appreciate that the form of any acceptance of preconditions by either side can be arranged with tact before a meeting.

5. I share Bitsios's concern that the Turks will get too used to the idea of having both *de facto* control of a large part of the island and, at the same time, a right to intervene in the affairs of the other half. But if, as part of a settlement, we could achieve real and major withdrawals of foreign forces from the Republic, I would hope that Ankara's influence would be lessened. The Turkish Cypriots may already be finding that being held on a tight rein by Ankara is a chastening experience. But their willingness to show more independence will not reveal itself outside a settlement. Nor is there any sign, despite budgetary pressures, of any weakening of the Turkish will to remain on the island for as long as they think they need to. I cannot see their being prepared to quit before they have achieved a real guarantee that their community will not be harassed. Guarantees of some kind for both communities must form part of a settlement.

6. I am deeply concerned that the stalemate in Cyprus may continue. I appreciate Mr. Bitsios's own concern over this and I am very grateful to him for taking me into his confidence. I welcome his own pragmatic

---

[4] Mr. Clerides appeared to admit this when, on 6 November, he stated publicly in the Argo Gallery, Nicosia, 'that through negotiations on an equal footing no negotiator ... can find a solution which requires Turkish consent and is not based on a federal independent state and moreover does not contain the element of geographical federation' (statement by Mr. Clerides, WSC 1/16).

[5] When, during a meeting with Mr. Callaghan on 20 November, Mr. Roussos spoke of Mr. Karamanlis's regret at the way in which HMG 'were putting forward the extreme Turkish position of a settlement based on a bi-regional federation', Mr. Callaghan explained that HMG 'did not espouse these ideas but ... did wish to talk realities'. 'A multi-cantonal system might', he said, 'be preferable but the question was whether it was attainable'. Mr. Callaghan added that he would be prepared to give diplomatic help at the right time, but that he 'was not willing to take an initiative' (telegram No. 394 to Athens of 20 November, WSC 1/16).

approach and positive resolve. It will be tragic for Cyprus if advances are not made to reach a lasting settlement. It will be necessary in the weeks ahead for all concerned to exercise discretion and to resist pressures to take up public postures which would aggravate the situation and only make progress more difficult. We shall hope to have an opportunity of speaking in this sense to President Makarios after his return from New York, and trust that the Greek Government will do the same.[6] Once the new Greek Government has assumed office,[7] I hope that it will be possible for an early start to be made on serious negotiations.[8]

---

[6] During a meeting with Archbishop Makarios and Mr. Clerides in London on 22 November, Mr. Callaghan argued in favour of a 'realistic approach' and pointed to the danger that in the absence of a settlement the Turks would consolidate their position (telegram No. 1055 of 22 November to Nicosia, WSC 1/16).

[7] The Greek national elections on 17 November resulted in a landslide victory for Mr. Karamanlis and his New Democracy (*Nea Dhimokratia*) Party. In a personal message to Mr. Karamanlis, drafted and despatched on the assumption that he would win the election, Mr. Wilson stated that he sincerely believed that public recognition of the fact that the Turks would not settle for anything less than a biregional federation 'might well prove the key to unlock the door to progress' (telegram No. 389 to Athens of 16 November, WSC 1/16). See No. 102.

[8] On 16 November, Mr. Richards put Mr. Callaghan's views to Mr. Bitsios. Mr. Richards subsequently warned Mr. Callaghan that in the absence of any firm timetable for substantive negotiations, the Greek Government would be unable to keep Archbishop Makarios away from Cyprus and that it was 'hopeless for them to attempt an indefinitely protracted role as intermediary between Clerides and Makarios' (Athens telegrams Nos. 648 and 649 of 18 November, WSC 1/16).

No. 100

Sir H. Phillips (Ankara) to Mr. Callaghan

No. 1539 Telegraphic [*WSC 1/16*]

Immediate. Confidential   ANKARA, *21 November 1974, 3 p.m.*

Repeated for information to Immediate Istanbul (for Ambassador), Priority Athens, Nicosia, Washington, Routine UKMIS New York.

For Goodison from Elgar.[1]
Nicosia tel[egram No.] 1296:[2]
Cyprus

1. We have had no opportunity to take sounding[s] of the new Government at worthwhile level on its Cyprus policy.[3] But as reported in Ankara tel[egram No.] 1495 to FCO,[4] it seems unlikely that they will be willing or confident enough to take major decisions. There is still general agreement among all shades of the political spectrum here, except the extremist NSP, that the policy adopted so far towards Cyprus is the right one and Prime Minister Irmak has said there will be no change. There is no indication of any deviation from line of bi-zonal federation. Position is as expressed in telegram under reference.[5]

2. The Turks feel they should be able to call the shots. Though Cyprus offers them some inconvenience, it is not a serious burden. There is much at stake also in terms of national pride and they will see no reason to give much away, especially at this time when Cyprus is the only unifying factor among the political parties.

3. From FCO tel[egrams Nos.] 394 to Athens[6] and 2366 to Washington[7] it appears that the Greeks are now wriggling desperately to get off the hook

---

[1] Mr. A.G. Elgar was Counsellor (commercial) in the British Embassy in Ankara.

[2] In this telegram of 20 November Mr. Olver reported that neither he nor the US Ambassador in Nicosia had 'the slightest indication of any Turkish wavering on bi-zonal federation as the basis for a Cyprus settlement'.

[3] See No. 99, note 3.

[4] In this telegram of 13 November Sir H. Phillips observed that the new Turkish Government was 'clearly intended as a holding operation' until elections were held in June, and that meanwhile no major decisions could be expected on either internal or external issues (WST 1/2).

[5] See note 2 above.

[6] See No. 99, note 5.

[7] This telegram of 19 November reported that, during a meeting that day with Sir J. Killick, Mr. Roussos had, after expressing Greek disappointment with HMG's 'insistence on a biregional federation', claimed that it had emerged from a conversation with Archbishop Makarios that Dr. Kissinger 'regarded a multi-cantonal solution as the preferred answer and one for which he could claim original paternity' (WSC 3/304/2).

of the bi-regional solution and seem to be liberally misinterpreting Dr. Kissinger and others in the process. It would be most unwise to encourage them to think they will get far with this in Ankara.[8]

4. Makarios. Obviously we can not prevent Makarios from returning to Cyprus or appear to be doing so.[9] And given that he does return[,] line proposed in Nicosia tel[egram No.] 1297 to FCO[10] seems right. But Makarios is very deeply distrusted indeed by the Turks. They had entertained hopes albeit unjustified, that he had been effectively removed from the scene. His reappearance, apparently supported by the Greek Government, will certainly do nothing to reassure them of his or Greek intentions. If they feel their hand is being forced they may well become more obstinate.

[8] *V. ibid.* Some confusion had arisen over US views on a Cyprus settlement. In a personal letter to Mr. Callaghan of 16 November Dr. Kissinger reported that he had derived the impression from a meeting with Archbishop Makarios on 13 November that the latter was reluctantly beginning to accept the idea of federation, but was insisting that this should be composed of a multiplicity of cantons. 'I understand', Dr. Kissinger observed, 'that since our meeting, Makarios has let it be known that the United States still holds open the idea of a multi-cantonal arrangement. I want to assure you that we support the bi-zonal concept as being the only practicable arrangement and on this I think we are in complete agreement' (WSC 3/304/2).

[9] During a press conference on 20 November, prior to his departure for meetings in London with Archbishop Makarios and Mr. Callaghan (cf. No. 99, note 6), Mr. Clerides affirmed that he 'was not prepared to undertake substantive negotiations with the Turkish side unless a document were drawn up defining the framework of negotiations, to be signed by the Greek Govt., Archbishop Makarios and the negotiator'. Further consultations were planned with Mr. Karamanlis and Archbishop Makarios in Athens. But Mr. Olver thought Mr. Clerides determined 'to resign if Makarios persist[ed] in returning without accepting a realistic negotiating line' (Nicosia telegrams Nos. 1302 and 1324 of 20 and 26 November).

[10] Mr. Olver suggested in this telegram of 20 November that it might be best if HMG were to concentrate on persuading Archbishop Makarios that he should use his influence to unify the conflicting strands of Cypriot opinion; that he should do nothing on his return which might add to Turkish suspicions regarding his intentions; and that HMG hoped that, given the Turkish commitment to a settlement based on a bi-zonal federation, he would 'not sacrifice a feasible solution in search of the ideal' (WSC 1/14).

No. 101

Mr. Callaghan to Sir P. Ramsbotham (Washington)

No. 2427 Telegraphic [*WSC 10/14*]

Immediate. Secret   FCO, *26 November 1974, 10.25 a.m.*

Defence Review: Cyprus

Please arrange to transmit the following message from me to Dr. Kissinger,

Begins.

Dear Henry,

In his message to the President of 20 November about the Defence Review,[1] the Prime Minister said that I should be replying more fully to your message of 16 November about Cyprus,[2] which Wells Stabler delivered in London.

First, let me say that we greatly welcomed the visit of Mr. Stabler and his colleagues. They gave our people a very clear presentation of the implications, as you saw them, of a decision by the British Government to withdraw from the Sovereign Base Areas in Cyprus. The British participants in Monday's discussions made an immediate report, and my Cabinet colleagues and I were thus able to take fully into account all your thoughts and concerns.[3]

Our conclusions with regard to Cyprus were that, although we shall embark almost at once on a rundown of our forces there—particularly airforce units—on the lines indicated to you by John Hunt and his team in Washington on 12 November,[4] we shall not in present circumstances proceed with our preferred policy of withdrawing from the Sovereign Base Areas altogether.[5]

The fact that the US Administration and you personally attach such importance to our presence in Cyprus, together with your argument about

[1] Mr. Wilson explained in this telegraphic message to President Ford that, while Britain was determined to pull its 'full weight in the common defence in Europe', it could not afford to 'keep forces stationed round the word and formally committed to non-NATO tasks' (DP 5/3).

[2] In this letter Dr. Kissinger emphasised that he believed that the elimination of the British SBAs in Cyprus 'could have a destabilising effect on the region as a whole, encouraging the Soviet Union and others to believe that the West had been weakened in that area, and damage Western flexibility to act in unpredictable situations'. He added that he considered it important 'to take no action at this time which could have a further unsettling effect on the situation in Cyprus'.

[3] On Monday 18 November Mr. Stabler and his colleagues met with Sir G. Arthur and other British officials to discuss the future of the SBAs (minute from Sir G. Arthur to Mr. Acland of 19 November, DP 5/3).

[4] See No. 98, note 14.

[5] See No. 82 and note 1 above.

the generally adverse effect of our withdrawal on the region as a whole, was the determining consideration.[6]

I would not pretend that we would accept without reservation each and every argument and point in your case, as presented by Mr. Stabler and his colleagues: and our people may well be discussing some of them further with yours. In the specific context of Cyprus, I am not entirely happy about the prospect which our decision to stay in Cyprus entails. Throughout the recent crisis, the existence of the Sovereign Base Areas has been a complicating factor in our efforts to discharge our role in relations to Cyprus and, as you know, I have been unhappy about my position of 'responsibility without power'. Even if we succeed in the end in achieving a Cyprus settlement requiring no external guarantees, the mere fact of our continued presence in the island, albeit technically not in the Republic itself, is bound, whatever we may say, to imply some kind of continuing special role and responsibility for the British Government.

[...][7]

I hope that this outcome will give you satisfaction and the feeling that, in matters of this sort, we continue to give full weight to the views and interests of the United States wherever these can, even at some cost, be reconciled with our own.[8]

Ends.

---

[6] Sir John Hunt minuted Sir G. Arthur on 21 November: 'At Cabinet yesterday morning (CC(74) 47th Conclusions, Confidential Annex) the Prime Minister referred to the fact that Dr. Kissinger [was] "emphatic" that we should retain the Sovereign Base Areas in Cyprus' although "'he would be less concerned at the prospect of a reduction in the size of our forces in Cyprus, provided we maintained our presence there". The summing up said "It was clear that we would encounter very considerable American opposition to withdrawal ... and the Foreign and Commonwealth Secretary would be considering the terms of a reply to be sent to Dr. Kissinger"'.

[7] A paragraph is here omitted.

[8] On 27 November, Dr. Kissinger replied to Mr. Callaghan's message: 'The decision to maintain the sovereign base areas on the island ... is welcome news indeed. I appreciate that the decision to stay in Cyprus was not an easy one, and I am thus especially grateful for the consideration that London was able to give to our views on this subject' (telegraphic letter from Dr. Kissinger to Mr. Callaghan of 27 November, WSC 10/14/75).

No. 102

Extract from Mr. Richards (Athens) to Mr. Callaghan

[*WSC 1/5*]

Confidential   ATHENS, *27 November 1974*

Summary ...[1]

Sir,

The Results of the Greek Elections ...[2]

Implications for British Policy

13. With the elections democracy is re-established in Greece on a legitimate footing.[3] Karamanlis is no longer heir to the junta. The result is as good for British interests as could have been hoped, not in the sense that it is a conservative conclusion but because it is a clear vote of endorsement of democratic stability and because Karamanlis over the issues which matter most to us will be more responsible and less emotional than would his rivals. This result comes after a period of seven and a half years during which Anglo-Greek relations have been correct rather than close and when Ministerial exchanges, public business and working contacts have remained at levels well below those which obtain with most European States. The time has surely now come for us to review this state of affairs.

14. I am under no illusion that Greece is in some way central to the preoccupations of Her Majesty's Government, and there are obvious limits to what the Greek Government can do for us or we for them. On Cyprus where both Governments are deeply involved, we share an interest in the attainment of a settlement which is acceptable to the Cypriot population of both communities and which can honourably be endorsed by the Greek Government. But there is a limit to the power we possess to bring about such a settlement or to persuade the Greek Government of the honourable nature of any settlement that could be had. Over the EEC our own position is delicate. We are somewhat limited as a result in the support which we can offer the Greeks or the concessions we can seek from them in return. Their NATO relationship is dominated by their American problem and while better relations on a governmental level might help secure us more public sector business, in the commercial field the main limitations on increasing our share of the Greek market lie in delivery dates

---

[1] Not printed.

[2] Paragraphs 1-12 and the Annex to this despatch, which analyse and describe the recent Greek elections and the domestic political situation in Greece, are not printed. Cf. No. 99, note 7.

[3] In paragraph 2 Mr. Richards described the election as 'the least corrupt in modern Greek history'. Mr. Karamanlis's New Democracy Party secured 54% of the vote and, because of the system of proportional representation, 220 of the 300 seats in Parliament.

and the capacity of British industry to supply the market, rather than in inter-Governmental dealings.

15. Nevertheless, as I wrote at the beginning of this despatch, restoration of Parliamentary democracy and the successful establishment of Karamanlis' Government as a result of these elections, is no small victory for the free Western system. Britain has a useful market here, alliance ties and a shared concern with Greece over Cyprus. To preserve and protect these interests we need to re-establish Anglo-Greek links on a more normal level. I will put detailed proposals before your department but in outline I consider that a series of quite modest developments would be preferable to any attempt to mount a spectacular goodwill visit at a senior Ministerial level at least at this stage.

16. The first and most appropriate field in which contacts might be enlarged is that of Parliament. Prior to 1967 joint Anglo-Greek Parliamentary Committees functioned and their restoration would be of value. It is true that with the unfreezing of Greece's Association Agreement European Parliamentary links with Greece (in addition to Greece's links with the Council of Europe) will be renewed, but these pose some party political and also European Community problems for our own Parliamentary purposes. The preponderance of the New Democracy Party in the *Boule* will present other problems, but so far as we can do so without political bias, it would be advantageous to have Parliamentary visits in both directions. A fairly early visit to Greece by British Parliamentarians as a mark of respect for the re-institution of Parliamentary life in Greece would seem particularly appropriate.

17. Renewed Parliamentary links would not exclude the possibility of Ministerial visits but on this I should prefer to start modestly. If a junior Minister, perhaps from the Department of Trade, could visit Greece during the next four months it might offer a basis on which to build future visits by senior Ministers, afford a fillip to our commercial interests here. The possibility of visits by Ministers or senior officials from the Foreign and Commonwealth Office must depend on the way things move over Cyprus: obviously any proposal by us of this kind would be liable in present circumstances to be construed as evidence that we are aiming at a more active role with regard to the issue that for the Greeks still looms larger than others in the field of foreign affairs. But if, for example, Sir T. Brimelow had occasion to pass this way in the course of some more general programme of travel, I do not think he need be inhibited by Cyprus from stopping here to make contacts. Indeed, as a general proposition we need now in my view to restore Athens as far and as fast as possible to the status of a capital which can be and is visited on the same basis as others in Europe with which we have common interests.

18. Outside the political field the question of military co-operation, both within the Alliance and in bilateral exchanges will require careful consideration. Although British Forces will no longer participate in NATO exercises in this area, I believe Karamanlis will attempt to stay as close to

the Alliance as internal political pressure permits and to this end our policy decision that Greece should not be forced to a 'take it or leave it' decision over NATO is undoubtedly helpful. What is required in my view is to re-establish and develop our working links with the Greek Services without too much flourish. To this end I see no reason why Royal Naval visits to the Ionian Islands, Crete and west coast ports should not begin as soon as is convenient. Initially, it may be prudent to avoid the Aegean, but in due course a visit to Piraeus by a major unit with Flag Officer embarked would strengthen the traditional bonds between the Royal Navy and the Hellenic Navy which suffered a setback as a result of the cancellation of the Royal Naval visit at short notice last March. Such a gesture would also help to extinguish the lingering suspicions of our connivance with the Turkish Armed Forces in Cyprus and it would certainly stimulate interest in defence sales, particularly for the frigate deal in which the Greeks have already shown an interest. On the army side, an invitation for a small delegation of middle-ranking officers to visit the UK to witness demonstrations at arms schools and to view British military hardware is also worth examining in the sales context. From small beginnings such gestures will hopefully lead on to bilateral exchange visits by Service Chiefs and so resume the pattern established up to the time of the Chief of the Defence Staff's visit in April 1973.

19. Less contentious but in some ways equally important are our cultural ties, British artistic, intellectual and literary contacts with Greece were extremely tenuous during the seven years of military rule. They are reviving and should be increased. With the British Council and with your department we have worked for a heavily British contribution to the 1975 Athens Festival and hope that this may result in a visit by the Royal Philharmonic Orchestra which would undoubtedly be appreciated not only for its own sake but as a sign of British recognition of the change that has taken place in Greece.

20 In the information field, I think we should increase the scope and amount of political material we issue here and that we should now revive the sponsored visits scheme. We should also seek ways of co-operating with the Greek Press Ministry over the whole field of training.

Conclusion

21. The conclusion must be 'so far so good'. The problems which Karamanlis now faces are more than sufficient to bring him down and, should things go badly, more than enough to bring back the army. The Communist Left is not dead.[4] Papandreou may have a field day over Cyprus, over the junta or the US bases;[5] the universities may not resume

---

[4] In paragraph 6 Mr. Richards reported that although the Communists had polled 'close to their hard-core 10 per cent', they might not be 'too disappointed as their hopes [lay] long in the future'.

[5] Mr. A.G. Papandreou, the leader and founder of the newly-formed PASOK (*Panellinio Sosialistiko Kinima*/the Panhellenic Socialist Movement), had campaigned on an anti-Western,

their former role as places of learning and a recession could bring new threats. No Cyprus solution acceptable to Greek opinion is in sight. But Karamanlis is now better placed to deal with these issues than would be any Greek leader in other circumstances. The re-establishment of democracy here is an achievement; its consolidation will be a major task. The prospects are dangerous but the obstacles no greater than those which have already, against most expectations, been triumphantly overcome.

22. I am sending a copy of this despatch to Her Majesty's Representatives in Bonn, Paris, NATO, EEC, Ankara, Nicosia, Washington, Rome and CBFNE.

I have, etc.,
F.B. RICHARDS

anti-American, anti-NATO and anti-capitalist ticket. But his party secured only 13.58% of the popular vote and twelve seats in Parliament.

No. 103

Letter from Mr. Morgan to Mr. Olver (Nicosia)

[*WSC 3/304/2*]

Confidential   FCO, *10 December 1974*

US Policy on Cyprus

1. Art Hartman called on John Killick on 9 December for a talk before the NATO Ministerial meetings take place in Paris this week, and we discussed Cyprus at some length. Alan Goodison and I were present.

2. Hartman's principal preoccupation was, of course, the Congressional moves to cut off military aid to Turkey.[1] He said that the purpose of Kissinger's statement last week (Washington telegram No. 11 to Paris)[2] was to tell the Congress that if military aid to Turkey ceased, American ability to influence Turkish policy on Cyprus was at an end and the US Government would conduct themselves accordingly. He admitted that the position might not be quite so clear cut as that, but the Administration was anxious to bring all possible pressures to bear on Congress. He explained on lines similar to those followed by Stabler in Washington telegram No.

---

[1] See No. 95, note 11.

[2] This telegram of 9 December reported that on 7 December Dr. Kissinger had told a press conference that it was 'absolutely essential' that the House of Representatives should follow the example set by the Senate on 4 December and authorise the postponement of the suspension of military aid to Turkey until 13 February 1975. Dr. Kissinger had said that the US did not approve Turkey's actions in Cyprus, but that US aid was justified because of Turkey's strategic importance (WST 3/304/1).

3934[3] that there was no hope of the House of Representatives going further than what had been achieved in the Senate—namely, an extension of the deadline to mid-February—and that he was in any case pessimistic about getting the necessary legislation through even to achieve that. The aid could therefore cease on 10 December. In fact, aid 'in the pipeline' could be delivered after that if the Turks were willing to pay the transport costs of the armaments in question. But this would clearly be contrary to the intentions of Congress and he did not know whether the President would be willing to authorise it. He believed that there was some change of attitude in Congress, given that they now realised that any unfortunate consequences of their legislation would be placed firmly at their door.[4]

3. In these circumstances, the United States were not well placed to take action. Furthermore, the Turkish Government was weak and the US Ambassador in Ankara had forecast that there would probably be no stronger Turkish Government for at least a couple of months.[5] Mr. Esenbel[6] had told him that the Turkish Government had had it in mind to make various gestures designed to facilitate negotiations and to help with Congress. They had, however, decided against this action on receiving the news of Archbishop Makarios' intention to return to the island.[7] Hartman added that in any case, the principal gesture would have been an announcement of troop withdrawals, which the Greek side had said they were not particularly interested in. What the Greeks wanted was greater flexibility from the Turks about the political content of talks about a settlement and the Americans had no evidence that the Turks were willing to discuss on any other basis than that of a biregional federation. (We agreed that in any case the Turks probably had reduced their forces in Cyprus by 1,500 or so men.)

[3] In this telegram of 6 December Sir P. Ramsbotham reported that on the previous day Mr. Stabler had told Mr. Wilberforce that he doubted if the House of Representatives would follow the Senate's example regarding aid to Turkey (*v. ibid.*). Mr. Stabler also stressed that this would only be an authorisation measure, and that it could not, without some appropriation measure, override the cut-off of aid on 10 December. Dr. Kissinger, Mr. Stabler observed, was worried about the effect this would have upon the Turkish attitude to Cyprus, since the Turkish Government could not afford to appear to be making concessions under US pressure (WSC 3/304/2).

[4] The US Congress finally agreed to defer the ban on military aid to Turkey until 5 February 1975.

[5] Cf. No. 100. None of the major Turkish political parties were represented in Prof. Irmak's Government and on 29 November its programme was defeated in the Assembly by 362 votes to 11. The Government thereupon resigned, but continued as a caretaker administration until a new Government could be formed.

[6] Mr. M. Esenbel, a former Turkish Ambassador to Washington, was Mr. Günes's successor as Turkish Foreign Minister.

[7] Archbishop Makarios returned to Cyprus on 7 December via RAF Akrotiri and a UN helicopter to Nicosia.

4. Our analyses of the situation in Cyprus coincided generally. Although we did not think the Turks likely to make any military moves without provocation, we agreed that we could not exclude the possibility that dissension in the Greek Cypriot community might lead to Turkish fears for Turkish Cypriots in the south and to consequent military action.[8] We agreed that the number of Turkish Cypriots in the south had declined considerably since the ceasefire. One danger, however, was Makarios' hankering for a continuance of the present situation. Hartman commented that the Archbishop had always said frankly that the worse the situation in Cyprus the better it was for him. Killick spoke of the dangers of any Turkish military move to rescue the refugees in the Western Sovereign Base Area and said he hoped that Dr. Kissinger would do his best to dissuade Mr. Esenbel from any such action. We had always made it clear to the Greeks that the refugees could not stay there indefinitely, but the present moment, when the Archbishop had just returned, was no time for us to take action to release them.[9] Hartman said that he had some evidence that there were differences of opinion within the Turkish military hierarchy; some were thinking that they had gone too far in Cyprus and were keener on a settlement than others.

5. Perhaps the most interesting thing Hartman said was that he had been trying to restrain Dr. Kissinger from intervening actively to promote a settlement, on the grounds that there were far too many uncertain factors at present. Killick told him that our Secretary of State did not want to intervene until the parties were readier to talk. We agreed that time was not on anyone's side and that what was wanted was greater flexibility, but that the most that could probably be obtained from the Turks next week was an assurance that they would not break off the talks between Mr. Clerides and Mr. Denktash. If the Greeks could be brought to tell the Turks that they were willing to negotiate on some geographical basis, this would be helpful. Hartman said he did not exclude the possibility that a settlement might eventually take the form of a geographical federation which was not based on complete separation of the two sides. He observed that although Karamanlis was realistic, we should have to wait and see how far he was willing to go in pressing Makarios to authorise realistic instructions to Clerides. Two features of the situation which were disquieting were that at his meeting with Dr. Kissinger in Rome, Mr. Bitsios had spoken much more with the voice of Makarios than with that of

---

[8] In a letter to Mr. J. Lynton Jones (SEED) of 28 November, Mr. A. Ibbott (First Secretary and Head of Chancery, Nicosia) noted that fears that the Turks might launch a third military operation continued to excite Greek Cypriot opinion. 'The Archbishop's return could', he suggested, 'in certain circumstances provoke a Turkish reaction.' But a week later Mr. Olver reported in Nicosia telegram No. 1376 of 6 December that while it was fairly clear that all mainland Turkish forces and Turkish Cypriot fighters had been placed on 'maximum alert', he thought these measures 'primarily precautionary' (WSC 1/10).

[9] See No. 91.

Karamanlis,[10] and that on his return, Makarios appeared to be deliberately ignoring and downgrading Clerides.

6. Killick and Hartman agreed to keep in touch in Brussels. Kissinger will be seeing the Greek and Turkish Foreign Ministers before Mr. Callaghan does so, and Hartman will arrange to let us have an early account of the meetings.

H.T. Morgan

[10] See No. 99, notes 1 and 2.

No. 104

Record of a meeting between Mr. Callaghan and Mr. Bitsios[1] at NATO Headquarters, Brussels, on 12 December 1974 at 6 p.m.

[*WSC 1/16*]

Confidential

Present:

The Rt. Hon. James Callagahan, MP	Mr. Bitsios
Sir John Killick	Private Secretary
Mr. P.J. Weston	

1. *Mr. Callaghan* said that Mr. Bitsios, having seen both Makarios and Clerides more recently than he had, would no doubt be more up to date. But his own impression was that Makarios had been thinking in a much longer perspective than Clerides who was naturally concerned with what could be done on a day to day basis. He had told Makarios that he thought the time had come to agree that there should be a geographical solution, with a federal umbrella; and that if Makarios wanted to pursue a cantonal solution that was for consideration. He had suspected that, at the joint meeting he had held in the FCO with Makarios and Clerides, Clerides had silently approved the line he was taking with the Archbishop. But Makarios remained unconvinced.[2]

2. Mr. Callaghan said he did not know how far the Athens meeting had gone toward agreeing on the next steps. He understood that Clerides wanted a mandate written down.[3] From the other side the impermanence of the Turkish Government was a problem and Denktash seemed to have no real authority. He was not optimistic after his conversation with Esenbel; the Turks wanted the Northern sector plus a large Turkish

[1] Following the Greek elections Mr. Bitsios was re-appointed Foreign Minister.

[2] See No. 99, note 6.

[3] See No. 100, note 9.

majority therein.[4] He was glad the Clerides/Denktash talks had been dealing with humanitarian problems, but would like them to move on to the political sphere.

3. The Soviet offer on Larnaca if accepted would still further complicate matters. He hoped for an interim solution on Nicosia airport.[5] On Turkish refugees he had just heard news about floods in the WSBA. He wondered whether on humanitarian grounds we could not now let some of the refugees go to Turkey. Otherwise the accusations would increase that we were holding hostages in miserable conditions.[6]

4. *Mr. Bitsios* said the Greek Government had been apprehensive about the Athens confrontation with Makarios. Their own starting point was that they knew what they could *not* accept, namely anything that smacked of partition. They could not accept that the Turks should have the right to bring about partition, whilst at the same time excluding *enosis* and refusing the Cypriots the right to self-determination. But they thought they could go ahead and meet the rest of the Turkish demands as far as structure was concerned. Three points had been agreed in Athens: (i) there must be a federal solution with cantons, in other words on a geographical basis (whether one called it 'multi-regional' was a matter of semantics). They had persuaded Makarios to come round to their view and had reached a common line on this. The division of area should approximate as far as possible to the respective percentages of the population. (ii) The readiness of the Greek Cypriots to start negotiations. (iii) Clerides should be entrusted with the actual negotiating. In the light of this, the return of Makarios to Cyprus took on another aspect, since his presence would be necessary if public opinion was to be won round for a solution on these lines. He was conscious of reluctance on the Turkish side. Were they willing to negotiate

[4] When during the morning of 12 December Mr. Callaghan discussed Cyprus with Mr. Esenbel, the latter insisted that the Turkish Cypriots must live together for their own security. 'The Turks', he said, 'should have a "crushing majority" in the North. This time they did not want a paper agreement as at Zurich, but real security in one single area' (record of meeting between Mr. Callaghan and Mr. Esenbel at UKDEL NATO on 12 December at 9.30 a.m., WST 3/548/2).

[5] The Soviet Union had apparently proposed that *Aeroflot* should use Larnaca airport. Mr. Callaghan told Mr. Esenbel that this would 'allow the Soviet Union to make an entry under the guise of a civil airline'.

[6] See No. 91. In telegram No. 287 to UKDEL NATO of 11 December Private Office informed Mr. P.J. Weston (Assistant Private Secretary to the Secretary of State) that Mr. Callaghan should be made aware 'that the situation of the refugees in the WSBA [had] deteriorated in the last few days, owing to heavy rain, accompanied by strong winds and a drop in temperature', and that attempts had been made 'to exploit the situation' with refugees expected to try to block the main road by a 'sitdown' at Paramali (WSC 19/1). Pressed by Mr. Esenbel on the subject of the refugees, Mr. Callaghan replied that this too should be a 'priority issue' once the Clerides/Denktash talks began. When Mr. Esenbel protested that the refugees could not be part of such a bargain, Mr. Callaghan explained 'it was not a question of the refugees being a bargaining counter, but the Greeks would see any move by us on the refugees as having political overtones' (see note 4 above).

or not? What was behind their hesitation? Was it internal political difficulties or a wish to consolidate their existing position?

5. *Mr. Callaghan* said Mr. Bitsios could help the parties to come to the negotiating table. The Turks had to be certain that Makarios would back Clerides. Had Makarios endorsed any document? *Mr. Bitsios* said he had every reason to believe this would be so. Clerides wanted a written mandate. Makarios could not get away from what had been agreed. There were verbatim records. Clerides was in fact now free to go ahead knowing that he had the Archbishop's backing. *Mr. Callaghan* said that if this were so and if Clerides were to move ahead along these lines, there might be a chance for others to put pressure on the Turks. But what about a move on the refugees? *Mr. Bitsios* said a move now might not have a good affect on the talks. He asked whether it would be possible to wait a week or so and what numbers had Mr. Callaghan in mind? *Mr. Callaghan* said he was thinking of certain specific categories whom the floods in the WSBA would provide a good excuse for letting go. He would wait until he had examined the detailed position on his return to London. *Mr. Bitsios* invited Mr. Callaghan to send him word when he had a clear picture. The airport question was very important. Clerides had proposed to Denktash that there should be joint Greek Cypriot/Turkish Cypriot work on the FIR[7] under UN/ICAO[8] supervision. Up to now Denktash had refused but not adamantly, and had referred to Ankara for instructions. *Mr. Callaghan* said he had told Esenbel all about this; the latter had said it was not a separate technical problem but a political issue which could be given priority when the talks began.[9]

6. Mr. Callaghan asked about the Treaty of Guarantee. *Mr. Bitsios* said the parties to the Treaty had not been able to discharge their duties under the Treaty. It was too early to talk of this now, but more objective guarantees would be necessary. *Mr. Callaghan* asked whether Clerides and Denktash would be able to carry on to the point of working out a structure, without the three guarantor powers joining in. *Mr. Bitsios* said yes, but the powers would have to come in over the international aspects. He added that the Greeks were against a bi-zonal arrangement, not simply for the political reason (partition) but for the humanitarian reason that a cantonal solution would allow more Greek Cypriots to return to their homes. He thought the Turks would be prepared to yield quite a lot of area. If 40 to 50,000 Greek Cypriots were to go to the city of Famagusta and another 30,000 to Morphou, then this would still allow the Turks to have a majority over the Greeks in some areas. There were some encouraging signs in that the Turks realised they could not exploit by

[7] Flight Information Region.

[8] International Civil Aviation Organisation.

[9] Mr. Esenbel agreed in principle that there should be negotiations on Nicosia airport, but he was not prepared to talk about modalities. Once the Clerides/Denktash talks started this, he said, could be a 'priority item' (see notes 4 and 6 above).

themselves the whole of the area they occupied. *Mr. Callaghan* said we must all encourage the two parties but it would be necessary to keep Makarios in a realistic frame of mind.[10] Mr. Bitsios said that one could not play games with Karamanlis. They now had an agreement which had been arrived at after Makarios had put all his ideas on the table. In answer to a question, Mr. Bitsios confirmed that the Greek Government kept Mavros regularly briefed on the situation: if they did not have a bi-partisan policy, at least Mr. Mavros was in effect in the position of being a 'loyal opposition'. In answer to another question he said he had not been surprised by the result of the referendum on the monarchy. The king had had very few chances.[11]

7. *Mr. Callaghan* said he hoped the Greek Government would strengthen its ties with NATO since all of us had big interests in common. He hoped Mr. Bitsios would be able to edge his way back and bring public opinion along. *Mr. Bitsios* said Mr. Callaghan would be aware of the reasons why the decision had been taken on that fateful evening. These reasons were still there.

[10] During his earlier meeting with Mr. Esenbel (*v. ibid.*) Mr. Callaghan argued that 'Makarios was the only man who could carry the Greek Cypriots with him', and that 'one possible advantage of his return to Cyprus was that he would see the reality of the situation on the ground and come to realise what Clerides could and could not do'.

[11] In a referendum held on 8 December on the future of the monarchy, 69.2% of the Greek electorate voted against, and 30.8% in favour, of the restoration of King Constantine II.

No. 105

Report by the Joint Intelligence Committee

JIC (75) 3

Secret   CABINET OFFICE, *13 February 1975*

Cyprus: The Year Ahead

PART II: Main Paper[1]

Introduction

1. This paper examines the future of Cyprus over the next 12 months. This is a particularly difficult time to be writing about this subject. The Clerides/Denktash talks are in a delicate and perhaps critical phase and their success or failure will have a major bearing on the island's future.[2]

[1] Part I, the summary, is not printed. It was signed by Sir G. Arthur on behalf of the JIC.

[2] Intercommunal talks between Mr. Clerides and Mr. Denktash were resumed on 14 January. As well as discussing a constitutional settlement for Cyprus, negotiations were begun on the re-opening of Nicosia international airport and Famagusta port to Greek and Greek Cypriot traffic, and a humanitarian sub-committee was established to investigate the issue of missing persons (Nicosia telegram No. 47 of 14 January, WSC 1/3). But progress remained slow,

The lack of a firm government in Ankara, the United States arms embargo,[3] and doubts about the intentions of Makarios and about the relative strengths and positions of the various factions on the Greek Cypriot side further complicate the position. Although it is premature to assess the long term effects on Anglo-Greek Cypriot relationships of the British decision to allow Turkish Cypriot refugees to leave the WSBA, the immediate effect has been very adverse. The demonstrations and violence which reached a peak on 21 January constituted a very serious direct threat to the security of the SBA's and British interests.[4]

Part 1: The General Situation
The Turkish Position
2. The immediate aim of the Turks has been to secure a militarily defensible zone in the North of the island in which the Turkish Cypriots could live safely. Their next objective has been to bring Turkish Cypriots to it from the South, notably the large number concentrated in the WSBA. With these, totalling approximately, 9,500, now on their way, the Turks are likely to turn their attention to the remaining Turkish Cypriots in the South, of whom there may remain about 8,000, some of them under UN protection, others in isolated but armed villages. Almost all will go North if given the chance. However, Turkish pressure for them to be moved may not be acute until the inefficient administration in the Turkish zone has managed to resettle the WSBA refugees. Exfiltration north of small groups of Turkish Cypriots will continue, but the Turkish Cypriots have orders not to leave village enclaves defenceless. When it comes, Turkish pressure for resumed northwards movement could be applied through the Clerides-Denktash talks, or by turning the screw on Greek Cypriots (about 12,500) still living in the Turkish zone. Only in the case of obstinate and prolonged Greek Cypriot resistance to any move northwards of Turkish Cypriots, or of a direct threat to the Turkish Cypriots in the South would they be likely to turn to more radical measures. If the Turks did attempt to remove any Turkish Cypriots from the South unilaterally, the risk of armed clashes with the National Guard and Greek Cypriot irregulars would be high. The consequent resurgence of violence would probably set back the prospect of political progress on the island by many months or even destroy it for the

---

and the talks were suspended on 13 February, following the proclamation by Mr. Denktash of a 'Turkish Federated State of Cyprus' (see note 5 below).

[3] See No. 103.

[4] On 15 January, Mr. Callaghan authorised the transfer to Turkey of 9,400 Turkish Cypriots from the WSBA. A massive airlift from Akrotiri to Adana took place during 18-27 January, whence the refugees were transferred to northern Cyprus. Greek Cypriot anger at HMG's decision grew when it became clear that the Turks would not reciprocate by granting permission for displaced Greek Cypriot refugees to return home. This resulted in strong protests by the Cyprus and Greek Governments and lengthy anti-British demonstrations in Nicosia and Athens (record of conversation between Mr. Callaghan and Mr. Menemencioglu on 14 January; Nicosia telegram No. 74 of 17 January; WSC 1/5).

foreseeable future. Given time, many of the Turkish Cypriots who want to go North may manage to do so independently.

3. Long term Turkish aims are more problematic. The presence of an interim government in Ankara has prevented the Turks from showing the flexibility needed for progress towards a settlement. But the Turks are inflexible at all times and may not be greatly affected even by the withdrawal of United States military aid. The main Turkish parties agree with the objective of a bi-regional federation in which the Turkish Cypriot part will enjoy not only security but a large degree of autonomy: this in turn implies a central government with strictly limited powers. However, the Turks wish Cyprus to retain ostensible sovereignty and independence as a sop to Greek Cypriot and world opinion, and also to forestall the prospect of double enosis. For strategic reasons, Turkey does not want its frontier with Greece to run through Cyprus. To achieve these aims Turkey will be prepared to give up some of the territory now held and to allow a certain number of Greek Cypriots back into the Turkish zone. The Turks are unlikely greatly to reduce their forces in advance of a settlement, and it is by no means certain that they are prepared to negotiate in a manner likely to produce one. They have shown this clearly by allowing Denktash to declare a new autonomous state for the Turkish held area.[5]

4. In the absence of a settlement and the definition of federal prerogatives, the Turks are introducing numerous administrative measures in the Turkish zone, modelled on mainland practice. We do not know of any decision or plans to annex this part of the island to mainland Turkey. But important decisions affecting the Turkish Cypriot part of the island are probably now taken on the mainland or by mainland representatives and that [*sic*] Denktash enjoys little freedom of manoeuvre. The Turkish Cypriots do not welcome this mainland dominance but there is little they can do about it. Increasing friction between Turks and Turkish Cypriots may well be a feature of the year ahead, but Denktash, because of the active opposition to him within the Turkish Cypriot community, will continue to need the steady support of Ankara.[6]

---

[5] Cf. No. 89, notes 19 and 20. At a special joint meeting on 13 February, the Executive Council and Legislative Assembly of the Turkish Cypriot Administration formally proclaimed a Turkish Cypriot Federated State in the part of Cyprus under Turkish occupation: the Autonomous Turkish Cypriot Administration should be 'restructured and organized on the basis of a secular and federated state until such time [as] the 1960 Constitution of the Republic ... is amended in a similar manner to become the Constitution of the Federal Republic of Cyprus and until the said Federal Republic is established' (Nicosia telegram No. 47 of 14 January, WSC 1/7).

[6] In a minute to Mr. Morgan of 28 February, Mr. Goodison commented that there had been considerable opposition to Mr. Denktash from the majority of members of the House of Representatives: 'One opposition group in particular led by Mr. Fuat Veziroglu, apparently gave Eçevit an 81-page memorandum centering [*sic*] on Mr. Denktash's proposals for a Council which, it was feared, would mean the end of the Turkish Cypriot House of Representatives'. The British High Commission in Nicosia also reported, Mr. Goodison minuted, 'significant

5. Though the Turks may have some economic worries, they have little reason to be unhappy with the military status on the island, and there is no effective pressure, apart perhaps from a need to restore or replace United States military aid, on them to agree with the Greek Cypriots other than on their own terms. They enjoy a preponderence of military strength over the Greeks, both on the island and elsewhere, and though they have no need to annex further territory, they will not hesitate to threaten or take reprisals if force is threatened or used against them. The Greek Cypriots may to some extent be able to use the presence of Turkish Cypriots in the South as a bargaining counter, but too much use of it could backfire by provoking the Turks into direct action (see paragraph 2 above). The United States arms embargo, if prolonged, will pose considerable difficulties for the Turks; but the pressure on them may not be severe for 3 to 6 months and longer if they can find alternative sources of supply and it could even make them more, rather than less, intransigent in Cyprus.[7]

6. The main current problem for the Turkish Cypriot section of the island is economic. It contains many capital assets in the form of land, agricultural equipment, factories and hotels, but neither the Turkish Cypriots nor mainland Turkey possess either the managerial skill and administrative capacity or even the semi-skilled manpower to operate and profit from these assets. Large numbers of mainland Turks may be settled in the North; but this might create internal friction with Turkish Cypriots; and would be yet another cause for continued Greek Cypriot resentment against both the Turks and the British. The invasion has already proved extremely costly and there may be the beginnings of a reaction in Turkey itself against 'sponging' by Turkish Cypriots on the Turkish taxpayer. Thus, even if there is a political settlement, the economy of the North of the island seems likely to remain stagnant for some time to come, war damage will not be repaired rapidly and the tourist industry will take a long time to recover. Libyan or other Moslem economic aid is a possibility but we know of no offers so far.

The Greeks and Greek Cypriots

7. At the Athens meeting of Greek and Greek Cypriot leaders, Archbishop Makarios conceded the principle of geographical federation,

opposition' to Mr. Denktash amongst the Turkish Cypriot community (minute to Mr. Morgan of 28 February, WSC 1/1).

[7] In his minute of 28 February (*v. ibid.*) Mr. Goodison argued that the suspension of US military assistance to Turkey would eventually greatly affect the Turks: 'The Turks' most immediate need will', he wrote, 'be for spare parts for aircraft, which may well be obtainable only from the US', and they were likely, he continued, to look to other NATO states, including Germany and France. They might also seek financial aid from Libya or Iran. Since he doubted whether any of these countries could provide more than a small proportion of Turkey's requirements, he thought the Turks might also look to Britain 'as a NATO ally' for help, and that they would be 'very resentful' if HMG declined.

and he has not so far reneged on this.[8] However, his public statements have been fairly tough on refusing to accept faits accomplis. If he did renege on the Athens agreement, it would halt the talks with the Turks in their tracks, and involve him in a split with Clerides. The Greek side is hoping for a cantonal rather than a purely bi-regional solution, which would enable more Greek Cypriot refugees to return to their homes and minimise the dangers of refugee backlash. This solution will be difficult, and may be impossible to sell to the Turks. The shape of an eventual settlement, like its timing, remains unclear; except that the Turks are determined to retain control of the Northern zone.

8. Whether or not the bulk of Greek Cypriots can reconcile themselves to agreement on Turkish terms there will remain trigger-happy elements at both ends of the Greek Cypriot political spectrum who will be unable to reconcile themselves to any likely solution. Although an uneasy peace has existed between the various factions since Makarios' return to the island, there can be no guarantee of its continuing indefinitely. It remains our view that frustrations on the Greek Cypriot side could ultimately vent themselves in some form of guerilla or terrorist campaign. This might be directed initially against targets in the North though ruthless Turkish measures would soon suppress it. There would also be a chance of action against Turkish Cypriots in the South, which would be met with massive military reprisals. But in the absence of satisfactory Turkish targets, the irreconcilable extremists might react to an unsatisfactory settlement by terrorist attempts against a Greek and Greek-Cypriot leadership thought to have connived in a sell-out. In this event, attempts might also be directed against the powers who sponsored a settlement, i.e. the Americans and/or ourselves. Attacks on British targets could be either on the island (e.g. the SBA's) or conceivably given the large Cypriot population here, in Britain itself or internationally. Such action by extremists might even develop in the absence of any settlement as a means of pushing Her Majesty's Government and the Americans to apply pressure on the Turks.

9. The composition of Makarios' new council of Ministers is similar enough to his pre-coup administration to discourage hopes that old problems may have been permanently buried; it is unlikely to satisfy extremists of the left or the right. Another potential cause of dissension is the constitutional 'requirement for elections' in July 1975 to the House of Representatives.

10. The economic outlook is dependent on political events. Even without a settlement, the Greek Cypriot economy has proved more resilient than was at first expected: loss of tourist and export income has been somewhat

[8] Talks in Athens between Archbishop Makarios, Mr. Clerides and the Greek Government were held from 29 November to 1 December 1974. Addressing a 'large and enthusiastic crowd in Constitution Square, the Cyprus President 'declared that he was ready to negotiate a solution with the Turkish Cypriots which would give them [the] right to self-government' without partition (Athens telegram No. 681 of 2 December, WSC 1/14).

offset by reduced import demand, and the central bank still has about C£100 million in foreign exchange reserves. If a settlement were achieved which returned new Famagusta with its hotels, some of the fertile central plain and perhaps also some Morphu citrus groves to the Greek Cypriots, there would be some grounds for optimism about the economic viability of their part of the island. Such a settlement would also reduce the political dangers stemming from a large reservoir of refugees (including those in the ESBA) whose discontent could be tapped by extremist groups wishing to make trouble. Failing such a settlement however, there could be an exodus of the best Cypriot business and administrative talent, discouraged both by the lack of prospects and the danger that renewed Turkish military activity would be provoked by Greek Cypriot extremists.

11. The Greek Government may be prepared to exercise discreet pressure on Makarios to reach a settlement soon, but they will be reluctant to do anything which exposes them to a charge of defection over the Cyprus problem. Their position is too weak to enable them to play any decisive role. They will try to avoid conflict with Turkey over Cyprus but may move towards confrontation elsewhere, e.g. over Aegean oil.

The Outlook

12. We think there is still some chance that a political settlement can be reached and sold to the Greek Cypriots, but it would probably have to concede at least the main substance of the Turkish demand for a bi-regional federation. In any case significant demographic changes are in progress despite the wishes of the Greek Cypriot administration. It remains equally possible that at some stage negotiations for a settlement will collapse, either because a significant number of Greek Cypriots will oppose a deal on Turkish terms or because Makarios himself will refuse to authorise the necessary concessions. However, perhaps the most likely hypothesis as matters stand is that for the next few months at least, the talks will fail to make progress on all but minor issues, but that neither side will be willing to break them off. An uneasy peace will continue on the island, with the Turkish mainland continuing to consolidate its hold on the North of the island and with the various Greek Cypriot factions, who have been badly rattled by the success of the Turkish invasion, continuing to present a low profile, unless they are tempted to profit from what is likely to be a sharp build-up of refugee pressure on the Government. The economic situation in the North will take a long time to improve but economic progress in the South may be faster if the Greek Cypriots adjust to the realities and if sufficient international help is forthcoming. Nevertheless there will be a significant reservoir of possibly violent discontent on the Greek Cypriot side.

Part II The British Presence
The SBAs

13. The British decision to agree to the transfer of the Turkish Cypriot refugees in the WSBA to Turkey has led the Greek Cypriots to vent some

of their pent up emotions which have been under restraint since the invasion. Their reaction has been violent and at the same time spontaneous and genuine. A serious deterioration in Anglo-Greek Cypriot relations may still be avoided provided Britain is seen to be pressing the Turks for some form of counter concessions and to be doing something about the undoubted plight of Greek Cypriot refugees on the island. But our action has nevertheless probably contributed to the myth, already firmly established in Greek Cypriot minds, that Britain has aided and abetted Turkey during the crisis, and at the very least has fallen down on her alleged obligations under the Treaty of Guarantee.[9]

14. We believe that over the next year, as economic and political problems in the South of the island magnify the frustration and anger of the Greek Cypriots, there will be a continuing danger of their turning on the British as a convenient scapegoat (and the SBAs and retained sites as a convenient target) for their problems and a more accessible and less dangerous one than Turkey or the Turkish Cypriots. This could happen spontaneously, but it would be more likely to grow out of official pressure on Britain by the Greek Cypriot administration to pay them the large sums of money which they were already demanding before the Turkish invasion as payment for facilities enjoyed by the British, and which they will now need more than ever to aid economic recovery. Makarios' recent reference to doubt over the future of the SBAs is seen as part of the pressure rather than a declaration of intent.[10] In such a situation there could be various forms of attack on our presence, from demonstrations outside British installations to mob violence and terrorist attacks. We think the risk of this will be higher if there is stalemate or breakdown in the Clerides/Denktash talks, than if a settlement is reached. The SBAs are vulnerable both physically and because they rely on Cypriot labour and to some extent on outside supplies of electricity.[11] Although there may be pressure from the Greek Cypriot Left for termination of the British presence, we think the Makarios Government will wish the presence to continue. It gives the Cyprus Government a lever for pressure on Britain and the financial advantages that it brings will be a disincentive to rash action.[12] Another

---

[9] See note 4 above and No. 96.

[10] In an interview with Mr. J. Sergeant of the BBC Archbishop Makarios suggested that 'the evacuation of the Turkish Cypriots and their transfer to the northern part of the island ... [was] contrary to the Treaty of Establishment and it create[d] problems as to the future of the British bases in Cyprus' (Nicosia telegram No. 106 of 24 January, WSC 10/9).

[11] In a letter to Mr. Goodison of 27 January, Sir S. Olver, who had just been appointed KBE, observed that the public in Cyprus had been shown how comparatively easy it was to interfere with the working of the SBAs. Previously, he noted, 'the SBAs had something of a mystique which has now vanished' (WSC 10/9).

[12] Sir S. Olver was less certain that the SBAs commanded the sympathy of the Cyprus Government. In his letter to Mr. Goodison (*v. ibid.*), he suggested that the 'hitherto general attitude to the SBAs as a reassuring background influence in Cyprus ha[d] fundamentally changed: to our "failure to act up to our role" as guarantor power has now been added this

deterrent would be uncertainty about Turkish reaction.[13] Nevertheless, in the last resort, popular pressures disregarding material interests might outweigh these considerations.[14]

15. We believe that the threat to the SBAs from the Turks is negligible so long as they believe that Britain intends to retain them. We have intelligence that they cover [*sic*] the ESBA and should they believe we are about to vacate it they may apply considerable pressure in support of their claims. They would also oppose any suggestion that Britain might give up the WSBA to the Greek Cypriots while retaining the ESBA.

16. British/Greek Cypriot relations have taken a blow. The threat to British lives, property and interests is direct and has manifested itself, and could be raised again at any time of great tension. But it will continue to be in the interest of the Cypriot Government to keep relations with Britain in reasonable repair, and to restrain popular violence as far as they are able. Against a reasonably peaceful background, apart from holding the ring and advising moderation on both sides, Britain seems unlikely to be able significantly to influence events in Cyprus over the next 12 months without calling up political measures, e.g. in the EEC or against Cypriot access to the United Kingdom which might be regarded as inappropriate and which might in any case stimulate anger which would again spill over into violence.

"pro-Turkish" and "partitionist" action by the WSBA'. He added that while he had always thought that Cyprus's leading politicians favoured Britain's continued presence in the island, '[t]hey don't any longer. The SBAs [critics argued] have proved a liability to Cyprus (the defence of the airport and Makarios' own rescue by RAF helicopter are quickly forgotten); they are pro-Turk; even the economic benefits from them are suspect in the light of the shaded Defence Review promises.'

[13] Sir S. Olver agreed that some capital could be gained by the Turkish threat to the ESBA. But he cautioned 'that frustration could easily reach a suicidal pitch where this sort of argument was lightly brushed aside: one has heard all too often the cry that it would be better if the Turks would finish it all off (*v. ibid.*).

[14] Although Sir S. Olver did not anticipate any dramatic developments against the SBAs in the short term, he nevertheless observed: 'some people are in a rash mood, and once this movement gathers force it will be very hard to stop. It is important that we should do whatever possible to win back goodwill while we still have room for manoeuvre' (Nicosia telegram No. 105 of 24 January, WSC 10/9).

Mr. Callaghan was inclined to take a firmer line. 'If the Greek Cypriots push us too hard', he commented, 'then I shall raise again the question of evacuating Cyprus. We are staying there in general Western interests—not our own: and the Greek Cypriots may have to face the alternatives of us pulling out *or* of replacement by a NATO force—neither of them desirable alternatives for the Greek Cypriots' (minute by Mr. Acland of 26 February, WSC 1/1). 'With respect', Mr. Goodison replied (see notes 6 and 7 above), 'I would suggest that our decision to stay in the SBAs was a response to a US request and not to an approach by anyone else based on general Western interests.' He added: 'Dr. Kissinger's interest in Cyprus, like his support for Turkey, seems to me to be related primarily to the Middle East problem and not to the Western Alliance'.

The UN

17. A United Nations presence will remain essential over the next 12 months, to police ceasefire lines, to prevent localised outbreaks of violence and to protect refugees and supervise their exchange. The United Nations is likely to play an important role in the situation leading up to a settlement, and possibly also in the guarantees for a future Cyprus Federation, if one is achieved. In this latter case, UNFICYP would have a new role of policing frontiers or buffer zones, at least until such time as the new arrangements were seen to be working successfully.

CHAPTER IV

Political Change in Portugal and Spain
1 May 1974–3 April 1975

No. 106

Letter from Mr. G.E. Clark[1] (Lisbon) to Mr. Goodison

[*WSP 1/1*]

Confidential   LISBON, *1 May 1974*

My dear Alan,

Events in Portugal

1. We have reported by telegram the salient events of the uprising in the Armed Forces which on 25 April swept away with astonishing rapidity Dr. Caetano's[2] regime and 45 years of government by stultification.[3] It is too early to give a comprehensive review of these events, their cause and results. For one thing I would not wish to duplicate the full reports which have no doubt appeared in the British press (but which we have not yet seen); for another, the events have by no means run their full course. It seemed worth attempting however to give you as balanced an assessment as we can at this stage of what has been achieved.

2. After the ineptitude of the isolated mutiny at Caldas da Rainha in March,[4] the professionalism and efficiency of the successful coup came as a

---

[1] First Secretary and Head of Chancery, in the British Embassy, Lisbon.

[2] Dr. M.J. das Neves Alves Caetano had been Portuguese Prime Minister since September 1968. His immediate predecessor, Dr. A. de Oliveira Salazar, had, following his appointment first as Minister of Finance (1928) and then as Prime Minister (1932), acquired dictatorial powers within an essentially corporatist New State/*Estado Novo*.

[3] Lisbon telegrams Nos. 98-101 of 25 April described how that morning elements of the Portuguese army had seized power in the name of the Armed Forces Movement (AFM)/*Movimento das Forças Armadas* (MFA). Dr. Caetano was subsequently forced to resign and the AFM announced the formation of a Council or Junta of National Salvation (JNS)/*Junta de Salvação Nacional* (JSN) headed by Gen. A.S. Ribeiro de Spínola. A former Deputy Chief of Staff of the Portuguese armed forces and prior to that Governor and Commander in Chief of Portuguese Guinea, Gen. Spínola had published in February a book, *Portugal e o Futuro* (*Portugal and the Future*), which argued that there could be no purely military solution to the wars in Portugal's overseas territories, and that if Portugal were not to lose its remaining possessions radical political changes at home were necessary. This explicit criticism of the Caetano régime, coupled with his subsequent refusal to swear an oath of allegiance to the Government, led to Gen. Spínola's removal from office on 15 March.

[4] On 16 March, following Gen. Spínola's dismissal (*v. ibid.*), 200 soldiers from army barracks at Caldas da Rainha, some 40 miles north of Lisbon, attempted to march on the capital. The column was easily turned back by units remaining loyal to the Government, and the junior

complete surprise. The Armed Forces won a virtually bloodless victory in a very short space of time. This indicates a degree of thoroughness in the preparation which is quite untypical of the Portuguese scene. But an equally important factor was the hollowness of the previous regime's pretensions. They were at loggerheads with almost every sector of the population: with the Armed Forces over the dismissal of Spínola and Costa Gomes;[5] with big business over spiralling labour costs; with the Church over missionary agitation in Mozambique; with the man in the street because of the high cost of bacalhau and inflation in general. Consequently when the crunch came virtually no-one was willing to stand up and be counted on their side. The old regime, which had seemed from the confident pronouncements of its heavily controlled press all too likely to last forever, collapsed like a house of cards at the first well co-ordinated putsch.

3. The Junta of National Salvation have banished Dr. Caetano and all his works as effectively as the summer sun disperses the early morning mist, but they have yet to contend with the forces which they have unleashed. The abolition of the censorship and the secret police, the release of political prisoners, the return of prominent exiles such as Mário Soares,[6] the possibility of political life outside the orthodoxy of the ANP[7] (also now abolished) have all created an unprecedented ferment and it is not clear where this may lead. The Portuguese have never been so animated as in the last few days, and while the general feeling is one of liberation, there is also an undercurrent which is more sinister. One of the last acts of the previous regime was as a precautionary measure to lock up prominent members of the extreme left, who were it was alleged plotting an uprising of their own for 1 May. To judge from the number of hammers and sickles daubed on the walls of the town and some of the manifestos now being distributed they are still plotting to that end. The Junta has declared 1 May an obligatory public holiday, and so far has shown no sign of wishing to ban the planned demonstrations. But it may find in them its own moment of truth: more troops have already been brought into the capital, and appeals for calm and criticism of 'undignified incidents' have already appeared in the press. Although the clean break with the practices of the past which the Junta announced in its first declaration of policy (Lisbon

officers who led the revolt were arrested. In a despatch of 26 March Mr. J.B. Ure, the British Chargé d'Affaires in Lisbon, noted that although this 'outburst of discontent' was on 'a puny scale', it had 'clearly shaken the Portuguese establishment to the core'.

[5] Gen. F. da Costa Gomes, a former Chief of Staff of the Portuguese armed forces, had been dismissed from office when in March he, like Gen. Spínola, refused to pledge allegiance to Dr. Caetano's Government.

[6] Dr. M.A.N. Lopes Soares was General Secretary of the Portuguese Socialist Party [PSP].

[7] *Acção Nacional Popular*. The ANP was the governing party of Dr. Caetano's régime. In elections to the Portuguese National Assembly in October 1973, the ANP won all 150 seats unopposed.

telegram No 106)[8] was undoubtedly sound, the Junta will probably find itself obliged to impose a measure of restraint if the situation is not to get out of hand.

4. Politically once the present euphoria dies down the new Regime faces a number of difficult and pressing problems. First and foremost is of course Africa, which indeed brought them to power.[9] It is one thing to declare that the wars should be brought to an end, and another to devise acceptable ways of doing so. General Spínola's book, and his conduct of affairs in Guinea when Governor, suggest that he would be prepared to go quite a long way towards internal self-government in the African territories,[10] but he has to devise means to sell this solution to the 'liberation movements' who have declared they want complete independence, and to the whites in Angola and Mozambique at least who will be reluctant to concede more than they have to the black majority. Yet if there is no progress on this front the young and middle ranking officers who supported the coup so enthusiastically will become disillusioned.

5. Secondly, there is the tricky question of how an authoritarian army is to hold the ring in a potentially anarchic situation where no one has experience of the restraints of ordinary democratic political life, and most of the politically active elements were forced by the policies of the previous regime to seek their expression in underground proscribed organisation whose *raison d'être* was (and is) conspiracy and violence. Thirdly, the Junta has declared that trade union activity may be resumed freely. Whatever other effects this may have it is bound to result in the short term in a further bout of wage inflation, as wages have hitherto been artificially depressed. Although there is some slack to be taken up as too much liquidity has recently been available, it will be difficult for the Junta to avoid aggravating the inflation by increasing the money supply to accommodate the higher wages, or alternatively if its advisers belong to the neo-classical school of monetary theory, creating a liquidity crisis, which will lead to bankruptcies, a collapse of business confidence and widespread unemployment. Either extreme looks bleak, and the middle track hard to find. Yet it must be found if the economic promises of the Junta are to be made good, and the ambition of General Spínola to make Portugal an integral part of a prosperous Western Europe fulfilled.

---

[8] In this telegram of 26 April, the JNS were reported to have declared that the provisional Government would support the 'implementation of preparatory economic, cultural and social measures guaranteeing effective exercise of the citizen's political freedom in the future'.

[9] By the early 1970s Portugal was struggling to hold on to its colonial possessions in Africa. The outbreak of guerrilla wars in Angola (1961), Portuguese Guinea (1962) and Mozambique (1964) had developed into national insurgencies, and by 1974 over 150,000 Portuguese troops were deployed in Africa. Despite this considerable investment of military resources, Portuguese forces remained stalemated in Mozambique and Angola and were actually facing defeat in Guinea.

[10] Gen. Spínola had proposed in his book the formation of a 'Lusitanian Federation' incorporating metropolitan Portugal and its overseas possessions.

6. On the military front, so far as we can tell the Army is solidly on the side of the Junta. The General officers who took the oath of allegiance to the old regime on 13 March command very little following among the rank and file, and have prudently gone to ground, or been removed by the Junta. The Navy too have now sought respectability by wholehearted support for the new regime, and as you will have seen from the Naval Attaché's account of the role of the frigate Gago Coutinho on 25 April,[11] only the brass hats supported the old order. About the Air Force there is less certainty. The paratroopers (an A.F. regiment) are entrusted with important guard duties now, but played no part in the uprising. As for the maintenance of public order referred to above, the Army has so far done well. It has fraternised with the people when appropriate, but when ugly scenes have developed it has maintained discipline and acted to prevent the worst excesses of mob violence. Psychologically its tactics are skilful. When for example an angry crowd attacked the offices of the extreme right wing newspaper Epoca the soldiers allowed the mob to overturn cars and smash windows, before they moved in to protect the individuals. The Army itself avoided becoming the focus of the mob's anger, and tensions were relieved without loss of life and with only modest damage to property. Whether these tactics will work on May Day, when at least some of those demonstrating will be aiming to provoke the Army, remains, at the time of writing, to be seen.

~~My dear~~[12]

Yours sincerely,

G.E. CLARK

[11] Not traced. The *Gago Coutinho* had been ordered by the Government to bombard the revolutionary forces amassing in the city centre. Although the ship's Captain was prepared, and gave the order, to fire on the insurgents, his crew were not. He was arrested by junior officers and the frigate's barrels raised skyward, indicating that it had no intention of intervening in the *coup*.

[12] In explanation of this slip of the pen, Mr. Clark noted at the bottom of this letter: 'The excitement is confusing. GEC.'

No. 107

*Record of a Conversation between Mr. H. Wilson and Dr. Soares at
10 Downing Street on Thursday, 2 May 1974 at 2.10 p.m.*[1]

[*WSP 3/548/4*]

Confidential

Present:

The Prime Minister	Dr. Mário Soares
Foreign and Commonwealth Secretary	Interpreter
Mr. Ron Hayward	
Mr. P.L. Carter	
Mr. T. McNally	
Lord Bridges	

The *Foreign and Commonwealth Secretary* summed up the position he had
reached in his talk with Dr. Soares over lunch. He intended to try to
strengthen Dr. Soares' position by announcing that the Government had
decided to accord recognition to General Spínola following the discussion
with Dr. Soares in London.[2] He had also suggested to Dr. Soares that it
was important for him to enter into discussions with the Americans, and
had undertaken to tell Dr. Kissinger that Dr. Soares was anxious to see
him. He had further said that we would be glad to see General Spínola as
a visitor in London. As regards the position of the Communists in the
future Portuguese Government, Dr. Soares had said that there would be
some Communist Ministers but they would not be permitted to hold
certain portfolios. His party would probably insist on the post of Prime
Minister (perhaps Dr. Soares himself), or the Prime Minister might be an
independent figure, or a Catholic: but the Catholics had no political
organisation and might end up as prisoners of the Communists. He would
not want to be Foreign Minister. The *Prime Minister* welcomed the timing of
British recognition, as this would show our full support for Dr. Soares. *Dr.
Soares* said this was certainly how the decision would be interpreted.
Replying to a question about the strength of his Party, Dr. Soares said that
hitherto the Party had operated illegally. Only now, with the first issues of
the Party paper appearing and the organisation on the ground beginning to
take shape, was it possible to evaluate Party strength. To judge from the

---

[1] Dr. Soares was in London at the invitation of Mr. R. Hayward, General Secretary of the
Labour Party.

[2] In a submission to Mr. Wiggin of 30 April, Mr. Goodison recommended HMG's early
recognition of the new régime in Portugal. It would, he argued, 'enable us to continue
conducting normal business with Portugal. But more importantly, it should encourage the new
régime to continue in the seemingly hopeful direction in which they have set out; liberalisation
at home and saner policies in Africa are certainly what HMG wishes to see' (WSP 2/2).

support given to him in public demonstrations, the Party was either in the strongest position, or sharing that position with the Communists.

Mr. McNally said that the Portuguese Socialists were in need of technical help, and Mr. Jack Jones[3] and the TGWU, as well as the Labour Party, might be able to help them over this. *Dr. Soares* said this would be very important. Senhor Alvaro Cunhal[4] had just returned to Lisbon, and the Communists had been given a lot of official support which provided them with big advantages.

The *Foreign and Commonwealth Secretary* said there were two things which needed action. First, there was the question of Party support; Dr. Soares should let the Labour Party know what he wanted. Secondly, as between Governments, he hoped General Spínola would tell the British Government what Portugal needed, so that Britain, Germany and the United States could help. *Dr. Soares* agreed that these were the main questions. On the first, financial support was very important: he was looking for a loan or grant. But he also needed technical assistance to help him to organise and project his electoral campaign. He would like soon to receive a delegation of the British Labour Party, including Members of Parliament; this should precede a planned visit from the Socialist International, for optical reasons. The *Prime Minister* said that Mr. Hayward would know how this help should be given, and the Foreign and Commonwealth Secretary (as Chairman of the Party) would also be able to provide assistance.

Turning to relations between Governments, *Dr. Soares* said that he fully accepted the urgency of the colonial problem which he was confident would be solved. If the British Government had any suggestions to make on this issue, for example as a result of their knowledge of American policy, he would be glad to receive them. The real issues lay in Angola and Mozambique, and he mentioned that there was some danger of a UDI[5] in Angola. The *Prime Minister* said that these problems were of the greatest interest to the British Government, and he would like further discussions about them in due course. The Foreign and Commonwealth Secretary would be able to speak with the benefit of his knowledge of American views. But in Africa (and this was particularly true of President Nixon's administration) the Americans tended to look to us for ideas, rather than to initiate their own. The Prime Minister supposed that the biggest problem would be how to handle Frelimo.[6]

Dr. Soares agreed that in Mozambique Frelimo was the single liberation movement, and that Portugal would have to negotiate with it. But there

---

[3] Mr. J.L. Jones was General Secretary of the Transport and General Workers' Union (TGWU) and Chairman of the Trades Union Congress (TUC) International Committee.

[4] General Secretary of the Portuguese Communist Party (PCP).

[5] Unilateral Declaration of Independence.

[6] *Frente Nacional de Libertação de Moçambique.*

were three competing movements in Angola: the MPLA[7] were recognised by the OAU,[8] but had serious problems with the followers of Holden Roberto[9] who was being promoted by Zaire and Ethiopia. Guiné was complicated because of the relationship with the Cape Verde islands; his Party's policy was to recognise the independence of the territory. The *Prime Minister* said that the British Government would wish to handle these matters within the United Nations context. This applied particularly to Rhodesia, an issue which had been made much more difficult for us because of Mr. Smith's ability to rely on his friends in Mozambique in the past.[10] He hoped to have thorough discussions of this whole area with the future democratic Government in Portugal. *Dr. Soares* expressed his general agreement with this view.

The *Foreign and Commonwealth Secretary* said that he would be glad to make British experience in decolonisation available to the new Portuguese Government, and invited Dr. Soares to send a delegation to the Foreign and Commonwealth Office to discuss the problem with his officials. *Dr. Soares* was grateful for this offer.[11] He thought that General Spínola would also be grateful for it, since the General's experience related only to Guiné. The *Foreign and Commonwealth Secretary* said that the British Government was anxious to help the Portuguese in any way they could: and thought that we could help each other over Rhodesia. *Dr. Soares* said that the situation in Africa was now very urgent, and was deteriorating each day.

The *Foreign and Commonwealth Secretary* asked Dr. Soares if he could tell General Spínola tactfully how much would depend on the position of the Socialist Party in his administration. *Dr. Soares* fully agreed, but thought that this might be better said by HM Ambassador than by himself. He expected that the Government would be formed within two weeks at the latest. The members of the junta were all men of goodwill but they had not political experience and did not know how to handle the Communists.[12]

---

[7] *Movimento Popular de Libertação de Angola.*

[8] Organisation for African Unity.

[9] Sr. H. Roberto was the leader of the *Frente Nacional de Libertação de Angola* (FNLA).

[10] In 1965 the white minority Government in Rhodesia, headed by Mr. I.D. Smith, renounced British sovereignty and issued a unilateral declaration of independence (UDI). The UN subsequently imposed mandatory economic sanctions on the rebel administration, but the Portuguese authorities in Mozambique had continued to allow Rhodesian commerce access to their Indian Ocean ports.

[11] In telegram No. 95 to Lisbon of 2 May Mr. Callaghan instructed Mr. N.C.C. Trench, the newly-appointed British Ambassador in Lisbon, that once he had 'completed the formality of recognition', he should seek an early meeting with Gen. Spínola and state HMG's readiness to 'to speak frankly to the new Portuguese Government about the problems we have ourselves experienced in the process of decolonisation and how we have overcome them' (WSP 3/548/4).

[12] In a personal message to Dr. Kissinger Mr. Callaghan reported on this meeting: 'Soares sees the Socialist Party as the only force in the country capable of resisting the Communists who he believes have the full backing of the Soviet Union. Soares pointed out that during yesterday's May Day demonstrations in Lisbon, which may have involved as many as a million

The *Foreign and Commonwealth Secretary* asked whether General Spínola would be receptive to British views passed to him through the British Ambassador. Dr. Soares replied 'enormously'. General Spínola wanted him to be an emissary to the British Government at this time. Replying to a question from the Prime Minister, *Dr. Soares* said that his relations with General Spínola were very good. He had already had previous contacts with the General; he had been 'conspiring' with the General before publication of the latter's book, and contacts had been made through the mediation of President Senghor[13] in Senegal. It had been easy to build on these previous indirect contacts since his own return to Lisbon. The junta now had the military situation under control, but he was apprehensive that the soldiers and sailors were being affected by the general atmosphere of jubilation in the capital, and that some were now adopting Communist slogans and symbols. The *Prime Minister* said this was what Dr. Soares had to watch. *Dr. Soares* was sure that the extreme right was not in a position to undertake a counter-coup now. But the Conservative press were trying to frighten the bourgeoisie, by exaggerating the current dangers: and he did not exclude the possibility that, if the economic situation were to deteriorate, there might be a counter-coup on Chilean lines. Hence the need to act as quickly as possible. He wanted, after his return to Lisbon and discussion with General Spínola, to announce at a press conference that Portugal's British friends wished to help Portugal in its present position in any way it could, by providing for example economic and technical aid. The *Foreign and Commonwealth Secretary* said that he would instruct HM Ambassador to get in touch with General Spínola, and to tell him of the views which he and the Prime Minister had expressed in this conversation, and of the determination of the British Government to help. He asked whether Dr. Soares could, before leaving London, send a message to General Spínola forewarning him of this approach, and *Dr. Soares* said that he would try to do so.

After the Prime Minister and the Foreign and Commonwealth Secretary had both renewed their congratulations to Dr. Soares on his success, and had given their best wishes to Portugal at this moment in her history, Dr. Soares left Downing Street at 2.45 p.m.

---

people, he himself was the only personality in a position to challenge the General Secretary of the Communist Party, Cunhal. He says that the right wing are in no state to stage a counter coup or even to constitute a viable political force at the moment.' (telegram No. 984 to Washington of 2 May 1974, WSP 3/304/1/74).

[13] M. L.S. Senghor was President of Senegal.

No. 108

Letter from Mr. J.A.N. Graham[1] (Washington) to Mr. Goodison

[*WSP 2/579/1*]

Confidential   WASHINGTON, *22 May 1974*

Dear Alan,

Greece, Portugal and The Alliance

At a lunch given by Mr. Rush, Deputy Secretary in the State Department, for Mr. Hattersley on Tuesday, 14 May,[2] there was an interesting general discussion about the problem presented to the North Atlantic Alliance by undemocratic member regimes. Mr. Hattersley made the point that many people in Britain, particularly those who did not remember the genesis of NATO or even the Hungarian and Czechoslovak crises, questioned its value if it tolerated, and indeed appeared to welcome to its counsels, such authoritarian regimes as those in Greece and Portugal. If NATO and what it stood for was to receive the support of people in our countries it was essential to show that we cared for and were doing something about the maintenance of freedom in all the members of the Alliance.[3]

2. Mr. Rush put the counter-argument. NATO was a defensive alliance whose object was to preserve its members from being taken over by Communism, from which there would be no return. As long as individual members of the Alliance retained the right to choose their own forms of government, it was not for the other members of the Alliance to interfere. We could take bilateral measures to bring home to such governments our distaste for their methods; but we would not achieve our purpose, and indeed might even strengthen them, if we attempted to take multilateral action or to throw them out of the Alliance. He doubted whether the recent *coup d'état* in Portugal would have happened had we tried to ostracise Portugal. Mr. Hattersley replied that that was a matter of argument, since it could be said that the *coup d'état* might have come earlier and might not

---

[1] Counsellor and Head of Chancery in the British Embassy, Washington.

[2] Cf. No. 13.

[3] In opposition, the Labour Party had been especially critical of the Portuguese Government and its African policies, and Mr. Wilson had suggested in July 1973 that 'in the absence of clear and indisputable repudiation of the brutalities inherent in Portugal's colonial policy, Portugal no longer had any claim to our support or welcome in NATO'. Although the new Labour administration was, as Mr. Goodison noted in a minute to Mr. Trench of 25 March, 'anxious to maintain in government, and be seen to maintain, the policies which it enunciated in opposition', in reality the only action taken to demonstrate HMG's disapproval of the Caetano régime had so far been the cancellation of a visit, planned for early April, of *HMS Arlingham* to Portimaõ (WSP 3/548/2).

have left the Communists in such a strong position to exploit it, had we exercised stronger pressure on Portugal at an earlier stage.[4]

3. At one point, Mr. Hartman suggested that it might be possible to found a right to offer advice, and even a right to interfere, on the implications of the internal policies of the individual members of the Alliance for their effectiveness as allies. For example, the Greek Government were weakening their armed forces by the wholesale retirement of officers; this gave the Alliance legitimate cause for concern. It was pointed out that, similarly, the Danish and, indeed, the Iceland Governments' policies had implications for the Alliance, which entitled the Secretary-General and other members to comment and remonstrate.

4. There was no conclusion to the discussion, except that it was generally agreed that our and the Americans' objectives were much the same, though we might differ over the means to achieve them.

Yours ever,
J.A.N. GRAHAM

[4] Gen. Spínola formally assumed the office of President of Portugal on 15 May, and a new provisional Government, headed by Prof. A. da Palma Carlos, and evenly divided between the Communists and Socialists on the one hand and centrists and independents on the other, was in place by 17 May. In conversation with Mr. Trench on 20 May, Dr. Soares, who was appointed Foreign Minister, expressed his concern that 'the emergence of the Communist Party [in Portugal] and the presence of Communist Ministers in the Government' would cause difficulties in NATO, and especially with the US. 'He wished', Mr. Trench informed Mr. Callaghan in telegram No. 151 of 20 May, 'to reassure you that they [i.e. Communist Ministers] were not there because the Provisional Government was a Popular Front government but because it was a truly national government. Their presence in the Government was necessary in order to guarantee peace in the labour field until the elections. The situation was similar to that in France and Italy in 1945/46 after Fascism had been overthrown. Despite these changes Portugal had not changed sides. She wished to maintain her traditional friendship with the United Kingdom and the United States, and to play her proper part in NATO and in Western Europe.'

The entry of the Communists into the Portuguese administration was considered a security risk in Brussels. In UKDEL NATO telegram No. 225 of 20 May, Sir E. Peck reported that the US were pressing for the withdrawal of ATOMAL clearance to Portugal (a NATO security classification to protect restricted information from US sources) and for a decision to refuse 'to communicate [to Portugal] any NATO documents above Confidential'. FCO officials were generally more sympathetic towards Portugal. On 21 May Mr. B.J. Everett (First Secretary, SED) noted on Sir E. Peck's telegram that this was 'hardly the time to be beastly to Portugal'.

No. 109

Letter from Mr. Trench (Lisbon) to Mr. Wiggin[1]

[*WSP 1/1*]

Confidential   LISBON, *5 June 1974*

Dear Charles,

I have not previously written to you since my arrival here for two main reasons. First, because I was given to understand that you would shortly be moving on to other things, and second, because the pattern of developments since 25 April has been such that it was impossible to attempt any overall analysis, and we could only keep the FCO informed of the course of events, with such comment as might help to provide some clarification in the short term. On the first count, I see from the records of the Secretary of State's talks with Dr. Soares at the end of May[2] that you are still in action on this front; and on the second, I thought that it might provide useful background if I were to give you some general impression of the new régime (or régimes, as some observers might prefer to say),[3] six weeks or so after what we now politely term 'the events of 25 April'.

2. The Portuguese are, by and large, a docile people, not unduly addicted to intellectual activity, and a paternalistic régime, such as that of Salazar in his early years, is not by its nature unwelcome to many of them. But the increasing rigidity of the régime, the excesses of the secret police and the burden of the colonial wars had combined to produce a great deal of discontent. So the sudden removal of all restraints naturally had a highly unsettling effect, and for the past six weeks we have seen demonstrations, strikes and political and industrial meetings following each other in rapid succession. At the same time the Junta of National Salvation (JSN), the Armed Forces Movement (AFM) and the new-born political parties have

---

[1] Mr. Wiggin was appointed British Ambassador to Spain in October 1974.

[2] Dr. Soares visited London during 24-28 May, primarily with a view to negotiating a ceasefire with representatives of the Guinean independence movement, the *Partido Africano de Independência de Guiné e Cabo Verde* (PAIGC). Talks with Mr. Callaghan and FCO officials on 26 May covered Portuguese plans for decolonisation in Africa and, more particularly, the impact of developments in Mozambique upon the political situation in Rhodesia and South Africa (record of conversation between Mr. Callaghan and Mr. Soares at No. 1 Carlton Gardens on 26 May at 5 p.m., WSP 3/548/6).

[3] As Mr. Clark explained in a letter of 22 May to Mr. Baker, the new interim constitutional arrangements, published on 16 May, offered 'plenty of scope for friction given the overlapping of responsibilities in the decision-making process between the Junta, the Armed Forces Movement and the Government'. The Junta was to continue in being as a watchdog to ensure the Government's programme was observed, and the Coordinating Committee of the AFM was to have a similar supervisory role. Seven members of the AFM were also to join a new Council of State when it was established. 'It therefore seems clear', Mr. Clark added, 'that having made the coup the military intend to try to keep the new Government on a tight rein.'

had to create almost from scratch some sort of upper echelon to direct the running of the country.

3. In these circumstances it is not surprising that confusion has been the most noticeable feature of the scene. Indeed, I doubt whether it is possible for anyone not immediately involved to realise the difficulties faced by the new régime, compounded by the customs of the country and the national character. When, for instance, I called on General Spínola at the Palace of Belém on 3 May, to convey our offer of help over decolonisation, Gerald Clark and I had to pick our way through groups of municipal councillors, countrywomen, trade associations, etc., all waiting to see the General to present their own particular problems; and as we left after some twenty minutes with him, we could hear in the next room the voices of the delegation that was to follow us. In the intervals of receiving official and unofficial callers, the General was taking part in meetings of the JNS to select Ministers for the Provisional Government, in interviews with those selected in order to discover whether they would be prepared to serve or not, and presumably also (though this was not publicly announced) in discussions with representatives of the AFM, who were determined to have a say in the manner in which their success was exploited.

4. Some commentators now blame the JNS for not having imposed a standstill on wages and prices the moment they came to power, and it is clear that the Junta themselves regret not having intervened earlier to put an end to the free-for-all to which the intoxicating cry of 'Freedom' understandably gave rise. But the fact of the matter is that in those early days there simply was not time for the Junta to attend to all the urgent problems that faced them, and indeed, one still has the feeling that the pressure of events is too much for them to cope with, though they are now trying to impose some degree of control over labour and the economy.

5. In foreign affairs the same break-neck pace has been apparent. Before Mário Soares had even taken formal charge of his Ministry, its officials learned through the grapevine that he was going at once on a journey abroad—no one knew where. The announcement that it was to Dakar came as a complete surprise, as did the news that meetings with the PAIGC[4] were to start in London on 25 May. When I later visited the Minister to try to extract from him some basic information about the forthcoming visit, the impression I received in his Private Office was one of people overwhelmed by the pace of events, and, of course, without any experience of dealing with the mechanics of such an operation—to take an elementary example, no one could tell me the flight number of the aircraft by which the Minister's party was to travel. As I sat in the waiting-room beforehand, figures popped in and out like characters in a bedroom farce. Col. Bruno[5] appeared with a journalist, tried to turn me out, apologised

---

[4] See note 2 above.

[5] Col. J. Almeida Bruno was a close associate of Gen. Spínola and member of the Portuguese Council of State.

profusely when I revealed my identity, and shot out again; an African was ushered in by a junior official, and both then retreated when they saw me; and so it went on, even in the Minister's room when he was talking to me, with people constantly coming and going, and carrying on conversations in the background.

6. Since then, Dr. Soares' hope of concluding an agreement with PAIGC in two days of negotiations has, not unexpectedly, been frustrated, and he has started on a fresh batch of talks, with Frelimo, though he has undertaken to return to London for the next round with the PAIGC, starting on 8 June. In the meantime, he has addressed a Socialist Party rally in Coimbra for an hour (on the day of his return from London), has had talks with the Netherlands Foreign Minister and Monsieur Edgar Faure,[6] attended a presentation of credentials, accompanied Mr. van der Stoel[7] in a call on the Prime Minister, and conferred with the President more than once. It is not surprising that he was looking exhausted when he left for Lusaka early yesterday, and one wonders how long he will be able to keep it up.

7. Equally important is the danger that, when the crucial point is reached in the various African talks, he will find himself at odds with General Spínola and many of those who are to the right of his own Socialist Party. There are hints of this in his conversations with the Secretary of State, and it certainly seems, to judge from the President's conversation with M. Faure, that General Spínola has not in any way modified the views expressed in his celebrated book, which do not altogether fit in with Dr. Soares' comments on African policy. So when Dr. Soares talked to the Dutch Foreign Minister two days ago about the need to find a formula which would satisfy the PAIGC without necessarily acceding in fact to all their demands, it may well be that he was mentally bracketing General Spínola, the Army and the Centre parties with the PAIGC.[8]

8. I suspect—though it is impossible to be sure at present, because the kaleidoscope is not yet stationary—that this situation typifies the régime as a whole, with each of its highly disparate elements pursuing its own aims and collaborating with the others only when the situation is so grave as to make concerted action essential—for example, over wage claims. As if this were not enough, the day to day administration of government and business is greatly handicapped by the wholesale dismissals and transfers which have been carried out, and which make it difficult for hard-pressed Ministers to secure the execution of decisions reached in the meetings

[6] President of the French National Assembly

[7] Mr. M. van der Stoel was the Netherlands Foreign Minister.

[8] As Mr. Baker explained to Mr. Clark, the Prime Minister was 'taking a keen interest in the course of events in Portugal', but was also 'getting impatient with General Spínola's failure to get a move on, set up a Government and decolonise'. 'There was', Mr. Baker added, 'a fear that he might be throwing it all away' (letter of 13 May).

which seem to occupy all their time when they are not making speeches or greeting the distinguished visitors who come to Portugal in a steady stream.

9. In short, the impression one gets is of an ant-heap which has been broken open. Frenzied activity is in progress and ants are scurrying in all directions, but it is not always possible for the observer to discern the pattern that directs their movements, and it is still more difficult to decide what is going on in the sections that have not been exposed to the light of day. As we have reported by telegram, it looks as though the AFM's activities were being damped down (though Col. Bruno would probably not agree—I gather that he rather fancies himself as a military 007),[9] but it will take some time to see how this works out. In a different field, there is much talk of the Portuguese Communist Party securing a grip on industry by extending the organisation which it had managed to preserve on a small scale during the previous régime. But we have no hard facts to go on, and in its public utterances the Party has been eminently sane and sensible, appealing to people not to let themselves be deluded by agitators of the extreme left (maoists, trotskyists and anarchists).

10. If and when the present frenetic activity of the JNS and the Provisional Government dies down, I hope that we shall be able to talk to their members in an atmosphere which enables them to look at problems in the longer term, rather than concentrating on one urgent subject at a time. We should then be able to form a more coherent picture. In the meantime we can only pick up information as best we may and try to put it in its place in the pattern.

Yours Ever,
N.C.C. Trench

[9] The codename of Ian Fleming's fictional British secret service agent, James Bond.

The strains upon the provisional Government, which Mr. Trench outlined in his letter of 5 June,[1] continued into July. Steep wage demands, threatening high inflation and a flight of foreign capital, undermined confidence in the Portuguese economy, whilst concurrent and widespread industrial unrest further deterred much needed foreign investment. Portugal did not, Mr. Trench noted in a letter of 10 July, 'have the money, the managerial skills or the administrators to enable it to absorb this sort of destructive process without suffering severely'. Indeed, he thought the economic chaos could only serve the interests of the PCP, which alone amongst Portugal's political parties was 'sufficiently well organised to take advantage of the resulting disarray'.[2]

[1] See No. 109.

[2] Letter from Mr. Trench to Mr. Wiggin of 10 July, WSP 1/1.

Displaying superior talents for 'publicity, coherence, appeal to the electorate and internal unity', the Communists also proved difficult partners within the coalition Government, impeding the reforms which the Prime Minister, Professor A. da Palma Carlos, felt essential for Portugal's future.[3] Frustrated by what he evidently saw as the extremist obstructionism rendering Portugal ungovernable, on 5 July he submitted to General Spínola proposals for constitutional reform, including a presidential election in the autumn and the postponement of elections for a Constituent Assembly until November 1976. These may have been meant to provoke the resignation of 'extremists' in the Cabinet. But, as Mr. Clark subsequently pointed out, it was also arguable that 'centrist' Ministers were putting forward measures which bore little direct relationship to the programme of the AFM, to which the Communists were able to look for support. In any event, when on 9 July General Spínola informed Professor da Palma Carlos that the Council of State had only in part accepted his proposals, the Prime Minister resigned.[4]

The ensuing political crisis was resolved with the appointment on 18 July of a new provisional Government, whose composition clearly reflected the wishes of the AFM. Led by Brigadier (subsequently General) Vasco dos Santos Gonçalves, it now included eight military officers (as opposed to just one previously), a number of whom were, according to Mr. Trench, believed to have 'extreme left-wing sympathies'.[5] The AFM had, he observed, 'moved from the sidelines into a position of direct and powerful involvement in the Government'. Meanwhile, General Spínola and his household appeared 'out of touch with the real feelings of the Movement'.[6] Commentators in London and Lisbon increasingly doubted whether the President's influence could effectively be brought to bear as a force for moderation. Few were therefore wholly surprised when in the early autumn another political convulsion provoked his resignation

[3] *V. Ibid.*
[4] Letters from Mr. Clark to Mr. Baker of 17 and 24 July, WSP 1/1.
[5] Lisbon tel. No. 228 of 18 July, WSP 1/1.
[6] Letter from Mr. Trench to Mr. Wiggin of 17 July, WSP 1/1.

No. 110

Mr. Trench (Lisbon) to Mr. Callaghan

[*WSP 1/12*]

Confidential   LISBON, *2 October 1974*

Summary ...[1]
Sir,

The Fall of Spínola

1. When I was in the Foreign and Commonwealth Office for the discussions on Africa some three weeks ago, I expressed my fear that the recent events in Mozambique[2] would destroy the fragile equilibrium of the political forces in Portugal and that within a short time there would be a different President, or a different Government, or both. I have since had the melancholy satisfaction of seeing my prediction borne out by events:[3] I shall now be dealing with the third President of the Republic and the fourth Portuguese Government to hold office since my arrival in Lisbon on the 8th of April. In the present despatch I shall attempt to put the latest developments in better perspective than has been possible in the telegrams which I have so far addressed to you. But first I must try to reconstruct the events leading up to the crisis.

2. The three months following the upheaval of the 25th of April were characterised by a steady increase in the powers of the extreme left wing elements in the Armed Forces Movement (AFM) and the Provisional Governments, at the expense of President Spínola and the more traditional

---

[1] Not printed.

[2] On 7 September the Portuguese Government signed an agreement with FRELIMO at Lusaka providing for the immediate establishment of a transitional government in Mozambique and the colony's complete independence by June 1975. A subsequent attempt by White Mozambicans to establish their own provisional government as a precursor to a UDI was quashed by Portuguese and FRELIMO forces. In a letter to Mr. D.C. Thomas (South West European Department (SWED)) of 25 September, Mr. Ure reported the Portuguese political establishment's discontent over the manner in which Dr. Soares and some of his colleagues had been 'forcing the pace over Guinea-Bissau and Mozambique'. Recent riots in Angola as well as the revolt in Mozambique had, in his opinion, 'clearly demonstrated the dangers which such "instant decolonisation" [could] provoke'.

[3] Mr. Trench's gloomy prognosis had not been shared by all in the FCO. In a minute of 9 October covering this despatch Mr. Thomas confessed to Mr. Morgan that for some time before the events of the end of September 'we had been receiving reports ... to the effect that a major confrontation between left and right was imminent and that the Portuguese Communist Party was organising itself clandestinely to "take over the country". Although the tensions within the armed forces and the government were obvious and the Communist Party was clearly making every effort to extend its influence, I confess I had tended to discount the more alarmist of these reports, on the grounds that they generally emanated from right-wing sources who could be expected to exaggerate the Red Menace. In the event they proved largely justified.'

elements in the Junta of National Salvation, in the Armed Forces as a whole and in the ranks of the politicians. However, as reported in correspondence with your Department, there had been indications in recent weeks that President Spínola was trying to reassert his authority. He undoubtedly vetoed the appointment of a number of Communist candidates for the important posts of Civil Governors; he flew to the Cape Verde Islands for talks with President Mobutu of Zaire—on his own initiative and without consulting his Foreign Minister—about the future of Angola, and he announced that he would take into his own hands the conduct of the negotiations for the independence of that territory. Concurrently with these moves, some observers believed that they could detect an increase in the support for President Spínola throughout the country. No doubt this was most pronounced in the political forces of the right and the centre, but it was also thought to enjoy the participation of many humble citizens who have become bemused and frightened in recent months by the alarming rise in the cost of living, by uncertainties about whether their jobs would survive the winter, by the deterioration in law and order, and by the unaccustomedly shrill tone of public debate. It is hard to say whether it was the vocal support which encouraged President Spínola to take a firmer line or whether it was his own visible initiatives which encouraged the popular support; in any event, President Spínola appeared to be in the process of checking the slide to the extreme left which had seemed to be taking place.

3. Events came to a head with the emergence of a movement calling itself 'The Silent Majority', who announced their intention to hold a large public rally in the capital in support of the President. It is difficult to analyse the support for this movement. It certainly included some elements of the extreme right wing; some of these, such as the former members of the Portuguese Legion, may possibly have made amateurish attempts to collect shotguns and other arms to protect themselves in 'an emergency'; others, like the big banking families, may have been handing out covert largess to tough gangs who were prepared to put up posters and distribute leaflets; others again were prepared to buy up blocks of tickets for the Lisbon bull-ring on the night of the 26th of September when President Spínola was due to make a public appearance there, in order to give him a noisy demonstration of support. But there were undoubtedly many—a majority within the movement if not within the nation—who merely wished to demonstrate peaceful support for the leader they trusted, and opposition to extremism. The (very amateurish) leaflets and posters distributed by the organisers specifically expressed adherence to the programme of the AFM.

4. By the end of last week it was clear that a major confrontation lay ahead. On the one hand President Spínola's supporters were determined to bring in the largest possible numbers from outside Lisbon to a demonstration before the Presidential Palace at Belem on the 28th of September. On the other, the greater part of the press (which is far from

impartial) was taking the line that the Silent Majority was a front for the forces of reaction. The Popular Democratic Party (PPD) had—after considerable fence-sitting—joined the Socialists and Communists in denouncing the Silent Majority, and evidence reached us that obstruction and threats of physical violence were being used all over the country to prevent supporters of the President from coming to Belem. A trial of strength was clearly about to be undertaken.

5. The crucial night was that of Friday 28th/29th September.[4] At about midnight, civilian members of the left-wing parties—under predominantly Communist direction—started erecting barricades on all the main roads into Lisbon to prevent the entry of Spínola's supporters for the following day's demonstration—which had, contrary to a report in The Times, been authorised by the Civil Governor. Inside Belem Palace (and our information is based largely on an account given subsequently to my Defence Attaché[5] by the Head of President Spínola's civil household) the President reacted sharply to this news. He summoned the whole Provisional Government, together with Brigadier Otelo Saraiva de Carvalho (the Commander of the Lisbon Garrison), and told them that it was up to them to restore law and order in the capital. He also issued a directive to the effect that the road-blocks should go. But about four o'clock in the morning it was clear that, despite the directive, the barricades remained in place and an ever increasing number of activists were manning them in defiance of President Spínola and his supporters. This, I believe, was the moment of truth. Spínola is said to have realised that with the civil and military commanders under his hand in the Palace, surrounded by his own loyal paratroopers and with military units in the capital who would unquestionably obey his commands, he could have forcibly removed the road-blocks. But he calculated that he could not have done so without loss of life, and—according to Colonel Dias de Lima—this he was unprepared to contemplate.

6. From that moment on the extreme left wing had everything its own way. Troops of the Lisbon area, apparently often helped by civilians of indeterminate status, carried out a clearly pre-arranged series of swoops on the houses of prominent figures of the right wing; some of these—like Dr. Franco Nogueira, Salazar's Foreign Minister—were taken from their beds at five o'clock in the morning. Only much later were the lists of those arrested published, and then it was clear that these included not only some possible plotters and activists (such as General Kaúlza de Arriaga),[6] but many others whose only offence was probably their potential as a rallying

---

[4] This is evidently an error since 27 September was a Friday. The reference is probably to the night of 27/28 September.

[5] Lt.-Col. T.E.H. Huggan.

[6] Gen. Kaúlza de Arriaga, formerly Commander-in-Chief of the Armed Forces in Mozambique, had a reputation as an inveterate right-wing plotter and had been behind an abortive attempt to overthrow the Caetano Government in December 1973.

point for traditional sentiment. Some of those arrested—like the wealthy Conde de Caria—seemed to have been included merely for their prominence and unpopularity as bankers or industrialists. By Saturday morning something close to panic was sweeping through the ranks of the Hundred Families who had for so long dominated the economic and social scene here.

7. By the end of the morning, President Spínola had been prevailed upon to issue a statement calling off the demonstration in his support, in order to avoid unpleasant incidents. This was backed up by more emphatic statements by the Government and Armed Forces Movement that the rally was cancelled. Warnings were put out urging people to keep away from Belem if they wanted to avoid violence and trouble. Later the same day further evidence of the prior preparations made by the Communist Party was provided by large-scale marches through Lisbon, on which Communist flags were carried and Communist slogans chanted. These processions were marshalled by Communist Party toughs carrying clubs, steel bars and other even more menacing home-made weapons. A sullenness and hatred were apparent which had been totally absent from the carnival-like demonstrations of the 1st of May. Meanwhile the Government-controlled radio—Emissora Nacional—which was the only one on the air, put out dramatic stories of the discovery of caches of reactionaries' weapons, one such story reporting the discovery of a sniper's rifle hidden opposite the house of the Prime Minister.

8. On the following day—Sunday, the 29th of September—the atmosphere of crisis was maintained. The radio warned the nation that a reactionary plot was attempting to reverse the results of the revolution. The road-blocks remained manned and those of my diplomatic colleagues who, like myself, attempted to reach points outside the centre of Lisbon, were subjected to searches of ourselves and our vehicles by motley pickets of self-appointed Representatives of the People, wearing Communist Party badges and arm bands, and supported, in some cases, by soldiers who often seemed to have little idea of what they were supposed to be doing and took their instructions from the civilian leaders. Conditions very close to total anarchy prevailed. There are well-documented cases of completely innocent travellers being robbed, threatened and insulted. Later in the day both the Co-ordinating Committee of the AFM and the Continental Operational Command[7] issued statements asking the populace to leave the road blocks to be manned by the military; the number of times this injunction had to be repeated, and the many hours which passed between the first announcement of the order and compliance with it, must have made the AFM realise how strong and independent was the grip of the Communist Party organisation.

[7] The military command structure established by the AFM on 8 July, usually known by its acronym, COPCON (*Commando Operacional do Continente*). This was an élite force of 5,000 men which functioned as an internal security service.

9. While on the Sunday evening the President, General Costa Gomes and the Armed Forces Movement were issuing a communiqué about being in agreement on the 'progress towards democracy', and while the Prime Minister was issuing reassuring statements about the crisis being concluded, we heard that the President was considering imminent resignation. His broadcast to the nation explaining the reasons why he could no longer carry on as President (my telegram No. 325)[8] was made at 11.20 a.m. on Monday, the 30th of September. Although the fact that he was expected to broadcast at 11 a.m. was widely known, his words cannot have been heard, nor his moving appearance on television seen, by any very large proportion of the population. The authorities declined to repeat or summarise General Spínola's remarks on the radio, until they were able to announce that General Costa Gomes had taken over the Presidency and to put Spínola's remarks in the context of general reassurances given by Costa Gomes.

10. With the resignation of President Spínola and with the apparent total victory of the extreme left, the authorities wasted no time in clearing the decks of those in high places who might be expected to impede their plans. The three more right-wing members of the Junta, including the foolishly outspoken General Galvão de Melo, were relieved of their places in that body, and Colonel Miguel, the Minister of Defence and widely believed to have been Spínola's candidate for the leadership of the second Provisional Government, was relieved of his portfolio, as was the Minister for Social Communication. The Council of State is to be re-constituted. The whole apparatus of government, both military and civil, thus appears to have been purged of all save those in sympathy with the aims of the left. Some of the traditionalist elements in the country are attempting to console themselves with the acceptance of the Presidency by General Costa Gomes, since he is a figure familiar to them (he held high office under Caetano before being dismissed with General Spínola) and is known to be respected in the higher ranks of those in the armed forces who are not associated with the left-wing of the AFM. But the recent record of General Costa Gomes suggests that he is adept at convincing all men of his friendship but less good at holding any determined line of his own, and he certainly has none of the personal appeal of his predecessor. Whatever else he may be, he cannot by any stretch of the imagination be envisaged as an inspiring leader of the nation.

11. Now that the dust has temporarily settled, it is natural to ask how much truth there was in the allegations that the Silent Majority was a

---

[8] In his resignation speech (reported in this telegram of 30 September), Gen. Spínola suggested that the principles of the AFM 'were in his view being betrayed and he therefore felt unable to continue as their guarantor'. An 'atmosphere of anarchy had', he claimed, 'arisen which was contrary to the original intention of the movement' and he 'did not feel able to associate himself with these revolutionary changes'.

cover for a violent reactionary plot.[9] Undoubtedly the right-wing contains firebrands who have been working themselves up for some time to a confrontation with the Left. Among the excitable Generals, the thwarted bankers and the young bloods of the upper classes there must have been some who were thinking in terms of forceful solutions. But the stories which were being broadcast about the discovery of caches of arms were very unconvincing and smacked strongly of fabrication: they were dramatic in content (one story spoke of a hearse full of arms nestling beneath 'the flowers of death'), but were quickly dropped from the news bulletins before serious investigation by journalists or others could disprove them.[10] At the moment of drafting this despatch a fresh and, on the face of it, even more improbable story has been issued about an attempt over last week-end to assassinate Spínola himself. On the other hand, at least some serious investigators have been convinced of the validity of the charges: the moderate left-wing newspaper *Expresso* has published circumstantial details of the arms finds and accepts the theory of a reactionary plot (though in this context it must be recalled that *Expresso* is the organ of the PPD,[11] which, after some hesitation, finally decided to condemn the Silent Majority—see para 4 above). All one can say with confidence is that, even if some of the stories were true, they were almost certainly exploited and made the subject of over-reaction by the left-wing of the AFM and the Communists.

12. There is no doubt that Portugal came very close to civil war on the night of the 27th/28th of September, when Spínola drew back from the use of force. Every hour and every day that passes since then seems to me to diminish the risk of such civil war. We know that there are many units of the Army and possibly also the Commander of the Air Force, who were loyal to Spínola and might have been inclined to take action on his behalf (I attempted to identify such units in my tel No. 328—not to all).[12] But with

---

[9] The Netherlands Ambassador in Lisbon was inclined to believe that the 'Silent Majority' was a cover for a plot by three right-wing generals (Gen. Silvério de Marques, Gen. Diego Neto, and Gen. Galvão de Melo), but Mr. Trench demurred: 'My own inclination is to believe that there was no plot, in the ordinary sense of the word, but that if the demonstration of support for Spínola had been a rousing success, the three right wing generals would have gone to Spínola and urged him to get rid of Álvaro Cunhal (the PCP Secretary-General and Minister without Portfolio) and the AFM left-wingers while his star was in the ascendant. Indeed, I think that it was this possibility which led the PCP to stake their all on preventing the demonstration from taking place' (letter from Mr. Trench to Mr. Morgan of 9 October).

[10] 'It is asking too much', Mr. Trench wrote in his letter of 9 October (*v. ibid.*) 'to believe that ten or twelve automatic pistols, a few dozen shot-guns and air rifles, some construction-workers' helmets, iron rods and unconvincing Molotov cocktails were really intended to overthrow the Gonçalves Government. The German Ambassador went so far as to say that the whole affair reminded him of the Reichstag Fire trial'.

[11] *Partido Popular Democrático*/Popular Democratic Party.

[12] Although Mr. Trench thought that a good many army and air force units would declare for Gen. Spínola in the event of a split in the AFM, he considered it 'unlikely that Spínola would allow himself to be adopted as a figurehead for any such movement: if he had intended

Spínola no longer in office and with the continued purging of the Centre and Right of the Armed Forces referred to above, and with the possibility of a fresh wave of arrests (which is widely feared by many), it seems that the moment for effective intervention is already past. At least the Extreme Left seem to think so. On the evening of the 30th of September they held a massive 'victory' celebration at São Bento.

13. If civil war has been avoided, one is left trying to assess the other possible developments. Unhappily, I cannot feel that what has been a victory for the Left is also a victory for civil liberty and democracy in Portugal. Over the past few days it has been clear that two different standards have been applied to the different ends of the political spectrum. The Right and Centre have been denied the opportunity of public demonstration and general publicity, on what appears less than adequate grounds; the Extreme Left, on the other hand, has been permitted to impose a degree of anarchy and intimidation on the rest of the population. There would appear to me to be at least as much evidence of Communist plotting, manipulation and resort to unconstitutional means as there has been evidence of this by the Right. The confiscation of the property of the alleged plotters—before any enquiry or trial—seems a particularly arbitrary act, designed further to intimidate opposition. The sight of the sullen marchers through the Lisbon streets last Saturday night, flanked by their menacing henchmen, was not a reassuring one for those who value democracy in Portugal.

14. At the moment of writing the nation is divided. The Right and Centre/Right are leaderless and in disarray. They have failed in their first attempt to make use of the democratic processes about which they have heard so much fine talk from the Communist Party and its allies (including members of the AFM), and they are the objects of continual abuse by the information media. The Centre Democratic Socialist Party (CDS)[13] has been silent, awaiting some indication of what liberty of action remained open to it without incurring charges of being reactionary. Its leader has told me that he is deeply anxious about the country's future. The Popular Democratic Party (PPD), while not joining in the 'victory' celebrations, has moved further from the Centre. The Socialists are seeking close identity with those who have dominated recent events, but must be uncomfortably aware that it is the Communists who have made the running and the Communist Party organisation which brought the activists out to the barricades.[14]

to do so he would have taken action a day or two ago while he had the capacity for effective intervention' (Lisbon telegram No. 328 of 30 September).

[13] *Centro Democrático Social*/Social Democratic Centre.

[14] Mr. Trench noted in his letter of 9 October (see notes 9 and 10 above), that at a meeting of EC Heads of Mission on 7 October no one agreed with the Italian Ambassador that recent events were evidence of a Soviet plot to install a communist government in Portugal. Nevertheless, he continued: 'There was general agreement that we were faced with the

15. The Prime Minister has reiterated that the Programme of the Armed Forces Movement remains unaltered and that it is still their intention to hold Parliamentary elections next spring. But nothing that has happened in the past few days is likely to cure those governmental ailments to which President Spínola drew attention in his resignation speech, and which have resulted in indecisive government (particularly in the economic and labour spheres) and disregard for those laws which have eventually found their way onto the Statute Book. The likelihood of foreign investment in the country, which all Ministers purport to desire (and which is in fact vital to economic recovery) is virtually non-existent in the present situation. During the next few months unemployment is likely to rise steeply and social unrest with it. It is scarcely conceivable that the Communist Party and the Maoist MRPP[15] will not take advantage of this.

16. The Foreign Minister has assured me that Portugal's foreign policy remains unchanged, but this begs the question of how such intractable problems as the decolonisation of Angola will be made any more soluble by the withdrawal of the one man—Spínola—who seemed to enjoy some measure of confidence from the white settlers. (In fact, it is not unreasonable to suppose that his disappearance from the scene makes an attempt at UDI more probable). So far as NATO is concerned, one is forced to wonder how long the Communist Party, confident in its newly-proven power, will continue to acquiesce in Portuguese membership.[16] And one can only view with apprehension the interaction of events in Portugal and in Spain after the death of Franco.[17]

possibility, if not the likelihood, of a popular front regime, given that the extreme left will presumably now try to destroy first the Centre Democratic Socialist Party (CDS) and then the Social Democrats (PPD) ... This is not to say that we all believe Costa Gomes, the new President, and Gonçalves to be in the pocket of the PCP, but we are uncertain of their ability to withstand the pressures which are bound to build up as unemployment increases and the promised elections approach—whether we shall actually see elections is a moot point.'

[15] *Movimento Reorganizativo do Partido do Proletariado*/Reorganising Movement of the Party of the Proletariat: a party largely composed of students, with a potential for disruption greater than its intrinsic political importance.

[16] During a recent trip to the United States Gen. Costa Gomes had 'gone out of his way to reassure those who feared that recent events were a prelude to Portugal leaving NATO', whilst Dr. Soares, according to Mr. Ure, 'was at pains to emphasise this aspect of recent developments when speaking yesterday to my Ambassador' (letter from Mr. Ure to Mr. Thomas, 23 October).

[17] Gen. Francisco Franco Bahamonde was Spanish Head of State. The lessons for Spain of Gen. Spínola's fall were, according to Mr. R.D. Wilkinson, Second Secretary in the British Embassy, Madrid, interpreted differently according to political persuasion. In a letter of 7 October to Mr. Everett (now in SWED), he noted that for the Spanish Right Portugal's experiment with democracy was 'undesirable in itself, was doomed to failure from the start. Once Pandora's box had been opened on 25 April it was inevitable that all order and respect for law and order would be blown away. It is simple folly to attempt to allow left wing parties, especially the communists, to operate freely. They are bound to use all means at their disposal to instal [*sic*] a dictatorship of the proletariat.' However, he added that more moderate opinion blamed Portugal's present situation on the 'suddenness with which the old order was

17. In short, I feel that the events of the past few days have solved none of Portugal's problems. They have brought the country close to civil war. They have left the country divided against itself. They have given an ugly foretaste of the efficacy and lawlessness of a Communist Party-controlled mob. Portugal may still achieve her democratic elections next spring and pass peacefully into the comity of free nations; but, if she does, she can hardly look back with pride on the 28th of September, as she can do on the 25th of April.[18]

18. I am copying this despatch to Her Majesty's Representatives in Madrid, Brussels (NATO), Luanda and Lourenço Marques; and to the Ministry of Defence (D13 West).

I have etc

N.C.C. Trench[19]

overthrown'. 'It is', he observed, 'argued that if only Portugal's leaders had had the wisdom to liberalise, then the foundations of a stable political system could have been laid, and forces other than the communist party could have had time to organise themselves and gather strength. Thus the moral for Spain is that *inmovilismo* is fatal, since when the reaction inevitably comes it sweeps away all moderate forces along with the old regime. The only wise course for Spain is one of gradual liberalisation.'

[18] On 14 October Sir J. Killick noted on Mr. Thomas's minute of 9 October (see note 3 above): 'The clear objective in Portugal is to make "socialism" irreversible. If the elections are ever held, they will merit close scrutiny. There will be more than a few shotguns in the cupboards of the extreme Left. I recollect, with little joy, that at my last talk with Mr. Hattersley before our election I said I would be surprised if Spínola was still on the scene in a year's time.' Mr. Thomas sidelined and initialled his agreement.

[19] In a letter to Mr. Trench of 7 October, written in response this 'admirable though melancholy despatch', Mr. Thomas observed that if, 'as you and we fear, the economic situation deteriorates sharply in the next month or two, the question where decisive political power now lies in Portugal may soon be put to the test'.

No. 111

Minute from Mr. D.C. Thomas to Sir J. Killick

[*WSP 1/1*]

Secret   FCO, *24 October 1974*

Portugal

1. The PUS is holding a meeting at 3.30 p.m. on Friday, 25 October[1] to discuss the outlook for Portugal in preparation for Mr Colby's[2] visit to

[1] This meeting, attended by Sir T. Brimelow, Sir J. Killick, Mr. Morgan, Mr. Baker and Mr. R.P.D. Chatterjie (Third Secretary, SWED), concluded that 'the outlook was confused and murky, but that it would be wrong and counter-productive to regard Portugal as a lost cause' (letter from Mr. Thomas to Mr. Ure of 28 October, WSP 3/548/2).

London on 28 October.³ The following note might serve as a basis for discussion.

The Outlook

2. The Assessment Staff are preparing a JIC report entitled 'Portugal: Will it go Communist?'⁴ Copies of the latest version reflecting (probably conflicting) comments by SWED and the Defence Intelligence Staff on an earlier draft should be available in time for the PUS's meeting.

3. In summary and simplistic terms one can envisage the following possible scenarios for developments in Portugal in the next year or two:

(i) A Communist takeover, possibly through control of the Armed Forces Movement⁵ or through the election of a popular front government.
(ii) A left-wing (but not overtly Communist) military dictatorship with some trappings of parliamentary democracy.
(iii) A democratic government of the centre-left, with the Armed Forces in the wings.
(iv) A right-wing counter-coup probably leading to
(v) a civil war, beginning as a struggle between factions in the Armed Forces and perhaps spreading to the whole country.

4. The Department's guess is that the apocalyptic extremes, although by no means impossible, are neither inevitable nor the most likely outcomes. Something along the lines of (ii) or (iii) above (which shade into each other) seems to us more likely: e.g. an elected left of centre government, perhaps with some Communist Party participation and tendencies to non-alignment in foreign policy, under the watchful eye of the Armed Forces. In that

---

² Mr. W.E. Colby was Director of the CIA.

³ Sir J. Killick thought the Americans 'disposed to take a gloomy view of the Mediterranean situation overall', and, as regards Portugal itself, he had 'the strong impression that, whatever their links with the former regime [might] have been, they [were] very lost and [had] not yet got their bearings with the new one'. The US were, he noted, 'more worried by the naivete and inexperience, especially in foreign policy, of the left wing of the AFM than by its extremist tendencies as such' (letter to Mr. Trench of 1 November).

⁴ The final version of this paper (JIC (74) (1A) 4) was approved by the JIC on 31 October. It concluded: 'though there remains a reasonable chance that democracy can be established in Portugal, there is now a real danger of a Communist takeover; this would not necessarily be at the first round, but could be after a period of coalition with the Communists or weak democratic government'. There was also, according to this assessment, a 'significant risk' of Portugal falling under the control of a neutralist government which wished to leave NATO.

⁵ The JIC assessment paper of 31 October (*v. ibid.*) assumed that much would depend on whether the Communists could control or outwit the AFM, and on whether the AFM could control the rest of the armed forces. If the Communists succeeded in the former case but the AFM could not achieve the latter, Portugal, the paper argued, might 'face a potential power struggle within the armed forces, possibly leading to internecine fighting and eventually even civil war'.

situation the threat of a Communist takeover would remain but might be contained.[6]

5. In the next six months leading to the General Elections the principal dangers are:

(i) A sharp deterioration in the already very serious economic situation, with destabilising social and political repercussions which could be exploited by the Communists and/or result in more directly interventionist and authoritarian measures by the government and the Armed Forces.

(ii) Emasculation of the moderate democratic parties of the centre-right (CDS) and centre-left (PPD) by intimidation, left-wing domination of the media, etc.

(iii) Repetition by the Communists and extreme left of their tactics on 28-30 September (street barricades etc), when they seized the initiative from the Armed Forces and held it until their objectives had been achieved.

6. It should be noted however that the Electoral Law, just published, reaffirms the commitment of the government and Armed Forces Movement to the holding of elections by 31 March, 1975 and its provisions (if observed) are designed to produce free elections.[7]

Implications for British Policy
7. HMG's basic interest [*sic*] are:-

(i) Positively, to encourage the development of healthy democratic institutions in a Portugal firmly aligned with the West; and
(ii) Negatively, to prevent Portugal falling within the Soviet sphere of influence.

8. The outlook is not encouraging (although General Costa Gomes, President of the Republic and Chief of the Armed Forces General Staff, has just publicly affirmed in Washington Portugal's continuing commitment to NATO);[8] but it would be wrong and counter-productive to regard

---

[6] In a letter to Sir J. Killick of 30 October Mr. Trench wrote that a wide range of opinions on Portugal's future were evident amongst Western European Ambassadors in Lisbon. He observed that while the 'pessimistic end of the spectrum' was represented by the views of his Swiss colleague, who was convinced that they were 'moving steadily towards a Czechoslovak finale', at the other extreme the Dutch Ambassador discounted the prospects of a Communist *coup*, and thought that the PCP would 'not want to spoil the chance of a Popular Front in France and Italy'.

[7] The JIC assessment paper of 31 October (see notes 4 and 5 above) predicted that the Communists 'might get not more than 15 per cent to 20 per cent of the vote' in these elections.

[8] Cf. No. 110, note 16. Dr. Soares was, however, unwilling to confirm Portugal's commitment to NATO on behalf of the PSP. An undated background brief for Adm. E.B. Ashmore, the First Sea Lord, stated: there was 'evidence that influential military men [in Portugal] have a naive perception of the nature of the Soviet threat to Western Europe and the realities of East-West relations. It is possible that Portugal will become less committed to NATO in the next

Portugal as a lost cause. On the contrary, within the limits of prudence we should seek to give the Portuguese Government the benefit of the doubt, responding as positively as we can to their requests for co-operation and assistance and demonstrating our confidence in them, with the aim thereby of increasing our ability to influence their actions.

9. We have two advantages which we should exploit to the full:-

(i) The 'old alliance': there is evidence that there still exists a fund of particular trust and goodwill towards Britain, especially in the Armed Forces.
(ii) A Labour Government.

What can we do?

10. Our ability directly to influence public opinion in Portugal or to counter the activities of the Communist Party is severely limited. But there are a number of areas inside and outside government in which we can and should try to exert our influence:-

Armed Forces: We have agreed to a Portuguese request (originally made by General Spínola, but since confirmed by General Costa Gomes) to train body guards for the President and the Prime Minister; the FCO have recommended that we should agree to three Portuguese officers from the embryonic military intelligence organisation to visit British military intelligence establishments. The British Defence Attaché in Lisbon appears to have good contacts with the new Portuguese military hierarchy. Given the political influence of the Armed Forces in Portugal, we should cultivate our relations with them and co-operate with them to the limit of our ability; conversely, if we rebuff approaches from the Portuguese Armed Forces the political consequences are likely to be disproportionately damaging. We must review our policy on arms sales to Portugal.

Portuguese Foreign Policy: We have already demonstrated our willingness to assist the Portuguese in the process of decolonisation; there are likely to be fewer opportunitites in this area in future. There is evidence that the Foreign Minister and a number of influential military men take a rosy and unsophisticated view of the realities of East/West relations. This is an area in which we should make a positive effort to educate them in our assessment of the nature of the Soviet threat, e.g. by means of a ministerial

year or two.' Dr. Soares's comments, reported in Lisbon telegram No. 350 of 16 October, 'to the effect that "as a socialist" he wondered whether the continued existence of NATO and the Warsaw Pact might not be prejudicial to détente' betrayed, according to Mr. Thomas, 'the woolliest of thinking', and he thought that 'one of the most useful things that we might do would be to try to get in some "re-education" of these people ourselves, before it is too late. We need to get across to key figures in the Government and the armed forces our view of the realities of East-West relations and the nature of the Soviet threat to Western Europe' (letter to Mr. Ure of 21 October, WSP 3/548/2).

visit and/or a visit to Lisbon by senior officials (I have floated this idea with HM Embassy at Lisbon and await their reactions).[9]

Political Parties: without appearing to dabble in domestic Portuguese party politics, we should do all we can to strengthen the moderate and democratic parties in Portugal. Offers of help from the Labour Party to the Portuguese Socialist Party [PSP] have been made at a high level, but to the best of my knowledge have not been followed up seriously on either side (a proposed visit by representatives of the PSP at the time of the British General Election was postponed at the last minute; and is due to take place at an unspecified date in the near future). The Conservative party have established links with the centre-right CDS and have offered them technical advice and assistance. We should consider sponsored visits to this country by leading members of the PSP, CDS and centre-left PPD, with a view to both giving them access to party political organisational expertise and increasing their international stature.

Trade Unions: The Communists are making a major effort to control trade unions in Portugal but this has met some resistance. The TUC are sympathetic, but so far, very cautious. Mr. Jack Jones has sponsored some practical assistance to the nascent Portuguese trade unions through the International Federation of Transport Workers. The newly appointed Labour Attaché at Lisbon should act as a channel for assistance to non-Communist trade unions, both on a bilateral basis and in concert with the ICFTU.[10]

Employers' Organisations: The CBI[11] are giving organisational advice to their Portuguese counterpart.

Economic: Lisbon telegram No. 362 of 24 October reports that M. Wellenstein's talks with Portuguese Ministers earlier this week showed that the Portuguese Government are looking to the EEC for economic aid.[12]

---

[9] Mr. Trench reacted very positively to this proposal. In his letter of 30 October (see note 6 above) he noted: 'the Centre Democratic Socialists (CDS) and the centre left PDD ("Socialism without Marxism") are both very nervous. They do not require any encouragement to oppose the forces of the extreme left, though they do need to improve their expertise in achieving this. The Socialist Party (PSP) under the peripatetic leadership of Mário Soares, is extremely frightened of the Communists and is very ready to work against them'. With specific reference to the PSP, Mr. Trench suggested that it would be particularly useful 'if someone of impeccable left-wing credentials could come here without any fanfares and talk in informal circumstances … to warn the moderate left against the techniques and take-over of the far left, and this might be done at a series of quiet meals at my house, or in restaurants, rather than in the formal surroundings of an official visit'.

[10] International Confederation of Free Trade Unions. 'Although', Mr. Trench noted in a letter to Sir J. Killick of 12 November, 'British trade unions as a whole don't seem to have been very keen to send anyone out here to show the Portuguese how to organise trade unions, some of them might be willing to organise a sort of propaganda mission for a few days' visit, which incidentally would give them a chance to see something of Lisbon and be wined and dined' (WSP 3/548/2).

[11] Confederation of British Industry.

General: We have discussed with IRD[13] and are consulting the Embassy about the (admittedly limited) possibilities for IRD operations in Portugal.[14]

The American Dimension[15]

11. US suspicions of the Portuguese are reciprocated in Portugal, where there are widespread fears or hopes, according to taste, of CIA intervention to prevent a Communist takeover. We have not yet seen reports of the outcome of General Costa Gomes' visit to Washington.[16] There is a risk that US/Portuguese negotiations over the Azores bases agreement may go

[12] In his meeting with M. E.P. Wellenstein, the EC's Director-General for External Relations, the Portuguese Minister of Finance explained that Portugal's balance of payments deficit was running at $500-600 million, and that while the country still had substantial reserves they would soon be exhausted if they were used to pay for the current deficits (Lisbon telegram No. 362 of 24 October, WSP 6/598/1).

[13] Information Research Department.

[14] In a letter to Mr. Thomas of 23 October, Mr. Ure suggested that carefully-targeted IRD pamphlets on 'Communist tactics in election rigging' and 'Communist subversion in the Armed Forces' could be usefully distributed in Portugal. 'We might', he continued, 'also be able to find a market for factual material about the way in which the Communist parties in Czechoslovakia and Hungary, etc., managed to clamber to power and kick away the ladder of future free elections.' However, Mr. Ure was equally aware that there was a risk of IRD material falling into the hands of Soviet diplomats in Lisbon who might then complain to Dr. Soares that the British Embassy 'was "working against the cordial relations being established between Portugal and the Soviet Union, etc. etc."'. Sir T. Brimelow shared these concerns. On 27 October, he noted on a minute from Mr. Thomas of 21 October 'what would be easy & helpful, given Portuguese good will, could be counter-productive if exploited by trouble-makers' (WSP 3/548/2).

[15] In a minute to Mr. Thomas of 28 October Mr. Tickell recalled that Mr. W.G. Hyland, Director of the Bureau of Intelligence and Research in the US State Department, had remarked to him that the US Embassy in Lisbon had 'been admirably plugged in to the Salazar régime', but that the Spínola government 'had baffled them and the present lot left them with virtually no contacts at all. So a trawl had been made through the Administration, and a few young men were discovered who knew some members of the new government ... [and in consequence they had been sent] to Portugal on vacation'. Mr. Tickell added: 'I do not know whether this will be good for the Portuguese tourist industry, but at least it illustrates US diplomatic methods' (WSP 3/304/1).

[16] Mr. Trench reported in a letter to Mr. Morgan of 12 November that Mr. Ure had learned from a conversation with Mr. R.S.F. Post, Counsellor in the US Embassy in Lisbon, and Mr. A.W. Lukens, Director of Iberian Affairs in the US State Department, that there were two schools of thought in Washington on policy towards the new Portugal. One 'advocated prompt and massive aid to prevent Portugal drifting towards Communism', whilst the other advised 'holding off until Portugal had demonstrated that she did not intend to become Communist-dominated'. According to this same source, the Americans had been impressed by the Portuguese President during his recent visit to Washington and, Mr. Trench added, 'whereas a few weeks ago they shared the general doubt as to whether he was a weak "front man" or a force for moderation in his own right, they have now come down conclusively in favour of the latter'. In mid-December the US Government announced a $20 million loan package for Portugal and, as Mr. J.E. Cornish reported from Washington on 20 December, 'the State Department, and Dr. Kissinger personally, were now a little less worried about the future of Portugal than they had been in September' (WSP 3/304/1).

sour if, as I should guess likely, the Portuguese pitch their price unrealistically high.[17] The Americans have already complicated matters for themselves and the rest of the alliance by insisting on Portuguese exclusion from the forthcoming NATO Nuclear Planning Group Ministerial Meeting.[18]

D.C. THOMAS

[17] The 1951 US-Portuguese Defence Agreement provided for American use of the Azores in time of a war involving NATO. A special clause, allowing the Americans to use the base at Lajes in peacetime, was reviewed on a five-yearly basis, but ran out in February 1974, following American use of the base to supply Israel with arms during the Arab-Israeli war of October 1973. A further temporary extension expired in July, but the Portuguese Government agreed to allow continued US use in advance of a final agreement. Although by the end of 1974 the Azores discussions had still not been concluded, they were no longer a serious sore-point in US-Portuguese relations (letters from Mr. J.E. Cornish to Miss A.J. Brimelow (SWED) of 23 August, WSP 3/304/1; letter from Mr. J.E. Cornish of 20 December (*v. ibid.*)).

[18] In the event, this meeting of the Nuclear Planning Group (NPG) in Rome was postponed because, as a background brief explained (see note 8 above), 'the Americans were unwilling to share top secret information with an unreliable member of the Alliance ... The trouble is that the Portuguese are extremely touchy, and any sign that they are being treated like second-class citizens will only strengthen the hand of those in Portugal who are hostile to NATO.' Cf. No. 108, note 4.

No. 112

Letter from Mr. Cartledge (Moscow) to Mr. Bullard

[*WSP 1/13*]

Confidential   MOSCOW, *20 November 1974*

Dear Julian,

Soviet/Spanish Relations

1. Recent changes of government in Portugal and Greece[1] have naturally led to speculation here about Soviet hopes or intention with regard to Spain.

2. Last year, the Soviet press was almost totally devoid of comment on Spain which, given the suitability of the régime as a propaganda target, was indicative of their acceptance of the *status quo*. There have recently been one or two articles in the Soviet central press which indicate that the line may be changing. I enclose a note of a conversation between Nigel Broomfield and Prat, the number 2 in the Spanish Trade Mission, which

[1] See No. 101.

shows that the Spaniards here consider that there has been a significant shift in the Soviet position on Spain.[2]

3. To complete the press picture, I should add that on 16 November *Pravda* carried a commentary entitled 'Without a Future' about the sacking of the 'liberal' members of the present Spanish cabinet.[3] This was taken as an indication that 'Spain is moving more and more to the right'. The two sentences which most caught my eye, however, were the following:

'The reasons for concern in Madrid are evident. The changed situation in Europe, in particular the collapse of fascism in Portugal and the fall of the military dictatorship in Greece, has underlined the isolation of the régime in Spain and added to the further activisation of the struggle of the democratic forces in the country against the dictatorship of Franco.'

The article ends predictably—'Neither terror nor repression can help to isolate Spain from the inevitable positive changes. The régime of Franco is an anachronism and does not have a future.'

4. If the analysis of recent Soviet actions put forward by Prat is right, and it seems a reasonable hypothesis, then it lends rather more than propaganda significance to the spate of Soviet references, most recently in Gromyko's speech of 6 November, about the effects of positive changes in Greece and Portugal and the view expressed in the Soviet rubric–'during a period of détente the political pendulum swings to the left' (para[graph] 2(*e*) of Moscow tel[egram] No. 1225).[4]

5. Seen from Moscow, the situation in the four countries which comprise the south-eastern and south-western fringes of Europe–Greece, Italy, Portugal and Spain–appears to offer good opportunities for the enhancement of Soviet influence with relatively little risk or even expenditure of diplomatic effort. This could offset the constraints of their bilateral relations with the USA (para[graph] 3 of your letter of 13 November, not to all).[5] In Greece, although the elections have put only a handful of communists into the Parliament, this can be seen as the first step along a road in which the Communist Party is able to organise itself legally and wait for increased support in the wake of the high level of inflation which the free market economies of the West are experiencing. In

[2] In conversation with Mr. N.H.R.A. Broomfield, First Secretary in the British Embassy, Moscow, Sr. J. Prat y Coll stated that he thought both the Soviet Union and the Spanish Communist Party 'were now actively preparing for the post-Franco situation in Spain'. He considered a recent wave of industrial unrest in Spain, due 'partly to Soviet financed subversion', symptomatic of a change in Soviet policy from 'knocking on the regime from outside to their more traditional method of internal tunneling [*sic*] and demolition from inside the country' (note of a conversation with Sr. Prat y Coll on 14 November, WSS 3/303/1).

[3] See No. 113, note 6.

[4] But in this telegram of 10 October Sir T. Garvey also suggested that détente had diminished Moscow's 'freedom to engage in large scale and blatant subversion in support of foreign policy' (ENS 2/1).

[5] Not traced.

Italy, the longer the present constitutional crisis continues the better it suits the communists who, while avoiding unpopularity through not being saddled with the responsibility of government can build up their negotiating position for whatever 'historic compromise' may eventually be offered.[6] In Portugal the break-through in relations has come, and although the elections in 1975 may enable the centrist parties to exclude the Communist Party from government (para[graph] 6 of Petrie's letter of 8 November to Thomas not to all)[7] the Communists, as the best-organised party in Portugal have the best long term prospects. This leaves Spain. It is clearly too early to make any confident predictions about what the situation might look like after the departure of Franco, but if they play their cards well the Communists must presumably have some chance of achieving popular recognition as in Greece, Italy, Portugal and France. However, this is something on which we would defer to the view of HM Embassy in Madrid.

Yours ever,
B.G. CARTLEDGE

---

[6] On 8 October the centre-left Italian Government, headed by Sig. M. Rumor, collapsed, but internal disagreements within the Social Democratic Party/*Partito Socialista Democratico Italiano* (PSDI) delayed the formation of a new centre-left government until 28 November.

[7] Not traced.

No. 113

Mr. Wiggin (Madrid) to Mr. Callaghan

[*WSS 1/1*]

Confidential   MADRID, *10 December 1974*

Summary ...[1]

Sir,

'Whither Spain? First Impressions from Madrid'

I have the honour to submit my first impressions. I have not been able to travel since arriving here two months ago, and they are necessarily impressions of Madrid. But for all the size and variety of this country, and the special and critical problems posed by certain regions, political power at present is centred on the capital.

---

[1] Not printed.

2. Spain's exceptional albeit uneven economic growth in recent years has not been accompanied by any real political evolution, though the Spanish media have in the past year or so been allowed a degree of freedom unprecedented in Franco's time. What is perhaps not quite so widely realised yet is the extent of the ferment unleashed by Carrero Blanco's assassination a year ago[2] and Franco's almost fatal illness last summer,[3] allied to the growing uncertainty about Spain's economic as well as political future. I have listened to a lot of people since my arrival. With rare exceptions the only serious topic they want to talk about is 'Whither Spain?'. They show little interest in foreign affairs except in so far as these may directly affect Spain's politico-economic prospects. But for a few professionals Gibraltar is on the back-burner, though that problem, until it is resolved, will remain a landmine in Anglo-Spanish relations regardless of the political colouring of any future Spanish Government.[4]

3. Also striking, and disturbing, is the degree of pessimism being expressed about the future by so many Spaniards ranging from the Right, through the Centre, to the democratic Left, more or less irrespective of age group and occupation. Their thesis is that world recession will prove the last straw for Spain in her present political plight. The pessimism is echoed by some, though by no means all, resident members of the British business and Press communities.

4. Personally, I believe it is being overdone. Economically, there are many countries even in Europe with more immediate problems. Politically, recent events have been widely interpreted as a serious set-back for those working for evolution. But I cannot see the more reactionary elements in the present régime succeeding in putting the clamps fully on again though I fear they will succeed for a period of time in frustrating the liberalisers. Indeed the régime as traditionally conceived can already arguably be classified as dead. I believe things have gone much too far for the

[2] Adm. L. Carrero Blanco, the Spanish Prime Minister, was assassinated by the Basque terrorist organisation, ETA (*Euzkadi ta Askatasuna*/Basque Homeland and Liberty), on 20 December 1973.

[3] Since the mid-1960s Gen. Franco had been displaying symptoms of Parkinson's disease and, by July 1974, the condition was quite advanced. His health was further compromised that summer by the development of a blood clot in his right leg, for which he was admitted to hospital.

[4] Gibraltar had since 1963 been subjected by Spain to an unofficial economic blockade, preventing the free movement of labour into the British colony and restricting the flight path to the isthmus. On 14 December 1973, following a debate on the dispute arising from Spanish claims to Gibraltar, the UN General Assembly adopted a Consensus Resolution looking forward to 'negotiations with a view to the final solution' of the problem. This HMG interpreted as meaning that the two Governments should continue by discussion to seek the elements of a negotiable agreement acceptable to all concerned. Talks were held at an official level in Madrid in May 1974, but the Spaniards insisted that there could be no alleviation of their restrictions in the absence of a British declaration, or statement of intent, recognising 'decolonisation' as the ultimate goal.

'movimiento'[5] in anything like its present form, let alone Franco's almost universally despised family, to enjoy power after he goes in anything but the short term. The Press still comments much as it did before Pio Cabanillas was sacked.[6] I can count on the fingers of two hands the number of Spaniards I have met—many of them traditionally loyal to Franco—who have said they welcomed Franco's decision to resume power; and most of those made clear that they took this view because they feared that he would otherwise make life even more difficult for Prince Juan Carlos,[7] whom they regarded as essential as a focus for orderly evolution.

5. How long the régime will continue to appear to stay alive is anybody's guess. There are rumours in this hotbed of rumour that even some very senior officers are beginning to ask themselves whether things can be allowed to continue as at present. But the probability is that nobody will do a Brutus and that, barring assassination, Franco will now hang on for as long as he is physically and mentally capable of going through the motions of government. While opinions on his mental and physical state differ—he is said to have his days—it seems to be no worse than it was before his illness.

6. It is in this uncertainty, with the prospect that Franco may linger on and on, that the main dangers lie. I do not believe, as so many Spaniards seem to, that the eventual choice after Franco must inevitably be an authoritarian régime of the extreme Left or (probably as a backlash) another of the extreme Right, with the army the main determining factor. There are certainly lessons for Spain in what has happened in Portugal but the two countries and peoples could hardly be more different given that they share the same peninsular [*sic*] and nearly the same language.[8] There

---

[5] The *Movimiento Nacional* (National Movement) was a coalition of Francoist forces and the sole official political organisation in Spain.

[6] Sr. Pio Cabanillas Gallas, one of Spain's most liberal Ministers, was dismissed as Minister of Information in October 1974, in part for his refusal to prevent the Spanish press from publishing details of a financial scandal involving Gen. Franco's brother.

[7] The son of Don Juan de Borbón y Battenberg, Count of Barcelona, the Bourbon claimant to the Spanish throne, Prince Juan Carlos was Gen. Franco's nominated successor. During Gen. Franco's illness in July and August 1974 he assumed the position of Head of State *ad interim*. Gen. Franco reassumed his powers on 2 September.

[8] Reporting on initial Spanish reactions to the Portuguese *coup* in April, Mr. Wiggin's predecessor, Sir J. Russell, suggested that 'the *Movimiento* must be shaken at the speed with which its Portuguese counterpart has been swept away; and the democratic Spanish opposition—such as it is—correspondingly heartened. There has never been much love lost between Madrid and Lisbon: but Spanish contempt for the Portuguese has always been nervously conditioned by a sneaking jealousy of the despised half-brother's success in retaining his vast overseas empire long after Spain has lost the last heritage of the Conquistadores. Schadenfreude at the probable break-up of the Portuguese colonies will now, however, be sharply countered by fears of liberal infection in the home continent. Franco cannot really be happy to see the Salazar/Caetano anachronism (a mummified replica of his own piece of taxidermy) so easily and suddenly overthrown by insubordinate officers: and dangerous liberals

is by now a vast middle class here, by no means confined to the white collar sector, with a lot to lose. And while one cannot assess current Spanish military thinking with confidence, the Spanish Army have not had to endure a colonial war of Portuguese proportions.[9] I would hazard a guess that the bulk of the military could by now be categorised as comparatively moderate reformists. Within the next few years the last of the old guard of Civil War and Blue Division[10] days will have been retired.

7. Yet the longer the present uneasy interregnum endures, with Franco switching on and off and decisions in every field of Government being postponed or blurred or sometimes reversed, the greater the risk that the democrats will eventually find themselves squeezed out. There is a clear trend towards the Left throughout the country. Unfortunately the democratic Left is fragmented, as are all democratic elements in this country of individuals. The Communists have kept their discipline and seem to be playing their hand quite cleverly. They have had some success in wooing democratic oppositionists, not only of the Left, into a degree of 'co-operation'. They never cease to criticise the 'sindicato' structure[11] in their propaganda as a mockery of trade unionism. But there is evidence that they regard that structure—which is not wholly dissimilar to the Russian—as well suited to their own purposes and are working hard, with some success, to penetrate it; so much so that some influential people in the establishment now incline to the view that the structure should be changed for that reason. At the other end of the spectrum, vested interests have been hard at work to try to ensure that power remains within the structure of the 'movimiento' after Franco's death. With Franco's backing they have already succeeded in largely frustrating Sr. Arias'[12] current attempt to legalise embryonic political parties. As already stated I believe those who still support the 'movimiento' must eventually fail. But they may well enjoy enough success for long enough to make the process of transition not merely difficult but actually dangerous.

8. If I may presume to summarise my understanding of Her Majesty's Government's policy towards Spain, it is that we want to see as soon as possible a democratic Spain, or at least a Spain progressing towards real

like Soares rapturously welcomed back from exile ... The wall is too near for the writing on it not to be alarming' (Madrid saving telegram No. 21 of 29 April, WSP 2/2).

[9] See No. 5, note 10.

[10] A Spanish volunteer force which fought with the Axis powers on the Eastern Front during the Second World War. Some 47,000 Spaniards participated in the Blue Division before, under intense Allied pressure, the unit was recalled to Spain at the end of 1943.

[11] The *Organización Sindical Española* (OSE) was the state union which operated throughout the Franco regime. Employers and workers alike were obliged to join the OSE, with all other unions prohibited.

[12] Sr. C. Arias Navarro succeeded Adm. Carrero Blanco as Prime Minister on 28 December 1973 (see note 2 above). Despite his reputation as right-wing hard-liner, Sr. Arias Navarro attempted to broaden the appeal of the Franco régime through the admission of liberal politicians to the Government and a raft of other policies designed to diffuse opposition.

democracy, while at the same time seeking to develop our trade relations and trying to keep Gibraltar in the background so long as no solution is in sight. (If and when Spain does become democratic, Gibraltar may well face us with more difficult problems than it does today, but that is another story).

9. I suggest the time has come when, to the extent that practical politics permit, we should be somewhat more adventurous in our contacts with Spaniards than we have tended to be hitherto, without, of course, forgetting important sectors such as the highly variegated yet very influential banking/industrial/commercial complex with which we have always sought to maintain close touch. This Embassy already has quite extensive contacts with members of 'illegal' democratic groups, and a few members thereof have been sponsored visitors to the UK lately. That process should be discreetly intensified. I have already met quite a number of oppositionists, and aim to keep in direct touch with the democratic opposition, whether Left, Right or Centre, more than my predecessors were able to do when the régime's grip was still tight and too obvious contacts could cause trouble for the Spaniards concerned as well as the Embassy.

10. But the process of widening contacts should not be confined to the declared opposition only. Under the surface at least things have been changing here rapidly. There are many elements still working within the establishment, particularly among the younger generations, who can fairly be described as *de facto* oppositionists. In marked contrast to 20 or even 10 years ago one finds many people in positions of authority who genuinely believe that there must be evolution. I hope that applications put forward by us for sponsored visits or the like will be considered case by case, not so much on the basis of past record and present position held but on the basis of the known current attitudes of the man or woman concerned.[13]

11. Last but by no means least we should do all we can to develop our contacts with the military, particularly the middle and junior officer ranks, who are increasingly being drawn from a very different social background

[13] 'This is almost certainly a reference to the case of Gabriel Cisneros, who was recommended, before Mr. Wiggin's arrival in Madrid, for a sponsored visit', noted Mr. Everett in a minute to Mr. Baker of 17 December. 'Cisneros is a "flier" in the Spanish Ministry of the Presidency (Prime Minister's Office) and an important liberalising influence both there and in the National Council of the Movement of which he is a member. It was because of the latter membership that Mr. Hattersley turned down our recommendation. Although we have not given up hope altogether, of getting him here, now is not the time (because of the fate of political associations) to return to the charge.' Sir J. Killick, in a minute to Mr. Goulding of 31 December, agreed: 'Mr. Wiggin is no crusader but is sensibly concerned to do everything within reasonable limits, and against the background of his full understanding of the domestic political situation here, to establish a wide range of contacts against the day when political change in Spain, however, modest, will enable us to put them to good use … I think our experience in Portugal has taught us that there are serious disadvantages in having only a narrow range of "opposition" contacts at a time when fundamental change takes place.'

to their seniors and predecessors, and who tend to keep their thoughts to themselves. Sooner or later the military, particularly the army, will have a decisive role to play whether by action, inaction or a mixture of both. I hope it will be possible for Spanish officers to be invited to attend courses in Britain from time to time and that we ourselves will be prepared to send officers to Spanish courses. There are clear signs that, notwithstanding Gibraltar, the Spanish authorities would not now be averse to this, which may in itself be an indication that the military, concerned about the future here, are seeking to develop their external links and to broaden their horizons.[14]

12. To sum up, I hope that any recommendations for extending our relations with Spain which we may put forward will be considered sympathetically as an investment in a future, as yet uncertain, which cannot be all that far away. They will not be dramatic. Their main purpose will be to place us in a better position to influence events here when the interregnum ends.[15]

I have etc.,
C.D. WIGGIN

[14] Junior and middle ranking officers, Sir. J. Killick noted (*v. ibid.*), could 'come to play a political role of crucial importance', Mr. Wiggin had, he thought, 'been rightly warned off for the moment', but, he continued, 'I would certainly hope that we might find it possible to move cautiously in the direction suggested by Mr. Wiggin in his paragraph 11'.

[15] 'Mr. Wiggin's despatch is interesting & strikes me as being a sound analysis', minuted Mr. Morgan on 24 December. 'It is', he added, 'a very different situation from the Portuguese one, and there is still a chance that the political centre can organize itself for Gov[ernmen]t, though time is against it. The approach to our own relations is right, I think.' The despatch was, according to Mr. S.J. Barrett (Head of SWED), 'included among the Secretary of State's slender and carefully selected box of Christmas reading' (letter to Mr. Wiggin of 13 January 1975, WSS 1/4).

No. 114

Mr. Trench (Lisbon) to Mr. Callaghan

[*WSP 3/548/3*]

Confidential   LISBON, *12 February 1975*

Summary ...[1]

Sir,

Secretary of State's Visit to Portugal

I have the honour to submit to you an account of your visit to Lisbon on 6-7 February, on which you were accompanied by Mr. P.J. Weston (Assistant Private Secretary), Mr. T. McNally (Political Adviser), Mr. S.J. Barrett (Head of South-West European Department of the Foreign and Commonwealth Office) and Mr. T.D. McCaffrey (Head of the News Department); the party also included Mr. N.B.J. Huijsman (of the Overseas Development Ministry) and Mr. P. Brazier (of the Central Office of Information).

2. It had been your wish and intention to make a visit to Portugal ever since Dr. Mário Soares suggested this to you in London a few days after the *coup d'état* of 25 April, 1974. When Dr. Soares became Foreign Minister of Portugal on 15 May, the invitation was formalised and you had hoped to take it up during the summer; however, events in Cyprus intervened and thereafter your own crowded programme and the fact that Dr. Soares was constantly absent from Portugal made it difficult to find a mutually acceptable date. With the first free elections for nearly half a century due to take place in Portugal in late March or early April this year,[2] it became clear that unless you were to visit Lisbon now, any later visit might attract the criticism that it was too near the polling date and liable to influence the course of those elections.

3. It was therefore a most welcome development when I was informed on 18 January that you might be able to come here at the end of the first week in February. I was, however, inhibited from immediately sharing this news with Dr. Soares by the fact that his party (the Portuguese Socialist

---

[1] Not printed.

[2] Under the original AFM programme elections for a constituent assembly in the spring were due to be followed by parliamentary elections in the autumn. Meanwhile, the provisional Government and the AFM were to continue to govern. But, as was pointed out in a brief prepared for Mr. Callaghan's visit, the internal situation was 'becoming polarised between on the one hand the Communists and the more radical members of the AFM leadership; and on the other democratic parties (themselves divided) and the more moderate members of the AFM'. The Communists had until recently been pressing for a postponement of the elections on the grounds that the population was 'not properly prepared'. By contrast, the PSP and the PPD had seemed to sense that the election would strengthen their position (Brief No. 2, attached to minute from Mr. Barrett to Mr P.J. Weston of 3 February).

Party—PSP) together with the only other non-Communist party represented in the Provisional Government (the Popular Democratic party—PPD) were going through a period of crisis and confrontation with the Armed Forces Movement (AFM) in connection with controversial trade union legislation;[3] it therefore seemed possible that these two parties might leave the Government and that, in those changed circumstances, a visit by you would have been inappropriate. Once this risk had receded it was possible to agree on the terms of an announcement.

4. But the doubts hanging over the visit were still not dispelled. On the night of 25 January the delegates to the Congress of the Centre Democratic Social Party (CDS) were subjected to harassment and overnight incarceration in their conference hall by violent and hostile crowds of Left-wing agitators in Oporto. Mr. Geoffrey Rippon, QC, MP (the Opposition spokesman on Foreign Affairs) and two other Conservative Parliamentarians narrowly escaped personal involvement in the unpleasantness, and the British information media reacted sharply with news stories and editorial comment suggesting that law and order in Portugal were precarious. It was necessary for the dust to settle after this furore before the announcement of your visit could be made on 29 January.

5. Even then, further problems loomed up in the final hours before your arrival, when there was widespread criticism here of the impending arrival of a NATO fleet, which was scheduled to put in to Lisbon at the conclusion of exercises off the coast of Portugal. The arrival date of the ships coincided with your visit and at one time seemed likely to provoke violent disturbances in the city, which would have been a most unfortunate accompaniment to your discussions. Once again, the crisis was averted; this time by a Government ban on street demonstrations (ignored by the Maoist MRPP, as it turned out) and a level-headed communiqué from the Portuguese Communist Party urging its members to desist from provocation of NATO personnel on shore-leave.

6. It was therefore not without anxieties that my staff and I went to meet your RAF Comet at Lisbon Airport on the afternoon of 6 February. Dr. Soares greeted you at the airport with unfeigned warmth and extended to you the courtesy of a military guard of honour—a gesture normally reserved for Heads of State or Government. You were immediately plunged into a programme of considerable intensity, arising necessarily from the unavoidable shortness of your visit.

7. You had come with four clear objectives to achieve in the brief time at your disposal. Firstly, you wished to support and encourage the forces working for representative democracy in Portugal and wishing to see Portugal linked with the rest of Western Europe; secondly, you wished to explore and influence the thinking of the Portuguese leadership, particularly the military men who are inexperienced and sometimes naïve;

---

[3] The proposed legislation related to the creation of a unified trade union structure.

thirdly, you wished to bolster Dr. Soares and the Portuguese Socialist Party as they faced the challenge from the extreme Left wing; and fourthly, you wished to derive what benefit you could for British business interests. Dr. Soares, for his part, was anxious to present your visit as further evidence that the new régime in Portugal was widely accepted by international opinion, and to strengthen his own standing in Portugal vis-à-vis his political opponents.

8. After a brief discussion of tactics with myself and your other advisers, you joined Dr. Soares at the Foreign Ministry for a private session at which you were accompanied by Mr. McNally. Thereafter, you proceeded to the first formal session of talks in the Foreign Ministry, which covered a wide range of international affairs. Dr. Soares clearly appreciated your frank briefing on East/West relations and the Middle East crisis, being particularly grateful for your first-hand account of the recent Washington meetings between President Ford and Dr. Kissinger on the one hand and Mr. Harold Wilson and yourself on the other.[4] Dr. Soares, for his part, gave you a frank and informative account of the problems facing Portugal in the task of rapid decolonisation. He explained the dangers of the time-scale originally envisaged by General Spínola and emphasised that the Portuguese Government's successful attempts to bring the three independence movements in Angola into harmony with each other had been the only alternative to early civil war in that territory—a danger which could still not be discounted in the longer term.[5] Dr. Soares also spoke with candour of the dilemma presented to his Government by the prospect of the Americans wishing to use the Azores bases in a further Middle Eastern war: were they to do so, Dr. Soares's painstaking work of re-establishing political relations with the African and Arab countries would be destroyed at a stroke; were Portugal not to allow the Americans such use of the bases, on the other hand, it would immediately provoke a confrontation between herself and the US.[6] You agreed with Dr. Soares

---

[4] Reporting his conversations with Dr. Kissinger during the previous week, Mr. Callaghan noted that UK and US views on East-West relations 'were broadly the same'. Both Governments thought Russia's recent abrogation of the US-Soviet trade agreement (see Volume III, No. 79, note 3) amounted only to a temporary setback for *détente*—'the backfiring of an engine which was otherwise working well'. Dr. Soares replied that he was 'glad to learn that Mr. Callaghan thought the Russians were still attached to *détente*'. Rumours about Mr. Brezhnev's health and the collapse of the superpowers' trade agreement had created fears of 'the possibility of a retreat from *détente*' which, he said, 'would have serious internal consequences for Portugal'. With the PCP's close links to Moscow, a lowering of tensions between the blocs would, he added, 'make Portuguese internal problems easier to solve and facilitate the implementation of democracy in Portugal' (record of a meeting between Mr. Callaghan and Mr. Soares at the Ministry of Foreign Affairs in Lisbon on 6 February at 6 p.m.).

[5] Agreement had been reached between the Portuguese Government and the three liberation movements in Angola which would lead to the country's independence in November.

[6] See No. 111, note 17.

that this was yet another reason for the overriding priority which must be given to establishing a durable peace in the Middle East. A full record of these talks is being forwarded to your department.

9. The principal social occasion of your visit was a dinner given in the handsome banqueting hall of the *Palacio das Necessidades* (Foreign Ministry) by Dr. Soares the same evening. He had invited most of the senior Ministers to his dinner, including prominent members of the Armed Forces Movement and also including Ministers representing the Portuguese Communist Party (Dr. Alvaro Cunhal) and the Popular Democratic Party (Dr. Magalhães Mota); the latter did not appear. You did, however, have an interesting talk with Dr. Alvaro Cunhal before dinner. Dr. Cunhal was at pains to emphasise that a Communist-dominated Portugal would still welcome British investment; he was categorical in his forecast that the elected Government would be a coalition one, and that the Communist Party would continue to play a part in such a coalition. When you reminded him that a large Communist Party in a foreign country had never been an impediment to good relations with the UK, and quoted to him the examples of France and Italy, Dr. Cunhal pointed out that in neither of these countries were the Communist Parties participating in Government and that he hoped this would not make a difference in the case of Portugal. His intention seemed to be, firstly, to emphasise the strength of his party and, consequently, to try to convince you that this should provide no grounds for undue anxiety. It was unfortunate that at the moment when you put to him a most significant question about a unitary trade union system, which would inevitably have led him on to the controversial ground of a one-party Government, you were interrupted by a summons to the dinner table.[7]

10. In fact, the summons came none too soon for most of the guests who had been waiting for nearly an hour while the Chief of the Army Staff (General Fabião) and the Military Governor of Lisbon (Brigadier Carvalho) were expected; their continued absence at a meeting of the Assembly of Delegates of the AFM not only delayed the commencement of dinner but caused obvious anxiety among some of your hosts. You were thus provided

[7] As a result of Dr. Cunhal's conversation with Mr. Callaghan, Mr. Ure and Lt.-Col. Huggan were invited to call on the Communist Minister for further talks on 18 February. Mr. Ure subsequently informed Mr. Barrett that according to Dr. Cunhal the PCP were 'in no way eager to seize control of existing businesses. Indeed, if the PCP were to find itself in a position to dominate economic events in the new Government, we would find it much more limited in its calls for nationalisation than had been the Labour Government in the UK after the Second World War. Public ownership was a process which should come slowly and naturally, not something that should be forced through with disregard to public and foreign confidence.' On the question of Portugal's membership of NATO, Dr. Cunhal was equally moderate: 'he did not believe Portugal's present allegiance to the Alliance increased the risk of world war or confrontation between NATO and the Warsaw Pact. Indeed, a precipitate removal of Portugal from the Alliance might alarm the Americans and thus increase–rather than diminish–the risks facing the world today' (letter of 19 February).

with an illustration of the nervousness which all members of the Provisional Government feel when they know that matters of paramount importance are being discussed—and often decided—in their absence by the Military.[8]

11. The texts of Dr. Soares's speech at dinner and your own response had been exchanged before the event. Inevitably, both explored the same theme: the complexity of democracy and the necessity of allowing different viewpoints and different parties to co-exist in a truly free society. Your speech struck the key-note of the visit and, in itself, went a long way to achieving your principal objective: the wide dissemination of a liberal democratic philosophy and the exposure of its incompatibility with Communist dogma. Dr. Soares heard you with visible pleasure and Dr. Cunhal with sphinx-like self-containment.

12. One problem had remained unresolved until after your arrival in Lisbon: this was whether or not you should consent to receive representatives of the CDS and the PPD, both of whom had asked to meet you. In the event, you decided that separate conversations with the leaders of these parties would have been inappropriate on an official visit of this nature, and might have given offence to Dr. Soares. You therefore deputed to your Political Adviser—Mr. McNally—the task of receiving representatives of the CDS, the PPD and the PSP. I understand that some points of interest emerged from these meetings, notably a confidential intimation from the CDS that they intended to establish electoral links with the Christian Democratic Party, and further evidence of the intransigence of the PDP towards conciliation either with the CDS or with the Socialists.

13. While these talks were under way, I was particularly glad that you yourself spared a few minutes to visit the Chancery of this Embassy and to meet almost all the members of my staff. The fact that you were willing to sacrifice some of your rare moments of free time here was very greatly appreciated, especially by those who had been involved in the rather hectic rush necessary to concert at short notice the practical arrangements for your visit, and by those who had had to remain on duty throughout the previous night.

14. Later in the morning I accompanied you on your call on General Costa Gomes, President of the Republic. According to the original programme, you should first have called on the Prime Minister, Brigadier Vasco Gonçalves, but pressure of work compelled the latter to cancel the engagement. Instead, and to the annoyance of both General Costa Gomes and Dr. Soares, he attended your audience with the President and, indeed, largely took the conversation out of the latter's hands. Considering the

---

[8] In a minute of 18 February on this despatch Mr. Morgan observed: 'There is obviously very little meeting of minds at present between the civilian ministers in Portugal & the AFM leaders. The latter's outlook is so obviously different & the naiveté & narrowness of vision sometimes frightening, as Mr. Trench's letters have shown. It will pay us to contribute our minds to the international education of the more intelligent ones like [Maj. E.A.] Melo de Antunes [Minister without Portfolio] & Alves.'

strains to which he has been subjected during the part fortnight, Brigadier Gonçalves was looking a good deal less tired and harassed than I had expected, but he soon embarked on his familiar denunciation of the way in which the foreign information media treated events in Portugal, and he singled out the BBC for special condemnation in this respect. At one point, indeed, it looked as though he was on the point of launching himself into one of his impassioned harangues, but he was brought back to earth by the good-humoured firmness with which you handled his complaints and outlined some basic facts about the nature of democracy. Nevertheless he continued to show great sensitivity to any hint of criticism, and the suavity of the interpreter's translation disguised the fact that some of his remarks, though not aimed directly at Dr. Soares (who was also present), were distinctly uncomplimentary to Portuguese politicians. He was also more than disingenuous in denying the existence of differences of opinion within the AFM and passing over in silence the alarm expressed not only by the CDS, but also by the PSP and PPD. On a personal basis, however, he was clearly trying to be friendly and at the end of the audience he apologised profusely to me for not being able to accept the invitation to your lunch party.

15. During the greater part of your call the President preserved an amiable silence, while occasionally his expression seemed to indicate a faint embarrassment at the views which his Prime Minister was expressing so vigorously. His own participation was largely confined to comments on the nature and attitude of the AFM. At lunch, however, Dr. Soares told me that he had been able to have a few words with General Costa Gomes after you had left, and that the President had been delighted with both the substance and the manner of your remarks to Brigadier Gonçalves (as indeed had Dr. Soares himself).

16. Meanwhile, Mr. Huijsman was having independent and useful conversations with the Economic Directorate of the Ministry of Foreign Affairs. He was able to explain the commitments which the British Government had already made regarding aid to Guiné-Bissau and Mozambique and to demonstrate our intention to co-ordinate these with the Portuguese and to study the possibilities of assisting—within the limits of our own economic difficulties—Portugal herself. These talks were a useful preliminary to more concrete discussions on a later occasion and will have helped to prepare the ground for a possible visit by the Minister for Overseas Development.

17. After your call on the President, you returned to the Foreign Ministry for the second and final session of formal talks with Dr. Soares and his advisers. Dr. Soares surprised us with a proposal that President Costa Gomes should visit the UK after a visit to France, probably in the first or second week of May this year. You pointed out the difficulties in this proposal but undertook to have it studied further in London, once the Portuguese Government had given us a more precise idea of possible dates. You then gave Dr. Soares an illuminating account of the British

Government's current thinking regarding the Rhodesian problem and of the conversations which you had had, in this context, during your recent African tour.[9] When the discussions turned to NATO questions, Dr. Soares reiterated the Portuguese Government's intention of adhering to their commitments, and his own personal support for Portugal's continued membership of NATO. A full record of this session is also being forwarded to your Department.[10] A communiqué summarising the achievements of the visit was agreed with the Portuguese and is attached as an annex to this despatch.[11]

18. Before ending your visit you gave a lunch at my Residence for Dr. Soares and other Portuguese Ministers and officials; the relaxed and friendly atmosphere on this occasion was—I think—a measure of the gratification which your appearance in Portugal at this juncture, and the forthright things you had to say both in public and in private, had given to your hosts. Dr. Soares was particularly pleased, and his impromptu arrangement of a brief tour to the Castelo São Jorge was a symptom of the general goodwill.

19. The Press too made the most of your visit. It received prominent front-page treatment, with photographs, in all sections of the Press except the Communist and near-Communist newspapers. Most responsible commentators accurately identified the objectives of the visit as being the strengthening of the forces of democracy within Portugal and her links with Europe and the West in general; some went further and saw the visit as providing moral support for Dr. Soares and the Portuguese Socialist Party. The preliminary progress in the field of aid, referred to above, was built up by the Press into a somewhat more definite proposition than had yet been established, but no harm was done by this. The generally constructive tone of the Portuguese Press was undoubtedly a reflection of the frank and pertinent briefing given to them by Mr. McCaffrey.

20. What should be our feelings at the conclusion of this visit? First, gratitude that you held firm in your intention to come to Portugal, despite the alarms of recent weeks, coupled with relief that the visit passed off without the accompaniment of a concurrent Government crisis or further disturbances in the streets of Lisbon. Peaceful as the city looked during your visit, experience since last April has shown that it is rare for two

---

[9] Mr. Callaghan had visited southern Africa in January to discuss developments in Rhodesia with the governments of Zambia, Tanzania and South Africa and to create a common front to pressure the Rhodesian Government into negotiations with black Rhodesians over constitutional reform. Despite, however, an apparent measure of consensus amongst the southern African leaders, Mr. Smith had remained unyielding (record of a meeting between Mr. Callaghan and Dr. Soares at the Ministry of Foreign Affairs in Lisbon on 7 February at noon).

[10] During this meeting Dr. Soares said that 'the existence of NATO was a necessary condition in the pursuit of *détente* and a factor in East/West relations. The PCP were realistic and although they were opposed in principle to NATO they recognised that Portugal could not leave the alliance' (*v. ibid.*).

[11] Not printed.

weeks to pass without some overt or barely concealed conflict taking place. Second, satisfaction at the achievement of the objectives of your visit; no one can doubt that the message you came here to put across has been heard in clear and friendly tones by the Government and people of Portugal; only time can tell whether the message will be heeded. Third—I suggest—some caution in assessing the impressions which you have taken away. Everyone whom you have met in the Portuguese Government has been putting his best foot forward for you during your visit. The Prime Minister gave an impression of relative stability and moderation; Dr. Soares was in one of his more self confident and optimistic moods—a remarkable contrast to his attitude 10 days ago; Major Vitor Alves—whom you sat next to during two meals—is always a reassuring interlocutor; and Dr. Cunhal, as always with foreign visitors, was on his best behaviour. I was delighted that all this should have been so. But Portugal can show a more sombre face, and I would not want you to carry home a conclusion that anxieties about free elections and the nature of the future régime in this country were things of the past.[12] You told us, Sir, at my Residence on return from dining with Dr. Soares, that we should not be narrow in our judgments of the Portuguese way ahead: our own concepts of democracy might be premature here, and there might well be a role for the continuing presence of the Armed Forces Movement in the machinery of Government. We shall certainly bear your words in mind during the coming months. But there are likely to be moments in the next year or two when it will be difficult to decide which course best accords with the future well-being of the Portuguese people, and to what degree it is permissible to adapt the democratic system to the country's special needs, without risking a relapse into authoritarianism.

21. I am copying this despatch to Her Majesty's Representatives at Washington, Brussels (NATO), Madrid, Luanda and Lourenço Marques.

I have, etc.,

N.C.C. Trench

[12] In a minute to Mr. Morgan of 17 February covering this despatch, Mr. Barrett noted: 'Mr. Trench rightly warns against taking too rosy a view of the situation in Lisbon. But I do not think that any of the party returned with an over-optimistic impression. The unsolved question of the relation of the AFM to the political parties; the political and economic content of the AFM's programme; the ever-present threat of demonstrations and intimidation; and the generally immature and fragile state of Portuguese democracy: these are all reasons for having at the most a cautious and highly qualified optimism about Portuguese prospects. This said, the policy conclusions remain unchanged, i.e. that support and encouragement to the democratic forces in Portugal remains the best course of action open to us unless and until it appears that undemocratic forces have triumphed.'

At midday on 11 March two companies of paratroops from Tancos, backed by two propeller-driven fighter/trainer aircraft, made an unsuccessful attempt to seize the barracks of a light artillery regiment stationed near Lisbon airport. Meanwhile, in the centre of Lisbon, a group of officers from the Portuguese National Republican Guard attempted to take control. But although they were able to imprison their commanding officer, their efforts were frustrated when their barracks were surrounded by left-wing groups and armoured vehicles. There were also unconfirmed reports of an attack on the COPCON[1] Headquarters in the city, and of troop movements elsewhere in the country. Nevertheless, by mid-afternoon such shooting as there had been had ceased, and the military authorities began to round up those suspected of being implicated in what was assumed to have been a right-wing plot. The failure of the coup gave rise to large left-wing demonstrations against 'reactionary forces', as civilians and soldiers of the political centre and right were illegally arrested and detained en masse. General Spínola, whom official broadcasts accused of involvement in the attempted coup, only just evaded capture when he and other officers escaped to Spain by helicopter.[2]

Mr. Trench subsequently reported that two hypotheses had been advanced to explain these events. The first, which he was personally inclined to favour, was that Spinolists in the armed forces had been quietly gathering strength and making preparations for a takeover sooner or later. The second was that AFM radicals and the Communists, 'alarmed by the signs that they were losing support within the armed forces, staged a fake Right-wing coup as a pretext for moving against Spínola and his sympathisers'. But, whatever the truth, the immediate consequence was, Mr. Trench observed, 'that the fragile balance at the centre of the power structure disappeared ... [t]he régime lurched violently to the Left, and the radicals, both civilian and military were able to profit from the disarray of their more moderate or conservative colleagues'. A Supreme Council of the Revolution, comprising members of the former junta, the former Coordinating Committee and representatives of the various armed services, was established with wide executive powers; the Prime Minister, General Vasco Gonçalves, was given full powers to reshuffle his Cabinet; and new measures to speed up the socialisation of the economy, including the nationalisation of the banks and insurance companies, were announced. The AFM thus appeared to acquire a more permanent role in the Portuguese political process. 'The assumption by the Movement of an overtly dominant position in political affairs has', Mr. Trench concluded, 'reinforced its non-democratic and authoritarian tendencies despite the AFM's spokesmen's continued insistence on the important contribution which the parties of all complexions have to make.[3]

---

[1] See No. 110, note 7.

[2] Despatch from Mr. Trench of 9 April 1975, WSP 1/1.

[3] *V. ibid.*

No. 115

Minute from Mr. Barrett to Mr. Morgan

[*WSP 1/1*]

Confidential   FCO, *17 March 1975*

The Situation in Portugal

1. My earlier minute of 11 March (dictated on the eve of the abortive coup) concluded that recent developments had perhaps increased the chances that a left-wing military régime with communist support would push the fledgling democracy out of the nest.[1] As a result of the fiasco of the coup, this prediction may already be on its way to fulfillment.

2. The events of 11 March gave the AFM radicals, with communist support, both reasons and a pretext for the following measures:

(*a*) Resolving the question of the future political rôle of the AFM by establishing a Supreme Council of the Revolution with comprehensive executive and legislative authority that will set it above the Constituent Assembly due to be elected on 12 April. There are now no civilian representatives on the state bodies set up by the AFM though there may continue to be some civilians in the provisional government.[2]

(*b*) A Government reshuffle, the details of which are expected in the next few days. It is rumoured that this will lead to the eviction of the PPD from the Government, the entry of the communist front MDP[3] party, and possibly the transfer of Dr. Soares from the Ministry of Foreign Affairs.[4]

---

[1] In this minute to Mr. Morgan, Mr. Barrett cited as 'worrying aspects of developments in Portugal': continuing disorders directed against democratic political parties; the inability of the police to intervene when disturbances occurred; the unresolved question of the 'institutionalisation' of the AFM; the postponement from 3 to 20 March of the official opening of the electoral campaign; and reports of 'rightist intrigues' and of a 'Spínolist revival' in the AFM. 'It would not be difficult', he warned Mr. Morgan, 'for the PCP and the radical left wing elements in the AFM to make common cause and find both reasons and pretext for postponing the elections.' Portugal could, he suggested, 'be quite near a situation where they will raise the cry of a danger to the achievements of the coup of 25 April as justification for intervention against the ordinary democratic processes'.

[2] In Lisbon telegram No. 152 of 14 March Mr. Trench expressed his concern about these developments. 'The balance of forces which made it possible to imagine that reasonably representative elections could take place has', he explained, 'been upset, and perhaps destroyed ... The checks and balances of the provisional constitutional arrangements have also been swept away by the introduction of the Higher Council of the Revolution. The promised re-shuffle of the Government will almost certainly do nothing to redress that balance.'

[3] *Movimento Democrático Popular*/Popular Democratic Movement.

[4] Gen. Vasco Gonçalves completed the reconstruction of his Government on 25 March. As a result, Maj. de Melo Antunes, an AFM moderate, replaced Dr. Soares as Foreign Minister.

(c) The nationalisation of banks and insurance companies. Although this is a measure that in Portuguese circumstances could be justified on its merits, its introduction at this stage, just a few weeks after the publication of [the] economic plan that excluded it, signifies a strong shift of economic policy towards the left. There is a risk of continuing economic dislocation, in which deterioration of foreign confidence in the Portuguese economy will be a factor.

3. The Armed Forces Movement have hinted that they will outlaw extremist parties of both right and left. If this measure is carried out, the CDS (together with the CDP) are likely to suffer the most since they, unlike the left-wing fringe, have substantial political backing. Although some who sympathise with the former regime have joined the CDS, the party as a whole is conservative rather than reactionary. Nevertheless there is reason to fear that the AFM will act on the principle of guilt by association and dissolve the CDS. A further pointer is that the PCP have begun to criticise the PPD for housing reactionary elements, no doubt foreshadowing the progressive increase of pressure and intimidation on all non-communist parties (including the PSP).[5]

4. Our Ambassador in Lisbon has reported that Dr. Soares is in a mood of resigned pessimism and has described the situation as being wholly in the hands of the new Supreme Council of the Revolution.[6] Dr. Soares has also suggested that although elections will still be held, the atmosphere would not be normal. The United States Ambassador in Lisbon had a similar interview with Dr. Soares.

5. It is possible to derive some slight encouragement from the announcements that the elections are still to be held on 12 April and that Portugal remains loyal to its international commitments (including for the time being membership of the North Atlantic Alliance). But even these signs may be deceptive; they could be a smokescreen behind which the extreme left-wing can more easily consolidate their position.

6. Nor should it be overlooked that prior to 11 March the moderate bulk of the AFM were beginning to show their strength, e.g. in elective bodies within the AFM. Although at present disrupted and confused, the

[5] On 18 March the Supreme Council of the Revolution announced that, along with two parties of the far Left, the MRPP and the Workers-Peasants Alliance, the Christian Democrats would be prohibited from participating in the elections (Lisbon telegram No. 163 of 19 March).

[6] When Mr. Trench called on Dr. Soares on 13 March, he found him 'particularly downcast' by the latest developments and their implications for the forthcoming election since 'a recent opinion poll had shown that the Socialist Party was well ahead of all the others'. Indeed, although Dr. Soares did not mention the fact, he personally was well ahead of other political figures, having almost twice as large a percentage as the Prime Minister. Dr. Soares said that the 'moderate parties as a whole were well ahead of the extreme Left' (Lisbon telegram No. 153 of 14 March).

moderates may yet succeed in making their weight felt, particularly if current policies lead to economic dislocation.[7]

NATO

7. Portuguese withdrawal from NATO would at this stage probably have more psychological and political impact than military importance. NATO would lose the IBERLANT[8] headquarters though this would not be a matter of major military significance. The Americans might lose the air facilities in the Azores (which they enjoy under a bilateral agreement) although they have to some extent already discounted this in the event of a new Arab/Israeli war. It is true that there is no effective Portuguese contribution on the major NATO fronts, but the loss of even a fringe member could do serious damage to Western confidence. If the situation deteriorated further and the Soviet Union acquired facilities in Portugal, this could present far-reaching problems for NATO. The Ministry of Defence have been asked to do a study of the implications of a Portuguese withdrawal from NATO and of a possible acquisition by the Soviet Union of facilities there.[9] Meanwhile, we can expect further problems within NATO on the release of information to the Portuguese authorities. A further point is that whether or not Portugal withdraws, the temper of the populace there may already be such that we could not rely on facilities there in a time of increased East/West tension.

Spain

8. The impact of recent events on developments in Spain is not easy to predict. In every respect Spain represents a more advanced society, yet the continuing absence of legitimisation of the regime by measures of liberalisation means that in the last resort only the armed forces in Spain can guarantee stability. It may be that fear of going the way of Portugal

[7] Mr. Clark was equally unwilling to assume that developments in the wake of the failed *coup* necessarily augured the beginnings of a Communist dictatorship, a prognosis he described as 'excessively gloomy'. In a letter to Mr. Baker of 18 March, he concluded that, after an 'initial show of bewilderment and despair', the moderate parties were 'fighting back'. The 'forces in favour of democracy and moderation have', he noted, 'not abandoned the field, and are doing their best to re-group. They were however dealt a severe blow by the foolishness and ineptitude of their more hot-headed supporters on 11 March.'

Mr. Trench was more pessimistic. 'I must confess', he wrote in a letter to Sir J. Killick of 19 March, 'that I am now even more deeply concerned about the future, because we are approaching a situation of anarchy, to all intents and purposes.' While he thought the AFM divided and the extent to which it could control the rank and file 'probably strictly limited', he considered the members of the PCP to comprise 'the only disciplined body in the country'. Indeed, his 'only cause for satisfaction' was that, with the moderates in the armed forces in disorder, a formal civil war seemed improbable. Rather, he suspected that Portugal was approaching a situation, similar to that which brought about the Salazar regime in the 1920s, in which 'groups of men [took] pot shots at each other in the streets, and no one could tell who was supporting what ideas against whom'.

[8] Iberian Atlantic Command.

[9] See No. 119.

will make it less easy for the would-be liberalisers to put across their point of view. We can probably expect that the Spanish regime will do its best to remove from the Spanish armed forces any elements that might be tempted to follow the pattern set by the Portuguese AFM.

Recommendations

9. In the present uncertain situation policy recommendations are particularly difficult. It is not easy to strike the right balance between:

(*a*) Our necessary reservations about the policy of the Portuguese military leadership and their extreme left-wing allies; and

(*b*) The need not to leave the field wide open for forces opposed to democracy.

Decisions on future actions and contacts will need to take account of the possibility that they may prove insufficient to halt the slide towards a fully established left-wing military regime operating with the support and under the influence of the PCP. Nevertheless our best guideline will still be to continue to befriend and seek to influence the Portuguese leadership as long as some prospect for democracy remains.

10. If this is accepted, certain specific recommendations follow:

(*a*) We should continue to take the attitude in public that we support and encourage the democratic forces in Portugal, saying that we hope that the elections will take place as planned.

(*b*) We should maintain our contacts with Dr. Soares and his party, as well as with the PPD. If it becomes clear that Dr. Soares is remaining Foreign Minister, a personal message from the Secretary of State might help him.

(*c*) We should go ahead with the projected visit of the Chief of Defence Staff to Portugal at the end of April. If the situation settles down, this could provide a useful opportunity for contact with the AFM. If it does not, the reasons for cancellation will be obvious and should not cause great embarrassment.

(*d*) As for the proposed invitation to the President of Portugal to pay a working visit here in May, we should seek Dr. Soares' views before issuing the invitation.

(*e*) We should continue to press the Ministry of Defence to invite the Army Chief of Staff, General Fabião, to pay a visit but should drop the idea of a visit by the COPCON Commander, Brigadier Carvalho.

(*f*) We should also consult Dr. Soares before putting to the Portuguese precise proposals for the projected aid mission. This would have the advantage that we should be able to take stock of developments in the field of economic policy before a final decision on the mission is taken.

(*g*) We should for the time being continue to help the Portuguese in matters of a mainly technical nature (e.g. training television staff, supplying information on organisation in the Army). But we should examine carefully any new proposals touching on security or other sensitive spheres.

(*h*) We should continue to exchange views with our allies in NATO and within the EEC and encourage Western governments to follow our approach.

S.J. BARRETT

No. 116

Mr. Callaghan to Mr. Trench (Lisbon)

No. 130 Telegraphic [*WSP 2/579/1*]

Flash. Secret   FCO, *21 March 1975, 11.30 p.m.*

Repeated to Immediate Paris, UKDEL NATO, for information to Immediate Washington, Bonn.

Portugal—Internal Developments

Schmidt[1] has telephoned Prime Minister to draw his attention to disturbing reports (by implication secret) from Lisbon which suggest that it is fairly certain that events there tomorrow or Sunday[2] will result in the introduction of 4 or 5 Communists into the Cabinet and the exclusion of close allies (by implication Soares).[3]

2. Schmidt said he had spoken to the Americans (whether Ford or Kissinger was unclear) who said this fitted their information and they intended to indicate to the Soviet Ambassador that they would view any developments of this kind with concern. Schmidt indicated that he intended to do the same 'in a very cautious way'.

3. Schmidt said he was also attempting to contact Giscard.

4. The Prime Minister has asked for an urgent assessment of these reports (first thing tomorrow 22 March) and for advice whether something should be said tactfully by us to Soviet Ambassador here.

[1] Herr H.H.W. Schmidt was German Federal Chancellor.

[2] i.e. 23 March.

[3] Sir N. Henderson, the British Ambassador in Bonn, informed Mr. Callaghan in telegram No. 253 of 22 March that Herr Schmidt's information about the situation in Portugal appeared to have reached him through party (i.e. SPD (*Sozialdemokratsiche Partei Deutschlands*)) channels, and that the Foreign Ministry was 'only partly in the picture'. A subsequent report from Lisbon indicated that following a complete breach between Dr. Soares and Gen. Vasco Gonçalves over the composition of the new Government, Dr. Soares had sent emissaries to Bonn to seek assistance from socialist friends abroad (Lisbon telegram No. 175 of 24 March).

5. Grateful for any comments and any indications of validity of Schmidt's report.[4]

---

[4] Mr. Trench was inclined to discount Herr Schmidt's warning. In Lisbon telegram No. 168 of 22 March he replied that it was proving more difficult to complete the reconstruction of the Portuguese provisional Government than at first expected, but that it seemed likely that the three existing parties would remain in the Government and 'be joined by the MDP/CDE [*Comissão Democrática Eleitoral* (Democratic Electoral Commission)], a body generally accepted to be a Communist front organisation'. He further noted in paragraph 4 of this telegram that, although German information on developments in Lisbon pointed 'generally in the right direction', it was 'exaggerated', and that he personally had reservations about the efficacy of speaking to the Soviet Ambassador. 'While the Communist party may take orders from Moscow the other crypto-communist parties', he observed, 'probably will not, and the Communist party itself is conscious of the dangers it runs from being outflanked by its more militant allies on the left' (WSP 1/1).

No. 117

Mr. D.A. Logan[1] (UKDEL NATO) to Mr. Callaghan

No. 139 Telegraphic [*WSP 1/1*]

Flash. Confidential   BRUSSELS, *22 March 1975, 12.30 p.m.*

Repeated for information to Flash Bonn and Lisbon, and Immediate to Washington, Paris, Moscow UKREP Brussels and Dublin.

Your tel[egram] No. 106:
Portuguese internal developments[2]

1. At German request the Secretary General called a private meeting this morning of the representatives of Belgium, France, Italy, Germany, United Kingdom, United States. We agreed with the Secretary General that the NATO Council could hardly be called together since this would mean having the Portuguese present and probably obliging him to defend his authorities.

2. German representative read a long report which he said came from a single very reliable source, and which suggested that Portugal was about to

---

[1] UK Deputy Permanent Representative to the North Atlantic Council (NAC).

[2] In this telegram, despatched at 10 a.m. on 22 March, Mr. Callaghan stated that HMG would welcome urgent discussions within NATO on the situation in Portugal. 'We understand', he added, 'that the State Department, while awaiting Kissinger's views on whether representations should be made to the Soviet Ambassador in Washington, hope that the NATO Council will act in some way' (WSP 2/579/1).

be taken over as Czechoslovakia had been after the war.[3] To balance this, I drew on Lisbon tel[egram] No. 168,[4] particularly paragraph 4.[5]

3. As regards action that might be taken it was agreed that bilateral approaches should be made to the Soviet Union. Bruce[6] (US) thought that they were already in train. De Rose (France) speaking personally thought a strong Communist presence in Portugal inevitable, even if the Soviet Union could be persuaded to halt their machine.[7] Was not a naked takeover better than gradual drift, which would comfort Mitterand[8] and the Italian left? But the position of the West at a CSCE[9] summit meeting would be highly embarrassing following a Communist takeover. Catalano[10] (Italy) doubted whether his Government could go so far, as de Rose has hinted, as to say to the USSR that they would not go to a CSCE summit in these circumstances[11] but there was general agreement that the Soviet Union should be warned of the effect on détente of a takeover.[12]

4. I suggested an approach to the Portuguese urging free elections[13] and warning them of the consequences on their relations with the West, particularly the Community, and on their economic development. Bruce read advice from the US Ambassador in Lisbon advising against action with the Portuguese which he thought likely to be counter-productive. We should play it cool and preserve what influence we had in the hope of using it effectively with whatever Government might emerge. We should work for free elections and an end to violence and subversion. The

[3] Sir N. Henderson reported in Bonn telegram No. 271 of 27 March that the Federal Government had secret information that the East Germans had passed 'large sums of money' to the Portuguese Communists.

[4] See No. 116, note 4.

[5] *V. ibid.* Mr. Trench also explained in this telegram that he had 'received no hint of a dramatic development on the lines presaged by Schmidt' either from the German Ambassador in Lisbon or from the Governor of the Bank of Portugal, both of whom he had recently met.

[6] Mr. D.K.E. Bruce was US Permanent Representative to the NAC.

[7] Count F. de Tricornot de Rose was France's Permanent Representative to the NAC.

[8] M. F.M.M. Mitterand was First Secretary of the French Socialist Party.

[9] Conference on Security and Cooperation in Europe. Stage II of the CSCE had begun in Geneva in the autumn of 1973. The Soviet Government was anxious to complete the negotiations with a European summit at Stage III. See Volume II.

[10] Sig. F. Catalano di Melilli was Italy's Permanent Representative to the NAC.

[11] See Volume II, No. 117.

[12] The JIC assessment paper of 31 October (see No. 111, notes 4, 5 and 7) maintained that the extent of Soviet aid to the Portuguese Communists did not then seem likely to be decisive, but that 'it would be critical in a civil war situation'. 'The chances of a Communist régime surviving in Portugal might', the paper concluded, 'depend critically on the extent of Soviet economic aid; and it is a least doubtful whether the Russians would be willing to take on an open ended economic commitment of this sort.'

[13] Mr. Trench reported in Lisbon telegram No. 167 of 20 March that it had been confirmed that elections were to take place on 25 April and that the official opening of the electoral campaign had been postponed to 2 April.

Portuguese leaders were excited and exhausted. Gonzales [*sic*] had told their Ambassador that he knew very well that the concern of the West was the presence of Communists in his Government: the US were obsessed about this. Reflecting as it did the picture presented in Lisbon tel[egram] No. 168[14] this advice was welcomed at the meeting but it was thought that it would be wrong to do nothing and that bilateral representations should be made in Lisbon on the lines I had suggested.[15]

5. At the end of the meeting Bruce read a telegram from the State Department instructing him to urge all NATO allies to make strong representations urgently with the Portuguese on the shift of power on the lines indicated in MIFT.[16] It was not clear whether these instructions took into account the advice of the US Ambassador in Lisbon. Bruce indicated that he did not agree with them.

6. This morning's meeting in NATO will not be made known to the countries not represented at it. The Secretary General will call a meeting at 4 p.m. of all representatives except Portugal when we shall go over the ground again in an attempt to coordinate and perhaps instigate action by other allies.[17]

[14] See notes 4 and 5 above.

[15] Mr. Callaghan subsequently instructed Mr. Logan to inform his NAC colleagues that HMG 'would be prepared to consider calling in the Soviet Ambassador if it [were] clear that the Americans [were] ready to authorise action in Washington'. He was also prepared to go along with selective bilateral démarches by the Ambassadors of the EC countries if there was a general feeling in favour of this course. But he thought that representations in Lisbon, unsupported by representations to the Soviet Union elsewhere, 'would have to be relatively low key and could hardly ensure that proper weight was given to any East/West considerations' (telegram No. 107 to UKDEL NATO of 22 March, WSP 2/579/1). Cf. No. 118.

[16] Mr. Bruce's instructions, as recorded in this telegram of 22 March, were to consult with the Secretary-General and those represented at this meeting, and to suggest parallel high-level démarches to the Portuguese authorities within the next 24 hours expressing concern about: (1) the 'leftist concentration of power' in Lisbon; (2) the reported impending appointment of additional Communist Ministers; (3) the 'impression that a radical military dictatorship' was being established; and (4) reports of Soviet overtures to the Portuguese. The démarches were also to indicate 'that these developments would adversely affect the character of the Alliance and fundamentally change Portugal's relationship to its allies' (WSP 2/579/1).

[17] During this meeting M. A.M. de Staercke, Belgium's Permanent Representative, stressed that it was important not to put the Soviet Union in the 'position of being arbiters of the situation' and, with French support, argued against giving the appearance of interference in Portugal's internal affairs (UKDEL NATO telegrams Nos. 141 and 142 of 22 March). Mr. Logan considered that there was 'no prospect of agreement in the Alliance for an official approach by NATO', and the next day he advised Mr. Trench: 'As I see it, it is not clear what representations to a reconstructed Portuguese Government including more Communists could be expected to achieve' (UKDEL NATO telegram No. 1 to Lisbon of 23 March, (WSP 2/579/1).

No. 118

Mr. Callaghan to Mr. Trench (Lisbon)

No. 132 Telegraphic [*WSP 3/548/1*]

Immediate. Confidential   FCO, *23 March 1975, 9.30 p.m.*

Repeated to Immediate UKDEL NATO, and for information to Immediate Moscow, Paris, UKREP Brussels, Dublin, Bonn and Washington.

My telegram No. 109 to UKDEL NATO:[1]
Portugal

1. Dr Kissinger and I discussed Portugal during his stopover in London this afternoon. I told him that it was not (not) my intention to summon the Soviet Ambassador but that in our view it would be useful to make representations to the Portuguese Government in Lisbon.

2. Please therefore seek an appointment tomorrow 24 March with the Portuguese President (or Prime Minister if you prefer) and speak to him on the following lines. As I said during my visit to Lisbon last month, the events of last April were received with particular joy in Britain. We have been saddened to see that recently in Portugal there has been violence and other events, including those of 11 March, that have no place in a democratic society. We are looking forward to the holding of elections on 25 April as an important step in the consolidation of democracy and as a landmark in the progress on the road towards a fairer society. We take the view that it is most important, not only for the Portuguese people, that these elections are held as planned and that the Portuguese democracy continues to develop. It is our hope and expectation that no changes will be made in Portugal before the elections that will prevent these from being held in a stable and balanced atmosphere, so that the Portuguese people can express their views freely and without fear, and in order that these views can be taken into account by leaders of the new Portugal. All who welcomed the new prospects opened by the events of April 1974 would be deeply disappointed and concerned if the promise of democracy were not fulfilled.[2]

---

[1] In this telegram of 22 March Mr. Callaghan expressed the view that while it was 'obviously going to be difficult and perhaps impossible to frame in good time a coherent approach by Western countries' towards Portugal, there was 'merit in each country taking account of the views expressed by the others and acting in the way it [considered] best' (WSP 2/579/1).

[2] These instructions, in concentrating on the importance of consolidating democracy in Portugal, reflected Mr. Trench's own advice that it 'could be counterproductive to speak to Costa Gomes or Gonçalves about Communists in the Government' (Lisbon telegram No. 174 of 23 March; telegram No. 133 to Lisbon of 24 March; WSP 2/579/1).

3. You should know that Dr. Kissinger gave me a message (text will be telegraphed to you separately) which he also is sending to the Foreign Ministers of the Federal Republic, France, Belgium, and Italy saying that Ambassador Carlucci is being instructed to make representations to the Portuguese President tomorrow 24 March, and urging them to instruct their Ambassadors to express similar concern to the Portuguese authorities.[3] There could be advantage in you and Carlucci going in together. If this is not possible, please decide with him how your separate representations can best be dovetailed so that you both take action on 24 March.[4] There is no objection to your informing your EEC or NATO colleagues of the sense of your instructions, but should not (not) hold up action to allow them to get their instructions.

4. Mr. Logan should tell his colleagues tomorrow of the action that is being taken.[5]

[3] Dr. Kissinger's instructions to Mr. F.C. Carlucci, US Ambassador to Portugal since December 1974, were on lines similar to the démarche suggested by Mr. Bruce to his NATO colleagues on 22 March (see No. 117, note 16). But there was no reference in this text to Soviet overtures to Portugal (telegram No. 135 to Lisbon of 24 March, WSP 3/304/1).

[4] Mr. Trench delivered this message alone to President Costa Gomes on the evening of 24 March, but subsequently reported that he had emerged from the meeting 'not much wiser'. The President had simply offered assurances that the AFM was determined to hold elections 'in an atmosphere of tranquillity and freedom', and that, once formed, the new Government 'would have no more influence on the elections than the previous one, since political power resided in the Revolutionary-Council'. Later that evening Dr. Soares remarked to Mr. Trench that on present calculations, six of the ten civilian Cabinet Ministers would go to the Communists or their allies, including Finance, Agriculture, Economic Affairs and Social Affairs, and that 'this would be an impossible situation' (Lisbon telegrams Nos. 178 and 179 of 24 March, WSP 2/579/1).

[5] On 25 March Mr. Callaghan told the Cabinet of this communication. He explained 'that the situation in Portugal was confused and potentially dangerous. The Armed Forces Movement was subject to internal stresses and was unpredictable. Reports within the past few days that changes would be made in the Portuguese Government which would represent a step towards the establishment of a totalitarian regime controlled by the Communists, had caused alarm within the North Atlantic Alliance. He had not supported suggestions that Soviet Ambassadors in Alliance capitals should immediately be called in to receive representations and had counselled against any action which could be regarded as interference in the composition of the Portuguese Government' (CC(75) 16th meeting, held on 25 March, WSP 1/1).

No. 119

Note by the Defence Policy Staff of the Chiefs of Staff Committee

DP Note 206/75 (Final) [*WSP 2/579/1*]

Secret   MoD, *26 March 1975*

A preliminary Assessment of the Military consequences
if Portugal withdraws from NATO

Introduction

The Higher Council of the Armed Forces Movement (AFM) recently stated that the Portuguese Government would honour its existing international obligations. There has, therefore, been no official suggestion that Portugal intends to withdraw from NATO. Nevertheless this possibility cannot be excluded as the internal situation in Portugal could deteriorate further very rapidly, and the fact that the Portuguese Government is considering a request to give the Soviet merchant fleet refuelling facilities in Madeira is symptomatic of the improving relations between Portugal and the Soviet Union.

2. It is believed, therefore, that it would be timely to consider the military consequences if Portugal should withdraw from NATO, and this preliminary assessment addresses:

(*a*) The military disadvantages which the United Kingdom and NATO would suffer from a Portuguese withdrawal from the Alliance.

(*b*) The possible military implications for NATO if the Portuguese regime decided to make facilities available to the Soviets.

PORTUGUESE WITHDRAWAL FROM NATO

Portuguese Armed Forces

3. From the point of Portugal's military contribution to Western defence in terms of men and material, the consequences of a Portuguese withdrawal from NATO would be limited. The bulk of Portuguese forces have for years been involved in fighting the African wars, and the Portuguese military contribution to NATO (details at Annex A)[1] has been, and still is, unimpressive.

4. In the current circumstances it is difficult to provide an accurate assessment of the state or strength of the Portuguese Armed Forces, as withdrawals from the overseas territories are still in progress and the final command and organisation structure is not yet clear. For some 14 years the Portuguese Armed Forces have been primarily organised for operations in Africa. They are neither trained nor equipped for European type operations in which NATO would be expected to engage. The efficiency of

---

[1] Not printed.

any Portuguese contribution to NATO is, therefore, very suspect until the Armed Forces are re-equipped, re-trained and re-organised.

5. Since 11 March, General Fabião, Chief of the Portuguese Army has admitted to the Defence Attaché in Lisbon that discipline has broken down in the Armed Forces. In the circumstances in which the current situation has developed, the indications are that morale is poor and unreliable except in a few units such as the paratroops. Any bonus which may accrue to the forces in metropolitan Portugal from overseas withdrawals will be offset by the lower efficiency and morale of the returning troops, and the inevitable economic pressure to reduce the size of the Armed forces as a whole.

6. Portugal has contributed one ship to STANAVFORLANT[2] for about five months each year. If this participation were to cease, there could be presentational connotations in relation to NATO solidarity, but there would be no significant operational effects.

Psychological Effect

7. Although the material effects of Portuguese withdrawal would be limited, the psychological effect on the Alliance, in the context of other events over the last twelve months, could be very serious. NATO's military capabilities have been progressively weakened by the force reductions of a number of nations. In particular there has been a marked deterioration in the Alliance's military posture in the Southern Region as a result of the Cyprus dispute, the intransigence of Greece and Turkey (including the withdrawal of Greece from the integrated military structure), the United Kingdom's Defence Review, and the emergency measures taken by Italy. The withdrawal of Portuguese bases and military facilities would aggravate this situation.

Bases

8. While the military contribution of Portugal is minimal, the loss of Portuguese bases would be much more serious. Madeira is a nominated NATO Island Command, and features in the Alliance's Maritime Contingency Force (MARCONFOR) plans for the Atlantic. However, probably the most important of the Portuguese bases is the Lajes airfield in the Azores, not only for its role in NATO Atlantic maritime operations but also because it is integral to US plans for military reinforcement of the Southern Region. This transit facility also played a valuable part in the American resupply of Israel during the October war, albeit because political difficulties within NATO precluded the use of suitable alternatives in Alliance countries. Nevertheless, another Arab/Israeli war could lead to greater US pressure on some of its NATO allies to facilitate reinforcement

[2] Standing Naval Force Atlantic.

of Israel if Lajes should not be available.[3] The US/Portuguese agreement covering the use of the Azores airfield éxpired in 1974, and negotiations for the renewal of the agreement are in progress. The lack of a formal agreement could make the US tenure even less secure if Portugal were to leave NATO.

9. Lajes also plays an important part in a number of United Kingdom contingency plans for the Caribbean area, in particular JTP[4] (Caribbean) 60 for the reinforcement of Belize. Under this plan Lajes would be the staging airfield for a force of six Harriers with supporting tankers and transport aircraft. The other strategic transport aircraft involved in the plan could be routed via Canada, provided diplomatic clearance was granted, but the feasibility of alternative routing of the Harriers would require further detailed study.

10. Equally, SACLANT's GDP[5] contains provision for American Maritime Patrol Aircraft (MPA) to deploy during a period of tension or hostility to the Portuguese mainland bases Espinho and Montijo. These airfields are also available to United Kingdom MPA for refuelling to extend their time on task. If these bases were not available, NATO's surveillance capability in the EASTLANT[6] and IBERLANT areas would depend on St Mawgan, much increased use of Gibraltar and continued US MPA operations from ROTA[7] in Spain, but would nevertheless be less flexible than formerly.

IBERLANT

11. The IBERLANT Maritime Headquarters (UK contribution is 12 officers and 48 ratings) is situated near Lisbon and it must be assumed that the facilities provided would no longer be made available in the event of Portuguese withdrawal from NATO. In the present political climate, it is likely that any proposal to resite the Headquarters in Spain would be strongly resisted in some quarters within NATO. However it must be expected that the US would apply greater pressure than hitherto for a closer association between Spain and NATO.

12. It is relevant that, during the consultations with the MNCs[8] on the United Kingdom's Defence Review, considerable concern was expressed about the position of GIBMED[9] and IBERLANT. The withdrawal of United Kingdom maritime forces from the Southern Region combined

---

[3] The authors of the JIC assessment paper of 31 October 1974 (see No. 111, notes 4, 5 and 7) speculated on the 'possibility of Arab money being used to persuade the Portuguese to deny the [Azores] bases to the West'.

[4] Joint Theatre Plan.

[5] Supreme Allied Commander Atlantic, General Defence Plan.

[6] Eastern Atlantic Command.

[7] The US naval base on Cadiz Bay.

[8] Major NATO Commands.

with the reluctance of the Mediterranean nations to deploy to the Western Mediterranean leaves, in effect, no forces available for the GIBMED area, and the solution may be for SACLANT to assume responsibility for GIBMED. In this case consideration could be given to absorbing IBERLANT into extended CENTLANT[10] and GIBMED areas with an enhanced role for the headquarters of COMGIBMED[11] at Gibraltar. If this could be achieved without any substantial increase in COMGIBMED's staff, such a solution could avoid any political difficulties with Spain that might arise from the establishment of a new or expanded NATO headquarters, and also ought not to aggravate the current accommodation problem in Gibraltar.

Other Facilities

13. Air staging, overflying and diversion facilities are made available to members of NATO throughout Portugal, including the Azores (paragraphs 8 and 9 above) and Madeira. Occasional air staging facilities have hitherto been available in the Cape Verde Islands. If the use of these facilities were to be denied to the United Kingdom, further doubts would be cast on the political reliability of the 'Cable Route' on which aircraft stage through Cape Verde. In normal circumstances, there would be no difficulty in obtaining clearance to use either Dakar or Freetown, but in times of tension it is possible that these alternatives might not be available. Thus, one of the alternative routes to the Indian Ocean area could be lost.

14. The radio facilities at Cape Verde have an important part to play in Naval Control of Shipping (NCS) in the area West of the African continent. However, it is possible that, as a result of reorganisation now contemplated, this role may be undertaken from United Kingdom stations in the future.

15. The United Kingdom maintains national stocks at the NATO POL[12] and ammunition facilities at Lisbon, which is one of the Alternate War Bases for Carrier Striking Group Two. Although these facilities are also available at Gibraltar, there would be some loss in flexibility. It would be inconvenient if single ships deploying to the Western Atlantic were unable to use the fuelling facilities in the Azores; those in the Cape Verde Islands are used only infrequently and their loss would not be significant.

16. There is also a submarine noise ranging area North East of the Azores. If this were not available, the facilities would have to be reprovided elsewhere or other alternative arrangements made.

NPG

17. Portuguese withdrawal from NATO would have a hidden bonus in removing any possible future problem over her membership of the NPG.[13]

---

[10] Central Atlantic Command.

[11] Commander, Gibraltar Mediterranean.

[12] Petrol, Oil and Lubricants.

[13] See No. 111, note 18.

The US were earlier not prepared to allow the Portuguese access to Alliance nuclear secrets while there were communists in the Government.

Financial Considerations

18. Withdrawal of the small Portuguese contribution (about £1M a year) to NATO common budgets would probably not pose great problems. On present plans, Portugal's contribution to NATO Infrastructure and the Military Budgets could be roughly balanced by the amount the Portuguese might expect to receive from NATO funds.

19. Nevertheless up to 1973, Portugal had received approximately £23M from Infrastructure funds toward the provision of facilities such as airfields, communications installations, War Headquarters, the POL and ammunition depots, and radio and navigation aids. Relocation of some of these facilities could lead to substantial costs in which the United Kingdom would share.

THE USE OF PORTUGUESE FACILITIES BY THE SOVIETS

General

20. While highly speculative, it cannot be discounted that, in the worst case, a Communist Government in Portugal might decide to grant military facilities to the Soviets, and that the Soviets might accept such an offer. It would not be appropriate to attempt to forecast possible Soviet reactions to such an offer, as this could be done only in a proper JIC assessment, and it is recommended that this should be undertaken. The subsequent paragraphs are intended to provide only an initial military and not a political assessment of the consequences of the use of Portuguese bases and facilities by the Soviets.

Peacetime

21. The major effect would be marked improvement in the capability of the Soviet forces to conduct surveillance operations in the Atlantic. Apart from Cuba and, to a lesser extent, Conakry, both of which are far from Europe, the Soviet forces currently have no access to any facilities in the Atlantic from which to operate or to support operations. The use of bases in Portugal, the Azores and Madeira would provide the Soviets with major facilities astride the main north/south shipping routes, and would greatly facilitate maritime operations in the Atlantic and the Mediterranean approaches. Furthermore, the problems of logistic support for Soviet units in the Atlantic would be considerably eased. The threat posed by Soviet submarines could be substantially increased by the use of these bases, particularly if refitting facilities in Portugal were used as in Yugoslavia recently.

22. Access to the Cape Verde Islands would complement current Soviet maritime operations from Conakry and, in conjunction with the use of bases in Madeira and the Azores, would provide the Soviet Navy with a complete chain of facilities covering the South Atlantic and trans-Atlantic trade routes.

23. Access to the Azores or Madeira could also permit the Soviets to instal [*sic*] fixed monitoring facilities for the US/West Indies/Ascension Island missile range.

Hostilities

24. Portuguese facilities would greatly facilitate Soviet surveillance operations in a period of tension, and could provide mounting bases for initial military operations at the outbreak of hostilities. However, it must be remembered that, in a period of hostilities, Soviet use of Portuguese facilities would be more vulnerable to pre-emptive operations or counter-attack than the use of bases behind the Iron Curtain. Equally, reinforcement and logistic support would present many difficulties, and it is debatable whether operations could be sustained if appropriate military measures were taken by NATO, albeit that this would require the diversion of NATO forces already committed to other tasks. However, an outline is given below of the possible uses the Soviets might make of Portuguese facilities.

25. Apart from the potent threat that could be presented, at least initially, by the presence of Soviet maritime forces close to NATO's sea lanes, an additional threat would be created for the Alliance if the Soviets chose to station aircraft at air bases in metropolitan Portugal. The NATO air defences, particularly those in Central Europe, are oriented mainly towards attack from the East and provision would have to be made to counter this new threat from the West and South.

26. The Soviets could use Portuguese bases for long range and tactical aircraft. These would threaten US bases in Spain, NATO forces in the Central Region, Southern Region, France, EASTLANT, IBERLANT and the Mediterranean approaches, in addition to hazarding US reinforcement and supply aircraft destined for Europe. It is not possible to forecast the weight of attack the Soviets might mount from Portuguese bases. However, it is reasonable to assume that the Soviets would consider that the chances of success from their main attacks from the East would be increased if NATO's air defences were confused by simultaneous attacks mounted from the West and South.

27. The use of Portuguese bases would also permit the Soviets to exploit more efficiently its methods of gathering intelligence on NATO. At the same time, it must be remembered that NATO would also benefit to some extent from closer observation of Soviet operations.

CONCLUSIONS

28. It is concluded that the withdrawal of Portuguese forces from NATO would have only a limited effect on the military capabilities of the Alliance, but could have a major psychological impact within NATO out of all proportion to the force contribution made by Portugal. If Portuguese bases and facilities were not available to the Alliance, this would affect not only NATO's surveillance capability in EASTLANT but also American plans

for the military reinforcement of the Southern Region. The latter effect would aggravate the recent deterioration in the Alliance's posture on the Southern Flank.

29. It is also concluded that it would be a matter of considerable concern to NATO if the Soviets were able to use facilities in Portugal. Apart from a marked improvement in Soviet capability to conduct peacetime surveillance and maritime operations in the Atlantic and the Mediterranean approaches, NATO's sea lanes would be threatened at least initially in a period of hostilities, and the concept of forward defence on NATO's Eastern front would have to cope with the potent additional and simultaneous threats which could be posed from the West and South. Nevertheless, although Portugal could become a weeping sore in NATO's flank, radical surgery at the outbreak of hostilities could prevent Soviet operations being sustained from Portuguese bases, and could to some extent mitigate the undesirable implications for NATO.

RECOMMENDATION

30. It is recommended that the JIC be invited to produce an assessment of possible Soviet reactions to any offer of the use of Portuguese facilities.[14]

A.S. MORTON
REAR ADMIRAL
ASSISTANT CHIEF OF
Defence Staff (Policy)

[14] Not traced.

No. 120

Submission from Mr. Barrett to Mr. Morgan

[WSP 3/548/1]

Confidential   FCO, *1 April 1975*

Future Policy towards Portugal

Problem

1. Recent developments in Portugal have shown how little influence the West has on the course of events there. What scope have we got? What should our policy and attitude be to:

(*a*) the new Portuguese Government (para[graph]s 7-9 and 12);
(*b*) the threat to NATO and the implications for the CSCE if Portugal goes Communist (para[graph]s 13-18);
(*c*) discussion of these questions within NATO and the EEC (para[graph]s 13-18 and 19-20);

415

(*d*) the projected visit here in mid-May by the Portuguese President (para[graph] 10);

(*e*) plans for visits to Portugal by the Chief of Defence Staff and by an aid mission from the UK (para[graph]s 10-11).

Background

The Situation in Portugal

2. The events of the last few weeks in Portugal have taken the country a long way from the democratic path. Immediately after the abortive coup of 11 March the Armed Forces Movement (AFM) set up a Supreme Revolutionary Council exercising all real legislative and executive power. The government announced by Prime Minister Gonçalves on 25 March has moved the balance of power in the administration dramatically towards the Portuguese Communist Party (PCP) and their close allies the MDP (Popular Democratic Movement). The PCP, the MDP and their sympathizers disguised as independent technocrats now control key ministries in the economic, financial and agricultural sectors. The AFM control the internal and information ministries. The Portuguese Socialist Party (PSP) and the Popular Democrats (PPD) have only one Ministry each (Justice and Social Affairs respectively), although they enjoy much greater support than the PCP and MDP. Dr. Soares has joined the leaders of the PCP, PPD, and MDP in the largely honorific position of Minister without Portfolio.[1]

3. The AFM still intend to hold elections on 25 April. It was never to be expected that these would be totally free or fair. But the intimidation of the centre and right-wing parties, the dissolution of the Christian Democrats (along with two extreme left-wing parties to which the PCP were opposed), the infiltration of Communist sympathizers into the media (and perhaps into the electoral machinery) have created an atmosphere in which the elections are unlikely to reflect popular feeling accurately. In any case the AFM and the present government will probably ignore any views which are contrary to their own approach to Portugal's problems. The possibility that the election will be cancelled or postponed yet again is not to be excluded. If this happened, the objective would be to strengthen the position of the AFM and PCP.

4. The Portuguese Foreign Ministry is now in the hands of Major Melo Antunes, one of the most influential figures in the AFM. He is a left-

---

[1] But in a despatch of 9 April Mr. Trench pointed out that, despite their initial disarray in the aftermath of the attempted *coup d'état*, the Socialists and the PPD had rallied and successfully resisted pressure from the Communists to reduce their representation in the Government. Moreover, Dr. Soares's move from the Foreign Ministry meant that he would be able to devote himself more fully to party affairs and the election campaign, and the establishment of an 'inner Cabinet', composed of the four Ministers without Portfolio and the military Ministers, left the PPD and the Socialists at the centre of Government. 'It is', Mr. Trench added, 'an ironic twist, finally, that the Government may now achieve the greater efficiency which Palma Carlos sought last summer, thereby hastening his own downfall' (WSP 1/1).

winger, but the Economic Plan which he introduced in February shows that he is also prepared to resist extremist solutions. He is intelligent and ready to modify his views to take account of other pressures and considerations.[2]

. 5. The future course of the Portuguese economy was also shifted to the left after 11 March when the AFM suddenly amended the Economic Plan announced a few weeks earlier by nationalising Portuguese banks and insurance companies (foreign companies are to be exempted but may be affected by measures that have still to be worked out). While much of the Plan and the later steps can be justified by a desire to end the concentration of economic power in the hands of a few, the actions of the Portuguese authorities are more a diagnosis of the problems they are facing than a contribution to their solution. Nor will foreign companies be reassured by the addition of problems of administrative confusion to those caused by a 30 per cent rate of inflation and rising costs. The Portuguese economy may not run into really heavy weather until 1976. But recent economic and political developments have made it more difficult for the Portuguese authorities to weather the storms ahead without resorting later to sterner political and economic measures.

Argument

6. Thus Portugal presents the picture of a left-wing military régime working closely with the PCP and its allies while maintaining some of the trappings of democracy in the form of PSP and PPD participation in the cabinet.

7. At present there is inside Portugal no sign of a force capable of diverting the AFM from its aim of being the agent of revolutionary change in Portugal. It is possible that either or both of the PSP and PPD will at some stage give up the shadow of power and withdraw from the government. This is perhaps more likely than that their showing in the elections (to the Constituent Assembly on 25 April and to the new legislation this autumn) will cause the AFM to reallocate political power in favour of the democratic parties. However, any falling off in Western support for the democratic parties in Portugal will only accelerate their demoralization or decline; while support for them will be justified as long as they genuinely represent democratic and ideological alternatives to the AFM and the PCP.[3]

---

[2] Mr. Morgan noted in the margin alongside this paragraph: 'He [Maj. de Melo Antunes] is, however, said to be more interested in ties with the Third World than with the West.'

[3] The new régime, noted Mr. Trench in his despatch of 9 April (see note 1 above), is 'clearly closer to the East European and Soviet *bloc* than its predecessor, and this has caused natural concern in the West ... Similarly, the Communist-dominated news media here have intensified their propaganda against the West, and particularly the Americans. On the other hand, the Italian and Spanish Communist parties seem to be by no means pleased by the turn which events have taken in Portugal, and it is believed that the Soviet Union has also advised a less impetuous advance, for fear of spoiling their game in a wider field.'

8. As to our attitude to the AFM and Prime Minister Gonçalves' government, it is no longer possible to sustain the view that they are on course towards democracy.[4] If we say that they are, we may discourage the democratic forces in Portugal with whom we have hitherto sought to work. Yet our attitude to the present régime must also recognise five other considerations:

(*a*) There is a real need to transform Portugal, politically, economically and socially;

(*b*) In a country as backward as Portugal radical change may have to be carried out by undemocratic agencies;

(*c*) If we ignore (*a*) and (*b*) and alienate the present Portuguese leadership, the Soviet Union and her allies (and perhaps the Arabs) will not hesitate to fill the vacuum at our expense;

(*d*) Portugal's African contacts may be of interest to us;

(*e*) We have important commercial interests in Portugal (in 1974 turnover in our bilateral trade was over £400 million).

Consequently, we need to balance our reservations about the nature of the régime and the direction in which it is heading by sufficient recognition of the nature of the problem Portugal faces. This may enable us to exert a small influence on developments there.

Policy on Contacts with Portugal

9. Accordingly, we should maintain contact with and support all who stand for or may sympathize with a more democratic and moderate approach. We shall want to encourage contacts with Portuguese parties corresponding broadly with those in our Parliament. Training courses for Portuguese working in radio, television and journalism may help to offset pro-Communist trends in the media. Wilton Park[5] and COI[6]-sponsored tours can go ahead provided our Embassy in Lisbon vouch for the usefulness of bringing the Portuguese in question to the UK. Portuguese attendance at the Royal College of Defence Studies could pose a certain security risk: if this can be tolerated by the Ministry of Defence, the balance is probably in favour of inviting Portuguese participation, mainly on the grounds that the exposure to Western influences should be

---

[4] In a letter of 9 April, written in reply to Mr. Trench's letter of 19 March (see No. 115, note 7), Sir J. Killick observed with regard to HMG's thinking on events in Lisbon: 'I am sure that any lingering optimism that Portugal was on a course towards democracy will have been dispelled by the reaction to the abortive coup; by the cynical reshuffle of the Portuguese Cabinet on 25 March; and by the dictatorial line the AFM is taking over the draft Constitution. This said, we are very conscious that *les absents ont toujours tort*, and I hope therefore that we shall be able to find something to maintain the British and Western stake in Portugal. We do not want to help to bring about the "worst case" by acting (or, still worse, speaking) as though it had already happened' (WSP 1/1).

[5] The FCO's Wiston House Conference Centre in West Sussex.

[6] Central Office of Information.

beneficial. But contacts in the sensitive fields of security and intelligence will need to be examined carefully in each case and submitted to Ministers.

Visits: The Portuguese President, our Chief of Defence Staff and our Aid Mission
10. Two urgent problems face us:

(*a*) Should we go ahead with plans for a visit to the UK in May by President Costa Gomes and with the idea that our Chief of Staff should visit Portugal for two days at the end of April? No 10 will have to approve an invitation.
(*b*) Should we abandon plans to send an aid mission to Portugal?

It is true that the Portuguese President has played an equivocal part in the formation of the new government. Despite his reputation as a moderate, he was apparently unwilling or unable to exercise much influence at a key moment. Against this, it is not in our interest to encourage a situation where the President is invited only by Communist countries. If he comes here, we will be able to explain frankly what our worries are and discuss ways in which democratic forces can be strengthened. There is always a risk that an invitation to President Costa Gomes will provoke public criticism in the UK, but this can be rebutted along two main lines:

(*a*) The President is personally acceptable;
(*b*) It is illogical to invite leaders of non-Communist countries and of Communist countries but not to invite leaders of countries that we want to prevent passing from the former to the latter camp.

But Field Marshal Sir Michael Carver's visit should not take place at the end of April on the grounds that it will be too soon after the elections when the military leadership will have much on their minds. It would in any case be better to space it out so that there is an interval between it and the President's visit. If President Costa Gomes cannot come in mid-May, then we should try to devise a better spaced timetable for his visit and that of the Chief of Defence Staff.

11. To withdraw the aid mission, after the Secretary of State's undertaking when he visited Portugal, would be resented by the new Portuguese Government, who are already sensitive to what they regard as a lack of economic support from Western countries. Such a step would put at risk any hopes of bringing influence to bear and could even endanger British commercial interests in Portugal. But there is no need to decide now whether or not the Minister of Overseas Development[7] should herself lead a mission. We should encourage the ODM[8] to continue to think in terms of a two-stage operation: an exploratory visit led by officials, followed

[7] Mrs. J. Hart.
[8] Ministry of Overseas Development.

by a later mission which Mrs. Hart might head if this seemed right nearer the time.

12. In contacts with the Portuguese and in public we should no longer speak in warm terms of their progress towards democracy. It is still appropriate to acknowledge the need for major changes in Portugal. But we should not hesitate to make clear our view that progress towards a stable, fair and democratic society depends on the leaders of Portugal harnessing the energies and will of the people, expressed through free elections and organised through democratic parties properly represented in the Government.[9]

The Soviet Rôle

13. Although the PCP have exploited the situation since April 1974, and will continue to do so, they were not the makers of the original coup. Their policy has been to support the AFM and to stress the identity of the AFM and the people. Despite Sr. Cunhal's links with the Soviet Union, it is probable that events in Portugal will continue to be home-grown rather than imported from the Soviet Union, though the Soviets may be able to exercise a restraining influence on the PCP's policy and tactics. Sir T Garvey is no doubt right when he argues in his telegram No. 476[10] that the Soviet Union will not want developments in Portugal to put at risk the final stage of the CSCE. But they will be aware too of the damage which events in Portugal could cause to the continuing development of détente in Europe. Accordingly, any attempt by the West to encourage the Russians to exert a moderating influence on the PCP would need to be placed in the context of the major questions of East/West relations, e.g. Stage III of the CSCE and its follow-up; and, more generally, the set back to East/West relations that would be caused by Communist subversion of democracy in Portugal.

East/West Relations, NATO and the CSCE

14. The Germans are right to suggest that the CSCE is particularly relevant.[11] All the participants see the Conference as an effort to establish

[9] This general approach was endorsed by Mr. Trench. In a letter to Sir J. Killick of 22 April he wrote: 'I understand Ministers' preoccupations about the rather erratic course that is being steered towards democracy here, but at the same time the Secretary of State himself said that we must not expect Portuguese democracy to be just like ours (no comment!)'. Whilst conceding that Portugal would 'continue to have upsets of various kinds and irregularities which will make us feel unhappy about the way things are proceeding here', he advised that 'the way to influence events is to butter up people who are likely to hold positions of strength'. Such a policy would inevitably mean 'that we shall put our money on a number of also rans', but by issuing invitations and sending distinguished visitors to Lisbon 'we shall at least be demonstrating our goodwill towards Portugal'.

[10] Not traced. Cf. Volume III, No. 78.

[11] On 24 March Herr K.-G. von Hase, the Federal German Ambassador in London, told Sir T. Brimelow that it was difficult to see how a third stage of the CSCE could take place 'if there were to be a major deterioration in the situation in Lisbon'. He further commented that public

for the future a pattern of good behaviour in Europe. The Russians, in particular Mr. Brezhnev, attach enormous importance to the Conference and to the Declaration of Principles which it will produce. They will not wish to prejudice the present work of the Conference nor tarnish its successful conclusion at summit level by drawing upon themselves, e,g. through public statements at Stage III, criticism of their own support for the subversion of democracy in Portugal. After Stage III, especially if the follow-up arrangements are not onerous, they may feel less restrained. But they will realize that the rest of Europe will see in their policy towards Portugal a test of their intention to implement the results of the CSCE and thus of their commitment to détente.

15. Whether or not any action with the Russians should be taken turns on an assessment of the consequences for the West if Portugal drifts further towards Communism. Five main possibilities can be distinguished:

(*a*) a continuation of the present state of affairs;

(*b*) the democratic parties withdraw from the government or are driven out; the AFM and PCP then govern alone;

(*c*) the PCP take over, neutralizing or absorbing all other forces in the country;

(*d*) Portugal leaves NATO;

(*e*) Portugal leaves NATO and gives military facilities to the Soviet Union.

Of these, (*a*) does not warrant a major change of attitude in East/West relations. (*b*) and (*c*) would have very important political consequences and would affect the position and tactics of communist parties in Western Europe (Italy and France in particular). (*d*) would have political and psychological repercussions but would not be of major military significance (which may be why the present Portuguese government have indicated that they will adhere to Portugal's international commitments, with any change coming in the context of the general international climate). (*e*) is perhaps the least likely as long as the Soviet Union follows a cautious line. However it would represent a major military threat which the Alliance would have to take seriously. It is therefore a vital Western interest that (*e*) should not happen. Thus, whereas from a political point of view (*b*), (*c*) and (*d*) are all undesirable, it is also a Western interest to avoid them because they would increase the risk of passing to (*e*).

16. If this is right, it is important that the Soviet Union should understand that (*e*) is unacceptable and that (*b*), (*c*) and (*d*) are undesirable because they would bring Europe several stages nearer (*e*). If Sir T Garvey is right in believing that the Soviet Union would not want to see events in Portugal prevent Stage III, then we should:

opinion in Germany was 'closely concerned' about Stage III and that there 'could be a feeling that events in Portugal could discredit the prospect' (telegram No. 169 to Bonn of 24 March, WSP 2/579/1). Cf. Volume II, No. 117, note 14.

(*a*) *before Stage III*, take advantage of suitable opportunities to make the point to the Soviet Union and her allies that a change in the situation in Portugal that resulted in a Communist takeover or Portugal leaving the North Atlantic Alliance would be bad for détente.

(*b*) *at Stage III or afterwards*, be ready to draw it to their attention that their policy towards Portugal will be a test of their intention to implement the results of the CSCE and thus of their commitment to détente. We should also be ready to make the point that the West would regard as incompatible with détente a situation in which Portugal gave military facilities to the Soviet Union; and that we would be bound to view very seriously any developments in Portugal that had a destabilizing influence, either politically or military, on Europe.

To be successful, action to this end would also need to be taken by the Americans and our principal allies in the North Atlantic Alliance. The measures envisaged might be enough to satisfy the Germans, who are concerned that events in Portugal may make Stage III unsellable to their public opinion; and also the French, who have told us that if the international strategic balance were upset (e.g. by the Soviet Union getting bases in Portugal) this would be intolerable and would require a diplomatic and possibly other reactions.

NATO Security

17. The government reshuffle of 25 March has reawakened NATO concern about Portuguese security. It has been reported in NATO that the NATO registry in Lisbon has been transferred from the Ministry of Foreign Affairs to the AFM headquarters. The question of Portuguese access to NATO classified material will have to be discussed by the Alliance in the light of these developments.

18. Portugal has already withdrawn from the Nuclear Planning Group and the practice is developing of showing sensitive papers to the Portuguese Ambassador to NATO on a personal basis (e.g. he is allowed to read them in the NATO headquarters but may not take them away). The Portuguese leaders are sensitive to discrimination against them and may genuinely be upset by the evidence of the lack of Western trust in them. Nevertheless, their naivety and inexperience cannot be allowed to endanger Western security unnecessarily. We will have to accept whatever limits to Portuguese access seems generally sensible to the Alliance and should ensure that NATO is aware of the political importance of how any decisions are presented to the Portuguese.

Portugal and the EEC

19. The scope and content of Portugal's relations with the Community offers little scope for the application of Western pressure.[12] Portuguese

---

[12] The West Germans had encouraged the Irish, who then held the EC Presidency, to draft a démarche for communication to the Portuguese authorities on behalf of the nine member

hesitations over the correct solutions to their internal problems has prevented the formulation of a general policy on Portugal's future relations with the EEC. The Portuguese have therefore only been able to produce a detailed shopping list based on the existing EEC-Portugal Free Trade Agreement. The most important requests concern loans from the EIB[13] and better conditions for Portuguese workers in the Community. The helpfulness or otherwise with which the Community reacts to these requests and other contacts will play a role in forming Portuguese attitudes, not least because the Portuguese themselves have been anxious to deal with the Community as such rather than with individual Western European states.

20. If matters go smoothly it will be less easy for Portuguese radicals to sustain a picture of the West reluctant to cooperate with them; but if the EEC makes difficulties or cannot be forthcoming, the Portuguese will be the more inclined to look for help outside the West. The best posture for the EEC is therefore one of sympathy and helpfulness, particularly on aid and workers conditions.

Recommendation

21. I *recommend* that:

(*a*) the general analysis and approach in this submission should be endorsed;

(*b*) we should be guided accordingly in discussions in the North Atlantic Council, within the European Political Cooperation machinery and bilaterally with our allies;[14]

(*c*) we should go ahead with the proposed invitation to the Portuguese President and with the first (official) stage of the aid mission; but should drop for the time being the idea of a visit to Portugal by the Chief of Defence Staff and decide later on a second stage of the aid mission which might be led by Mrs. Hart.

22. WOD, EESD and EID(E)[15] agree.

S.J. BARRETT

---

states, expressing concern 'that the path to a free pluralistic democracy in Portugal [was] in jeopardy and that as a consequence a close link of Portugal with Western Europe could be endangered'. But, evidently much to Bonn's disappointment, the French objected to this course, fearing that such action might be counter-productive since it could be construed in Lisbon as interference in Portugal's internal affairs (minute from Mr. Morgan to Mr. Barrett of 24 March, WSP 2/579/1; Bonn telegrams Nos. 271 and 278 of 27 and 28 March, WSP 1/1).

[13] European Investment Bank.

[14] Mr. Morgan sidelined this paragraph and noted: 'first at the Political Directors' meeting in Dublin on 8 April.'

[15] European Integration Department (External).

No. 121

Minutes by Mr. Morgan, Sir J. Killick and Mr. Hattersley on future policy towards Portugal[1]

[WSP 3/548/1]

Confidential   FCO, *2-7 April 1975*

Private Secretary[2]

1. I agree with Mr. Barrett's general analysis and approach; and with his recommendations, except that I now have doubts about the invitation to President Costa Gomes (see below).

2. I am struck by the increasing resemblances to the 'Peruvian model'[3] in all that we have seen and heard during the past fortnight. The effective leaders of the AFM are military-authoritarian in outlook. They do not really believe in freedom of choice or speech but are morbidly sensitive to opposition or public criticism, especially from abroad. They are resentful against the old ruling class and eager to destroy all its works; but they lack the experience and talent to build a new system. They have dreams of a 'Portuguese way' not communist (not Moscow-communist anyhow) but certainly not capitalist. In all this they are exactly like the Peruvian Generals. The big difference, of course, is that they still make a show of governing with the political parties; but they regard them 'as a bunch of squabbling nuisances' (the US Ambassador's conclusion from his interview with Costa Gomes in Lisbon tel[egram] No. 184).[4] They do, however, respect the discipline, dedication and organisation of the orthodox Communists: General Carvalho told Mr. Ure that he regarded them as the only real civilian patriots. This is reflected in the new appointments. Nevertheless, if they want to get rid of the parties, I think their instinct may well be to get rid of the whole lot and have a purely military Government at the top level, as in Peru, an option which Mr. Barrett does not consider in his para[graph] 15. The question is whether their troops would support them against the organised street forces of the Communists.

---

[1] These minutes accompanied Mr. Barrett's submission at No. 120.

[2] Mr. Acland.

[3] On 3 October 1968 the Peruvian Government had been overthrown by a military *coup*. Gen. J. Velasco Alvarado, the leader of the revolutionary Junta, assumed the duties of President and appointed an all-military Cabinet with Gen. E. Montagne Sánchez as Prime Minister.

[4] In this telegram of 26 March Mr. Trench reported on Mr. Carlucci's interview with President Costa Gomes that afternoon, during which the US Ambassador had delivered Dr. Kissinger's representations (see No. 118, note 3). In response to Mr. Carlucci's request for a clarification of the situation, President Costa Gomes had said 'that events had moved further to the left than could have been foreseen, for two reasons: (*a*) the panorama of the West presented to Portugal; and (*b*) the West's failure to provide assistance' (WSP 3/304/1).

3. Anyhow, with all the reins of civil and legislative power in the hands of the AFM and those of economic administration in the hands of the Communists, it is clear that we cannot expect the democratic parties to wield any real influence in the foreseeable future.

4. In these circumstance, I cannot see how we or our Western allies can do anything but wait, basically, for Portugal to get through its revolutionary period in its own way. Even if capital and credit were much less tight than they are, we could not buy them round to our way of thinking: their capacity to absorb aid is bound to be very limited. All we can do is support our political friends as far as we prudently can and make sure that the option of collaboration with the West is kept clearly and effectively open, by the kind of action that Mr. Barrett suggests.

5. Sooner or later the AFM will be disillusioned about Soviet aid and will fall out with the Communist parties (it has already done so with the Maoists). We should use all discreet influence to bring this about while there are still some options open. But we must I think be very cautious about direct political intervention. The recent representations by us and others at Chancellor Schmidt's urging did not provoke too much resentment and just may have helpfully influenced the formation of the new Government. We obviously cannot make a habit of it. Nor will the nationalistic leaders of the AFM welcome curtain lectures by the Nine, at least until economic relations with the Community are seen to be developing profitably.

6. I agree with Mr. Barrett on the CSCE problem. I don't think the Germans will play for anything less. Even so, we may be faced with awkward decisions if there is another lurch to the left in Portugal that can't reasonably be pinned on the Russians.[5] I also agree as regards NATO, where we must be concerned not to burn any boats till we have to. On the other hand, we should not wait for Mr. Barrett's para[graph] 15 (*e*)—Portugal out of NATO and giving military facilities to the Soviet Union—to take us by surprise. Surely we should make a contingency study with the US and others of what we should actually do if this case arose; and our eventual warnings to the Soviet Union should be tailored to the conclusions reached.

7. The invitation to President Costa Gomes now presents a difficult problem. He has come disappointingly out of the recent conversations with

---

[5] In a minute to Sir J. Killick of 3 April Mr. Cable expressed his concern that both Mr. Barrett's submission and Mr. Morgan's minute seemed to miss 'the relevance of Portugal to détente'. 'I do not', he observed, 'think we can rely merely on stage 3 of the CSCE (which may be over in a few months anyway) to deter the Soviet Union from exploiting the situation in Portugal. I think the Western Allies (and above all the United States) should make a point of saying at every appropriate opportunity to the Russians and East Europeans that détente must be reciprocal and indivisible. If they want the West to refrain from interfering in Eastern Europe and to respect this as a Soviet sphere of influence, they must adopt a similar attitude in Western Europe. Eastern European regimes are likely to remain politically vulnerable long enough for this to constitute an effective and durable argument.'

Western ambassadors in Lisbon. He is neither a strong man nor all that moderate. We are likely to get less out of his visit than we at one time hoped. If it is to go through as now planned, we must give a hostage to political fortune by inviting him *before* the elections and receiving him here only three weeks after them. Is it worth the risk that the elections will leave a bad taste, that Costa Gomes will be unpopular here in consequence, and that the visit will turn out counterproductive? The Prime Minister has doubts. So has The Queen (Sir M Charteris' letter of 31 March to Mr. Curle).[6] Dr. Soares, who started the idea, has lost interest and has told us merely to consult his successor. The foreseeable profit no longer seems to match the possible inconvenience. I agree with Mr. Barrett that we have no reason to cold-shoulder Costa Gomes, but I believe we could achieve all that is necessary now by taking advantage of the first Ministerial contact with Major Melo Antunes, the new Foreign Minister, to say that we should welcome a visit by Costa Gomes but can't fit it in before the autumn at the earliest.

H.T. MORGAN

2 April 1975

Private Secretary

1. I agree too with this general approach and with Mr. Morgan's further comments. I agree in particular about the desirability of postponing any visit by President Costa Gomes.

2. More generally, this whole problem seems to me to involve unavoidable difficulties and risks. Mr. Hattersley may like to have a discussion. I think it reasonable to assume that the AFM will not be and cannot be totally taken over by the PCP. Equally we must be realistic and accept that the influence of the PSP cannot hope to be decisive and may very well decline. Having clearly in view our basic interest in keeping Portugal in NATO and reasonably pro-Western we must do everything possible to cultivate a positive relationship with the AFM which emerges more and more clearly as the decisive force in Portugal. For so long as possible we shall obviously wish to do this without prejudice to our link with the PSP, but we may have to face a situation of choice, with the PSP no longer participating in government. In such circumstances, there will be strong reasons for continuing to work with and on the AFM. The basic essential seems to me to be to gain time for them to become disenchanted

---

[6] In this letter to the Vice-Marshal of the Diplomatic Corps, Sir M. Charteris, the Private Secretary to the Queen, indicated Buckingham Palace's concern that, despite the diplomatic advantages to be had from a visit from President Costa Gomes, it might be poorly perceived by the general public, particularly if the forthcoming Portuguese elections were seen to have been rigged (WSP 3/548/9).

with the Portuguese Communists (and with Moscow). In any case, there is a lot to be said for suitable exploitation of military links with the AFM, and Mr Trench's telegram No. 196 (just received) must, I think, lead to the conclusion that the CDS's visit should go ahead.[7] I in any case was not totally convinced by the argument in Mr. Barrett's paragraph 10. There is something to be said for striking while the iron is hot and maintaining what contact we can, especially if the President's visit is put off.

3. Meanwhile, with our basic aims still in mind (and although I agree in general with Mr. Barrett's paragraph 12), we must do everthing [*sic*] we can to avoid as it were publicly expressing a vote of 'no confidence' in the democratic attributes of the AFM. To judge from the latest remarks of Melo Antunes in Dar es Salaam,[8] he at least is still finding it possible to reconcile the idea of greater 'non-alignment' with membership of NATO. We should continue to express our desire for a pluralistic democratic approach without implying that the AFM have abandoned it. Otherwise we risk driving the AFM further and faster down the wrong road.

4. I also see some difficulty with the suggestion (paragraphs 13 and 16 of Mr. Barrett's minute) that we should commit ourselves officially to the proposition that a Communist takeover in Portugal, or Portuguese departure from NATO, are by definition unacceptable to the West and bad for détente. The proposition is of course true, but we cannot rule out the possibility that these things might be 'the choice of the people'; we can only object to attempts to bring them about by outside interference or by undemocratic and/or violent internal methods. On the other side of the coin, we must surely adopt the position that the question whether or not Portugal remains in NATO is a matter for decision by the Portuguese government strictly speaking this is no less true of any decision to grant military facilities to the Soviet Government.

[I had dictated the foregoing before reading the text, sent to me by the Portuguese Ambassador, of an interview given by Brigadier Gonçalves to the 'Süddeutsche Zeitung'. This reinforces my point in various respects, e.g.:

'We are for pluralism of democratic and patriotic forces.'

'[In reply to a question about NATO] ... We will honour all treaties and this is exactly what we are doing. Any alternative can only be

---

[7] In this telegram of 2 April Mr. Trench suggested that 'when the military in the Revolutionary Council still have the final word, we should do what we can to get on the right side of them'.

[8] In his meeting with President J.K. Nyerere of Tanzania on 1 April, Maj. de Melo Antunes had suggested that Portugal's support for 'non-aligned socialism' could be reconciled with its 'continued adherence to NATO'. Yet, as Mr. Trench pointed out, it had to be remembered that Maj. de Melo Antunes represented 'one of the more intelligent, balanced and pragmatic of the leaders of the Armed Forces Movement (AFM) and that there are others, such as the Prime Minister, who are a good deal more extreme' (Lisbon telegram No. 205 of 4 April, WSP 10/2).

brought about by the Portuguese people. But we realise in what part of the world we are living, we know our geographical position.'

'[In reply to a question about US intervention in Portugal] ... We hope that there may be no foreign interference of any kind. But should this happen, then we would fight for national independence.']⁹

5. I have against this background rather strong reservations about any further action vis-à-vis the Soviet Government. What the Secretary of State said to Kosygin in Moscow was in my view exactly right¹⁰ and we should leave it at that. The threat to the CSCE and détente in general arising from the Portuguese situation must be self-evident in Moscow. I am less than convinced that it is either realistic or well-advised to talk to Moscow in a manner which implies that they have any responsibility for or effective control over internal developments in Portugal. I am in particular strongly opposed to establishing any direct link between developments in Portugal and the successful completion of CSCE. While I would not exclude the possibility that developments in Portugal might in fact in the worst case make the holding of a third stage at the summit out of the question, I believe it would be most unwise to state this as a proposition at any foreseeable stage. CSCE now has in my view a momentum and significance of its own and is not something which can effectively be used as a bargaining counter in this way. I would wish to keep open the option of using the third stage of CSCE as a forum in which we might ventilate developments in Portugal to our advantage. To this extent I have reservations about what Mr. Barrett proposes in his paragraph 16. The Federal German Government has already shown itself ill-advised over Portugal and I think that we should resist any further German attempts to use CSCE as a lever in this way.¹¹ I doubt if Dr. Kissinger will be ready to do so. Meanwhile I see every advantage in continuing to bring home to the Soviet Government *indirectly* how much importance we attach to the continued uninhibited application of the pluralistic democratic process in Portugal without necessarily pointing the finger at anybody or asserting that the process has already been seriously prejudiced. I have taken this

⁹ The square brackets appear in the filed copy of this document.

¹⁰ In February Mr. Callaghan had accompanied Mr. Wilson on a visit to the Soviet Union. During a Kremlin lunch on 14 February he told Mr. A.N. Kosygin, the Soviet Prime Minister, about the considerable concern in Portugal over PCP intentions and the fears there of a *coup* from the left. Mr. Callaghan pointed out that the AFM and the other political parties needed reassurance in particular on Soviet policies and the line the Soviet Government was taking with Dr. Cunhal: 'if democracy were not allowed to prosper in Portugal', then, Mr. Callaghan stated, 'the future of détente and the CSCE would be jeopardised'. Mr. Kosygin assured Mr. Callaghan that the 'Soviet Government had no desire to see the PCP leave the Portuguese Government and wanted to see them continue to cooperate with other political forces' (Moscow telegram No. 1 to Lisbon of 14 February, WSP 1/6). Cf. Volume II, No. 112, and Volume III, No. 74.

¹¹ Cf. No. 116, and No. 120, note 12.

line recently with the Polish Deputy Foreign Minister and also with Academician Inozemtsev[12] in the confident expectation that my remarks will be reported back. (In all this, my concern is not with Anglo-Soviet relations or Soviet sensitivities as such. My fear is, again, that such action will certainly become known to the AFM, and contribute to their going down the wrong road.)

6. Finally, our chief concern must be not only to avoid appearing to express 'no confidence' in Portugal but also to avoid laying ourselves open to the charge that we have failed to do all we could to help. Thus, I entirely agree that the aid mission should go ahead; if the visit of the CDS is to be called off, it should be on Portuguese initiative and not ours; we should continue to take a generally helpful line about Portuguese relations with the EEC. Mr. Barrett's paragraph 20 is absolutely right, but has general application going beyond just the EEC.

7. At the same time, we cannot afford to take practical NATO considerations lightly (Mr. Barrett's paragraphs 17 and 18) and Mr Morgan's suggestion of a private contingency study with the US and selected others seems to me a good idea.

8. I am incidentally assuming that we cannot effectively hope for any earlier direct contact with the new Portuguese Foreign Minister than at the NATO Ministerial meeting at the end of May.

JOHN KILLICK
3 April 1975

Secretary of State

1. I have reservation [*sic*] about creating a Portuguese/CSCE link *in advance* of further hard evidence of unacceptable interference—partly as I want our room to manoeuvre kept as wide as possible, partly because I do not want us to mutter threats we will not carry out.

2. In the meantime—a little less fulsome talk (me in particular) about the 'new democracy' and of the help we can give to the real democratic parties.

3. The CGS [*sic*] should go (the balance is tipped by the Ambassador's telegram). The President should not come—at least not yet.

4. If the worst happens and the Russians get military bases in Portugal what do we do (repeat do)?

These comments seem a great deal more illiterate when typed up than they did when I wrote them on the submission. I hope you can follow my drift.[13]

---

[12] Mr. N.N. Inozemtsev was Director of the Institute of World Economics and International Relations, Moscow.

[13] The last two sentences were added in manuscript.

ROY HATTERSLEY[14]

7 April 1975

[14] On 10 April, after seeing No. 120 and the above minutes, Mr. Callaghan noted on Mr. Hattersley's minute: 'Yes, thank-you. This is a useful series of notes and can form the background to our actions—i.e. Mr. Barrett as modified by Mr. Morgan and Sir J. Killick. I don't know the answer to Point 4.'

No. 122

Sir T. Garvey (Moscow) to Mr. Callaghan

No 511 Telegraphic [*WSP 3/303/1*]

Routine. Confidential   MOSCOW, *3 April 1975, 8.45 a.m.*

Repeated for information to Lisbon, Washington, Bonn, Paris, NATO Brussels.

Portugal

1. My Portuguese colleague[1] has recently returned from Lisbon where he went for consultation just before 11 March *coup*. He saw President, Cunhal, Soares, Melo Antunes and several others: and yesterday had one and a half hours here with Gromyko. He is a bourgeois democrat and, I think, an honest man but with touches of naivety.

2. His main impressions after 5 months absence were:

(*a*) the physical and mental weariness of those whom he had seen. Everyone was very tired: and
(*b*) the growing climate of violence, particularly among the young. The risks of irrational action were, he thought, increasing because people had begun to lose their heads.

3. Neves had noted a growth of anti-Western sentiment partly engendered by departure of foreign industrialists who had closed their factories, and by cancellation of foreign orders. Though reasons for this were comprehensible, resultant unemployment had made things worse. If West wanted to help, it should make a few bets and risk losing its money.[2]

[1] Sr. M. Neves, Portuguese Ambassador in Moscow.

[2] The same point was made by the Portuguese Ambassador in London, Sr. A.P. Fernandes Nogueira, in a meeting with Sir J. Killick on 17 April. Sir J. Killick, however, responded by explaining that the bulk of the economic investment in Portugal must come from the private sector, and that this 'could not just be turned on and off like a tap'. Unheralded nationalisations of the banks, insurance companies and other businesses had created a situation in which 'the climate for foreign investment was at the very least something of a questionmark' (letter from Sir J. Killick to Mr. Trench of 22 April, WSP 3/548/1).

4. Conversely, Soviet Union, as source of new things and ideas, attracted wide interest.

5. Armed Forces Movement (AFM) were 'furious' with Maoist far Left, had the means of caning them and would probably do so one day. But AFM were themselves strongly 'progressive' and in spectrum of Portuguese Left Wing Communist Party were thus not notably revolutionary.

Soviet Union

6. Neves had sent message saying he was back in Moscow and Gromyko had promptly summoned him and, I gather, been given substance of foregoing account. Gromyko expressed serious anxiety about course of events and repeated to Ambassador assurance offered before latter's departure of Soviet non-intervention in Portuguese affairs. Neves has long believed that Soviet interests (CSCE summit, relations with West European Communist Parties etc) exclude risk of Soviet-inspired takeover in Portugal. Gromyko has further reinforced him in this view.[3] So also has reaction of Spanish Communist Party whose pitch has been queered by events in Portugal.[4] Ambassador had been meant to travel back to Moscow with Major Martines [*sic*],[5] Portuguese Minister of Labour, who spent last week here, but, having stayed behind to see new Foreign Minister, caught up with him before he returned home. Martines [*sic*] ostensibly came to look at Soviet manpower arrangements but probably I suspect to obtain Soviet assistance over closed factories and lost orders (para[graph] 3 above). He raised this with Kosygin who reportedly asked for a list and offered to help.

8.[*sic*] Neves said in confidence (which please respect) that an unofficial envoy from Portuguese Communist Party had separately been in Moscow last week, but whether on summons from Moscow or on Portuguese initiative he could not tell. Man's name is Pato, apparently a member of

---

[3] In conversation with Sir T. Garvey on 26 February, Sr. Neves had suggested that 'so long as the Soviet Government was firmly committed to détente, the prospects of real Moscow-inspired trouble in Portugal could be discounted: but, if the Russians changed course, Portugal must look out for squalls' (undated minute from Sir T. Garvey to Mr. Broomfield). 'If Mr. Neves' account is accurate', noted Mr. Cartledge, Head of EESD since January 1975, 'Mr. Gromyko is by no means insensitive to Western reactions to the developing situation in Portugal. This testifies to the value of referring, particularly in Ministerial conversations with Soviet or East European opposite numbers, to the adverse consequences for détente of a deterioration in the Portuguese internal situation. This message is evidently getting through' (minute of 10 April).

[4] During a lunch on 1 April, Mr. Broomfield's Portuguese counterpart, Sr. M. Curto, suggested that 'precipitate action in Portugal by the Communists would probably prejudice the chances of other Communist parties in Western Europe'. The 'main prize for the Russians', Sr. Curto argued, 'was a Communist take-over, in the medium term, in Spain which would fundamentally alter the East/West balance in Europe. This might be put back a number of years, and the life of Franco's regime and its successor prolonged, if there were disruptions and a forced take-over by the Communists in Portugal' (letter from Mr. Broomfield to Mr. R.A. Burns (EESD) of 2 April).

[5] Maj. J. Costa Martins, the Portuguese Minister of Labour.

PCP's central committee. Natural choice would have been Ingles, resident long-term PCP representative in Moscow, who returned to Portugal a few months back and has all the contacts. But Pato had been sent. According to Portuguese First Secretary (Broomfield's letter of 2 April to Burns EESD)[6] he saw Ponomerev.[7]

NATO/EEC

9. Recent American and, particularly, German representations in Lisbon had been taken amiss less because of their content than their manner. So, likewise, had measures taken since last winter for 'courteous exclusion' of Portugal from NATO meetings. This played into hands of those in Portugal, and they existed, who would like to take Portugal out of Alliance. Melo Antunes had however told him that Portugal would stand by her treaty engagements.

[6] See note 4 above.

[7] Prof. B.N. Ponomarev was Secretary of the Central Committee of CPSU.

CHAPTER V

Political Change in Portugal and Spain
18 April 1975–29 April 1976

No. 123

Minute from Mr. Tickell to Mr. Morgan

[*WSS 2/579/1*]

Secret   FCO, *18 April 1975*

NATO and the Mediterranean

1. Yesterday Mr. Hockaday (Deputy Under-Secretary of State (Policy and Programmes) in the Ministry of Defence) held a meeting for Mr. [H.] Bergold (Deputy Assistant Secretary of Defense in the Bureau of International Security Affairs in the [US] Department of Defense). The Ministry of Defence will be producing a full record of the meeting but you may care to have a note of what seemed to me to be the main points at once.

2. The purpose of Mr. Bergold's visit to London was to acquaint us with the results of his recent visits to Lisbon, Madrid, and Athens and to express anxiety about the implications of developments in the Mediterranean for the Alliance.

Lisbon

3. Mr. Bergold said that he had found the atmosphere in Lisbon greatly changed within the last few months, and most disagreeable. Anti-Americanism was of course very evident, but he did not know how deep it went. Mobs could be whistled up from side streets at a moment's notice for any purpose. It was hard to tell how much the Government was in control of events. Certainly he doubted if the forthcoming elections would produce a fair result: the Communists would have to be included in the new government if Portugal was to continue to be governed.

4. Mr. Bergold said that he had seen some of the 24 in the Revolutionary Council, and some of the 200 in the Assembly of the Armed Forces Movement. He had found their views on foreign policy very neutralist: they did not want Portugal to be too closely associated with either power block. At the same time they said they did not want to upset Portuguese obligations to NATO. But they dropped a broad hint that Portuguese departure from NATO might only be a matter of time. If in the Autumn the new government moved in that direction, the Armed Forces Movement would not object. In the meantime overt discrimination against Portugal within NATO would only accelerate matters. We had a

long—now familiar—discussion about the difficulties which Portugal created for the Alliance. I noticed that Mr. Bergold was clearly against any move to eject Portugal in present circumstances, and seemed to think that the decision whether to stay or go must rest with the new Portuguese Government. After tolerating a virtual Fascist government in Portugal for 25 years, the Allies could hardly push Portugal out when she moved Left.

5. We touched briefly on the problem of the Azores. In reply to a question about whether there was any possibility of the Azores becoming independent, Mr. Bergold said that the Americans had naturally considered the idea but had concluded that it was not a starter. As it happened the population on the island harbouring the present US base was particularly sleepy and prone to lotus eating. Moreover the base was now much less important to the United States than it had been. Resupply of Israel could, for example, now take place without use of the Azores as a staging post.

Madrid

6. Mr. Bergold described the present impasse in the US/Spanish negotiations over the US bases on the lines already reported in Sir E Peck's letter of 10 April to Sir J Killick.[1] He laid particular stress on the emotional heat behind Spanish demands for some explicit link with NATO. Those concerned in Madrid wanted to set Spanish policy on a firmly Atlantic/European course before General Franco went. If nothing happened there would be a danger of the successor government, overwhelmingly preoccupied as it would be with domestic problems, locking itself into its present sterile position, or worse doing something really silly. Mr. Hockaday spoke on the lines of the Secretary of State's recent remarks to the US Ambassador in London,[2] emphasising our inability to do anything explicit before General Franco's departure, but our readiness for contingency planning at official level with the United States to prepare for that event. He also emphasised the political difficulty which the Government would have in apparently coming to terms with General Franco.

---

[1] The US had enjoyed access to military facilities in Spain since 1953 under a series of bilateral executive agreements, the most recent of which had been concluded in 1970 and was due to expire in September 1975. In his letter Sir E. Peck reported on a briefing given by Mr. Bergold to NATO representatives on 10 April regarding the current state of negotiations, which had begun in the previous November, for a new executive agreement. The Spanish negotiators had, according to Mr. Bergold, complained that while Spain contributed to Western defence through allowing the US to use facilities in support of NATO, it 'received no security guarantee from the United States nor NATO', and that the risks Spain ran 'as a result of this discrimination were incompatible with such benefits as she received from the agreements with the US'. The Spaniards had stopped short of demanding full membership of NATO, but Mr. Bergold believed they 'wanted some new arrangements to be worked out which would be politically acceptable, conceivably some form of Associate Membership'.

[2] Mr. E.L. Richardson was US Ambassador in London. A record of these remarks has not been traced (see No. 124).

7. I referred to Gibraltar. Had the Spaniards mentioned Gibraltar? Did they realise that an explicit link with NATO was out of the question in present circumstances?[3] It was not only a question of Britain. The views of other members of the Alliance were well known. Mr. Bergold replied that the Spaniards had not mentioned Gibraltar but he thought that they realised they had got into a thoroughly false position in this respect. He thought himself that an amicable settlement of the Gibraltar question would form part of an eventual package to bring Spain into the Atlantic/European family. As for the explicit link, Spanish national pride was heavily engaged, and reason was not paramount. Feelings were running higher on this point than he had ever known. He suspected that if the Spaniards did not obtain some sort of satisfaction they would seek to punish NATO by demanding removal of some of the NATO facilities from the US bases.[4] He then read out a formidable list of what the Americans feared the Spaniards might do. I asked Mr. Bergold how he thought the other members of NATO should react. There were a number of possibilities for quiet co-operation with Spain (including that mentioned by M de Staercke[5] at NATO) but an explicit link was out. No doubt the Americans found it tedious to be used by the Spaniards as their stalking horse.

8. Mr. Bergold said he thought that the Spaniards might soon be mounting a diplomatic effort to bring home their points to the European members of the Alliance. President Ford would probably raise the matter at the NATO Summit meeting, and might visit Madrid on his way to or from Brussels. Speaking personally I said that there seemed to me to be dangers in raising the matter in too strong terms at the NATO Summit. News of it would probably leak, and a rebuff would make the Spaniards more sensitive than ever. Would it not be better for discussion at NATO to be kept at a lower level? The whole problem needed much more thought than had so far been given to it. There was no getting round the European political realities. Mr. Bergold agreed. He said that his visit should be regarded as part of the process of consultation between the United States and its leading European Allies.

9. I should add in parenthesis that Mr. [A.G.] James (US Embassy) also discussed this point with me to-day. He said that he thought it almost

[3] See No. 113, note 4. A background briefing paper of 2 May, prepared for Mr. Wilson's forthcoming visit to Washington (see note 9 below), pointed out that HMG 'might be able to trade off the prospect of a Spanish link with NATO against Spanish agreement to lift the pressure on Gibraltar'.

[4] In telegram No. 81 to Madrid of 30 April Mr. Callaghan commented on this point: 'This seems an unlikely tale, and scarcely in the Spanish interest.'

[5] During Mr. Bergold's NATO briefing on 10 April (see note 1 above), M. de Staercke suggested that while the political difficulties of Spanish association with NATO remained 'insuperable', it should be possible for Gen. A. Haig, in his dual capacity as Supreme Allied Commander Europe and Commander of US forces in Europe, 'to give Spain greater knowledge of the mission allotted to American forces in Spain'.

certain that President Ford would raise the matter at NATO. The Americans were very exercised about the problem. What Mr. Richardson had told the Secretary of State last week was a considerably diluted version of his instructions. He added that Mr. Richardson had been pleased by the Secretary of State's interest in Anglo/American exchanges on the official level about what should happen after General Franco's departure. But of course what the Americans were interested in was something rather sooner. The State Department shared Mr. Bergold's view that it was important to get Spanish foreign policy on the right lines now if it was to survive the difficulties of the period after General Franco went.[6]

Athens

10. Mr. Bergold said that the current US/Greek negotiations over US bases in Greece were proceeding in slow time and at a low level. The Greek negotiators seldom had proper instructions, and the Americans got most of their information directly from Greek Ministers. The Greeks wanted to get the Americans out of the most important mainland base and seemed ready to expand facilities in Crete where local political pressure was less. But Mr. Bergold was relatively optimistic and thought that the Greeks would eventually compromise. For their part (and he told us this in strict confidence) the Americans were ready to bargain with their home porting facilities.[7]

General

11. Mr. Bergold also described the current situation in Washington over aid to Turkey. He said he thought there were little prospects of early change. Senator Mansfield, who was on the side of the Administration, had decided that the best tactic was to move slowly. Members of Congress still wanted to punish the Administration for its earlier disregard of the law, and to use the lever they had created for themselves against the Administration. He was more optimistic about the possibilities of a more even traffic in arms between the United States and Europe, and welcomed the information Mr. Hockaday gave him about the Defence Secretary's initiative on the subject within the Eurogroup.[8]

C.C.C. TICKELL[9]

[6] Mr. Callaghan had, according to Mr. P.J. Weston, already suggested that there might be advantage in asking Mr. Wiggin to return to London at some suitable juncture to talk about HMG's attitude towards Spain once Gen. Franco was no longer in power. 'I think', Mr. Weston noted, 'he is interested in the problem of how we should be approaching our relations with the sort of sensible and influential people in Spain who might be expected to become prominent after Franco's demise and in the whole question of Spain's relationship with NATO' (minute to Mr. Baker of 15 April).

[7] Cf. No. 88.

[8] See Volume I, p. 90.

[9] On 22 April Mr. Callaghan, who was due to accompany the Prime Minister on a visit to Washington on 7 May (cf. Nos. 125 and 126), noted on the copy of this minute returned to Mr.

Tickell: 'Very interesting. Will you bring me up to date (esp. on Spain) before we touch down in Washington. We may be able to influence Pres. Ford a little.'

No. 124

Mr. Callaghan to Sir N. Henderson (Bonn)

No. 238 Telegraphic [WSS 2/579/1]

Immediate. Secret   FCO, *30 April 1975, 11.45 p.m.*

Repeated for information to Immediate Madrid, Washington and UKDEL NATO

Sir E. Peck's letter to Sir J Killick of 10 April:[1]
Spain and NATO

1. As you know the US Ambassador raised the relationship between Spain and NATO with me on 11 April.[2] He said that current Spanish/American negotiations over renewal of the bases agreement had given rise to the question of some possible form of Spanish association with NATO. He suggested that NATO Governments should examine the possibilities of moves in this direction. He thought this could have a bearing on whether the Americans were allowed to stay in their bases, and that it might have a beneficial effect on moderate influence in Spain.

2. I told Mr. Richardson that we would be ready for British and American officials to talk about the kind of scenario which, after Franco had gone, might make possible some kind of reconciliation between Spain and NATO. But there could be no question of doing anything while Franco lived. There had for long been great depth of feeling in Britain about Spain which would make it impossible for HMG to consider such a step. Mr. Richardson mentioned the possibility of Spanish participation in joint naval exercises: I said this was not a starter.

3. On 28 April the Minister of the US Embassy[3] called on the PUS on instructions to follow up this conversation in stronger terms. He said that after 5 inconclusive rounds of negotiations there was increasing doubt about whether the bases agreement could be renewed before it expired in September, unless the Spaniards were given some satisfaction over their wish for public recognition of their contribution to Western defence. He had been instructed to ask for HMG's support in multilateral discussion within the Alliance of possible means of bringing Spain closer to the

---

[1] See No. 123, note 1.

[2] *V. ibid.*, note 2.

[3] Mr. R.I. Spiers.

Alliance with a view to eventual membership. Text of a paper outlining US views is contained in MIFT (not to Washington, who we understand already have a copy).[4] Spiers said this paper was being handed over in similar démarches to all other NATO members. He added that he was also instructed to ask for bilateral discussion with HMG about the possibilities both of Anglo-Spanish cooperation on politico/military matters and of contacts between Spain and the integrated NATO structure. He handed over a list of possibilities (text in my second IFT, not to Washington).[5]

4. Spiers explained that the Americans had also proposed bilateral talks on this subject to the FRG[6] (but to no other Government). They had received a non-committal response, though they were told that Genscher[7] was personally interested in the memorandum. In reply Sir Thomas Brimelow rehearsed the difficulties for us over any form of military association with Spain, but promised to study the American proposals carefully.[8]

5. This subject may be discussed when the Prime Minister and Secretary of State are in Washington on 6 and 7 May. Before this we should be grateful for some idea of the German reaction. You could tell them that the proposal raises major difficulties for us. We would have to take into account not only the strong feeling of this country about the Franco régime, but also the Spanish attitude over Gibraltar. A number of other NATO Governments (e.g. the Netherlands and Norway) would almost certainly have similar problems about any link between Spain and NATO.

6. Pfeffer (Federal Ministry of Foreign Affairs)[9] who was here last week told us privately that Genscher, when recently in Spain, had been told that the Spaniards were seeking a couple of agreements: one with the

[4] The US memorandum communicated in this telegram of 30 April expressed the US Government's belief 'that Spain's relationship to NATO should be examined under present circumstances with the objective of bringing Spain closer to the Alliance, with a view to eventual membership'. It argued that Spain would be aided in 'following a stable, moderate course' if it were brought into the NATO framework as early as circumstances permitted.

[5] This second memorandum (communicated in telegram No. 240 to Bonn of 30 April) listed as possible areas for bilateral cooperation with Spain: closer contacts between British and German delegations to NATO and the Spanish Embassy in Brussels; an exchange of visits between the Spanish military and their counterparts in Britain and Germany; the presence of Spanish observers at their military exercises; training for British and German forces at Spanish facilities; and steps towards a closer Spanish/NATO relationship, including 'some form of favourable public allied reference to the importance of Spain to NATO'.

[6] Federal Republic of Germany.

[7] Herr H.-D. Genscher was West German Foreign Minister.

[8] Mr. Wiggin had, however, little doubt that the Spaniards would be content to settle with the US on a bilateral basis if the Administration could overcome its problems with Congress and deliver enough on the bilateral security guarantee and military supply fronts. 'I do not', he noted, 'believe the Spanish Government will burn their boats this year' (Madrid telegram No. 107 of 30 April).

[9] Herr F. Pfeffer was Head of the NATO Department of the West German Foreign Ministry.

Americans to renew the base agreement, and the other with NATO to cover the primarily NATO functions of the US bases. The Germans had the impression that the second agreement might be seen as a special endorsement of the first. Pfeffer gave the impression that, although Genscher personally was in favour of some arrangement with Spain, he would not want to get out of line with the other allies. Schmidt's views were uncertain. But Pfeffer thought that Schmidt would be more inclined towards Spain than Brandt,[10] and that the German position might therefore change.[11]

[10] Herr W. Brandt was German Federal Chancellor, 1969-74.

[11] Herr G. van Well, the Political Director of the West German Foreign Ministry, told Sir N. Henderson on 30 April that Herr Genscher's visit to Madrid had confirmed the Foreign Ministry in the view that it would be 'unwise to leave till after Franco's departure from the scene the process of closer cooperation with the Spanish authorities', and that in general they felt 'it would be desirable for the Western European countries to take an active interest in Spain so as to try to avoid a repetition of what had occurred in Portugal'. He further explained that Herr Genscher believed in the need for closer contact with Spain, and that Herr Schmidt was more cautious (Bonn telegram No. 364 of 30 April).

Elections for a Constituent Assembly were held in Portugal on 25 April 1975. These, according to Mr. Trench, were 'a major political milestone, in spite of sustained efforts by the Armed Forces Movement and the left-wing parties to play down their significance in advance'. The events of 11 March had provided the 'extremist wing' of the AFM with a pretext for emasculating the political right and centre-right in Portugal and for forcing the main parties into a 'Constitutional Pact'. This ensured the Movement's primacy, regardless of the outcome of elections for at least 3-5 years, and preserved the wide-ranging powers of the self-appointed Council of the Revolution as an agreed essential part of any constitution the Assembly might devise. The AFM also announced that the election result would not affect the composition or policies of the Government and encouraged voters to cast blank votes as an expression of support for the armed forces. Indeed, as Mr. Trench pointed out, some members of the AFM 'took to describing the elections as a mere "pedagogic" exercise, or as being no more significant than a gigantic "opinion poll"'. Nevertheless, in the approach to polling day, 'it was more and more widely believed that the extreme left-wing wanted to have the elections postponed or even abandoned, for fear that the results would show how narrow their popular base really was'.[1]

The battle lines of the campaign itself were quickly defined by the 'Communists and their allies on the one hand, and the non-communist parties, including the Socialists, PPD and CDS, on the other; with the latter group advocating the need for a pluralistic democratic system in the liberal European tradition'.[2] Yet, despite 'the wild rumours and widespread anxiety' which characterised the campaign, voting day itself was, Mr. Trench

[1] Despatch from Mr. Trench of 6 May, WSP 1/1.

[2] *V. ibid.*

reported, 'a model of sobriety and calm'.[3] A turnout of nearly 92% produced a resounding victory for the moderate left, with the Socialists winning nearly 38% and the PPD over 26% of the vote, and the PCP polling less than 13%. The blank votes amounted to 7%. Mr. Trench was, nonetheless, unsure as to whether this result would embolden the AFM's left-wing radicals, who would regard Dr. Soares's success 'as a threat to their own position', or 'stiffen the resolve of more moderate members of the Movement to stand up and be counted'. Certainly, he felt that Dr. Soares and his allies faced a difficult problem in judging just 'how far they [could] assert themselves against the AFM and the extreme left-wing'. An open confrontation with the extreme left could, he feared, 'produce intolerable strains of which the fledgling Portuguese democracy is the most likely early victim'. The conduct and results of the election were an 'encouraging event', which might have helped tipped the scales in favour of the non-communist political forces, but the latter remained 'in a highly perilous position', and on the basis of their past performance Mr. Trench doubted if the West could 'rely on their judgement and fortitude to see them through'.[4]

[3] Lisbon telegram No. 247 of 26 April, WSP 1/1.
[4] See notes 1 and 2 above.

No. 125

Sir P. Ramsbotham (Washington) to Mr. Callaghan

No. 1659 Telegraphic [*WSP 3/304/1*]

Routine. Confidential   WASHINGTON, *9 May 1975, 11.52 p.m.*

Repeated for information to Lisbon, UKDEL NATO, Moscow, Madrid, UKREP Brussels

Talks in Washington:[1]
Portugal

1. In your talk with Kissinger here after dinner on 7 May, you found his views on Portugal to be as apocalyptic as ever. You confirmed to him your view that Dr. Soares remained our best hope, and that the large vote for the Socialists in last month's elections should serve to encourage the moderates who made up one of the strands in the Armed Forces Movement. While you were by no means sanguine that the Communist Party would not continue to manipulate the situation, or that there would not be a further slippage away from Portugal's links with the West, it was still well worth our while doing what we could now to support the moderates. In particular, you spoke in favour of closer links between

[1] Mr. Wilson and Mr. Callaghan visited Washington on 7-8 May after attending the Commonwealth Heads of Government Conference at Kingston, Jamaica.

Portugal and the European Community. I also mentioned the recent successful visit to Lisbon of the Chief of the Defence Staff (Lisbon telegram to you No. 253).[2]

2. Dr Kissinger remained sceptical, and said that he would hold back two steps behind the Europeans. He was particularly concerned about the effect on other countries with large Communist parties, especially Italy and France, if Portugal, with its increasingly neutralist leanings, stayed on in NATO. You raised the question of whether it would be wise to discuss the MBFR Option III in NATO next month in view of the Portuguese security situation.[3] Kissinger appeared indifferent to this problem: the Russians, he said, would know about Option III already.

3. At a lunch yesterday with Sonnenfeldt[4] and Hartman, I mentioned this conversation and asked why Kissinger was so exceptionally gloomy about Portugal and so convinced that it was doomed to go Communist. Hartman has now telephoned me to say that he had spoken with Kissinger, who wanted to assure me that his gloom was confined to his analysis and did not imply that the United States had any separate policy or plan of action which differed from those of its allies. He was simply sceptical of the value of efforts to improve matters.

4. Kissinger's belief that the situation in Portugal is bound to get worse is based partly on the view, which Hartman also expressed to me, that the present Portuguese leaders are an unfortunate combination of zeal and naivety. One example quoted was Jesuino,[5] the Minister of Social Communication, who is now visiting the United States as an official guest and is having talks in the State Department and with Congress, where his naivety apparently succeeded in turning off even Senator Kennedy.[6] (Costa Martins, the Minister of Labour, will be here next week.) Hartman added that Coutinho,[7] who is increasingly influential, seemed to have persuaded the Armed Forces Movement that the Portuguese people needed guidance in their political activity, and that a one-party system would be the best way of bringing this about. Hartman therefore thought that the likely future for Portugal was a left-wing dictatorship rather than a plurality of parties. Kissinger and Hartman think that Soares is faced with the choice

[2] The visit to Portugal by Sir M. Carver at the end of April was described by Mr. Trench in this telegram of 3 May as 'a signal success from the point of view of Anglo-Portuguese and NATO-Portuguese relations' (WSP 10/5).

[3] Option III was a nuclear weapons reduction package which the Americans and their Western allies thought might be offered to the Soviet Union as a means of breaking the deadlock in the ongoing Mutual and Balanced Force Reductions (MBFR) talks in Vienna. See Volume III, Nos. 20, 22 and 23.

[4] Mr. H. Sonnenfeldt was Counsellor in the State Department.

[5] Capt. J. Correia Jesuino.

[6] Senator E.M. Kennedy (Democrat, Massachusetts).

[7] Adm. A.A. Rosa Coutinho was executive officer of the Council of the Revolution. He was formerly High Commissioner in Angola, where White settlers dubbed him the 'Red Admiral'.

of being knocked off his perch by the Armed Forces Movement for insubordination, or else of compromise with the Communists, which would be fatal to him.

5. I should add that the above pessimistic view of the future of Portugal is not shared at all levels of the State Department, nor by the US Ambassador in Lisbon, who has just been here on a visit.

No. 126

Minute from Mr. Barrett to Mr. Morgan

[*WSS 2/579/1*]

Confidential FCO, *9 May 1975*

Spain: Discussions in Washington

Spain and NATO were not discussed when the Prime Minister and the Secretary of State met the President and Dr. Kissinger at the White House. However, the Secretary of State has given me the following brief account of a conversation he had with Dr. Kissinger at the Residence on the evening of 7 May. A more detailed record will be coming from Sir Peter Ramsbotham in due course.[1]

It was agreed with Dr. Kissinger that Sir P. Ramsbotham and Mr. Sisco should discuss possibilities for closer relations with Spain after the departure of Franco. This would be on the basis that the point should be got across to the Spanish that there would be all to play for if Franco could be got rid of in the near future. Apparently in parallel the American Ambassador in Madrid[2] (for whom Dr. Kissinger has a high regard) and Mr. Wiggin should make contact to discuss the same range of matters, with a view to a possible meeting between the Americans and ourselves in London.[3] (Mr. Wiggin's return to London for consultations could be helpful here.) The Secretary of State has also given his blessing for increasing contacts on a Party basis and has asked Mr. McNally to pursue this.

He has ruled out military contacts with Spain. He has in mind not only the great difficulties this would cause in the UK but also the fact that

---

[1] In Washington telegram No. 1641 of 9 May Sir P. Ramsbotham recalled that, during his conversation with Mr. Callaghan, Dr. Kissinger 'did not press the case for an association of Spain with NATO and seemed reconciled to our position that no such moves were possible during the Franco régime'.

[2] Mr. Stabler was appointed US Ambassador to Spain in March 1975.

[3] According to Sir P. Ramsbotham (see note 1 above), Dr. Kissinger had 'warmed' to Mr. Callaghan's suggestion that 'we should have a bilateral exchange of views on the scenarios which, after Franco [had] gone, might make possible some kind of reconciliation between Spain and NATO.' The talks, which it was agreed should initially take place between their respective Ambassadors to Spain, were however subsequently postponed until after President Ford's visit to Madrid on the weekend of 31 May (Madrid telegram No. 121 of 12 May).

whereas the Spanish militarily [*sic*] may indeed have a role to play in the post-Franco situation, they are unlikely to follow the example set by their Portuguese opposite numbers.[4] He summed up by saying he wished us to be active in our contacts with Spain. Subject to the point about military contacts and the need to consider very carefully proposals for contacts at Ministerial level, this is the basis on which we can go ahead.[5]

Gibraltar was not discussed in Washington, both in the sense that our continuing difficulties over this question were not raised and in the sense that it was apparently not mentioned as an obstacle to increasing contacts with Spain. Nevertheless you may feel that a certain caution may be necessary.

S.J. BARRETT

[4] Sr. M. Fraga Iribarne, Spain's Ambassador in London, was of much the same opinion. During lunch with Sir J. Killick on 7 May he said: 'Parallels and links between Spain and Portugal existed but should not be exaggerated. First of all, Portugal was spectacularly poor ... Moreover, the Spanish Army had not been through an experience equivalent to Portugal's African war' (letter from Sir J. Killick to Mr. Wiggin of 9 May, WSS 3/548/1).

[5] The Americans had found other allies equally unenthusiastic about their proposals. On 8 May Mr. James of the US Embassy in London admitted to Mr. Tickell that they 'had been getting a lemon from most of the European Governments to whom they had suggested some form of explicit link [between Spain and NATO] ... In no capital had the Americans obtained any promises of support' (minute from Mr. Tickell to Mr. Morgan of 12 May).

No. 127

Mr. Trench (Lisbon) to Mr. Callaghan

No. 273 Telegraphic [WSP 1/1]

Immediate. Confidential   LISBON, *22 May 1975, 4.50 p.m.*

Repeated for information to Priority Washington, Moscow, UKDEL NATO, Madrid, MoD D13 (west).

My tel[egram] No. 271:[1]
Political Crisis

1. A long meeting of the Council of the Revolution on 21 May, which ended only in the small hours, was devoted to the crisis precipitated by the closing down of 'República'; the communiqué issued after the meeting mildly deplored the exploitation of this affair for political ends.

2. At his press conference on 22 May Dr. Soares said that the Socialist Party (PS), as the representative of 40% of the Portuguese people, was no longer prepared to tolerate the undemocratic activities of the Communists and other left-wing minority groups aimed at taking over the trade unions and local authorities, and Communist manipulation of the media. The closing down of 'República' had been the last straw. The Socialists were also very concerned about the tendency to write off the political parties as irrelevant to the revolutionary process. They still regard their participation in the Government as having symbolic importance, even though the Armed Forces Movement (AFM) no longer consulted the parties in the Government on matters of major national interest. Nevertheless, Dr. Soares confirmed that the Socialists were boycotting Cabinet meetings pending satisfactory settlement of the República issue. He said that he and Salgado Zenha had presented the Socialist case to the President, and were also seeking an early meeting with the Council of the Revolution for the same purpose.

3. The Socialists have called a rally this evening, at which they hope there will be a convincingly large turn-out in their support. This is very much a last ditch effort, and it seems doubtful whether the PS have any

---

[1] On 19 May the editorial staff of the Lisbon Socialist evening newspaper, *República*, were locked-in by the newspaper's pro-Communist printing workers, who demanded the replacement of the editorial staff, and nominated their own interim editor. The Socialist Party organised a large demonstration outside the newspaper's offices, but Dr. Soares, who led the demonstration was refused access to the building. In Lisbon telegram No. 271 of 20 May Mr. Trench reported that the Socialists had decided to 'stand and fight' over the closing down of *República*, and that Dr. Soares and Sr. F. Salgado Zenha, the Socialist Minister of Justice, intended to boycott Cabinet meetings pending a satisfactory settlement of the dispute.

coherent plan about what they should do next if the rally is successful.[2] There could in any event be serious trouble as a result.

4. Although events are moving faster than I thought desirable in the immediate wake of the elections (my manuscript letter of 5 May to Sir J. Killick not copied)[3] it must be recognised that the PS have had a very difficult hand to play. On the one hand it seemed unwise for them to stick their necks out too far and too fast, since the AFM and the Communist Party (PCP) were obviously extremely touchy as a result of their electoral failure. On the other hand, some of their supporters in the provinces were already beginning to question the value of voting for the PS, if the latter constantly gave way before PCP encroachments.

5. After their humiliation at the intersindical rally on 1 May,[4] the PS could not be expected to take the 'República' incident lying down, and the issue is one on which they will enjoy wide support (outside the Council of the Revolution and the extreme left-wing parties and groups).

6. It is tempting to see the [1] May and República cases as part of a cunningly orchestrated PCP plot designed to bring matters to a head (cf. 11 March), but we have no evidence of this. It may also be, of course, that in view of continuing AFM talk about the irrelevance of the political parties, Soares feels that if he does not make a stand now the PS (and PPD) will be pushed onto the sidelines.[5] In this connection it is of interest that Cunhal is also showing signs of alarm at the AFM's increasing tendency to attack the political parties generally (notably in a speech at Vila Franca last weekend, now given prominence in the latest edition of Avante). Whether this will lead to a Communist concessions [*sic*] on the point Soares considers important is another question.

---

[2] In the event this demonstration was well attended and passed off peacefully. But the Council of the Revolution issued a statement deploring party strife and calling for renewed national unity. The Communists declared that the anti-Communist line of the Socialists would make the present system of coalition government impossible (Lisbon telegram No. 274 of 23 May).

[3] Not traced.

[4] The Communists successfully outwitted the Socialists and the PPD in the arrangements to celebrate May Day, excluding both parties from participation.

[5] Mr. Trench reported in Lisbon telegram No. 275 of 27 May that there was still no sign of a compromise allowing the Socialists to return to full participation in the Government. Indeed, when the Assembly of the AFM met on 26 May it discussed, but did not adopt, two propositions put to it by the Council of the Revolution calling for the creation of local Revolutionary Councils of Workers, Soldiers and Sailors, or for the creation of Committees for the Defence of the Revolution. 'The aim of both propositions' Mr. Trench observed, 'was to create an immediate and more effective link between the AFM and the people so as to avoid "the party polemics which were distracting the revolutionary process from its regular course".'

No. 128

Letter from Mr. Morgan to Mr. Wilberforce (Washington)

[*WSP 3/548/14*]

Confidential. Eclipse   FCO, *30 May 1975*

Portugal

1. Alan James of the American Embassy called on me yesterday to tell us in confidence about the reaction from Washington to Elliot Richardson's report of his conversation with the Secretary of State about Portugal on 19 May.[1] It consisted of six points which Kissinger wanted to be made to us in reply. James was speaking in confidence because the Embassy had decided that the points might not be well received and should not be put to us officially. In view of the contact which Kissinger had had with Mr. Hattersley in Ankara[2] and would be having with the Secretary of State in Brussels, they felt there was no need for them to reply at Ministerial level.

2. The points were as follows:-

(i) Kissinger had not given Portugal up for lost, but he made a considerably more pessimistic analysis than we did, and one which looked more realistic every day;

(ii) He and Ford had no intention of snubbing the Portuguese in Brussels;

(iii) He was baffled to think how the Alliance could for long accommodate a country that looked likely to end up somewhere between Yugoslavia and Algeria;

(iv) He failed to see how aiding or fraternising with the radical leadership could help to strengthen the moderates. Nevertheless, he saw nothing else to be done at present and would follow the general NATO line, though the US would keep a step or two behind the Europeans;

---

[1] Mr. Richardson called on Mr. Callaghan on 19 May to brief himself on British views on the 'forthcoming crescendo of meetings', including the NATO Heads of Government meeting scheduled for the end of the month at Brussels. During the ensuing discussion Mr. Callaghan remarked that Dr. Kissinger had something of a 'blind spot' over Portugal: 'He hoped that Dr. Kissinger could be persuaded not to ignore the Portuguese at the NATO summit. A few minutes spent with them in Brussels could strengthen the hand of the moderates in Portugal. As he understood the situation, the members of the Armed Forces Committee still represented a wide spectrum of political views. Until the situation had been lost one must assume that it could be won' (record of a meeting between Mr. Callaghan and Mr. Richardson at the FCO on 19 May at 5 p.m., WSP 3/304/1).

[2] Dr. Kissinger and Mr. Hattersley both attended the 22nd session of the Council of Ministers of CENTO which was held in Ankara on 22-23 May.

(v) If Soares were to be excluded in one way or another from the political scene, would the Europeans try to find 'another moderate guy'?;[3]

(vi) If Portugal were irretrievably lost, it would at least administer a salutary shock to other Europeans.[4]

3. I said that whilst I appreciated the Embassy's delicacy, I doubted whether our Ministers would have been at all upset by this reaction. In fact Kissinger had made point (iv) above verbatim across the table to Mr. Hattersley at the CENTO meeting, and it had certainly been taken in good part.[5] We were not at all happy with the situation, or about the adequacy of our policy, which was the general policy of the Nine; but, like Kissinger, we could think of nothing better to do in practice. Basically, we were hoping to help maintain Portuguese links with the West and give some support to the moderates in the political parties of the AFM until the military leadership began to come to terms with the facts of life and therefore to be disillusioned with the Communists. We fully realised that the Communists might beat us to the post or that the military themselves might go the other way; and our helpful attitude was quite clearly and explicitly linked to the survival of people like Soares.

4. I gave James an account of the discussion in the EEC Council Meeting at Dublin on 26 May about aid for Portugal: and I told him that Mr Hattersley had said in terms to the meeting that in our view the approach agreed in Dublin would remain valid only so long as the AFM could reasonably be given the benefit of [the] doubt.[6] If we found the

[3] In a telephone conversation with Mr. P.J. Weston on 27 May Dr. Soares, who had travelled to Paris for the Ministerial meeting of the Organisation for Economic Cooperation and Development (OECD), repeated to Mr. Weston a warning, already delivered to Dutch and German representatives, that Portugal was in a 'very grave crisis'. He said that the Communists were 'mounting an offensive aimed at a complete take-over and the Socialists were in danger of being hounded from the Government', and urged Mr. Callaghan to 'be firm both in NATO and in the Community context', and to point out the dangers to the Alliance's southern flank (minute from Mr. Weston to Mr. Callaghan of 27 May).

[4] On 5 June Mr. Wilberforce observed in his reply to Mr. Morgan's letter that the 'short-temperedness' of Dr. Kissinger's message 'no doubt reflected a momentary fit of exasperation over the way in which we were combining with his own officials to urge on him a course of action in which he did not believe'.

[5] In a minute to Mr. T.J. Clark (Assistant Head of Middle East Department) of 28 May Mr. Goodison noted that during the restricted session in Ankara Dr. Kissinger had said that the Americans viewed events in Portugal more seriously than the Europeans, but 'their view was not necessarily an incentive to action'. 'He believed', Mr. Goodison continued, 'the danger lay not in a communist takeover, but a Yugoslav-type government which would remain a member of NATO largely in order to ensure its protection against the United States, whom it conceived of as an enemy. Such a development would hold dangers for Italy, Greece and Spain.'

[6] Agreement by the Council to open negotiations with Portugal on trade and 'industrial, technological and financial co-operation' was coupled with an undertaking to begin preliminary arrangements for a ministerial meeting between the EC and Portugal 'with a view to

democratic parties being shut out of politics, we might want to cut the approach off short. James thanked me for the information about Dublin and said that he would let the State Department know what I had told him, without however referring to what he had told me.

Yours ever,
H.T. Morgan

strengthening their ties and furthering Portugal's development' (UKREP Brussels telegram Nos. 2447 and 2529 of 22 and 28 May, MWE 3/354/1; Council of the European Communities Press Release, 343rd meeting of the Council, Dublin, 26 May, MWE 1/20).

No. 129

Letter from Sir. J. Killick to Mr. Trench (Lisbon)

[*WSP 2/579/1*]

Personal and Secret   FCO, *5 June 1975*

My dear Nigel,

You will be receiving various records and bits and pieces about various exchanges with the Portuguese in the margin of the NATO Summit. I did not participate in all of them but nonetheless you may like to have my somewhat subjective overall impression which you will not readily gain from just reading the records.

2. My feeling is that we (i.e. the UK) did a much better job with Gonçalves and Rosa Coutinho than any of the other Allies.[1] The Americans were not as well placed as we and were I think disposed to be much too tough, even though Kissinger appeared receptive to the Secretary of State's urging that we, as friends of Portugal, could afford to speak strongly while the Americans—on the assumption that they wished to try, despite their forebodings, to keep Portugal in the Alliance—should try to

---

[1] During their meeting with Gen. Vasco Gonçalves and Adm. Rosa Coutinho at Brussels on 30 May both Mr. Callaghan and Mr. Wilson complimented the AFM on its achievements in Portugal and the speed with which it had moved towards decolonisation in southern Africa. Mr. Callaghan then expressed his concern about political developments in Portugal, adding that the recent elections reflected 'no great desire in Portugal for communism or for a one-party State' and that he hoped the AFM would help Portugal 'develop into a democracy'. The meeting, which concluded after fifty minutes, was evidently regarded as a success by the Portuguese, the latter's delegation confiding to Mr. P.R.H. Wright (Private Secretary to Mr. Wilson since December 1974) that Gen. Vasco Gonçalves 'had much appreciated the frank talk' and that 'the attitude shown by the British Government was in marked contrast with the attitude shown by the Nordic countries and others. The meeting between General Gonçalves and Chancellor Schmidt that morning had been little more than a "dialogue of the deaf"' (note of a meeting between Mr. Wilson and Gen. Gonçalves at NATO on 30 May at 12 noon, WSP 3/548/1).

offer the Portuguese something positive in addition to firm criticism.[2] The fact is, I am afraid, that I am less than convinced that the Americans really want to keep the new Portugal in the alliance even though their attempts to bring Spain closer have for the moment run into a dead end.[3]

3. The other Western Social Democrats were, I thought, all too brutal. The Danish Permanent Representative—my former colleague from Moscow—told me that their bilateral with Gonçalves had ended near disastrously with a great harangue from the Portuguese side. The Danes had had to get up and leave to meet another engagement before Gonçalves had finished. In the actual NATO sessions themselves, we took a much more oblique and restrained line about the application of the democratic principle in the area of the southern flank of NATO while the others put much more bluntly the question whether a dictatorship of the Left could remain within the Alliance.

4. The trouble is of course, between ourselves, that although this probably leaves us better placed with the Portuguese than anybody else, our capacity to deliver the kind of outside assistance they are liable to ask us for is unlikely to measure up to their expectations.[4] No doubt they will demand money rather than technical assistance; are our Unions really best placed to give them the sort of advice they want? and so on. (Incidentally, when I was in Bonn on 25-26 May I met Dingels, the International Secretary of the SPD, who spoke most scathingly of the Labour Party's failure to do anything effective about Portugal. 'Only we and the Swedes have done anything worthwhile' he said.) To revert to the Americans, although I had hoped to have a talk with Hartman about the Azores in particular, he did not actually participate in the NATO Summit and Sonnenfeld [*sic*] was pretty inaccessible for bilateral talks throughout. However, I expect to be seeing one or other if not both of them at a

[2] In conversation with Dr. Kissinger after the OECD dinner (cf. No. 128, note 2) on 27 May, Mr. Callaghan suggested 'that while it would be right to be firm with the Portuguese, the United States ought to offer a degree of encouragement. It would be far better if closer friends of the new Portugal like the United Kingdom were to "take the Portuguese to the cleaners". This would come much better from them tactically' (minute from Sir J. Killick to Mr. Acland of 29 May).

[3] On 18 June, Mr. Hattersley, then visiting Washington, was told by Mr. Sonnenfeldt of the US Administration's concern lest the leftward trend in Europe move in the direction of neutralism. Mr. Sonnenfeldt 'made the point that a dictatorship of the left of the kind that was coming about in Portugal and was impregnated with neutralist ideas while still paying lip-service to NATO membership was more incompatible with the essential defence purposes of NATO than dictatorships of the right had been' (Washington Saving telegram No. 71 of 20 June, WSP 3/548/14).

[4] According to Mr. Trench one of Gen. Vasco Gonçalves's most frequent complaints was 'the "economic boycott" or "economic sabotage", of Portugal by international capital'. As Mr. Trench pointed out, these allegations 'failed to take account of the world economic situation, the general lack of liquidity and so forth'. '[O]ne's best course', Mr. Trench suggested, 'is probably to agree with him and say that this makes HMG all the more understanding of Portugal's problems' [letter to Sir J. Killick of 13 May).

Ditchley Conference this coming weekend, and will try again then.[5] Meanwhile, I took the opportunity of a 'wash-up' meeting with Alan James of the US Embassy to mention my misgivings about the American attitude both on Portugal generally and on the Azores in particular. I spoke on the lines of paragraph 6 of my letter of 19 May and he, apparently genuinely, expressed full agreement.[6] He showed no knowledge, if he has any, of any plans of a more disturbing nature which might be current in Washington but this proves nothing since it would in any case be abnormal for Washington to keep the American Embassy here informed.[7]

Yours ever,
JOHN KILLICK[8]

[5] Sir J. Killick discussed the Azores, and the American attitude towards the islands in the event of a Communist take-over in Portugal, at some length with Mr. Sonnenfeldt when the latter visited Ditchley Park Conference Centre on the weekend of 8-7 June. In a minute to Mr. Goodison of 9 June Sir J. Killick observed that Mr. Sonnenfeldt had said there was evidence of a 'solid separatist movement in the Azores' which, because of the 'significant number of people of Azorean origin which lived in the United States, particularly in New England (this was news to me) ... [had] to be taken seriously'. Sir J. Killick had protested that 'it would be one thing for the United States to contemplate doing something about the Azores after Portugal had gone irretrievably Communist and had left the Alliance and there were signs of Soviet wish to secure facilities on Portuguese territory; it would be quite another thing for the Americans to intervene in the Azores while Portugal remained a member of the Alliance.' Although Mr. Sonnenfeldt insisted there would be 'no intervention', Sir J. Killick was 'left with the strong impression that the CIA [were] probably already becoming involved'. The Foreign Editor of the *New York Times* subsequently remarked to Sir J. Killick with regard to the Azores that 'he believed that the Administration wanted to create a sort of Atlantic Taiwan' (WSP 3/548/14).

[6] In this letter to Mr. Trench, Sir J. Killick warned that US support for Azorean independence 'could very well put paid to the prospects for democracy in Portugal for a long time and drive her out of the Alliance for good (to say nothing of any effects it might have in the Middle East)' (WSP 1/13).

[7] Sir J. Killick subsequently recalled that at the Ditchley Park conference (see note 4 above) the Americans (Mr. Sonnenfeldt and Mr. R.F. Ellsworth (Department of Defense)) had spoken in 'gloomy terms about Portugal', suggesting that events there might have a 'spin off in Italy' and elsewhere. 'A full take-over by the Portuguese Communist Party supported by the Soviets might', they had indicated, 'be a healthy shock for the West but seemed the least likely outcome. The more likely would be a more radical regime with continuing and increasing Communist participation.'

[8] In a post-script Sir J. Killick responded to an earlier letter by Mr. Trench on the future of the Anglo-Portuguese Society, arguing that the leadership and style of the Society ought to be 'revamped' to reflect the 'new Portugal'.

No. **130**

Minute from Mr. Tickell to Sir J. Killick

[*WSS 2/579/1*]

Confidential   FCO, *24 June 1975*

Spain and NATO

It may be worth recording a brief discussion I had with Mr. Hartman and later Mr. Sonnenfeldt at the State Department in Washington on 18 June.[1]

2. I asked Mr. Hartman how President Ford's visit to Madrid had gone.[2] He said that little or nothing had been done as unfortunately General Franco had had one of his good days and had put on an astonishing performance, considering his age and Parkinson's Disease. Although the General had initiated little himself (and had inhibited others from doing so), his replies to the President had been models of brevity and good sense.

3. On the negotiations for the renewal of the US bases in Spain, Mr. Hartman said that the Spaniards were still insisting on an explicit link with NATO. At this point Mr. Sonnenfeldt interrupted to say that he had had very recent information to show that they were beginning to weaken.[3] But Mr. Sonnenfeldt then launched into a diatribe against the Europeans for their attitude. What would we say if the Americans lost vital facilities and NATO defence was prejudiced as a result?[4] I explained once more the underlying elements in the European position, and said that in any case it was hard to take Spanish threats literally. The Spanish interest was so obviously to re-enter the European family sooner or later that they would scarcely cut off their noses to spite their faces. Mr. Sonnenfeldt replied that if the European Community could have an association agreement with

---

[1] Mr. Tickell accompanied Mr. Hattersley on a visit to Washington during 18-20 June. Cf. No. 129, note 3.

[2] President Ford paid a 24-hour visit to Spain over the weekend of 31 May.

[3] In a letter to Mr. R.P. Flower (SED) of 5 June Mr. R.D. Wilkinson (Second Secretary in the British Embassy, Madrid) noted that the Americans considered the decision to retain the presence of US forces in Spain had been taken at the highest level in the Spanish Government, and that they took it for granted that the bases agreement would be renewed, although they did not discount the possibility that there might be further hard-bargaining ahead.

[4] On 22 May Dr. Schlesinger told a restricted session of NATO's Defence Policy Committee (DPC) Ministerial meeting that the US/Spanish bilateral agreements had assisted in maintaining deterrence and increasing the flexibility of US forces. He stated that 'the facilities in Spain provided support for US Polaris/Poseidon submarines in the Mediterranean under SACEUR's command, for tanker aircraft to support the operational readiness of US aircraft deployed in Europe through exercise facilities available in Spain'. If these facilities were lost, he thought, the US would have to redeploy some forces, but others would have to be completely withdrawn (UKDEL NATO telegram No. 239 of 22 May).

Spain why shouldn't NATO? Was commerce so different from defence? I replied that obviously it was. The Community had association agreements with a large number of countries, including Algeria, and the United States had commercial arrangements with the Soviet Union. NATO was a body with democratic standards and had only just signed up on the Ottawa Declaration.[5] As all had said in notably moderate terms at the NATO summit, an agreement with Spain in present circumstances would make nonsense of Article 12 of the Ottawa Declaration.[6]

4. Mr. Hartman then referred to the possibility of the Americans making some unilateral statement in the new US/Spanish agreement about the value of Spain to Western defence. What would we think of that? Speaking personally, I said that while much would depend on the drafting, the Americans were entitled to say what they thought right in a bilateral agreement provided they did not claim to speak for NATO. Mr. Hartman said that he was not sure that the Spaniards would think a clause to this effect enough. But the Americans were certainly doing their best on these lines. The Americans feared that the Spaniards might ask for a security guarantee, and here the Americans would have trouble with Congress not—as in the case of the Europeans—because of the ideological aspect but because no-one in Washington wanted the government to enter into new military commitments.[7]

C.C.C. TICKELL

[5] Article 12 of the Declaration on Atlantic Relations, approved at the NAC meeting in Ottawa on 19 June 1974 and signed by NATO Heads of Government in Brussels on 26 June 1974, recalled that the signatories proclaimed their 'dedication to the principles of democracy, respect for human rights, justice and social progress'. See *Selected Documents Relating to Problems of Security and Cooperation in Europe 1954-77*, Cmnd. 6932 (London: HMSO, 1977), pp. 184-86.

[6] At the Ministerial meeting of the DPC on 22-23 May (cf. note 4 above) Dr. Schlesinger had urged his colleagues to acknowledge in their communiqué the 'relevance for the Alliance of the US/Spain agreement'. But of the other NATO Defence Ministers only the German showed any enthusiasm for this proposal. The Danish, Dutch and Norwegian Ministers argued that any hint of association between Spain and NATO would produce a very hostile reaction in their countries, and Mr. Mason made it clear that HMG would not agree to any links between Spain and NATO 'at least until Franco's departure from the scene'. At the restricted session of the NATO summit on 30 May Mr. Wilson also insisted on the need for internal changes in Spain: 'When as we all hoped democracy became a reality there, we should', he said, 'be among the first to hold out the hand of welcome' (telegram No. 128 to UKDEL OECD of 28 May; UKDEL NATO telegram No. 275 of 30 May).

[7] On Spanish reactions to US efforts to secure for Spain a greater degree of politico/military acceptance by NATO, Mr. Wilkinson observed that the general impression given was that the Americans had 'done their best, but that success was not possible given the traditional West European attitudes towards Spain', and that President Ford's visit 'coming immediately after the NATO summit provided some consolation for the Spanish establishment' (see note 3 above).

No. 131

Report by the Joint Intelligence Committee

JIC (75) 17

Confidential   CABINET OFFICE, *26 June 1975*

The Outlook for Portugal and its Relationship with the Western Alliance

PART I: SUMMARY[1]

Introduction

1. Portugal's relationship with the Western alliance will depend to a large extent on the interplay between developments in Portugal itself and Western reactions to them: events since the armed forces' coup of April 1974 have raised the question not only whether Portugal will remain a member of NATO, but also whether it will be to the advantage of the alliance that she should. In this paper we try to assess how the political balance of forces in Portugal may develop over the next year or two and then consider the foreign policy implications.

The Internal Outlook

2. The internal situation in Portugal is unstable, with a deepening crisis of political authority and public order compounded by major economic problems.[2] Formally, the Armed Forces Movement (AFM) has political control and the political parties are committed to accepting this for the next 3-5 years. But the AFM is deeply divided and its capacity to govern is suspect. Its commitment to a pluralist democracy (which, as has become increasingly clear, conflicts with the ideological attitudes of some of its leaders) has released political forces which challenge its own authority and legitimacy: the massive majority obtained by the social democratic parties, led by the Socialists (PSP), in the Constituent Assembly elections in April revealed a situation in which the distribution of political power in Portugal varies inversely with electoral support. At the same time, the AFM's promotion of the concept of a revolutionary 'armed forces-people alliance' poses a wider threat to social stability and civil liberties.

3. The PSP's bid for political influence commensurate with its electoral backing can be exploited as anti-revolutionary by its opponents and risks bringing it into an open confrontation with the Communist Party and the AFM, which it would lose. But it cannot afford to let its case go by default. Its room for manoeuvre is limited. The Communist Party (PCP) has identified itself from the start with the AFM and has exploited its

[1] Part II, the Main Report, is not printed.

[2] In a letter to Mr. Goodison of 18 June, Mr. Trench bemoaned the continued 'drift to the left' in Portugal. He observed, with regard to communist influence over the news media, that any 'tendency which does not echo the prevailing policy is denounced as "fascist", "reactionary", "counter-revolutionary", etc.' (WSP 1/1).

organisational strength and discipline to gain a dominating position in the trade unions, local authorities and the media. Its influence with the AFM is very great, but it cannot dictate policy and its position is not impregnable: if it overplays its campaign against the Socialists it risks running foul of the AFM's growing impatience with party political in-fighting.

4. The AFM is divided on how to reconcile revolution and democracy. Broadly there are three trends—

(i) a 'moderate' approach which favours a continuing role in government for the political parties under AFM control;

(ii) a pro-communist approach; and

(iii) a 'radical' populist approach, which would bypass or eliminate the political parties (probably including the PCP) and establish mass revolutionary organisations directly linked with the AFM.

5. The increasingly bitter party political struggle has strengthened the hand of the radicals in the AFM; but at present the majority of the AFM evidently prefers to persevere with pluralism, at least in name. Continuing friction between the PSP and the AFM (and its exploitation by the communists) could quite quickly provoke the AFM to more drastic measures against the social democratic parties; but for the time being both sides may draw back from a final rupture. If the Constituent Assembly is able to complete its work, local authority and legislative assembly elections should follow; these would be likely to intensify the polarisation of Portuguese politics between communists and anti-communists. But the prospects of free legislative assembly elections or, if they take place, of the AFM accepting the results seem questionable.

6. The only forecast we can make with any confidence is that the AFM will not voluntarily relinquish power in the foreseeable future. It may aim to retain more or less democratic institutions under its overall control, as envisaged in the constitutional pact signed with the main political parties before the April elections. But it is likely also to promote mass organisations closely linked with the armed forces as a counterweight to the established political parties. If so, this could lead to a further slide to the authoritarian left, with the exercise of 'pluralist' democracy becoming progressively restricted to a popular revolutionary front comprising the communists and organisations representing the 'AFM—People Alliance'. A further possibility (despite its recent disavowal) might be an exclusively military government, which a majority of the AFM may come to see as a means of reducing the power of the Communist Party. For its part, the PCP is likely to aim to extend and consolidate its influence to the point where it can dictate to the AFM without appearing openly to challenge its authority. Although critical situations could arise in which the PCP might attempt to seize outright control, we think it unlikely that either the PCP or the AFM would risk a direct confrontation in the near future.

7. Besides the struggle for political power, the AFM faces other serious problems. There is a considerable risk of civil war in Angola, which could

have far-reaching repercussions in Portugal.[3] Separatist agitation in the Azores is a lesser problem, but if it persists it could act as a catalyst for wider unrest on the mainland. At home, the economic situation is very serious and deteriorating; the most urgent needs are for increased productivity and new investment, but the prospects for both are poor and the manner in which state control has been extended to cover about half the industrial and services sector of the economy seems likely to hinder rather than help early recovery.[4] The outlook, therefore, is sombre.[5] The AFM is likely to remain in control of the organs of power, but may not be able to control the economic and social consequences of the revolution it is trying to bring about. The prospects for the evolution of a Western social democracy are poor. Communist influence is likely to remain strong as long as the PCP identifies with the AFM, but its position is not invulnerable. The AFM may be forced increasingly to carry out a populist revolution by authoritarian means. The consequences could be a new left-wing military dictatorship, or a drift into anarchy.

The External Outlook

9. The ideological and emotional sympathies of the leaders of the AFM encourage them to identify with the Third World and the non-aligned; and though they see practical reasons for preserving their links with the West, their attitude to their traditional allies is schizophrenic. Suspicion of the United States is widespread. Relations with Western Europe are likely to be conditioned by the Europeans' willingness to help Portugal on Portuguese terms, and will be vulnerable to Portuguese sensitivity to real or imagined interference in their domestic affairs.

10. By contrast, the Portuguese are susceptible to Russian and East European blandishments and have a simplistic view of East-West détente. Events in Portugal are running the Russians' way; but though they can be expected to take advantage of opportunities to extend their influence there,

---

[3] The Main Report further explained that failure to avert a civil war in Angola, where Portugal with its residual responsibilities for security might be unable to avoid involvement, would be a severe blow to the credibility of the AFM. Moreover, the possible return to Portugal from Angola of several hundred thousand settlers, many bitter at what they regarded as betrayal by the AFM, would exacerbate employment problems and wider political and social tensions.

[4] During talks with Maj. de Melo Antunes, who visited London on 27 June, Mr. Callaghan pointed to the problems faced by British firms whose operations in Portugal were being hampered by industrial unrest and worker occupation of premises. 'Our firms', Mr. Callaghan remarked, 'were not all angels, and those who had lagged behind had to come into line with modern labour practices. But they needed reasonable stability and reasonable prospects of making a reasonable return' (record of conversation between Mr. Callaghan and Maj. de Melo Antunes at the FCO on 27 June at 3.30 p.m., WSP 3/548/13).

[5] According to Mr. Trench (see note 2 above) the arrival of white colonists fleeing Angola, coupled with the 'polarisation between North and South in Portugal', accentuated the already dangerous situation. And despite his own earlier discounting of a civil war, he now thought a division taking shape and the point was approaching when 'real trouble [might] break out'.

they are unlikely to run high risks for a quick success in the near future, and certainly not before the conclusion of CSCE. For the time being it probably suits the Russians for Portugal to remain an awkward, divisive and insecure member of NATO.[6]

Possible developments in Portugal's relationship with NATO

11. Portugal's direct military contribution to NATO is negligible.[7] Of much greater significance are the bases and facilities available to NATO in Portugal and the Azores. If these were denied to NATO they could to some extent be reprovided elsewhere at some cost, but maritime flexibility and reinforcement capabilities (especially to the Southern Region) would suffer. If these facilities were made available to the Russians, the Soviet maritime and air threat would be substantially increased, but they would be vulnerable to attack.

12. The Portuguese Government and the AFM have reaffirmed their intention of remaining a member of NATO. Although there are reasons for doubting it, we believe that on balance this statement of intent can be accepted at its face value: partly because the Portuguese do not want gratuitously to jeopardise their prospects of receiving Western aid, partly because they do not want to disturb the balance of power in Europe and the climate of détente which they aim to promote.

13. But Portuguese membership creates serious problems for NATO. The nature of the régime is likely to be a standing source of friction between Portugal and her allies; the Communist Party's strong position in the Portuguese government could set an awkward precedent for other member countries with large communist parties; and neutralist Portuguese attitudes could be contagious.[8] Developments in the Azores and perhaps Angola could also cause tensions between Portugal and other NATO members, notably the United States.[9] But the most immediate problem is the greatly increased threat to the security of NATO documents and communications posed by extensive communist penetration of the

[6] On the Soviet Government's objectives with regard to Portugal, the Main Report commented: 'in the longer term, assuming that there is not an outright communist takeover in Portugal, they may aim to engineer Portugal's withdrawal from NATO in such a way that they could present it as a logical consequence of détente and of the alliance's internal contradictions'.

[7] The Main Report put this point more vividly: 'Portugal has always been a sleeping partner in NATO ... In addition, the authoritarian nature of the Salazar and Caetano régimes and, since 1961, their commitment to a series of colonial wars in Africa in support of policies which were repugnant to many of Portugal's allies became an increasing political liability, in terms both of internal alliance solidarity and of NATO's image in the world at large.'

[8] The Main Report argued that the continued membership of NATO by a Portugal strongly susceptible to Communist influence would make it more difficult for other member states with large communist parties (i.e. France and Italy) to resist pressures for communist participation in government. Portugal's advocacy of neutralist policies in NATO would also encourage existing neutralist tendencies in the Netherlands, Scandinavia, Greece and perhaps Turkey.

[9] In this context the Main Report envisaged the prospect of civil war in Angola and possibility of the Portuguese supporting the Soviet-backed MPLA.

Portuguese government machine and armed forces: we believe that all classified NATO information supplied to Lisbon must be assumed to be compromised.[10] Some measures have been taken in NATO to limit the potential damage, but the problem is likely to persist as both a security and a political issue. Sooner or later the alliance is likely to have to weigh up the balance of disadvantage between tolerating an insecure and politically unreliable Portugal and setting conditions for Portugal's continued membership which the Portuguese could not accept. Assuming that it had not already fallen under communist control, Portugal's expulsion or withdrawal under pressure from NATO would be likely to accelerate the unravelling of the alliance, especially on the southern flank.[11] In those circumstances we think it unlikely that the AFM would switch to open alignment with the Warsaw Pact; unless they believed that there was a real threat of Western military intervention, they would be more likely to take their stand on non-alignment.

R.A. Sykes[12]
Chairman, on behalf of
the Joint Intelligence
Committee

[10] On this the Main Report elaborated: 'The Portuguese NATO registry was transferred early this year from the relatively secure Foreign Ministry to the intelligence and security division of the Armed Forces General Staff; there have been a number of purges and reorganisations of the armed forces' security organisation and we have no reason to believe that this key target is any more immune to communist penetration than other sectors of the armed forces.'

[11] This, the Main Report commented, 'would be very difficult to stop, particularly in a post-CSCE atmosphere of détente'.

[12] DUS since May 1975.

No. 132

Mr. Trench (Lisbon) to Mr. Callaghan

No. 409 Telegraphic [WSP 1/1]

Immediate. Confidential   LISBON, *12 July 1975, 10.05 a.m.*

Repeated for information to Priority UKDEL NATO, Paris, Washington, Copenhagen, The Hague, Bonn, Rome, Moscow, UKDEL Strasbourg, UKREP Brussels, MoD (D13 west), Routine Madrid, Saving Luxembourg.

My tel[egram] No. 401 (not to Moscow):
Portuguese Political Crisis[1]

1. Mário Soares came to my house late last night. He said that (as has been only too clear for some time) there was an almost total breakdown of governmental authority, at both the military and civilian levels. The military were divided amongst themselves, with many of them wishing to get rid of the Prime Minister,[2] while responsible civilian members of the Govt. were becoming increasingly alarmed and considering resignation. Soares mentioned in this context Silva Lopes (Foreign Trade, formerly Finance), Oliveira Baptista (Agriculture, formerly close to the Communists but now said to be disillusioned by Communist-inspired farm seizures in the Alentejo), Cravinho (Industry) and Almeida Santos (Inter-territorial Co-ordination).

2. Soares was aware that PPD Ministers had put conditions for remaining in the Govt., but thought it unimportant whether they stayed or

---

[1] On 9 July the AFM Assembly published radical proposals, which in Mr. Trench's words, called for the 'complete purging of the state apparatus, its decentralisation and the creation of a new apparatus on a popular base in the interests of the working masses' (letter to Mr. Goodison of 16 July). These threatened severely to curtail the functions of the Constituent Assembly and the role of political parties, and two days after their appearance Dr. Soares announced that the Socialists were leaving the Government, ostensibly because of the continuing political deadlock over the editorship of *República* (cf. No. 127). In Lisbon telegram No. 401 of 10 July Mr. Trench reported that during a dinner that evening with Sr. D. Freitas do Amaral, the leader of the CDS, the latter had expressed the view that if the AFM declaration were literally carried out, it would 'mean the end of democracy (in the Western sense) in Portugal'. He further forecasted a major economic crisis in the autumn, adding that he 'could not exclude the possibility of a civil war breaking out at this stage'.

[2] In a retrospective despatch of 17 September Mr. Trench identified two main strands of opposition to Gen. Vasco Gonçalves within the AFM: those inspired by Maj. de Melo Antunes, 'who clearly believed the Revolution was going too far and too fast to be either successful in practical terms or politically acceptable to the Portuguese population and to Portugal's traditional allies'; and those associated with Gen. Saraiva de Carvalho, who, though Marxist in inclination, were suspicious of the élitism of the PCP, and demanded a far greater degree of popular participation in the political process than had so far been possible.

not.[3] If they did, many of their supporters would ally themselves with the Socialists (PS). The Socialists in the Constituent Assembly would not give up their seats.

3. Asked how he saw the immediate future, he said that it was unpredictable. There seemed to be three possibilities:-

(a) Government by the military, assisted by technocrats;

(b) Government by the military in alliance with the Communists (PCP and MDP);[4]

(c) Government by the Communists alone.

He thought (c) unlikely. He added that, if the PS were forced into active opposition, the Armed Forces Movement (AFM) would find itself in trouble. The Party was united and in militant mood. The AFM realised this, hence a conciliatory interview just given to an evening paper by Ramiro Correira, a left-wing member the Council of the Revolution.

4. Asked how the Western powers could help in the present situation, Soares said that three ways were open in the diplomatic sphere, NATO and EEC. In the first, it was essential to show that the West was aware of the danger to democracy presented by the situation in Portugal. It would be disastrous if the country became a second Cuba, for Spain would be the next to succumb and, with Tito[5] no longer the man he was, Yugoslavia might follow. The PCP leader, Cunhal, was an agent of the Soviet Union: the Western powers should refuse to attend a CSCE summit, so long as the Soviet Union was attacking Europe in the south-west flank.

5. I interjected that most informed observers tended to think that the Russians were not altogether happy about the way things were going here and did not want their policy of détente spoiled by events in Portugal. Soares replied that Cunhal would not have dared to go so far, against the opinion of all other European Communist parties, unless he had Soviet support. Moreover Brezhnev had taken a very hard line over Portugal with Willy Brandt.

6. Second, NATO should carry out military manoeuvres to demonstrate its anxiety over developments here (presumably Soares envisages NATO

[3] The PPD formally left the Government on 17 July. On the dissolution of the coalition Government, Gen. Vasco Gonçalves was invited to form a new administration (Lisbon telegram No. 428 of 17 July).

[4] In his letter to Mr. Goodison of 16 July (see note 1 above) Mr. Trench observed: 'The North/South polarisation [of Portuguese politics] ... is being supplemented by social polarisation in which the "povo" [people] is increasingly coming to mean "the masses" and the Communist parties, while the entire middle class find themselves excluded from the description ... If, as seems likely, the Communist Party (PCP) delegates leave the Constituent Assembly, then the sense of separation between the "povo" and the rest will be increased.'

[5] Marshal J.B. Tito was President of Yugoslavia.

naval exercises in the vicinity). The Portuguese military believed that NATO was prepared to accept anything without demur.

7. The West should continue to promise aid, but on condition that Portugal followed a democratic course.

8. I asked whether he thought it still useful for us to invite leading personalities, e.g. Saraiva de Carvalho and Cravinho, to visit the UK. He said that it was—particularly the military, and he undertook to provide me with a list of the 'floating vote' officers whom it was especially important to influence, Carvalho was the number one priority (though he realised that we could not have asked him before inviting Fabião). He could not think why the West was allowing the Communist countries to make all the running in exchanges of visits, cultural manifestations, etc.

9. It was well past midnight, and Soares was obviously exhausted, so I did not go into the points raised in any detail, except on the question of Soviet support for the PCP. In this context I must note that, although the PCP has undoubtedly been working hard, and often successfully, in the trade unions, agricultural areas of the south and the information media, it is generally believed that the Party has lost ground in recent months—and Soares indeed admitted this when I put it to him. What observers, including the foreign press, refer to as communist action is often the work of irresponsible groups—UDP,[6] MRPP, PRP (BR),[7] LUARN[8] [*sic*] etc—with extreme left-wing tendencies but very vaguely formulated ideas. Though ready to exploit openings made by them, the PCP must regard these groups generally as anathema. One has only to talk to one's East European colleagues to sense this.

10. Apart from the practical difficulties of arranging NATO exercises on the spur of the moment, I do not (repeat do not) believe that ostentatious manoeuvres would have the effect desired by Soares—they might well push the AFM's 'floating voters' in the wrong direction. But, provided that the crisis atmosphere subsides, I would see no harm in NATO ships calling at Portuguese ports in the normal course of events, and I very much favour NATO countries exchanging visits of appropriate officers of the services (Soares was exaggerating the inactivity of the West in this sphere, but it is undeniable that the activity of the East Europeans in sending delegations of all kinds, and the partiality of the news media, give the impression that the West is a very long way behind).[9]

---

[6] *União Democrática Popular*/Democratic People's Union.

[7] *Partido Revolucionário do Proletariado (Brigadas Revolucionárias)*/Revolutionary Party of the Proletariat (Revolutionary Brigades).

[8] *Liga da União e de Acção Revolucionária (LUAR)*/League of Revolutionary Union and Action.

[9] In the concluding paragraph of his letter to Mr. Goodison of 16 July (see notes 1 and 4 above), Mr. Trench commented on the widespread political disaffection in Portugal: 'So we are faced with a scenario which is either totally gloomy or highly dangerous, depending on whether one considers the slide to Communist-dominated military rule to be likely to progress unresisted, or to provoke effective opposition.' As to what 'constructive action' HMG could

11. I have been trying for some time to get an appointment with Carvalho to discuss the political situation. There is no knowing at present when I shall be successful, but it would be very valuable if I could be authorised now to sound him about possible dates for a visit, and the type of programme he would like. I am not for the time being pursuing the question of visits by the civilian Ministers suggested at an earlier date, as their chances of survival are problematical.

take, he confessed, 'that, beyond the very limited types of action which we have been discussing—visits, aid, etc.—I do not see there are many options open to us'.

No. 133

Submission from Mr. Goodison to Mr. Morgan

[*WSS 3/548/1*]

Confidential   FCO, *14 July 1975*
                      Policy towards Spain

Problem

1. Franco is unlikely to last long. He may step down soon, possibly even on 18 July. Even if he lingers on in power we will enter a new period in which the uncertainties of the future will dominate the current situation in Spain. What policies should we follow to prepare for the period after his departure, and to deal with it when it arrives?

Background and Argument

2. By agreement between the Secretary of State and Dr. Kissinger, Mr. Wiggin and the US Ambassador in Madrid have been discussing these matters.[1] Their discussions have been held up by the US/Spanish Bases talks. Their next meeting is on 18 July.

3. I do not think we should wait for completion of their discussions in Madrid before reporting to Ministers, and seeking their views on policy. Time is going by. There is a possibility that Franco will step down on 18 July, the anniversary of the start of the civil war that brought him to power (though I should add that neither Mr. Wiggin nor Mr. Stabler thinks this likely). Even if he does not, there remains the possibility that he might die, or be incapacitated, at any moment.

4. I attach the current British Embassy draft for a joint paper.[2] The American Embassy may well disagree with some of it, but it gives us our Embassy's view of how the land lies in Spain at the moment.

---

[1] See No. 126.

[2] Not printed. This analysis of the current situation in Spain pointed out that, despite rumours of Gen. Franco's impending departure, there was 'no hard evidence that he [would] go or be pushed until death or total incapacity intervene[d]'. It concluded that when Prince

5. I also attach Mr. Wiggin's own recommendations for policy.[3]

6. There will be advantage in coordinating our policy with the Americans when they are ready to do so, but there is no reason why our policies need to be identical. The Americans may wish to pursue a more forward policy with the present régime than we can contemplate. We may feel able to build closer links than they dare with respectable opposition groups of the democratic left. Our policies could well be complementary.

7. Much of what Mr. Wiggin recommends is in line with policy that we are already pursuing, in accordance with the Secretary of State's general guidance (sidelined passage in Mr. Barrett's minute of 9 May).[4] For instance, Mr. Hattersley recently received four visitors from the social democratic USDE.[5] Mr. McNally has it in mind that, in the autumn, the Secretary of State might receive visitors from the PSOE[6] if a visit can be arranged. We could pay similar attention to visitors from the Christian Democrats. All of these groups are opposed to the Communists and have, so far, steered clear of the Communist-inspired Junta Democrática.

8. We have, over the last year or so, been somewhat hesitant in inviting as sponsored visitors to the UK Spanish officials who have political positions or a Movimiento past. I think, now that Franco is on his last legs, we should accept the suggestion in paragraph 8 of Mr. Wiggin's recommendations and accept such visits, provided that the visitor is a convert to democracy.[7]

9. The only recommendation with which I think we will have difficulty is in paragraph 12 of those recommendations. Mr. Wiggin recommends intensification of contacts with the Army and the military in general.[8] The

Juan Carlos came to the throne he was likely to attempt to put through a programme of gradual democratic reform, whose success would depend on the support of the armed forces, favourable economic circumstances, and the absence of serious disturbances. But the paper added that the support of the armed forces might not prove durable once reform encountered serious opposition, and that bleak economic prospects meant that disturbances could not be discounted.

[3] Not printed. Mr. Wiggin, who largely dictated this paper before departing on leave, recommended that HMG remain in a position to do business with the Franco régime, but that they should assume that its immediate successor would be Prince Juan Carlos supported by the military and many elements of the existing régime. 'There is', he concluded, 'nothing dramatic we can do to contribute to healthy evolution in Spain. We must beware preaching to them, particularly when our own problems are so manifest. We should not hope for too much too soon here.'

[4] See No. 126. The third paragraph was sidelined.

[5] *Unión Social Democrática Española*/Spanish Social Democratic Union.

[6] *Partido Socialista Obrero Español*/Spanish Socialist Workers Party.

[7] In paragraph 8 of his paper (see note 3 above) Mr. Wiggin recommended that HMG 'intensify [their] relations with people within the régime ready to work for change, e.g. by inviting them to the U.K.'. He added that, while Ministerial visits might not be practical politics before Gen. Franco went, there were 'plenty of radically-minded officials'.

[8] *V. ibid.* Mr. Wiggin suggested that 'it would be very valuable if more could be done in this area by way of e.g. visits, exchanges of staff courses, and if possible arms sales'.

Secretary of State has so far ruled out military contacts with Spain. It is impossible to deny the difficulties to which the Secretary of State draws attention, nor, on the other hand, the importance of the role that the military will play in Spain after Franco. Though the Secretary of State is surely right in saying that they are unlikely to emulate the military in Portugal, they will nevertheless have the last word on many important decisions, particularly the wide range of crucial matters, such as whether the Communists should be allowed to operate as a legal party, that will have a direct bearing on the maintenance of public order. Thus, while official contacts with the Spanish military will for the moment remain politically unacceptable, I believe that it is important for us to seek unofficial ways to build up our contacts. Specifically, I think it would be useful for Mr. Wiggin to make a point of cultivating the Spanish military. I also think it would be useful, and should not lead to unacceptable publicity in the United Kingdom, for senior British officers to visit Madrid ostensibly on private visits, and for Mr. Wiggin and members of his staff to take the opportunity to introduce them to members of the Spanish Armed Forces at informal dinners. This could be done at whatever level—Chief of Staff or far below—Mr. Wiggin thought most useful. I see no reason why it should not lead to similar informal contacts in London when Spanish officers happen to be holidaying here.[9]

10. Some leading members of the British Conservative Party are already making contacts in Spain on the lines recommended. It would be useful to encourage this.

Recommendation

11. I *recommend* that we should, for the moment, base our policies on Mr. Wiggin's suggestions, taking into account paragraphs 6, 7, and 8 above. Specifically, I *recommend* that we should:-

(*a*) seek the views of Mr. Wiggin and the MoD on the suggestion in paragraph 9 above, and if they agree act on it;

(*b*) continue to receive the democratic left when they visit London, but deal with members of the Junta Democrática individually rather than collectively;

(*c*) be prepared to accept as sponsored visitors radically-minded individuals, even if they are officials of the present régime; and

[9] On 16 July Mr. Morgan noted on this submission: 'The question of military contacts is delicate, but we are playing for high stakes in all this & to develop some contact with the Spanish military could turn out to be extremely valuable. I hope Ministers may not feel that their political difficulties absolutely rule out such discreet contacts as Mr. Goodison suggests.' Mr. Hattersley was, however, wholly opposed to the idea, 'partly because in covert operations of this kind the possible gains rarely outweigh the penalties of discovery' (minute from Mr. C.V. Anson (Assistant Private Secretary to Mr. Hattersley) to Mr. Goodison of 21 July).

(*d*) ask Mr. Wiggin to identify further likely equivalents for the Liberal and Conservative parties (paragraph 9 of his recommendations),[10] and then encourage them to build up links with his candidates.

12. I propose to inform Mr. Wiggin of the decisions taken on this submission, so that he can take them into account during his further exchanges with the Americans in Madrid, and to submit them again on any significant points that arise from further exchanges.[11]

A.C. GOODISON

[10] In this paragraph (see note 3 above) Mr. Wiggin suggested: 'It would be useful if the British Conservative and Liberal Parties could be encouraged to build up links with those who look like emerging as broadly their Spanish equivalents.'

[11] With the exception of those in paragraphs 9 and 11(*a*), Mr. Hattersley supported Mr. Goodison's recommendations. The submission and its attachments formed the basis of an Office meeting on 25 July when, with Mr. Hattersley's approval, it was agreed that they should be put to Mr. Callaghan after his summer break (letter from Mr. Baker to Mr. R.L. Wade-Gery (British Minister in Madrid) of 28 July).

No. 134

Mr. I.J.M. Sutherland[1] *(Moscow) to Mr. Callaghan*

No. 1026 Telegraphic [*WSP 2/5*]

Confidential   MOSCOW, *18 July 1975, 8.45 a.m.*

Repeated for information to Priority Lisbon, Washington, Routine UKDEL NATO, Paris, Bonn, Rome, The Hague, Madrid and UKREP Brussels.

Lisbon telegrams [Nos.] 409[2] and 425-27:[3]
Portuguese Political Crisis

1. The views reported in telegrams under reference assume that the Soviet Union is paying and directing the Portuguese Communist Party (PCP), who would not go further or faster than Moscow allows.

[1] Minister in the British Embassy, Moscow.

[2] No. 132.

[3] In these three telegrams of 16 July Mr. Trench reported on a conversation he had had that day with Dr. E. Rui Vilar, a former Minister of Economy, and on another which the Netherlands Ambassador had had on 15 June with Maj. V. Alves. Dr. Rui Vilar had told Mr. Trench that he thought that the Soviet Union and its allies would 'find it amazing if the West accepted a CSCE agreement now, when the communists were clearly trying to undermine the West in the Iberian Peninsula'. Maj. Alves had also suggested that 'the proposed Helsinki summit meeting would be very useful card to play'.

2. While we can take for granted that Moscow is paying the PCP and must assume that it can directly influence not only the PCP but probably also elements within the AFM, I know of no evidence that could be used to prove this incontrovertibly.[4]

3. In the absence of usable evidence, an attempt at this eleventh hour to make the Helsinki Summit dependent on Soviet undertakings about Portugal would almost certainly prove impracticable and might well be counter-productive: the West, unable to prove its case, would eventually have to climb down in the face of Soviet denials.

4. The Russians may have an interest in delaying too sharp [a] swing towards Communist control in Portugal for détente reasons especially until SALT II[5] has been concluded, which should be in the autumn: they will also fear adverse repercussions on other West European CP's[6] (para[graph] 6 below). But they must all the time be weighing the balance of advantage between achieving a communist bridgehead in Western Europe, with all its strategic and political implications, and the risk of preventing further successes for their détente policy. It is in our interest and that of our NATO Allies to make the Russians take the latter consideration as seriously as possible. If we do not try to do so, we shall not only be taking risks about Portugal: but also indicating to the Russians much more generally that we may lack the determination to resist Soviet moves to exploit internal situations in the West to shift the balance of power.

5. If attempts to use the Helsinki Summit are ruled out, we need to consider what alternatives exist. Approaches to the Russians by HMG, and others except USA, are unlikely to elicit a Soviet response, except perhaps the kind of denial that Kosygin gave you in February (Moscow telegram No. 1 to Lisbon of 14 February).[7] But the Americans have more leverage. Subject to events in Portugal, a possible move, as seen from here, might be for Kissinger to make a serious and private attempt to convince the Russians that a communist takeover in Portugal against the wishes of the majority of the population will place in question the major issues of US-Soviet relations.[8] This could be backed by public statements by the

---

[4] Already in a minute of 4 June Mr. Morgan had opined on developments in Portugal: 'We are lucky all this is happening in the period of détente. We have a convincing report from the Portuguese Ambassador in Roumania that the Communists did actually contemplate a coup before the elections, but found no support in Moscow or E. Europe for it & so desisted' (WSP 3/548/1)

[5] The second round of US/Soviet Strategic Arms Limitations Talks. See Volume III, No. 1, note 12.

[6] Communist Parties.

[7] See No. 121, note 10.

[8] But on 23 July Mr. Sonnenfeldt told Mr. J.O. Moreton (British Minister in Washington) that Americans were 'anxious to avoid raising false hopes over the extent to which they might be able to influence Russian actions in Portugal. Although the Soviet Union was certainly playing a role, there were many other factors at work.' Two days later Dr. Kissinger revealed at a press conference that he and President Ford had warned the Soviet Union that active

Americans and ourselves, and other Western speakers, at Helsinki and on other suitable occasions.[9]

6. One brake upon unqualified and open Soviet support for communist control is their general commitment to popular front tactics elsewhere in Europe. With the departure of the socialists and popular democrats from the Government in Lisbon, the interest which Moscow has had in preserving at least the façade of a multi-party front has evaporated. But they must be seriously concerned at reactions elsewhere particularly by the parties in Italy and France and amongst the electorates in these countries and possibly Greece, especially in advance of the meeting of the European Communist parties. One Soviet political theorist lately returned from Portugal (Rubinsky of IMEMO)[10] has maintained to me that the situation in Portugal is *sui generis* in that the AFM is now a truly revolutionary movement and that the pattern is Latin American rather than European. He added that the Italian and French parties would understand this. I doubt if they will, or indeed that the Russians really believe that they can divorce Portugal from their international party interests elsewhere in Europe. The Russians therefore should also take some heed of what is said by the left in Italy and France.

---

involvement in the political affairs of Portugal would 'violate the spirit of détente'. But he added that the Soviet Union could not be blamed for the current turmoil in Portugal which was due to Portugal's previous involvement in Africa and the unpopularity of the Caetano régime (Washington telegrams Nos. 2458 and 2497 of 23 and 25 July).

[9] Already at a European Council meeting on 16-17 July Mr. Wilson and President Giscard d'Estaing had agreed to take the lead in a joint approach to Mr. Brezhnev at the CSCE summit (planned for 30 July) on the situation in Portugal (see Volume II, No. 138, note 8). Sir J. Killick thought a senior Ministerial approach was definitely required. 'It is worth noting', he minuted Mr. Cartledge on 21 July, 'that, without seeking to indict the Russians, I have been banging on about Portugal, and underlining the implications for détente, for quite a while now [with East European diplomats] ... Not that it does a lot of good at my level.' He suggested that Mr. Wilson should include a passage on Portugal in his opening speech at the CSCE summit. Others, he thought, would 'be sure to follow his lead', whereas 'if he doesn't say something, it could have the wrong effect. But heaven knows what the situation will be on the ground in Lisbon by 30th July.'

[10] Mr. J.I. Rubinsky was a head of department in the *Instit Mirovoi Ekonomiki Mezhdunarodnykh Otnoshenii* (IMEMO)/Institute of World Economy and International Relations.

No. 135

Mr. Callaghan to Mr. Trench (Lisbon)

No. 337 Telegraphic [*WSP 1/1*]

Confidential   FCO, *25 July 1975, 11.00 a.m.*

Repeated for information to Immediate Washington, Moscow, UKDEL NATO, and to Priority Madrid, Paris, Bonn and The Hague.

Your tel[egram] No. 453:[1]
Political Crisis

1. Please seek an early opportunity to speak to Sn. Machado or Soares, to discuss their predicament in the light of your tel[egram]s [Nos.] 453, 446,[2] 445,[3] and 409.[4]

2. You should assure them that their difficulties will be in the forefront of our minds in the run-up to Stage III in Helsinki on 30 July, at Stage III itself and in its aftermath. We shall be doing our best to help them.

3. We greatly regret the events that led to their withdrawal, and that of the PPD from the Government, but fully understand why they felt compelled to resign. We hope that a new government will emerge, if not in the immediate future or in the first instance at any rate before long, that will contain adequate representation of the moderate elements in Portugal that represent the wishes of the people in Portugal. Their cause will continue to have our support, both bilaterally and in the Community.

4. The Prime Minister and I look forward to meeting Soares in Stockholm at the meeting called by Olof Palme for 2 August. For your own

---

[1] In this telegram of 23 July, Mr. Trench transmitted a request from Dr. Soares, passed that afternoon by his *Chef de Cabinet*, Sr. V. Sá Machado, to Mr. Ure, that Mr. Callaghan send 'an urgent message to Brezhnev or other Soviet leaders, making the Helsinki summit dependent on their desisting from encouraging a Communist takeover in Portugal'.

[2] Mr. Trench reported in this telegram of 23 July the latest public reaffirmation by the Socialists and the PPD of their refusal to serve in the Government.

[3] This telegram of 22 July recorded a clandestine meeting that evening between Sr. Sá Machado and Mr. Ure. 'The gist of his [Dr. Soares's] message', observed Mr. Trench, 'was that he expected a left-wing coup within the next few days, with the acquiescence, if not encouragement, of the President.' According to Sr. Sá Machado, Dr. Soares feared that an attempt would then be made (using the pretext of an alleged US-inspired 'reactionary plot') to arrest himself and his colleagues. He was determined not to be caught, and 'would start an uprising at whatever risk'. In the event of a civil war, Dr. Soares said he looked to HMG and the international labour movement for support, 'money and even arms'. Mr. Ure pointed out that 'intervention of this kind hardly seemed realistic in the present world conditions'. But while Mr. Trench considered Dr. Soares possibly 'unduly alarmist', he thought there was 'nothing inherently impossible in his story of a planned coup' especially in view of the numerous anti-communist incidents reported during the past few days.

[4] No. 132.

information we are considering asking Palme to announce the meeting soon.[5]

5. As regards the CSCE, a decision has of course been taken to hold Stage III from 30 July. We do not think that it would help the democratic parties in Portugal if the West were to try to put pressure on the Soviet Union by blocking Stage III. In particular we do not see how a link with Stage III could provide any guaranteed long-term effects in Portugal. Since the Portuguese Prime Minister is prepared to go to Helsinki, and in the absence of useable evidence of Soviet interference in Portugal,[6] we believe that to hold up Stage III would itself be seen as intervention in Portuguese internal affairs. Nor should we lose sight of the element of 'intervention' that could be alleged about the Stockholm meeting. One Western objective at the CSCE has been to acquire leverage with the Russians in exactly this sort of situation. For the West to refuse to go to Helsinki would not simply anger the Russians, but would also risk removing the constraint on their actions which we hope that the Conference will have provided and which we hope follow-up to it will continue to provide (e.g. when the Declaration of Principles has been signed). (For your own information it could well jeopardise our other interests in the process of détente.) There would be no guarantee that our action would have any positive effect on events in Portugal, and a risk that it might make matters worse.

6. You have, however, discretion to tell Soares that following discussion of the Portuguese situation at the European Heads of Government meeting in Brussels on 16/17 July the Prime Minister and Giscard agreed to take the lead in making a joint approach to Brezhnev at Helsinki.[7] We intend furthermore to make it clear bilaterally to the Russians that we shall regard developments in Portugal as a major test of Soviet good faith in accepting the commitments to be signed at Helsinki, and of the significance and value of the CSCE in promoting détente in Europe. In doing so, we shall have to be careful to avoid implying or uttering threats of consequences which we cannot carry out, and equally revealing to the Russians how far they can risk going (i.e. an approach to Moscow could do harm—para[graph] 5 of your tel[egram No.] 453).[8]

---

[5] Herr O.J. Palme, the Swedish Prime Minister, had called for a meeting European socialist leaders in Stockholm.

[6] Mr. Callaghan told the Cabinet on 24 July that there 'was no doubt that the Soviet Union was supplying substantial funds to the Portuguese Communist Party, so Mr. Brezhnev had it partly in his power to control the situation as evidence of his wish for genuine détente' (CC(75) 37th meeting held on 24 July),

[7] See No. 134, note 9, and Volume II, No. 138.

[8] See note 1 above. In paragraph 5, Mr. Trench wrote that he appreciated that HMG could produce no proof of Soviet meddling in Portuguese affairs and that matters in Portugal might well not be moving in a way which accorded with Soviet wishes. But, he added, 'it is difficult to believe that an approach to Moscow could do any harm, especially if made by several governments more or less simultaneously'. Mr. Sutherland was more cautious. In Moscow telegram No. 1056 of 26 July, he argued that to accuse Moscow and the Portuguese indigenous

7. We will also be making our views public, in whatever way seems most appropriate and likely to help. For your own information, this is an awkward question further complicated by the uncertainty about who on the Portuguese side will be at Helsinki. A decision may need to wait until nearer Stage III, when we have a clearer idea of the situation on the ground in Portugal.

8. We fully agree with you and your US colleague on the subject of extraordinary NATO manoeuvres.[9] You should tell Soares that we do not think that a show of force by NATO would be helpful. Indeed it might well prove to be counter-productive by laying the moderates in Portugal open to charge of association with the threat of foreign intervention. If he raises ships visits you could say that, similarly, an increase in the number of visits by NATO ships to Portuguese ports would provide the extremists with an excuse and greater opportunities for creating unpleasant incidents and for scaremongering. On the other hand we intend to keep up our normal rate of visiting on the principle of business as usual with our ally, except when (as now) periods of tensions could make visits counter-productive.

9. You should use the statement issued after the Heads of Government Meeting in Brussels on 16/17 July (UKREP Brussels tel[egram] No. 3519 of 17 July to FCO) to reply to Soares on the Community's attitude to Portugal.[10]

10. It was unfortunate that the visit by General Fabião due to start on 20 July had to be cancelled.[11] If conditions allow we intend to press ahead with trying to arrange a programme of visits by Portuguese leaders to the UK, in order to impress on them the value and relevance of a democratic system to Portugal.

11. You could draw as you feel appropriate on the PPD's analysis while speaking to Soares of [*sic*] Sá Machado. While it is not for us to tell Soares how to play his hand we agree with the PPD in considering that the AFM might have found it much easier to remove Gonzales [*sic*] if Soares had not felt obliged to call so publicly for his removal.[12] But Soares may well have

communists of 'interfering with and opposing the development of democracy of Portugal' would be counter-productive. 'Although incontestable, if put directly to Brezhnev it will', he wrote, 'surely provoke a tirade about democracy under Caetano, "rightist plots" and the principle of "non-interference in internal affairs"'(WSP 2/5).

[9] See No. 132.

[10] The text of this statement read: 'The European Council reaffirms that the European Community is willing to discuss closer economic and financial cooperation with Portugal. It also points out that the European Community–in accordance with its European policy and history to date–can only support a pluralist democracy' (WSP 6/598/1).

[11] Gen. Fabião's visit had been cancelled in the wake of July's political crisis in Lisbon (see No. 132, note 1).

[12] Dr. Soares called for Gen. Vasco Gonçalves's dismissal in a speech on 19 July. Four days later, Sr. A. Gouveia, who had close contacts with senior figures in the PPD, informed a member of Mr. Trench's staff that 'the general consensus in the PPD leadership was that

been forced into this by his supporters. We hope that Soares's short-term difficulties will not make him lose sight of the strength of his position in the country.[13]

Soares had made a tactical mistake by demanding the removal of Vasco Gonçalves': it had made the AFM close ranks round him and put more moderate members of the Council of the Revolution, who would have preferred to see the Prime Minister go, in a difficult position since they would wish to avoid siding openly with the Socialists. Sr. Gouveia believed that Gen. Vasco Gonçalves would be able, with difficulty, to form a government whose civilian members would be Communists, but he also indicated that the PPD leadership did not share the Socialists' fear of a communist-inspired wave of arrests (Lisbon telegram No. 450 of 23 July).

[13] Mr. Ure communicated the views expressed in this telegram to Sr. Sá Machado on the afternoon of 25 July (Lisbon telegram No. 465 of 25 July).

No. 136

Record of meeting between Mr. Wilson and the President Costa Gomes at the Finlandia Hall, Helsinki, on 1 August 1975 at 12.30 p.m.[1]

[*WSP 2/5*]

Confidential

Present:

The Prime Minister
The Foreign and Commonwealth Secretary
Mr. J.T.W. Haines
Mr. P.R.H. Wright
Mr. P.J. Weston

President Costa Gomez [*sic*]
Mr. S. Scadura Cabral, Deputy Director-General for Political Affairs, Ministry for Foreign Affairs
Mr. R.G. de Brito Ecunha, Chief of Protocol a.i.,[2] Ministry of Foreign Affairs

The *Prime Minister* said he was very glad to have an opportunity to meet the President. He had met the Portuguese Prime Minister at the NATO Council in Brussels and Major Antunes had visited London.[3] He spoke for the British Government and all the British people, together with Portugal's other friends, in saying that we were gravely disturbed by recent events in Portugal and the continuing march of events from day to day. We had

[1] Mr. Callaghan and President Costa Gomes had joined other European leaders in Helsinki for Stage III of the CSCE. See Volume II, Nos. 138 and 139.

[2] *ad interim.*

[3] See No. 131, note 4.

been heartened by the revolution 16 months ago. He trusted that the commitment that Portugal's leaders had given to pluralist democracy still held firm. We wanted to make clear our strong desire to give all the support and assistance we could toward the achievement of this commitment. The President would have seen the statement released by the European Council in Brussels on 16/17 July.[4] All the Nine had been unanimous in linking closer economic and financial cooperation between the EEC and Portugal with the development of a pluralist democracy in Portugal. The President would realise that the Community was not willing to finance a dictatorship of any kind. But we looked forward to a closer, and warmer, cooperative relationship with a Portugal moving on the path of democracy based on the people's choice in elections. The Council of Foreign Ministers had looked forward to seeing Major Antunes on 22 July, for they would have considered that meeting (as indeed the Prime Minister considered the present meeting) as to the advantage of Portugal, in the sense that it provided an opportunity for Portugal to explain internal developments to her allies and friends; the Prime Minister reminded the President that Britain was Portugal's oldest ally (having been such for 602 years). When Dr. Caetano was in London, he himself had protested strongly and had told the British Government of the day that they should cancel the arrangements for the invitation to Caetano.[5] The Prime Minister said he had been attacked for taking this line; as it so happened this was in the very week when the news had been received about the Wiriamu [*sic*] massacres in Mozambique.[6]

Both Portugal and the United Kingdom were not only friends and allies but also members of NATO. The President would be aware that Article 2 of the North Atlantic Treaty committed all members of the Alliance to democracy. We had been greatly encouraged by the beginnings of the revolution and the speed and determination with which decolonisation had been put into effect in Mozambique and Angola (as indeed the President had mentioned in his speech to the Conference that morning). But we were now gravely disturbed and would like to do all we could to help Portugal on the path to democracy. We were not concerned with who the leaders of Portugal were or which party or group they belonged to. That was for the Portuguese people to decide. But we were disturbed at the increasing signs that the freely expressed will of the Portuguese people was being rejected. He hoped that the President would be able to reassure not just him, but

[4] See No. 135, note 10.

[5] See Volume II, No. 138, note 12.

[6] On 10 July, 1973, *The Times* had published evidence from a Roman Catholic missionary group that, on 16 December 1972, Portuguese forces had attacked the Mozambique village of Wiriyamu, massacring over 400 of its inhabitants. *The Times*'s article led to pressure on the Conservative Government to cancel Dr. Caetano's official visit to London to mark the 600th anniversary of the Anglo-Portuguese alliance. In the event, the visit went ahead as planned on 16-18 July.

her other friends and allies in Helsinki about Portugal's intentions. He regretted having to speak so frankly but he considered the situation to be so serious that it was preferable to avoid disguising one's feelings in unclear language.

President Costa Gomez [*sic*] thanked the Prime Minister for his frankness. He had to say with equal frankness that the UK and her other allies in NATO or elsewhere in Europe were looking at the matter from a distorted point of view. There was no doubt that following the revolution on 25 April 1974 there had been a certain distortion and lack of balance in the social situation in Portugal. But it had not up to now reached a point where they were concerned that it might lead to violence. He had had the opportunity of stressing on a number of occasions, and indeed it was stated in the political and social action programme of the AFM and the Revolutionary Council, that Portugal intended to establish a pluralist socialist system where all individual liberties would be fully assured and protected. He knew that there had been criticism that the Portuguese mass media were dominated by a certain party. But in his opinion this was unfair, because he could say that the freedom of the press was so open and so full that in fact everyone could speak and criticise as they wanted. This had been one of the main motives of the revolution so far as decolonisation was concerned, because up till then the Portuguese press had not assisted in the normal process of democratisation. The freedom of the press in Portugal had indeed caused the régime some difficulties, e.g. in Angola, which they could have avoided if the press had been more directed and had not favoured one or other of the liberation movements in Angola. He knew that the majority of European countries were surprised because they had not reorganised or restructured the Government immediately after the first free elections in Portugal. He recalled, however, that the pact signed with the parties had established that the elections were only for the purpose of electing deputies to a constituent assembly and it was agreed that the Government would remain up to the time of legislative elections. Unfortunately inter-party fighting had taken the Portuguese Socialists out of the Government and they had been followed by the PDP. This had forced the leadership to choose another Government consisting of people who were not openly affiliated with political parties.[7]

---

[7] Following the meeting of the AFM Assembly on 25 July it was announced that the supreme direction of the revolution would henceforth be vested in a triumvirate composed of President Costa Gomes, the Prime Minister Gen. Vasco Gonçalves and Gen. Saraiva de Carvalho, and that the Council of the Revolution would henceforth have no more than a consultative status. Meanwhile, in his speech to the AFM Assembly President Costa Gomes acknowledged that the forces of revolution had outrun the sentiments of the majority of the population and urged a more cautious pace. But Mr. Trench saw little cause for optimism. 'On balance', he observed in Lisbon telegram No. 466 of 26 July, 'I see little comfort for Soares (and his democratic associates) in these latest developments. We have yet to see any evidence of Costa Gomes attempting to implement his own reasonable sentiments' (WSP 1/1).

On the Prime Minister's reference to dictatorship, he felt obliged to say very frankly that if they had had any interest in establishing a military dictatorship they would have done so on 25 April when they were backed by 90% of the country. But he himself and the great majority of members of the Revolutionary Council were opposed to the institution of any dictatorship, whether military or imposed by any party. They knew that they were going through a difficult moment because their economy was in recession. But he foresaw that if they could master the economic crisis they would be able to lead the Portuguese to the final aim of a pluralist socialism and thereby attain a political form where they would be able to remain both in NATO and in other organisations of which they were members. He had noticed that, possibly because the situation in Portugal had been seen from a particular angle, Europe and the Western world in particular had closed the door to Portugal in the economic field. Obviously this had produced certain effects on their economy, as he had told President Ford when he had visited the United States. He thought it would greatly improve the social situation in Portugal if her friends in the West had helped her at the right time.

The Prime Minister said that when he had met the Portuguese Prime Minister in Brussels, the latter had made very clear the grave economic problems which, as he put it, were due to the fact that under the dictatorship preceding the revolution Portugal had slipped back 50 years in development. He had talked with the Portuguese Prime Minister about the extensive land holdings in Portugal etc, and he fully recognised that there were problems. He would like to ask the President some questions. First, about the freedom of the press which the President had mentioned. What about the newspaper República, which was not being printed or read? Secondly, if what he himself had said to the President at this meeting had been said publicly, would the Portuguese press have printed it? The UK press often said nasty things about the British Prime Minister, because as a free press they were entitled to do so. Thirdly, when the President talked about social democracy did he mean that the Government would be chosen by the vote of the people? He himself had been beaten in 1970 by the Conservatives and had had to accept that. He had then won two elections in 1974. Did President Costa Gomez' [*sic*] definition mean a democracy where the party which gained a majority in the election could govern even without the approval of the present rulers?

President Costa Gomez [*sic*] said they had all regretted the República affair because what had at the start been a conflict between the workers and the management had turned into a conflict between the PSP and the workers. It was a complicated matter which had dragged on for a long time. On several occasions they had been on the verge of a solution but for ridiculous and incredibly futile reasons the problem had not been solved in the way they had wanted. What had finally happened had not pleased them, but at the time they thought it was the only solution which would obviate the need to resort to violence against the workers. It could not be denied that newspapers had their own political orientation and often had to give in to pressure from the workers. But there was no doubt that it was not the government or any official body which had limited the freedom of the press. He thought it would be necessary to pass legislation to make the newspapers and broadcasting more responsible. He had had contacts with all parties represented in the former government (amounting to 80% of the vote) and they had agreed that responsible people from the political parties and officials from the Ministry of Social Communications should study the problem thoroughly and put forward proposals for a solution. As for his ideas of democratic socialism he thought that as soon as legislative elections had taken place the winning party would be invited to form a Government by itself or in coalition (the *Prime Minister* interjected: invited by the President?) by the President. In the pact with the parties they had agreed that certain Ministries should be headed by military men, i.e. the Ministries of Defence, Interior and Information, and that this should be for a period of 3 years. *Mr. Callaghan* said he remembered the pact well. Would the Assembly meet in September and draw up a Constitution? Would it prepare elections? When would these take place? *President Costa Gomez* [*sic*] said the Assembly was even now at work on the specific task of elaborating the Constitution. It had been foreseen that it would take three months but they could be given an extra two months in case of need. It had also been agreed with the parties that the first elections after the promulgation of the Constitution would be for local Councils. After that they would have legislative elections and proceed to the election of a President of the Republic. *The Prime Minister* asked whether when he spoke of social democracy he meant socialism in the sense of a socialist like Dr. Soares (who had got the biggest vote) or in the Communist sense? *President Costa Gomez* [*sic*] said that in theory he meant democracy as seen by Soares but he had to say frankly that sometimes the leadership of the PSP had confused the people in the country a little with its speeches and statements and had got away from the very principles of the socialist party. *The Prime Minister* asked whether the AFM had the popular support of the country and if so how they knew that this was so. How had it been tested? *President Costa Gomez* [*sic*] said that on 25 April 1974 90% of the country had supported the AFM in the revolution. Today that support had obviously decreased, but he could say that a majority of the country were still with the revolution because of all the contacts between the military and people in the country. These proved that people still welcomed the military. He could say that they had made an important contribution in the social programme carried out by the AFM especially in the less developed rural areas. He was referring to new roads, new schools and the electrification of small villages, and other tasks e.g. in the health field which had assisted in ensuring that the AFM were welcomed by the rural population as they worked together in common. *Mr. Callaghan* said that nothing the Prime Minister had said called in question our basic position that the people of Portugal were free to choose their own Government. But we felt that the right of choice was not at present being demonstrated. *President Costa Gomez* [*sic*] said the Portuguese revolution had two parallel lines. There was the electoral line, which they used to get information in order to know exactly what the political tendencies were in the country. Then there was the revolutionary line by which they intended to establish a direct link between the AFM and the people, aimed at discovering deficiencies and identifying the aims and aspirations of the people. They would use that line to understand better what the country really wanted. They all thought that the two lines would ultimately converge and were not incompatible. One line had a political finality, the other a social finality. In conclusion *Mr. Callaghan* mentioned briefly labour unrest, lockouts and other problems which existed for firms in Portugal. *The Prime Minister* told the President he would like to write him a letter about this.

As the meeting ended, the *Prime Minister* said that the President had illustrated the two lines of the Portuguese revolution with his hands. The question was which hand would ultimately be round the people's throats?

The meeting ended at about 1 p.m.

No. 137

Minute from Mr. Hattersley to Mr. Callaghan

[*WSS 3/548/1*]

Confidential   FCO, *12 August 1975*

We have both been considering future British policy towards Spain with the end of the Franco era and the dispute between us and Spain over Gibraltar very much in mind.

2. You will recall that you agreed a submission in which it was suggested that whilst the future status of Gibraltar should be 'kept on the back boiler'[1] it was essential for a dialogue to begin between the two governments both to avoid criticism in the United Nations and to ensure that our relationship with the post-Franco Government was not prejudiced by our apparent obduracy over this issue.[2] This minute does not directly

---

[1] In the margin Mr. Callaghan queried Mr. Hattersley's metaphor, adding 'burner'.

[2] In this submission of 26 February to Mr. Morgan, Mr. Barrett accepted that there was little room for manœuvre. He also acknowledged the difficulties of reconstituting formal talks with Spain on the issue: they would inflame Gibraltarian suspicions whilst, with little prospect of success, their failure might only strengthen the position of the Spanish hard-liners. Nevertheless, Mr. Barrett advised that some form of dialogue with Madrid over Gibraltar was desirable. Such talks, even if low key, were, he contended, 'the best way of keeping the temperature down', both bilaterally and at the UN. Moreover, Gibraltar was also inextricably entwined with the domestic situation inside Spain. Those Spaniards who were moderates on the question of the Rock represented the 'more progressive elements' in Madrid, and it was, Mr. Barrett suggested, 'in our interest to see them strengthened; helpful talks would achieve this. Conversely, it would

concern the Gibraltar question but I am of course conscious that in all our dealings with Spain we have to bear in mind complications that arise because of the Gibraltar dispute. I am minuting you separately on our policy towards Gibraltar.[3]

3. Formally and publicly we are committed to keeping Spain at arms length until Franco goes. I have no doubt that that is right. But I am equally sure that we have to prepare ourselves to respond suitably to the new circumstances in Spain immediately Franco has gone. Officials believe that the government most likely to succeed Franco will be formally headed by Juan Carlos; that it will be authoritarian in character; that it will make some progress towards liberalisation of the régime; that its real intentions will not be articulated by its spokesmen who will need to overstate both the enthusiasm for liberalism and the determination to preserve the framework of the old order. Furthermore, the post-Franco régime will be heavily dependent on the support and the goodwill of the army.

4. Whilst that seems the most likely outcome of the turbulence that will follow Franco's death or resignation, there is obviously the possibility that the Communist Party will be able to so disrupt society and confuse the agencies of law and order that Juan Carlos and his supporters may not automatically succeed. There is even the likelihood of a 'popular' government being formed in which the Communist Party would once again have an interest disproportionate to their numerical support. Officials suggest that this is less likely in Spain than in Portugal because of Spain's comparative prosperity but there is growing evidence of increasing Communist activity. Wischnewski[4] told Sir Nicholas Henderson some weeks ago that there are 100,000 organised Communists in Spain. When I saw Wischnewski in Athens last month he told me that the Communist Party in Spain was 'very active and gaining more and more influence'. We have no real information how far it has infiltrated the army but we do know that it is doing its best to prepare for Franco's passing. The Spanish Social Democrats (USDE) who came to see me ten days ago expressed the same fear. My visitors did not represent the most energetic social democrats and they did nothing to assure me that they were in any position to combat or counteract the work the Communists were about to do.

not be to our advantage to give these elements the impression that our Gibraltar policy was irredeemably anti-Spanish and unconstructive' (WSB 3/548/1). See No. 113, note 4.

[3] Mr. Hattersley pressed in this minute of 15 August for consideration of Britain's general policy towards Gibraltar, observing: 'Whilst the Department argue persuasively that in the end it will in some way have to be linked with Spain, almost every individual decision that we take ties the Gibraltarians more closely to the UK and makes the achievement of the eventual solution more difficult.' A more cautious Mr. Callaghan noted on this minute: 'By all means re-examine it provided you do it *privately*, but don't forget the result of the last (Gibraltar) Referendum! LJC, 1/9.' In a referendum held in September 1967 Gibraltarians had voted almost unanimously in favour of remaining British.

[4] Herr H.-J. Wischnewski was Minister of State in the West German Foreign Ministry.

5. In this situation I wonder if we are right to stand so aloof from Spain. I am conscious that the only positive suggestion made in this area by the Department (holidays by British Service officers in Spain which might be used as an opportunity for contact between the British army and the Spanish armed forces) were severely criticised by me.[5] Whilst I do not retract my objections to that scheme I think it is worth at least examining whether we ought not to do all we can to prepare ourselves for what might happen after Franco's death. After Franco goes responsibility for law and order will fall upon the army and we ought to consider what sort of relationship we can build up with the Spanish armed forces. If a non-representative Communist Party tries to take politics into the streets it will be the army which has to resist them. Equally the move away from right wing authoritarianism towards a genuinely pluralistic democracy could only come about with army support. In short, the army seems likely to be crucially important during the early post-Franco days and I do not think we should allow ourselves to be isolated from any hope of influencing their attitude.[6]

6. At the moment there is a great deal of analysis going on in the Department and we are doing something to develop our contacts with various groups who may assume importance post-Franco. But we lack an overall plan of action. I would like to think that we had at least considered exactly and precisely what we should do immediately on Franco's death and how we should respond to a number of situations which might then result. It may be that the wisest course is to do little—though myself I doubt it. But if we are to adopt this course I think we should do so as a conscious act of policy rather than let it simply come about because we had not considered what our response should be. I think it also worthwhile at least considering whether or not we could make more extensive contact even before Franco's death. Clearly it is impossible to do or say anything which in any way endorses his régime. But I wonder if it is possible to make clear in advance that since everyone knows substantial changes in Spain are certain soon to come, we naturally want to encourage the democratic forces which seem likely to emerge after Franco goes and that in order to do so we are making official and quasi-official contacts of a sort we have not previously thought right.[7] I do not think that a suitably

[5] See No. 133, note 9.

[6] Mr. McNally minuted Mr. Hattersley on 5 August: 'Given the Portuguese experience I am attracted by the idea of contacts with the Spanish Army. I see the difficulties about formal invitations to the UK, but I am wondering whether such meetings could be arranged on "neutral territory", such as seminars in third countries, where we could ensure that the right British and Spanish Army officers met.' As Mr. Goodison later pointed out in a minute to Mr. Morgan of 15 September, Portuguese officers had been known to the British through their NATO links, yet, despite the potential importance of members of the military in Spain's future, the UK had as yet had only 'scanty contacts' with them.

[7] Mr. Baker nicely summarised the problem in the penultimate paragraph of his letter to Mr. Wade-Gery of 28 July (see No. 133, note 11). 'It may be', he ruminated, 'that if Spain becomes

worded public statement explaining that intention would cause intolerable resentment even in Franco's Spain. A recent letter from the Embassy in Madrid records that such open preparations are being made by Spanish politicians.[8]

7. I regard an open statement of our intention as an essential element in this plan as it would protect us from later ill-judged and ill-intended criticism. Our position would be made easier if the PSOE actually made it known that they would like the Government to make exploratory contacts. The PSOE Delegation to the Labour Party Conference might well be prepared to make the point publicly.

8. If you agree, I would like to consider with officials how we should prepare for and respond to the change in the Spanish regime that will follow Franco's death or retirement and let you have some suggestions.[9]

ROY HATTERSLEY

liberal enough to be really comfortable for us to embrace she will rapidly become too unstable to be much use, while if she remains stable she will not be very liberal (Portugal has reminded us how much easier it is to topple over from authoritarian right to totalitarian left than to achieve stable democracy after an authoritarian past ... Ministers may be willing in the lurid light of Portugal to give a post-Franco Spain that is moving pretty slowly the benefit of the doubt, and to establish early working relations in the hope of encouraging progress, rather than waiting to see how things go before committing themselves.'

[8] In a letter to Mr. Flower of 31 July, Mr. Wilkinson reported that, across the various supreme bodies of the state, main-stream Falangists were 'in the ascendant', and that 'the possibility that Juan Carlos may come to power and find virtually all the important political posts in the hands of men of that stamp is beginning to look increasingly strong', whilst Sr. Arias was 'beginning almost to look like a relic from an earlier political period' (WSS 1/1). On a minute from Mr. Flower of 15 August, Mr. Baker noted on 18 August: 'If Franco lingers on what we will be looking at is an elegant way of ignoring him'. Mr. Goodison added on 20 August: 'we have ignored Franco inelegantly for forty years. Though the Spaniards do not like it, we have nevertheless gone some way in their eyes to acquiring a prescriptive right to do so'.

[9] Mr. Callaghan noted on this minute: 'Pl go ahead. Are any Spaniards coming to Conference? We might see them there? LJC, 1/9'. The Labour Party held its party conference at Blackpool from 29 September to 3 October.

No. 138

Submission from Mr. Baker to Mr. Goodison

[*WSP 6/598/1*]

Confidential   FCO, *22 August 1975*

Problem

1. The Secretary of State has commented recently 'I think we must prepare for real and quick help to Portugal if the moderates win'.[1] How can we best give effect to this?

Background and Argument

2. There is a good chance that the Communists will lose a lot of their current power and their position at the centre of things in the near future and that the power they currently wield will be redistributed to less extreme revolutionaries[2] such as Crespo[3] and Antunes, though these leaders may well have to share it with others, such as Carvalho, whose unorthodox policies have extreme and authoritarian aspects that may provide the Communists with an opportunity to recoup much of what they are currently losing.

3. The democratic political parties, in particular the Socialist Party and the PPD, may well have a position in the new government, though it is perhaps unlikely that they will enjoy much power for the time being, and their long-term prospects of gaining it are not good, though not to be discounted.

4. Crespo repudiates the label 'moderate', not merely in public, and his views on Portugal and NATO are thoroughly uncomfortable.

---

[1] Minute of 15 August from Mr. P.J. Weston to SED.

[2] The announcement on 8 August of the formation of the fifth Provisional Government, had in Mr. Ure's words 'looked like a victory for Vasco Gonçalves'. He remained Prime Minister and all the new Ministers were either Communists or supporters of affiliated parties. But his authority had already been challenged by the publication on the previous evening of a letter to President Costa Gomes from Maj. de Melo Antunes and eight other senior figures in the AFM, complaining of the country's decline into 'anarchy' and rejecting the East European model for Portugal. The Triumvirate subsequently denounced the 'divisionism' of the document, and the nine signatories were suspended from the Supreme Council of the Revolution (Lisbon telegrams Nos. 506-08 of 8 August). The Communists were nonetheless forced on to the defensive, anti-Communist demonstrations continued in northern Portugal, the Melo Antunes group seemed close to agreement with Gen. Carvalho, and pressure mounted for the removal of the Prime Minister (Lisbon telegrams Nos. 537 and 538 of 21 and 22 August, WSP 1/1).

[3] Rear-Adm. V. Crespo, the former Commander of Portuguese forces in Mozambique, was one of the signatories of the open letter to President Costa Gomes (*v. ibid.*). But at a NATO luncheon on 12 August Rear-Adm. Crespo insisted that he was not a 'moderate' but a 'revolutionary', and stated that in his view it was 'not appropriate for Portugal to remain an active partner in the Alliance' (Lisbon telegram No. 518 of 12 August, WSP 1/1).

5. Antunes is sensible and solid, but probably keener, if it came to a choice, on the imposition of social justice than the introduction of electoral democracy.

6. Portugal could conceivably throw up a régime so democratic as to deserve our unstinted support. This is unlikely. If it occurred it would greatly increase the amount of money that it would be appropriate to provide, and we might well have great difficulty in meeting our share.

7. More likely is a régime which our interests would make us wish to support, but whose professed policies and actions would fall short of the degree of democracy that would make such support readily defensible to the electorates of Northern Europe. This difficulty will be partly lessened if Dr. Soares is included, since he will call loud and clear for unstinted financial support. But this brings us back to the problem of money.

8. We are too poor to do much ourselves. Logically, we should leave it to others to make the running. But our special links with Portugal lay a certain responsibility on us. We should therefore be ready to encourage our allies to help. The Germans and French are the key.

9. The Community must adopt a stance which has a helpful effect in Portugal, can readily be defended against the accusations, already being levelled by the Russians, that we are seeking to intervene inside Portugal, and encourages the Portuguese, but does not lead to exaggerated hopes.

Recommendation

10. I *recommend* that we should instruct HM Ambassadors in the capitals of the Nine to seek urgently the agreement of the governments to which they are accredited for the following policy.

11. (i) As soon as a new, more moderate, government emerges the Presidency should announce that the Council of Ministers are looking forward to resuming at an early date the dialogue with the Portuguese. Specifically, the Council of Ministers looks forward to the meeting with the Portuguese Foreign Minister which the Portuguese had to postpone.

(ii) At that meeting the Council of Ministers should make their position clear to the Portuguese, and it should be as follows. We have no wish to interfere in Portugal's internal affairs. But Portugal is our friend, neighbour and ally, and we wish to help the Portuguese to build a just and prosperous society. We recognise that Portugal may develop a form of democracy which is not identical to that in any of the Western European countries (which after all are all different). But the Community is a collection of electoral democracies and our electorates will not allow us to support a country which is not poverty stricken (like India) and not democratic. We are not taking a moral stand, but drawing Portugal's attention to a fact of life.

We have grave doubts about a 'direct democracy' which attempts to operate without secret ballots or seeks to bypass independent political parties. Nor do we believe that the military, in any country, have any particular right to hold sway unless the people grant them that right through a genuinely democratic process, including the exercise of choice in properly conducted secret ballots. (We make these points not through a wish to interfere, but because we want the Portuguese authorities to understand clearly the kind of considerations that our electorates will bring to bear on the question whether and to what extent they are willing to help Portugal).[4]

All of this said, we realise that, under the impact of the Communists, Portugal has wasted a year and a quarter, and cannot now build democracy in a day. We are ready to make available (say) 100 million units of accounts now, to be devoted to projects agreed by the Portuguese and the EIB. If events in Portugal continue to move in a direction that will enable us to defend to our electorates continuing help, we will give them continuing help.

We do not wish to exaggerate the amount of help we can give. It will be primarily up to the Portuguese to create the stable climate in which outside investment can be attracted and production can prosper. But if they help themselves we will do our best to help them.

(iii) The exact amount to be made available in the first instance could be as high as 200 million units of account if the régime is heading in a sufficiently democratic direction.

12. EID(E) and FRD[5] concur.[6]

---

[4] In a note of 26 August Sir J. Killick suggested the insertion here of the following additional paragraph: 'Apart from these political considerations, there is the important practical matter of the application of economic assistance. Aid from Governments or from the Community must demonstrably be seen to be put to effective use, and not vitiated at the receiving end. Of course, it is entirely for the Portuguese Government to decide how to organise and run its economy, but if aid is to flow from outside and be properly used the Portuguese side of the equation must be planned with this in mind. This is particularly so since Governmental and Community action can meet only a small fraction of the need; the main answer must come through private investment and the restoration of trade.'

[5] Financial Relations Department.

[6] Mr. Goodison also agreed with Mr. Baker's assessment and recommendations. He noted on 25 August: 'the only course we can take to provide help for a better Portuguese government is to move the Community to action, and that the measured action proposed by Mr. Baker is the most which the character of such a government is likely to make defensible. We should share these thoughts with our partners.' But Sir T. Brimelow was more sceptical, questioning whether the envisaged injection of funds into Portugal would really 'save the day and not merely be money down the drain' (annotated minute of 26 August). 'I have no confidence that it would save the day', replied Mr. Baker in a minute to Mr. Goodison of 27 August, 'but I am completely confident that in the circumstances envisaged it would be helpful ... and that to refuse to help would be harmful. I am equally confident that we would be in a position in which inaction would not be merely wrong but also very uncomfortable.' He added: 'The commodity bought would be time. Whether the Portuguese people would be able to use it to avoid tyranny is uncertain; the conclusion is not foregone.' In telegrams Nos. 434 and 435 to Bonn of 29 August Mr. Callaghan sought the views of the West German and other EC governments on the possibility of providing early economic aid to Portugal if the moderates came to power. He suggested that the Portuguese might be told that if there were in Portugal 'a government which the electorates of the EEC countries could regard as democratic and as well-

R.H. BAKER

disposed towards the development of cooperation with the EEC, Community help could and would be available' (WSP 6/598/1).

No. 139

Mr. Callaghan to Mr. Trench (Lisbon)

No. 397 Telegraphic [WSP 1/1]

Immediate. Secret   FCO, *26 August 1975, 12.45 p.m.*

Repeated for information to Washington, Bonn and The Hague.

Portugal: Internal Situation

Following from PUS

1. The Minister in the US Embassy, Spiers, called on me this morning on instructions to discuss the situation in Portugal. It was the view of the US Embassy in Lisbon and the State Department that the moderates['] momentum was being lost and that Western countries should take, [*sic*] immediately any action they could to strengthen the resolve of Costa Gomes to move things in a moderate direction. The US Government hoped that we would instruct you to reiterate to Costa Gomes the fact that aid from the Community would be dependent on pluralistic democracy,[1] and to make again to him the points made by the US Ambassador, Carlucci, when he saw him on 22 August.

2. The points made by Carlucci on 22 August were as follows:–

(*a*) Present analysis indicates that Portugal today is in the hands of a narrowly-based repressive group enjoying the support of only 20 per cent of the country and opposed by the remaining 80 per cent.

(*b*) Throughout the West the question therefore is being asked, 'Is Portugal really deserving of our support? Or is the Portuguese Government seeking Western financial aid to construct a society modelled along totalitarian communist lines?'

(*c*) Sooner or later these same questions also must be asked in NATO where the contradiction between Portugal's membership in the Alliance and its communist-influenced and narrowly-based Government will have to be faced.

(*d*) Unless Portugal embarks clearly on the road to a democratic form of government, and sets forth a clear programme to implement the original objectives of the revolution, the United States will not be able to justify

[1] See No. 138 and No. 140, note 6.

to its own people continued—much less expanded—support for Portugal of any kind.

(*e*) Noting the opinions Costa Gomes has expressed in public and private, we believe that he must recognise that his decisions can determine whether Portugal achieves its goal of a pluralistic, democratic kind of socialism.

3. Spiers stressed that Carlucci's contacts with the Melo Antunes group were strictly confidential and must be protected. The Melo Antunes group had urged that the United States should get the British, Federal German and Dutch Ambassadors to make immediate démarches to Costa Gomes supporting these points. US representatives in Bonn and The Hague would be speaking today on the same lines as Spiers.

4. An aide to Costa Gomes had told Carlucci that the President asked Gonçalves to resign on 23 August. Late on 25 August Gonçalves was apparently insisting that he should be made Chief of Staff of Armed Forces as compensation. This was completely unacceptable to the moderates. They are 'acutely conscious that the crunch point has come' and convinced that Allied démarches would strongly influence Costa Gomes, but to be effective the démarches must take place immediately.

5. In response to Costa Gomes' request for US help for evacuation and resettlement costs for Angolan refugees, Carlucci told him that the US would help but only if Gonçalves were not involved in any way: if the Government were to be helped it would have to be one with which they could work.

6. We told Spiers that we would need to consult the Secretary of State and this might not be easy, since he is holidaying in Ireland, and would also need to consult you first. We said that paragraph 2 would probably not cause much difficulty, apart from point (*c*). The Secretary of State might be reluctant to introduce this thought as a threat: we had consistently taken the line that it was tactically right to treat Portugal as a normal NATO ally as long as we possibly could.

7. We also commented that we should be telling Costa Gomes nothing that he did not know already. The Secretary of State might wish to be sure, before authorising a démarche, that Antunes and his colleagues had taken full account of the risks attached to a series of démarches, and the propaganda that could be made of them by their opponents, and had concluded that the advantages outweighed these risks. The precedents from the last series of démarches, in March, were not good. A series of démarches might increase Costa Gomes' wish to move, but lessen his ability to do so.

8. We showed Spiers your tel[egram] No. 539 describing your conversation with the President, commenting that Washington would no

doubt be informing the State Department.[2] Washington should also enquire whether the American approach has Kissinger's personal authority.[3]

9. We do not wish to omit any action which might promote democracy in Portugal. But we do not want to take the action proposed by the Americans if its effect is likely to be to strengthen the Communists' hands by an appearance of Western threats. Nor can we urge Costa Gomes to take action if he genuinely believes it will lead to an avoidable civil war. When you saw Costa Gomes on 22 August, you spoke well, and asked him the single most pertinent question, why he did not now remove Gonçalves.[4] But I believe that the Secretary of State will be anxious to keep in step with the Americans if at all possible, and inaction, even if it may be correct, is not comfortable.

10. The central question is whether three démarches on these lines would help or hinder.[5] On this you should consult your FRG, Dutch and US colleagues urgently, raising with Carlucci in particular the question whether Antunes has given full thought to the point in para[graph] 7 above.[6] If he does not know, Antunes should be asked by one of you.

11. It occurs to us that, if there are to be démarches, they should perhaps be represented as enquiries on the part of Portugal's allies, which might help lessen partly the adverse effects. But you will be able to judge whether this device (which Costa Gomes might at some point deny) is much use given the state of the media in Portugal.

[2] In this telegram of 22 August, Mr. Trench reported a conversation that morning with President Costa Gomes on the political situation in Portugal in general and differences within the AFM in particular. When pressed by Mr. Trench about what steps he would take to overcome the present crisis, President Costa Gomes replied 'that the key to his actions was his intention to avoid civil war at all costs', first by unifying the AFM and then by arranging a truce between the main political parties.

[3] In Washington telegram No. 2783 of 26 August Mr. Moreton confirmed 'that Kissinger was fully behind the proposal for a triple démarche though he had not approved the instructions *verbatim*'.

[4] Mr. Trench reported in his telegram No. 539 (see note 2 above) that in response to this question President Costa Gomes had 'admitted that the Prime Minister was a very controversial personality' and that, besides having lost the support of the AFM, he was opposed by both the Socialists and the PPD. 'The implication', Mr. Trench observed, 'was that the Prime Minister was indeed a liability in the present situation, but I could not induce the President to be more explicit.' Mr. Carlucci subsequently informed Mr. Trench that he had learned that the President had agreed to dismiss Gen. Vasco Gonçalves by 27 August.

[5] Mr. Baker doubted the value of the proposed démarches. Indeed, he thought that President Costa Gomes would already have removed Gen. Vasco Gonçalves, if he believed Maj. de Melo Antunes and Gen. Fabião able to enforce the decision. He admitted, however, that Maj. de Melo Antunes was 'on the spot' and had called for a démarche, and that in these circumstances HMG could not refuse it (minute to Mr. Goodison of 27 August, WSP 3/548/1).

[6] Mr. Trench confirmed, in Lisbon telegram No. 550 of 27 August, that the Mr. Carlucci had assured him that Maj. de Melo Antunes 'had taken fully into consideration' the points raised in paragraph 7 and 'had concluded that the advantages outweighed the risks'.

12. Grateful for your views by immediate telegram as soon as possible.[7]

[7] The Dutch and German Ambassadors in Lisbon were, according to Lisbon telegram No. 550 (*v. ibid.*), already on the point of making representations to President Costa Gomes regarding Gen. Vasco Gonçalves, and the French Ambassador told Mr. Trench that he too felt that the 'West should put maximum pressure on the President now'. But, following his conversation with President Costa Gomes on 22 August, Mr. Trench thought that to take 'a forceful line, similar to that of the Americans, would be a mistake given the limited extent of any contribution to economic aid for Portugal that [HMG were] likely to be able to make'.

Sir T. Brimelow agreed that 'it might be a mistake to take too hard a line with the President', particularly as it could enable Maj. de Melo Antunes's opponents to claim that the President was 'under such pressure from NATO/EEC Governments that he [was] no longer acting freely in the interests of his country'. Nevertheless, he considered that HMG had to respond to Maj. de Melo Antunes's request, and he instructed Mr. Trench to call on the President again to 'try as far as possible to support the points made by Carlucci', whilst tempering the language and omitting any reference to NATO membership (telegram No. 403 to Lisbon of 28 August). On the evening of 29 August, before Mr. Trench had the opportunity to carry out these instructions, it was announced that Gen. Vasco Gonçalves was to be replaced as Prime Minister by Adm. J.B. Pinheiro de Azevedo. In consequence, Mr. Trench confined his meeting with the President on the morning of 30 August to seeking further enlightenment on the situation as it had been developing (Lisbon telegram No. 561 of 30 August)

No. 140

Extract from Minute by Sir. J. Killick[1]

[WSP 3/303/1]

Confidential   FCO, *1 September 1975*

At short notice, the Soviet Chargé[2] invited me to a farewell lunch on Friday, 29 August. Contrary to my expectations, it turned out to be *à deux* and not a great gathering with speeches, etc. Semenov appeared genuinely to have no particular axes to grind and mercifully refrained for once from making propaganda points. We only had about an hour and I was not able to cover all the ground I would have wanted. (I was amused when he was called to the telephone in the middle to take a call from Moscow and was obviously very torn between the need to go to the phone and his evident wish not to leave me alone in the dining room. The call turned out to be about the IPU[3] delegation's programme, so he said.)

2. We opened with expressions of mutual esteem and some general talk about the nature of diplomacy. Semenov said he had learned two things from working with Yakov Malik:

[1] This minute was addressed to EESD and copied to SED. In October Sir J. Killick succeeded Sir E. Peck as UK Permanent Representative to NATO, Brussels.

[2] Mr. Semenov.

[3] Inter-Parliamentary Union.

(*a*) that things never work out as expected;

(*b*) that if there was ever a choice between taking action whose prospects were doubtful or speculative or doing nothing, inaction should always prevail.

I said I found this interesting but would certainly add the precept that no diplomat should ever tell a lie. I had throughout my career often been evasive or told a great deal less than the truth, but I had never told an untruth. [...][4]

Portugal

5. This said, I turned to Portugal, saying that in accordance with my own precept, I had been telling the full truth when Semenev had asked me the other day about the situation there.[5] I did indeed wish I knew. One thing was, however, very clear to me and I said this as a simple matter of fact and not as a British official on instructions. Developments in Portugal were most disturbing to British Ministers, whatever one might think the facts to be (and we would no doubt disagree about them).[6] There was no doubt that the impression which Portuguese events were making on Labour Party Ministers was beginning to raise the broader question of the future of détente.[7] They saw a situation in which the will of the Portuguese people,

[4] The next two paragraphs are omitted. They cover recent developments in the Middle East and UK-Soviet bilateral relations.

[5] During a conversation with Sir J. Killick on 26 August Mr. Semenov had enquired as to what was going on in Portugal. Sir J. Killick subsequently minuted to Miss S.J. Lambert (Western European Department (WED)) that he had replied, 'with complete sincerity, that I wished the hell I knew'.

[6] See No. 139, note 7. Initially, one of the main obstacles to the formation of a new administration under Adm. Pinheiro de Azevedo, was the opposition of the Socialists and the Melo Antunes group to the appointment of Gen. Vasco Gonçalves as Chief of Staff of the armed forces. As Mr. Trench pointed out in Lisbon telegram No. 563 of 30 August, if the Socialists refused to collaborate in the Government and combined forces with 'the nine' (the Melo Antunes group), they would have to face the prospect of a civil war. However, in a meeting with Sr. Sá Machado on the morning of 30 August, Mr. Trench and the Netherlands and US Ambassadors in Lisbon expressed their unanimous personal view 'that the time had come when the PS must make a stand, whatever the consequences'. If, they concluded, 'yet another compromise was attempted, especially accompanied by the transfer of Gonçalves to so vital a position as Chief of Staff of the Armed Forces, the chances of a truly democratic solution in Portugal would be virtually eliminated'. In telegram No. 407 to Lisbon of 1 September, Mr. Callaghan stated that he agreed generally with these conclusions.

[7] Mr. D.I. Miller of Research Department raised the issue of outside involvement in Portugal's domestic affairs in a minute of 20 August. After citing a Chinese description of the Americans and Russians quarrelling over Portugal 'like two dogs over a bone', he noted: 'Our own impression is that the Portuguese bone is remarkably devoid of alien toothmarks, whatever the allegations and counter-allegations of interference in Portugal's internal affairs (largely confined to statements about feeding PCP funds e.g. the "Shelepin cheque", and unspecified activities by the CIA).' Mr. Broomfield suggested two alternative interpretations of Soviet policy towards Portugal. In a letter to Mr. S.L.J. Wright (EESD) of 17 September, he argued that Soviet money for the PCP and the absence of concern in Soviet press comment until very late

expressed in free and fair elections, in the shape of a pluralistic democratic approach, was not being reflected in practice. Mário Soares, a fellow Socialist, was being called a counter-revolutionary and accused of aiding and abetting fascist reaction.

6. Semenov remarked that Mrs. Hart having visited Portugal, had expressed the opinion that fascist reaction was indeed the threat. Soares was not a 'proper Socialist'. I said that I doubted whether many of Mrs. Hart's colleagues would agree with her. We certainly did not discount the danger of counter-revolution and wanted the revolution to succeed. But the danger, and the risk of failure, would only be increased if the Portuguese people and the democratic politicians for whom they had expressed support were frustrated.

7. Semenov pointed out that the political parties had agreed with the AFM before the election that its purpose was solely to create a Constituent Assembly and not a Parliament or Government. I acknowledged this, but pointed out that the role and power of the Constituent Assembly had been severely curtailed and that the AFM, with Communist support and participation, were showing every sign of intending to continue arbitrary rule indefinitely. In this they were themselves divided, but those elements which disagreed with the present course were also being pushed out.

8. Semenov said that the Portuguese Communist Party had all along offered dialogue and cooperation to the other parties. I said that this was true, but that I could well understand Soares's hesitation over embarking on a course in which the dice seemed to be loaded against him. What about his proposal for eight-sided talks among the Communist and Socialist Parties of Portugal, Spain, Italy and France? Semenov said that the situation in Portugal was nothing to do with outside parties. I said that I did not share this view. They, like we, were watching developments with close concern. In this respect, the Zarodov article in Pravda was surely relevant. No doubt he would say that the article was of no significance, but what was significant to me was the reaction to it of the Communist Parties in Spain, Italy and France.[8] Semenov said the article was indeed not only of no particular significance, but it had been seriously misinterpreted.

---

in the day might imply Soviet approval of 'Cunhal's activism'. But, he added, one could also 'postulate that the Russians all along were privately urging moderation on Cunhal, in the interests inter alia of détente and Berlinguer [Secretary of the Italian Communist Party], while publicly appearing to be at one with the PCP, so that the latter could not blame Moscow later for advocating gradualism when a total take-over might have been achieved'. The Soviet role in Portugal was, he concluded, 'important, both in understanding Portugal and in forecasting Soviet tactics if communist opportunities occur in other Western countries. In particular, if the Russians first whipped Cunhal on and later reined him in, the Western representations to the Russians may have had some effect and should be repeated if similar situations arise again.'

[8] In an article, published in *Pravda* on 6 August, Mr. K.I. Zarodov criticised Communist parties abroad which were prepared to 'dissolve' themselves in alliances with Social Democrats. See Volume III, No. 81, particularly notes 6 and 8.

9. He finally showed great interest in whether Soares had recently visited this country. I said that so far as I knew our last contact with him had been at the meeting of Social Democratic leaders in Stockholm following the Helsinki summit. Mr. Callaghan had not even met him during the May meetings of OECD, etc in Paris.

10. Finally, Semenov enquired whether we had yet asked for *agrément* for a new Ambassador in Moscow. I said, genuinely, that I did not know. Semenov was clearly aware that it is to be Mr. Howard Smith, and I made no attempt to deny this.[9]

JOHN KILLICK

[9] Mr. H.F.T. Smith was appointed British Ambassador to the Soviet Union in January 1976. He was subsequently appointed KCMG.

No. 141

Mr. Callaghan to HM Representatives Overseas

Guidance No. *159 Telegraphic* [*WSP 1/1*]

Confidential   FCO, *7 October 1975*

Developments in Portugal

1. The situation in Portugal has changed rapidly and radically in recent months. The Sixth Provisional Government, which took office on 19 September, marks the first notable reversal of the previous trend towards domination by the Communists and others on the extreme left.[1] This is, therefore, an appropriate time to take stock of developments and give you some indication of current British policy towards Portugal.

2. The following analysis of the situation may be used with reliable contacts; and unattributably at your own discretion. Paragraphs 11 to 17 on British policy towards Portugal may be drawn on freely.

3. In September 1974 President Spínola tried to halt any further drift to the left in Portugal and called for a march by the 'Silent Majority'. Street barricades were erected and there was virtual mob control of Lisbon for a day and a half by those who were opposed to the march. President Spínola discovered he did not have the support of the Armed Forces Movement (AFM) in his stand and resigned.[2] He was replaced as President by General

[1] The new Government of National Unity, headed by Adm. Pinheiro de Azevedo, could, as Mr. Trench claimed in Lisbon telegram No. 626 of 20 September, be represented as a success for the Socialists as they had achieved their objective of having the distribution of Ministerial portfolios more or less proportional the to the April election results.

[2] See No. 110.

Costa Gomes, Chief of the Defence Staff. Colonel (now General) Gonçalves continued as Prime Minister and the previous Government survived with a more left-wing and military emphasis.

4. On 11 March 1975, at a moment when the moderates were beginning to assert themselves with some success, there was an attempted right-wing coup, the circumstances of which have never been fully explained.[3] Following this, Spínola fled to Spain and thence to Brazil. The AFM also dissolved their existing political structures (which included civilian representatives on the 'Junta of National Salvation') and set up in their place a single body, the Supreme Revolutionary Council, based entirely on the military, which was to exercise all legislative and executive power. Gonçalves and his allies tightened their grip, and reconstituted the Government, and Dr. Soares (the Socialist leader) was moved from the position of Foreign Minister to be a Minister without Portfolio.

5. In the elections for a Constituent Assembly on 25 April there was a turn-out of 92% and the results showed an overwhelming victory for the democratic parties. (Results were: Portuguese Socialist party 37.8%: Popular Democratic Party 26.38%: Social Democratic Centre 7.65%: Portuguese Communist Party 12.53%: Portuguese Democratic Movement 4.12%: Others 4.53%). Prior to the election, however, the political parties had been forced to sign a constitutional pact, the important points of which were that the new constitution would be drawn up in conjunction with the AFM, and that during a transitional period of three to five years effective political power and direction of policy would remain with the AFM and its organs.

6. On 11 July, following a decision by the AFM General Assembly to support the establishment of Radical Populism, Dr. Soares and the Socialist Ministers withdrew from the Fourth Provisional Government.[4] The question of the freedom of the media had been a central issue for some time. The Socialists had been deprived of control of their newspaper 'República' and the Catholic Church of its radio station 'Radio Renascensca'. The Popular Democrat Ministers followed the Socialists out of the Government, which was dissolved on 17 July. A ruling Triumvirate consisting of President Costa Gomes and Generals Gonçalves and Carvalho (the latter being the Commander of Copcon, the internal security force) was announced on 26 July and was entrusted with the 'supreme direction of the Revolution'.

7. General Gonçalves finally managed to form another Government—The Fifth Provisional—which was announced on 8 August and consisted of radical technocrats and military officers. But internal disagreements in the AFM grew and came increasingly into the open. Three groups could be identified: Prime Minister Gonçalves and the pro-Communist faction: the 'moderates', (the Antunes Group), who believe that Portugal should ultimately become a socialist society but with full

[3] See No. 115.
[4] See No. 135.

democratic freedoms: and the radical populists associated with General Carvalho, who believe in a grass-roots, workers' committee, form of Socialist rule. Pressure from the 'moderates' and from the Socialist Party, together with widespread anti-Communist demonstrations in Northern Portugal, increased pressure on Gonçalves.

8. After much debate in the AFM, it was announced on 29 August that General Gonçalves would be replaced as Prime Minister by Admiral Azevedo, Chief of Staff of the Navy. Gonçalves was to become Chief of Staff of the Armed Forces, a position held by President Costa Gomes, but this was opposed by the 'moderates' and others. The 'moderates' rallied support particularly in the Army and the Air Force, and Gonçalves was forced to decline his new post on 5 September. He was also removed from the Supreme Revolutionary Council. The Fifth Provisional Government resigned at the same time.

9. After hard bargaining, particularly between the three main political parties, the Sixth Provisional Government, under Admiral Azevedo, took office on 19 September. In addition to representatives of the AFM, three of whom (Major Antunes who returns as Foreign Minister, Major Alves and Rear-Admiral Crespo) are leaders of the 'moderates', and independent technocrats, the new Government also contains members of the three political parties that obtained most votes in the elections for the Constituent Assembly last April. The distribution of the portfolios to those parties reflects the support they obtained in those elections. Thus there are four Socialist Ministers, two Popular Democrats and one Communist. The distribution of the posts of Secretaries of State (Junior Ministers) has followed the same lines. In addition to emphasising the importance of establishing their own authority in the country, the new Government's programme lays stress on the importance of democratic freedoms. It pledges, for example, to ensure democratic practices in trade unions, pluralism in the media and the replacement of unrepresentative local authorities. It also refers to the importance of strengthening relations with the EEC and EFTA.[5] The Prime Minister has declared that the aim is socialism, not social democracy.

10. In the coming weeks the priority tasks of the new Government will be to consolidate their authority and to begin to tackle Portugal's severe economic problems.[6] Another essential, and difficult, task will be the

[5] European Free Trade Association.

[6] During a meeting with Mr. Trench on 25 September, Maj. de Melo Antunes, who had been re-appointed Foreign Minister, insisted that Portugal was 'at a turning point'. 'Everything', he said, 'now depended on a solution, as rapidly as possible, of the economic problem—in terms of the living standards of the man in the street as well as in the general sense. It was therefore essential that the friends of a democratic Portugal should come to the country's help as rapidly as possible' (Lisbon telegram No. 633 of 25 September).

restoration of discipline in the armed forces.[7] The Government may well be helped in these tasks by the fact that the Supreme Revolutionary Council of the AFM has been re-constituted and its composition now favours the 'moderates'. The formation of a new 'intervention group' (additional to COPCON) and the military occupation of radio and TV stations show the determination of Portugal's leaders to establish their authority and end instability in the country. But they are already running into trouble with extreme left wing opposition in some military units and in the populace. The outlook is still uncertain.

HMG's Policy Towards Portugal

11. HMG's policy has been, and remains, to foster the development of democracy in Portugal. Our bilateral technical assistance programme and any European Community aid to Portugal should be seen in this context.

12. We have tried to promote contacts with political and military leaders in Portugal whereby we can explain our view of the importance and relevance of democratic freedoms. The Secretary of State paid an official visit to Portugal from 6-7 February 1975; the Chief of Defence Staff paid a brief visit to Lisbon at the end of April where he saw Portuguese leaders; Mr. Ron Hayward, General Secretary of the Labour Party, was there for a Socialist Conference early in July. Prominent Portuguese visitors to the UK in 1975 have included the former Labour Minister, Major Martins, in March, Foreign Minister Major Antunes in June, and former Ambassador-at-large Major Alves in early July. The Portuguese Chief of Army Staff, General Fabião, was due to visit Britain in July but had to cancel because of the Government crisis in Portugal.[8] It is hoped to reinstate this visit. Dr. Soares visited Britain earlier this month for the meeting of Socialist leaders held on 5 September at No 10 to discuss Portugal, and again to attend the Labour Party Conference in Blackpool.

13. Following the Secretary of State's visit in February it was decided to establish a modest technical assistance programme to Portugal. An ODM mission to Lisbon in June established with the Portuguese that the main areas of interest were public health, management training, highway development, fisheries (especially pollution), planning, renewable natural resources, and social development. Exchanges of experts in some of the above fields are taking place and others are planned. The Portuguese have also nominated some candidates for training in the UK and we expect others to be nominated in due course.

14. In addition, HMG have provided one RAF vc10 for the months of September and October to help in the Portuguese airlift from Angola.

---

[7] There were, Maj. de Melo Antunes told Mr. Trench, 'grave difficulties over discipline, both military and social, and in getting the people to understand how the democratic system should work' (*v. ibid.*).

[8] See No. 135, note 11.

15. The European Community attitude towards Portugal was set out in the following statement after a meeting of the European Council on 16/17 July:

'The European Council reaffirms that the European Community is willing to discuss closer economic and financial cooperation with Portugal. It also points out that the European Community—in accordance with its European policy and history to date—can only support a pluralist democracy.'

Urgent discussions are now taking place within the Community about aid to Portugal, and the Foreign Minister, Major Antues, is to meet members of the Council of Ministers on 7 October.

16. Portugal's leaders have reaffirmed the country's continued respect for international obligations and treaties, including NATO. We welcome this.

17. HMG have welcomed the new (Sixth) Government in Portugal which reflects popular opinion to a much greater degree than before, and whose composition and programme offer firmer grounds for hopes that Portugal will now attain a period of greater stability. This is essential to free Portuguese energies to tackle the daunting problems facing the country, particularly in the economic field, and to allow progress along the road towards democracy.[9] HMG do not underestimate the magnitude of these problems.[10] We shall continue to offer what help we can, without, of course, interfering in Portugal's internal affairs.[11]

---

[9] In a despatch of 17 September commenting on the fall on Gen. Vasco Gonçalves, Mr. Trench speculated 'the future looks as uncertain as ever'. He added: 'The coalition which combined to oust Gonçalves are agreed on relatively little else but that they prefer the democratic option. That was the main feature of General Spínola's first government in May 1974, and, as we have seen, the cement was too weak.'

[10] Mr. Trench reported in his despatch of 17 September (*v. ibid.*) that although it was 'generally agreed that the dangers of a Communist takeover by stealth' had been averted, there remained 'the possibility that they [would] try to achieve by force what they [had] failed to win by legitimate (or quasi-legitimate) means'. With this Mr. Goodison evidently agreed. In a letter to Mr. Trench of 6 October he reasoned that Portugal's future would hinge on the restoration of discipline in the army, the 'wresting of control of the unions away from the Communists', and putting an end to the communist control of the media.

[11] In his letter to Mr. Trench of 6 October (*v. ibid.*) Mr. Goodison observed: 'I sympathize with your strictures on the Portuguese tendency to go for consensus at any price, even the price of total inactivity and the breakdown of government. But I suppose that it is partly due to this tendency that there has been so little bloodshed so far. It can perhaps also be said in their defence that time has been bought, at a very heavy price in economic and political chaos, in which there has finally emerged in the AFM a consensus on the need to give the Portuguese people roughly what they have asked for.'

No. 142

Sir J. Killick (UKDEL NATO) to Mr. Callaghan

No. 481 Telegraphic [WSS 3/548/1]

Secret   BRUSSELS, *7 November 1975, 4.45 p.m.*

NATO consultation on Spain

1. At US instigation the Secretary General today called a private meeting of Permanent Representatives to discuss the Spanish situation. Luns recalled that the Allies had in the past had differing views about how best to bring Spain into the mainstream of Western political, economic and defence affairs. The time now seemed right to being [*sic*] a confidential exchange of views and information on the subject.[1]

2. Streator[2] (US) then made a statement. The basic US objective was to strengthen political and security relationships with a Spain more closely linked to the Atlantic community. The US favoured a gradual evolution towards a pluralist society and while not favouring any particular party, believed that a future Spanish Government was likely to follow a conservative line. Communist participation in government would be undesirable. The US hoped that continued US-Spanish co-operation in many fields would help the Spaniards in the transition by playing a stabilising role. The US would counsel against hasty changes which might risk severe reaction. In contact with Spaniards, including the military, US sympathy over the delicate problem of political liberalisation would be made clear, but nevertheless the US would urge the necessity of gradual liberalisation. She would keep in touch with all democratic opposition parties and hope that they would take a full part in the process of transition and be realistic in not seeking sweeping changes. The US hoped that the European leaders would adopt a similar gradualist approach to their relations with Spain rather than hold back in the hope that full parliamentary democracy could be instituted soon. Streator also urged that the Europeans should take part in Franco's funeral and in Juan Carlos' investiture in such a way as to avoid recrimination about the past and to offer encouragement for the future. The US hoped that today's meeting would be part of a continuing quiet process of exchange of views and information. Streator also spoke of the new general framework agreement on US bases in Spain. (For details see MIFT.)[3] Its main purposes had been

---

[1] During October Gen. Franco suffered a series of heart attacks. On 26 October medical bulletins admitted for the first time that he was seriously ill, and on 30 October Prince Juan Carlos assumed the functions of Head of State.

[2] Mr. E.J. Streator was US Deputy Permanent Representative to NATO.

[3] According to this telegram of 7 November, Mr. Streator recalled a press statement of 4 October that general agreement had been reached between the US and Spain. US-Spanish

to preserve a useful defence relationship and to serve as a supportive framework for a post-Franco government.

3. Emphasising that I was without instructions but in the belief that I was reflecting HMG's general views, I said that you would probably agree with many of the basic considerations in US thinking. In particular HMG would certainly wish to encourage democratic development and avoid the danger of communism. But I saw important differences on timing and tactics. I recalled what the Prime Minister had said at the spring NATO Heads of Government meeting in particular that an essential pre-condition for a closer Alliance relationship with Spain was the fulfilment by the Spanish Government of the objectives in Article 2 of the North Atlantic Treaty and paragraph 12 of the Ottawa Declaration.[4] The disappearance of Franco made these objectives attainable but was unlikely to achieve them overnight, for the reasons Streator had given.[5] There was also the problem of Gibraltar, which would be no less difficult for us with a new régime.[6] Serious consideration had, I knew been given in London to contacts with democratic elements in Spain but the domestic political problems facing HMG on this issue should not be underestimated. The executions had increased them.[7] Any special gesture in connexion with the funeral/accession was, I believed, ruled out, and might well be counter-

defence cooperation was, he said, 'based on the belief that Spain should be admitted to NATO' and that it was 'important to encourage the Spanish Government to think in terms of a Western defence framework'. The preamble of the framework agreement therefore recognised *inter alia* the part Spain played in the security arrangements of the north Atlantic area and the Mediterranean. A further supplemental agreement was to cover US bases in Spain.

[4] See No. 130, note 5.

[5] In a letter of 11 November Mr. R.A. Hibbert (AUS) advised Sir J. Killick that HMG hoped to be able 'to make a positive contribution to a satisfactory evolution of events in Spain' by: (1) speeches displaying sympathetic interest in, and encouragement to, the Spanish nation and the new régime in any moves to liberalise or reform; (2) working for closer ties between Spain and Western organisations; (3) visits in both directions; (4) encouraging contacts between British political parties and Spanish political groups; and (5) encouraging other contacts (WSS 1/2).

[6] Talks on Gibraltar were held in Madrid on 9-11 September, following contacts between Mr. Wiggin and Sr. N. Aguirre de Carcer, the Director-General for European Affairs in the Spanish Foreign Ministry, with a view to settling the terms of reference for further possible conversations (WSB 3/548/1).

[7] Following the murder by terrorists of nine Spanish policemen, the authorities in Madrid took swift retaliatory action. Anti-terrorist legislation was introduced by decree, providing for trial by court marshal of anyone accused of killing a policeman and a mandatory death sentence for those convicted. On 18 September eleven members of ETA and the Maoist organisation FRAP (*Frente Revolucionario Antifacista y Patriotica*) were tried and condemned to death. Gen. Franco confirmed the death sentence on five of these, and the executions were carried out on 27 September. This provoked widespread international criticism of Spain, and EC Ambassadors were temporarily withdrawn from Madrid for consultations. In a letter of 8 October to Sr. Arias Navarro, the Prime Minister expressed HMG's hope that in meeting the threat of violence the Spanish Government would be able 'to give full weight to humanitarian considerations and to the principles of human rights, in particular the right to a fair and public hearing and the guarantees necessary for the defence of those charged' (WSS 1/7).

productive because of reactions in Britain.[8] Personally I thought each ally should develop its relations with a new Spain separately and at its own pace, with continuing discreet exchanges of views and information. The Alliance as a whole should not for the foreseeable future be involved, and the question must not be put on its agenda. In this sense, I took note gratefully of Steator's information about the US-Spanish agreement, and in particular his point that it did not affect Spain's relations with the Alliance or its members, but would make no further comment.[9]

4. The Norwegian, Danish, Dutch, Greek and Italian representatives also spoke in favour of caution in dealings with a new Spanish Government and thought their own Governments were likely to adopt an attitude of wait and see. De la Ferrière[10] (France) recalled that his own Government had already demonstrated the importance it attached to bringing Spain into the democratic community. He felt, however, that it would be well to leave Spain largely alone for a period after the disappearance of Franco so that she could decide for herself how to go forward. During that period any outside interventions should be very carefully judged. But France would be ready to take part in consultation at NATO or other fora. Krapf[11] (FRG) said that the Association of European Social Democratic and Christian Democratic Parties under their respective chairmen Herr Brandt and Signor Forlani[12] were already getting together with a view to sinking their own political differences in order to help their Spanish opposite numbers resist a possible communist advance. (Krapf requested that this information should be treated with particular discretion.)

5. As regards representation at Franco's funeral, my Netherlands, Norwegian and Danish colleagues made clear that no higher level of representation than Ambassadors in Madrid was likely. Bacon[13] (Canada) spoke similarly but indicated that the Canadians were still considering whether a different level of representation would be appropriate at Juan Carlos' investiture. De Staercke (Belgium) said that Alliance Ambassadors should consult on the spot in Madrid about this aspect. I should be grateful

---

[8] Mr. Hibbert informed Sir J. Killick in his letter of 11 November (see note 5 above) that the FCO expected HMG to be represented at Gen. Franco's funeral by a Cabinet Minister and the Queen by the Ambassador. They hoped that the accession ceremony could be treated as a State occasion and that it would turn out to be appropriate for a member of the Royal Family to attend.

[9] But in a minute to Mr. Callaghan of 6 November Mr. Hattersley argued: 'It is obviously in the interest of the Western Alliance that everything is done to bring Spain into a close relationship. That is true whether the alternative to incipient democracy is a Communist backed Government, political confusion or an indefinite continuation of a quasi-Fascist regime. For the sake of Spain and Europe we need to make the best of whatever hopeful signs emerge.'

[10] M. J.G. de la Ferrière was French Deputy Permanent Representative to NATO.

[11] Herr F. Krapf was West German Permanent Representative to NATO.

[12] Sig. A. Forlani was Italian Minister of Defence.

[13] Mr. T.C. Bacon was Canadian Deputy Permanent Representative to NATO.

for confirmation that no special representative will attend on behalf of HMG.

6. All concerned laid great emphasis on the need to keep not the substance but the fact of NATO consultation on what is for many allies a sensitive domestic political issue highly confidential. It was therefore agreed that the next discussion of Spain should take place at the Permanent Representatives lunch (Ambassadors only) on 12 November.[14] Streator indicated, however, that the US Ambassador was taking a parallel initiative with Allied Ambassadors in Madrid.

[14] During this discussion Sir J. Killick drew briefly on Mr. Hibbert's letter of 11 November (see notes 6 and 9 above). Dr. Luns confirmed that direct exchanges would continue on the matter (UKDEL NATO telegram No. 489 of 13 November, WSS 1/2).

No. 143

Letter from Mr. Hibbert to Mr. Wiggin (Madrid)

[*WSS 3/548/1*]

Confidential

FCO, *1 December 1975*

Dear Charles,

Policy towards Spain[1]

In recent months considerable thought has been given to the policy HMG might adopt towards Spain in the post-Franco era.[2] In this process the analysis and recommendations put forward by you and your American colleague and enclosed in your letter of 9 September were very helpful.[3]

2. Much will have to be decided from day to day in the light of what the new régime says and does, but Ministers have expressed themselves in principle in favour of the approach set out below.

3. The period in which we now find ourselves following General Franco's death is likely to be confused and difficult in the extreme. It will be important to encourage as far as possible those Spaniards who wish

[1] A draft of this letter was submitted to Mr. Hibbert under a covering minute from Mr. Goodison of 21 November. An abbreviated version was conveyed to President Ford as a personal message from Mr. Wilson (telegram No. 2644 to Washington of 22 December).

[2] Gen. Franco died during the early hours of 20 November, and two days later Prince Juan Carlos was proclaimed King by the Spanish *Cortes*.

[3] Mr. Wiggin concluded his discussions with Mr. Stabler on 30 August. The 'final' versions of the two joint papers on the current situation in Spain and future policy resembled closely the British Embassy drafts of mid-July (see No. 133, notes 2, 3, 7, 8 and 10). The only substantive difference between the British and the American approach was Mr. Wiggin's reluctance to exclude eventual contacts with the Spanish Communist Party, if it 'came to play a major role within a future system' (letter from Mr. Wiggin to Mr. Goodison of 9 September).

Spain to move in a liberal direction and towards the rest of Europe. If the new Spanish Government is seen to be moving generally in the right direction it may prove to be appropriate to give them the benefit of the doubt if they make a slow start in some respects. But giving them the benefit of the doubt is likely to take the form of welcoming specific encouraging signs rather than declaring broad approval for the new régime. It cannot expect a blank cheque. In other words there will have to be some encouraging signs from Spain before there can be encouraging words from Britain.

4. The central difficulty will be how to deal with pressure whether from within Spain or without either to withhold words of welcome when advances in Spain fall short of expectation or to over-react to initial acts by the King which are cosmetic rather than substantial. It has to be recognised, even if it cannot be put bluntly in public, that King Juan Carlos has a very hard row to hoe, and that he will not achieve anything unless he steers a course which, while disappointing everybody, disappoints nobody more than they can bear. Ministers will want to give careful consideration to the way they react to initial policy pronouncements by the King and his government.[4]

5. Tactics will clearly have to be chosen with care in order not to offend Spanish pride by appearing to patronize or interfere in their domestic affairs. As far as possible any appearance of taking sides among the all too many political groups should be avoided.

6. It should nevertheless be possible to make a positive contribution to satisfactory developments by:

(i) speeches displaying sympathetic interest, and encouragement to the Spanish nation and the new régime, in any moves to liberalise or reform, and particularly in any moves to permit political parties legal existence and to move towards a parliamentary system;

(ii) efforts to establish closer ties between Spain and Western organisations. The NATO and EEC partners should be ready to meet the Spaniards at whatever the speed at which they are able to move towards a rapprochement. It would be wrong to give them the impression that there could be any question of bending the rules, e.g. of the Council of Europe, NATO or the EEC, to allow them entry, or of wanting them in before they have achieved a satisfactory degree of democracy. It is more a case of indicating that, as they move towards a

---

[4] But on 21 November Mr. McNally noted on Mr. Goodison's covering minute (see note 1 above): 'My own fear is that contrary to what is [here] suggested ... there will be pressure on us from the Opposition, from our American, French and German allies, and perhaps even from within the Office to over-react to initial cosmetics by Prince Juan Carlos. Reactions to initial policy pronouncements must be subject to the most careful political scrutiny and initial involvement with the régime must only be undertaken after careful thought.'

more democratic system, so it will be possible to build up closer links, and so to arrive at realistic planning for eventual membership;[5]

(iii) Visits, in both directions: the level will of course depend on the degree of political progress in Spain;

(iv) encouragement to British political parties to establish contacts with as broad as possible a spread of Spanish political groups, and to urge on those groups the need to work together for the common interest and eschew sectional policies (but this presupposes the legitimisation of political parties and political activity in Spain);

(v) encouragement of other contacts, e.g. trade union and inter-Parliamentary contacts.

7. There have already, as you know, been some Party contacts. It may be necessary to consider if and how the Liberals can be brought into the act.

8. Your Service Attachés have contacts with the Spanish military authorities which, considering the cool state of Anglo-Spanish relations and the related difficulties, nevertheless provide a useful basis from which to expand. It may be impossible to arrange immediate military exchanges, and it would certainly be necessary to watch the level of any such exchanges with care. Similarly, as regards arms sales, it is impossible to expect to be able to move suddenly to a much more permissive policy. But military exchanges and increased arms sales could be one of the directions in which movement might be possible provided things were going in the right direction politically in Spain.[6]

9. It has to be recognised that Gibraltar will continue to hamper the development of Anglo-Spanish relations. It nevertheless cannot be ruled out altogether that the Spanish may finally wake up to the truth that the way out of this age-old *impasse* is for them to build links with the Gibraltarians instead of isolating and antagonising them. That this is indeed the way out of the *impasse* should be more obvious than ever in the wake of the Defence Review. The line to take is that the United Kingdom genuinely wishes to

[5] The US Government took a rather different view of how best to handle the new régime in Spain. In his reply to Mr. Wilson's message of 22 December (see note 1 above), delivered to the Prime Minister on 23 January 1976, President Ford argued that the Spaniards 'should not be pressed to move more rapidly than the political pressures permit'. He was wary of using 'liberalization as a price Spain must pay' for closer ties with Europe, and suggested that it would be 'more effective to emphasize the benefits of full participation in European affairs ... rather than to threaten continued exclusion from NATO and the European Community' (telegram No. 36 to Washington of 23 January 1976, WSS 21/304/548/1).

[6] In his minute to Mr. Callaghan of 6 November (see No. 142, note 9) Mr. Hattersley had contended: 'Because of the crucial role that the armed forces will play whatever form of Government follows Franco[,] it is essential to make what contacts we can with the Spanish army. It may be impossible to arrange immediate exchanges and we would have to watch the level of such exchanges with care in any case. However we must do nothing to further alienate ourselves from Spanish military opinion and the MOD must be ready to respond quickly to our needs when Franco goes.'

pursue a solution that will be acceptable to all and hopes that Spain will follow a course which will make this possible.

Yours ever,
R.A. HIBBERT

Portugal's sixth Provisional Government faced a difficult task in re-establishing order and discipline in the country's domestic affairs. Communist dominance of the press and the trades unions, and their continued influence over the Portuguese armed forces, led Mr. Trench to conclude 'that the Government['s] grasp of authority was tenuous'.[1] The Communists and other parties of the extreme left continued to dominate the media; they accelerated the pace of agrarian reform; and instigated the illegal occupation of farms, extending their operations to foreign-owned properties. Governmental authority was further eroded when, on 12 November, a mass demonstration by construction workers in Lisbon effectively besieged the Prime Minister in the Parliament building for thirty-six hours. Admiral Pinheiro de Azevedo's appeals to COPCON and the police to rescue him were of no avail, and he was only released after promising to concede the workers' demands. After this, Mr. Trench observed, it was 'no longer possible seriously to maintain the fiction that the Government was in control of the country', and on 19 November the Provisional Government announced that they were suspending their activities 'until such time as the President of the Republic could ensure that the necessary military support was afforded to them for the fulfilment of their proper role'.[2]

With this 'dangerous gamble', the position of the moderates looked very uncertain. Consideration was given to relocating the Government and the Constituent Assembly to the north of the country, where local military units could be relied upon for support. There was even talk of using the air force, which remained loyal to the Government, to take action against dissident military units, and civil war seemed close. During the next few days farmers in the centre of the country blocked rail and road access to Lisbon and threatened to cut off electricity and water supplies to the capital, in protest against the chaos resulting from the actions of the extreme left. Then, in the early hours of 25 November, parachute troops, incited by left-wing elements, seized the air force bases at Tancos, Monte Real and Montijo and occupied an air force headquarters. Soldiers from the Light Artillery Regiment also joined in the insurrection, cutting off the capital from the north of the country and surrounding the airport, whilst other disaffected troops occupied television studios. In Lisbon President Costa Gomes appeared reluctant to move against the rebels lest bloodshed precipitate civil war. Only when appeals from the rebels for mass demonstrations failed did forces loyal to the Government feel able to act. Rebel positions, including those in the radio and television stations, were quickly recaptured and by the late evening it was clear that the rebels were losing ground everywhere. By 27 November all serious resistance had ended and the more prominent leaders of the

---

[1] Despatch from Mr. Trench to Mr. Callaghan of 10 December 1975, WSP 1/1.

[2] *V. Ibid.*

attempted coup arrested. Generals Fabião and Carvalho were relieved of their commands and COPCON dissolved.

No. 144

Letter from Mr. Goodison to Mr. Ure (Lisbon)

[*WSP 020/303/1*]

Confidential   FCO, *12 January 1976*

My dear John,

The Mutiny of the 25ᵗʰ November

I have thanked the Ambassador orally for his useful despatch[1] on this important and topical subject. It is being given priority printing.

2. The most interesting question, which has given rise to some discussion here, is the role of the PCP in these events. I note that paragraph 10 of the despatch says that it is not yet possible to determine their role with any degree of accuracy, and Nigel Trench repeated this view when he called the other day. There can be little doubt that the PCP has been fomenting disaffection in the armed forces and we agree with you that had the mutiny succeeded the PCP leadership would have been ready to exploit it. But we judge that the Soviet Union would not favour civil war in Portugal, given the damage which this could do to its détente image and to the prospects of other Western Communist Parties, and we therefore believe the Russians will have advised the PCP against fomenting insurrection, as distinct from disaffection.[2] That the PCP acted in accordance with this principle, whether they were so advised or not, is demonstrated by their failure to bring their civilian supporters onto the streets—the arguments that Government control of the media prevented their broadcasting an appeal and closure of the banks prevented their subsidizing a Rentacrowd mob surely underestimate the capacities of their organisation. What has been described as their hesitation seems to us to have been an unreadiness, a reluctance to become involved in direct insurrectionary action because they

---

[1] Mr. Trench's despatch of 10 December summarised the recent history of the sixth Provisional Government and analysed the political impact of events of 25 November (see preceding editorial note). Already, in a letter to Mr. Baker of 4 December 1975, Mr. Ure had reflected on the significance of the mutiny. 'Everyone', he noted, 'has been greatly heartened by the fact that this round appears to have been a decisive victory to the forces of moderation, law and order, and resistance to Communism. There is an atmosphere of immense relief in Lisbon itself' (WSP 1/1).

[2] Mr. Cartledge agreed. He suggested that there was 'no doubt that the events in Portugal during the last twelve months had caused the Russians considerable embarrassment' and that in recent months Moscow had 'been firmly of the view that their interests would best be served by not encouraging the PCP to be too militant' (minute to Mr. Hibbert of 15 January).

did not believe it could succeed in doing other than open the way to counter-revolution. We conclude that whatever action individual members of the Communist Party may have been involved in, the leadership of the PCP was not the instigator of the actions of the dissident units.[3] Certainly the failure of the mutiny has been very damaging to the PCP, and it is not unreasonable to suppose that they might have foreseen this. Thus, the PCP were not in control of events; and this must be a black mark for Cunhal. It is doubtful whether the proposed Governmental enquiry will add much to this analysis.[4]

3. It is a very welcome development that action has already been taken to overcome some of the basic problems to which paragraphs 17-19 of the despatch rightly point.[5] The economic measures are of particular importance.

4. I am sure that the Ambassador is right about the need for patience with the Portuguese Government in the coming months, and HMG will no doubt wish to continue to be helpful and patient. That patience may however still need to be accompanied on occasion by friendly pressure on the Portuguese Government to act quickly and sensibly. After all the West are being asked to help bale out the Portuguese economy.[6] In addition, HMG have a responsibility towards the British farmers and businessmen who have patiently held on through recent months of uncertainty. HMG will not expect miracles from the Portuguese. Ministers are aware, for example, that agrarian reform is a delicate and difficult issue, and that this makes it unlikely that there will be early satisfactory solutions to the problems of British farmers. But there are Parliamentary pressures on

[3] Mr. Trench had reported in his despatch of 10 December 1975 (see note 1 above) that Dr. Soares believed the PCP the 'main instigator' of the mutiny. But Mr. Hibbert was not convinced. In a minute to Mr. Cartledge of 2 January 1976 he recalled that in recent months 'Soviet influence and the influence of others in Eastern Europe and in the Communist movement in general … [had] been thrown in the direction of dissuading the PCP from thinking that a Leninist revolution could be carried out in Portugal'.

[4] Published on 20 January, the 'preliminary' report described the rebellion as 'the culmination of a sustained campaign by the PCP and its supporters in the armed forces, in concert with other extreme left-wing groups and unions, to seize power'. COPCON was also alleged to have played 'a central role' in the plot (Lisbon telegram No. 37 of 20 January, WSP 014/1).

[5] The problems Mr. Trench listed in these paragraphs (see notes 1 and 3 above) were: divisions amongst the political parties in Government; the role of the AFM; economic difficulties (including the effects of nationalisation, labour unrest, unemployment, and low foreign exchange reserves); and a 'thirst for worker participation in industry and commerce and for peasant land-ownership which, if gratified, will result in yet more inefficiency, but which, if left ungratified, may produce further explosive situations'.

[6] But, Mr. Ure reminded Mr. Goodison in a letter of 29 January, 'the hard fact is that the UK has not so far done any very conspicuous baling and there are limits to the amount of capital we can make out of what we have done'. It was, he contended, 'unrealistic to think that we have any special leverage in this respect' (WSP 014/1).

Ministers here which mean that they cannot appear to be neglecting those problems.

Every good wish for the New Year:[7] hoping to see you soon,

Yours Ever,
A.C. GOODISON

[7] Mr. Ure was far from optimistic about Portugal's immediate future. Rumours of left- and right-wing plots still abounded and the 'relative calm prevailing in military, political and social circles [had] become increasingly uneasy'. Meanwhile, the Portuguese Government had 'proved rather disappointing in the slowness with which it [managed] to cope with the fundamental economic and social problems besetting the country': agrarian reform, unemployment, food shortages and Angolan refugees were all problems the authorities were struggling to surmount (letter to Mr. Goodison of 5 February, WSP 014/1).

No. 145

Letter from Sir J. Killick (UKDEL NATO) to Mr. Goodison

[*WSS 022/579/1*]

Confidential.   BRUSSELS, *18 February 1976*

Dear Alan,

1. As I foreshadowed to you on the telephone, Nuño Aguirre[1] paid a brief call on me yesterday afternoon following a visit to Ed Streator, the Acting US Permanent Representative.

2. We chatted for about half an hour but did not touch much on the question of Spain and NATO (which I have dealt with in my telegram No. 2 Saving).[2] He was more interested in my views on the development of Anglo/Spanish relations. I of course disclaimed any knowledge of or responsibility for current British policy and said I could only make purely personal comments. Although nobody sought to draw close parallels between Portugal and Spain, I believed that developments in Portugal had created a certain disposition in London to move as quickly as possible towards the establishment of working relations with the new Spanish

[1] See No. 142, note 6.

[2] In this telegram of 18 February, Sir J. Killick reported a dinner conversation, two days earlier, between Dr. Luns, and the new Spanish Foreign Minister, Sr. J.M. de Areilza y Martínez de Rodas, the Count de Motrico. Sr. Areilza had then 'expressed satisfaction with the new Spanish/American Treaty arrangements and particularly with the references to collaboration and to NATO. Spain was not asking for membership of NATO because she wanted first to be sure that she would be welcome. But the King and the new Government were very eager to integrate the new Spain into the democratic structure of Europe ... as a deterrent to reactionary tendencies and as a safeguard against any threat to democratic developments'.

Government. I could not quantify precisely what this meant in time-scale nor what was required to satisfy British domestic opinion that real progress towards democracy was being made in Spain. But what I felt would tell with British Ministers was the possible danger of reaction against present trends whether from the right or the extreme left. I assumed (and Aguirre agreed) that it was very difficult to make any estimate of the possible Communist threat. Aguirre said that there would be no question of giving passports to a short list of particularly prominent people still in exile whose return might have a particularly unsettling effect domestically. Carrillo[3] was one of these. He outlined the programme over the next twelve months, including the various elections which were planned, and suggested that we ought to see merits in this staged process since it would give the Socialists and others in Spain the opportunity to establish and organise themselves whereas the Movimiento was and remained strong.

3. I added that the special complication of Gibraltar was a factor which had to be born [*sic*] in mind. In reply to Aguirre's question I said it was my understanding, as Charles Wiggin would no doubt have told him, that the Secretary of State did not wish to make this Item One of the Agenda for the London talks although he was prepared to discuss it if Areilza wished.[4] When Aguirre asked how much of an obstacle I thought it would prove to be, I said frankly that this would depend entirely on how it was handled from the Spanish side. Aguirre said he had been charged by his Minister with personal responsibility for handling the problem and I said this was a good thing. He should bear in mind that the British Government had been having some very uncomfortable experiences recently and were sensitive to harassment. Our difficulty with Iceland was a case in point;[5] the Government in the interests of its domestic image needed to show that it was standing up to this sort of thing and protecting national interests. It followed that it would be a mistake to raise the Gibraltar issue in this kind of way. My personal hope remained (and Aguirre agreed) that if Spanish association with or accession to the EEC could be brought about, the way might be open for the economic integration of the Rock with the Campo.[6] The ultimate solution still

[3] Sr. Santiago Carrillo Solares was General Secretary of the *Partido Comunista de España* (PCE)/Communist Party of Spain.

[4] Sr. Areilza, who in January had visited Bonn, Paris and Luxembourg, primarily to pursue his ideas about the development of Spain's relationship with, and eventual membership of, the EC, had also indicated his desire to visit London. Mr. Callaghan had agreed, commenting: 'Provided the Spaniards keep quiet on Gibraltar' (submission from Mr. Goodison to Mr. Hibbert of 8 January, WSS 026/548). The visit was arranged for 2 March. See Nos. 146 and 148.

[5] See Volume II, No. 42, note 9. Royal Naval frigates were despatched to protect British fishing vessels when, in the autumn of 1975, Icelandic gunboats began to harass British trawlers fishing in waters over which Iceland claimed jurisdiction.

[6] i.e. the hinterland.

seemed to me to be through improved Spanish cultivation of the population of the Rock.

4. On this, Aguirre said that he had been very pleased with the success of the opening of telephone etc communications over the Christmas period[7] but nevertheless he had been attacked from several quarters for this demonstration of 'softness'. He remained vulnerable to this sort of criticism but did not propose to be deterred. He found it much easier to work with Areilza than with his predecessor.[8] He now had in mind further similar moves, particularly in the cultural field, such as opening the frontier so that Gibraltarians could participate in such things as the Fiesta at La Linea. Beyond this he also envisaged the re-opening of contacts with Joshua Hassan,[9] but this time purely on the basis of oral exchanges and without pieces of paper being slapped on the table. If such oral exchanges opened up certain areas of agreement, these could be reflected on paper thereafter.

5. On the question of Spanish membership of NATO I said that I had heard it suggested that Soviet reactions to the expansion of the Alliance in this way might be very negative. Had the Spanish Government had anything to this effect directly from the Russians? Aguirre said they had heard nothing. It had been asserted by Brandt that Brezhnev had said something to this effect in an exchange between the two, and the Spanish side had raised this during their visit to Bonn with van Well. Van Well had looked up the Brezhnev/Brandt record and had assured the Spaniards that there was no trace of any such remark by Brezhnev. I said I found this interesting because my own assumption would be that while the Russians would certainly not welcome Spain's accession to the Alliance, they probably accepted privately that Spain lay essentially in the Western 'sphere of influence' and would not do anything serious to prevent a development of this sort.

6. I cannot imagine that there is anything in the foregoing which you do not know already, but you will appreciate that the hallowed practice of your faithful servant in acting as an SED desk officer dies hard!

Yours ever,
JOHN KILLICK

[7] Telephone links between Gibraltar and Spain were restored for ten days over Christmas, the first time since 1969 and for longer than at any time since they were severed. The Spaniards were also talking of a further relaxation of restrictions, especially on cultural contacts.

[8] Sr. P. Cortina Mauri was Spanish Foreign Minister from January 1974 until December 1975.

[9] Chief Minister of Gibraltar.

6. But public affirmation of this kind could be dangerous in Gibraltar, and to make too much of the EEC point could run the risks in paragraph 3 above. GGD[5] agree with the concept of persuading the Gibraltarians that their future lies in economic co-operation with Spain, but suggests that it would be premature and possibly counter-productive to pursue this at this juncture. HMG are, of course, publicly pledged not to enter into any arrangements under which the people of Gibraltar would pass under other sovereignty against their wishes. Our large aid programme and other efforts (e.g. to maintain the RN[6] Dockyard) have been directed to fulfilling our parallel pledge to sustain their economy. The governing Gibraltar Labour Party [GLP] recognises the need for an ultimate accommodation with Spain, but in view of TGWU and Integration with Britain Party pressure in the opposite direction, the GLP must be able to convince the electorate at the mid-1976 elections that they are also committed to seeing that HMG's pledges are fulfilled, and capable of ensuring this. Gibraltar Ministers have consequently concurred with HMG's policy of avoiding confrontation with the Unions in e.g. negotiations under the Scamp Report[7] which are nearing completion, and have joined for tactical reasons in an opposition request for a permanent economic link with Britain.

7. GGD consider that, at least until after the election, we should avoid any sign of back-sliding from our pledges to maintain Gibraltar's economic position, since this would be seized upon by the Opposition as an ideal basis for campaigning for a permanent link with Britain, to rally support against any *rapprochement* with Spain, to discredit Gibraltar Ministers' present position and possibly to succeed in the election—although their present assessment is that the Opposition would prefer not to come to power but rather to pursue obstruction.

8. As GGD see it, it would still be appropriate for the Secretary of State to urge economic co-operation with Gibraltar on Sr. Areilza (the Maxwell Stamp Survey of the economic prospects of South-West Spain including Gibraltar, about to be published, may provide a natural talking point),[8]

[5] Gibraltar and General Department

[6] Royal Naval.

[7] Sir J. Scamp, Associate Professor of Industrial Relations at the University of Warwick, had reported on parity of wages and salaries for local workers in Gibraltar, recommending that these should in principle be the equivalent to 80% of UK rates for corresponding employees. In May this was agreed by the local branch of the TGWU.

[8] This report, *Gibraltar: British or Spanish? The Economic Prospects*, was written by independent economists from Britain and Spain and was published in February 1976. Although the report concluded that the political integration of Spain and Gibraltar could not occur unless 'the necessary political conditions existed', it nevertheless stressed the economic advantages that this would bring Gibraltarians and warned of 'the prospect of more serious economic and social problems in the long run' if the Rock remained isolated from its hinterland (letter from Mr. A.R. Thomas (Head of Chancery in the British Embassy, Madrid) to Mr. Baker of 18 March, WSB 3/548/1).

load the policy of democratisation with one more burden than it is able to bear. Nor could we be sure that our partners in Europe would see things our way; they might well say that the chance of promoting democracy in Spain and welding Spain into Europe was more important than getting Gibraltar's frontier opened. This is thus delicate ground, but advantageous to us if trod carefully.

4. It seems to us that it would be preferable to invite Sr. Areilza to open the discussions. He will do so by explaining what Spain wants: entry to the EEC and eventually NATO. It is after he has asked for our support that the Secretary of State will be best placed to explain his views and to ask pointed questions about the Spanish Government's plans for internal reform. Then we recommend that the Secretary of State should explain that there is an anomaly in the Spanish attitude, as long as they are knocking at the great gates of Europe asking for them to be opened for Spanish entry and themselves keeping closed the gates of Gibraltar. We do not suggest that this latter point need be laboured. We should avoid raising the sovereignty issue, but should say that if Spain opens the gates, this would give Gibraltar the possibility of diversifying and expanding its economy, and of ending the current narrow dependence on the economic link with the UK. Of course, it may be that Sr. Areilza will raise the subject of Gibraltar without any initiative on our side. If Sr. Areilza should fail to volunteer anything encouraging on the topic of Gibraltar, it will be the more important for the Secretary of State to raise it, in order to be able to say afterwards that he has pressed for a new approach by Spain.

5. One reason why Mr. Hibbert is anxious that this point should be made to Sr. Areilza is that he, like Gibraltar and General Department, is concerned that the TGWU extremists may gain support in the Gibraltar elections due in June, through their campaign for a permanent link with the UK and parity of wages, secured by threats of industrial action. He believes that their campaign will fail if HMG tell the Gibraltarians frankly that they have an artificial economy; that HMG are, of course, committed to a policy of sustaining and supporting it as long as Spanish restrictions last; but that in the long term they would be wise to look for a more natural growth of the economy through economic co-operation with Spain.[4] Mr. Hibbert considers that HMG can only publicly affirm in Gibraltar that this is their policy if the Spanish Foreign Minister has been firmly faced with the need for economic co-operation with Gibraltar as a concomitant of his wish for economic co-operation with the Community.

[4] However, Mr. H.S.H. Stanley (AUS) questioned the wisdom of 'arm-twisting in Gibraltar ... until we were much more satisfied that Spain really was becoming the kind of decent place with which we could envisage a future for Gibraltar'. The UK could not, he argued, 'push Gibraltar into the arms of a Spain which is distasteful to us any more than we can allow Gibraltar to impede our relations with a Spain we accept' (minute to Mr. Goodison of 19 February).

6. But public affirmation of this kind could be dangerous in Gibraltar, and to make too much of the EEC point could run the risks in paragraph 3 above. GGD[5] agree with the concept of persuading the Gibraltarians that their future lies in economic co-operation with Spain, but suggests that it would be premature and possibly counter-productive to pursue this at this juncture. HMG are, of course, publicly pledged not to enter into any arrangements under which the people of Gibraltar would pass under other sovereignty against their wishes. Our large aid programme and other efforts (e.g. to maintain the RN[6] Dockyard) have been directed to fulfilling our parallel pledge to sustain their economy. The governing Gibraltar Labour Party [GLP] recognises the need for an ultimate accommodation with Spain, but in view of TGWU and Integration with Britain Party pressure in the opposite direction, the GLP must be able to convince the electorate at the mid-1976 elections that they are also committed to seeing that HMG's pledges are fulfilled, and capable of ensuring this. Gibraltar Ministers have consequently concurred with HMG's policy of avoiding confrontation with the Unions in e.g. negotiations under the Scamp Report[7] which are nearing completion, and have joined for tactical reasons in an opposition request for a permanent economic link with Britain.

7. GGD consider that, at least until after the election, we should avoid any sign of back-sliding from our pledges to maintain Gibraltar's economic position, since this would be seized upon by the Opposition as an ideal basis for campaigning for a permanent link with Britain, to rally support against any *rapprochement* with Spain, to discredit Gibraltar Ministers' present position and possibly to succeed in the election—although their present assessment is that the Opposition would prefer not to come to power but rather to pursue obstruction.

8. As GGD see it, it would still be appropriate for the Secretary of State to urge economic co-operation with Gibraltar on Sr. Areilza (the Maxwell Stamp Survey of the economic prospects of South-West Spain including Gibraltar, about to be published, may provide a natural talking point),[8]

[5] Gibraltar and General Department

[6] Royal Naval.

[7] Sir J. Scamp, Associate Professor of Industrial Relations at the University of Warwick, had reported on parity of wages and salaries for local workers in Gibraltar, recommending that these should in principle be the equivalent to 80% of UK rates for corresponding employees. In May this was agreed by the local branch of the TGWU.

[8] This report, *Gibraltar: British or Spanish? The Economic Prospects*, was written by independent economists from Britain and Spain and was published in February 1976. Although the report concluded that the political integration of Spain and Gibraltar could not occur unless 'the necessary political conditions existed', it nevertheless stressed the economic advantages that this would bring Gibraltarians and warned of 'the prospect of more serious economic and social problems in the long run' if the Rock remained isolated from its hinterland (letter from Mr. A.R. Thomas (Head of Chancery in the British Embassy, Madrid) to Mr. Baker of 18 March, WSB 3/548/1).

even though they advocate that there should be no reference publicly to that proposal before the Gibraltar General Election.

9. I share Gibraltar and General Department's views. I think the Secretary of State ought not to let the opportunity pass to appeal for the gates to be opened. At the same time, we must recognise that, as yet, we know little of Sr. Areilza's Gibraltar policies; it is conceivable, though unlikely, that he will agree to a relaxation of restrictions; in that case the content of the Ministers' conversation will have to become public.[9] It is also possible that, for their own purposes the Spaniards will reveal whatever the Secretary of State says on Gibraltar; but this is, in my view, a risk worth running.

9. I should be grateful for directions on the proposal in paragraph 4 above before we draft the Steering Brief for the visit.[10]

A.C. Goodison

[9] In his minute of 10 February (see note 3 above), Mr. Goodison noted that Sr. Areilza had already 'told Mr. Wiggin that he [was] reconsidering his predecessors' policies towards Gibraltar; a sign of this was the temporary restoration of telephonic communications over Christmas' and the 'mild language' used by the King and the Prime Minister in recent references to Gibraltar. Nevertheless, Mr. Goodison concluded, there was 'no prospect of an agreement on substance in the near future'.

[10] Mr. Campbell expressed his agreement with the proposal made in paragraph 4 in a minute of 20 February, and the next day Mr. Hattersley, to whom this submission was also addressed, endorsed Mr. Goodison's views.

No. 147

Mr. Wiggin (Madrid) to Mr. Callaghan

No. 69 Telegraphic [WSS 014/2]

Immediate. Confidential MADRID, *26 February 1976, 12 noon*

Repeated for information to Saving EEC Posts, UKREP Brussels, UKDEL NATO, Lisbon, Washington and Governor Gibraltar (Personal).

Spain's Political Evolution

1. King Juan Carlos's first Government[1] has now been 3 months in office. Although almost all the Ministers are conservative by conviction and some are authoritarian and oligarchical in temperament, most people here do not now doubt the wish of the majority of them to transform Spain's

[1] On becoming King, Juan Carlos confirmed Sr. Arias Navarro as Prime Minister, but asked that he form an administration from which liberal policies and constitutional reform could be expected. A key figure in the new Government was the Minister of the Interior, Sr. Fraga Iribarne, formerly Spain's Ambassador in London.

institutional system over the coming two years into something qualitatively approximating to the democracies of Western Europe. Franco's dictatorship used to be defended by the argument that democracy as we know it was totally unsuitable for Spain. The change wrought by his death is well illustrated by the fact that that argument has been discarded so soon and so openly by a Government whose members virtually all occupied Ministerial or Official posts under him at one time or another.

2. The reformers within the Government have decided to avoid a clean break with the past. Their hope is to prevail upon the existing institutions to sanction their own transformation. The Government regard this as the only way to avoid the danger of backlash, in particular from the armed forces where many senior officers retain strong emotional attachment to the memory of Franco's regime.[2] In deference to military opinion in particular, separatism (as opposed to regionalism) and communism are to remain illegal. The calculations of the more articulate reformist Ministers, such as Fraga and Areilza, are probably that change is inevitable post-Franco: that controlled evolutionary change, provided momentum is maintained, is the best safeguard against a major explosion: and that those who stage-manage the change should be well placed to retain democratic power thereafter. They are also convinced that EEC membership is both politically and economically necessary for Spain within the next 5-10 years. They are aware that the achievement of democracy is a necessary pre-condition: but they are anxious, given the latent depths of xenophobia here, to avoid any suggestion that either democracy or EEC membership (or any formal link between the two) is being foisted on Spain at the insistence of foreigners. They attach perhaps somewhat less importance to joining NATO, though similar considerations apply: and Areilza himself would like to find useful military work for potentially idle military hands post-Sahara.[3]

3. The King has clearly decided, at least for the present, not to play the forward role some expected of him before his accession. He seems content to concentrate on symbolic activities and to leave the main work of government to his Ministers. But his power of intervention could be a crucial factor in a crisis. His advisers show awareness that he may need to use it before he can reach the safe haven of constitutional monarchy. With

[2] In a despatch of 5 May, addressed to Mr. C.A.R. Crosland, Mr. Callaghan's successor as Foreign and Commonwealth Secretary, Mr. Wiggin later explained that 'Franco's régime had been set up and staffed by the winning side in a Civil War', and that Francoist sympathisers could be expected to 'try to hold up change' by courting the Spanish armed forces 'as the one organisation possessing the strength and discipline to impose its will'. 'If changes came too quickly', he observed, 'then the shock might provoke a reaction from vested interests enjoying at least tacit military support.'

[3] On 14 November 1975 Spain had agreed to hand over its Western Saharan territory (formerly the colony of Rio de Oro) to joint Moroccan-Mauritanian control by the end of February 1976. Algeria denounced this agreement as an outrage, proclaimed its support for Saharan independence, and fighting soon broke out between Algerian and Moroccan forces.

this in mind they hope to strengthen his popular appeal, as well as keeping fresh his special relationship with the armed forces.[4]

4. Apart from the repeal of the bulk of Franco's notorious anti-terrorist decree-law of August 1975,[5] the Government's tangible progress has so far been limited. Given their intention of submitting nearly all reforming legislation to the Cortes for approval, advance is bound to be slow. Meanwhile they face the continuing problem of how far to bend, stretch or even ignore existing laws. They have survived a series of challenges in the form of strikes and demonstrations without having yet been blown off their political course, though they have probably deepened their economic policy problems in the process. Police behaviour is in general distinctly more restrained than in Franco's day, although the government's desire to show that they retain control has led to a periodic readiness to sanction methods reminiscent of the old régime. (Inevitably the degree of common sense and restraint shown by security authorities on the spot has also varied widely.) The government's approach to protest meetings, censorship, and opposition activities generally has been similarly uneven. But the overall atmosphere remains very much freer and there have been mercifully few casualties whether by terrorist or police action. The democratic opposition are making full use of the greater liberty accorded them. In spite or because of the proliferation of would-be political parties, they are beginning to take the prospect of eventual elections seriously.

5. The King's recent visit to Catalonia was on balance a success. Timed to coincide with a number of minor but nevertheless significant devolutionary measures it has served to show that the Government are aware of regional feeling and prepared to make concessions to it. But other recent items of news have been less promising and have served to underline just how difficult the Government's task is. The sacking last week of the premises of a Catholic labour organisation in Madrid shows that right-wing violence is far from eliminated as a potential source of disorder. The imposition of a £7,500 fine on a well-known Communist, arrested for taking part in a university discussion at which a Christian Democrat and a Socialist also participated without any reprisals, has emphasised how many problems will be raised by the attempt to keep communism illegal and has high-lighted the danger that such discrimination will merely add to its glamour. (The arrest and fine have been privately categorised to me as 'stupid' by Areilza's deputy and close associate.) The announcement that the deliberations of the Mixed Commission on constitutional reform[6] will

---

[4] In his despatch of 5 May (see note 2 above), Mr. Wiggin observed: 'Personally, I believe the threat of direct military intervention on the side of reaction to be more apparent than real. But appearances count in the Spanish political jungle.'

[5] See No. 142, note 7.

[6] A Mixed Commission, consisting of nine members of the Government and nine members of the Cortes who were also members of the National Council of the Movement, was

be secret is also bad news, since it may help the reactionaries on that body to resist change without exposing themselves to hostile public opinion.

6. The situation in Spain remains wide open. The chances of the evolutionary reformers succeeding cannot be rated higher than evens. Many informal observers rate them lower. But they remain the country's best and perhaps only hope of orderly transition.[7]

FCO please pass to all saving addressees.

established in January to discuss reform of Spain's Fundamental Laws, including changes in the structure of Parliament, as well as laws on freedom of assembly and association.

[7] Mr. Wiggin enlarged upon this point in his despatch of 5 May (see notes 2 and 4 above): 'Even if the present Government are brought down by the weight of their hesitations and internal contradictions, the far right should find it impossible to turn back the clock unless a really severe deterioration in public order swings the military their way.' The 'extremes of the left and right will continue each in their own way to oppose the evolutionary concept, ... [but] as yet I see no reason to despair that the evolutionaries will somehow be able to muddle through into a new situation at least approximating to democracy. This may be wishful thinking. But I can visualise no alternative type of régime which would enjoy a better chance of achieving democracy with Spain as divided and fragmented as it is.'

No. 148

Record of a meeting between Mr. Callaghan and Sr. Areilza at the FCO on 2 March 1976, at 11 a.m.

[*WSS 026/548/1*]

Confidential

Present:

The Rt. Hon. James Callaghan MP
Mr. E.A.J. Fergusson[1]

HE Señor Don Jose
Maria de Areilza[2]

Southern Africa and Rhodesia
1. *Mr. Callaghan* apologised that their meeting after lunch would have to be curtailed because he had to make a statement in the House of Commons on Rhodesia, following Lord Greenhill's visit.[3] The situation was difficult.

[1] Principal Private Secretary to Mr. Callaghan since October 1975.

[2] Sr. Areilza's visit to London was one in a series which he was making to EC capitals with a view to explaining his Government's reform policies and winning support for Spain's forthcoming application for EC membership.

[3] Lord Greenhill, Sir T. Brimelow's immediate predecessor as PUS, was sent to Salisbury (Rhodesia) as a HMG's special envoy for talks with Mr. Smith on 26-27 February (see No. 107, note 10).

Sr. Areilza referred to the newspaper reports of the speech by Agôstinho Neto of the MPLA that they would give support to the liberation movements in Rhodesia and Namibia. *Mr. Callaghan* said that the Rhodesian Europeans seemed to be confident that they could hold the situation but there was a risk that the situation might deteriorate rapidly as in Angola. He did not think that they could hold out. Our interest was to try to ensure that there could be a peaceful transition to majority rule and the best hope of stability would be if Mr. Ian Smith were to listen to our advice. There were substantial numbers of Rhodesian guerillas in Mozambique. He personally thought that it would be very serious if, in the African context, we had to find ourselves on the same side as guerillas supported by Russian and Chinese arms. But it was hard to bring pressure on the Rhodesians. Smith was a stubborn man and even the South Africans had been unsuccessful in pressing him to shift from his position—though it was not clear that they had tried hard enough. *Sr. Areilza* referred to his conversations with Dr. Kissinger in December 1975. At that time Dr. Kissinger had been seriously concerned by the growing extent of Cuban involvement. He already took for granted to [*sic*] loss to the West of Angola and was talking about recognition of the MPLA. He had said that it was a serious danger to the balance of power in Southern Africa that 12,000-15,000 armed Cubans should be let loose. Dr. Kissinger had asked about Cuban involvement in the Saharan dispute;[4] at that time there had only been a few of them on the Algerian side but now there were some 2,000 supported by sophisticated armaments. Dr. Kissinger had said that he did not expect the Cubans to return from Angola; they would stay on in Africa as a destabilising force. *Mr. Callaghan* said that the Angolans needed expert support from the Cubans to stiffen their administration. However, he believed that in the long run the Africans' own personality would predominate. Pressure on the Soviet Union was only of limited effectiveness; they had come into the scene late in the day and the Cubans had involved themselves on their own initiative.

2. *Sr. Areilza* said that Agôstinho Neto had told Major Antunes in January that the MPLA intended to pursue non-aligned policies, especially in the trade field, and they looked forward to future co-operation with Portugal, with the West and even with the US. *Mr. Callaghan* commented that Neto might feel that way but there were other elements in the MPLA who would disagree. We must wait and see.

Portugal

3. *Sr. Areilza* said that he had met Major Antunes in January on the Portuguese frontier. They had had a long and important talk and had agreed on measures to avoid a repetition of the serious incidents of

[4] See No. 147, note 3.

September 1975.[5] He had been impressed by Antunes and his report of the pact between the Armed Forces Movement and the political parties and the assurance from the AFM that they would not step into the Party struggle but would stay outside as guarantors of democratic order. Relations with Spain and Portugal would be based on the principle of non-interference. The Spanish had prevented General Spínola from staying in Spain and had resisted requests that they should provide training facilities for right wing counter-revolutionaries. Major Antunes had been most co-operative and they had agreed that plans should be drawn up for future collaboration. Antunes had spoken of the Portuguese Communists; Cunhal had had two options, either to accept the pact between the parties and the AFM and to participate openly in the political struggle or to revert to clandestine activity. He had chosen the former. This was a helpful development.

Spanish Internal Policy

4. *Sr. Areilza* said that he wanted the countries of Western Europe to understand the effect in Spain of the change from 40 years of immobile dictatorship to the new monarchy. It was a major task to move in the direction of a democratic state. Spain would not leap forward suddenly; this would entail the risk of a break-down like that in Portugal. But he wanted to explain both the aims of the régime and the limits to what was possible. General Franco had filled the power vacuum so fully that political institutions had not been able to develop. The King now wanted to push for reforms leading to the establishment of representative democracy. He believed that this was the essential element of democratic progress. But the Spanish wished to make political progress without losing all social and economic discipline. Three major political changes were foreseen, two of them requiring changes in the constitution which would be put to a Referendum and the third which required only Government decree.

5. The first change would be to permit party political development within the framework of new laws and a revised constitutional system. Discussion was proceeding in a mixed commission which would shortly present draft legislation to the Government permitting liberty of association in political parties to all those over the age of 18. There would be three constraints:

(*a*) Totalitarian parties either to the right or left would not be permitted.
(*b*) Violence as an instrument of political activity must be eschewed.
(*c*) No party would be permitted which aimed at the break-up of the Spanish State.

---

[5] On 27 September 1975, in reaction to the execution of five terrorists in Spain (see No. 142, note 7), Portuguese mobs attacked and burnt the Spanish Embassy in Lisbon without intervention by either Portuguese armed forces or police.

These changes in the law would be intended to help the development of Socialist, Christian and Liberal parties, to the exclusion of the totalitarian extremists (Communists and Fascists).

6. It was planned to have elections to a bicameral legislature. The lower house would be elected by universal suffrage. The second chamber would offer representation to regions (such as the Basques and Catalans), city councils and economic interests. The proposals for parties and for elections would be put to the people for decision by Referendum.

7. The third area of change would be to breathe life into the laws affecting civil liberties which had been promulgated under General Franco but which had never been developed. These would cover freedom of expression, political meetings etc. This would not need a Referendum.

8. The electoral law was under examination. The Government hoped to find a method, perhaps by using UK or German experience, to avoid the proliferation of parties which was the weakness of other Western democratic systems. The present phase would last until the Referendum in the autumn this year, leading to a general election in spring 1977. At that time he hoped that it would be possible to say that Spain had a Parliament elected by popular vote and a legal system guaranteeing civil liberties.

Trades Unions

9. *Sr. Areilza* said that, because he had known that Mr. Callaghan would be keenly interested in this, he had spoken to his 'Ministerial colleague' [the Minister of Syndical Relations] to brief himself on the Government's intentions. Trades Union law in Spain was not a part of constitutional law and could therefore be changed by Governmental decree. Under General Franco the Trades Unions had been a part of the bureaucracy and had been run by Government officials. This did not mean that there had been no improvements in social security and related measures but the political structure of Trades Union activity had been undeveloped. The Government now wanted to develop worker activity on a 'horizontal basis' separating it from the Council of Employers so that the two groups could be free to negotiate with each other on wages, conditions of service etc. Within the broad horizontal structure of worker organisations the Trades Unions would be free to organise themselves on an industry by industry basis as they wished. He went on to describe the difficulties of the present formal and informal Trades Union structure and the opportunities which this gave to the Communists to infiltrate both parts. If revised Trades Union regulations were to be established. [*sic*][6] It was essential for the Trade Unionists themselves to participate in drawing up their own rules. The government would call together a General Congress of Trades Unionists in June to discuss Trade Union reform. Proposals would be put to them but the delegates to the Congress would be allowed to participate in the decisions about how the new proposals could be implemented. *Mr.*

[6] The punctuation here is unclear.

Callaghan referred to the letter which he had received that morning from the General Secretary of the TUC and said that it would be helpful if the Spanish Government could study ILO[7] Convention 87 on freedom of association and ILO Convention 98 on the right to organise and bargain collectively and see whether it would be possible for the Spanish Government to ratify them. *Sr. Areilza* took careful note.

10. *Mr. Callaghan* said that he would speak with all candour and frankness. The events of the last 40 years had gone very deep. Public opinion would lag behind in its attitude to Spain whatever changes took place and formal changes would in any case take time to have an effect on the real situation. There would be continuing hostility, doubt and suspicion of the Spanish Government. Those who wanted to see an improvement in relations would have to convince those who were doubtful. The Spanish Civil War had been a traumatic experience for the generation of Britons who were now in control of affairs. For instance he had never visited Spain and would not go so long as General Franco lived. There were many like him. He realised that many of the younger generation flocked to Spain for their holidays. They were more flexible in their attitudes but fundamental changes of view would be slow to develop. He hoped that those like the Foreign Minister, Sr. Fraga and others like them, would be successful in bringing Spain into the spirit of Western democracy. He well understood the difficulties and he saw also that if they were not successful the Communists might fill the vacuum. He had told the House of Commons that we should be prepared to give assistance to Spain, but so far as attitudes were concerned the Walls of Jericho did not fall at the first sounding of the trumpets. Excessive expectations would only lead to disappointment. This was why the Spanish Government must not hurry too much in their application to the EEC. It would provoke the reaction 'show us first what you have done'. Speaking for the Government, he said that as they saw movement in Spain in the right direction it would help them to convince public opinion that closer relations with Spain were desirable. He repeated that it would be wrong to under-estimate the extent of, and how formidable and deep rooted were opposition to a non-democratic Spain.

11. *Sr. Areilza* said that he was aware that this was not an easy problem. There were after all opponents to their plans in Spain, e.g. on the right wing. They were not rushing, pushing, demanding or seeking anything at this stage in respect of membership of the EEC. He had wanted to explain their intentions so that the British Government could learn what was going on without distortion. The next steps might take up to 18 months. They were not in a hurry as he had told the Commission and NATO. Political evolution in Spain would take time and he knew that when ultimately they sought entrance to the EEC, negotiations would take a further period of years. He was presenting the case and he hoped that the UK could help

[7] International Labour Organisation.

them overcome the difficulties. It was in the wider interests of Western Europe that Spain should be stable and that there should not be revolutionary disturbances. *Mr. Callaghan* said that the visit had been well timed. He hoped that in a few months time when Spanish policy had been seen to have changed course it would be possible to be more positive. It would be a tragedy if Spain were to return to dictatorship either of the left or of the right.

12. *Sr. Areilza* said that he wished to draw attention to the programme for the release of political prisoners. In the next six months all but 120 or so of the 660 prisoners would be released, the remainder being those who had been tried and convicted of criminal offences. Changes in the criminal code would mean the disappearance of the charges against most of them. There would be an amnesty for the prisoners released and their police and penal records would be destroyed save for a small number (about 6) of special cases.

13. *Mr. Callaghan* suggested that, as a way of influencing British public opinion, it would be worth explaining the progress which was being made on e.g. Trades Union reform either by inviting Trades Unionists to Spain or by sending an emissary to explain the proposals to the British Trades Unions.

Naval Collaboration

14. *Sr. Areilza* said that the Minister of the Navy had telephoned him the day before to ask him to raise the possibility of renewed collaboration between Britain and Spain in the field of naval construction and exchanges of technology. The Spaniards were looking for small aircraft carriers (6,000 tons), for frigates and for mine sweepers and thought that construction might take place in the UK or in Spain—in the latter case, using British advanced technology. The Minister for Navy was anxious to diversify Spanish procurement from exclusively US sources. He was most insistent that as soon as the climate was propitious he would like to send a naval mission to explore the possibilities. *Mr. Callaghan* said that he could not give an answer on the spot. His first thought was that when the plans for democratic development had been made public it would be easier to move forward. Naval construction was a slow moving affair and there could be no harm in waiting until July. He would not rule out the suggestion in principle; he would be happy for us to co-operate in the right circumstances. When he could say to the Trades Unions that concrete benefits would accrue, e.g. to employment and when the plans for political advancement had unfolded it would be much easier to take steps of this kind.

Gibraltar

15. *Sr. Areilza* referred to the discussions in Madrid between Mr. Wiggin and Sr. Aguirre. He had looked carefully at their outcome and thought that there were possibilities of progress. Although (see the King's Accession

Statement)[8] public opinion required certain things to be said, his personal view was that we should explore how Spain, the UK and the population of Gibraltar could be brought together. His feeling was that if and when Spain had moved in a democratic direction and was seen to be part of Western Europe, of the EEC, of NATO, it would be much easier to reduce the tension between Gibraltar and Spain. *Mr. Callaghan* said that his formal position must remain that we should be guided by the wishes of the people of Gibraltar. However, speaking very privately, he agreed that the best hope lay in the integration of a democratic Spain in Europe and he quoted the adage that one could more easily catch flies by honey than by vinegar. Gibraltar could survive the current situation but its economic advancement would be easier if relations with Spain improved. A move towards democracy in Spain would facilitate solutions. We would certainly not do anything to manipulate public opinion in a contrary direction. *Sr. Areilza* recognised that the main problem was the attitude of the Gibraltarians. He had already authorised one or two small gestures and was considering further steps, e.g. over telecommunications. *Mr. Callaghan* referred to the landing difficulties at Gibraltar airport. *Sr. Areilza* said that they would try to improve access for holiday makers. They wanted to make contact with the leaders of Gibraltar opinion. He asked for assurance that we should not oppose such contact. *Mr. Callaghan* said that we should certainly not oppose such contacts. He would say to the Gibraltarians that gestures from the Spanish should be met by gestures from the Gibraltarians. We had no interest in hostilities between Gibraltar and Spain. Looking forward 10 years to a time when a democratic Spain had entered the EEC and NATO what interest could we have in keeping control of a solid piece of rock? We had joint interests, given that Spain were to evolve on the hoped-for lines. Whatever the situation in the past that was our policy now. *Sr. Areilza* referred to the possibility of developing a large scale international airport as a joint venture in the hinterland between Gibraltar and Spain. This followed ideas which he had had for Franco/Spanish collaboration over a regional airport at St Jean de Luz which he had espoused when he had been Spanish Ambassador in Paris. *Mr. Callaghan* said that ideas of this kind were valuable in that they could influence the Gibraltarians. At the next elections both major parties were formally committed to integration with the UK. Spanish policy should aim at making them see the advantages of alternatives. *Sr. Areilza* said that he knew Sir Joshua Hassan. Helping him was possibly the best path. *Mr. Callaghan* said that democratic progress in Spain was the answer.

16. *Sr. Areilza* said King Carlos sent his personal regards. They had been very glad that Prince Philip had attended the coronation. *Mr. Callaghan* sent

[8] In this speech, made before the *Cortes* on 22 November 1975, King Juan Carlos declared that he 'would not be faithful to the tradition of my blood if at this moment I did not recall that for generations as Spaniards we have fought to restore the territorial integrity of our soil. With full convictions, the King takes on this objective' (*The Times*, 24 November 1975).

his respects in return. But as Sr. Areilza would have seen he had got into trouble over our representation at General Franco's funeral.[9] He wound up by saying that the Government would proceed with caution. They had to carry public opinion with them. They would not lag behind it; they would do their best to lead public opinion but they could not move so far forward that they got out of sight. He wished Sr. Areilza good fortune. *Sr. Areilza* said that it would be a hard struggle. They wanted to develop a constitutional opposition but one which would accept the democratic rules. There had been a wave a [*sic*] strikes. Some of the grievances had been justified (e.g. on salaries) but there had been a good deal of manipulation by the Communists. The right wing were in some respect an easier problem since at present they still gave loyal support to the aspirations of the King.[10]

17. The private discussions ended at 12.00 hrs and the Ministers were then joined by officials (see separate record).[11]

[9] Britain had been represented at Gen. Franco's funeral on 23 November 1975 by Lord Shepherd of Spalding, the Lord Privy Seal and Leader of the House of Lords, and Mr. E.W. Griffiths, MP, the former Conservative Minister for Sport. Mr. Wiggin represented the Queen.

[10] In telegram No. 14 Personal to Madrid of 4 March, which summarised the results of Sr. Areilza's visit, Mr. Callaghan wrote: 'Altogether the atmosphere was cordial and the Spaniards were successful in giving their impression that the Spanish Government genuinely wish to bring Spain out of the Franco era. But Sr. Areilza spoke much as expected. The Spanish Government's room for manoeuvre is very limited and the prospects of their success are hard to assess. Any real improvement in relations must await definite and public moves towards democracy, and these will take time.'

[11] Not printed. This meeting was additionally attended on the British side by Mr. Wiggin, Mr. Campbell, Mr. Goodison, Mr. McCaffrey, Mr. McNally and Mr. H.J. Arbuthnott (First Secretary, EID(E)). The talks dealt with Spain's commercial arrangements with the EC (record of meeting between Mr. Callaghan and Sr. Areilza at the FCO on 2 March at 12 noon).

APPENDIX I

Mr. Olver (Nicosia) to Mr. Callaghan

[*WSC 1/10*]

Confidential   NICOSIA *2 December 1974*

Summary ...[1]

Sir,

The Coup against Makarios

In early August, when it seemed that a genuine ceasefire might be achieved, I commenced a draft of a despatch on the disaster which had overtaken Cyprus since the *coup d'état* of 15 July. That draft began with the words: 'While memories are still reasonably fresh and before some new crisis engulfs us I shall endeavour in this despatch to convey some of my main impressions and an account of the principal events of the last few weeks in Cyprus'. Months have now passed. Memory has become dimmed and events have multiplied many-fold. I therefore propose in this despatch to deal with the causes, the course and the consequences of the 15 July *coup*. In a subsequent despatch I shall deal with the Turkish military intervention.[2] In these despatches I can only hope to give the broadest possible picture of events. Many details will be perforce omitted. The full record nevertheless remains in the telegraphic exchanges that took place at the time.

2. It is all too easy to forget that the tragedy that has befallen Cyprus in recent months had its immediate origins in the *coup d'état* inspired by Athens on 15 July: 'the senseless *coup* attempted by the dictatorship' as Mr. Karamanlis described it in his broadcast of 15 August. This event set in train the whole sequence of events from which Turkey has taken such determined and callous advantage. But the basic origins of the crisis go back beyond 15 July, 1974. It now seems doubtful whether Archbishop Makarios ever really intended to operate effectively the Constitution which he accepted in 1960. This Constitution gave Cyprus independence from Britain and the Archbishop supreme power in the Republic. But it did not provide a direct path to Enosis (in fact it specifically excluded this), and it gave to the Turkish Cypriot community a position which the Archbishop and the Greek Cypriot community regarded as privileged and thus unfair. Throughout the succeeding years the Turkish Cypriots were made to feel unwelcome and opportunities taken to undermine their position. The fault did not however lie only with one side. The more pressure the Greek Cypriots applied, the more arrogant and demanding the Turkish Cypriots themselves became. The prolonged intercommunal talks between Mr. Clerides and Mr. Denktash never really got to grips with the central problem which was, and remains, the almost total lack of trust between the leadership of the two communities and the absence of any real confidence by either side in the basic good intentions of the other. The long drawn out arguments about

[1] Not printed.
[2] Not printed.

local autonomy and other constitutional devices never made any noticeable impression on this central problem.

3. Archbishop Makarios must himself assume the major responsibility for the failure to bridge the gap between the two communities. He had the power and the ability, had he chosen to use them, to lead the Greek Cypriot community to a just and acceptable settlement with the Turkish Cypriots. Concessions would have been necessary and generosity would have to have been shown. The Greek Cypriots, with the probable exception of the powerful though numerically small EOKA fringe, would have followed Makarios' lead. Sadly, he lacked the statesmanship and the wisdom that his country needed. Cyprus is now paying the price for his failure.[3]

4. The Archbishop's lack of resolution, a fatal weakness of wishing to keep all options open and to be all things to all men ultimately provoked the *coup* of 15 July. He delayed his campaign to stamp out the EOKA terrorist movement until it was too late. He allowed relations with Athens to turn so sour that they curdled. He trusted to fate, which let him down. By mid-July Makarios had lost a great deal of his appeal and attraction to many Greek Cypriots. He still stood head and shoulders above any other political figure and would have won any ballot handsomely. But his image had been badly tarnished by the excesses of his armed supporters. The tales of torture in the central prison and in the Paphos Gate police station may have been somewhat exaggerated, but there was sufficient evidence to cause grave disquiet. The Archbishop condemned these excesses but took no effective action to prevent them.

5. In retrospect one can now see the letter sent by Makarios to the Greek régime in Athens on 5[2] July, as the inevitable final step.[4] In it he accused the Colonels in humiliating language of responsibility for all the interfactional misfortunes of Cyprus. He called for the immediate withdrawal of all Greek mainland officers serving with the Greek Cypriot National Guard. The letter was published immediately it was delivered. Athens was faced with the choice of abasing herself before the priest that they had never liked or trusted, or of disposing of him. The temptation and the provocation were too great. The *coup* was launched.

6. It began at 8.30 a.m. on 15 July with a murderous assault on the Presidential Palace by artillery at point blank range.[5] Makarios, in true-Houdini style, escaped from the inferno.[6] The conspirators were either unaware of his escape or fearful of its consequences. The Cypriot people were therefore informed of his death and, after some delay, of the swearing in of Nicos Sampson as President of the Republic.[7] This particular piece of news was received with incredulity by many. The subsequent

---

[3] Mr. J. Lynton Jones observed in a minute to Mr. M.C.S. Weston of 23 December that although he accepted that culpability for the *coup* 'must be laid at the Archbishop's door', he thought Mr. Olver had failed 'to draw sufficient attention to the rôle of the Colonels'. He surmised: 'For there can be no doubt now that the Greeks were behind the *coup*–however unthought-out and irrational a response it may have been to the Archbishop's ultimatum.' Mr. Weston annotated: 'I am doubtful about some of the statements on the background to the *coup* (paragraph 2) but I generally agree with the conclusions.'

[4] See No. 17, note 1.

[5] See Nos. 18 and 19.

[6] See No. 20.

[7] See No. 20, note 2.

announcement of the new Ministerial team confirmed the initial view that the *coup* had thrown up a collection of nonentities who could never provide a credible or enduring Government.

7. The *coup* itself was conducted with vigour and efficiency. The key posts in the capital were captured with the minimum of force. The radio and television station, the central telephone and telegraph office, the police headquarters and the airport were all occupied during the morning. The main resistance in Nicosia came from a contingent of the Police Tactical Reserve who had established a fortress in the Nicosia premises of Kykko Monastery: the building and the PTR took heavy punishment.[8] Supporters of the Archbishop also managed to hold out for some time in the Archbishopric, an elegant building inside the walls of the Old City. Eventually this building also fell—to reveal a cache of some thousands of small arms and ammunition.

8. At the time there was endless speculation as to the extent of the involvement in the *coup* of the Greek National Contingent stationed in Cyprus. It soon became clear that, just as the political inspiration for the *coup* came from Athens, so its military direction came from mainland Greeks in Cyprus. One small incident is indicative. During the fighting around Nicosia Airport, a number of wounded were taken to the medical centre at UNFICYP Headquarters which adjoins the airport. One of the casualties, more seriously wounded than the others, was flown to the British Military Hospital at Dhekelia. The soldier in question revealed that he was a member of the Greek mainland contingent. Two days after his transfer to Dhekalia the soldier in question was removed abruptly and without warning by a National Guard ambulance even though, given his medical condition, he should have remained in hospital. This incident reveals a guilty conscience and a desire where possible to cover up the tracks of mainland Greek involvement. Any suggestion therefore that the *coup* was an entirely indigenous Cypriot uprising against Makarios must be discounted—though once the bandwaggon began to roll many leapt enthusiastically on to it and others fell quietly into line behind.

9. A *coup* has always been a possibility and most observers of the Cyprus scene were agreed that the attitude of the National Guard would be crucial to the success and failure of any move against Makarios. If the National Guard on direction from Athens, stood aside, the Archbishop would easily have weathered almost any storm: and it was thought likely that, even if Athens wished to use the National Guard against the Archbishop, divided loyalties would render it a broken reed for their purpose. In the event, the National Guard rank and file obeyed their Greek officers—and Makarios was swept away. Greek Cypriot members of the National Guard who were not prepared to follow the lead of Athens were either confined to their barracks or sent off on harmless exercises to get them out of the way. No units of the National Guard came to Makarios' aid.[9] His own armed supporters (the Presidential Guard, the Police Tactical Reserve, the Communist Party AKEL, the armed groups of Dr. Lyssarides, etc.) were no match for the National Guard and put up little if any resistance. The announcement of Makarios' death also took the heart out of such resistance as there was. By the time that his survival and presence in Paphos was confirmed by broadcasts from that town,

[8] See No. 18.
[9] Cf. No. 17.

521

the military and the new puppet régime were in firm control throughout the rest of the island. Makarios by then had no hope of victory and like the good tactician he has always been, he decided to withdraw and live to fight another day.

10. At this point I would wish to pay special tribute to the Near East Air Force by the arrangements made for the Archbishop's departure from Cyprus. The request from the Archbishop was conveyed to me by General Prem Chand, the Officer Commanding UNFICYP at noon on 16 July. At 4.15 p.m. the Archbishop was lifted from the UNFICYP Camp in Paphos by a helicopter of Number 84 Squadron, prior authority having been given by Her Majesty's Government. It was made clear to the Archbishop in advance that he would not be allowed to remain within the SBA but would be immediately flown out of Cyprus. By 5.00 p.m. GMT the Archbishop and a small personal retinue had left Akrotiri *en route* for Malta and London. The whole operation was carried out with calm efficiency. The actual rescue from Paphos was not without danger. The UN Camp was by then within range of National Guard Units and the Royal Air Force crew undoubtedly put their lives at risk to save that of the Archbishop.

11. One of the more disturbing features of the *coup* was the appearance on the streets of Nicosia and the other main towns of bands of young men heavily armed, in assorted uniforms and driving commandeered cars and lorries. Road blocks appeared on all the main roads and it seemed at one stage as if some at least of these wild young men would get out of control and try to wreak vengeance upon their political opponents. This did not in practice happen on any large scale. Undoubtedly some old scores were settled and we shall probably never know how many lost their lives in this way. Furthermore a number of Makarios' supporters spent a few uncomfortable days in jail before being released. Sampson claims much credit for the moderation shown and there is no reason to doubt that he was able to exercise a restraining influence. There were however other influences at work. The Greek mainland officers managed to maintain an admirably tight hold on the National Guard and on many of its irregular supporters. Secondly the Turkish invasion on 20 July united all factions of the Greek Cypriot community against the common enemy.[10] One of the first acts after the invasion was the release of all pro-Makarios supporters from the Central Jail in Nicosia so that they could join in the fight against the Turks.

12. One question that must be asked is whether the *coup* could have succeeded and led to a lasting solution to the Cyprus problem had there been no Turkish military intervention. The answer must I think be 'No', given the origins of the *coup* itself, the background of the puppet civilian régime and above all the fact that Archbishop Makarios had escaped and was at large, still recognised by the world as lawful President of Cyprus. Sampson was personally held in little respect by the majority of Greek Cypriots. He was regarded with positive hatred and distrust by the Turkish Cypriots who remembered only too well his leading role in the assault on the Turkish Cypriot suburb of Ormophita in 1967. To the Turks, Sampson meant Enosis and their elimination. He or they would have to go. Since they had no intention of leaving and since Ankara had the military strength and the political will to 'rescue' Cyprus from its own folly intervention became inevitable. Speculation whether, even without the Turkish intervention, Sampson would have been succeeded by Clerides, and what the

[10] See Nos. 30 and 31.

latter might then have achieved, comes up also against the Archbishop's presence in the wings.

13. Sampson has recently published his own version of his role in the *coup*. He alleges—and this could well be true—that he had no advance notice of the *coup* and that he was the fourth person invited to assume the Presidency, the others being the Chief Justice, Mr. Michael Triantafyllieds; a former (and now reappointed) Minister of Health, Mr. Zenon Severis and Judge L. Loizou. Sampson claims that he reluctantly accepted the call in order to prevent violent internecine clashes between the various Greek Cypriot factions and that in this he was successful. Fanciful though his account may appear it tends to confirm the view formed at the time that whilst the military operation was successfully planned and well executed, the political foundations of the *coup* were virtually non-existent. If the Chief Justice was indeed the first choice for the Presidency why launch a *coup* at a time when he was known to be absent in Strasbourg attending a Council of Europe Meeting. It did not make sense.

14. There was much about this *coup* that did not make sense. Did the instigators really believe that Sampson was a credible President who could command the loyalty of Greek Cypriots and the trust of Turkish Cypriots? Did they totally ignore the probable reaction at Ankara to a military takeover by the National Guard, which had for many years been the main breeding ground for the Enosis movement and the main recruiting ground for EOKA? The miscalculations were enormous: the consequences disastrous.

15. The immediate consequences [*sic*] was the Turkish intervention of 20 July.[11] I shall deal with this in a subsequent despatch. It would however be appropriate here to consider some of the longer term consequences of the action initiated by the Colonels in Athens on 15 July. As far as they themselves were concerned, the most direct consequence was their own downfall, the return of Mr. Karamanlis and the restoration of democracy in Greece.[12] This however is probably the only favourable outcome. For the rest the *coup* brought death and destruction to Cyprus. It gravely affected relations between Greece and the US, and Turkey and the US. The cohesion of the South-Eastern flank of NATO has been prejudiced.[13] A US Ambassador has been murdered.[14] The Turkish Army is entrenched in strength in Northern Cyprus. The economy of Cyprus has been shattered, and refugee camps have become an accepted feature of its landscape. The Soviet Union, by pursuing a policy of masterly inactivity, have been able to pose as the only true supporters of Cypriot independence and have appreciably improved their standing with the Greek Cypriot majority.[15] All of this has resulted from 'the senseless *coup*'.

16. It is however just possible that one further lasting benefit may result from the events initiated on 15 July. Many Greek Cypriots, in all stations and walks of life, are claiming that, left to themselves, the two communities could co-exist peacefully and urging that efforts for a peace settlement should work towards this. A number of the more intelligent Greek Cypriots have admitted to us the responsibility of the

[11] *Ibid.*
[12] See Nos. 39, 93 and 102.
[13] Cf. No. 77.
[14] See No. 84, note 5.
[15] Cf. No. 95.

Government (and I would add of the Archbishop personally) over the years 1960-1974 for the failure to make the fairly painless sort of political gesture to the Turks which could have bought a settlement in 1964, 1968 or on several occasions thereafter. Much of this is alas an emotional and perhaps ephemeral post-hoc rationalisation on the Greek-Cypriot part. For them, the *coup* followed by the war has been cathartic. I fear that on the Turkish Cypriot side, there has been no catharsis: that, for the politicians at least, power is proving heady stuff. But if the negotiations for a settlement do not get too bogged down and do not produce too much bitterness, it is perhaps just possible that out of the evil precipitated by the *coup* may be born a lasting solution to the Cyprus problem.

17. I am sending copies of this despatch to Her Majesty's Ambassadors at Athens, Ankara and Washington, to the UK Permanent Representative at the UN in New York, the Permanent UK Representative on the North Atlantic Council and to the Commander, British Forces Near East.

I have, etc.,

S.J.L. OLVER

Report by the Joint Intelligence Committee

JIC (76) 3

Secret. UK Eyes A   CABINET OFFICE, 29 April 1976

The Outlook for the Southern Flank of NATO

PART I: SUMMARY[1]

Introduction

1. In this paper we examine the outlook for the southern flank of the North Atlantic Treaty Organisation (NATO), defined as the whole of southern Europe and the Mediterranean sea area.[2] We first survey the current regional politico-military balance between East and West; against this background we identify possible developments in the area for the next 2-3 years and assess their political and military implications for the Western Alliance.

I. THE CURRENT EAST/WEST BALANCE

Soviet objectives

2. Within the framework of detente, conceived by the Russians as a low-risk offensive policy designed to bring about a steady and controlled shift in the balance of power in Soviet favour while minimising the risks of confrontation with the United States, we assess Soviet objectives as being—

   i. To extend Soviet power and influence throughout the Mediterranean area and to secure acceptance of the Soviet Union's status as a superpower having a right to say in all important regional issues;

   ii. To undermine the hitherto preponderant influence of the United States and to encourage the fragmentation of the Western Alliance in the area;

---

[1] Part II, the Main Report, is not printed.

[2] Already during the autumn of 1975, at the Prime Minister's suggestion, a paper had been prepared by the FCO, with MoD assistance, on the 'Problems of NATO's Southern Flank' (OPD (75) 41). The paper, dated 11 November 1975, was presented by Mr. Callaghan to the Cabinet Defence and Oversea Policy Committee on 13 November 1975. Mr. Mason then explained that, following the Defence Review, the UK's military effort would be concentrated on the central region of NATO, in the eastern Atltantic and in the home base; the rundown of Britain's defence presence in Malta would be complete by 1979, more than half of its forces would have left Cyprus by the spring of 1976, specialist reinforcement forces were being cut, and by the end of 1976 it would have no maritime forces in the Mediterranean declared to NATO. 'The only effective action we could take', he added, 'would be political and diplomatic' (OPD (75) 13th Meeting, WDN 26/46).

iii. To counter the NATO (primarily United States) naval presence in the Mediterranean, in order both to deter a NATO maritime strategic strike against the Soviet Union and to limit the West's room for manoeuvre militarily and politically;

iv. To achieve the traditional Russian aim of secure naval passage from the Black Sea into the Mediterranean and thence to the Atlantic and India Oceans;

v. In the longer term, to shift the balance of military power in the area decisively in favour of the Soviet Union.[3]

The Military Balance

3. A static numerical comparison of the regional combat-ready forces available to NATO and the Warsaw Pact in peace-time suggests that the position is generally more favourable to NATO in the Southern than in the Northern and Central Regions of Allied Command Europe. But this is misleading. The area of NATO's Southern European Command (comprising Italy, Greece, Turkey and the whole of the Mediterranean sea area) is highly fragmented both strategically and in terms of command structure. The land areas to be defended in effect constitute separate sub-theatres, heavily dependent on timely external reinforcement. The most recent military assessment by major NATO commanders (with which we agree) draws attention to deficiencies in manning levels, equipment and war reserve stocks which seriously weaken the defensive capabilities of the indigenous land and air forces. At sea, the Italian Navy provides a valuable supplement to the United States Sixth Fleet, but the Greek and Turkish Navies are of very limited effectiveness. Additional French naval units are being deployed in the Mediterranean, they do not form part of the NATO military structure, but the Russians must take them into account.

4. The Italian, Greek and Turkish Governments have embarked in [*sic*] modernisation programmes for their armed forces, but all are subject to internal economic and political constraints and Greece and Turkey depend on external military aid. Following the Cyprus crisis of 1974, Greece has virtually withdrawn from the integrated NATO military structure and United States military assistance to Turkey has been interrupted by the action of the United States Congress. Increased defence expenditure by Greece and Turkey has been motivated more by the threat each perceives from the other than by the common Soviet threat.

5. Against this background, the United States/Soviet naval balance in the Mediterranean is of crucial importance: the trend since 1964, from the United States dominance to the present state of approximate parity, has been the most significant

---

[3] 'Many of the factors making for instability in the Mediterranean area', noted the Main Report, 'derive from essentially national or regional causes rather than the relationship between NATO and the Warsaw Pact; many are a function of more or less widespread economic, social and poitical trends in which East/West relations constitute only one, sometimes marginal, element. At the same time the Mediterranean is an area of high and increasing strategic importance—militarily, politically and economically—in the relationship between the Eastern and Western alliances in general and between the two superpowers in particular ... In the wider East/West competition for global power and influence in an increasingly fluid international system, the Mediterranean area has particular significance, encompassing as it does members of the "four worlds"—industrialised Western countries, Socialist countries, rich oil-producers and non-oil-producing developing countries—covering a broad and changing spectrum of internal social and political development and of external interests and alignments.'

military development in the area. In a time of international tension (eg the Arab/Israel war of October 1973) the Soviet Mediterranean squadron is capable of being reinforced so as to provide a viable counter-force to the Sixth Fleet. At present Soviet naval force levels in the Mediterranean are fairly steady but their fighting quality (notably missile capabilities) has been steadily improved. For the time being, however, the Soviet Mediterranean Squadron lacks organic air support, although the first Kiev class aircraft carrier is expected to be deployed in the area later this year equipped initially with anti-submarine helicopters and in due course with VSTOL[4] aircraft; it also lacks secure shore facilities in the Mediterranean. In time of war its operational flexibility would be constrained so long as the Soviet Union were denied control of the three maritime points of access to the Mediterranean.

6. In addition to its overriding deterrent role and other tasks, the United States Sixth Fleet has a vital function in providing military cohesion for the Alliance in the Mediterranean area. United States naval striking power includes 5 ballistic missile firing submarines as well as 2 aircraft carriers and an amphibious force. For the geographical and operational diversity of its tasks the Sixth Fleet is not large; but it constitutes a powerful deterrent force, and together with indigenous naval forces (for all their shortcomings) should be capable of dealing with the Soviet Mediterranean Squadron in war.

The Political Balance

7. The cumulative effect of the military deficiencies of the countries of NATO's Southern Region undermines the credibility of the Alliance's regional military posture. Significant improvements will depend largely on the extent to which political solidarity can be strengthen. But events in the Eastern Mediterranean, Portugal and Italy have brought intra-Alliance relationships under increasingly severe strain over the past two years; in particular their interplay with political developments in the United States has damaged America's regional image and influence and soured United States relations with a number of Southern European countries.[5]

8. Soviet promotion of detente has contributed to the malaise on NATO's southern flank by encouraging an atmosphere in which some Southern European countries feel it safe to pursue perceived national interests at the expense of wider Alliance interests, and in which local communit [*sic*] parties have gained political respectability. But in general developments favourable to the Soviet Union have taken place without overt Soviet intervention and the Russians have so far done little to exploit them. The volatile

[4] Vertical Short Takeoff and Landing.

[5] The Main Report further explained: 'In Greece, Portugal and probably Spain, the United States has suffered from its identification with former unpopular regimes. The Cyprus crisis and its aftermath provoked strong anti-American reactions, though for opposite reasons, in both Greece and Turkey. The United States Administration's efforts to improve their relations with both countries by means of new, even-handed bilateral defence co-operation agreements could still be frustrated by Congress. More generally, the aftermath of Vietnam and Watergate—not least the public spectacle of the Americans' own search for scapegoats for past mistakes by United States governments and their agencies and the continuing debate about the purposes and conduct of United States external policy—has diminished respect for and confidence in the United States and encouraged the anti-Americanism always latent in Europe.'

condition of Southern Europe could nevertheless encourage the Soviet Union to take advantage of opportunities to pursue more forward policies in the Mediterranean area (although the Russians have problems of their own on the Warsaw Pact's southern flank).[6]

9. While strains within NATO have multiplied, Western influence in the Mediterranean outside the NATO area has increased since the shocks of October 1973 and is capable of further consolidation. But the Western position in the Middle East and North Africa will remain vulnerable to the consequences of a new Arab/Israeli crisis, sharpening inter-Arab disputes and renewed confrontation between oil producers and consumers.

II. Possible Challenges to NATO

A. Greece/Turkey/Cyprus

10. The longstanding disputes between Greece and Turkey over Cyprus and the delimitation of territorial waters and air space in the Aegean came to a head in 1974 and have dominated all aspects of the two countries' relations with each other and with the rest of the Alliance ever since. In practice the terms and timing of a Cyprus settlement will largely be dictated by Turkey; but for various reasons of internal and external policy the Turkish Government shows no real will to conciliation, and we see little prospect of an early settlement. The longer the present deadlock persists, the greater will become the danger of renewed inter-communal tensions in Cyprus further exacerbating relations between Greece and Turkey. The Aegean dispute is potentially even more dangerous, since it involves conflicting claims to sovereignty in an area where the armed forces of the two countries are in direct confrontation. Though each side remains preoccupied by its perception of the threat posed by the other, military tension between Greece and Turkey has abated over the past year. Both sides (but especially Greece) have good military reasons for avoiding war and we believe that they will go to considerable lengths to do so. But the degree of mutual distrust is such that we cannot rule out the risk that hostilities could arise from miscalculation or irrational behaviour.

11. There is a standing risk that persistent deadlock in the Greco-Turkish disputes or new setbacks for one side or the other may be ascribed to the ineffectiveness or partiality of the Alliance and that the aggrieved party may question whether continued membership of NATO is in its national interest. The Turkish Government has consistently maintained that Congressional interference with the United States military assistance to Turkey has not affected its loyalty to NATO; given Turkish distrust of the Soviet Union, a reversal of Turkey's conscious orientation to the West would require a fundamental change of political outlook. But if Western support fell short of Turkish expectations the ensuing disenchantment, combined with internal political instability, could induce drift towards non-alignment.

---

[6] These were listed in the Main Report as 'the maverick nationalism of Romania, Yugoslav determination to maintain its own brand of non-alignment and the unrelenting hostility of Albania'.

12. Further Greek humiliation at the hands of Turkey would greatly strengthen anti-NATO feeling in Greece. Even if relations with Turkey improved, the re-integration of the Greek armed forces in the NATO military structure would be a highly divisive issue and although the present Greek Government would favour it, they might well decide not to risk it. In or out of the NATO military structure, Greece will pursue her aspirations to membership of the European Economic Community (EEC) in order to strengthen her links with Western Europe.

13. If Greece and/or Turkey were to leave NATO the military consequences for the Alliance would be serious but, provided they remained non-aligned and denied bases and facilities to the Soviet Union, need not be disastrous.[7] The repercussions for the political morale of the Alliance would, however, be very damaging.

B. Italy

14. In Italy, the prospect that the Italian Communist Party (PCI) may soon achieve participation in government by democratic means poses what is potentially the most serious challenge to NATO's political cohesion. We do not regard the PCI's 'historic compromise' as a foregone conclusion; but the probability of its coming about after the forthcoming Italian general elections in sufficiently high to be taken seriously.[8]

15. Whatever the PCI's real attitude to Italian membership of NATO, there are a number of reasons for expecting that, initially at least, the PCI in government would abide by its public undertakings to respect Italy's existing international commitments, leaving it to the rest of the Alliance to take the initiative in deciding how to adjust to the new situation.[9] It might be argued that the Alliance had no choice but to accept the verdict of the Italian electorate and to give the PCI the chance to prove its avowed commitment to pluralist democracy and independence from Moscow. But the risks would be very grave: there would be no guarantee that the PCI would not revert to classic communist methods in order to seize power outright or that the Soviet Union would not find ways of reasserting its control over the party; the PCI's success would be likely to strengthen anti-NATO and anti-democratic forces in other Western countries (notably France) and undermine Western solidarity and strength of purpose vis-a-vis the Soviet Union; most seriously, Western European toleration of communist success in

---

[7] In addition to the loss of the indigenous forces of the two countries, the Main Report also cited 'the loss of important forward bases ... and some unique intelligence-gathering facilities' as the main military consequences of a Greek or Turkish withdrawal from the Alliance. 'The operational flexibility of the United States Sixth Fleet in the Eastern Mediterranean would be seriously impeded; and the West would lose the ability to control the passage of Soviet warships through the Turkish Straits which Turkish co-operation now gives it. Of the two, the loss of Turkey would be strategically much the more serious. But if Greece alone were to leave NATO, this would leave Turkey isolated on the extreme south-eastern flank of the Alliance.'

[8] Since 1974 there had been much talk in Italy about an 'historic compromise', i.e. the association of the Communists with Government. Communists were encouraged by the municipal and regional elections in June 1975 in which the PCI polled an unprecedented 33% share of the vote, compared to the Christian Democrats' 35%, and the Socialists' 13%.

[9] 'In some ways', suggested the Main Report, 'this would undoubtedly suit the Russians too. Italy's disruptive potential within the Alliance, and the opportunities it would offer for Soviet penetration and subversion could bring them significant gains.'

Italy could call into question United States' willingness to maintain its support of European defence at a credible level.

16. The fundamental dilemma facing the Alliance could be brought to a head quickly by practical problems relating to such matters as the security of sensitive NATO documents and communications. However delicately handled, these would be likely to sour Italy's relationship with her allies, to strain Alliance cohesion and sooner or later to force the issue of Italy's continuing membership of NATO.[10]

C. Portugal

17. The Portuguese Communist Party's bid to seize power received a severe and possibly decisive setback last November. The new political balance of power favours the evolution of a social democratic system under some degree of military supervision; but the underlying political, economic and social problems may be beyond the capacity of Portugal's embryonic democratic institutions and quarrelsome political parties. Continuing political instability is likely and could lead the armed forces to reassert their authority. But Portugal's position in NATO appears secure in the medium term; her military value to the Alliance will continue to rest on NATO's access to bases and facilities in mainland Portugal and the Azores, which are important for maritime surveillance and control of the Atlantic and for United States reinforcement of Europe.

D. Spain

18. Because of her geographical position, her defence relationship with the United States and her actual and potential economic strength, Spain's internal political development and external alignment are of obvious concern to the Alliance. The present Spanish Government intend to seek membership of NATO (as well as the EEC). From the point of view of the Alliance there are strong strategic arguments for this; but the uncertainties surrounding Spain's political future are such that it is at best an open question whether closer Spanish association with NATO will prove politically feasible or desirable; and while they persist, these uncertainties will make it more difficult for NATO members to arrive at a common approach to their individual and collective dealings with Spain. For the United Kingdom, Gibraltar will continue to be a complicating factor. On the other side of the coin, a social democratic Spanish regime or, *a fortiori*, one further to the left might not want to join NATO, preferring to rely on the EC as the vehicle for its integration with Western Europe.

---

[10] In the Italian General Election of 20 June the PCI gained 34.4% of the votes cast (7% more than in the previous General Election of 1972). But, while the Socialists polled less than 10% of the votes, the Christian Democrats still managed to secure 38.7% (the same as in 1972). The new single-party Government, headed by the Christian Democrat leader, Sig. G. Andreotti, was therefore only able to implement its programme with Communist and Socialist consent. Sir G. Millard, who was about to retire as HM Ambassador in Rome, forecast in his valedictory despatch of 25 September: 'But with all due allowance made for change, Italy is likely to remain a basically conservative society, in which the majority have much to lose and set high value on their freedom. It is a country in quite rapid evolution; it remains my judgement that it is not ripe for Marxist revolution, whether by violent or by parliamentary means' (WRJ 014/2).

E. *Yugoslavia*

19. Developments in Yugoslavia after Tito's departure could provide a crucial test of the Soviet attitude to détente, with important repercussions for the security of NATO's southern flank and for East/West relations in general. On balance we would expect the Russians to have considerable reservations about provoking a crisis in Yugoslavia; but if one were to develop, eg out of a disputed succession to Tito and/or severe economic difficulties (and we cannot rule this out), then they would be likely to seek to exploit it to their own advantage.[11] Spanish entry into NATO (or the imminent prospect of it) could be exploited by the Russians to justify a harder line towards Yugoslavia. But their assessment of the likely United States reaction would be the most critical external factor determining Soviet behaviour. Any United States Administration could be expected to exert pressure on the Russians to discourage Soviet meddling; but we do not believe that the United States would commit itself to any direct military involvement in Yugoslavia; nor do we see any prospect of military intervention by NATO.[12]

20. The incorporation of Yugoslavia into the Warsaw Pact and access to Yugoslav facilities by Soviet naval and air forces would change the regional balance in Soviet favour. The threat to Italy would be increased, Greece and Turkey would be isolated further and Soviet maritime capabilities in the Mediterranean would be strengthened significantly. The Russians would also be better placed to assert their authority elsewhere in Eastern Europe, especially Romania.

F. *The Middle East and North Africa; Cyprus; Malta*

21. Developments in the Middle East could have important repercussions for NATO. Another Arab/Israel war would pose new dangers of United States/Soviet confrontation, use of the oil weapon by the Arabs and strains in United States/European relations. On the other hand progress towards an Arab/Israeli settlement would require United States/Soviet collaboration and could bring the two superpowers into uneasy partnership as the ultimate arbiters of peace in the Eastern Mediterranean. Meanwhile the Soviet Union will persist in its efforts to expand its influence in the Arab world, with mixed success. Their exclusion from Egypt[13] will cause the Russians to renew their hitherto unsuccessful efforts to gain access to naval

---

[11] In an economic crisis, the Main Report argued, the Russians 'might well exert economic pressure on the Yugoslavs; they might also try to manipulate tensions between the Republics and within the Party in the hope of engineering a change in the central Party leadership. In a crisis of succession they would use their influence in support of pro-Soviet elements. They could use the threat of military intervention as a means of reinforcing their pressure for change, although we continue to believe that the arguments for military intervention would prevail only if the Russians were prepared to risk a major international confrontation. If there were civil war, however, the Russians would be under a very strong temptation to give indirect military support to one side against the other.'

[12] The paper presented to the Cabinet Defence and Oversea Policy Committee on 13 November 1975 (see note 2 above) recommended that Western countries develop their relations with Yugoslavia wherever possible in order to help 'strengthen the central Government and increase the value to the Yugoslavs of their connections with the West'.

[13] On 18 July 1972 President A. Sadat had instructed the Soviet Union to remove its 20,000 military advisers and experts, accusing the Soviet Union of failing to provide promised armaments.

facilities in Algeria or Libya; if they succeed, the military implications for NATO would be serious. We do not foresee the Russians gaining military access to Cyprus or Malta[14] in the period under review.

III. The Outlook

22. Overshadowing the individual challenges facing NATO on its southern flank is the wider problem of international economic recession. Prolonged economic dislocation could have profoundly destabilising effects; it is already a crucial factor in the political difficulties affecting Italy, Portugal and Spain. But even in conditions of sustained economic recovery, pressure on Western European defence budgets will persist, with the risk that NATOs' military capabilities will be weakened without compensating negotiated reductions by the Warsaw Pact.

23. NATO's southern flank will remain politically volatile and the Western position in the area will continue to be accident-prone. But the most notable characteristic of the complex of problems facing the Alliance is the extent to which their outcome will depend on Western rather than Soviet actions and attitudes. The most difficult of these problems is how the Alliance should respond to the advance towards a share in governmental responsibility in Italy and France by communist parties which proclaim their commitment to the rules of parliamentary democracy and their independence of Soviet control. The fundamental question how far communist participation in government is compatible with membership of NATO is bound to be divisive and in particular is likely to impose severe new strains on relations between Western Europe and the United States.

24. These strains may be compounded by several factors. One is the American tendency to view regional problems in terms of their implications for the bilateral superpower relationship with the Soviet Union in a way which can lead to misunderstanding and mutual irritation between the United States and Western Europe. Another is the element of uncertainty introduced into the calculations of America's allies and adversaries alike by the United States Congress' assertion of an active role in the conduct of foreign policy. A new consensus on foreign policy between Congress and Administration could emerge quite quickly after the Presidential elections; but Congressional influence will remain strong and the European allies may have to adjust to a narrower and more selective pursuit of American overseas interests, even in relation to NATO. The United States is unlikely to reverse its calculation that the preservation of Western Europe's security is essential to the security of the United States itself. But, depending in part on Soviet actions, European toleration of the increasing

---

[14] The UK/Maltese Military Facilities Agreement was due to expire in 1979. When it did, the Main Report speculated, 'Mr. Mintoff (or the Nationalists, if they have won power) will extract the best possible price from NATO for denying Malta to the Soviet Navy. Facilities in Malta would be a very considerable benefit to the USSR. But given Mintoff's publicly reiterated aversion to both superpowers' intervention in the Mediterranean, and the Nationalists' adhesion to the West, we believe that things would have to go very badly wrong before the Russians gained a military foothold in Malta (and so long as the Chinese retain their current influence in Malta they would be likely to try to dissuade the Maltese from allowing the Russians in).'

influence of indigenous communist parties could revive pressures in the United States for a reduction of the American contribution to European defence.

25. Within the relatively short time-scale of this paper we do not foresee significant changes in the main thrust of Soviet foreign policy, whether or not there are changes in the leadership. The Russians will remain ready to exploit targets of opportunity which may arise on NATO's southern flank; but they will also remain wary of risking a direct confrontation with the United States.

26. Looking further ahead, a tendency may develop for Southern European countries to give increasing priority to regional concerns, to dissociate these from the larger issues of East/West relations and to regard a shift towards non-alignment as politically desirable. This need not be regarded by the countries concerned as implying dissociation from the West, particularly if it were accompanied by continuing or closer association with the EEC. But if such a trend were to develop unchecked, it could lead to an unravelling of the southern flank of the Alliance (which would extend to other areas) and a deterioration of NATO's collective political and military strength which would not be matched by any similar weakening of the Warsaw Pact. The extent to which this challenge can be overcome will be largely up to the Alliance itself.

R.A. SYKES
CHAIRMAN, ON BEHALF OF THE
JOINT INTELLIGENCE COMMITTEE

Index of Main Subjects and Persons

This index is designed to be used in conjunction with the Chapter Summaries. References in this index are to page, rather than document numbers.